From the employees at Tie,

April 19, 1985.

Ed Stubbs

Ben Thomas

SOFTWARE
ENGINEERING
ECONOMICS

Barry W. Boehm

Director, Software Research and Technology
TRW, Inc.

SOFTWARE ENGINEERING ECONOMICS

Prentice-Hall, Inc., Englewood Cliffs, New Jersey 07632

Library of Congress Cataloging in Publication Data

BOEHM, BARRY W. (date)
    Software engineering economics.

    (Prentice-Hall advances in computing science and
technology series)
    Bibliography: p.
    Includes index.
    1. Electronic digital computers—Programming—
Economic aspects.   2. Electronic digital computers—
Programming—Economic aspects—Case studies.   I. Title.
II. Series.
QA76.6.B618   001.64′25′0681   81–13889
ISBN   0–13–822122–7   AACR2

Editorial/Production Supervision
    and Interior Design: *Lynn S. Frankel*
Cover Design: *Carol Zawislak*
Manufacturing Buyer: *Gordon Osbourne*

**Prentice-Hall Advances
in Computing Science and Technology Series**
Raymond T. Yeh, editor

Printed in the United States of America

10   9   8   7   6   5   4

ISBN   0-13-822122-7

Prentice-Hall International, Inc., *London*
Prentice-Hall of Australia Pty. Limited, *Sydney*
Prentice-Hall of Canada, Ltd., *Toronto*
Prentice-Hall of India Private Limited, *New Delhi*
Prentice-Hall of Japan, Inc., *Tokyo*
Prentice-Hall of Southeast Asia Pte. Ltd., *Singapore*
Whitehall Books Limited, *Wellington, New Zealand*

To
Sharla, Romney, and Tenley

CONTENTS

Chapter 2 Case Study 2: An Urban School Attendance System   10

Chapter 3 The Goals of Software Engineering   14

PART II THE SOFTWARE LIFE-CYCLE: A QUANTITATIVE MODEL   29

Chapter 4 The Software Life-Cycle: Phases and Activities   35

Chapter 5 The Basic COCOMO Model 57

Chapter 6 The Basic COCOMO Model: Development Modes 74

Chapter 7 The Basic COCOMO Model: Activity Distribution 97

Chapter 15   Figures of Merit   223

Chapter 16   Goals as Constraints   243

PART IVB   THE DETAILED COCOMO MODEL   **344**

Chapter 23   Detailed COCOMO: Summary and Operational Description   **347**

Chapter 24   Detailed COCOMO Cost Drivers: Product Attributes   **371**

Chapter 25   Detailed COCOMO Cost Drivers: Computer Attributes   **400**

PART IVC SOFTWARE COST ESTIMATION AND LIFE-CYCLE MANAGEMENT   532

Chapter 30 Software Maintenance Cost Estimation   533

Chapter 31 Software Life-Cycle Cost Estimation   556

Chapter 32 Software Project Planning and Control   591

Chapter 33   Improving Software Productivity   **641**

INDEX   **751**

PREFACE

A course in engineering economics has become a fairly standard component of the hardware engineer's education. So far, the opportunities for software engineers to take a similar course tailored to software engineering economics have been rare. As a result, I think most software engineers miss out on a chance to acquire and use a number of significant economic concepts, techniques, and facts which can play a vital part in their future careers—and a vital part in making our software easier to live with and more worthwhile.

Not surprisingly, then, the major objective of this book is to provide a basis for a software engineering economics course, intended to be taken at the college senior/first-year graduate level. This objective has led to two subsidiary objectives:

1. To make the book easy for students to learn from;
2. To make the book easy for professors to teach from.

I have also tried to make the book serve a third objective:

3. To provide help for working professionals in the field.

Since these aims are sometimes at variance with each other, I have added notes to the student, professor, and practicing software engineer as a starting point for dealing with the contents of the book.

The basic structure of the book is shown in Figure A. Part I contains introductory material which provides a context, motivation, and framework of software engineering goals for the material to follow. Parts II and III cover two complementary topics: a quantitative model of the software life-cycle in Part II, and the fundamentals of engineering economics as they apply to software projects in Part III. Part IV then provides the detailed techniques for software life-cycle cost estimation which underlie the simpler cost models in Part II, and which further support the software engineering economic analysis techniques in Part III.

Figure A also shows the primary questions addressed in each part of the book. Thus, for example, Part IV addresses not only questions of software cost estimation and understanding software cost-influence factors, but also such questions as, "How can we use this understanding to improve our visibility and control of software projects, and to improve software productivity?"

Figure B shows how each part of the book is organized into components and individual chapters. This figure is reproduced at the beginning of each major component (Part openings) of the book. For example, Figure B indicates the successive levels of detail provided in the hierarchical software cost estimation model called COCOMO, for COnstructive COst MOdel. The top level of the hierarchy is Basic COCOMO, a simple formula estimating the cost of a software project solely as a function of its size in delivered source instructions, presented in Chapters 5, 6, and 7. The next level of the hierarchy is Intermediate COCOMO, presented in Chapters 8 and 9. It estimates the cost of a software project as a function of size and a number of other software cost driver attributes, such as personnel experience and capabilities, computer hardware constraints, and degree of use of modern programming practices. The most accurate and detailed level of the hierarchy is Detailed COCOMO, presented in Chapter 23 with elaborations in Chapters 24 through 27. It uses the cost driver attributes to estimate the software product's costs by individual phase, subsystem, and module.

The term "constructive" used to describe COCOMO derives from the detailed explanations in Chapters 24–27 of how the various software cost driver attributes influence the amount of effort required to complete each phase of the software life-cycle. The model not only provides estimating formulas, but it also provides the best explanation possible for *why* the model gives the results it does. The detailed material in Chapters 24–31 also discusses the frontiers of our knowledge of software life-cycle cost estimation, and provides an extensive agenda of suggestions for further research which can extend our knowledge of the software life-cycle and its economic properties.

For providing me with encouragement, insights, and data, I feel deeply indebted to many people. I wish I could name them all.

At TRW, I have benefited from a great deal of management insight and support from Simon Ramo, C. W. (Bill) Besserer, Bob Williams, and Ed Goldberg, and a wealth of technical information and insight from Tom Bauer, Mike Cozzens, Myron Lipow, Fred Manthey, Nancy Mikula, Eldred Nelson, Ron Osborne, and Tom Thayer; from

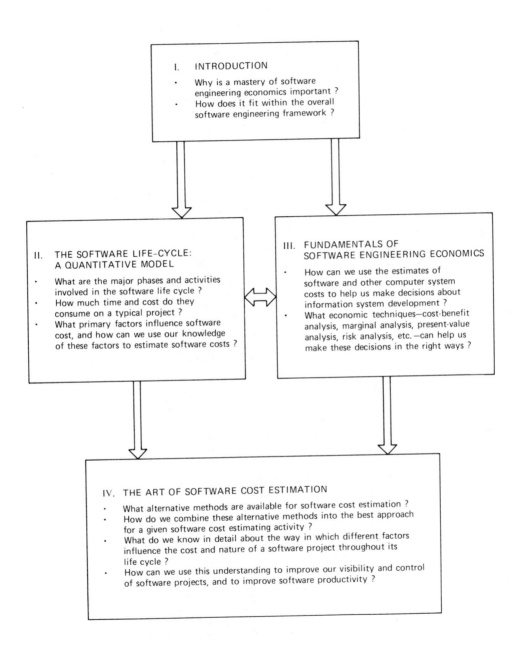

I. INTRODUCTION

- Why is a mastery of software engineering economics important ?
- How does it fit within the overall software engineering framework ?

II. THE SOFTWARE LIFE-CYCLE: A QUANTITATIVE MODEL

- What are the major phases and activities involved in the software life cycle ?
- How much time and cost do they consume on a typical project ?
- What primary factors influence software cost, and how can we use our knowledge of these factors to estimate software costs ?

III. FUNDAMENTALS OF SOFTWARE ENGINEERING ECONOMICS

- How can we use the estimates of software and other computer system costs to help us make decisions about information system development ?
- What economic techniques—cost-benefit analysis, marginal analysis, present-value analysis, risk analysis, etc. —can help us make these decisions in the right ways ?

IV. THE ART OF SOFTWARE COST ESTIMATION

- What alternative methods are available for software cost estimation ?
- How do we combine these alternative methods into the best approach for a given software cost estimating activity ?
- What do we know in detail about the way in which different factors influence the cost and nature of a software project throughout its life cycle ?
- How can we use this understanding to improve our visibility and control of software projects, and to improve software productivity ?

FIGURE A   Book Structure—Major questions addressed

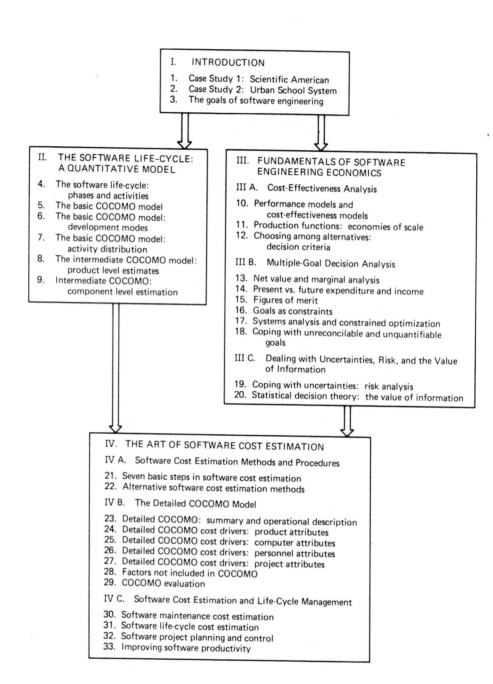

I. INTRODUCTION

1. Case Study 1: Scientific American
2. Case Study 2: Urban School System
3. The goals of software engineering

II. THE SOFTWARE LIFE–CYCLE:
A QUANTITATIVE MODEL

4. The software life-cycle:
   phases and activities
5. The basic COCOMO model
6. The basic COCOMO model:
   development modes
7. The basic COCOMO model:
   activity distribution
8. The intermediate COCOMO model:
   product level estimates
9. Intermediate COCOMO:
   component level estimation

III. FUNDAMENTALS OF SOFTWARE
ENGINEERING ECONOMICS

III A. Cost-Effectiveness Analysis

10. Performance models and
    cost-effectiveness models
11. Production functions: economies of scale
12. Choosing among alternatives:
    decision criteria

III B. Multiple-Goal Decision Analysis

13. Net value and marginal analysis
14. Present vs. future expenditure and income
15. Figures of merit
16. Goals as constraints
17. Systems analysis and constrained optimization
18. Coping with unreconcilable and unquantifiable
    goals

III C. Dealing with Uncertainties, Risk, and the Value
of Information

19. Coping with uncertainties: risk analysis
20. Statistical decision theory: the value of information

IV. THE ART OF SOFTWARE COST ESTIMATION

IV A. Software Cost Estimation Methods and Procedures

21. Seven basic steps in software cost estimation
22. Alternative software cost estimation methods

IV B. The Detailed COCOMO Model

23. Detailed COCOMO: summary and operational description
24. Detailed COCOMO cost drivers: product attributes
25. Detailed COCOMO cost drivers: computer attributes
26. Detailed COCOMO cost drivers: personnel attributes
27. Detailed COCOMO cost drivers: project attributes
28. Factors not included in COCOMO
29. COCOMO evaluation

IV C. Software Cost Estimation and Life-Cycle Management

30. Software maintenance cost estimation
31. Software life-cycle cost estimation
32. Software project planning and control
33. Improving software productivity

FIGURE B Book structure—Parts and chapters

ex-TRW'ers Bert Abramson, Tom Bell, John Brown, Kurt Fischer, Bob Page, and Win Royce; and particularly from Ray Wolverton.

Within the field of quantitative software analysis, I have had many enjoyable, stimulating, and valuable exchanges with Prof. Vic Basili of the University of Maryland, Dr. Les Belady of IBM, Tom DeMarco, Tom Gilb, the late Prof. Maurice Halstead of Purdue University, Capers Jones of ITT, Prof. Manny Lehman of Imperial College, London, Dick Nelson of RADC, Bob Park of RCA, Dr. Montgomery Phister, Jr., Larry Putnam of Quantitative Software Management, Inc., and Claude Walston of IBM.

In other areas, I feel fortunate to have learned much from discussions with Dr. Gerald Weinberg of Ethnotech, on software psychology; with Dr. Dave Parnas of the Naval Research Labs and IBM, Dr. Harlan Mills of IBM, and Prof. Tony Hoare of Oxford University on software methodology; and from numerous informal tennis-court seminars on economics and statistics from Dr. Charles Wolf of Rand and Prof. Carl Morris of the University of Texas.

In preparing this book, I must first acknowledge the essential contributions of Karl Karlstrom of Prentice-Hall and particularly Prof. Richard Hamming of the U.S. Navy Postgraduate School, who more or less goaded me into writing it. My secretaries, Merilyn Gripenwaldt and Kay Clyne, have been exceptionally supportive and helpful. Ms. Lynn Frankel of Prentice-Hall has made the book a great deal better as its editor. I received many valuable suggestions from the reviewers of the manuscript, particularly Prof. Lee Cooprider of USC, Prof. Richard Fairley of Colorado State University, Prof. Ellis Horowitz of USC, Brian Kernighan of Bell Labs, Prof. Tim Standish of University of California, Irvine, and David Weiss of the Naval Research Labs.

Finally, for the many necessarily anonymous contributors of software data, a special note of thanks and a wish that they could be recognized directly as well. And I owe my family more than I could ever express in words.

A NOTE TO THE STUDENT

There is a good chance that, within a few years, you will find yourself together in a room with a group of people who will be deciding how much time and money you should get to do a significant new software job. Perhaps one or two of the people in the room will know software well, but most of them will not. They will be higher-level managers, business analysts, marketing specialists, product-line planners, and the like. Generally, they will discuss issues and make decisions in terms of such concepts as marginal return on investment, cost-benefit ratio, present value, and risk exposure.

There will also be a number of highly interested people who won't be in the room. These include the people who will be working for you or with you on the software job, and the people who will have to use the software that your team is going to produce. Whether they know it or not, their fate over the next few months or years will depend a good deal on how well you and the non-software people in the room can produce a realistic decision on the appropriate scope, budget, and schedule for your software job.

The non-software people in the room won't be able to do this by themselves; they won't have the feel for the technical software tradeoffs that you do. So it will be extremely important for you to be able to communicate with them, and understand the economic concepts that underlie the ways they have learned to think and to make decisions. If you can do this, you will have a chance to change what is often an adversary relationship between software people and business-oriented people into a relationship of mutual understanding, commitment, and trust.

In this book, I have tried to provide you with the essential concepts and techniques you will need to be able to think in economic terms as well as to think in programming terms. Besides the practical utility of these concepts, I hope you will find them as stimulating as I have in providing a new perspective on our field of computers and information processing. I've found them very helpful in illuminating such questions as:

- Why does information have value?
- Why do people commission software products?
- How do people decide what information processing products they want?
- Why is the software life-cycle organized the way it is?

And, as with other pursuits, the better we can understand why the software engineering field exists, the better we will become in practicing it.

A NOTE TO THE PROFESSOR

In this note—well, actually, with this note and the material in the book—I hope to convince you of three things:

1. Software engineering economics is a stimulating and satisfying topic to teach and study.
2. This book can be used successfully either for a one-quarter or one-semester course on software engineering economics, or as a secondary text for more general software engineering courses.
3. Software engineering economics is a significant and fruitful research area.

First, I think you will find software engineering economics an enjoyable and rewarding subject to teach. The basic relationships in microeconomics form a nice, clean, mathematical discipline. The material on risk and the value of information provides a stimulating perspective on why so many people feel they need the computers, software, and processed information our field produces. And the material on factors influencing software costs helps to explain a good many current software engineering guidelines and their impact on the software life-cycle.

Further, I don't think that one has to immerse oneself in industrial practice and jargon to find relevant examples and applications of software engineering economics. When I was at USC, I was impressed with the wide variety of computer and software applications being developed around the university, and—particularly in these days of tight university budgets—the degree of concern with computer and software costs. Accordingly, I have tried to keep the book free of industrial jargon, and to include a good many university-oriented questions and examples in order to keep the material in a familiar context.

The fundamental material in the book can be covered fairly well in a one-quarter or one-semester course. The primary learning objectives I have used in teaching such a course are to enable the student to:

- Identify the factors most strongly influencing software costs, and use these to determine the estimated costs of a software project.
- Understand the fundamental concepts of microeconomics as they apply to software engineering.
- Apply economic analysis techniques to software engineering decision situations.

An outline for a fairly ambitious one-quarter course I have given using the book is provided below:

Week	Book Chapters	Topics
1	1–4	The Software Life-Cycle: An Economic Perspective
2	5–6	Simple Software Cost Models
3,4	7–9	Intermediate-Level Software Cost Models: Factors Influencing Software Costs
5	10–12	Cost Effectiveness Analysis: Production Functions, Economies of Scale, Choosing Among Alternatives
6	—	Review, Midterm Exam
7	13–15	Multiple-Goal Decision Analysis: Net Value, Present Value, Figures of Merit
8	16–18	Multiple-Goal Decision Analysis: Constraints, Systems Analysis, Unquantifiable Goals
9	19–20	Risk, Uncertainty, and the Value of Information
10	21–22	Practical Software Cost Estimation Techniques
11	31–32	Case Study: Software Life-Cycle Cost Analysis and Control
12	—	Final Exam

For the first time teaching a software engineering economics course, the above volume of material is probably better suited to a one-semester course. A satisfactory one-quarter course could cover only the material through Chapter 18, and still satisfy the basic learning objectives reasonably well.

Such a course can be taught at either an upper-level undergraduate or a first-year graduate level. The only prerequisites are a general familiarity with the programming process (the equivalent of about two years' worth of computer science courses) and a familiarity with the basics of differential calculus. For exercising the software cost estimation models, a hand calculator with exponentials (an X^y key) is strongly recommended, although I have included curves which allow the student to work the models without a calculator, but with much less accuracy and facility.

Finally, I hope you'll get far enough into the subject of software engineering economics to become intrigued with some of the fundamental research questions it raises about the nature of the software development process, such as:

- Why does software development cost as much as it does?
- What factors make the cost of software go up or down, and how do they interact?
- What activities consume most of the cost?
- How can new software techniques reduce software cost?

In Part IV of this book, I have presented and analyzed a data base representing the costs and development attributes of 63 software projects, in an attempt to answer the question:

"How can we explain this project data in a way that will help future projects estimate and understand their software costs?"

The resulting set of cost models presented in the book represents a first step toward answering this question, but a tremendous amount of valuable research still remains to be done. A number of significant new insights can be achieved simply by further analysis of the existing 63-project data base. And a great deal more insight can be achieved through collection and analysis of further observational and experimental data. Most of the chapters in Part IV contain a final section on "Topics for Further Research" indicating some of the most promising directions we can go in illuminating the fundamental questions above. I hope you or your students will give them a try.

A NOTE TO THE PRACTICING SOFTWARE ENGINEER

During your software engineering experience, I would imagine that you have evolved a number of personal guidelines for estimating software costs and for dealing with software product and project decisions. I think you'll find this book helpful in calibrating your own rules of thumb with other people's experiences, and in providing you with some additional useful techniques for dealing with software cost estimation and software engineering decisions. I hope, also, as you go through the book, you can enjoy an experience as stimulating and rewarding as mine has been, as I began to see how various, seemingly unrelated techniques and decision guidelines I had been using in practice were actually parts of a unified framework of economic principles.

Depending on your primary interests and needs for information, you may wish to concentrate on selected portions of this book rather than read it from cover to cover. For some of the likely interests you may have, here are the most appropriate parts of the book to read.

- If you are primarily interested in improving your (organization's) ability to estimate software development costs, your best bet is to begin with Chapters 21 and 22 on software cost estimation techniques, followed by Chapters 4–9 on the software life-cycle and on the Basic and Intermediate COCOMO models.

* If you are further interested in estimating maintenance and other software-related costs, read Chapters 30 and 31.

* If you are further interested in implementing a detailed software cost estimation model and tailoring it to your organization's experience, read Chapters 23 and 29.

• If you are primarily interested in the effect of a particular software attribute (such as project personnel capability, use of modern programming practices, or language level) on software costs, read the appropriate section in Chapters 24–28.

• If you are primarily interested in improving your ability to perform software economic decision analyses, read Chapters 10–18.

• If you are primarily interested in software project planning and control techniques, read Section 31.6 and Chapter 32.

However, even if you are primarily interested in a particular topic, I would especially recommend your reading the introductory material in Chapters 1–3 and Chapter 33 on improving software productivity. These chapters provide a context and an approach for realizing a more effective, satisfying, and productive environment within which to practice your software engineering activities.

I. INTRODUCTION

1. Case Study 1: Scientific American
2. Case Study 2: Urban School System
3. The goals of software engineering

II. THE SOFTWARE LIFE-CYCLE:
A QUANTITATIVE MODEL

4. The software life-cycle:
phases and activities
5. The basic COCOMO model
6. The basic COCOMO model:
development modes
7. The basic COCOMO model:
activity distribution
8. The intermediate COCOMO model:
product level estimates
9. Intermediate COCOMO:
component level estimation

III. FUNDAMENTALS OF SOFTWARE
ENGINEERING ECONOMICS

III A. Cost-Effectiveness Analysis

10. Performance models and
cost-effectiveness models
11. Production functions: economies of scale
12. Choosing among alternatives:
decision criteria

III B. Multiple-Goal Decision Analysis

13. Net value and marginal analysis
14. Present vs. future expenditure and income
15. Figures of merit
16. Goals as constraints
17. Systems analysis and constrained optimization
18. Coping with unreconcilable and unquantifiable
goals

III C. Dealing with Uncertainties, Risk, and the Value
of Information

19. Coping with uncertainties: risk analysis
20. Statistical decision theory: the value of information

IV. THE ART OF SOFTWARE COST ESTIMATION

IV A. Software Cost Estimation Methods and Procedures

21. Seven basic steps in software cost estimation
22. Alternative software cost estimation methods

IV B. The Detailed COCOMO Model

23. Detailed COCOMO: summary and operational description
24. Detailed COCOMO cost drivers: product attributes
25. Detailed COCOMO cost drivers: computer attributes
26. Detailed COCOMO cost drivers: personnel attributes
27. Detailed COCOMO cost drivers: project attributes
28. Factors not included in COCOMO
29. COCOMO evaluation

IV C. Software Cost Estimation and Life-Cycle Management

30. Software maintenance cost estimation
31. Software life-cycle cost estimation
32. Software project planning and control
33. Improving software productivity

Part I

INTRODUCTION: MOTIVATION AND CONTEXT

The objective of this book is to equip you to deal with software engineering problems from the perspective of human economics as well as from the perspective of programming. Part I focuses on two case studies which illustrate the importance of the human economics perspective in software engineering practice.

The first case study, in Chapter 1, describes two successive attempts to develop an information processing system for the magazine *Scientific American*. The first attempt was structured from a pure programming perspective, with no consideration of economic issues. Its result was a nicely programmed system whose performance left *Scientific American* worse off than when it started. The second attempt was structured from both a programming perspective and an economic perspective. Its result was a well-programmed system satisfying all of *Scientific American*'s operational goals: reduced costs, faster subscription processing, fewer errors, reduced personnel turnover, and fewer customer complaints.

The second case study, in Chapter 2, illustrates the need for an economic perspective that goes beyond the narrow profit-and-loss concerns of the countinghouse. It describes a proposed design for an education information system for a large urban school district. The design did an excellent job of satisfying the school district's financial goals, but only at the cost of some of the school district's human goals, such as providing local attendance-clerk jobs for disadvantaged mothers with children attending the schools. This second case study demonstrates that software engineering economics cannot limit itself to pure quantitative, profit-maximizing *material economics,* but can and should be applied in the broader context of *human economics.*

Chapter 3 presents an overall goal structure and procedure for integrating our programming, economic, and human concerns into a practical approach to software engineering, within which we can apply the software engineering economics techniques presented in the remainder of this book. This approach is called GOALS, for Goal-Oriented Approach to Life-cycle Software. Chapter 3 presents the GOALS approach, provides examples of its use, and discusses its role within the overall context of software engineering.

Chapter 1

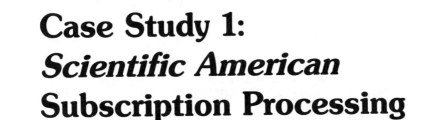

Case Study 1: *Scientific American* Subscription Processing

1.1 THE OLD SYSTEM

In the late 1960s, *Scientific American* magazine found itself with a robustly expanding number of subscriptions, an increasing subscription data processing workload, and a slow, cumbersome, unreliable manual system for subscription fulfillment.

The system being used at the time is summarized in Fig. 1–1. Incoming mail first came to the cashier's cage, where cash, checks, and money orders were sorted out. The remaining items were divided into orders and nonorders (complaints, changes of address, etc.). At this stage the items were manually counted and totaled to serve as a control for the subsequent steps.

The subsequent steps were performed by people operating at a sequence of work stations in the Subscription Fulfillment Department. These people sorted the orders by transaction type (new, continuing, gift), coded them for entry, and batched them for subsequent punched card processing. After being keypunched, the orders were processed by unit-record equipment (card-oriented tabulators, printers, sorters, etc.) to produce an initial set of bills and mailing labels. The subscriber cards were then

3

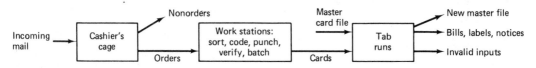

FIGURE 1-1 *Scientific American:* The old system

manually inserted into a punched card master file, which would be periodically processed to produce monthly mailing labels, annual renewal notices, etc.

This labor-intensive system became increasingly slow, expensive, unreliable, and unable to keep up with the seasonal peaks in subscription processing. The resulting delays caused an increasing number of customer complaints, and *Scientific American*'s management decided to follow the lead of many larger-circulation periodicals which had automated their subscription-processing functions.

1.2 THE PROGRAMMING SOLUTION: TOP-DOWN STEPWISE REFINEMENT

Scientific American contracted with a software house to develop a computerized system tailored to its needs. The software house personnel usually approached jobs from the programming perspective. Their previous training and experience were focused on deriving programming solutions from clearly formulated programming problems.

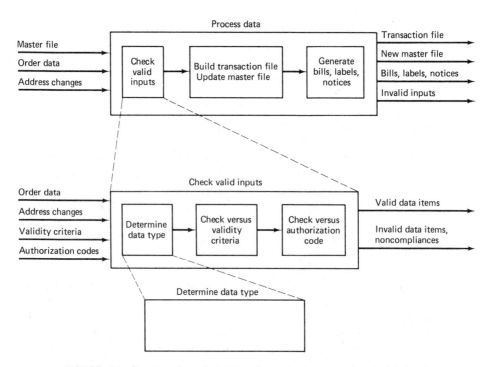

FIGURE 1-2 Programming-oriented top-down development: A typical example

So, in the *Scientific American* situation, they analyzed the situation, identified a part that had a programming solution, and applied a programming solution.

In fact, the righthand portion of Fig. 1–1 (processing and updating a master file) looks like one of the familiar starting points in current texts on top-down structured programming via stepwise refinement. As seen in Fig. 1–2, the subsequent steps in top-down stepwise refinement are to refine the top-level function in Fig. 1–1 (Process data) into a sequence of lower-level functions (Check valid data, etc.), and to continue to refine functions to lower and lower levels (Determine data type, etc.) as necessary.

The programming solution developed by the software house is shown in Fig. 1–3. It replaced the tab run data processing step with an IBM 360/30 processor programmed along the lines of Fig. 1–2. Let us look at how this solution worked out at *Scientific American*.

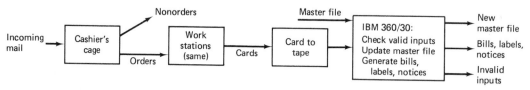

FIGURE 1-3 *Scientific American:* The programming solution

1.3 THE PROGRAMMING SOLUTION: RESULTS

The main results were

- Costs went up
- Reliability and quality of service went down
- More clerical people were required
- Employee morale went down
- Employee turnover went up

The main reason for these results was that the programming solution overlooked some key operational elements of the problem. The overlooked factors contained significant performance and economic implications. For example, trivial input errors would cause the program to reject entire batches of input, or cause a complete stop of an entire update run. When this happened, the transaction input listing had to be found and manually checked for errors. Correcting these errors involved another cumbersome process of updating the transaction file. In the old tab run system, these errors were usually discovered and fixed on the spot by the operators, who had extensive experience on errors to expect and how to fix them.

In order to avoid as many of these time-consuming errors as possible, *Scientific American* imposed additional levels of controls on the manual processing steps leading up to the computer runs. Added checks were performed to avoid problems such as renewals of nonexistent subscriptions. More complicated input forms and control sheets were developed to handle exception conditions. These all led to the added personnel, costs, delays, and reduced staff morale.

1.4 THE ECONOMIC–PROGRAMMING APPROACH

Fortunately, at this point *Scientific American* hired a person who was able to approach the problem from both the programming perspective and the economic perspective. He analyzed the overall user system with a more user-oriented, top-down approach. This involved considering the following sequence of questions:

1. What objectives is the user trying to satisfy?
2. What decisions do we control which affect these objectives?
3. What items dictate constraints on our range of choices?
4. What criteria should we use to evaluate candidate solutions? How are the criterion values related to the decision variables involved in candidate solutions?
5. What decision provides us with the most satisfactory outcome with respect to the criteria we have established?

Based on the answers to these questions, he was able to define and develop a more cost-effective solution for *Scientific American*'s needs. Below is a summary of the answers he determined.

1. What objectives is the user trying to satisfy?

   For *Scientific American,* the primary objectives were to increase subscription fulfillment speed and reliability, and to reduce costs, staff level and turnover, and customer complaints. Answering this question also involved gathering and analyzing data on primary sources of costs, errors, delays, and frustrations.

2. What decisions do we control which affect these objectives?

   For *Scientific American,* these decisions included not only computer decisions, but also decisions to use separate postal boxes for different types of orders, neatly transferring the job of sorting to the U.S. Postal Service.

3. What items dictate constraints on our range of choices?

   For *Scientific American,* there were some significant constraints, such as the need to preserve audit trails on financial transactions. However, this step was just as important for the number of items that were not identified as constraints. There were no requirements to preserve the cumbersome front-end processing sequence or to use only one post office box number, for example.

4. What criteria should we use to evaluate candidate solutions? How are the criterion values related to the decision variables involved in candidate solutions?

   Criteria important to *Scientific American* included the cost of subscription processing, the time required to respond to subscriber changes, error rates, and personnel staff level and turnover rates. In determining how these related to candidate solutions, the analysts performed comparative cost analyses similar to those described later in this book. They found that the manual

preprocessing was a major trouble spot, and that the processing workload was insufficient to justify a dedicated IBM 360/30.

5. What decision provides us with the most satisfactory outcome with respect to the criteria we have established?

The decision made by *Scientific American* was to implement the system summarized in Fig. 1–4. Separate post office box numbers were used for different types of orders, thus accomplishing a basic sort of the inputs at the post office. The first step performed at *Scientific American* was the opening of envelopes and entry of orders by a clerk using a dedicated minicomputer-based intelligent terminal. This terminal was programmed to permit interactive validation of entries; inputs were checked by the minicomputer within the terminal and flagged immediately for correction by the order-entry clerk. Entries were frequency-optimized, so that the most frequent transaction (standard order renewal) required only 21 key strokes. The resulting inputs were recorded on tape cassettes, which were taken daily to a service bureau for processing.

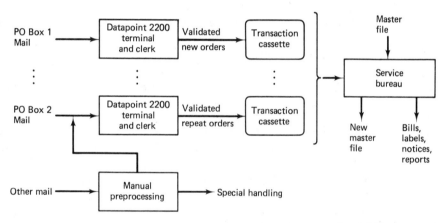

FIGURE 1-4 *Scientific American:* The economic–programming solution

1.5 RESULTS OF THE ECONOMIC–PROGRAMMING APPROACH

The sequence of questions above constitutes the essence of the economic-oriented systems analysis approach discussed in Chapter 17 of this book. The result at *Scientific American* was to install five minicomputer-based intelligent terminals, at $10,000 each, to eliminate the IBM 360/30 at a savings of roughly $9,000 per month, and to obtain service bureau processing at roughly $7,000 per month. The resulting system required significantly fewer people, so that *Scientific American* was able to amortize their investment in the terminals by the end of the first year of operation. At the end of the year the results were as follows:

- The number of clerical workers was reduced from over 40 to fewer than 20
- Clerical errors were reduced to a small fraction of the number of unavoidable "subscriber errors" (for example, duplicate orders or payments)
- Virtually all transactions were handled in less than a week, compared to frequent delays of over a month in the previous system
- The new system was handling a 33 percent increase in workload
- Subjective responses from the clerks indicated an increased feeling of job satisfaction. The single-step order entry gave them a more meaningful job to perform, with more opportunity to exercise their own judgment in handling problems and exceptions.

Thus, the economic–programming approach led to a solution meeting or exceeding all of *Scientific American*'s improvement objectives, where the pure programming solution had only succeeded in making things worse for *Scientific American*.

1.6 GENERAL DISCUSSION

The main value of the economic–programming approach to *Scientific American* was that it allowed the analysts to see the problem from more than one perspective. Consider the following saying:

> *Give a man a hammer, and he will begin to see the world as a collection of nails.*

This is what happened with the first solution at *Scientific American*. The programmer-analysts identified the portion of the problem that was a programming problem (their "nail") and proceeded to hammer it in with a programming solution.

As you begin to confront practical software engineering situations, you will find that they contain both programming problems and nonprogramming problems: operational problems; budget problems; schedule problems; problems in determining the relative priorities of users' needs. Bypassing the nonprogramming problems to concentrate on the programming problems will almost always lead to trouble later on.

The economic perspective provided in this book will help you to analyze software engineering situations and formulate more satisfactory economic–programming solutions. However, there is one additional perspective which is essential to successful software engineering. It will be the subject of the next chapter.

1.7 QUESTIONS

1.1. Suppose you had been the analyst on the second approach to solving *Scientific American*'s problem. What alternative solutions might you have considered?

1.2. Suppose you had been the *Scientific American* employee responsible for establishing and monitoring the work done by the software house. What could you have done to detect and correct the problems introduced by the software house solution?

1.3. Can you think of any other software applications which were designed and developed from a pure programming-oriented viewpoint? What were the results?

1.4. Mary Jones in the Accounting Department tells you that she has a file of personnel records, and asks you to develop a program to compute the median age of the personnel in the file. Here are four different ways you might respond:

(a) Invoke a sort routine which sorts the personnel file by increasing age. Count the number, N, of personnel records in the file. Find record $N/2$ in the sorted file, and extract its value for "age."

(b) Note that in *The Art of Computer Programming* [Knuth, 1973], Vol. III, pp. 209–220, the problem of obtaining the median is a special case of the problem of finding the tth largest of N numbers, and that R. W. Floyd has formulated a recursive method of obtaining the median in an average of $\frac{3}{2} N + \mathcal{O}(N^{2/3} \log N)$ comparisons. Spend a couple of weeks attempting (unsuccessfully) to improve on Floyd's algorithm, a day programming Floyd's algorithm, and then return to Mary Jones with some questions on the size and format of her file.

(c) Ask Mary how soon she needs the results, how much she is willing to pay for them, how many records, N, her personnel file has, and how often she will be making such runs. If N is large, and she wants results often, quickly, and cheaply, ask her if she would be satisfied with the mean value, which is much easier and cheaper to calculate. If not, work with Mary to tailor an approach to obtaining the median which is the best compromise between her various objectives.

(d) Compute the mean age, and print it out as the median. It's much easier to program, and Mary Jones will probably never notice the difference.

Rank the responses in the order of their relative concern with programming considerations, economic considerations, or other important considerations. If you were the programmer, which approach would you prefer? If you were Mary Jones, which approach would you prefer?

1.5. Suppose a user comes to you with a mathematical function and asks you to develop a program to compute the maximum value of the function. How would you respond to this request?

Chapter 2

Case Study 2: An Urban School Attendance System

2.1 PROGRAMMING ASPECTS

In the early 1970s, a team of analysts from a consulting company produced a design for a school attendance processing system, as one portion of an overall educational information system for a large urban school district. The programming aspects of the design were good: a modular, functionally-oriented program structure, and a data structure well matched to the school district's anticipated distribution of data base update, query, and batch reporting workload.

2.2 ECONOMIC ASPECTS

The economic aspects of the design were also very good; the predicted net savings to the school district amounted to several millions of dollars per year. A huge part of the savings came from the redesign of the school attendance system, which at the time was a manual system requiring up to nine attendance clerks at some schools.

The new design employed computer-readable mark-sense cards to collect attendance data and a remote data entry/printer station at each school. This system would produce faster, more consistent attendance reports while reducing the number of attendance clerks required at each school to two.

2.3 HUMAN RELATIONS ASPECTS

The reduction in number of attendance clerks now required was the major human relations flaw in the design. It turned out that most of the attendance clerks whose jobs would be eliminated by the new system were working mothers from disadvantaged areas of the city, often with children in the schools in which they worked. The attendance clerk positions were virtually their only opportunity both to work at a productive job and to keep their families together. Without these jobs, most of the mothers would have been required either to get remote jobs and lose a lot of contact with their children, or to go on the welfare rolls.

Although the narrow definition of the functions of a school system would not include providing respectable, convenient jobs for needy people, the school system administrators and the school board wisely recognized that this function was serving a valuable community need. Therefore, they strongly vetoed the automated attendance-keeping portion of the system design.

The major fault of the design team was to overconcentrate on the programming and quantitative economic aspects of the design. In the process, the more significant human relations aspects of the design for an important segment of the community were missed completely.

2.4 LESSONS LEARNED

I was a participant on this design team, and I can remember that initially this failure came as a painful blow to my self-esteem. I had been an enthusiastic follower of and participant in various "Impact of Computers on Society" activities sponsored by professional societies, which were largely speculative discussions of the long-range impact of computers on society in the large. By participating in these discussions, I felt that I was doing my bit for society. And here I was jolted into the realization that the "Impact of Computers on Society" was nothing more than the sum total of the day-to-day activities of analysts and programmers like myself, and that I didn't seem to be very good at recognizing or seeking out the significant social implications of my own designs.

On reflection, though, the main lesson learned from this experience was very positive and encouraging. It was that:

> *Each of us as individual software engineers has an opportunity to make a significant positive impact on society, simply by becoming more sensitive to the long-range human relations implications of our work, and by incorporating this sensitivity into our software designs and products.*

It takes some practice to do this well, and to learn how to balance human relations concerns with programming and quantitative economic concerns. The big thing to remember in doing so is to keep our priorities straight between programming, budgetary, and human considerations.

2.5 GENERAL DISCUSSION

The case study above shows that there is a significant difference between the *human–economics* approach to a problem and the classical *material–economics* approach. Material economics is the purely quantitative approach to economic decisionmaking initiated by Adam Smith and others in the eighteenth and nineteenth centuries and refined into a highly formalized discipline by John Keynes and others in the twentieth century. Its main guiding principles are:

- All decision criteria can be expressed in terms of a dollar equivalent.
- Organizations should make decisions in ways which maximize their dollar profit.

The main advantages of material economics are that it makes decision problems relatively easy to analyze and resolve, and that it makes it relatively easy to perform quantitative planning and control of activities. The analysis performed on the school attendance system is a good example of this.

Material economics is based on the assumption that if people and organizations act according to its guiding principles, the greatest number of people will benefit. This assumption is expressed in such concepts as Adam Smith's "invisible hand," which acts to keep wages and prices in an equilibrium acceptable to both employees and employers, or in statements such as Charles Wilson's "What is good for General Motors is good for the United States."

Recently, many people have been questioning the validity of this assumption. Books such as E. F. Schumacher's *Small Is Beautiful* [Schumacher, 1973] provide convincing evidence that the material-economics approach leads to decisions which have dangerous long-range consequences (for example, depletion of limited natural resources or degradation of everyone's environmental quality), or which force people into frustrating and meaningless work situations, such as the "cog in the assembly line" type of job (exemplified by the sequence of manual clerical processing steps in *Scientific American*'s old subscription-processing system).

Another trend which undermines the validity of the basic material–economics assumption is the global trend away from a primarily production-oriented economy toward a primarily service-oriented economy. As the basic objective of a service is to satisfy people, it is clear that the material–economics approach needs to be extended to consider the more qualitative human relations aspects involved in evaluating the effectiveness of a service.

Software engineering is playing a central role in the transition to a service-oriented economy. Thus, it is important that software engineering economics emphasize a human–economics approach, in which the purely quantitative dollar-oriented, material–economics approach is extended to include qualitative human relations considerations in economic decisionmaking. That is what we will try to do in this book.

2.6 QUESTIONS

2.1. What steps might the designers of the school attendance system take to identify the concern with the loss of attendance clerk jobs and factor it into their system design?

2.2. Given a requirement that no clerical jobs be eliminated at any school, how could the designers apply computing power to make the clerical jobs more satisfying and productive?

2.3. A few years ago, there were a number of attempts to apply material–economics techniques to improve school and college education (for example, to maximize performance on standardized tests per dollar input into the educational system). How well do you think such an approach would work? What problems might it create?

2.4. [Docherty, 1977]. A Swedish bank developed a computerized teller operation based on a management assumption that 80% of the tellers were uninterested in their work. Therefore, the system was designed to make minimum job demands on the tellers who would be using it. In general, the programming and material-economics aspects of the system were quite satisfactory.

After a year's operation, a remarkable change in the bank tellers' attitudes toward their work was discovered, largely by noticing trends in the bank's employee suggestion program.

Before the computer system was installed, the tellers suggested changes that would improve customer services. Thus, they tended to see themselves as "minibankers," whose primary concern was to satisfy the bank's customers.

After the computer system was installed, most of the tellers' suggested changes concerned added codes, new forms, or new displays to expedite computer operations. Within a year, the "minibankers" had been turned into computer peripherals, whose primary concern was to keep the computer system running efficiently. At this point, the bank's management became worried about what this was doing to their business because of the evident deterioration in customer relations.

From the changing pattern of employee suggestions, do you think that the tellers were actually uninterested in their work? What might be done at this point that would help the tellers again act as "minibankers" rather than computer peripherals?

Suppose you were a software engineer in an organization whose management proposed a similar system, based on similar assumptions about their employees. What could you do to convince them that such a system would be unsatisfactory for the organization?

Chapter 3

The Goals of Software Engineering

3.1 INTRODUCTION

On Separation of Concerns

The main conclusion of Chapters 1 and 2 is that good software engineering must accommodate human and economic concerns as well as programming concerns.

However, even without these other concerns, programming is already extremely complex. The best minds in the programming field counsel us that even further simplification, or *separation of concerns,* is necessary to make most programming problems tractable [Dijkstra, 1976]. If this is true, how can we justify making the software engineering job even more complex by requiring the consideration of additional human and economic concerns?

The answer is twofold:

1. We can't afford not to. Chapters 1 and 2 show the typical unsatisfactory results stemming from the neglect of human and economic concerns in software engineering.

2. We can largely retain the benefits of both approaches by embedding separation-of-concerns programming activities in a software engineering control loop which involves periodic review and iteration of the programming products with respect to a more general goal structure.

The essential components of this control loop are shown in Fig. 3–1. This approach to software engineering is called GOALS, for Goal-Oriented Approach to Life-cycle Software. As shown in Fig. 3–1, it is a fairly general approach which is not particularly specific to software. Its software orientation is provided by a hierarchical software engineering goal structure (shown later in this chapter as Figure 3–5) which encompasses the major goals generally desired both in the software product and in the software process.

In order to make this approach work, we need to know how to determine preferred or satisfactory courses of action with respect to a number of conflicting goals. This is what the engineering economics material in Part III will provide: techniques for

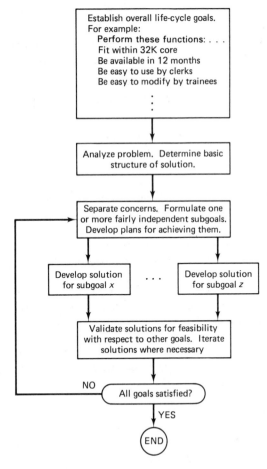

FIGURE 3-1 The GOALS approach

cost-effectiveness analysis, present value analysis, and other systems analysis techniques for goal reconciliation and multiple goal decisionmaking.

Contents of this Chapter

This chapter provides the conceptual framework within which to apply the software engineering economics techniques covered in the body of the book. The chapter addresses the following questions:

- *What is software engineering?* Section 3.2 provides a definition and a discussion of its implications.
- *Why are the human and economic aspects of software engineering so important?* Chapters 1 and 2 presented two particular cases in which they were important. Sections 3.3 and 3.4 provide evidence of their importance in general.
- *Why is a multiple goal approach necessary?* Sections 3.5 to 3.7 give examples showing why a plurality of goals is necessary for both the software product and the software process.
- *How can we cope with the broad range of goals involved in software engineering?* Sections 3.8 and 3.9 present the hierarchical software engineering goal structure and the GOALS approach, with some brief examples of its use.

3.2 SOFTWARE ENGINEERING: A DEFINITION

Our definition of *software engineering* is based on the definitions of *software* and *engineering* given in the current edition of *Webster's New Intercollegiate Dictionary* [Webster, 1979]:

- *Software* is the entire set of programs, procedures, and related documentation associated with a system and especially a computer system.
- *Engineering* is the application of science and mathematics by which the properties of matter and the sources of energy in nature are made useful to man in structures, machines, products, systems, and processes.

Since the properties of matter and sources of energy over which software has control are embodied in the capabilities of computer equipment, we can combine the two definitions above as follows:

- *Software engineering* is the application of science and mathematics by which the capabilities of computer equipment are made useful to man via computer programs, procedures, and associated documentation.

Discussion

This definition of software engineering contains two key points which deserve further discussion. First, our definition of software includes a good deal more than just computer programs. Thus, learning to be a good software engineer means a good deal more than learning how to generate computer programs. It also involves learning the skills required to produce good documentation, data bases, and operational procedures for computer systems.

The second key point is the phrase "useful to man." From the standpoint of *practice,* this phrase places a responsibility upon us as software engineers to make sure that our software products are indeed useful to people. If we accept an arbitrary set of specifications and turn them into a correct computer program satisfying the specifications, we are not discharging our full responsibility as software engineers. We must also apply our skills and judgment to the job of developing an appropriate set of specifications, and to the job of ensuring that the resulting software does indeed make the computer equipment perform functions that are useful to society. Thus, concerns for the social implications of computer systems are part of the software engineer's job, and techniques for dealing with these concerns must be built into the software engineer's practical methodology, rather than being treated as a separate topic isolated from day-to-day practice.

From the standpoint of *learning,* the phrase "useful to man" implies that the science and mathematics involved in software engineering covers a good deal more than basic computer science. For something to be useful to people, it must satisfy a human need at a cost that society can afford. The science and mathematics of human economics presented in this book provides an opportunity to learn some ways to handle the cost and human-needs aspects of a software engineering problem, and to integrate them with the computer science aspects.

3.3 SOFTWARE TRENDS: COST

The way we perform software engineering determines the cost and the quality of the software produced. This makes software engineering important because of the following two trends:

1. Software is a large and increasingly costly item.
2. Software makes a large and increasing impact on human welfare.

These trends are covered in the next two sections.

The annual cost of software in the U.S. in 1980 was approximately 40 billion dollars, or about 2% of the Gross National Product. Its rate of growth is considerably greater than that of the economy in general. Compared to the cost of computer hardware, the cost of software is continuing to escalate along the lines predicted in Fig. 3–2 [Boehm, 1976].

By now, the trend in Fig. 3–2 has become so pronounced that we can often consider the hardware as a kind of packaging for the software, which is the portion of the computer system which largely determines its value. Thus, today, the computer system that we buy as "hardware" has generally cost the vendor about three times as much for the software as it has for the hardware. Most thorough "hardware" procurements are primarily software purchases, as the buying evaluations place more weight on the software aspects than on the hardware aspects. (For an example, see

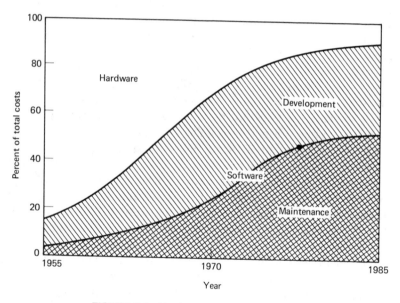

FIGURE 3-2 Hardware/software cost trends

Chapter 15.) A number of new computer systems (for example, Amdahl, Magnuson, Cambridge, and National Semiconductor) offer a product that is largely IBM software repackaged for a different mainframe. And the IBM software rental for a basic IBM 4331 system can be greater than the rental cost for the hardware [Lundell, 1979].

With respect to the overall computer and information processing industry of the future, computer software will be the dominant portion of an industry expected to grow to 8.5% of the Gross National Product by 1985 [Dolotta and others, 1976] and to 13% of the GNP by 1990 [Steel, 1977].

This growth in demand for software creates a tremendous challenge for the software engineering profession. The challenge is twofold: first, to significantly increase software development productivity; and second, to increase the efficiency of software maintenance. As shown in Fig. 3–2, the portion of effort spent on software maintenance is greater than that spent on software development. The data point for 1978 comes from a recent survey of 487 data processing installations, in which the mean percentages of effort were 43.3% for development, 48.8% for maintenance, and 7.9% for other miscellaneous activities [Lientz–Swanson, 1978].

3.4 SOFTWARE TRENDS: SOCIAL IMPACT

The growth in the demand for software results largely from the fact that as computer hardware becomes increasingly inexpensive, reliable, and plentiful, we find it more and more advantageous to automate the machine-like portions of human jobs.

Figure 3–3 illustrates this trend. It summarizes the results of three studies ([AFIPS–Time, 1971; Boehm, 1973; Dolotta and others, 1976]) on the growth of computer usage and its human impact. The most striking implication of the studies is that, by 1985, roughly 40% of the American labor force will be relying on computers and software to do their daily work, without being required to have some knowledge of how computers and software work. Thus, this 40% of the labor force will be trusting implicitly in the results produced by computer software.

Computers and software are making an even deeper impact on our personal lives. With every passing day, more and more of our personal records, bank accounts, community services, traffic control, air travel, medical services, and national security are being entrusted to the hopefully reliable and humane functioning of computers and software. And the potential threats to our personal welfare via computer crime [Parker, 1976], massive data banks [Westin–Baker, 1972; Ware and others, 1974], or computer systems that make people think and act like computers [Weizenbaum, 1976; Docherty, 1977], become more and more difficult to contain.

This increasing impact on human welfare presents several tremendous challenges for the software engineering profession. They are to develop and maintain software which ensures that computer systems are:

- Extremely reliable
- Humane
- Easy to use
- Hard to misuse
- Auditable

and that keep people, rather than computers, in the driver's seat.

These challenges, plus the economic productivity and maintainability challenges identified in the previous section, provide the main motivation for the goals of software engineering discussed in the next section.

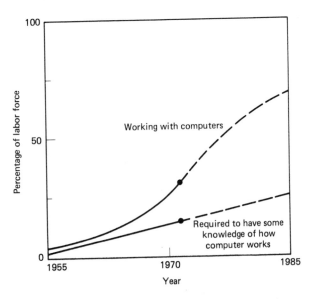

FIGURE 3-3 Growth of reliance on computers and software

3.5 THE PLURALITY OF GOALS

It would be convenient if we could set up a single overall goal for software engineering such that, if we satisfied this goal, we would satisfy all of the above challenges in the process. This is the usual situation with which you are familiar as a student. Most tests and homework assignments have a single, well-defined scale for measuring how well you do on them, and your grade in the course is generally determined by a simple weighted sum of your grades on each activity.

Unfortunately—or, on second thought, fortunately—the world of software engineering is not so simple. A number of the challenges above are in conflict with each other: for example, software development speed, program efficiency, extreme reliability, ease of use, and ease of maintenance. If we concentrate on any one of these, the others are likely to suffer.

3.6 AN EXAMPLE: WEINBERG'S EXPERIMENT

A good example of this goal conflict is provided in Table 3–1, which shows the result of a programming experiment performed several years ago [Weinberg-Schulman, 1974]. In this experiment, five teams were given the same programming assignment, but each team was given different directions about what to optimize while doing the job. One team was asked to complete the job with the least possible effort, another team was to minimize the number of statements in the program, another was to minimize the amount of memory required by the program, another was to produce

TABLE 3–1 Experiments Show that Programming Team Performance Is Highly Sensitive to Given Objectives[a]

Team objective: Optimize	Resulting Rank on Performance[b]				
	Effort to Complete	Number of Statements	Memory Required	Program Clarity	Output Clarity
Effort to complete	1	4	4	5	3
Number of statements	2–3	1	2	3	5
Memory required	5	2	1	4	4
Program clarity	4	3	3	2	2
Output clarity	2–3	5	5	1	1

[a] Weinberg-Schulman, 1974
[b] 1 = Best

the clearest possible program, and the final team was to produce the clearest possible output.

When the programs were completed and evaluated, the results were remarkable:

- Each team finished first (or, in one case, second) with respect to the objective they were asked to optimize.
- None of the teams performed consistently well on all of the objectives.

Note in particular the performance of the first team: the team asked to do the job with the least possible effort. Although this team finished first on effort to complete and second in *productivity* (lines of code produced per man-day), they finished next-to-last in the number of statements and amount of memory required to do the job, last in the clarity of their program, and third in the clarity of their output.

The primary conclusions we can draw from the results of Weinberg's experiment are:

1. *Programmers have very high achievement motivation.* If you define *good achievement* in terms of what you want from the project, programmers will generally work very hard to give you what you asked for. This is borne out by the survey data presented in Chapter 33 on factors that tend to motivate data processing people.
2. *Different software objectives do indeed conflict with each other in practice.* In particular, as seen from the first team's performance, pure concentration on minimizing the software *development* budget and schedule is likely to have bad effects for software *life-cycle* budgets, schedules, and effectiveness, because of the penalties paid in other important software dimensions.
3. *Successful life-cycle software engineering requires continuing resolution of a variety of important but conflicting goals.*

3.7 THE PLURALITY OF SOFTWARE ENGINEERING MEANS

It would also be convenient if we could present a single rule (for example, "Thou shalt program without the GO TO") which would simultaneously satisfy all of the software goals and challenges identified above. Again, (un)fortunately, the world of software does not seem to be so simple.

As a matter of fact, the situation is more like the one presented in Fig. 3–4. The software engineer is being continually bombarded with different suggested rules: Do the job top-down; prove everything correct; do the job outside-in; use independent verification and validation; do the job twice; etc. Each of these suggested rules responds to some of the challenges, but does nothing about others and actually impedes progress toward meeting some of the other challenges.

Proving everything correct, for example, does a great deal to meet the challenge of high reliability, but it does nothing to meet the challenge of making software easy for people to use, and (at least with today's technology) it often slows down

FIGURE 3-4 Sorting out software advice

our attempts to meet the challenge for higher software life-cycle productivity.* As another example, "build it twice" is a good approach for meeting the challenges of user satisfaction and application system efficiency in unfamiliar situations: The first attempt provides us with practical insights that can make the second attempt much more satisfactory. But in a situation that is already familiar, requiring programmers

---

* This is particularly true in highly volatile situations, in which a modified version of the software must be developed before the proof of the original version is complete. In these situations, much of the effort of proving the correctness of the out-of-date program goes to waste.

to build it twice will generally waste their time and frustrate their desire for achievement.

Thus, the most important software engineering skills we must learn are the skill involved in dealing with a plurality of goals which may be at odds with each other, and the skill of coordinating the application of a plurality of means, each of which provides a varying degree of help or hindrance in achieving a given goal, depending on the situation. *

The software engineering goal structure and the GOALS approach discussed in the next two sections provide a framework for acquiring these skills. The rest of the book will cover the software engineering economics skills themselves.

3.8   THE SOFTWARE ENGINEERING GOAL STRUCTURE

Figure 3–5 presents a hierarchical goal structure for successful software engineering. It indicates that if we wish to be fully successful in software engineering, we need to pay attention to two primary subgoals

1. Achieving a successful software *product.*
2. Conducting a successful software development and maintenance *process.*

Each of these subgoals has three similar components

a. Human relations
b. Resource engineering
c. Program engineering

Here again, successful software engineering is the result of achieving an appropriate balance between these subgoals, for both the software product and the software process.

Below each component is listed a number of more specific subgoals. Each of these subgoals is defined, discussed, and briefly illustrated in Appendix B.

3.9   THE GOALS APPROACH TO SOFTWARE ENGINEERING

The GOALS (Goal-Oriented Approach to Life-cycle Software) approach to software engineering is the process by which the software engineering goal structure of Fig. 3–5 can be used to guide how we specify, develop, and maintain software. The overall approach was illustrated in Fig. 3–1; a more specific stepwise procedure is shown in Table 3–2.

---

* At least, I have come to this conclusion after having spent a good deal of effort trying to prove the statement false by formulating a single unifying principle (e.g., the software-first approach, model-driven software) which could serve as the master key to all software engineering problems. Each of these attempts has been cordially but convincingly demolished by colleagues who have pointed out situations in which the principle was either not general enough to apply, or too general to provide useful guidance.

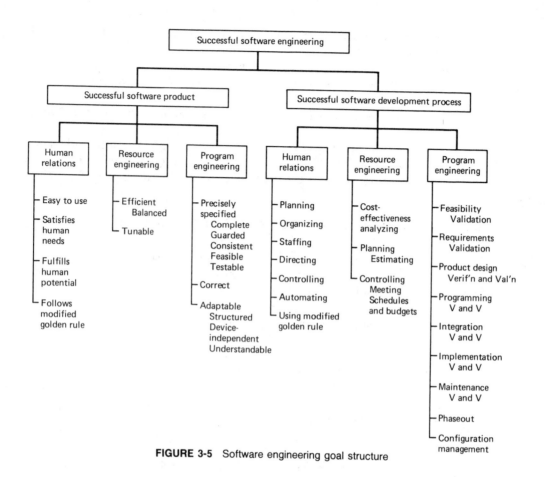

FIGURE 3-5 Software engineering goal structure

TABLE 3-2 The GOALS Approach to Software Engineering

1. Define the major goals to be achieved by the software product and the software process.
2. Use the software engineering goal structure (Figure 3–5) as a check list to assure that you have identified all your major goals.
3. Define the means by which you will achieve the goals. This includes defining a plan for:
   - *Who* is responsible for achieving each goal.
   - *When* and *where* the goals will be achieved.
   - *How* the goals will be achieved. This includes the definition of any additional sets of subgoals required, and their sequencing.
   - *What assumptions* must be valid in order to achieve the goals.
   Several levels of subgoals may be necessary to define the means in enough detail to keep the process under control.
4. Follow your plan through the achievement of your next process subgoal (or set of subgoals, if some can be worked in parallel).
5. Review both your product and process status with respect to all of your defined goals and subgoals.
6. Iterate your goals and plans as necessary.
7. Continue to perform steps 4 to 6 for successive process subgoals until the process is complete.
8. Independent of the above steps, periodically review your progress with respect to the entire software engineering goal structure. Iterate your goals and plans as necessary.

TABLE 3–3 Examples of the GOALS Approach

Step	Product Goals		Process Goals	
	Quantitative	Qualitative	Quantitative	Qualitative
1. Define goals	Decrease subscription processing cost per transaction by 25%	Improve school employees' jobs	Develop software in 12 months	Career development for test personnel
2. Define means	Automate tabulator operations	Automate attendance processing	Detailed development schedules, activity networks	Training sequence, job assignments
4. Complete next subgoal	Top levels of program design	Efficient attendance-processing design	Complete product design	Complete product design
5. Goal review	Most of cost still spent preprocessing; tab automation may increase cost per transaction	Job elimination instead of job improvement	Check schedule, completion of all milestone products: find test-plan items missing	Check test personnel readiness, performance: find people unfamiliar with test activity network techniques
6. Iterate	Analyze, redesign preprocessing, computer processing	Expand attendance-office functions, e.g., counseling assistance	Focus effort on missing test-plan items	Provide assistance, on-the-job training in preparing test activity networks
8. Review in regard to goal structure	Check plans for relocating displaced clerical staff	Check that operating budget stays realistic	Check rumor that key developer is unhappy, about to leave	Review project and career progress with test personnel

Figure 3–1 and Table 3–2 provide a somewhat abstract formulation of the GOALS approach. To provide a better feel for how the approach works in practice, Table 3–3 provides example steps that we would perform with respect to four representative goals during the product design phase of the software life-cycle. The first two examples show how the GOALS approach would have helped *Scientific American* and the urban school system project avoid their problems.

- *A quantitative product goal:* Decrease subscription processing cost per transaction by 25%.
- *A qualitative product goal:* Improve school employees' jobs.

- *A quantitative process goal:* Develop the software in 12 months.
- *A qualitative process goal:* Provide for career development for the test personnel.

In Table 3-3, the "next set of subgoals" that are completed at the end of step 4 are the product design subgoals, the overall product design, the overall product test plan, a set of draft users' manuals, and a development plan.

From Table 3-3, step 5, we can see some typical results that arise from a review of progress with respect to the product and process goals. The *Scientific American* goals review would have detected that the proposed software design did not lead to the cost reduction goal; the urban school system goals review would have detected that the proposed attendance system design did not lead to the employee job improvement goal, etc.

The GOALS approach is a form of *management by objectives* [Drucker, 1954] where the objectives consist of the multivariate goals of software engineering represented in the goal structure of Fig. 3-5. Thus, the benefits of the GOALS approach are similar to those of other management by objectives approaches. The primary benefits are:

- Establishing explicit personal commitments to product and process goals.
- Providing a framework for checking the completeness of the goals.
- Establishing a well-documented sequence of subgoals required to achieve the goals.
- Providing early warning if some subgoals are not being achieved.
- Providing checkpoints for reconciling quantitative and qualitative goals.

The set of subgoals provided for the program engineering of the software process is different from the other sets of subgoals, in that it represents a *sequence* of subgoals to be addressed in turn. These subgoals represent the key milestones of the software life-cycle, which will be the subject of the next part (Chapters 4 to 9) of this book.

3.10 QUESTIONS

3.1. Define *software* and *software engineering*. Chart the top three levels of the Software Engineering Goal Structure.

3.2. One view of the future of computer hardware and software is that the hardware will perform the same function as the paper in a book: it will be indispensable to the overall product, but the idea content (the software) will be what gives the product its value. For what classes of future computer hardware do you think this might be true? For what classes of computer hardware do you think this will more likely be untrue?

3.3. Figure 3-2 indicates that, globally, 80% of the hardware–software dollar is currently going to software. If you were planning a life-cycle budget for a new computer system, would you allocate 80% of the budget for software? What factors might make you allocate the life-cycle budget differently?

3.4. Perform a survey of several local computer-using organizations to determine their relative expenditures on hardware and software. How do they compare with Fig. 3-2? How much of their "hardware" expenditure do you think is actually being spent on vendor software?

3.5. *(Research Project)* Perform a survey of computer vendors to determine their relative expenditures on hardware and software for their products.

3.6. Evaluate a software product you use with respect to the product goals in the Software Engineering Goal Structure. What do you think may have been the cause of any deficiencies?

3.7. Your software team is about to complete the product design of a microprocessor-based patient-monitoring system for the Santa Maria Hospital. Four of your goals for the project are given below. Prepare a table similar to Table 3–3 which indicates the kinds of problems that a GOALS review of the product design activity might detect and correct.

(a) Keep the program within 32K of core memory.

(b) Develop a product easy to modify by trainees.

(c) Assure the correctness of the life-control portion of the software.

(d) Use the project as a means of educating the programming staff in microprocessor software development.

I. INTRODUCTION

1. Case Study 1: Scientific American
2. Case Study 2: Urban School System
3. The goals of software engineering

II. THE SOFTWARE LIFE-CYCLE:
A QUANTITATIVE MODEL

4. The software life-cycle:
phases and activities
5. The basic COCOMO model
6. The basic COCOMO model:
development modes
7. The basic COCOMO model:
activity distribution
8. The intermediate COCOMO model:
product level estimates
9. Intermediate COCOMO:
component level estimation

III. FUNDAMENTALS OF SOFTWARE
ENGINEERING ECONOMICS

III A. Cost-Effectiveness Analysis

10. Performance models and
cost-effectiveness models
11. Production functions: economies of scale
12. Choosing among alternatives:
decision criteria

III B. Multiple-Goal Decision Analysis

13. Net value and marginal analysis
14. Present vs. future expenditure and income
15. Figures of merit
16. Goals as constraints
17. Systems analysis and constrained optimization
18. Coping with unreconcilable and unquantifiable
goals

III C. Dealing with Uncertainties, Risk, and the Value
of Information

19. Coping with uncertainties: risk analysis
20. Statistical decision theory: the value of information

IV. THE ART OF SOFTWARE COST ESTIMATION

IV A. Software Cost Estimation Methods and Procedures

21. Seven basic steps in software cost estimation
22. Alternative software cost estimation methods

IV B. The Detailed COCOMO Model

23. Detailed COCOMO: summary and operational description
24. Detailed COCOMO cost drivers: product attributes
25. Detailed COCOMO cost drivers: computer attributes
26. Detailed COCOMO cost drivers: personnel attributes
27. Detailed COCOMO cost drivers: project attributes
28. Factors not included in COCOMO
29. COCOMO evaluation

IV C. Software Cost Estimation and Life-Cycle Management

30. Software maintenance cost estimation
31. Software life-cycle cost estimation
32. Software project planning and control
33. Improving software productivity

Part II

THE SOFTWARE LIFE-CYCLE: A QUANTITATIVE MODEL

This part of the book discusses the software life-cycle, from the earliest exploratory phases in which the feasibility of a new software product is addressed, to the phaseout stage at which the software product is discontinued. The life-cycle is presented quantitatively, in terms of the amount of time and effort required to complete each phase.

The quantitative life-cycle relationships are organized into a hierarchy of software cost-estimation models bearing the generic name COCOMO, for COnstructive COst MOdel. We will start with the simplest model, Basic COCOMO, which estimates software development effort and cost solely as a function of the size of the software product in source instructions. Then we will discuss an intermediate model, which estimates software development effort as a function of the most significant software cost drivers besides size.

These cost drivers include various product attributes (for example, complexity and required reliability), computer hardware attributes (execution time and storage constraints), personnel attributes (personnel capability and experience with the application or computer system), and project attributes (schedule constraints and use of software tools). Later, in Part IV of the book, we will present an even more detailed and accurate model, in which the effects of these attributes on each individual life-cycle phase are represented. We will also discuss at that time the observational evidence underlying each of the COCOMO cost-estimating relationships, and the overall calibration of the model.

IMPORTANCE OF SOFTWARE COST ESTIMATION

The reason for this strong emphasis on software cost estimation is that it provides the vital link between the general concepts and techniques of economic analysis and the particular world of software engineering. There is no good way to perform a software cost-benefit analysis, breakeven analysis, or make-or-buy analysis without some reasonably accurate method of estimating software costs, and their sensitivity to various product, project, and environmental factors.

Software cost-estimation techniques are also important because they provide an essential part of the foundation for good software management. Without a reasonably accurate cost-estimation capability, software projects often experience the following problems:

1. Software project personnel have no firm basis for telling a manager, customer, or salesperson that their proposed budget and schedule are unrealistic. This leads to optimistic overpromising on in-house software development, low-balling on competitive software contract bids, and the inevitable overruns and performance compromises as a consequence.
2. Software analysts have no firm basis for making realistic hardware–software tradeoff analyses during the system design phase. This often leads to a design in which the hardware cost is decreased, at the expense of an even larger increase in the software cost.
3. Project managers have no firm basis for determining how much time and effort each software phase and activity should take. This leaves managers with no way to tell whether or not the software is proceeding according to plan. That basically means that the software portion of the project is out of control from its beginning.

AN EXAMPLE

An example illustrating these problems is given in Fig. II–1 [Devenny, 1976], which shows the comparative progress of software cost estimates and actual project expenditures over the development cycle of a recent U.S. Air Force command-and-control software project. The specific project and customer are not significant, as this job's history is little different from many others in government and industry around the world, except perhaps that the Air Force has more carefully recorded and analyzed its history in an attempt to avoid similar future problems.

The initial estimate for the software job was roughly $1,500,000. After a round of competitive "best and final" estimates, the winning bidder's estimate for the job

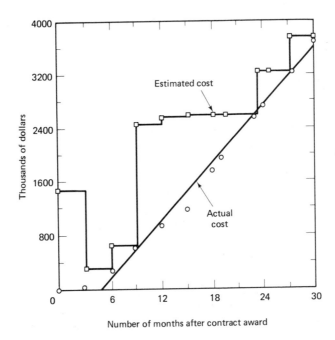

FIGURE II-1 Example software project cost history

was about $400,000, based more on optimistic assumptions and claims than on any sound software cost-estimation rationale.

The subsequent history of the project was a continuing series of realizations—at the $400-K level, at the $700-K level, at the $2500-K level, and at the $3200-K level—that the current budget was running out, but the job was not finished. Each time this happened, an increased budget and schedule was negotiated, finally resulting in a total project cost of about $3700 K, almost ten times the early optimistic estimate. Even in the later stages of the project, the cost-to-complete estimates were highly inaccurate.

"Negotiating an increased budget and schedule" sounds like a cut and dried business exercise, but it covers a great deal of painful and frustrating human drama which everybody involved wishes they had never gotten themselves into. For example:

- The users have made plans to phase out their existing operation: reassigning personnel, ordering new equipment and facilities, cutting off old supplies, integrating new operations within their system. They will not enjoy the job of reworking these problems even once.
- Project software performers are urged to work harder to compensate for problems they didn't create.
- The money to rescue the project must come from somewhere. Sometimes it comes from corporate profits or tax revenues, and people are fired from their jobs for failing to meet financial objectives. Sometimes it comes from other budgets (for

example, research, training, travel), with bad effects on people's morale and on future opportunities.
- Other projects with agreements to use this project's personnel are forced to delay their development schedules. This makes them less efficient as well as late, and often creates a similar domino effect which propagates to other projects.

All of these effects create frustration, antagonism, and sometimes lawsuits for the people caught up in the process. Much of this can be avoided by the use of reasonably accurate software cost-estimation, cost-monitoring, and project control techniques, providing a much more effective base for positive project achievement and job satisfaction.

SOFTWARE COST MODELING ACCURACY

Note particularly the term *reasonably accurate* used above in describing the software cost-estimation capabilities. It is important to recognize that we can't estimate the cost of producing 100,000 source instructions of software as accurately as we can estimate the cost of producing 100,000 aspirin tablets, 100,000 ketchup bottles, or 100,000 transistor radios. There are many reasons for this; some of the main ones are

- Source instructions are not a uniform commodity, nor are they the essence of the desired product.
- Software requires the creativity and cooperation of human beings, whose individual and group behavior is generally hard to predict.
- Software has a much smaller base of relevant quantitative historical experience, and it is hard to add to the base by performing small controlled experiments.

Given these and other drawbacks, it is perhaps surprising that any viable cost-estimation capability exists for software. However, over the past few years, a number of valuable studies and data collection efforts have provided the basis for some cost models which are, again, reasonably accurate.

Today, a software cost estimation model is doing well if it can estimate software development costs within 20% of the actual costs, 70% of the time, *and* on its own home turf (that is, within the class of projects to which it is calibrated).* Currently, the Intermediate and Detailed COCOMO models do approximately this well (within 20% of the actual costs, 68 to 70% of the time) over a fairly wide range of applications: a sample of 63 completed projects covering the areas of business, control, man-machine, scientific, support, and systems software. This is not as precise as we might like, but it is accurate enough to provide a good deal of help in software engineering economic analysis and decisionmaking.

---

* This means that the model's estimates will often be much worse when it is used outside its domain of calibration. Two previous versions of COCOMO ran into this difficulty, requiring further iteration of the model to account for the discrepancies and to expand COCOMO's applicability.

OUTLINE OF PART II

Chapter 4 provides the basic foundation of definitions of software life-cycle phases and activities which we will need to assure that our software cost estimates are meaningful. Further, it provides an economic rationale which explains why the software life-cycle phases are best ordered into the classic "waterfall" model of software development, and under what conditions it makes economic sense to deviate from this model.

Chapter 5 presents a simple model, Basic COCOMO, for estimating the cost and schedule of the most familiar type of software project, and for estimating the phase distribution of effort and schedule, including the annual maintenance effort. Chapter 6 extends the Basic COCOMO model to cover the three primary modes of software development, and discusses the model's accuracy with respect to the CO-COMO data base of 63 completed software projects (good enough for rough early estimates, but not accurate enough for definitive budget negotiations or detailed project planning). Chapter 7 presents the COCOMO model for estimating the distribution of effort among the major project activities within each life-cycle phase. It also shows how these activity distributions can be used to generate first-cut organization charts for the various phases of the project.

Chapter 8 presents the next level in the COCOMO hierarchy of cost-estimation models, Intermediate COCOMO, which incorporates the effect on software costs of a number of product, computer, personnel, and project attributes besides size. Intermediate COCOMO also covers the important case of estimating the cost of adapting existing software for use in a new product. Chapter 8 also discusses the accuracy of Intermediate COCOMO with respect to the projects in the COCOMO data base: sufficiently accurate for most detailed budget negotiation and project planning activities. Chapter 9 shows how Intermediate COCOMO can be used as a *micro* (many-component) cost-estimation model as well as a *macro* (overall-product) model, and presents several examples including the transaction processing system which will be used as the basic example for Part III of this book.

Chapter 4

The Software Life-cycle:
Phases and Activities

4.1. INTRODUCTION

This chapter provides definitions of the basic software life-cycle phases and activities. We begin by presenting the "waterfall" model of software development used as the basis of the software product program engineering goal sequence in the previous chapter (Fig. 3–5), along with an economic rationale for the sequencing of the various phases. We then discuss various refinements of the idealized waterfall model, including the concepts of prototyping incremental development, software scaffolding, and anticipatory documentation. The chapter concludes with detailed definitions of the endpoints of each phase, and of the activities carried out within each phase.

4.2 THE WATERFALL MODEL

The waterfall model of the software life-cycle is illustrated in Fig. 4–1. The original version was presented in [Royce, 1970], and was foreshadowed in various U.S. Air Force and industry publications such as [Air Force, 1966] and [Rosove, 1967]. The major overall features of the waterfall chart in its current form are the following:

- Each phase is culminated by a verification and validation (V & V) activity whose objective is to eliminate as many problems as possible in the products of that phase.
- As much as possible, iterations of earlier phase products are performed in the next succeeding phase.

The successful completion of one of the life-cycle phases in the waterfall chart corresponds to the achievement of the counterpart goal in the sequence of program

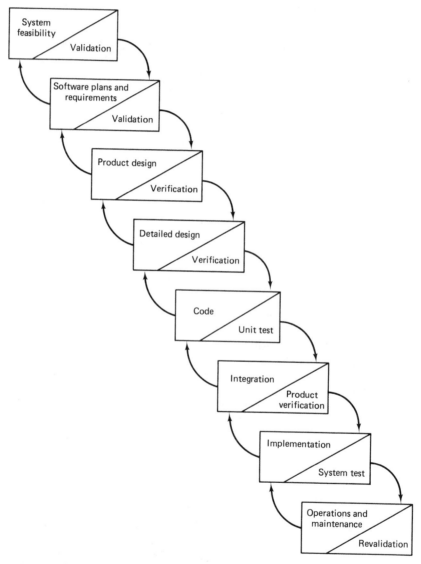

FIGURE 4-1 The waterfall model of the software life-cycle

engineering goals for the software process defined in the previous chapter (Fig. 3–5). These subgoals are defined as the achievement of the following:

1. *Feasibility.* Defining a preferred concept for the software product, and determining its life-cycle feasibility and superiority to alternative concepts.
2. *Requirements.* A complete, validated specification of the required functions, interfaces, and performance for the software product.
3. *Product Design.* A complete, verified specification of the overall hardware–software architecture, control structure, and data structure for the product, along with such other necessary components as draft user's manuals and test plans.
4. *Detailed Design.* A complete, verified specification of the control structure, data structure, interface relations, sizing, key algorithms, and assumptions of each program component (routine with ≤ 100 source instructions).
5. *Coding.* A complete, verified set of program components.
6. *Integration.* A properly functioning software product composed of the software components.
7. *Implementation.* A fully functioning operational hardware–software system, including such objectives as program and data conversion, installation, and training.
8. *Maintenance.* A fully functioning update of the hardware–software system. This subgoal is repeated for each update.
9. *Phaseout.* A clean transition of the functions performed by the product to its successors (if any).

The process of achieving these sequential* subgoals is closely bound to two additional program engineering subgoals—verification and validation (V & V) and configuration management (CM)—which are addressed in each phase of the software life-cycle. Their roles are described below.

10. *Verification and Validation.* An integral part of the achievement of each program engineering life-cycle subgoal is the verification and validation that the intermediate software products do indeed satisfy their objectives. We define the terms verification and validation as follows:

    Verification: To establish the truth of correspondence between a software product and its specification (from the Latin *veritas,* "truth").
    Validation: To establish the fitness or worth of a software product for its operational mission (from the Latin *valere,* "to be worth").

    Informally, these definitions translate to:

    Verification: "Are we building the product right?"
    Validation: "Are we building the right product?"

---

* To say that these goals are approached in pure sequence for the entire project is a convenient oversimplification. There are several situations in which it is cost-effective to modify the sequence, including prototyping (discussed in Section 4.3), incremental development (Section 4.4), and advancemanship (Section 4.4).

11. *Configuration Management* (CM). Successful achievement of this subgoal implies that the project is able at any time to provide a definitive version of the software product, or of any of the controlled intermediate products (called *baselines*) such as the requirements specification. These baselines and the life-cycle *milestones* at which they are established are fundamental to the GOALS approach. They form a vital unifying link between the management and control of the software *process,* and the management and control of the software *product.* The milestone–baseline process generally works in the following way [TRW, 1973]:

    (a) An initial version of the intermediate or final software product is developed.

    (b) This initial version is verified and validated, and iterated as necessary.

    (c) A formal product review (for example, a Software Requirements Review) determines whether or not the product is in satisfactory shape to proceed to the next phase (that is, whether or not the milestone has been reached). If not, the process reverts to step 1.

    (d) If the product is satisfactory, it is baselined (put under a formal change control process).

The baselining of the product has the following three main advantages:

1. No changes are made thereafter without the agreement of all interested parties.
2. The higher threshold for change tends to stabilize the product.
3. The controller of the configuration management process (for example, the Project Librarian) has, at any time, a definitive version of the product.

The configuration management subgoal is pursued concurrently with the other sequential program engineering life-cycle subgoals.

4.3 ECONOMIC RATIONALE FOR THE WATERFALL MODEL

The economic rationale for the subgoal-at-a-time waterfall model is based on two major premises. They are

1. In order to achieve a successful* software product, we must achieve all of the subgoals at some stage anyway.
2. Any different ordering of the subgoals will produce a less successful software product.

---

* A successful software product is one which meets its desired level with respect to all the goals in the software product goal structure in Fig. 3–5.

Premise A: Necessity for All Process Subgoals

For premise A, clearly subgoal 5 (Coding) and all the later subgoals (except Phaseout) are necessary to achieve any sort of functioning product. The key question is whether the earlier subgoals (Feasibility, Requirements, Product Design, and Detailed Design) are necessary. For many small, simple software products, it is possible to achieve an acceptable result with relatively little formal attention to these earlier subgoals, because the developer already has a clear understanding of what the user needs, and because the consequences of each programming decision are easy to foresee. However, this sort of informal approach often leads to highly unacceptable results, which can often be anticipated and avoided if the earlier subgoals have been thoroughly satisfied.

On larger, more complex projects, the lack of thorough attention to the earlier subgoals has almost always led to serious deficiencies in the success of the software product and process. Some examples are

- In two large command-control systems, the software had to be 67% and 95% rewritten after delivery because of mismatches to user requirements [Boehm, 1973].
- Lack of appropriate requirements and early feasibility analyses have led to total cancellation of many projects whose successful completion was found to be totally infeasible. Some of the more expensive examples are the $56 million Univac-United Airlines reservation system [Av Week, 1970] and the $217 million Advanced Logistics System [Congress, 1976].*

Analysis of these and other software situations have led all the recent major government studies of software problems [Boehm–Haile, 1972; Asch and others, 1975; Kossiakoff and others, 1976; Merwin, ed., 1978] to the conclusion that these earlier subgoals are essential to software product success.

Premise B: Sequential Approach to Process Subgoals

The economic rationale behind premise B is primarily presented in Fig. 4–2 [Boehm, 1976]. The solid line in this figure shows a summary of current experience on larger projects at IBM [Fagan, 1976], GTE [Daly, 1977], the Safeguard software project [Stephenson, 1976], and several TRW projects on the relative cost of correcting software errors (or making other software changes) as a function of the phase in which the corrections or changes are made. If a software requirements error is detected and corrected during the plans and requirements phase, its correction is a relatively simple matter of updating the requirements specification. If the same error is not

---

* On the Univac-United system, the initial invalidated estimate for the number of instructions executed per transaction was 9000. By the time the project was cancelled, the number had reached 146,000.

On the Advanced Logistics System, the initial unvalidated specification required 90% of the transactions to be performed in real time. During the review leading to project cancellation, the actual percentage of transactions for which users needed real-time response was determined to be about 10%.

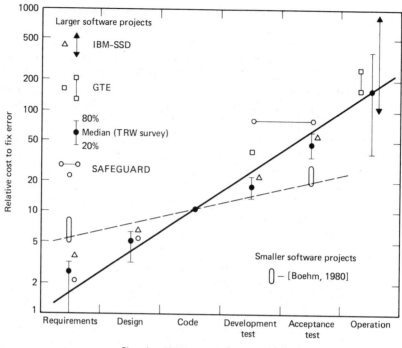

FIGURE 4-2 Increase in cost-to-fix or change software throughout life-cycle

corrected until the maintenance phase, the correction involves a much larger inventory of specifications, code, user and maintenance manuals, and training material.

Further, late corrections involve a much more formal change approval and control process, and a much more extensive activity to revalidate the correction. These factors combine to make the error typically 100 times more expensive to correct in the maintenance phase on large projects than in the requirements phase.*

The dotted line in Fig. 4–2 shows the escalation in cost-to-fix versus phase for two smaller, less formal software projects analyzed in [Boehm, 1980]. It indicates that the degree of support for premise B is less for such projects than it is for larger, more formal projects. There were two main reasons for this reduced effect in the projects studied:

1. The smaller size meant that there was a relatively smaller inventory of items to fix in the later phases.
2. The reduced formality meant that if a fix appeared to be very time-consuming, the project could generally decide to implement a simpler fix, an option not as easily available on more formal projects.

---

* The total economic impact of leaving errors to be found after the software has become operational is actually much larger, because of the added operational costs incurred by the error. See [Boehm, 1973] and [Myers, 1976] for examples.

Although the effect for such smaller projects is less pronounced, the 4:1 escalation in cost-to-fix between the requirements phase and the integration and test phase still supports premise B. It also places a considerable premium on the value of early requirements and design specification and validation, even for small projects.

Premise B thus says that if we proceed to write code without having performed the earlier requirements and design activities, there will be many more requirements and design errors in the resulting product. By Fig. 4–2, these errors will be much more expensive to correct in the later phases, leading to a less successful software project and product.

Deviations from the Sequential Approach: Prototyping Tradeoffs

It is important to note that Fig. 4–2 provides a *relative* rather than an absolute rationale for the purely sequential approach to the successive software process subgoals. In fact, it provides a tradeoff curve which indicates when it may be more cost effective to proceed with development of a first-cut prototype product rather than spend more effort pinning down requirements in full detail.

For example, consider an interactive user-application system (a decision support system for command and control or medical diagnosis). Here, the analysis of just what information processing is required may consume much more than 100 times the cost of fixing the requirements specification once the analysis is complete. If the same result could be obtained (often more reliably) by the option of developing a first-cut prototype system and letting the users try it, even the 100:1 increase in software correction cost would not keep this option from being preferable to the pure sequential approach. (An even stronger case for the prototype approach can be made for small, informal projects with their 4–6:1 cost-to-fix increase, and for problem domains in which rapid-prototyping capabilities are available.) These tradeoff curves thus provide us with a more quantitative approach to resolving the build-it-twice issue raised in Section 3.7. This issue can be explored further via questions 4–5 and 4–6 at the end of this chapter.

4.4 REFINEMENTS OF THE WATERFALL MODEL

Two refinements of the idealized waterfall model must be presented here, both because of their intrinsic importance to software engineering and their impact on the time and phase distribution of software cost and effort. These refinements are *incremental development* and what we shall call *advancemanship*.

Incremental Development

Incremental development is a refinement of both the build-it-twice full prototype approach and of the level-by-level, top-down approach discussed in the initial *Scientific American* project in Chapter 1. It holds that, rather than the two approaches above, we should develop the software in *increments of functional capability*.

Incremental development has been used successively as a refinement of the water-fall approach on extremely large software products such as the $100 million Site Defense system [Williams, 1975] and on small software products such as a 3K-source statement version of the COCOMO software cost-estimation model to be described later in this book.*

Figure 4–3 shows how the development of the COCOMO model was broken down into three successive increments. Increment 1 (the rectangles) provided a basic capability to operate and gain experience with the model: a bulk input option, the basic algorithms required to compute cost estimates, and a basic printout of the results. Increment 2 added some valuable production-mode capabilities such as the ability to file and retrieve previous runs and an input by address mode for selective modification of inputs. Increment 3 added various nice-to-have features such as query-directed input for new users and added computational features such as schedule calculations and activity breakdowns.

The main advantages of incremental development over the total build-it-twice approach and the pure level-by-level, top-down approach are the following:

- The increments of functional capability are much more helpful and easy to test than the intermediate level products in level-by-level top-down development.
- The use of the successive increments provides a way to incorporate user experience into a refined product in a much less expensive way than the total redevelopment involved in the build-it-twice approach.

The implications of incremental development to software cost estimation are primarily in the time-phasing of project effort. A modification of the waterfall chart to cover incremental development is shown in Fig. 4–4. The main result of this modification is to level out the labor distribution curve on software projects. Instead of the classical Rayleigh curve distribution of labor over time, illustrated in Fig. 4–5a [Norden, 1958; Aron, 1969; Putnam, 1978], one has a more flattened labor distribution curve, such as the curve shown in Fig. 4–5b for a recent incrementally developed radar data processing project.

Advancemanship

In a political or advertising campaign, the advance man is the person who gets everything ready before the main body of people arrive in town. This person makes sure that, by the time the others arrive, all the potential logistical, political, and support problems have been smoothed out so that the main body of people can achieve their objectives efficiently and successfully. The same sort of advancemanship is essential to a software development project or campaign. For a software project, it takes two main forms, which we call *anticipatory documentation* and *software scaffolding*.

---

* See [Basili–Turner, 1975] and [Parnas, 1976] for guidelines on incremental development.

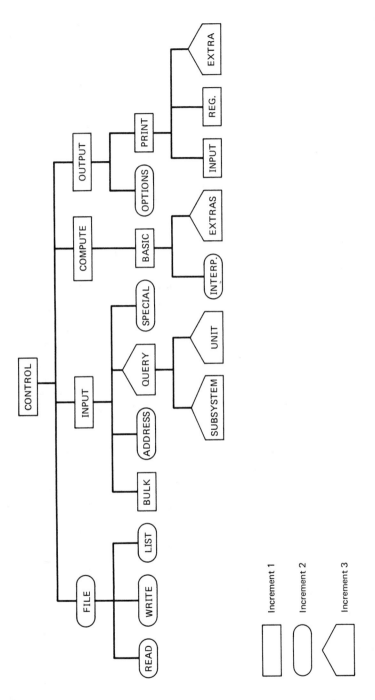

FIGURE 4.3 Integration strategy: Software cost model

Increment 1

Increment 2

Increment 3

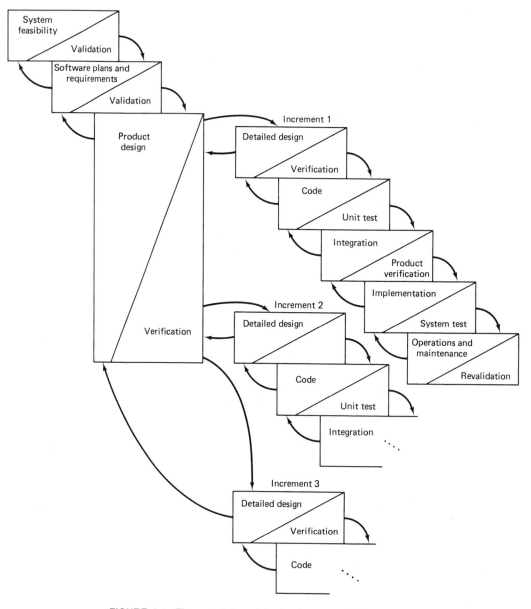

FIGURE 4-4 The waterfall model using incremental development

Anticipatory documentation. Anticipatory documentation is advance documentation prepared for two main reasons:

1. To define detailed objectives and plans for future software development activities (development plans, test plans, conversion plans) as part of the GOALS approach summarized in Table 3–2 of Section 3.9.

2. To produce early versions of user documentation (for example, a draft users' manual to be available for review by the end of the Product Design phase). This has the powerful advantage of giving the users a chance to look at how the system will affect them, *in their own terms,* and to negotiate the necessary changes before the changes become expensive—as they will later on, as shown by Fig. 4–2. (It also has the advantage of a better guarantee that adequate user documentation will be produced along with the code.)

Scaffolding. Scaffolding refers to the extra products that must be developed to make the main job of software development and V & V go as smoothly and

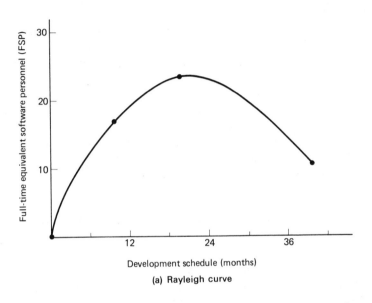

(a) Rayleigh curve

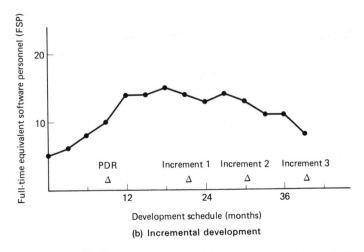

(b) Incremental development

FIGURE 4-5 Rayleigh-curve and incremental development labor distributions

efficiently as possible. As indicated in [Brooks, 1975], it can include dummy software components or stubs, miniature files, or other simulated portions of the future operational environment. Further, it can include auxiliary programs such as test data generators, postprocessors, cross-reference generators, conversion aids, standards checkers, or requirements and design language processors.

Software Economics Implications

Anticipatory documentation and scaffolding tend to have two major economic implications for the software life-cycle:

1. They reduce overall costs, primarily by reducing the entropy [Jensen–Tonies, 1979] involved in the software life-cycle: those activities which consume people's energy and talent with no constructive result. The magnitude of this reduction is estimated by the COCOMO model (Chapters 8 and 27) via the Tools and Modern Programming Practices factors.
2. They tend to front-load the software labor distribution. Acquiring test tools or writing test plans and draft users' manuals tends to increase the costs of the requirements and design phases and significantly decrease the costs of the testing and maintenance phases. The magnitude of these effects is estimated by the full phase-sensitive COCOMO model described in Chapter 23.

4.5 DETAILED LIFE-CYCLE PHASE DEFINITIONS

Table 4–1 extends the basic definitions of the software life-cycle phases given in Section 4.2 by providing detailed definitions of the endpoints marking the end of one phase and the beginning of the next phase. For incremental development, the definitions refer to the phase boundaries for each increment.

4.6 DETAILED PHASE/ACTIVITY DEFINITIONS

The cost models in this book estimate not only the total amount of effort required in each life-cycle phase, but also how that effort is distributed between eight major project activities:

- Requirements Analysis
- Product Design
- Programming
- Test Planning
- Verification and Validation
- Project Office Functions
- Configuration Management and Quality Assurance
- Manuals

For these activity estimates to be meaningful, we need definitions of the functions included within each activity. This section defines the project functions included in each activity (Table 4–2), and the tasks performed under each activity during each phase (Table 4–3).

To illustrate the use of Tables 4–2 and 4–3, let us consider a representative phase/activity item. In the basic cost-estimation model to be presented in Chapter 7, 6% of the programming phase of a project is devoted to something called CM/QA. From Table 4–2, we see that CM/QA stands for configuration management and quality assurance, and that it includes product identification, change control, program development library operations, standards development and monitoring, and technical audits. From Table 4–3, we see that these CM/QA functions are performed on the requirements, design, and code during the programming phase, along with operation of the program development library.

4.7 THE SOFTWARE WORK BREAKDOWN STRUCTURE (WBS)

For project budgetary planning and control purposes, it is very useful to organize project activity elements into a hierarchical structure called a work breakdown structure (WBS). Figures 4–6a and b present a software WBS which is sufficiently detailed and modular to cover most software project situations. It is composed of two hierarchies, which can be connected in whichever way best fits the project. These two hierarchies are:

Fig. 4–6a: *The Product Hierarchy,* which indicates how the various software components (routines, modules, subsystems, and so on) fit into the overall software system.

Fig. 4–6b: *The Activity Hierarchy,* which indicates the various activities which may deal with a software component.

The product hierarchy reflects the basic structure of the software product, as determined by the software designers. Portions of the activity hierarchy may be applied at any level of the product hierarchy for which they are appropriate. Thus, for example, a management or SX1 work element may apply to the management of the entire project (S1), or it may refer to the management of subsystem SS_{AB} (SAB1), or to the management of any other subsystem. The appropriate WBS element identifier is obtained by substituting the letter identifier in the activity hierarchy for X in SX1; thus, SAB1 (X = AB) is the WBS element for tracking the management costs for subsystem SS_{AB} and S1 (X = null) is the WBS element for tracking the management costs for the entire software system SS.

In practice, WBS elements—in both the product hierarchy and the associated activity hierarchies for each component—are defined only down to the level necessary for cost reporting and control.* An example WBS is given in Fig. 4–7 for a 40

---

* Some reasonable thresholds for establishing separate WBS elements in terms of percentage of total effort or number of man-months are:
• For small (7 man-month) projects: at least 7% or 0.5 man-month
• For medium (300 man-month) projects: at least 1% or 3 man-months
• For very large (7000 man-month) projects: at least 0.2% or 15 man-months

TABLE 4-1 Definition of Phase Endpoints

1. *Begin Plans and Requirements Phase.* (Completion of Life-Cycle Concept Review)
   - Approved, validated system architecture, including basic hardware–software allocations.
   - Approved, validated concept of operation, including basic human-machine allocations.
   - Top-level life-cycle plan, including milestones, resources, responsibilities, schedules, and major activities.

2. *End Plans and Requirements Phase. Begin Product Design Phase.* (Completion of Software Requirements Review)
   - Detailed development plan—detailed development milestone criteria, resource budgets, organization, responsibilities, schedules, activities, techniques, and products.
   - Detailed usage plan—counterparts of the development plan items for training, conversion, installation, operations, and support.
   - Detailed product control plan—configuration management plan, quality assurance plan, overall V & V plan (excluding detailed test plans).
   - Approved, validated software requirements specification—functional, performance, and interface specifications validated for completeness, consistency, testability, and feasibility.
   - Approved (formal or informal) development contract—based on the above items.

3. *End Product Design Phase. Begin Detailed Design Phase.* (Completion of Product Design Review)
   - Verified software product design specification.
     - Program component hierarchy, control and data interfaces through unit[a] level.
     - Physical and logical data structure through field level.
     - Data processing resource budgets (timing, storage, accuracy).
     - Verified for completeness, consistency, feasibility, and traceability to requirements.
   - Identification and resolution of all high-risk development issues.
   - Preliminary integration and test plan, acceptance test plan, and user's manual.

4. *End Detailed Design Phase. Begin Code and Unit Test Phase.* (Completion of design walkthrough or Critical Design Review for unit)
   - Verified detailed design specification for each unit.
     - For each routine ($\leq$ 100 source instructions), specifies name, purpose, assumptions, sizing, calling sequence, error exits, inputs, outputs, algorithms, and processing flow.
     - Data base description through parameter/character/bit level.
     - Verified for completeness, consistency, and traceability to requirements and system design specifications and budgets.
   - Approved acceptance test plan.
   - Complete draft of integration and test plan and user's manual.

5. *End Code and Unit Test Phase. Begin Integration and Test Phase.* (Satisfaction of Unit Test criteria for unit)
   - Verification of all unit computations, using not only nominal values but also singular and extreme values.
   - Verification of all unit input and output options, including error messages.
   - Exercise of all executable statements and all branch options.
   - Verification of programming standards compliance.
   - Completion of unit-level, as-built documentation.

6. *End Integration and Test Phase. Begin Implementation Phase.* (Completion of Software Acceptance Review)
   - Satisfaction of software acceptance test.
     - Verification of satisfaction of software requirements.
     - Demonstration of acceptable off-nominal performance as specified.
   - Acceptance of all deliverable software products: reports, manuals, as-built specifications, data bases.

TABLE 4–1 *(Cont'd)*

7. *End Implementation Phase. Begin Operations and Maintenance Phase.* (Completion of System Acceptance Review)
   - Satisfaction of system acceptance test.
     - Verification of satisfaction of system requirements.
     - Verification of operational readiness of software, hardware, facilities, and personnel.
   - Acceptance of all deliverable system products: hardware, software, documentation, training, and facilities.
   - Completion of all specified conversion and installation activities.
8. *End Operations and Maintenance Phase (via Phaseout)*
   - Completion of all items in phaseout plan: conversion, documentation, archiving, transition to new system(s).

[a] A software unit performs a single well-defined function, can be developed by one person, and is typically 100 to 300 source instructions in size.

TABLE 4–2 Activity Definitions

Requirements analysis	Determination, specification, review and update of software functional, performance, interface, and verification requirements. Covers all SX21 WBS[a] elements in Figure 4–6b, except SX212 (Requirements validation).
Product design	Determination, specification, review and update of hardware–software architecture, program design, and data base design. Covers all SX22 WBS elements in Figure 4–6b, except SX222 (Design V & V).
Programming	Detailed design, code, unit test, and integration of individual computer program components. Includes programming personnel planning, tool acquisition, data base development, component level documentation, and intermediate level programming management. Covers WBS element SX3.
Test planning	Specification, review, and update of product test and acceptance test plans. Acquisition of associated test drivers, test tools, and test data. Covers all SX4 WBS elements except SX413, 414, 423, 424.
Verification and validation	Performance of independent requirements validation, design V & V, product test, and acceptance test. Acquisition of requirements and design V & V tools. Covers WBS elements SX212, 222, 413–4, 423–4.
Project office functions	Project level management functions. Includes project level planning and control, contract and subcontract management, and customer interface. Covers WBS element SX1.
Configuration management and quality assurance (CM/QA)	Configuration management includes product identification, change control, status accounting, operation of program support library, development and monitoring of end item acceptance plan. Quality assurance includes development and monitoring of project standards, and technical audits of software products and processes. Covers WBS elements SX23, 24, 25.
Manuals	Development and update of users' manuals, operators' manuals, and maintenance manuals. Covers WBS element SX51.

[a] WBS stands for work breakdown structure, a concept which is defined and discussed in Section 4.7.

TABLE 4-3 Project Tasks by Activity and Phase

Activity	Phase			
	Plans and Requirements	Product Design	Programming	Integration and Test
Requirements analysis	Analyze existing system, determine user needs, integrate, document, and iterate requirements	Update requirements	Update requirements	Update requirements
Product design	Develop basic architecture; models, prototypes, risk analysis	Develop product design; models, prototypes, risk analysis	Update design	Update design
Programming	Top-level personnel and tools planning	Personnel planning, acquire tools, utilities	Detailed design, code and unit test, component documentation, integration planning	Integrate software, update components
Test planning	Acceptance test requirements, top-level test plans	Draft test plans, acquire test tools	Detailed test plans, acquire test tools	Detailed test plans, install test tools
Verification and validation	Validate requirements, acquire requirements, design V & V tools	V & V product design, acquire design V & V tools	V & V top portions of code, V & V design changes	Perform product test, acceptance test, V & V design changes
Project office functions	Project level management, project MIS planning, contracts, liaison, etc.	Project level management, status monitoring, contracts, liaison, etc.	Project level management, status monitoring, contracts, liaison, etc.	Project level management, status monitoring, contracts, liaison, etc.
CM/QA	CM/QA plans, procedures, acceptance plan, identify CM/QA tools	CM/QA of requirements, design; project standards, acquire CM/QA tools	CM/QA of requirements, design; code, operate library	CM/QA of requirements, design; code, operate library; monitor acceptance plan
Manuals	Outline portions of users' manual	Draft users', operators' manuals, outline maintenance manual	Full draft users' and operators' manuals	Final users', operators', and maintenance manuals

man-month project to develop an energy model of about 10,000 instructions. It shows some activities applied at more than one level of the product hierarchy. Management is applied both to the overall project (S1) and to the computation subsystem (SB1). System engineering is applied both to the overall project (S2, with components S21 and S22) and to the energy module (SBA2).

Uses of the Software WBS

One main use of the software WBS is to help define just what costs are being estimated by a software cost-estimation model. Without such definitions, software cost estimates and data lose precision and meaning. The dotted lines in Fig. 4–6b show that the software development costs estimated by the COCOMO model presented in this book cover all of the work performed in the first five major activity elements (SX1–SX5), with the exception of feasibility studies—the work performed in the feasibility phase of the software life-cycle—and requirements analysis, which is estimated as a separate quantity apart from software development.

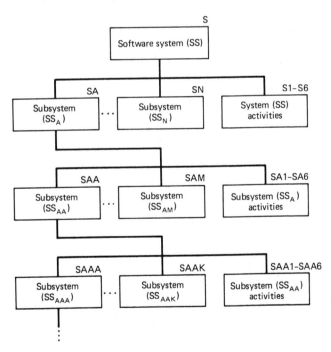

FIGURE 4-6(a) Software work breakdown structure: Product hierarchy

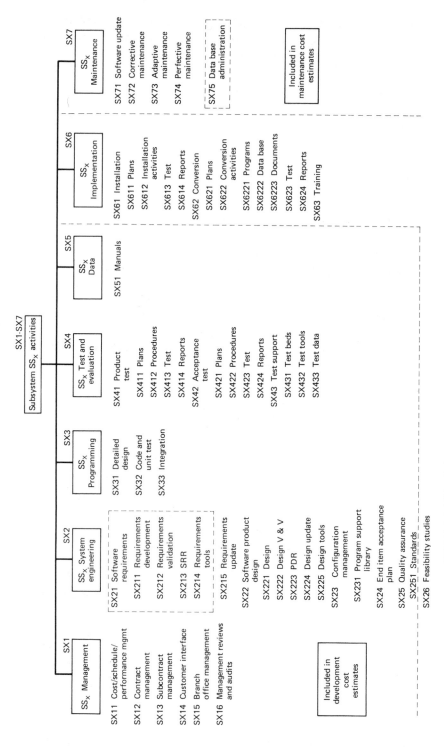

FIGURE 4-6(b) Software work breakdown structure (WBS): Activity hierarchy

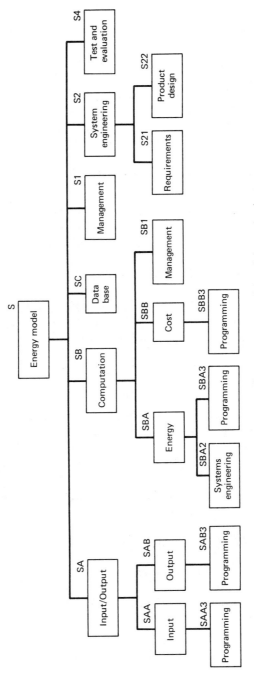

FIGURE 4-7 Example software work breakdown structure

The other main use of the WBS is to serve as the basis for software cost collection and reporting. Each of the WBS elements can be given a project budget and a job number for people to use in reporting the amount of time they have spent on different project activities. This data can be processed by a project management information system to give managers an understanding of how the expenditure for each task is progressing with respect to its budget. More detailed explanations of how this works are given in Chapter 32.

Further, if an organization collects its software costs according to a standard WBS, it will be accumulating an extremely valuable data base on its software cost distribution, which can be used to refine and tailor a general cost-estimation model to the particular features of the organization.

4.8 SOFTWARE MAINTENANCE

Software maintenance is defined as the process of modifying existing operational software while leaving its primary functions intact. The definition *includes* the following types of activity within the category of software maintenance:

- Redesign and redevelopment of smaller portions (less than 50% new code) of an existing software product
- Design and development of smaller interfacing software packages which require some redesign (of less than 20%) of the existing software product
- Modification of the software product's code, documentation, or data base structure

This definition *excludes* the following types of activity from the category of software maintenance:

- Major redesign and redevelopment (more than 50% new code) of a new software product performing substantially the same functions
- Design and development of a sizable (more than 20% of the source instructions comprising the existing product) interfacing software package which requires relatively little redesign of the existing product
- Data processing system operations, data entry, and modification of values in the data base

Software maintenance can be classified into two main categories:

1. Software *update*, which results in a changed functional specification for the software product.
2. Software *repair*, which leaves the functional specification intact.

In turn, software repair can be classified into three main subcategories [Swanson, 1976]:

2a. Corrective maintenance (of processing, performance, or implementation failures)

2b. Adaptive maintenance (to changes in the processing or data environment)

2c. Perfective maintenance (for enhancing performance or maintainability)

4.9 QUESTIONS

4.1. Many of your courses have prerequisites: courses which must be passed before you can take the course in question. To what extent is the satisfactory completion of a software requirements specification a prerequisite for performing software design and programming?

4.2. Define the eight major phases of the software life cycle.

4.3. The solid-line cost-to-fix curve in Fig. 4–2 is based on data from medium-to-large software projects. Give reasons why you think the steep slope of the curve would increase or decrease on:

(a) small projects (similar to the dotted line in Fig. 4–2)

(b) projects fully using structured programming methods

(c) software being developed for a complex distributed microprocessor system

(d) projects using application generators or other rapid-prototyping capabilities

4.4. *(Research Project)* Consider your answers to Question 4.3 as hypotheses to test via observation and experiment. Collect and analyze data to test these and related hypotheses about the cost-to-fix curve. Formulate and test an underlying model of the software development process which explains your results.

4.5. Suppose you are a project manager for Structured Software, Inc., and your team is currently specifying the man-machine interface requirements for a large urban fire department command and control system. The project's cost-to-fix curve is given by the solid line in Fig. 4–2. You have three options:

(a) *Build and Fix.* Pick the most convenient man-machine interface to develop. Build the resulting software product, try it, and fix the resulting problems you find in practice.

(b) *Sample Protocols.* Develop some sample protocols and scenarios of the product in use. Try them with the fire department personnel in the requirements phase; find and fix the resulting problems. Build the resulting product; find and fix the remaining problems.

(c) *Full Requirements Analysis.* Perform a very detailed analysis of the man-machine interface. Find and fix most of the problems in the requirements phase, leaving only a few problems to fix during operations.

Each of these options has a different distribution of problems found and fixed during the requirements phase and the operations phase. The number of problems found and fixed, and the associated costs per problem, are given in Table 4–4. What are the overall costs of eliminating man-machine interface problems for each option? Which option is best from a cost standpoint? What other factors might be important in choosing which option to use?

4.6. In Question 4.5, how would your answers to the first two questions change in each of the following situations:

(a) The cost-to-fix per problem in the operations phase were $10,000?

(b) The cost-to-find per problem in the requirements phase were $6000 for option b and $10,000 for options a and c?

TABLE 4–4

Option	Requirements Phase			Operations Phase		
	Problems Found and Fixed	Cost to Find per Problem	Cost to Fix per Problem	Problems Found and Fixed	Cost to Find per Problem	Cost to Fix per Problem
(a) Build and fix	0	$5000	$100	100	0	$5000
(b) Sample protocols	70	$3000	$100	50	0	$5000
(c) Full requirements analysis	100	$5000	$100	10	0	$5000

(c) Option b finds 50 problems in the requirements phase and 70 problems in the operations phase?

4.7. The use of incremental development depends a great deal on a factor called *software breakage:* the amount of software which is broken because of unforeseen incompatibilities, and must be replaced during the development of a later increment. Suppose you were the Manager of Electronic Test Operations for VLSI, Inc., and you had two software development options for developing a new product test support system:

(a) Developing the entire software package for $150,000, and then having to spend $75,000 revising it to reflect lessons learned in test operations.

(b) Developing the software in three $50,000 increments, with added breakage costs of $20,000 in the increment just previous, and $10,000 in earlier increments (that is, the cost of breakage in increment 1 during development of increment 3).

What are the total costs for each option? Which is best? Which would be best if the breakage costs were $30,000 per completed increment for all previous increments?

4.8. Define the eight major software project activities.

4.9. Your company, Query Systems, Inc., is developing a small (2500 instruction 6 man-month) data base query software product for a real estate company. The project is estimated to have the following characteristics:
- Project management: 1 man-month
- Product system engineering: 1 man-month (25% requirements, 75% product design)
- Test and evaluation: 1 man-month (33% each for product test, acceptance test, and test tools)
- Query subsystem: 2 man-months (30% system engineering, 70% programming)
- Update subsystem: 1 man-month (30% system engineering, 70% programming)

Set up a work breakdown structure for tracking and controlling project costs. Use the 7% (0.5 man-month) minimum threshold for WBS elements.

Chapter 5

The Basic COCOMO Model

5.1 INTRODUCTION

Some Estimating Equations and Issues

This chapter presents an equation for estimating the number of man-months (MM) required to develop the most common type of software product, in terms of the number of thousands of delivered source instructions (KDSI) in the software product:

$$MM = 2.4(KDSI)^{1.05} \qquad (5\text{--}1)$$

It also presents an equation for estimating the development schedule (TDEV) in months:

$$TDEV = 2.5(MM)^{0.38} \qquad (5\text{--}2)$$

However, before we can put these equations to much practical use, we need to resolve a number of significant definitional issues, such as:

- *Which instructions count as delivered source instructions?* For example, do they include comments, which often comprise over half the source text for the program?
- *Which man-months are included in the estimate?* For example, do they include the effort of program librarians, secretaries, computer operators, and janitors?
- *Which phases are included in "development"?* For example, do they include the plans and requirements phase and the implementation phase?
- *What classes of projects are covered by the estimating equations?* Do they cover all types of project environments, projects which are poorly managed, frequently redirected, etc.?

Some of these issues have been largely covered by the phase, activity, and work breakdown structure definitions given in the previous chapter. The others will be covered in Section 5.2 before we proceed to discuss the equations themselves.

Versions of the COCOMO Model

The COnstructive COst MOdel (COCOMO) provided in this book exists in a hierarchy of increasingly detailed and accurate forms. The equations above present the top-level model, Basic COCOMO, in the version applicable to the large majority of software projects: small-to-medium size products developed in a familiar in-house software development environment. Other aspects of Basic COCOMO, including phase distributions of effort, schedule, and activities, are covered in the next three chapters.

Basic COCOMO is good for quick, early, rough order of magnitude estimates of software costs, but its accuracy is necessarily limited because of its lack of factors to account for differences in hardware constraints, personnel quality and experience, use of modern tools and techniques, and other project attributes known to have a significant influence on software costs. Chapters 8 and 9 will present Intermediate COCOMO, which includes such factors in terms of their aggregate impact on overall project costs. A later part of the book (Part IV) will present the detailed COCOMO model, which accounts for the influence of these additional factors on individual project phases.

5.2 DEFINITIONS AND ASSUMPTIONS

The software life-cycle phase and activity definitions required by COCOMO were presented in the previous chapter. Below are some additional definitions and assumptions underlying the use of COCOMO.

1. The primary cost driver is the number of delivered source instructions (DSI) developed by the project. These are defined as follows:

   Delivered. This term is generally meant to exclude nondelivered support software such as test drivers. However, if these are developed with the same care as delivered software, with their own reviews, test plans, documentation, etc., then they should be counted.

Source Instructions. This term includes all program instructions created by project personnel and processed into machine code by some combination of preprocessors, compilers, and assemblers. It *excludes* comment cards and unmodified utility software. It *includes* job control language, format statements, and data declarations. *Instructions* are defined as *lines of code* or *card images.* Thus, a line containing two or more source statements counts as one instruction; a five-line data declaration counts as five instructions.

2. The development period covered by COCOMO cost estimates begins at the beginning of the product design phase (successful completion of a software requirements review; Table 4–1), and ends at the end of the integration and test phase (successful completion of a software acceptance review). Costs and schedules of other phases are estimated separately.

3. COCOMO cost estimates cover those and only those activities indicated on the software work breakdown structure (WBS) shown in Fig. 4–6b. Thus, for example, the development estimates cover management and documentation efforts, but exclude some efforts which take place during the development period, such as user training, installation planning, and conversion planning. Chapter 31 provides some estimating relationships which cover these activities.

4. COCOMO estimates cover all direct-charged labor on the project for the activities indicated in assumption 3 above. Thus, they include project managers and program librarians, but exclude computer center operators, personnel-department personnel, secretaries, higher management, janitors, and so on.

5. *A COCOMO man-month consists of 152 hours of working time.* This has been found to be consistent with practical experience with the average monthly time off due to holidays, vacation, and sick leave. To convert a COCOMO estimate in man-months to other units, use the following:

Man-hours: multiply by 152
Man-days: multiply by 19
Man-years: divide by 12

6. COCOMO estimates assume that the project will enjoy good management by both the developer and the customer. For example, the amount of nonproductive slack time is kept small by the manager and the customer.

7. COCOMO assumes that the requirements specification is not substantially changed after the plans and requirements phase. Some refinements and reinterpretations will be inevitable, but any significant modifications or added capabilities should be covered by a revised cost estimate.

8. The detailed COCOMO model assumes that the influence of the software cost drivers is phase dependent. Basic COCOMO and Intermediate COCOMO do not, except for distinguishing between development and maintenance.

9. The phase costs include all costs incurred during the phase. Thus, as seen in Fig. 5–1, the costs of updating the integration and test plan and completing the acceptance test plan are included in the detailed design phase costs.

Figure 5–1 also summarizes the underlying software development process model which COCOMO assumes will be used on the project. This process emphasizes the following major features:

1. Careful definition and validation of the software requirements specification by a relatively small number of people prior to significant work on the full system design.

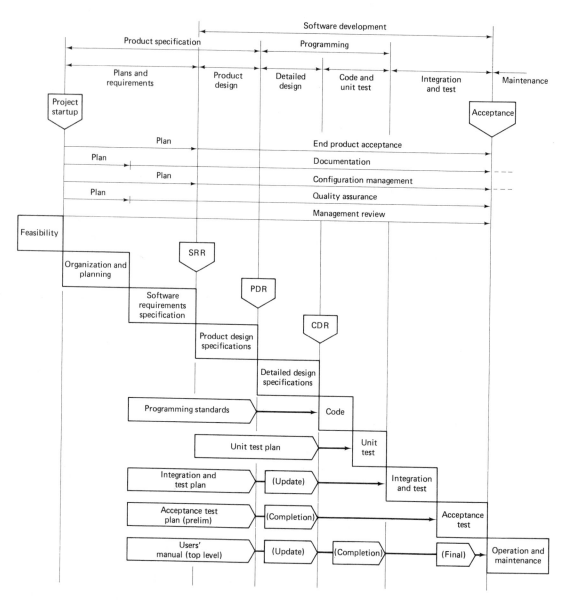

FIGURE 5-1 Software project phases, activities, and milestones

2. Careful definition and validation of the software system design down to the unit level (see Table 4–1) by a somewhat larger, but still relatively small group of people, prior to significant work on detailed design and coding.
3. Detailed design, coding, and unit test performed by a larger group of programmers in parallel, working within a firmly baselined system design framework, often with respect to a planned incremental development.
4. Integration and test of each increment is based on a significant amount of early test planning, and the elimination of almost all intraunit faults via thorough walkthroughs and unit testing.
5. Much of the documentation effort (for example, draft users' manuals) is performed early, in order to provide users (and developers) some early feedback on the operational nature of the product.

Man-Month versus Dollar Estimates

COCOMO avoids estimating labor costs in dollars because of the large variations between organizations in what is included in labor costs (unburdened by overhead costs? burdened? including pension plans? office rental? profits?), and because man-months are a more stable quantity than dollars, given current inflation rates and international money fluctuations.

In order to convert COCOMO man-month estimates into dollar estimates, the best compromise between simplicity and accuracy is to apply a different average dollar per man-month figure for each major phase, to account for inflation and the differences in salary level of the people required for each phase. For example, an average man-month might cost $6000 for the plans and requirements and product design phases, $5000 for the detailed design, code, and unit test phases, and $5500 for the integration-and-test and maintenance phases.

5.3 DEVELOPMENT EFFORT AND SCHEDULE

We have now established enough of a framework of software life-cycle definitions to give us a clear idea of what we are estimating when we arrive at an estimate. This section provides the fundamental COCOMO effort and schedule equations for the most common type of software project: the small-to-medium size product developed in a familiar, in-house, organic software development environment. For this form of organic-mode software development, this section also presents tables for estimating how the effort and schedule are distributed by phase.

The Basic COCOMO Effort and Schedule Equations: Organic Mode

Here again are the estimation equations presented at the beginning of this chapter. The basic effort equation for an organic-mode software project is:

$$MM = 2.4(KDSI)^{1.05} \qquad (5-1)$$

The quantity KDSI is the number of thousands of delivered source instructions in the software product, as defined in Section 5.2. The quantity MM is the number of man-months estimated for the software development phase of the life-cycle, subject to the definitions and assumptions given in Section 5.2. A graph of the estimates given by the basic effort equation, and the corresponding productivity estimates in DSI/MM, is given in Fig. 5-2.*

The basic schedule equation for an organic-mode software project is:

$$TDEV = 2.5(MM)^{0.38} \qquad (5\text{–}2)$$

The quantity TDEV is the number of months estimated for software development, using the same definitions and assumptions as for the basic effort equation. A graph of the estimates given by the basic schedule equation is given in Fig. 5-3.

Example Estimates

Du Bridge Chemical, Inc., a large chemical products company, is planning to develop a new computer program to keep track of raw materials. It will be developed by an in-house team of programmers and analysts who have been developing similar

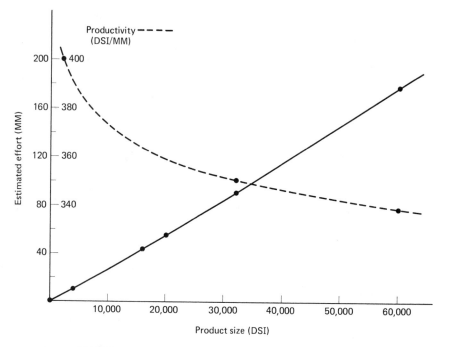

FIGURE 5-2 Basic COCOMO effort estimates: Organic mode

* In using COCOMO, you will find it valuable to have a calculator which performs exponentiation functions. However, curves such as those in Fig. 5–2 are provided so that you can still use the model without such a calculator.

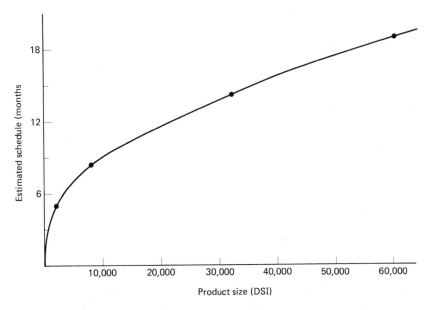

FIGURE 5-3 Basic COCOMO schedule estimates: Organic mode

programs for several years. Thus, it is a good example of an organic-mode software project. An initial study has determined that the size of the program will be roughly 32,000 delivered source instructions (32 KDSI). From our basic equations, we can then estimate the following characteristics of the project:

$$\text{Effort:} \quad MM = 2.4\,(32)^{1.05} = 91 \text{ man-months}$$

$$\text{Productivity:} \quad \frac{32,000 \text{ DSI}}{91\text{MM}} = 352\,\frac{\text{DSI}}{\text{MM}}$$

$$\text{Schedule:} \quad TDEV = 2.5\,(91)^{0.38} = 14 \text{ months}$$

$$\text{Average staffing:} \quad \frac{91 \text{ man-months}}{14 \text{ months}} = 6.5 \text{ FSP}$$

The quantity FSP stands for Full-time-equivalent Software Personnel, a measure of the equivalent number of people working on the project at a given time.

Project Profiles

Table 5–1 gives similar profiles for a set of standard-size organic-mode projects:

Small:	2,000 DSI
Intermediate:	8,000 DSI
Medium:	32,000 DSI
Large:	128,000 DSI

TABLE 5-1 Overall Project Profiles: Organic-Mode Projects

Product Size	Effort	Productivity	Schedule (months)	Average Staffing
Small: 2 KDSI	5.0 MM	400 DSI/MM	4.6	1.1 FSP
Intermediate: 8 KDSI	21.3 MM	376 DSI/MM	8.0	2.7 FSP
Medium: 32 KDSI	91.0 MM	352 DSI/MM	14.0	6.5 FSP
Large: 128 KDSI	392.0 MM	327 DSI/MM	24.0	16.0 FSP

Thus, we can see that a small project is essentially a one-person job,* while a large project requires an average staffing level of 16 people. In the next section, we will see how these people are typically distributed throughout the software development cycle.

5.4 PHASE DISTRIBUTION

Table 5-2 presents the percentage distribution of the basic software effort and schedule within the phases of the development cycle defined in Table 4-1 and Fig. 5-1. The phase distribution varies as a function of the size of the product. Larger software projects require relatively more time and effort to perform integration and test activities, and are able to compress the programming portion of the schedule by having larger numbers of people programming components in parallel. Smaller software projects have a more uniform, flat distribution of labor throughout the development cycle, and have relatively more resources devoted to the phases other than integration and test. (Both large and small organic-mode software projects have relatively flat labor distributions compared to the other modes of software development, to be discussed in Chapter 6.)

As an example of the use of Table 5-2, consider the medium size (32 KDSI) Du Bridge Chemical, Inc., raw materials inventory project, which we determined from the Basic COCOMO effort and schedule equations above would require a 91-MM effort and a 14-month schedule. Suppose we wanted an estimate of the amount of time, amount of effort, and average number of full-time-equivalent software personnel (FSP) we would need for the programming phase of this project. By the effort portion of Table 5-2, the programming phase requires 62% of the total effort, or:

$$(0.62)(91MM) = 56MM$$

By the schedule portion of Table 5-2, the programming phase requires 55% of the total schedule, or

$$(0.55)(14 \text{ months}) = 7.7 \text{ months}$$

* Note that the 5 man-month estimate for a small project refers to the development of a 2000-DSI *software product,* including thorough documentation, testing, error-proofing, user-tailoring, etc. Many people have developed 2000-DSI *personal software* programs without such product features in fewer man-months. As indicated in [Brooks, 1975], a software product requires about three times as much effort to complete as an equivalent-sized personal software program.

TABLE 5–2 Phase Distribution of Effort and Schedule: Organic Mode

Phase	Product Size			
	Small (2 KDSI)	Intermediate (8 KDSI)	Medium (32 KDSI)	Large (128 KDSI)
Effort				
Plans and requirements	6%	6%	6%	6%
Product design	16	16	16	16
Programming	68	65	62	59
Detailed design	26	25	24	23
Code and unit test	42	40	38	36
Integration and test	16	19	22	25
Total	100%	100%	100%	100%
Schedule				
Plans and requirements	10%	11%	12%	13%
Product design	19	19	19	19
Programming	63	59	55	51
Integration and test	18	22	26	30
Total	100%	100 %	100%	100%

The average number of people (FSP) required for the programming phase is

$$\frac{56\ \text{MM}}{7.7\ \text{months}} = 7.3\ \text{FSP}$$

5.5 NOMINAL PROJECT PROFILES

Similarly, we can calculate the effort, schedule, and average FSP required for the other phases of the medium size (32 KDSI) project by using the percentages in Table 5–2. This information, and its counterparts for the other standard size projects, is presented in Table 5–3. The basic project profiles in Table 5–3 also contain additional information such as the average labor on the project in FSP, the average labor per phase as a percentage of project average labor, and the overall project productivity (total DSI/total effort for development in MM).

From Table 5–3, we can begin to get a feel for the relative sizes of the different phases and projects, and for the magnitude of some of the effects of going from smaller scale to larger scale projects. For example, if we are going to develop a product that is four times larger than our largest product so far (say, 32 KDSI versus 8 KDSI), we should expect our overall project productivity in DSI/MM to drop to 94% of our previous productivity (352 DSI/MM versus 376).

This decrease in productivity on larger projects is called a *diseconomy of scale*

TABLE 5-3. Basic Project Profiles: Organic Mode

Quantity	Product size			
	Small (2 KDSI)	Intermediate (8 KDSI)	Medium (32 KDSI)	Large (128 KDSI)
Total Effort (MM)	5.0	21.3	91	392
Plans and Requirements	0.3	1.3	5	24
Product Design	0.8	3.4	15	63
Programming	3.4	13.8	56	231
Detailed Design	1.3	5.3	22	90
Code and Unit Test	2.1	8.5	34	141
Integration and Test	0.8	4.1	20	98
Total Schedule (months)	4.6	8	14	24
Plans and Requirements	0.5	0.9	1.7	3.1
Product Design	0.9	1.5	2.7	4.6
Programming	2.9	4.7	7.7	12.2
Integration and Test	0.8	1.8	3.6	7.2
Average Personnel (FSP)				
Plans and Requirements	0.6	1.4	2.9	8
Product Design	0.9	2.3	5.6	14
Programming	1.2	2.9	7.3	19
Integration and Test	1.0	2.3	5.6	14
Project Average (FSP)	1.1	2.7	6.5	16
Percent of Project Average				
Plans and Requirements	60%	55%	50%	46%
Product Design	84	84	84	84
Programming	108	110	113	116
Integration and Test	89	87	85	83
Productivity (DSI/MM)	400	376	352	327

in economic terms. Economies and diseconomies of scale will be discussed further in Chapter 11. The main reasons why larger software products incur diseconomies of scale are the following:

1. Relatively more product design is required to develop the thorough unit-level specifications required to support the parallel activity of a larger number of programmers.
2. Relatively more effort is required to verify and validate the larger requirements and design specifications.
3. Even with a thoroughly defined specification, programmers on a large project will spend relatively more time communicating and resolving interface issues.

4. Relatively more integration activity is required to put the units together.

5. In general, relatively more extensive testing is required to verify and validate the software product.

6. Relatively more effort will be required to manage the project.

We can also see from the percent of average portion of Table 5–3 that the shape of the labor curve for larger projects does have a somewhat higher peak of parallel effort in the programming phase than do the smaller projects. This is illustrated in Fig. 5–4, which compares the labor curves (relative to average personnel level) for small, medium, and large organic-mode projects.

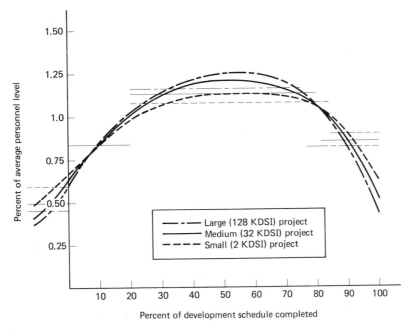

FIGURE 5-4 Basic labor distribution: Organic mode projects

5.6 THE RAYLEIGH DISTRIBUTION

The COCOMO average labor level estimates for each software development phase yield the straight line, step-function labor distributions shown in Fig. 5–4. Actually, the level of full-time-equivalent software personnel active on a project tends more to follow a continuous curve, particularly on large projects, where the instantaneous full-time commitment of a large number of people is an unlikely event. Examples of such curves are also shown in Fig. 5–4.

There is a mathematical function which, if properly used, yields good approximations to the actual labor curves on many types of software projects, including the organic-mode projects illustrated in Fig. 5–4. This function is the Rayleigh distribution function, given in terms of the COCOMO variables FSP and MM by the formula:

$$FSP = MM \left(\frac{t}{t_D^2}\right) e^{-\left(t^2/2\, t_D^2\right)} \tag{5-3}$$

The variable t represents the month for which the FSP level is being calculated, and the quantity t_D represents the month at which the project achieves its peak effort.

It has been shown by Norden [Norden, 1958; Norden, 1970] that the Rayleigh distribution gives a good approximation to the labor distributions for many types of research and development activities. Norden's results were extended by Putnam [Putnam, 1976; Putnam, 1978], who showed that the labor distributions for a number of software projects were approximated rather well by the Rayleigh distribution. Putnam has also derived relationships between software development effort and software development schedules, based on analysis of the Rayleigh distribution. These topics will be discussed in Chapters 6 and 27.

Application to Organic-Mode Software Development Projects

Figure 5–5 shows the Rayleigh distribution as calculated for the medium-size (32 KDSI) Du Bridge Chemical software development project, with MM = 91 and $t_D = 7$ months, or half of the 14-month estimated development time.

It is evident that the shape of the Rayleigh distribution in Fig. 5–5 is not a close approximation to the shape of the labor distribution curves for any of the organic-mode software projects shown in Fig. 5–4. This is largely because an organic-mode software project generally starts with a good many of the project members at work right away, instead of the slower buildup indicated by the Rayleigh distribution; and also because of the long tail off to the right of the Rayleigh distribution.

However, the central portion of the Rayleigh distribution provides a good approximation to the labor curves of organic-mode software projects. If we use only the

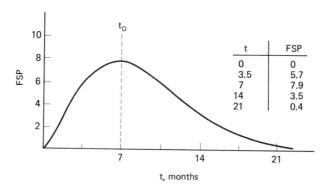

t	FSP
0	0
3.5	5.7
7	7.9
14	3.5
21	0.4

FIGURE 5-5 Rayleigh distribution for $t_D = 7$, MM = 91.

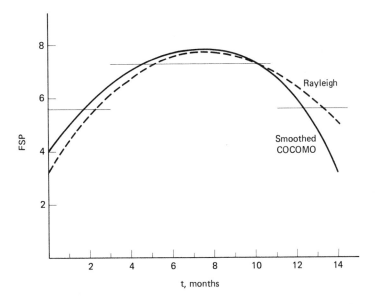

FIGURE 5-6 Rayleigh approximation to COCOMO estimates for Du Bridge chemical project (32 KDSI, 91 MM, 14 months development)

portion of the Rayleigh distribution between 0.3 t_D and 1.7 t_D to represent the full development cycle from 0 to TDEV in the Basic COCOMO model, we arrive at the labor estimating equation:

$$\text{FSP} = \text{MM} \left(\frac{0.15\,\text{TDEV} + 0.7t}{0.25\,(\text{TDEV})^2} \right) e^{-\frac{(0.15\,\text{TDEV} + 0.7\,t)^2}{0.5(\text{TDEV})^2}} \tag{5–4}$$

As seen in Fig. 5–6, this equation provides a reasonably good approximation to the smoothed labor distribution obtained from the Basic COCOMO estimate for the medium-size, 32-KDSI Du Bridge project. The only appreciable difference is the slower tail off of the Rayleigh distribution at the end of the project, and there are many projects for which this slower tail off is an appropriate approach. Thus Eq. 5–4 can be used as a reasonably effective means for estimating the personnel level at any given point of an organic-mode software development project.

5.7 INTERPOLATION

Suppose we are planning the programming phase of a project to produce a software product sized at 12,800 DSI. The total development effort and schedule are easy to compute:

$$\text{Effort} = 2.4(12.8)^{1.05} = 35\ \text{MM}$$
$$\text{Schedule} = 2.5(35)^{.38} = 9.7\ \text{months}$$

To obtain estimates for the programming phase, we use Table 5–2. Since our project is not a standard size project, we must interpolate within Table 5–2 to obtain the values we need.

We begin by determining that our 12.8-KDSI project is 20% of the way from the standard 8-KDSI intermediate project to the standard 32-KDSI medium project. By linear interpolation, the percentage value for programming effort on our 12.8-KDSI project will be 20% of the way from the 65% for the 8-KDSI project to the 62% for the 32-KDSI project, or 64.4% (see Fig. 5–7).

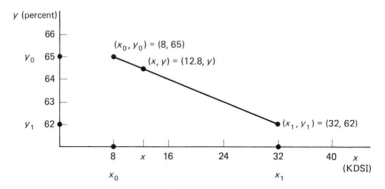

FIGURE 5-7 Linear interpolation

More generally, if we have two points in a table, (x_0, y_0) and (x_1, y_1), and we wish to find the value of y corresponding to a point x between x_0 and x_1 ($x_0 \leq x \leq x_1$) by linear interpolation, we can use the following formula:

$$y = y_0 + \left(\frac{x - x_0}{x_1 - x_0}\right)(y_1 - y_0) \tag{5-5}$$

Substituting our values above, we see indeed that

$$y = 65 + \frac{12.8 - 8}{32 - 8}(62 - 65) = 65 + (0.2)(-3) = 64.4$$

This linear interpolation formula is the one to be used on all COCOMO tables. The same formula can also be used for *extrapolation* outside the ranges of the CO-COMO tables (for example, to scope projects of 1000 DSI or 1,000,000 DSI), but this must be done at the estimator's risk, as the COCOMO model has not been calibrated outside the given limits. *In particular, one must be very wary of using COCOMO, or any algorithmic cost estimation model, for products below 2000 DSI,* as personal differences tend to dominate any other effects on small projects.

At any rate, we can proceed to analyze our 12,800-DSI project. By a similar interpolation in the schedule portion of Table 5–2, we determine that the programming phase will consume 58.2% of the overall project schedule. We can then compute the programming phase effort, schedule, and average FSP level:

5.8 BASIC SOFTWARE MAINTENANCE EFFORT ESTIMATION

The Basic COCOMO estimate for annual software maintenance (as defined in Section 4.8) is calculated in terms of a quantity called

Annual Change Traffic *(ACT): The fraction of the software product's source instructions which undergo change during a (typical) year, either through addition or modification.*

For example, suppose that the 32-KDSI Du Bridge Chemical software product had 4000 DSI added and 2400 DSI modified during its first year of maintenance. Then

$$ACT = \frac{4000 + 2400}{32,000} = \frac{6400}{32,000} = 0.20$$

The COCOMO equation for estimating basic annual maintenance effort $(MM)_{AM}$, given the estimated development effort $(MM)_D$, is

$$(MM)_{AM} = 1.0 \, (ACT) \, (MM)_D \tag{5-6}$$

Since a full-time software person (FSP) contributes 12 man-months in a year, we can easily compute the FSP level required for maintenance, $(FSP)_M$, as

$$(FSP)_M = (MM)_{AM}/12 \tag{5-7}$$

For example, consider the maintenance of the 32-KDSI Du Bridge software product discussed above, with an ACT of 0.20. Its development required 91 MM, from Table 5.3. Its maintenance effort for the first year is then

$$(MM)_{AM} = (0.2) \, (91) = 18 \text{ MM}$$

and the number of FSP required to maintain it is

$$18/12 = 1.5 \text{ FSP}$$

5.9 QUESTIONS

5.1. Compute the total effort, schedule, and overall project productivity associated with the development of organic-mode software products of the following sizes: 5000 DSI; 20,000 DSI; and 50,000 DSI.

5.2. Define the following: COCOMO, DSI, FSP, MM, ACT, TDEV, $(MM)_{AM}$.

5.3. Suppose you are planning the maintenance of a 10-KDSI organic-mode payroll processing software product, assuming that it will annually add 3000 DSI and modify 2000 DSI. How many man-months will be required for annual maintenance, and what FSP level of effort should be anticipated?

5.4. Suppose your maintenance activity involved the same number of instructions as in Question 5.3, but that the base size of the payroll software product was 32,000 DSI or 128,000 DSI. What FSP level of effort would be required to maintain these products? What does this imply about the relative effort required to maintain large versus small products?

5.5. Compute a basic project profile (Table 5–3) for a 20-KDSI product.

5.6. Compute a basic project profile for an 80-KDSI product.

5.7. Determine the number of man-months, $(MM)_{CUT}$, required to perform the code and unit test phase of small, intermediate, medium, and large organic-mode software projects, respectively. Compute the productivity $DSI/(MM)_{CUT}$ for each size project. What do you conclude about the relative productivity of code and unit test activities on large and small projects?

5.8. Compute the number of instructions developed per person $[DSI/(FSP)_{CUT}]$ during the code and unit test phase of small, medium, and large projects.

5.9. Suppose your estimate of the size of a software product is multiplied by 2. What is the relative effect on the estimated effort and time required to develop the product?

5.10. State the assumptions underlying the Basic COCOMO model.

5.11. Graph the modified Rayleigh distribution (Eq. 5–4) for the personnel level of a large (128-KDSI) organic-mode software project, and compare it with the Basic COCOMO estimate shown in Fig. 5–4.

5.12. Perform the comparison in Question 5.11 for a small (2-KDSI) project.

5.13. Colonel Mac's fast food chain has automated its point-of-sale terminal operation, and is now planning to develop an inventory control software system to better control food supplies. A commercial software house has already developed a similar system, comprising roughly 50,000 DSI, and offers to tailor it to Colonel Mac's needs for $500,000. How does this price compare with the estimated cost for Colonel Mac's to develop its own 50-KDSI inventory control system, assuming it would be done as an organic-mode project with software personnel costing an average (including overhead) of $5000 per MM?

5.14. Colonel Mac's expects that its annual change traffic for maintenance of the inventory control system will be about 15% per year. The commercial software house offers to provide this level of maintenance service to Colonel Mac's for $135,000 per year. Assuming the same in-house labor costs for Colonel Mac's as in Question 5.13, how does this offer compare with in-house development and maintenance on an overall life-cycle (acquisition plus maintenance) cost basis, assuming a six-year maintenance life span? Assuming a 12-year maintenance life span?

5.15. Perform a similar analysis, assuming that Colonel Mac's labor costs would be $5500 per MM during the product design phase; $4000 per MM during the programming phase; \$4500 per MM during the integration test phase; \$5000 per MM during the first year of maintenance; and 10% higher each year thereafter.

5.16. The example in this question shows how sensitive software productivity figures can be to definitions. Below are some typical size and effort figures for a large software product:

Applications software	100 KDSI
Support software	250 KDSI
Test drivers	50 KDSI
Additional comment cards	40%
Total development effort	1200 MM
Code and unit test effort	250 MM
Management, clerical effort	20%

Compute the project's productivity using the following definitions:

1. $\text{Productivity} = \dfrac{\text{Noncommented applications software}}{\text{Total development effort}}$

2. $\text{Productivity} = \dfrac{\text{All developed software, including comments}}{\text{Code and unit test effort, excluding management and clerical}}$

Chapter 6

The Basic COCOMO Model: Development Modes

6.1 INTRODUCTION

The Basic COCOMO model presented in the previous chapter provides basic effort and schedule estimates for the most common mode of software development: the small-to-medium size product developed in an in-house, familiar, organic software development environment.

One significant conclusion reached in the research and data analysis culminating in this book is that there are several modes of software development. These different software development modes have cost-estimating relationships which are similar in form, but which yield significantly different cost estimates for software products of the same size.

In this chapter, we provide estimating relationships for the two other main modes of software development: the ambitious, tightly-constrained *embedded* mode, and an intermediate mode called the *semidetached* mode.

Section 6.2 presents the basic effort and schedule equations for each mode. Section 6.3 describes each of the modes in terms of their distinguishing features, and discusses the differences in project activities experienced by projects of different modes. Section

6.4 presents the COCOMO data base of 63 projects, and shows how well the Basic COCOMO effort and schedule estimating equations are corroborated by the project data. Finally, Section 6.5 presents and discusses tables for estimating the phase distribution of effort and schedule for the three development modes.

6.2 BASIC EFFORT AND SCHEDULE EQUATIONS

Table 6–1 presents the Basic COCOMO effort and schedule equations for the organic, semidetached, and embedded modes of software development.

TABLE 6–1 Basic COCOMO Effort and Schedule Equations

Mode	Effort	Schedule
Organic	$MM = 2.4(KDSI)^{1.05}$	$TDEV = 2.5(MM)^{0.38}$
Semidetached	$MM = 3.0(KDSI)^{1.12}$	$TDEV = 2.5(MM)^{0.35}$
Embedded	$MM = 3.6(KDSI)^{1.20}$	$TDEV = 2.5(MM)^{0.32}$

Examples of the estimates given by these equations are given in Table 6–2, which summarizes the estimated project effort, productivity, development schedule, and

TABLE 6–2 Basic COCOMO Estimates for Standard-Size Products

Effort (MM)	Small 2 KDSI	Intermediate 8 KDSI	Medium 32 KDSI	Large 128 KDSI	Very Large 512 KDSI
Organic	5.0	21.3	91	392	
Semidetached	6.5	31	146	687	3250
Embedded	8.3	44	230	1216	6420

Productivity (DSI/MM)	Small 2 KDSI	Intermediate 8 KDSI	Medium 32 KDSI	Large 128 KDSI	Very Large 512 KDSI
Organic	400	376	352	327	
Semidetached	308	258	219	186	158
Embedded	241	182	139	105	80

Schedule (months)	Small 2 KDSI	Intermediate 8 KDSI	Medium 32 KDSI	Large 128 KDSI	Very Large 512 KDSI
Organic	4.6	8	14	24	
Semidetached	4.8	8.3	14	24	42
Embedded	4.9	8.4	14	24	41

Average personnel (FSP)	Small 2 KDSI	Intermediate 8 KDSI	Medium 32 KDSI	Large 128 KDSI	Very Large 512 KDSI
Organic	1.1	2.7	6.5	16	
Semidetached	1.4	3.7	10	29	77
Embedded	1.7	5.2	16	51	157

average development personnel level for each software development mode, for the following standard size products:

Small:	2 KDSI
Intermediate:	8 KDSI
Medium:	32 KDSI
Large:	128 KDSI
Very large:	512 KDSI

Figures 6–1 and 6–2 show the estimated effort and schedule for the three modes as a function of product size. Figure 6–3 shows estimated schedule versus development effort. The major trends seen in progressing from the organic to the embedded mode in Table 6–2 and Figs. 6–1 through 6–3 are:

- For software products of the same size, the estimated effort is considerably greater and the estimated productivity is considerably less for the embedded mode.
- For larger products, the dropoff in productivity (diseconomy of scale) is greater for the embedded mode.
- The estimated schedule as a function of product size is about the same for all three modes.

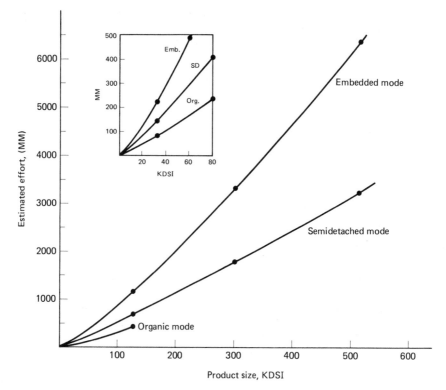

FIGURE 6-1 Basic COCOMO effort estimates: Three development modes

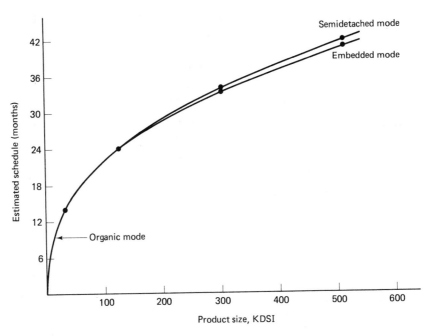

FIGURE 6-2 Basic COCOMO schedule estimates: Three development modes

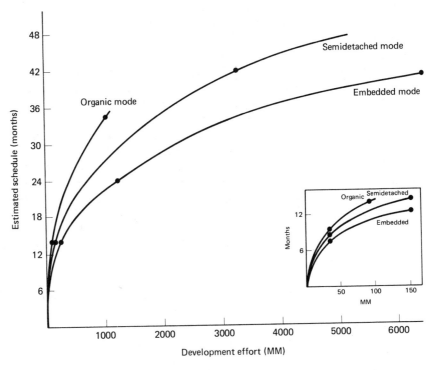

FIGURE 6-3 COCOMO schedule estimates: Three development modes

- For software projects requiring the same amount of development time, the embedded-mode project will consume more effort.

The next two sections describe the modes in more detail and discuss the main reasons for these trends.

6.3 THE THREE COCOMO MODES OF SOFTWARE DEVELOPMENT

It is clear from Table 6–2 that it is important for a software engineer to be able to distinguish between the different modes of software development. For example, if we are required to develop a medium size, 32-KDSI software product in an embedded-mode environment, and we instead estimate and staff the project as if it were an organic-mode activity, we will seriously underestimate the amount of effort required for the project (91 MM versus 230 MM). We will also schedule project personnel in a way that will make it difficult to recover gracefully, once we find the project is different in nature. (This has happened on a large number of software projects.)

The Organic Mode

In the organic mode, relatively small software teams develop software in a highly familiar, in-house environment. Most people connected with the project have extensive experience in working with related systems within the organization, and have a thorough understanding of how the system under development will contribute to the organization's objectives.

This means that most of the project people can usefully contribute to the project in its early stages, without generating a great deal of project *communications overhead* in finding out what the project is all about and what everybody else is doing. This accounts for the relatively flat labor distributions shown for organic-mode projects in Chapter 5. It also means that larger projects experience relatively little loss in productivity due to communications overhead.

An organic-mode project is relatively relaxed about the way the software meets its requirements and interface specifications. If a situation arises where an exact correspondence of the software product to the original requirements or interface specification would cause an extensive rework, the project team can generally negotiate a modification of the specifications that can be developed more easily, and that will not be too difficult for the user to accommodate. This is another reason for both the higher productivity and the smaller diseconomy of scale on an organic-mode project.

Other factors characteristic of organic-mode software projects are:

- A generally stable development environment, with very little concurrent development of associated new hardware and operational procedures.
- Minimal need for innovative data processing architectures or algorithms.
- A relatively low premium on early completion of the project.

- Relatively small size. Very few organic-mode projects have developed products with more than 50 KDSI of new software. (Larger organic-mode products often may be developed by using existing software.)

These factors also tend to correlate with higher project productivity and smaller project diseconomies of scale.

The Semidetached Mode

The semidetached mode of software development represents an intermediate stage between the organic and embedded modes. "Intermediate" may mean either of two things:

1. An intermediate level of the project characteristic.
2. A mixture of the organic and embedded mode characteristics.

Thus, with respect to the feature "experience in working with related software systems," any of the following could be characteristic of a semidetached mode project.

- The team members all have an intermediate level of experience with related systems.
- The team has a wide mixture of experienced and inexperienced people.
- The team members have experience related to some aspects of the system under development, but not others.

With respect to its conformance to functional and interface specifications, a typical semidetached-mode project might be a transaction processing system with some very rigorous interfaces (for example, with the terminal hardware or the government audit requirements) and some very flexible interfaces (for example, with the nature and format of operator display messages and sales trend reports). This partial flexibility explains the derivation of the term semidetached. The size range of a semidetached mode product generally extends up to 300 KDSI.

The Embedded Mode

The major distinguishing factor of an embedded-mode software project is a need to operate within tight constraints. The product must operate within (is embedded in) a strongly coupled complex of hardware, software, regulations, and operational procedures, such as an electronic funds transfer system or an air traffic control system. In general, the costs of changing the other parts of this complex are so high that their characteristics are considered essentially unchangeable, and the software is expected both to conform to their specifications, and to take up the slack on any unforeseen difficulties encountered or changes required within the other parts of the complex.

As a result, the embedded-mode project does not generally have the option of negotiating easier software changes and fixes by modifying the requirements and interface specifications. The project must therefore expend more effort in accommodating changes and fixes (remember the cost-to-fix curves in Fig. 4–2?). It must also expend more effort in assuring that the software actually meets the specifications (higher V & V costs) and in assuring that changes are made correctly (higher configuration management costs). These factors contribute both to lower productivity and to greater diseconomies of scale on larger projects.

The embedded-mode project is generally charting its way through unknown territory to a greater extent than the organic-mode project. This leads the project to use a much smaller team of analysts in the early stages, as a large number of people would get swamped in communications overhead.

Once the embedded-mode project has completed its product design, its best strategy is to bring on a very large team of programmers to perform detailed design, coding, and unit testing in parallel. Otherwise, the project would take much longer to complete, which would be bad for two main reasons:

- The product would have to absorb more changes.
- The product would be further out-of-date when delivered. (Generally, the premium for early completion of embedded-mode projects is much higher, often because of a need to get an entire hardware–software complex in operation as soon as possible.)

This strategy leads to the higher peaks in the personnel curves of embedded-mode projects, and to the greater amount of effort consumed compared to an organic-mode project working to the same total development schedule.*

Summary

A summary of the comparative features of the organic, semidetached, and embedded modes of software development is given in Table 6–3, with typical examples of software projects characteristic of each mode.

A summary of another type is given in Table 6–4, which shows the main differences in project activities due to the mode of software development as a function of the development phase. Table 6–4 provides a better understanding of why the diseconomies of scale are greater for embedded-mode projects: larger projects have proportionally more internal and external interfaces to control and rework.

A final way to summarize the differences is to provide an example of how each of the three modes would accommodate a functionally similar software routine: a routine to predict the position of an airplane from various sensor data.

> *Organic Mode* (Aircraft postflight data reduction): "We know from the last ten years of programming these algorithms just how well they'll do in predicting the airplane's position. If something extraordinary happens and the error or computing time is a good deal larger than usual, the data analysis people will just have to make do."

---

* The organic-mode project thus also has the advantage of having had most of its programmers participate in the earlier stages of analysis, leading to further productivity advantages.

TABLE 6–3 Distinguishing Features of Software Development Modes

Feature	Mode		
	Organic	Semidetached	Embedded
Organizational understanding of product objectives	Thorough	Considerable	General
Experience in working with related software systems	Extensive	Considerable	Moderate
Need for software conformance with pre-established requirements	Basic	Considerable	Full
Need for software conformance with external interface specifications	Basic	Considerable	Full
Concurrent development of associated new hardware and operational procedures	Some	Moderate	Extensive
Need for innovative data processing architectures, algorithms	Minimal	Some	Considerable
Premium on early completion	Low	Medium	High
Product size range	<50 KDSI	<300 KDSI	All sizes
Examples	Batch data reduction	Most transaction processing systems	Large, complex transaction processing systems
	Scientific models	New OS, DBMS	Ambitious, very large OS
	Business models	Ambitious inventory, production control	Avionics
	Familiar OS, compiler	Simple command-control	Ambitious command-control
	Simple inventory, production control		

Semidetached Mode (Aircraft flight-training simulator): "We need a fair amount of accuracy for this flight simulator, and the sensor inputs are somewhat different from our previous experience, but our main concern will be in getting the simulated aircraft position computed in time for each display cycle. If we have to reduce accuracy to meet the time constraints, we can live with that."

Embedded Mode (Aircraft on-board collision avoidance system): "With this new radar, we're going to have to experiment with various algorithms to find one with adequate accuracy and speed. If we don't find a satisfactory algorithm, we'll have to rework the entire collision-avoidance approach in the on-board computer, and we may run into problems with the FAA flight-safety guidelines."

A large software project may contain several subprojects operating in different modes (embedded-mode mission control software; organic-mode support software.) Further, if the subprojects are not closely interrelated and do not cause each other

TABLE 6-4 Project Activity Differences Due to Software Development Mode

Mode	Phase			
	Requirements and Product Design	Detailed Design	Code and Unit Test	Integration and Test
Embedded	Extensive rework to accommodate specification changes Thorough specification, validation of requirements and interfaces Extensive analysis, prototyping of high-risk elements	Very formal configuration management, interface control	Extensive rework to accommodate code changes	Extensive requirements, interface testing
Semidetached	Intermediate level of above effects			
Organic	Relatively little rework to accommodate specification changes Fairly general specification, validation of requirements and interfaces Occasional analysis, prototyping of high-risk elements	Fairly informal configuration management, interface control	Moderate rework to accommodate code changes	Moderate requirements, interface testing

82

diseconomies of scale, their costs should be estimated as several smaller projects rather than as one large project with its corresponding large diseconomy of scale.

6.4 DISCUSSION OF THE BASIC COCOMO EFFORT AND SCHEDULE EQUATIONS

The COCOMO Data Base

The Basic COCOMO estimating equations (and the other COCOMO estimating equations) have been obtained by analyzing a carefully screened sample of 63 software project data points. Table 6–5 summarizes the nature of the COCOMO data base; more detailed information is given in Chapter 29.

As can be seen from Table 6–5, the distribution of projects in the COCOMO data base is not perfectly representative of the current universe of software projects (there aren't enough COBOL data points, for example) or of the likely future universe of software projects (there aren't enough microprocessor data points, for example). However, the data base does have some representative points from all of the major sectors of the software world, and there have been no examples of data from a particular

TABLE 6–5 The COCOMO Data Base

	Number of Data Points	Productivity Range (DSI/MM)
Entire Data Base	63	20–1250
Modes: Organic	23	82–1250
Semidetached	12	41–583
Embedded	28	20–667
Types: Business	7	55–862
Control	10	20–304
Human-Machine	13	28–336
Scientific	17	47–1250
Support	8	82–583
Systems	8	28–667
Year developed: 1964–69	3	113–775
1970–74	14	20–485
1975–79	46	41–1250
Type of computer: Maxi	31	28–1250
Midi	7	114–583
Mini	21	20–723
Micro	4	41–379
Programming Languages: FORTRAN	24	28–883
COBOL	5	55–862
Jovial	5	45–583
PL/1	4	93–1250
Pascal	2	336–560
Other HOL	3	124–300
Assembly	20	20–667

sector being especially out of line with the COCOMO estimates. Further, the data base has one other major advantage: all of the data entries are carefully and consistently defined with respect to the meaning of "delivered source instructions," "development," "man-months," and the like.

Effort Equations: Estimates versus Actuals

Figure 6–4 is a plot of the Basic COCOMO estimated man-months versus the actual project man-months for the 63 projects in the COCOMO data base. The plot for a perfect estimation model would have all the data points on the diagonal estimates-equals-actuals line.

The results here do not look too bad, as there are no data points at the extreme opposite corners of the ideal diagonal line. But we should not become too optimistic based on the appearance of these results, which are plotted on a logarithmic scale. From a practical prediction standpoint, it is important to note that the Basic COCOMO estimates are within a factor of 1.3 of the actuals only 29% of the time, and within a factor of 2 only 60% of the time.

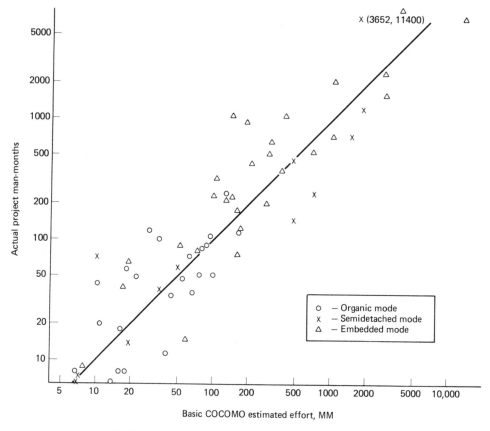

FIGURE 6-4 Basic COCOMO effort estimates vs. actuals

Effort Equations: Comparisons by Mode

Figure 6–5 shows the performance of each of the Basic COCOMO estimating equations for the three development modes. The three lines show the estimated man-months for each development mode as a function of delivered source instructions in thousands (KDSI). The points in Fig. 6–5 show the corresponding actual project sizes and man-months for the projects of each mode.

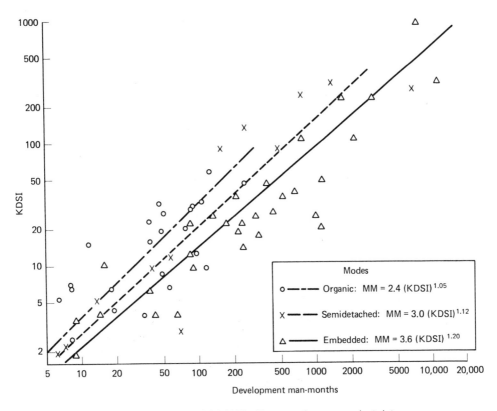

FIGURE 6-5 Basic COCOMO effort equations vs. project data

The major conclusions that we can draw from Figs. 6–4 and 6–5 are:

1. The differences in productivity and in scale effects between the three modes are clearly distinguishable (Fig. 6–5). This point can be argued somewhat for the semidetached-mode data, but the differences between the organic- and embedded-mode data are quite clear.
2. The Basic COCOMO estimating equations are not optimal least-squares fits to the data points (Fig. 6–5). In fact, for the current sample of data points, the optimal least-squares fits would produce a wider variation between the three modes. These optimal-fit equations are not used as the Basic COCOMO equations for the following reasons:

- Simplicity. The simple coefficients and exponents are easier to remember and work with.
- Stability. The estimating equations do not change each time a new project is added to the data base.
- Consistency with the more detailed COCOMO estimating relationships presented later in the book.

3. The estimating equations are not very accurate (Figs. 6–4, 6–5). As mentioned above, they estimate the actual data points within a factor of 1.3 only 29% of the time, and come within a factor of 2 only 60% of the time. This is consistent with the use of these equations only for rough early estimates of software effort and costs.

4. The estimating equations are at least as accurate as any other one-variable fit to the data. The results are as good as can be expected, as there are a number of factors besides size that determine the amount of effort required to develop a software product. We will see that the Intermediate COCOMO model presented in Chapter 8 produces a much more accurate fit to the data by including a number of those other factors in its estimating relationships.

Effort Equations: Comparison with Other Models

A number of other software cost models and studies have derived effort equations of the same form as the Basic COCOMO effort equations. Their results are summarized in Table 6–6.

Unfortunately, the different estimating equations in Table 6–6 cannot be compared too closely, because they are based on different—and often unstated—assumptions and definitions (whether or not to include comment cards, requirements analysis effort, management costs, and so on).

However, the overall spectrum of models displays an interesting variation of conclusions on the prevalence of economies of scale (exponents less than 1.0), or

TABLE 6–6 Comparison of Effort Equations

Reference	Effort Equation
[Walston–Felix, 1977]	$MM = 5.2 \, (KDSI)^{0.91}$
[Nelson, 1978]	$MM = 4.9 \, (KDSI)^{0.98}$
[Freburger–Basili, 1979]	$MM = 1.48 \, (KDSI)^{1.02}$
COCOMO: Organic Mode	$MM = 2.4 \, (KDSI)^{1.05}$
[Herd and others, 1977]	$MM = 5.3 \, (KDSI)^{1.06}$
COCOMO: Semidetached Mode	$MM = 3.0 \, (KDSI)^{1.12}$
[Frederic, 1974]	$MM = 2.43 \, (KDSI)^{1.18}$
COCOMO: Embedded Mode	$MM = 3.6 \, (KDSI)^{1.20}$
[Phister, 1979]	$MM = 0.99 \, (KDSI)^{1.275}$
[Jones, 1977]	$MM = 1.0 \, (KDSI)^{1.40}$
[Walston–Felix, 1977a]	$MM = 1.12 \, (KDSI)^{1.43}$
[Halstead, 1977]	$MM = 0.70 \, (KDSI)^{1.50}$
[Schneider, 1978]	$MM = 28 \, (KDSI)^{1.83}$

diseconomies of scale (exponents greater than 1.0) in software production. A large project has a number of unavoidable diseconomies of scale (more effort per instruction required for product design, integration, communications overhead, and so on), but a number of opportunities to achieve economies of scale as well (by investing in items such as automated aids and standards that can be more than amortized over the large base of project activities). The Basic COCOMO equations indicate that the diseconomies of scale outweigh the economies of scale most for embedded-mode projects, but all three COCOMO equations occupy an intermediate position with respect to the wide range of exponents in the other models.

Schedule Equation: Estimates versus Actuals

Figure 6–6 shows the comparison between the COCOMO development schedule estimates versus the actual development schedules in months for the 63 projects in the COCOMO data base. Figure 6–7 shows the performance of each of the estimating equations for the three development modes as compared to the project data points for the corresponding modes.

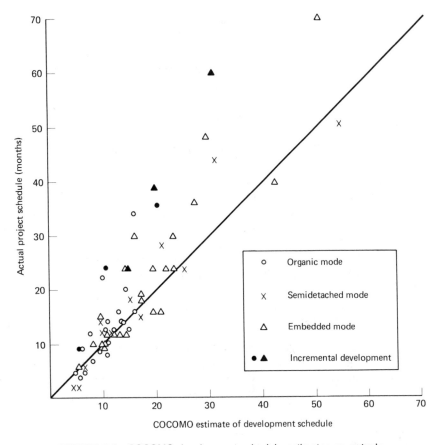

FIGURE 6-6 COCOMO development schedule estimates vs. actuals

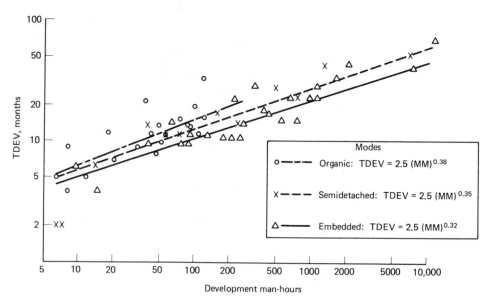

FIGURE 6-7 COCOMO schedule equations vs. project data (excluding incremental development projects)

The main conclusions that we can draw from Figs. 6–6 and 6–7 are similar to the conclusions we reached from the effort equations and data:

1. The differences between the three modes are clearly distinguishable (Fig. 6–7), although less so for the semidetached mode.
2. The schedule equations are reasonable but not optimal least-squares fits to the data (Figs. 6–6, 6–7).
3. The schedule estimating equations are somewhat more accurate than the effort equations. The estimates are within 20% of the actuals 58% of the time. Still, there is a wide variation between projects, particularly from a number of projects whose schedules were overly long due to frequent customer redirection and inadequate planning.*
4. The schedule equations clearly underestimate the time required for a project using incremental development (Fig. 6–6).

Schedule Equations: Comparisons with Other Models

Table 6–7 compares the Basic COCOMO schedule estimating equations with similar equations derived from other sources. These results display a remarkable agreement, particularly considering that some of the models do not precisely define the beginning point and endpoint of the development period. To date, no one has

---

* For example, one project added three months to its schedule because nobody began assembling test data until it was time to start testing. As a result, the test team could make little progress until the test data was ready, a three-month task which could have been done easily in advance.

come up with a good explanation for this relation in terms of project phenomena: it is one of the most intriguing research issues in the software cost estimation area.

TABLE 6–7 Comparison of Development Schedule Equations

Reference	Development Schedule Equation
[Freburger–Basili, 1979]	$TDEV = 4.38 \ (MM)^{0.25}$
COCOMO: Embedded mode	$TDEV = 2.5 \ (MM)^{0.32}$
[Putnam, 1978], Minimal schedule	$TDEV = 2.15 \ (MM)^{0.333}$
COCOMO: Semidetached mode	$TDEV = 2.5 \ (MM)^{0.35}$
[Walston–Felix, 1977]	$TDEV = 2.47 \ (MM)^{0.35}$
[Nelson, 1978]	$TDEV = 3.04 \ (MM)^{0.36}$
COCOMO: Organic mode	$TDEV = 2.5 \ (MM)^{0.38}$

6.5   PHASE DISTRIBUTION OF EFFORT AND SCHEDULE

Percentage Distributions

Our previous discussion of the differences in software development activities between the organic, semidetached, and embedded modes (as in Table 6–4) would lead us to expect that these project modes would differ considerably in their estimated phase distribution of effort and schedule. This is indeed the case, as we can see from Table 6–8, which shows the estimated percentage distribution of project effort and schedule for the three modes.

As compared to the phase distributions for the organic mode, which we previously discussed in Sections 5.4 and 5.5, here are the main differences in the effort and schedule distributions for the semidetached and embedded modes:

1. The embedded-mode project consumes considerably more effort in the integration and test phase. This results from the need to follow and verify software requirements and interface specifications more carefully in the embedded and semidetached modes.
2. The embedded-mode project consumes proportionally less effort in the code and unit test phase. This results from the proportionally higher effort required for the other development phases. Does this mean that the embedded-mode project spends less *actual* effort in the code and unit test phase than the organic-mode project? No, because of the higher total development effort in the embedded-mode project, as we can see below, using the medium size (32-KDSI) project as an example.

Mode	Development Effort (MM)	Percent Code and Unit Test (%)	Code and Unit Test Effort (MM)
Organic	91	38	35
Semidetached	146	33	48
Embedded	230	28	64

Effort distribution		Small 2 KDSI	Inter-mediate 8 KDSI	Medium 32 KDSI	Large 128 KDSI	Very Large 512 KDSI
Mode	Phase					
Organic	Plans and requirements (%)	6	6	6	6	
	Product design	16	16	16	16	
	Programming	68	65	62	59	
	Detailed design	26	25	24	23	
	Code and unit test	42	40	38	36	
	Integration and test	16	19	22	25	
Semidetached	Plans and requirements (%)	7	7	7	7	7
	Product design	17	17	17	17	17
	Programming	64	61	58	55	52
	Detailed design	27	26	25	24	23
	Code and unit test	37	35	33	31	29
	Integration and test	19	22	25	28	31
Embedded	Plans and requirements (%)	8	8	8	8	8
	Product design	18	18	18	18	18
	Programming	60	57	54	51	48
	Detailed design	28	27	26	25	24
	Code and unit test	32	30	28	26	24
	Integration and test	22	25	28	31	34
Schedule distribution		2 KDSI	8 KDSI	32 KDSI	128 KDSI	512 KDSI
Organic	Plans and requirements (%)	10	11	12	13	
	Product design	19	19	19	19	
	Programming	63	59	55	51	
	Integration and test	18	22	26	30	
Semidetached	Plans and requirements (%)	16	18	20	22	24
	Product design	24	25	26	27	28
	Programming	56	52	48	44	40
	Integration and test	20	23	26	29	32
Embedded	Plans and requirements (%)	24	28	32	36	40
	Product design	30	32	34	36	38
	Programming	48	44	40	36	32
	Integration and test	22	24	26	28	30

The main reasons why the embedded-mode project has to spend more effort in the code and unit test phase were shown in Table 6–4: more rework to accommodate specification changes, more formal product controls, and more rework to accommodate code changes.

3. The embedded-mode project consumes considerably more schedule in both the plans and requirements phase and the product design phase. This is because of the project's need for more thorough, validated requirements and design

specifications, and the greater need to perform these phases with a relatively small number of people.

4. The embedded-mode project consumes considerably less schedule in the programming phase. This results from the strategy of employing a great many people programming in parallel, in order to reduce the project's overall schedule (and thereby reduce the number of product changes which must be accommodated during development).

Use of Tables

Table 6–8 is used in the same way as Table 5–1 (phase distributions for organic-mode projects). Thus, the distribution percentages for products of nonstandard sizes are similarly obtained by interpolation. For example, the estimated percentage of the development schedule required for integration and test of a 20-KDSI embedded-mode project (halfway between 8 KDSI and 32 KDSI) is 25% (halfway between 24% and 26% in Table 6–8).

Basic Project Profiles

In Chapter 5, we constructed basic project profiles for the various size organic-mode projects, in order to get a feel for how the amount of time, effort, and average personnel in the different development phases varies with the size of the product being developed. In Table 6–9 we present basic project profiles for the medium-size (32-KDSI) projects in all three software development modes, in order to provide a feel for how the distribution of time, effort, and personnel varies with the development mode.

It is particularly illuminating to compare the average personnel figures for the organic and embedded modes. A medium-size organic-mode project can be handled smoothly by a relatively small (less than eight) group of people, most of whom work on the project throughout the entire development cycle. A medium-size embedded-mode project, on the other hand, requires an average of 22 people during its programming phase, most of whom did not participate in the earlier phases.

Looking further into these two projects, we see that the embedded-mode project required 9.3 months to complete its plans and requirements phase and product design phase, while the organic-mode project required only 4.4 months (largely because of the more familiar organic operating environment). Furthermore, the embedded-mode project is generally the one with the high premium on early completion.

At the beginning of the programming phase, the embedded-mode project still has 188 man-months of effort remaining. Even if a reduction in team size to 8 FSP could reduce the remaining effort to 120 MM (a very optimistic assumption), the project would then require (120 MM)/8 FSP = 15 months to complete, rather than the 9.2 months required to complete the job by staffing up to an average of 22 FSP in the programming phase.* For most embedded-mode projects, the value to the

---

* There is, of course, a limit to how far we can squeeze the schedule by adding more people. This topic is discussed in Chapter 27.

TABLE 6–9 Basic Project Profiles: Medium-Size Projects

Quantity	Organic	Mode Semi-detached	Embedded
Total effort (MM)	91	146	230
Plans and requirements	5	10	18
Product design	15	25	42
Programming	56	85	124
Detailed design	22	37	60
Code and unit test	34	48	64
Integration and test	20	36	64
Total schedule (Months)	14	14	14
Plans and requirements	1.7	2.8	4.5
Product design	2.7	3.6	4.8
Programming	7.7	6.8	5.6
Integration and test	3.6	3.6	3.6
Average personnel (FSP)	6.5	10.4	16.4
Plans and requirements	2.9	3.6	4.0
Product design	5.6	6.9	8.8
Programming	7.3	12.5	22.1
Integration and test	5.6	10.0	17.8
Percent of average personnel			
Plans and requirements	45	35	24
Product design	84	66	54
Programming	113	120	135
Integration and test	85	96	108
Productivity (DSI/MM)	352	219	139
Code and unit test only (DSI/MM)	941	667	500

organization of getting the system into operation 6 months earlier is worth much more than the 68 man-months that might be saved by going to a smaller team size.

Manpower Distribution Curves and the Rayleigh Distribution

The resulting Basic COCOMO-estimated personnel distribution curves for the medium-size organic, semidetached, and embedded-mode projects are shown in Fig. 6–8, normalized with respect to the average personnel level for each project. The relatively slower, low-level start and the higher peak personnel requirement of the embedded mode is clearly evident from Fig. 6–8. (These characteristics are even more pronounced for very large embedded-mode projects, as can be seen from a similar comparative graph of embedded-mode projects of different sizes in Fig. 6–9.)

Figure 6–8 also shows the normalized Rayleigh curve:

$$FSP = 13,300 \left(\frac{t}{60^2} \right) e^{-t^2/2(60)^2}$$

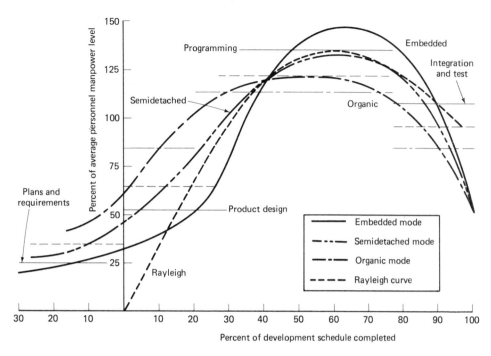

FIGURE 6-8 Basic COCOMO personnel distribution: Medium (32 KDSI) projects

whose peak effort occurs at the 60% point in the development schedule (the constant 13,300 normalizes the curve to account for the portion of the distribution left out beyond the 100% point in Fig. 6–8). Again, the Rayleigh curve is a reasonably good fit for portions of the manpower distribution (particularly for the semidetached mode), with the main exception of its zero-level behavior at the start of the project.

Thus, for practical use, we would have to tailor a portion of a Rayleigh curve to a particular mode and a particular portion of the development cycle, as we did in Chapter 5 for the organic mode. In general, it is easier and more realistic to develop a project labor plan from the average personnel per phase information given by the COCOMO model, plus as much information as you can obtain about the future availability of people to support the project and their needs for advance training, combined with your knowledge of the project's strategy for incremental development, need for early development of special support software, and so on. These topics are covered in detail in Chapter 32.

A Final Perspective

These last points provide us with a valuable final perspective for this chapter, on the use of analytic models in project personnel planning.

The models are just there to help, not to make your management decisions for you.

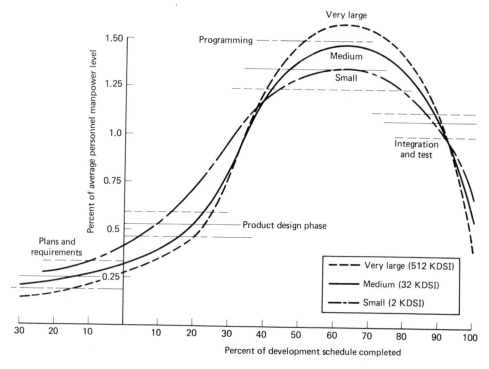

FIGURE 6-9 Basic personnel distribution: Embedded-mode projects

If you become a software project manager, and the COCOMO model or the Rayleigh distribution says you should bring another 10 people onto the project next week, while your designers say they won't be able to use any more people for another month, by all means wait another month.

6.6 QUESTIONS

6.1. The Hunt National Bank is embarking on a number of software development projects. Indicate whether each project is characteristic of the organic, semidetached or embedded mode:

(a) A program to print various straightforward summaries of information from a daily tape of international money market transactions.

(b) A high-volume, real-time national electronic funds transfer system.

(c) A major next generation central financial management system, integrating and extending several existing programs and files.

(d) A model predicting near-term trends in demand for various bank services, based on existing bank transaction summary files.

(e) An experimental on-line transaction processing system for bank tellers.

(f) A simple on-line query system to support loan applications, based on the bank's loan files and a standard data base query package.

6.2. Indicate what additional circumstances would make each of the above projects characteristic of a different development mode.

6.3. Compute the estimated effort, development schedule, productivity, and average project personnel level for 5-KDSI projects in each of the organic, semidetached, and embedded development modes.

6.4. Compute the estimated effort, schedule, and average manpower required to perform the integration and test phase for 5-KDSI projects in each of the organic, semidetached, and embedded development modes. Give reasons why the personnel level for integration and test of an embedded-mode project would be higher than for the other modes.

6.5. Compute the estimated effort in man-months required to complete a 32-KDSI project, using each of the estimating equations in Table 6–6. Why do you think there is so wide a variation between the estimates produced by the models?

6.6. Compute the estimated schedule in months required to complete a 100 man-month project, using each of the estimating equations in Table 6–7.

6.7. If the size of a software product (in KDSI) is doubled, by what factor is the estimated development effort increased for each of the organic, semidetached, and embedded modes?

6.8. Compute Basic Project Profiles along the lines of Table 6–9 for each of the standard size (2, 8, 32, 128, and 512 KDSI) embedded-mode projects.

6.9. Compute Basic Project Profiles along the lines of Table 6–9 for each of the standard size semidetached-mode projects.

6.10. Graph the Rayleigh distributions for the following parameters:

$$MM = 14400, \qquad t_D = 65$$
$$MM = 15700, \qquad t_D = 60$$

How well do these curves match the personnel distribution curves for the small and very large embedded-mode personnel distributions in Fig. 6–9?

6.11. An even simpler effort estimation equation for organic-mode projects is the linear equation:

$$MM = 2.7 \, KDSI$$

Compute its estimate of development man-months for projects with sizes 2, 8, 32, and 50 KDSI. How well do they compare with the estimates given by the Basic COCOMO estimating equation for the organic mode?

6.12. Perform similar comparisons to those in Question 6–11, using the following linear effort estimating equations:

$$\text{Semidetached mode:} \quad MM = 4.0 \, KDSI$$
$$\text{Embedded mode:} \quad MM = 6.0 \, KDSI$$

6.13. *(Research Project)* A simple form of the development schedule equation is:

$$TDEV = 2.5 \sqrt[3]{MM}$$

Formulate an explanation of this cube root equation in terms of software project phenomena. Conduct experiments or observations to verify your explanation.

6.14. List software project or product factors which lead to:

- Economies of scale on larger projects
- Diseconomies of scale on larger projects

6.15. *(Research Project)* Formulate and test hypotheses with respect to economies or diseconomies of scale on software projects (for example, effects of tool investment, communications overhead, added integration effort, etc.).

Chapter 7

The Basic COCOMO Model: Activity Distribution

7.1 INTRODUCTION

We now have some basic techniques for estimating the overall effort, cost, and schedule required to develop and maintain a software product, and for estimating how the effort, cost, and schedule are distributed across the various project phases. In addition to this information, we will often find it necessary to estimate how the effort is distributed among the primary software life-cycle activities: design, programming, test planning, etc. For example:

- In preparing detailed personnel plans for a software project, we need to know what special talents the project will need at what times.
- In staffing the project, we need to be able to work out individual assignments and responsibilities with prospective team members.
- In organizing the project, we need to tailor the organizational structure of the project to the size of the teams devoted to the various project activities. Particularly on large projects, the organizational structure will need to be modified several times during the software life-cycle as the pattern of project activities changes.

- In controlling the project's progress, we need a frame of reference for determining whether we are putting the right amount of effort into each activity.

In this chapter, we present project activity distribution estimating relationships for each of the software life-cycle phases. We then provide some guidelines for the overall organization of a software project, and show how these and the activity distribution estimates may be used to derive a basic project organization chart for each phase of the project.

Throughout the chapter, we will illustrate the use of these techniques with an overall project case study requiring the use of each of the Basic COCOMO estimating relationships presented in this and the previous two chapters. We then conclude our discussion of the Basic COCOMO model with a discussion of its relations to similar models, and of its limitations, many of which will be covered by the Intermediate COCOMO model to be presented in Chapters 8 and 9.

7.2 ACTIVITY DISTRIBUTION BY PHASE

Tables 7–1, 7–2, and 7–3 show how the software project effort in each life-cycle phase is distributed among the eight major activities:

- Requirements Analysis
- Product Design
- Programming
- Test Planning
- Verification and Validation
- Project Office Functions
- Configuration Management and Quality Assurance
- Manuals

The constituents of these phases were defined in Section 4.6. Separate tables are provided for the embedded, semidetached, and organic modes. We will discuss the use of the tables with respect to the embedded mode (Table 7–1); the other tables are used in the same way.

As seen in Tables 7–1 through 7–3, the distribution of effort by activity varies with the size of the project. The standard size projects used for the elements of the tables are:

- S: Small (2 KDSI)
- I: Intermediate (8 KDSI)
- M: Medium (32 KDSI)
- L: Large (128 KDSI)
- VL: Very Large (512 KDSI)

TABLE 7-1 Project Activity Distribution by Phase: Embedded Mode

Phase	Plans and Requirements					Product Design					Programming					Integration and Test					Development					Maintenance				
Product Size	S	I	M	L	VL	S	I	M	L	VL	S	I	M	L	VL	S	I	M	L	VL	S	I	M	L	VL	S	I	M	L	VL
Overall Phase Percentage	8	8	8	8	8	18	18	18	18	18	60	57	54	51	48	22	25	28	31	34										
Activity percentage																														
Requirements analysis	50	48	46	44	42	10	10	10	10	10	3	3	3	3	3	2	2	2	2	2	4	4	4	4	4	6	6	6	5	5
Product design	12	13	14	15	16	42	42	42	42	42	6	6	6	6	6	4	4	4	4	4	12	12	12	12	12	11	11	11	11	11
Programming	2	4	6	8	10	10	11	12	13	14	55	55	55	55	55	32	36	40	44	48	42	43	43	44	45	38	39	39	40	41
Test planning	2	3	4	5	6	4	5	6	7	8	4	5	6	7	8	3	3	4	4	5	4	4	5	6	7	3	3	4	5	6
Verification and validation	6	7	8	9	10	6	7	8	9	10	8	9	10	11	12	30	28	25	23	20	12	13	14	14	14	12	13	14	14	14
Project office	16	14	12	10	8	15	13	11	9	7	9	8	7	6	5	10	9	8	7	6	10	9	8	7	6	10	9	8	7	6
CM/QA	5	4	4	4	3	4	3	3	3	2	8	7	7	7	6	10	9	9	9	8	8	7	7	7	6	8	7	7	7	6
Manuals	7	7	6	5	5	9	9	8	7	7	7	7	6	5	5	9	9	8	7	7	8	8	7	6	6	12	12	11	11	11

TABLE 7-2 Project Activity Distribution by Phase: Semidetached Mode

Phase	Plans and Requirements					Product Design					Programming					Integration and Test					Development					Maintenance				
Product Size	S	I	M	L	VL	S	I	M	L	VL	S	I	M	L	VL	S	I	M	L	VL	S	I	M	L	VL	S	I	M	L	VL
Overall Phase Percentage	7	7	7	7	7	17	17	17	17	17	64	61	58	55	52	19	22	25	28	31										
Activity percentage																														
Requirements analysis	48	47	46	45	44	12.5	12.5	12.5	12.5	12.5	4	4	4	4	4	2.5	2.5	2.5	2.5	2.5	5	5	5	5	5	6.5	6.5	6.5	6	6
Product design	16	16.5	17	17.5	18	41	41	41	41	41	8	8	8	8	8	5	5	5	5	5	13	13	13	13	13	12	12	12	12	12
Programming	2.5	3.5	4.5	5.5	6.5	12	12.5	13	13.5	14	56.5	56.5	56.5	56.5	56.5	33	35	37	39	41	45	45	44.5	44.5	44.5	41.5	41.5	41	41	41
Test planning	2.5	3	3.5	4	4.5	4.5	5	5.5	6	6.5	4	4.5	5	5.5	6	2.5	2.5	3	3	3.5	4	4	4.5	5	5.5	3	3	3.5	4	4.5
Verification and validation	6	6.5	7	7.5	8	6	6.5	7	7.5	8	7	7.5	8	8.5	9	32	31	29.5	28.5	27	11	12	13	13.5	14	11	12	13	13.5	14
Project office	15.5	14.5	13.5	12.5	11.5	13	12	11	10	9	7.5	7	6.5	6	5.5	8.5	8	7.5	7	6.5	8.5	8	7.5	7	6.5	8.5	8	7.5	7	6.5
CM/QA	3.5	3	3	3	2.5	3	2.5	2.5	2.5	2	7	6.5	6.5	6.5	6	8.5	8	8	8	7.5	6.5	6	6	6	5.5	6.5	6	6	6	5.5
Manuals	6	6	5.5	5	5	8	8	7.5	7	7	6	6	5.5	5	5	8	8	7.5	7	7	7	7	6.6	6	6	11	11	10.5	10.5	10.5

TABLE 7-3 Project Activity Distribution by Phase: Organic Mode

Phase	Plans and Requirements	Product Design	Programming	Integration and Test	Development	Maintenance
Product Size	S I M L	S I M L	S I M L	S I M L	S I M L	S I M L
Overall Phase Percentage	6	16	68 65 62 59	16 19 22 25		
Activity percentage						
Requirements analysis	46	15	5	3	6	7
Product design	20	40	10	6	14	13
Programming	3	14	58	34	48 47 46 45	45 44 43 42
Test planning	3	5	4	2	4	3
Verification and validation	6	6	6	34	10 11 12 13	10 11 12 13
Project office	15	11	6	7	7	7
CM/QA	2	2	6	7	5	5
Manuals	5	7	5	7	6	10

Activity distributions for projects of other sizes are obtained by linear interpolation within Tables 7–1 through 7–3.

To explain Table 7–1, let us look first at the leftmost column of numbers. This column indicates that, on a small (2 KDSI) project, 8% of the total effort will be required to complete the plans and requirements phase. Of this 8% share, 50% (or 4% of the total project) will be devoted to performing requirements analysis tasks: analyzing the existing system, determining user needs; and integrating, documenting, and iterating the requirements. Another 12% of the 8% share (or 1% of the total project) will be devoted to performing product design tasks during the plans and requirements phase: investigating the basic hardware–software product architecture, and performing sensitivity and risk analyses to assure that the requirements are feasible. Another 2% of the 8% share will be devoted to programming preparation tasks, etc.

In the next column of Table 7–1, we can see that the activity distribution is somewhat different for an intermediate (8 KDSI) project during the plans and requirements phase. For the intermediate project, only 48% of the effort in the plans and requirements phase is devoted to requirements analysis, while 13% is devoted to product design tasks. The reason for this difference is that larger projects tend to need more effort to investigate the feasibility of the requirements by performing product design functions than do smaller projects. The other portions of Table 7–1 have similar interpretations.*

As an example of the use of Table 7–1, let us compute the activity distribution for the product design phase of a very large (512 KDSI) embedded-mode project. From Table 6–2, we find that the total development effort and schedule for a very large embedded-mode project are 6420 MM and 41 months, respectively. From Table 6–8, we find that the corresponding effort and schedule percentages for the product design phase are 18% and 38%. Thus the project will require

$$(6420 \text{ MM})(0.18) = 1156 \text{ MM}$$
$$(41 \text{ months})(0.38) = 15.6 \text{ months}$$

to complete the product design phase. This means that an average of 1156/15.6 = 74 people (FSP) are at work during the product design phase. From Table 7–1, we can find out what to expect these 74 people to be doing.

Using the rightmost (VL) subcolumn of the product design column in Table 7–1, we see that 10% of the 74 people, or roughly 7 people, will be performing requirements analysis functions; 42% of the 74 people, or 31 people, will be performing product design functions, and so on. The number of people involved in each of the eight activities is given below:

---

* The tables show particularly that software development consists of a great deal more than writing code. From Table 7–1, a medium-sized embedded-mode project devotes only (54%)(55%) = 30% of its effort to programming activities during the programming phase. Further, almost half of this 30% is devoted to detailed design, and the remainder split about evenly between coding and unit testing. This means that only about 8% of the project's effort is devoted to writing code.

Requirements analysis	7 FSP
Product design	31
Programming	10
Test planning	6
Verification and validation	7
Project office functions	5
CM/QA	2
Manuals	5

If we want further information on what these people will be doing, we can consult the task breakdown by activity in Table 4–3.

7.3 BASIC COCOMO CASE STUDY: THE HUNT NATIONAL BANK EFT SYSTEM

The Hunt National Bank has just completed the feasibility phase for a high-volume, real-time Electronic Fund Transfer (EFT) system to handle the bank's nationwide fund transactions. The bank's management has decided to develop an initial increment of the system to perform basic EFT functions for its Northeast region. Even with this specialization, though, the project is a very ambitious venture into a new area, with a number of constraints imposed by the system's interfaces with the bank's other regions and other fund-handling functions.

Suppose that we have been asked to develop a life-cycle plan for the product's development and maintenance. So far, we have determined four key findings about the expected nature of the product:

- From Table 6–3, we have determined that the project's characteristics indicate an embedded-mode development.
- We expect the initial product's size to be 80 KDSI.
- We expect the annual change traffic (ACT) to be 15%.
- We expect the project to be a reasonably standard case with respect to other cost drivers (personnel, environment, etc.).

This last finding means that we can reasonably use the Basic COCOMO model to determine estimates on the expected nature of the product's life-cycle.*

First, we use the embedded-mode equations of Table 6–1 to determine the required product development effort and schedule.

$$\text{Effort} = 3.6 \ (80)^{1.20} = 692 \text{ MM}$$
$$\text{Schedule} = 2.5 \ (692)^{0.32} = 20 \text{ months}$$

---

* In Chapters 23–27 on the Detailed COCOMO model, we will find that a project's distribution of effort may be strongly influenced by other cost drivers (for example, very high required reliability strongly increases test phase costs).

Note that if a typical burdened man-month will cost $6000, the total labor costs for developing the initial system will be $4,152,000.

Next, we use Table 6–8 to determine how the effort and schedule is distributed among the various development phases. We note that our 80-KDSI product is exactly halfway between the standard medium (32-KDSI) product and the standard large (128-KDSI) product, so we will interpolate halfway between these columns in the embedded-mode portions of Table 6–8. This means, for example, that the effort required for the plans and requirements phase of our medium-large project is 8% of the total development effort, or $(692)(.08) = 55$ MM. Similarly, we can determine the estimated effort, schedule, and FSP level for each phase, as given in Table 7–4.

TABLE 7–4 EFT System: Phase Distribution of Effort and Schedule

Quantity		Plans and Requirements	Product Design	Programming	Integration and Test
Effort	(Percent)	8	18	52.5	29.5
	(MM)	55	125	363	204
Schedule	(Percent)	34	35	38	27
	(Months)	6.8	7.0	7.6	5.4
Average number of personnel	(FSP)	8.1	17.9	47.8	37.8

We can compute the estimated annual maintenance effort from Eqs. (5–6) and (5–7), given that ACT = 15%.

$$(MM)_{AM} = (.15)(692) = 104 \text{ MM}$$
$$(FSP)_M = 104/12 = 8.7 \text{ FSP}$$
$$\text{Annual cost} = (104 \text{ MM})(\$6000/\text{MM}) = \$624,000$$

Finally, we can compute the distribution of effort among the major activities for each phase, using Table 7–1. Once again, we interpolate midway between the percentages for the medium and large projects. For example, the requirements analysis activity requires 45% of the personnel required for the plans and requirements phase, or $8.1(.45) = 3.6$ FSP. Similarly, we can determine the estimated activity distribution for the other activities and phases, as given in Table 7–5.

7.4 DERIVING BASIC PROJECT ORGANIZATION CHARTS

A project organization chart tells how the project manager has delegated authority and responsibility for project functions to the people identified in the chart. It is a valuable asset in clarifying project responsibilities and in complying with principles of good project management (such as, "unity of command" and "parity of authority and responsibility" [Koontz–O'Donnell, 1972]).

TABLE 7-5 EFT System: Activity Distribution by Phase

	Plans and Requirements		Product Design		Phase Programming		Integration and Test		Maintenance	
Activity	Percent	FSP	Percent	FSP	Percent	FSP	Percent	FSP	Percent	FSP
Requirements Analysis	45	3.6	10	1.8	3	1.4	2	0.8	5.5	0.5
Product Design	14.5	1.2	42	7.5	6	2.9	4	1.5	11	1.0
Programming	7	0.6	12.5	2.2	55	26.3	42	15.9	39.5	3.4
Test Planning	4.5	0.4	6.5	1.2	6.5	3.1	4	1.5	4.5	0.4
Verification and Validation	8.5	0.7	8.5	1.5	10.5	5.0	24	9.1	14	1.2
Project Office	11	0.9	10	1.8	6.5	3.1	7.5	2.8	7.5	0.6
CM/QA	4	0.3	3	0.5	7	3.4	9	3.4	7	0.6
Manuals	5.5	0.4	7.5	1.4	5.5	2.6	7.5	2.8	11	1.0
Total	100	8.1	100	17.9	100	47.8	100	37.8	100	8.7

With the aid of a few guidelines discussed below, the Basic COCOMO estimates can be used to generate draft project organization charts for the various phases of the software life-cycle.

A Generalized Software Project Organization Chart

Figure 7–1 presents a generalized software project organization chart which can be tailored to fit particular project needs by merging adjacent functions. The Staff and Planning and Control functions, plus the Project Manager, correspond to the Project Office Functions activity in the COCOMO model. System Engineering includes the Requirements Analysis, Product Design, and Manuals activities in the COCOMO model. Verification and validation in the organization chart also includes the Test Planning activity in the COCOMO model. $SS_1 \ldots SS_n$ refers to the programming of software subsystems 1 through n. Implementation refers to conversion, installation, training, and related implementation-phase activities as defined in Table 4–1.

Adjacent functions in the organization chart are generally easier to merge with each other than nonadjacent ones, because of a greater similarity between the objectives, tasks, and skills required to perform the functions. Thus, for example, CM/QA fits together better than CM/V&V, because of the close kinship of the status accounting, standards issuance and monitoring, and auditing tasks of the CM and QA activities.

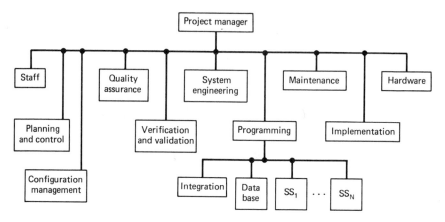

FIGURE 7-1 Generalized software project organization chart

Organization Chart Tailoring Guidelines

Table 7–6 presents a set of guidelines for tailoring the generalized organization chart in Fig. 7–1 to the needs of a particular project or project phase. The term *guidelines* rather than *rules* is used, because project management and organization are human affairs, and not exercises in abstract logic. Various human relations considerations—customer preferences, personal preferences or weak spots, personality conflicts, career development considerations—may make it preferable to deviate from

TABLE 7–6 Organization Chart Tailoring Guidelines

---

1. Merge adjacent functions in the generalized organization chart in Fig. 7–1.
2. Merge a function staffed by less than 2 FSP into a neighbor, unless:
   (a) It represents the manager of a set of subordinate functions, or
   (b) It is staffed by at least 0.5 FSP, and will be growing to a full function in the following phase
3. Split a function into a manager and a set of subordinate functions if it has more than 7 FSP.
4. Keep the span of control (number of functions managed) of any manager to no more than 7 functions.
5. If any of the guidelines conflicts with common sense, disregard the guideline and use common sense.

---

the guidelines in Table 7–6.* In fact, Guideline 5 is the only one which should be treated as a rule.

Example: The Hunt National Bank EFT Project

As an example, let us tailor an organization chart for the product design phase of the medium-large (80-KDSI) embedded-mode Hunt National Bank EFT project used as a case study in the previous section. Its personnel distribution by phase and activity was detailed in Table 7–5. From the product design column of Table 7–5, we see that the project office activity has an average of 1.8 FSP for the phase. We will assume that 1.0 FSP is a full-time project manager and the other 0.8 FSP is devoted to Staff and Planning and Control functions. This is less than 2 FSP, but is greater than 0.5 FSP, and will be growing to more than 2 FSP in the following phase, so we set up this activity as a separate function.

Its neighboring functions in Fig. 7–1, the CM and QA functions, have an average of only 0.5 FSP for the phase, but will grow to 3.4 FSP in the next phase, according to Table 7–5. This would also be enough to rate a separate organizational function by Guideline 2. However, since both this and the neighboring Planning and Control function are so small, it is often appropriate to bend the guidelines and merge them, producing a Staff function for the organization chart with a manpower level of 1.3 FSP.

The test planning and V & V activities in Table 7–5 combine to a level of 2.7 FSP, and thus merit a separate V & V function in the organization chart. Similarly, the 2.2 FSP devoted to programming leads us to define it as a separate function.

The requirements analysis, product design, and manuals activities in Table 7–5 add up to a personnel level of 10.7 FSP for the System Engineering function. We have three options for this function.

1. Following Guideline 3, split it into a manager, a 6.5-FSP Product Design function, and a 3.2-FSP Requirements and Manuals function.
2. Following Guideline 3, split it into a manager and two System Engineering functions for two portions of the product.

* The "magic number seven" used in Guidelines 3 and 4 is generally qualified by the phrase "plus or minus two." As such, it is the result of considerable management experience and scientific observation; see [Miller, 1956].

3. Bend Guideline 3 and use a somewhat large single System Engineering function.

Of these three options, Option 1 is the least attractive, due to the close interaction between the product design activity and the other two activities. Option 2 is preferable if there is a natural division of the product into two System Engineering functions; otherwise (barring any other special circumstances), Option 3 would be preferable.

Assuming Option 2 is chosen, Fig. 7–2 shows the resulting organization chart for the product design phase, with approximate staffing levels for the functions in parentheses.

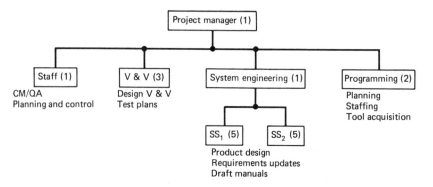

FIGURE 7-2   EFT system: Product design phase organization chart

Organization Charts and Decisions for Other Phases

Similar draft organization charts for the other phases of the medium-large EFT project, based on the personnel levels in Table 7–5, are given in Fig. 7–3. Again, the charts are simply drafts to be altered wherever it makes sense. In some cases, this has already been done in Fig. 7–3; here are some notes explaining the exceptional or borderline situations.

1. In the plans and requirements phase, we could merge the Staff and V & V functions into a single function. In this case, we did not do this because of the broader variety of functions which would then be encompassed under a single manager, and because of the subsequent split of these functions into three separate functions in the following phase.

2. In the programming phase, there are a number of options for dividing the programmers into teams:
   (a) 3 teams of roughly 8 people each
   (b) 4 teams of roughly 6 people each
   (c) 5 teams of roughly 5 people each
   (d) 6 teams of roughly 4 people each
   (e) 8 teams of roughly 3 people each
   The most important consideration in making this decision is to organize the teams along clear lines of the software product functions, using the same

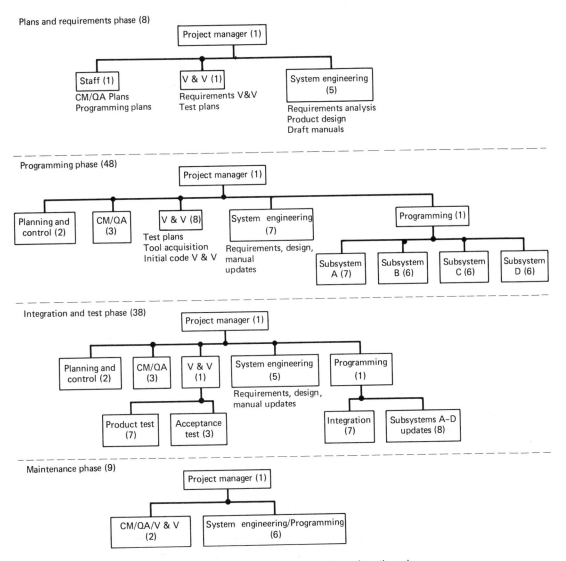

FIGURE 7-3 EFT system: Organization charts for other phases

principles of cohesion, coupling, and information hiding as are used in good software design (see [Daly, 1979], for example). The other main consideration is the following secondary guideline:

- A small number of larger teams is easier to manage than a large number of smaller teams.

To see why this is the case, suppose you were the programming group manager during the programming phase of the EFT project, and you find you must accommodate a new requirement for government financial reporting which affects several portions of the software product. In general, you would find it much easier if you could identify two team leaders (or, better yet, one) and have them work out the necessary product and project changes, than if you had to involve five or six team leaders in accommodating the change. (Of course, there are limits and exceptions to this guideline, as with the others.)

3. For simplicity, the Manual Updates activity was identified with the System Engineering function in the programming and integration-and-test phases. Often, it makes sense to include all or part of this activity in the Programming function, particularly where programmers have a good deal of dead time waiting for the results of computer runs or waiting to respond to problem reports from the V & V team.

4. In the maintenance phase, a 2 FSP System Engineering function could be split off from the Programming function. Where possible, however, it is preferable to integrate these functions and give everybody a chance to do some analysis and design. In many situations, it is preferable to organize the maintenance-phase system engineering and programming activities along major product subsystem lines or along customer organization lines. A good discussion of these and related issues is given in *The Organization of the Data Processing Function* [Withington, 1972].

7.5 DISCUSSION OF BASIC COCOMO PHASE AND ACTIVITY DISTRIBUTIONS

Rayleigh Curve Comparisons

The Basic COCOMO models have an overall personnel distribution by phase that is fairly similar to the Rayleigh curve model used in [Putnam, 1978] and [Norden, 1958]. A comparison of the distributions was given in Fig. 6–8 and discussed in Section 6.5. The main differences appear to be the following:

- The COCOMO model defers adding large numbers of people to the project until full completion and V & V of the product design; thus, its approach to maximum staffing is considerably later and steeper than with the Rayleigh curve, especially on large projects.
- The COCOMO model reflects a continuing slow buildup of personnel during the plans and requirements phase, while the Rayleigh curve starts with zero personnel at the beginning of the product design phase and quickly builds a large organization. ([Putnam, 1978] adds another small Rayleigh curve at the front end to account for this effort.)

The modeling of personnel distribution during the maintenance phase is also different, but this discussion will be postponed until Chapter 30.

Phase/Activity Distributions

The activity distributions by phase in COCOMO reflect those of earlier phase/activity breakdowns developed by [Wolverton, 1974] and [Jones, 1977]. The Wolverton breakdown provides more detail (eight phases and up to 25 activities per phase), but the breakdown percentages have been subsequently found to be specific to relatively large projects within a somewhat narrow range of cost drivers, characteristic of near real-time, high-reliability government projects.

The Jones breakdown is similar in form to Tables 6–8 and 7–1, 7–2, and 7–3, in that the percentages are presented as a function of project size. The Jones model is similar to Basic COCOMO, but not to Intermediate and Full COCOMO, in that it does not modify the breakdowns as functions of other cost drivers (such as higher test costs as functions of higher required reliability and restricted computer access).

The Jones model activity distributions appear at times inconsistent with the data used to calibrate COCOMO. For example, the percentage of effort for requirements specification is given as 8% for a very large project, 2% for a medium project, and 31% for a small project. With respect to the COCOMO model and project data base, the corresponding percentages are more consistent: 6% for an organic-mode project, 7% for a semidetached-mode project, and 8% for an embedded-mode project.

7.6 LIMITATIONS OF BASIC COCOMO

One of the limitations of Basic COCOMO (and of all other phase-distribution models to date) is that it does not accommodate *highly sequential forms of incremental development*. The effort distribution estimates hold up reasonably well, but the schedule calculations must be done differently. This topic is discussed in more detail in Section 29.4.

Another limitation is that Basic COCOMO calculates estimates of *average* staff levels in each phase. This means that there are discontinuities in personnel level at the boundaries between phases that must be smoothed out, such as is done in Figs. 5–6, 6–6, and 6–7. This transition effect also makes some of the organization charts more approximate, particularly for the programming activity during the integration and test phase (see Fig. 7–3). At the beginning of the phase, there are a large number of programming personnel performing integration, while near the end of the phase there are none.

The major limitation of Basic COCOMO is that it does not incorporate the effect of any software cost drivers other than delivered source instructions (DSI), and also annual change traffic (ACT) for maintenance. The effect of such additional cost drivers as hardware constraints, personnel factors, and environmental attributes will be incorporated in the Intermediate COCOMO model discussed in the next chapter.

7.7 QUESTIONS

7.1. Project Zenith is a new government project to develop a Prototype Community Information Utility, based on a citywide two-way home cable-TV network in the large Midwestern city of Zenith. Project Zenith will provide Zenith residents with a wide variety of education, polling, shopping, financial, information, news, and entertainment services in the home. The initial operational capability version of the Project Zenith software is a very large (512-KDSI) embedded-mode product, requiring interface compatibility with a number of private, community, regional, and national institutions. Suppose you are developing an overall budget for the programming phase of Project Zenith. How many people (FSP) will you need for the eight major activities? At an average cost of $6000 per FSP per month, how many dollars should you budget for each activity?

7.2. Suppose you are developing a CM/QA plan for Project Zenith. How many people (FSP) will you need to perform CM/QA activities for the four phases of software development?

7.3. Suppose you have agreed to develop the required manuals for Project Zenith. How many FSP will you need in each development phase? At an average cost of $5000 per FSP per month, how many dollars should you request to do the job?

7.4. On the Project Zenith manuals job in the previous question, suppose instead that your average labor cost is $5000 per FSP per month for the first year and increases at a rate of 10% per year for each succeeding year ($5500 in year 2; $6050 in year 3, and so on). In this case, how many dollars should you request to do the job?

7.5. What will be the total effort required to run the Project Zenith software project office during development? What will be the personnel level for the project office during maintenance, assuming ACT = 15%?

7.6. Compute the activity distribution by phase, along the lines of Table 7–5, for Project Zenith. Assume ACT = 15% for maintenance. Develop corresponding organization charts for the various phases of the project.

7.7. Compute the activity distribution by phase, along the lines of Table 7–5, for a 320-KDSI semidetached-mode software development project.

7.8. You are planning to develop a 32-KDSI semidetached-mode software product to perform packet-switched communications functions for Megabit Computer-Communications Company's new network. However, Megabit advises you that they wish to perform all the software CM/QA functions as part of their overall CM/QA activity. By what percentage should you reduce your quoted software cost to Megabit?

7.9. Construct a table similar to Table 7–5 in which the columns are the activity distributions for the programming phase of organic, semidetached, and embedded-mode 32-KDSI software development projects. Compare the coding productivity, or lines of delivered code per man-month of programming activity during the programming phase, for the three modes.

7.10. Suppose you are asked to perform the test planning and V & V activities during the maintenance of a 32-KDSI organic-mode software package for producing environmental impact reports, with an ACT of 15%. Should you agree to do the job alone, or should you ask for some help?

7.11. Note from the organization charts for the programming phase and integration and test phase for the Hunt National Bank EFT project in Fig. 7–3, that the Project Office is not the only source of people performing management functions on the project. Including Project Office personnel and the Programming Manager as fully dedicated management personnel, and the leaders of six to eight person teams as half-time management personnel, how many FSP are performing management functions during the programming phase of the Hunt EFT project? How much is this in terms of percentage of total personnel? How does this compare with the percentage of total staff devoted to management functions on a small (2-KDSI) embedded-mode project?

7.12. Formulate additional organization chart tailoring guidelines based on the exception conditions discussed in the Hunt EFT organization chart development. Do you think that such detailed tailoring guidelines are better than the ones in Table 7–6?

Chapter 8

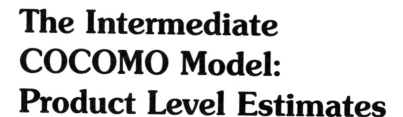

The Intermediate COCOMO Model: Product Level Estimates

8.1 INTRODUCTION

In the last three chapters, we presented the Basic COCOMO model, which estimates the effort required to develop a software product, using only a single predictor variable (size in delivered source instructions) and three modes of software development. As we saw in Fig. 6–4, this level of model is good enough to explain a good deal of the variation in software project costs. However, its accuracy is only good enough to make it useful in the rough early stages of software product definition. With respect to the COCOMO data base, the Basic COCOMO estimates were within a factor of 1.3 of the actuals only 29% of the time, and within a factor of 2 of the actuals only 60% of the time.

   In the next two chapters, we present the Intermediate COCOMO model, a compatible extension of Basic COCOMO whose greater accuracy and level of detail make it more suitable for cost estimation in the more detailed stages of software product definition. Intermediate COCOMO incorporates an additional 15 predictor variables which account for much of the software project cost variation left unexplained by

Basic COCOMO. With respect to the COCOMO data base, Intermediate COCOMO estimates are within 20% of the project actuals 68% of the time.

The Intermediate COCOMO Cost Driver Attributes

There are many candidate factors to consider in developing a better model for estimating the cost of a software project. The pioneering System Development Corporation studies of the mid-1960s [Nelson, 1966; Weinwurm, 1970] investigated 104 different factors, all of which are to some extent plausible determinants of software development costs. These included such factors as the type of application; the number of input and output types; the percent of input-output, control, or mathematical instructions in the program; the average experience of analysts and programmers; the computer configuration and programming language used; the number of agencies requiring concurrence on product decisions; and the number of person-trips required for project activities.

Subsequent studies, such as [Walston–Felix, 1977], have identified additional factors which also influence software costs, such as the program flow complexity, the presence of classified security constraints, and the uses of such techniques as structured programming, inspections, top-down development, and chief programmer teams.

In order to reduce this large number of candidate factors down to a relatively manageable number of factors which can be used for practical software cost estimation, we have subjected the candidate factors to two main tests:

- *General Significance.* This tends to eliminate factors which are significant only in a relatively small fraction of specialized situations: such as the number of person-trips or the presence of classified security constraints.
- *Independence.* This tends to eliminate factors which are strongly correlated with product size (for example, number of input and output types), and to compress a number of factors which tend to be highly correlated on projects into a single factor (such as use of structured programming, inspections, and so on, into a single "use of modern programming practices" factor).

The resulting set of 15 factors, or cost driver attributes,* used in the Intermediate COCOMO model are grouped into four categories: software product attributes, computer attributes, personnel attributes, and project attributes. They are listed below.

- *Product Attributes*
    RELY Required Software Reliability
    DATA Data Base Size
    CPLX Product Complexity

---

* Detailed discussions on the productivity influences of each of the COCOMO cost driver attributes are provided in Chapters 24 through 27. Chapter 28 discusses why some other fairly significant candidate variables were not included in COCOMO.

- *Computer Attributes*
  - TIME Execution Time Constraint
  - STOR Main Storage Constraint
  - VIRT Virtual Machine Volatility*
  - TURN Computer Turnaround Time

- *Personnel Attributes*
  - ACAP Analyst Capability
  - AEXP Applications Experience
  - PCAP Programmer Capability
  - VEXP Virtual Machine Experience*
  - LEXP Programming Language Experience

- *Project Attributes*
  - MODP Modern Programming Practices
  - TOOL Use of Software Tools
  - SCED Required Development Schedule

Each of these cost driver attributes determines a multiplying factor which estimates the effect of the attribute on software development effort. These multipliers are applied to a nominal COCOMO development effort estimate to obtain a refined estimate of software development effort. A similar process is carried out to determine a refined estimate of the software maintenance effort.

Chapter Preview

This chapter presents the Intermediate COCOMO effort multiplier tables and their associated definitions. It provides a number of examples that show how the tables can be used to estimate product level software development and maintenance effort and cost.

The examples also illustrate how Intermediate COCOMO can be used to help resolve a number of common software acquisition and project management decisions. They show how the use of Intermediate COCOMO can contribute to:

- The performance of software project sensitivity analyses
- A better understanding of the software job to be done

In this chapter, we also present techniques for dealing with software development situations in which portions of the project are adapted from previously existing software products. Finally, we summarize the correlation of Intermediate COCOMO estimates with the actual project data in the COCOMO data base, and conclude that the 15 additional cost driver attributes in Intermediate COCOMO indeed account for most of the variance not explained by the Basic COCOMO model.

* For a given software product, the underlying virtual machine is the complex of hardware and software (OS, DBMS, etc.) it calls upon to accomplish its tasks.

8.2 INTERMEDIATE COCOMO: SOFTWARE DEVELOPMENT EFFORT ESTIMATION

Nominal Scaling Equations

An Intermediate COCOMO software development effort estimate begins by generating a nominal effort estimate, using scaling equations of the same form as those used in Basic COCOMO. This nominal estimate is then adjusted by applying effort multipliers determined from the project's ratings with respect to the other 15 cost driver attributes.

The Intermediate COCOMO scale factors (exponents) for the three software development modes are the same as in Basic COCOMO, but the coefficients are different.* Table 8–1 presents the nominal effort estimating equations used for Intermediate COCOMO.

Figure 8–1 provides a graphical comparison of the Intermediate COCOMO nominal effort estimates for the three modes.

TABLE 8–1 Intermediate COCOMO Nominal Effort Estimating Equations

Development Mode	Nominal Effort Equation
Organic	$(MM)_{NOM} = 3.2 \ (KDSI)^{1.05}$
Semidetached	$(MM)_{NOM} = 3.0 \ (KDSI)^{1.12}$
Embedded	$(MM)_{NOM} = 2.8 \ (KDSI)^{1.20}$

Software Development Effort Multipliers

Table 8–2 presents the Intermediate COCOMO software development effort multipliers. Each cost driver attribute has a set of multipliers which are keyed to a set of project ratings for the attribute. The basic rating scales for each attribute are explained in Table 8–3.†

To explain the use of Tables 8–2 and 8–3, let us consider the development of a set of 32-KDSI semidetached software products which have different requirements for software reliability because of the nature of their expected operational use. The nominal effort equation for the semidetached mode in Table 8–1 estimates that $3.0(32)^{1.12} = 146$ MM are required to develop a 32-KDSI semidetached-mode product, independent of any considerations of the product's required reliability. Here are the adjusted estimates for the set of different products.

---

* An earlier version of Intermediate COCOMO used the same coefficients as were used in Basic COCOMO, but it did not work well. The main reason was that the aggregate effect of the effort multipliers was not the same in the three modes. Thus embedded-mode projects had Intermediate COCOMO estimates that were too high, and organic-mode projects, estimates that were too low.

† Detailed definitions of the rating scales for each attribute are given in Chapters 24 through 27.

TABLE 8-2 Software Development Effort Multipliers

Cost Drivers	Ratings					
	Very Low	Low	Nominal	High	Very High	Extra High
Product Attributes						
RELY Required software reliability	.75	.88	1.00	1.15	1.40	
DATA Data base size		.94	1.00	1.08	1.16	
CPLX Product complexity	.70	.85	1.00	1.15	1.30	1.65
Computer Attributes						
TIME Execution time constraint			1.00	1.11	1.30	1.66
STOR Main storage constraint			1.00	1.06	1.21	1.56
VIRT Virtual machine volatility[a]		.87	1.00	1.15	1.30	
TURN Computer turnaround time		.87	1.00	1.07	1.15	
Personnel Attributes						
ACAP Analyst capability	1.46	1.19	1.00	.86	.71	
AEXP Applications experience	1.29	1.13	1.00	.91	.82	
PCAP Programmer capability	1.42	1.17	1.00	.86	.70	
VEXP Virtual machine experience[a]	1.21	1.10	1.00	.90		
LEXP Programming language experience	1.14	1.07	1.00	.95		
Project Attributes						
MODP Use of modern programming practices	1.24	1.10	1.00	.91	.82	
TOOL Use of software tools	1.24	1.10	1.00	.91	.83	
SCED Required development schedule	1.23	1.08	1.00	1.04	1.10	

[a] For a given software product, the underlying virtual machine is the complex of hardware and software (OS, DBMS, etc.) it calls on to accomplish its tasks.

TABLE 8-3 Software Cost Driver Ratings

Cost Driver	Very Low	Low	Nominal	High	Very High	Extra High
Product attributes						
RELY	Effect: slight inconvenience	Low, easily recoverable losses	Moderate, recoverable losses	High financial loss	Risk to human life	
DATA		$\frac{\text{DB bytes}}{\text{Prog. DSI}} < 10$	$10 \leq \frac{D}{P} < 100$	$100 \leq \frac{D}{P} < 1000$	$\frac{D}{P} \geq 1000$	
CPLX	See Table 8–4					
Computer attributes						
TIME			≤50% use of available execution time	70%	85%	95%
STOR			≤50% use of available storage	70%	85%	95%
VIRT		Major change every 12 months Minor: 1 month	Major: 6 months Minor: 2 weeks	Major: 2 months Minor: 1 week	Major: 2 weeks Minor: 2 days	
TURN		Interactive	Average turnaround <4 hours	4–12 hours	>12 hours	
Personnel attributes						
ACAP	15th percentile[a]	35th percentile	55th percentile	75th percentile	90th percentile	
AEXP	≤4 months experience	1 year	3 years	6 years	12 years	
PCAP	15th percentile[a]	35th percentile	55th percentile	75th percentile	90th percentile	
VEXP	≤1 month experience	4 months	1 year	3 years		
LEXP	≤1 month experience	4 months	1 year	3 years		
Project attributes						
MODP	No use	Beginning use	Some use	General use	Routine use	
TOOL	Basic microprocessor tools	Basic mini tools	Basic midi/maxi tools	Strong maxi programming, test tools	Add requirements, design, management, documentation tools	
SCED	75% of nominal	85%	100%	130%	160%	

Ratings

[a] Team rating criteria: analysis (programming) ability, efficiency, ability to communicate and cooperate

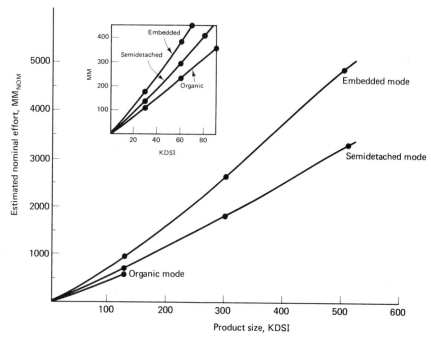

FIGURE 8-1 Intermediate COCOMO: Nominal effort estimates

1. A 32-KDSI prototype or feasibility demonstration model of a natural language or voice input system would have a very low required reliability, as it is not intended for production use, and the effect of a software fault is simply the inconvenience to the developers to fix the fault (Table 8–3). The adjusted effort estimate, from Table 8–2, for a product of this nature is

$$(146 \text{ MM})(0.75) = 110 \text{ MM}$$

2. A 32-KDSI long-range planning model or climate forecasting model would have a low relative required reliability, because their operational impact is generally long-range, and most faults would incur low-level, easily recoverable losses to users. The adjusted effort estimate here is

$$(146 \text{ MM})(0.88) = 128 \text{ MM}$$

3. A 32-KDSI management information system or inventory control system is representative of the large class of software with nominal required reliability. The effect of a fault in such systems is often nontrivial, but generally recoverable without extreme penalty. No adjustment is made for nominal ratings; thus the estimated effort for this system remains at 146 MM.

4. A 32-KDSI banking, credit authorization, or electric power distribution control system would have a high required reliability. The effect of software

faults in such systems can be major financial losses or massive human inconvenience. The adjusted effort estimate here is

$$(146 \text{ MM})(1.15) = 168 \text{ MM}$$

5. A 32-KDSI military command and control system or a nuclear reactor control system would have a very high requirement for software reliability. Here, the effect of a software fault could be the loss of human lives. The adjusted effort required to achieve the desired reliability is

$$(146 \text{ MM})(1.40) = 204 \text{ MM}$$

The reasons why it takes more man-months to develop a software product with higher required reliability are summarized in Table 8–5. This table indicates the typical sources of reduction or addition of effort in each development phase as a function of the required level of reliability. Thus, for example, in the integration and test phase of a software product with very low required reliability, Table 8–5 indicates that less effort is devoted to test procedures, requirements testing, quality assurance, configuration management, stress testing, off-nominal testing, and detailed as-built documentation. On the other hand, a product with very high required reliability will require much more than the usual effort for these activities, plus added effort to deal with an independent verification and validation agent.

Table 8–5 is an example of the tables provided in the Detailed COCOMO model provided in Part IV of this book. Detailed COCOMO contains phase-dependent effort multipliers, indicating the relative effort required to perform each software development phase as a function of the cost driver attribute ratings. The tables similar to Table 8–5 are provided in order to explain why a software project would take more or less effort in each phase because of the cost driver rating.

Another table "borrowed" from Part IV is Table 8–4, which provides a set of objective scales for various types of software as a frame of reference for assigning software complexity ratings. Thus, for example, a program to compute income taxes, based on a straightforward set of tax equations, would be given a very low or low rating from the Computational Operations scale, depending on the nature of the equations. If the income tax computation involved interpolation in a set of tax tables, the program would be given a nominal rating.

Figure 8–2 provides a graphical comparison of the relative magnitude of the Intermediate COCOMO effort multipliers for each factor. It provides a better intuitive feel for which factors cause major cost swings (Analyst Capability, Programmer Capability, Execution Time and Storage Constraints, Complexity, and Required Reliability), and which factors cause relatively minor cost swings.

Phase and Activity Distribution of Effort and Schedule

Intermediate COCOMO uses the same estimating relationships for development schedule, phase distribution, and activity distribution as those used in Basic COCOMO. That is

TABLE 8-4 Module Complexity Ratings versus Type of Module

Rating	Control Operations	Computational Operations	Device-dependent Operations	Data Management Operations
Very low	Straightline code with a few non-nested SP[a] operators: DOs, CASEs, IFTHENELSEs. Simple predicates	Evaluation of simple expressions: e.g., $A = B + C * (D - E)$	Simple read, write statements with simple formats	Simple arrays in main memory
Low	Straightforward nesting of SP operators. Mostly simple predicates	Evaluation of moderate-level expressions, e.g., $D = SQRT$ $(B**2-4.*A*C)$	No cognizance needed of particular processor or I/O device characteristics. I/O done at GET/PUT level. No cognizance of overlap	Single file subsetting with no data structure changes, no edits, no intermediate files
Nominal	Mostly simple nesting. Some inter-module control. Decision tables	Use of standard math and statistical routines. Basic matrix/vector operations	I/O processing includes device selection, status checking and error processing	Multi-file input and single file output. Simple structural changes, simple edits
High	Highly nested SP operators with many compound predicates. Queue and stack control. Considerable intermodule control.	Basic numerical analysis: multivariate interpolation, ordinary differential equations. Basic truncation, roundoff concerns	Operations at physical I/O level (physical storage address translations; seeks, reads, etc). Optimized I/O overlap	Special purpose subroutines activated by data stream contents. Complex data restructuring at record level
Very high	Reentrant and recursive coding. Fixed-priority interrupt handling	Difficult but structured N.A.: near-singular matrix equations, partial differential equations	Routines for interrupt diagnosis, servicing, masking. Communication line handling	A generalized, parameter-driven file structuring routine. File building, command processing, search optimization
Extra high	Multiple resource scheduling with dynamically changing priorities. Microcode-level control	Difficult and unstructured N.A.: highly accurate analysis of noisy, stochastic data	Device timing-dependent coding, micro-programmed operations	Highly coupled, dynamic relational structures. Natural language data management

[a] SP = structured programming

TABLE 8–5 Project Activity Differences due to Required Software Reliability (acronyms are explained in Appendix C)

Rating	Rqts. and Product Design	Detailed Design	Code and Unit Test	Integration and Test
Very low	Little detail Many TBDs Little verification Minimal QA, CM, draft user manual, test plans Minimal PDR	Basic design information Minimal QA, CM, draft user manual, test plans Informal design inspections	No test procedures Minimal path test, standards check Minimal QA, CM Minimal I/O and off-nominal tests Minimal user manual	No test procedures Many requirements untested Minimal QA, CM Minimal stress, off-nominal tests Minimal as-built documentation
Low	Basic information, verification Frequent TBDs Basic QA, CM, standards, draft user manual, test plans	Moderate detail Basic QA, CM, draft user manual, test plans	Minimal test procedures Partial path test, standards check Basic QA, CM, user manual Partial I/O and off-nominal tests	Minimal test procedures Frequent requirements untested Basic QA, CM, user manual Partial stress, off-nominal tests
Nominal	Nominal project V & V			
High	Detailed verification, QA, CM, standards, PDR, documentation Detailed test plans, procedures	Detailed verification, QA, CM, standards, CDR, documentation Detailed test plans, procedures	Detailed test procedures, QA, CM, documentation Extensive off-nominal tests	Detailed test procedures, QA, CM, documentation Extensive stress, off-nominal tests
Very high	Detailed verification, QA, CM, standards, PDR, documentation IV & V interface Very detailed test plans, procedures	Detailed verification, QA, CM, standards, CDR, documentation Very thorough design inspections Very detailed test plans, procedures IV & V interface	Detailed test procedures, QA, CM, documentation Very thorough code inspections Very extensive off-nominal tests IV & V interface	Very detailed test procedures, QA, CM, documentation Very extensive stress, off-nominal tests IV & V interface

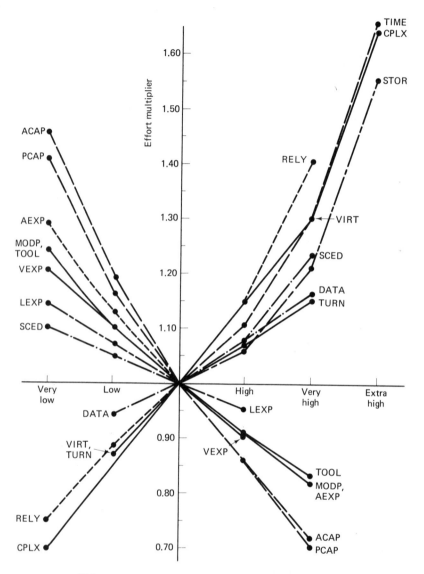

FIGURE 8-2 Intermediate COCOMO effort multipliers

- The estimated development schedule, TDEV, is calculated from the Intermediate COCOMO estimate of development effort in MM, using the equations in Table 6–1.
- The percentage distribution of effort and schedule by phase is obtained as a function of mode and product size, using Table 6–8.
- The percentage distribution of effort by activity and phase is obtained as a function of mode and product size, using Tables 7–1 through 7–3.

8.3 A PRICING EXAMPLE: MICROPROCESSOR COMMUNICATIONS SOFTWARE

Suppose we are negotiating with the Megabit Communication Company over the price to develop a 10-KDSI embedded-mode software product to perform communications processing functions on a commercial microprocessor. The nominal effort equation for the embedded mode (Table 8–1) estimates that a nominal 10-KDSI project requires $2.8(10)^{1.20} = 44$ MM for development, and we now wish to determine the effect of various non-nominal features of our project on the overall development effort and cost. For example, communications processing software generally rates very high on the complexity scale (see the Device-Dependent Operations column in Table 8–4), but we plan to use analyst and programmer personnel with high capabilities, which should balance the tendency to increase costs due to complexity. However, they will make our average personnel costs $6000 per month (per person, including overhead), and we wish also to find out how much the development is estimated to require in dollars.

TABLE 8–6 Cost Driver Ratings: Microprocessor Communications Software

Cost Driver	Situation	Rating	Effort Multiplier
RELY	Local use of system. No serious recovery problems	Nominal	1.00
DATA	20,000 bytes	Low	0.94
CPLX	Communications processing	Very high	1.30
TIME	Will use 70% of available time	High	1.11
STOR	45K of 64K store (70%)	High	1.06
VIRT	Based on commercial microprocessor hardware	Nominal	1.00
TURN	Two-hour average turnaround time	Nominal	1.00
ACAP	Good senior analysts	High	0.86
AEXP	Three years	Nominal	1.00
PCAP	Good senior programmers	High	0.86
VEXP	Six months	Low	1.10
LEXP	Twelve months	Nominal	1.00
MODP	Most techniques in use over one year	High	0.91
TOOL	At basic minicomputer tool level	Low	1.10
SCED	Nine months	Nominal	1.00
	Effort adjustment factor (product of effort multipliers)		1.17

Our estimate of the situation, with respect to each of the cost drivers, is summarized in Table 8–6, along with the resulting cost driver rating (from Table 8–3) and corresponding effort multiplier (from Table 8–2). We note that the 1.30 increase due to very high complexity is more than balanced by the 0.86 and 0.86 reductions due to high analyst and programmer capability. Overall, however, when we multiply all the effort multipliers together, the resulting overall effort adjustment factor is 1.17, representing a 17% increase over the nominal effort. The resulting adjusted estimate of the software development effort and cost is:

Man-months: (44 MM)(1.17) = 51 MM

Dollars: (51 MM)($6000/MM) = $306,000

Sensitivity Analysis

The Intermediate COCOMO model enables us to perform sensitivity analyses with respect to the cost driver attributes, which allow us to estimate the effect on software development cost of changes in the cost driver rating levels.

For example, suppose we had an option to staff the project with less expensive but less capable personnel. With this option, our manpower costs would be $5000 per month instead of $6000 per month, and the Analyst Capability (ACAP) and Programmer Capability (PCAP) ratings would be nominal instead of high. These ratings correspond to software development effort multipliers of 1.00 each, rather than the 0.86 multipliers obtained with the high ratings (from Table 8–2). This means that the COCOMO estimate must be adjusted to eliminate the 0.86 reduction factors; the resulting modified estimate would be

Effort adjustment factor = 1.58

Man-months: (44 MM)(1.58) = 70 MM

Dollars: (70 MM)($5000/MM) = $350,000

Thus, we see that the advantages of using more capable personnel more than outweigh (by $44,000) the effect of the higher salaries we would pay them.

As another example, suppose that for $10,000 Megabit could buy 96K words of memory for the microprocessors to be used, rather than 64K. This would change the main storage constraint to 45K/96K = 0.47 or 47%, for a nominal rating rather than a high rating for the STOR cost driver. The resulting effort multiplier would be 1.00 rather than 1.06, and the modified estimate would be

Effort adjustment factor = 1.10

Man-months: (44 MM)(1.10) = 48 MM

Dollars: (48 MM)($6000/MM) = $288,000

This is a software cost savings of $18,000, which more than compensates for the added $10,000 in hardware costs. Thus, when we negotiate with Megabit, we can propose this option as a way of reducing the software costs and sharing the resulting savings.

As a final example, suppose that a new, cheap microprocessor becomes available which delivers equivalent hardware performance to the one we have selected, at a price of $20,000 less for the quantity needed. However, this new microprocessor has only a bare minimum of tool support: its compilers, assemblers, and loaders are primitive and unreliable, and it does not have the maintenance and diagnostic aids available on our current choice of microprocessor. As a result, the Tools rating becomes very low instead of low, with an effort multiplier of 1.24 instead of 1.10. The modified software development cost estimate would be

$$\text{Effort adjustment factor} = 1.32$$

$$\text{Man-months:} \quad (44 \text{ MM})(1.32) = 58 \text{ MM}$$

$$\text{Dollars:} \quad (58 \text{ MM})(\$6000/\text{MM}) = \$348,000$$

The added software cost of $42,000 does not justify the purchase of the cheaper microprocessor.

Other examples of sensitivity analyses which can be performed via Intermediate COCOMO are given in the questions at the end of this chapter.

8.4 A MANAGEMENT EXAMPLE: REDUCED COST-TO-COMPLETE

The Problem

Suppose we have decided to proceed with Megabit Communication Company on the microprocessor communications software project discussed in the previous section, using the option of buying more memory and reducing the software development cost to $288,000. We complete the product design phase of the project right on budget, with an expenditure of $52,000 (18% of total development cost as predicted by Table 6–8).* This leaves us with a cost-to-complete of $236,000.

At this point, Megabit informs us that they are running short of funds, and only have $200,000 (15% less money) to pay to complete the software development. What can we do about this? The Intermediate COCOMO model provides us with a way to determine and evaluate our options. We need to identify the possible ways to modify the cost drivers on the project so that we reduce the estimated project cost by 15% (at this early stage, this is essentially equivalent to reducing the cost-to-complete by 15%).

Solution 1: Reduce Project Size

The most satisfactory solution is to reduce the size of the product to be developed by eliminating some of its functions or deferring their development until some later time. This means that we need to determine what product size in DSI would reduce the nominal development effort by 15%, from 44 MM to 37.4 MM (reducing the

---

* Intermediate COCOMO uses the same estimating relationships as Basic COCOMO for estimating phase and activity distributions, and for estimating the development schedule from the estimated number of development man-months.

nominal estimate by 15% would also reduce the adjusted estimate by 15%, if we kept all of the other factors the same).

If we apply the effort equation (Table 8–1) to a product with 8700 DSI, we find that it yields a nominal effort estimate of 37.5 MM. This means that if we can find a way to reduce the size of the product by 1300 DSI and still satisfy Megabit's basic needs, we will be able to meet the reduced development budget.*

Other Possible Solutions

The Intermediate COCOMO model (Table 8–2) indicates several other possibilities to reduce project expenditures by roughly 15%.

1. Reduce the required reliability from nominal to low. This would reduce project costs by 12% (0.88 versus 1.00). This solution is not recommended unless there is a corresponding change in the intended use of the product; otherwise, it will simply lead to higher levels of expenditure and disruption in the operations and maintenance phase.
2. Increase analyst capability or programmer capability from high to very high (bring on the superstars). Either of these measures would reduce project costs by about 17–19% (0.71/0.86 = 0.83; 0.70/0.86 = 0.81). The usual difficulty with this solution is finding (or making available) the superstars.
3. Increase applications experience from nominal to very high or virtual machine experience from low to high (bring on the experts). Either of these measures would reduce project costs by about 19% (0.81 versus 1.00 or 0.90 versus 1.10). Again, finding the people and making them available would be the main difficulty.
4. Find a way to provide an interactive software development support system for the project. This would reduce the computer turnaround rating from nominal to low, at a savings of 13% (0.87 versus 1.00).
5. Reduce the real-time performance requirements for the system. Suppose that the 70% execution time constraint is based on Megabit's desire for a 2-msec average processing time per message handled. If Megabit is willing to settle for 3-msec average processing time instead of 2 msec, the execution time constraint becomes (70%) × (2 msec/3 msec) = 47%, reducing the TIME rating from high to nominal, with a savings of 10% (1.00/1.11 = 0.90).

Other Candidates

The other COCOMO cost drivers are not good candidates for helping out in this situation. Some (data base size, main storage constraint, schedule) are already at their minimum levels. For some, it is hard to achieve instant improvements (use of tools and modern programming practices). Some are largely beyond the developer's control (complexity and virtual machine volatility). And one (language experience) has a savings potential of only 5%.

---

* This assumes that the costs required to reorient the project are negligible. This will not always be the case.

Choice of Solution

Again, the most appropriate solution is to eliminate or defer some of the functions to be developed. Next best would be to reduce the real-time performance requirements, particularly if they were rather arbitrarily determined. The other solutions depend upon the availability of suitable personnel or interactive software development facilities.

The actual solution chosen is thus likely to result from a negotiation between our people and Megabit's people, based on the factors above. Intermediate COCOMO can provide a valuable service, both in helping the developer and customer to identify possible solutions to the budget problem, and in helping them negotiate a mutually acceptable revision of their development plan.

8.5 ADJUSTED ESTIMATE OF ANNUAL MAINTENANCE EFFORT

The effort multipliers in Intermediate COCOMO can be applied to the maintenance phase as well as to the development phase.

For most of the cost drivers, we can safely assume that the effort multipliers are the same for maintenance as for development (that is, the ones given in Table 8–2). For these cost drivers, we can simply compute adjustments due to differences in the cost driver ratings: maintenance personnel with more (or less) experience than the development personnel; better (or worse) computer response time during maintenance, etc.

Cost Driver Not Used for Maintenance Phase: SCED

One of the development cost drivers, SCED (Required Development Schedule) is only a factor during development. The fact that some of the software was developed on a different schedule does not make a perceptible difference in the relative effort required to maintain it. Thus, the SCED effort multipliers are adjusted back to 1.00 for the maintenance phase.

Modified Effort Multipliers: Required Reliability

Two of the cost drivers, RELY and MODP, have different productivity multipliers due to differences in their relative impact on development and maintenance. For RELY (Required Software Reliability), the cost driver rating is assumed to be the same for development and for maintenance. Thus, for example, one should not expect to develop software with low reliability (many faults) and then expect it to operate with few faults (high reliability) during maintenance. The RELY productivity multiplier table is presented below as Table 8–7.

TABLE 8–7 RELY Maintenance Effort Multipliers

Very Low	Low	Nominal	High	Very High
1.35	1.15	1.00	0.98	1.10

The trend shown in Table 8–7 is the net effect of two trends:

1. The lower the required reliability, the less effort is required to maintain the required level.
2. The lower the required reliability, the more effort is required to fix latent faults in the software, and to update a software product with inaccurate documentation and code.

Modified Effort Multipliers: Modern Programming Practices

The effect of using Modern Programming Practices (MPP's) (structured code, top-down design and development, walkthroughs, program support libraries, and anticipatory documentation) during development (and maintenance) has a twofold effect on the required level of software maintenance:

1. The more MPP's used, the greater the savings in maintenance effort.
2. The more MPP's used, the easier it is to maintain large products with the same efficiency as small products (the smaller are the diseconomies of scale for software maintenance).

This twofold effect is evident in the MODP maintenance productivity multipliers presented in Table 8–8.

TABLE 8–8   MODP Maintenance Effort Multipliers

Product Size (KDSI)	Rating				
	Very Low	Low	Nominal	High	Very High
2	1.25	1.12	1.00	0.90	0.81
8	1.30	1.14	1.00	0.88	0.77
32	1.35	1.16	1.00	0.86	0.74
128	1.40	1.18	1.00	0.85	0.72
512	1.45	1.20	1.00	0.84	0.70

8.6 EXAMPLE: MICROPROCESSOR COMMUNICATIONS SOFTWARE MAINTENANCE

As an example of the use of the software maintenance effort multipliers, let us take the Megabit microprocessor communications software product originally defined in Table 8–6, with the STOR rating reduced to nominal by our acquisition of additional main memory. The development of this 10-KDSI software product required 48 MM, at a cost of $288,000.

Let us calculate the annual effort and cost required to maintain this product, under the following assumptions:

- The product will be maintained by analysts and programmers with nominal rather than high capabilities, at a reduced personnel cost of $5000 per MM.
- The virtual machine volatility will be low rather than nominal.
- The virtual machine experience will be nominal rather than low.
- The annual change traffic will be 20%.

The nominal annual maintenance effort $(MM)_{NAM}$ is calculated from the nominal development effort (44 MM for a 10-KDSI product) and the annual change traffic (0.20) as

$$(MM)_{NAM} = (0.20)(44 \text{ MM}) = 8.8 \text{ MM}$$

The adjusted annual maintenance effort $(MM)_{NAM}$ is calculated via the effort multipliers determined from

- Table 8–7 for RELY
- Table 8–8 for MODP
- Using 1.00 for SCED
- Table 8–2 for the other cost drivers

Table 8–9 summarizes the resulting development and maintenance ratings. These yield a maintenance effort adjustment factor of 1.14.

TABLE 8–9 Microprocessor Communications Software Maintenance Ratings

Cost Driver	Development Rating	Maintenance Rating	Maintenance Effort Multiplier
RELY	Nominal	Nominal	1.00
DATA	Low	Low	0.94
CPLX	Very high	Very high	1.30
TIME	High	High	1.11
STOR	Nominal	Nominal	1.00
VIRT	Nominal	Low	0.87
TURN	Nominal	Nominal	1.00
ACAP	High	Nominal	1.00
AEXP	Nominal	Nominal	1.00
PCAP	High	Nominal	1.00
VEXP	Low	Nominal	1.00
LEXP	Nominal	Nominal	1.00
MODP	High	High	0.88
TOOL	Low	Low	1.10
SCED	Nominal	———	1.00
		Effort Adjustment Factor	1.14

Thus, the adjusted annual maintenance effort is

$$(8.8 \text{ MM})(1.14) = 10.0 \text{ MM}$$

or an average staff level of $10/12 = 0.83$ FSP. At $5000 per MM, the annual maintenance cost is $50,000.

Six-Year Life-Cycle Sensitivity Analysis:
Required Reliability

If we were to operate and maintain the resulting software product for six years, our resulting life-cycle cost would be

$$\$288\text{K} + 6(\$50\text{K}) = \$288\text{K} + \$300\text{K} = \$588\text{K}$$

Suppose we had decided to develop and maintain the software with a very low required reliability rather than nominal. Would the savings in development cost pay off over the six-year product lifetime? To determine this, we compute a revised development cost estimate of

$$(\$288\text{K})(0.75) = \$216\text{K} \qquad \text{(from Table 8–2)}$$

and a revised maintenance cost of

$$(\$300\text{K})(1.35) = \$405\text{K} \qquad \text{(from Table 8–7)}$$

for a revised life-cycle cost of $621K. Clearly, given the length of the life-cycle and the level of annual change traffic in this situation, it does not pay to develop unreliable software here. In other situations, it might; see Questions 8.14 and 8.15 below.

8.7 INTERPOLATION AND EXTRAPOLATION

Tables 8–2, 8–7, and 8–8 may be used for interpolation in the same way as the phase and activity tables in Chapters 6 and 7. Thus, for example, the effort multiplier corresponding to an execution time constraint of 90% (halfway between very high and extra high in Table 8–3) would be 1.48 (halfway between very high and extra high in Table 8–2). Similarly, the effort multiplier corresponding to an 80th-percentile analyst capability (one-third of the way between high and very high in Table 8–3) would be 0.81 (one-third of the way between high and very high in Table 8–2).

Some of the entries are defined with $\leq$ signs. This means that the rating applies to all less-than situations, and that the equals-to value is used for interpolation. For example, a main storage constraint of 40% implies an effort multiplier of 1.00; a 60% constraint implies an effort multiplier of 1.03.

Extrapolation outside the effort multiplier tables is not recommended, as effects outside the given ranges are highly situation dependent and hard to predict. In particular, the required development schedule rating should never be below the very low 75% of the nominal development schedule; experience has shown that it is virtually impossible to compress the nominal schedule more than 25% (see Chapter 27).

8.8 ESTIMATING THE EFFECTS OF ADAPTING EXISTING SOFTWARE

Adaptation Considerations

Up to now, we have been estimating software costs based on the assumption that all of the delivered source instructions (DSI) in the software product are being specified and developed from scratch. This is often not the case. Many software products consist of a combination of newly developed software and previously developed software which is adapted for use in the new product.

How should we account for this adapted software in our software development estimates? Clearly, we don't want to include its DSI count in the same way we do for newly developed software. For example, suppose we use a simple input-output routine which is part of our computer center's standard library of utilities, and count it as part of our product's DSI for estimation purposes. We are then increasing the size of the product by several hundred DSI, which will increase the estimated development effort by several man-months. But, in fact, our use of the I/O routine does not at all increase the amount of effort required to develop the software.

On the other hand, we don't want to disregard adapted software completely. In many cases, it will require us to spend a good deal of product effort in:

1. Redesigning the adapted software to meet the objectives of the new product
2. Reworking portions of the code to accommodate redesigned features or changes in the new product's environment (hardware, operating system, compiler, and so on)
3. Integrating the adapted code into the new product environment and testing the resulting software product

Thus, we want a technique for estimating adaptation effects which is sensitive to each of these three sources of adaptation effort. This is the basis of the adaptation estimating equations used in the COCOMO model.

The COCOMO Adaptation Estimating Equations

The effects of adapted software are handled in COCOMO by calculating an equivalent number of delivered source instructions (EDSI), which will be used in place of DSI in the other COCOMO estimating relationships. EDSI is calculated from the following estimated adaptation quantities:

- ADSI *Adapted DSI.* The number of delivered source instructions adapted from existing software to form the new product.
- DM *Percent Design Modified.* The percentage of the adapted software's design which is modified in order to adapt it to the new objectives and environment. (This is necessarily a subjective quantity.)
- CM *Percent Code Modified.* The percentage of the adapted software's code which is modified in order to adapt it to the new objectives and environment.
- IM *Percent of Integration Required for Modified Software.* The percentage of effort required to integrate the adapted software into an overall product and to test the resulting product as compared to the normal amount of integration and test effort for software of comparable size.

The equations for calculating EDSI involve an intermediate quantity, the *adaptation adjustment factor* (AAF), as follows:

$$AAF = 0.40(DM) + 0.30(CM) + 0.30(IM) \qquad (8\text{--}1)$$

$$EDSI = (ADSI)\frac{AAF}{100} \qquad (8\text{--}2)$$

The rationale underlying Eqs. (8–1) and (8–2) will be explained in more detail below, but first let us look at some examples of the use of the adaptation equations.

Example 1: The I/O Routine (Transparent Utility Software)

The input-output routine discussed above is an example of transparent utility software, which is usually adapted into a software product with essentially zero added effort. For the I/O routine, the COCOMO adaptation quantities are

$DM = 0.$ (no change in the I/O routine's design)
$CM = 0.$ (no change in the I/O routine's code)
$IM = 0.$ (no effort required to integrate the I/O routine)

Thus AAF = 0 and EDSI = 0, meaning that no effort will be added to the COCOMO estimate because of its use of the transparent utility routine.

Example 2: Simple Conversion

Suppose we are converting a 50-KDSI organic-mode Fortran electronic circuit analysis program from a Univac 1110 computer to an IBM 3033. Typically, for this situation, we would have

$DM = 0$ (no change in the program's design)
$CM = 15$ (perhaps 15% of the lines of code will change because of compiler

idiosyncrasies, operating system interfaces, job control language changes, and so on)

IM = 5   (a small amount of effort required to integrate the above changes)

The resulting adaptation calculations would be

$$AAF = 0.40(0) + 0.30(15) + 0.30(5) = 6$$

$$EDSI = 50,000 \left(\frac{6}{100}\right) = 3000$$

Using the Basic COCOMO organic-mode estimation Eq. (5–1), the resulting conversion effort would be

$$MM = 2.4(KEDSI)^{1.05} = 2.4(3)^{1.05} = 7.6 \ MM$$

The resulting *conversion productivity rate* would be

$$\frac{50,000 \ DSI}{7.6 \ MM} = 6580 \ DSI/MM$$

Example 3: More Complex Conversion

Suppose that the overlay structure of the electronic circuit analysis program and the change from a 36-bit Univac 1110 word size to a 32-bit IBM 3033 word size require some redesign of the program for efficiency and accuracy considerations. Typically, for this situation, we would have

DM = 15   (some changes in overlay structure, numerical algorithms, and related logic)
CM = 30   (in this range, code changes often run about twice the rate of design changes)
IM = 20   (largely to accommodate overlay changes)

The resulting conversion effort estimate would be

$$AAF = 0.40(15) + 0.30(30) + 0.30(20) = 21$$

$$EDSI = 50,000 \left(\frac{21}{100}\right) = 10500$$

$$MM = 2.4(10.5)^{1.05} = 28 \ MM$$

The resulting conversion productivity would be

$$\frac{50,000 \ DSI}{28 \ MM} = 1800 \ DSI/MM$$

Example 4: Extensive Rework, Complex Interfaces

Suppose we had developed the 10-KDSI communications processor software for Megabit Communications Corp. along the original lines indicated in Section 8.3. Subsequently, the Hunt National Bank asks us how much it would cost to adapt this software for uses in their Electronic Fund Transfer system. In this situation, we might estimate

DM = 35   (considerable modification of the design to accommodate different message formats, protocols, and equipment)

CM = 60   (many of the design changes will have side effects requiring additional code modifications)

IM = 140   (the software will have to be integrated and tested within an entirely new environment)*

The resulting adaptation calculations would be

$$AAF = 0.40(35) + 0.30(60) + 0.30(140) = 74$$

$$EDSI = 10,000 \left(\frac{74}{100}\right) = 7400$$

Using the Intermediate COCOMO nominal effort estimating equation for embedded-mode software, as before (Table 8–1), we have

$$(MM)_{NOM} = 2.8(7.4)^{1.20} = 31 \text{ MM}$$

Using the effort adjustment factor calculated in Table 8–6, we have

$$(MM)_{EST} = 31(1.17) = 36 \text{ MM}$$

At an average personnel cost of $6000 per MM, our estimated cost is

$$(36 \text{ MM})(\$6000/\text{MM}) = \$216,000$$

Example 5: Component Adaptation

Suppose we are developing a communications processor software product for the Brazilian telecommunications agency. Since the host computer and the various communications protocols are considerably different from those on the software we developed for Megabit Communications Corp., we are not able to use much of the Megabit software for the Brazilian application. However, we find that a 1000-DSI

---

*There is no reason why the values of DM, CM, and IM cannot be greater than 100. In fact, it frequently happens that one spends more effort adapting a piece of existing software to one's needs than it would have taken to develop a new piece of software.

message routing module can be adapted without too much trouble. Its adaptation parameters for use in the Brazilian application are:

DM = 5   (some small changes to accommodate a different routing doctrine for acknowledgements)

CM = 15   (some code changes to reflect the design changes, and to accommodate the different computer)

IM = 25   (the message routing module is fairly self-contained, but we anticipate some extra effort in working with the Brazilian test data and programs)

The resulting adaptation calculations would be:

$$AAF = 0.40(5) + 0.30(15) + 0.30(25) = 14$$

$$EDSI = 1000 \left(\frac{14}{100}\right) = 140$$

For an adopted software component, we would then add this 140 EDSI to the size of the remainder of the Brazilian application software (say, 8,000 DSI), to obtain a total equivalent size of 8,140 EDSI. Assuming the same Embedded development mode, 1.17 Effort Adjustment Factor, and \$6000/MM labor cost as in the Megabit development, we would then have:

$$(MM)_{NOM} = 2.8(8.14)^{1.20} = 35 \text{ MM}$$

$$(MM)_{EST} = 35(1.17) = 41 \text{ MM}$$

$$Cost = (41 \text{ MM})(\$6000/MM) = \$246,000$$

Rationale Behind the COCOMO Adaptation Estimating Equations

The coefficients in the Adaptation Adjustment Factor (AAF) estimating equation (8–1) are determined from the general average fractions of effort devoted to design, code, and integration-and-test given by the COCOMO model in Table 6–8:

Design: 40%

Code: 30%

Integration and test: 30%

These phase fractions vary somewhat as a function of the product's size and development mode, but as the AAF calculations are not extremely sensitive to moderate variations in the coefficients, the averaged values are used for simplicity. An installation whose phase distributions are considerably different might consider an alternate formula—for example, for small embedded-mode jobs:

$$AAF = 0.40(DM) + 0.40(CM) + 0.20(IM)$$

Adaptation Estimates: A Note of Caution

No quantities are as easy to underestimate as are the estimates of how much one will have to change an existing piece of software to get it to work successfully in a new product environment. Two useful general guidelines in making adaptation estimates are

1. Be very conservative.
2. Take a small, representative piece of the existing software and work out in detail what you will be doing to adapt it. In general, you will be surprised at how many side effects and complicating factors pop up in the process.

8.9 DISCUSSION OF THE INTERMEDIATE COCOMO EFFORT EQUATIONS

The cost driver attribute multipliers used in the Intermediate COCOMO effort equations are averaged values of the multipliers used in the Detailed COCOMO model covered in Part IV of this book. Detailed COCOMO has a separate set of cost driver attribute multipliers for each software development phase; they were determined through a four-step process.

1. Review of data and literature to identify the most significant candidate cost driver attributes
2. A two-round Delphi group-consensus activity involving ten experienced software managers to determine initial values for the multipliers
3. Calibration of the multipliers using a 36-project subset of the COCOMO data base
4. A small final adjustment of the multipliers to correct some discrepancies in the phase distribution of effort, using a 56-project subset of the COCOMO data base.

The Detailed COCOMO phase-dependent multipliers were then averaged across the various development phases to produce the Intermediate COCOMO multipliers, which are applied uniformly across the software development cycle.

Intermediate COCOMO Estimates versus Actuals

Figure 8–3 is a plot of the Intermediate COCOMO estimated man-months versus the actual project man-months for the 63 projects in the COCOMO data base. It shows a striking improvement over Fig. 6–4, the corresponding plot for Basic COCOMO. The large variations between the Basic COCOMO estimates and the project actuals are mostly eliminated by the use of the cost driver factors in Intermediate COCOMO. The Intermediate COCOMO estimates are within 20% of the actuals 68% of the time; this is sufficiently accurate for most practical estimation purposes. Also, the estimates are roughly equally accurate for all three software development modes.

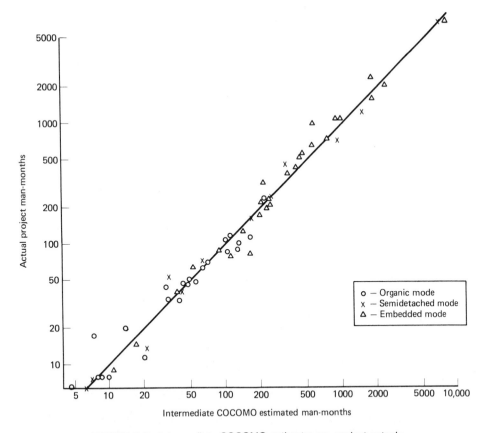

FIGURE 8-3 Intermediate COCOMO estimates vs. project actuals

Intermediate COCOMO Nominal Effort Equations versus Actuals

Figure 8–4 shows the source of the different nominal effort estimating equations used for the three development modes by Intermediate COCOMO. It shows the residual effect due to product size which remains after we normalize the project effort figures by removing the effects of the other Intermediate COCOMO cost driver attributes.

Specifically, Fig. 8–4 contains a plot of product size in KDSI versus the normalized effort parameter

$$(MM)_{NOM} = \frac{\text{Project man-months}}{\text{Effort adjustment factor}}$$

where the effort adjustment factor is computed from the cost driver attribute ratings for each project in the COCOMO data base (these ratings are given in Table 29–1).

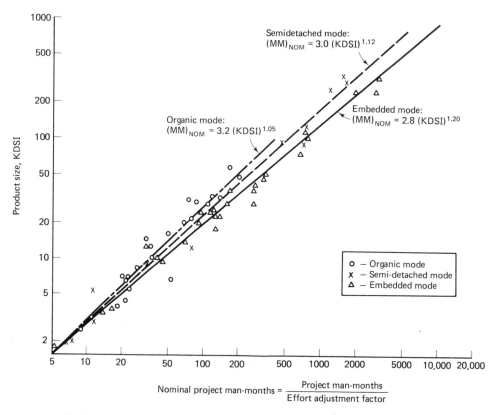

FIGURE 8-4 Intermediate COCOMO nominal effort equations versus project data

When the effects of the factors other than size are normalized out, the data in Fig. 8–4 clearly fall into groups which are reasonably well-characterized by the Intermediate COCOMO nominal effort estimating equations: the lines shown in Fig. 8–4.

More detail on the calibration and validation of Intermediate COCOMO is given in Chapter 29. Of particular note, Chapter 29 covers the topic of calibrating Intermediate COCOMO to the experience of a particular installation. For various reasons, primarily differences in definitions, a given installation's experience may not correspond with the projects in the COCOMO data base, in which case a calibrated version of COCOMO will give better results for the installation.

The Weighted Delivered Source Instructions Metric

One way of looking at the difference between Basic COCOMO and Intermediate COCOMO is the following:

- Basic COCOMO assumes that every source instruction (in a given development mode) is equally easy to produce. Intermediate COCOMO recognizes that source instructions produced under very high reliability requirements, time and storage constraints, and so on, are relatively harder to produce, or "heavier to move into place," than an equal number of nominally rated source instructions.

Thus, Intermediate COCOMO uses the cost driver attribute ratings to produce a new metric, *weighted delivered source instructions,** which by Fig. 8–4 is seen to correlate much more closely to project effort in man-months for the projects in the COCOMO data base than did the unweighted deliverable source instructions plotted in the Basic COCOMO data analysis in Fig. 6–5.

8.10   QUESTIONS

8.1. A nominal 128-KDSI embedded-mode software product requires 950 MM and 22 months for development. Using Intermediate COCOMO, how many man-months will the development require if the required development schedule is:

$16\frac{1}{2}$ months	(75% of nominal)?
19 months	(85%)?
29 months	(130%)?
35 months	(160%)?

8.2. Enumerate the Intermediate COCOMO cost drivers by product attributes, computer attributes, personnel attributes, and project attributes.

8.3. A nominal 10-KDSI embedded-mode software product requires 44 MM to develop, or $220,000 at a personnel cost of $5000 per MM. The amount of main storage needed by the program is 61K words. The project has options to buy hardware with various amounts of main storage; the resulting hardware costs and main storage constraints are given in the table below.

Option	Main Storage	Storage Constraint	Hardware Cost
1	64K	0.95	$150,000
2	72K	0.85	$160,000
3	88K	0.70	$180,000
4	128K	0.48	$220,000

What are the total hardware–software costs for the various options? Which is the best buy?

8.4. Suppose you are managing the development of a 32-KDSI, organic-mode sales information system; the nominal development effort estimate is 122 MM. You have the option

* Here, weighted delivered source instructions are defined as

$$\text{WDSI} = (\text{KDSI})^{e_i} \prod_{j=1}^{15} (\text{EM})_j$$

where e_i is the exponent used for the ith development mode, and $(\text{EM})_j$ is the effort multiplier determined for the jth cost driver attribute.

of staffing the project with high capability programmers at an average project labor cost of $5500 per MM, or with very low capability programmers at an average cost of $4000 per MM. Assuming all of the other cost driver ratings are nominal, how much would each of these options cost?

8.5. A nominal 23-KDSI semidetached-mode product requires 100 MM to develop. How much effort would the development require if all the cost drivers had their most expensive ratings? How much would the development cost if all the cost drivers had their least expensive ratings? Compute the weighted DSI metric for these two extreme cases.

8.6. What activities account for the increased cost of a product with higher required reliability?

8.7. Suppose you have two 10-KDSI organic-mode programs to develop. Both are nominal, except that one has very high complexity and the other very low. You also have two teams of analysts and programmers, one with very high analyst and programmer capabilities and the other with very low. You have two staffing options:
(a) Staff the very high complexity job with the very high capability personnel, and vice versa.
(b) Staff the very high complexity job with the very low capability personnel, and vice versa.
What is the total effort required to develop the two programs for the two options? How do you think the two options would compare with respect to the likely morale and job satisfaction of the two teams?

8.8. In the Megabit microprocessor communications software example in Section 8.3, suppose that we could increase the system's throughput by 5% by microprogramming the control operations. How much would this add to the software development effort and cost by increasing the complexity of the software?

8.9. In the Megabit microprocessor communications software example in Section 8.3, suppose that Megabit required that the software be available in 7 months, about 80% of the 8.8 months computed from the basic schedule equation. How much would this requirement add to the development cost? Suppose the customer required the software in 5 months. What does COCOMO say about estimating the cost of this requirement?

8.10. Which cost drivers have different effort multipliers for development and maintenance? Which development cost drivers are not used for maintenance?

8.11. A nominal 40-KDSI semidetached-mode intelligent terminal software product requires 187 MM for development. If the average applications experience was two years rather than three years, how would this affect the amount of development effort?

8.12. For the nominal 40-KDSI intelligent terminal software product above, how would the amount of development effort be affected if the main storage constraint were 62%? 76%? 93%?

8.13. Compute life-cycle costs for the Megabit communications software product analyzed in Section 8.6 for the other possible ratings for required reliability: low, high, and very high.

8.14. Suppose the annual change traffic in the Megabit example of Section 8.6 was 2% rather than 20 percent. How would the life-cycle costs compare for required reliability ratings of very low, low, and nominal? How realistic do you think an ACT estimate of 20% is for a very low reliability product?

8.15. Suppose the product lifetime for the Megabit example of Section 8.6 was one year rather than six years. How would the life-cycle costs compare for required reliability ratings of very low, low, and nominal?

8.16. Suppose you are planning the life-cycle of a new Master Claims Processing System for the Allweather Insurance Co. It is estimated to be a nominal, semidetached-mode, 150-KDSI product with an annual change traffic of 15% and a product lifetime of 10 years. For $1,000,000, you can run a training program for all project personnel which will increase your modern programming practices rating from nominal to high. Compute the resulting life-cycle savings, at $6K/MM. Are they worth the $1,000,000 investment?

8.17. Suppose you are preparing a life-cycle plan for an organic-mode prescription information system for the pharmacy of the Santa Maria Hospital. It has an estimated size of 25-KDSI, an annual change traffic of 15%, and an operational lifetime of seven years. It has the following characteristics

RELY–high	AEXP–high
DATA–very high	PCAP–nominal
CPLX–nominal	VEXP–high
TIME–nominal	LEXP–high
STOR–high	MODP–high
VIRT–low	TOOL–high
TURN–nominal	SCED–nominal
ACAP–high	

Using an average personnel cost of $6000 per MM, compute the development cost and the life-cycle cost for the product.

8.18. Compute the phase and activity effort distributions for the Santa Maria Hospital prescription information system's development and maintenance.

8.19. How would the life-cycle cost of the Santa Maria Hospital prescription information system compare if the required reliability had been nominal or very high? Given the potential risks to human life or health if the wrong prescription is issued, which do you think would be the appropriate choice for required reliability?

8.20. Assign Intermediate COCOMO cost driver attribute ratings to a software project with which you are familiar, and compute the resulting estimated development effort.

8.21. Suppose that the 50-KDSI, organic-mode electronic circuit analysis program discussed in Examples 2 and 3 in Section 8.8 is being adapted to a Honeywell 8/70 computer. The Honeywell computer also has a 36-bit word size, eliminating the need to rework the numerical algorithms, but some rework is still necessary to accommodate the overlay structure. The resulting estimated adaptation parameters are

$$DM = 10, \quad CM = 15, \quad IM = 10$$

What is the corresponding estimated effort required for conversion?

8.22. In discussing our communications software adaptation options with the Hunt National Bank (Example 4, Section 8.8), it appears that some small changes in the design of the Hunt EFT system could reduce our adaptation effort. The resulting estimates of our adaptation parameters are

$$DM = 20, \quad CM = 40, \quad IM = 70$$

What is the corresponding reduced cost to adapt the communications software to the EFT system?

8.23. Pick a program with which you are familiar and use Intermediate COCOMO to estimate the effort required to convert it to run on a different computer system.

8.24. *(Research Project)* Develop extensions to the complexity metrics and related software work/effort models in [Halstead, 1977; McCabe, 1976; and Putnam, 1978] based on the weighted delivered source instruction metric (and counterpart metrics such as weighted complexity, weighted program volume, etc.).

Chapter 9

Intermediate COCOMO: Component Level Estimation

9.1 INTRODUCTION

Up to now, we have been dealing with *macro* cost estimation models, which are the most common software cost models used today (for example, the Putnam SLIM model [Putnam, 1978; Putnam-Fitzsimmons, 1979] and the RCA PRICE S model [Freiman-Park, 1979]). These models assume that the cost driver attributes are applied uniformly across the entire software product: for example, that the people working on each component are equally capable and experienced, and that each component is equally complex. This approach is adequate for rough early estimates of the cost of an entire software product, but it has clear limitations once we begin to define the components of the product.

For example, we may wish to assign the high complexity parts of a job to our high capability people (with higher labor costs per person), and the low complexity parts of the job to people with less capability and experience. Assessing the effect of such a strategy is difficult and sometimes risky if we are working at the level of overall product averages.*

In this chapter, we present a form and a set of procedures for using Intermediate COCOMO at the software product component level. This allows us to use Intermediate COCOMO easily and consistently through all stages of software product definition: as a *macro* model during the rough early stages, and as a *micro* model in the later, more detailed stages.

---

* A striking example of this risk is given as Question 9.9 at the end of this chapter.

9.2 THE COMPONENT LEVEL ESTIMATING FORM (CLEF)

Experience has shown that it is highly useful to collect and record intermediate level software cost estimating information on a standard form organized for the purpose. The Component Level Estimating Form (CLEF) is shown in Fig. 9–1. The procedures for using the CLEF to generate software cost estimates are straightforward; they are given in Table 9–1.

The use of the CLEF and the procedures are also illustrated in Fig. 9–1, using a simple refinery process control system as an example. The procedure steps, as applied to the example, are explained below.

Steps 1 and 2. The process control software product consists of three major components (described in columns 1 and 2 of the CLEF):

1. A Process component, which performs the basic process control operations. It operates on sensor data (such as temperature, pressure, fluid flow) to keep the refinery running efficiently and to determine any potential trouble conditions. We estimate its size as 7000 DSI.*
2. An OPSYS component, which performs operating system functions: sensor polling, emergency interrupt processing, scheduling, and computer resource management. We estimate its size as 5000 DSI.
3. An I/O component, which performs input-output functions: receiving and preprocessing sensor inputs, transmitting refinery commands, equipment status monitoring, and operator terminal displays, queries, and commands. We estimate its size as 10,000 DSI.

Steps 3, 4, and 5. The total size of the product is 22,000 EDSI (22 KEDSI). We use the total size in the organic-mode nominal effort equation (at the bottom of Table 9–1) to compute the nominal number of man-months required to develop a 22-KEDSI product

$$(MM)_{NOM} = 3.2(22)^{1.05} = 82 \text{ MM}$$

We then use this figure to compute the nominal productivity for a 22-KEDSI product

$$(EDSI/MM)_{NOM} = \frac{22,000 \text{ EDSI}}{82 \text{ MM}} = 268 \text{ EDSI/MM}$$

We enter these quantities in rows 11, 12, and 13 of column 2 on the CLEF.

Step 6. The nominal effort required to develop each component is computed from its size and the nominal product productivity and entered in column 20. For example, we compute the nominal effort for the PROCESS component as

---

* None of the software is being adapted from existing software, so DSI and EDSI are identical for this case.

Project: REFINERY PROCESS CONTROL   Analyst: Q. SMITH   Date: 4/1/6-

(1) COMPONENT	(2) EDSI	(3) AAF	(4) RELY	(5) DATA	(6) CPLX	(7) TIME	(8) STOR	(9) VIRT	(10) TURN	(11) ACAP	(12) AEXP	(13) PCAP	(14) VEXP	(15) LEXP	(16) MODP	(17) TOOL	(18) SCED	(19) EAF	(20) MM NOM	(21) MM DEV/AM	(22) EDSI/MM ACT	(23) $K	(24) $/EDSI
1. PROCESS	7 000	1.0	HI 1.15	LO 0.94	HI 1.15	HI 1.11	N 1.0	N 1.0	LO 0.87	HI 0.86	N 1.0	N 1.0	N 1.0	N 1.0	HI 0.91	N 1.0	N 1.0	0.94	26	24	292	5.5 / 132	19
2. OPSYS	5 000	1.0	HI 1.15	LO 0.94	VHI 1.30	HI 1.11	N 1.0	N 1.0	LO 0.87	HI 0.86	LO 1.13	HI 0.86	LO 1.10	LO 1.07	HI 0.91	N 1.0	N 1.0	1.21	19	23	217	6.0 / 138	28
3. I/O	10 000	1.0	N 1.0	LO 0.94	N 1.0	N 1.0	N 1.0	N 1.0	LO 0.87	N 1.0	N 1.0	N 1.0	LO 1.10	N 1.0	N 1.0	N 1.0	N 1.0	0.92	37	30	333	5.0 / 156	15
4.																							
5.																							
6.																							
7.																							
8.																							
9.																							
10.																							

11. Total EDSI: 22 000

12. (MM)NOM: 82

13. (EDSI/MM)NOM: 268

Totals: 77   286   420   19

Schedule (Months): 13

Development Mode: Organic

FIGURE 9-1 COCOMO software cost model: Component-level estimating form (CLEF)

147

TABLE 9–1 Procedures for Using the Component Level Estimating Form (CLEF)

1. Identify all of the software product's components in column 1.
2. Estimate the sizes in DSI of all the components. If the component is not being adapted from existing software, enter its size in column 2 (EDSI). If it is being adapted, compute its adaptation adjustment factor (AAF) by the equation given below, enter it in column 3, then compute the Equivalent DSI (EDSI) and enter it in column 2.
3. Add up the total EDSI for the product and enter it in row 11, column 2.
4. Use the appropriate nominal effort equation for the specified development mode (given below) to estimate the nominal amount of development effort $(MM)_{NOM}$ as a function of total EDSI and enter it in row 12, column 2.
5. Compute the nominal productivity $(EDSI/MM)_{NOM} = $ (total EDSI)/(MM_{NOM}) and enter it in row 13, column 2.
6. For each component, compute $(MM)_{NOM} = EDSI/(EDSI/MM)_{NOM}$ and enter it in column 20.
7. Provide cost driver ratings (columns 4 to 18) for all components, using the rating scales in Table 8–3.
8. Enter the corresponding effort multipliers for all components in columns 4 to 18 using Table 8–2.
9. For each component (row), compute the effort adjustment factor (EAF) as the product of the effort multipliers in columns 4 to 18 and enter it in column 19.
10. Multiply $(MM)_{NOM}$ (column 20) for each component by its EAF to produce the adjusted estimate for $(MM)_{DEV}$, which is entered in column 21.
11. Add up the total adjusted man-month estimates for all components and enter that in row 11, column 21.
12. Use the appropriate basic development schedule equation for the specified development mode (given below) to compute the number of months required for product development and enter it in row 12, column 21.
13. For each component and for the entire product, compute the estimated productivity EDSI/MM $= EDSI/(MM_{DEV})$ and enter it in column 22.
14. Estimate the average manpower cost ($K/MM) for each component and enter it in column 23.
15. Compute the dollar cost for each component $K = (MM_{DEV})($K/MM)$ and enter it in column 23 (lower half).
16. Add up the total product development cost in $K and enter it in row 11, column 23.
17. For each component and for the entire product, compute the cost per instruction $/EDSI $=$ (1000)($K)/EDSI and enter them in column 24.

Adaptation Equations (COCOMO Eqs. 8–1, 8–2)

$$AAF = 0.4 \text{ (Percent design modified)}$$
$$+ 0.3 \text{ (Percent code modified)}$$
$$+ 0.3 \text{ (Percent integration modified)}$$
$$EDSI = \text{(Adapted DSI)(AAF)}/100$$

Effort and Schedule Equations (COCOMO Tables 8–1, 6–1)

Development Mode	Nominal Effort	Schedule
Organic	$(MM)_{NOM} = 3.2(KEDSI)^{1.05}$	$TDEV = 2.5(MM_{DEV})^{0.38}$
Semidetached	$(MM)_{NOM} = 3.0(KEDSI)^{1.12}$	$TDEV = 2.5(MM_{DEV})^{0.35}$
Embedded	$(MM)_{NOM} = 2.8(KEDSI)^{1.20}$	$TDEV = 2.5(MM_{DEV})^{0.32}$

(KEDSI = thousands of EDSI)

$$(MM)_{NOM} = \frac{7,000 \text{ EDSI}}{268 \text{ EDSI/MM}} = 26 \text{ MM}$$

Step 7. We now rate each of the three components with respect to the 15 cost driver attributes, using the rating scales in Table 8–3. In general, it is best to do this step one cost driver at a time rather than one component at a time, because the process of comparing the cost driver ratings across all of the components tends to produce a more consistent and well-understood set of ratings. These ratings are entered in the upper half of the appropriate component row for each of the cost driver columns (4 through 18).

For example, the PROCESS and OPSYS components are required to have a high reliability, because their malfunctioning is highly likely to lead to serious trouble and financial loss for the refinery, with perhaps some human safety concerns also (but not enough to require very high reliability). The I/O component's faults are generally not so critical, and their effects are generally easier to control and compensate for, leading to a nominal rating being entered in column 4.

Another example is provided by columns 6, 11 and 13 (complexity, analyst capability, and programmer capability). We estimate that the PROCESS component will have a high complexity (from Table 8–4, considerable intermodule control and basic numerical analysis operations), and we plan to assign high capability analysts and nominal capability programmers to this component. We estimate the OPSYS component will have a very high complexity (from Table 8–4, use of reentrant code and fixed-priority interrupt handling), and we plan to assign high capability programmers and analysts to this component. We estimate the I/O component to have nominal complexity (from Table 8–4, use of device selection, status checking, and error processing, and mostly simple nesting of structured programming operators), and we plan to assign nominal capability programmers and analysts to this component.

Step 8. Once we have assigned ratings for each cost driver and each component, we can use Table 8–2 to determine the corresponding effort multipliers, which we enter in the lower half of the component-row for columns 4 to 18. For example, in column 6, the high complexity PROCESS component receives an effort multiplier of 1.15; the very high complexity OPSYS receives a 1.30; and the nominal complexity I/O component receives an effort multiplier of 1.00.

Step 9. We compute the overall effort adjustment factor (EAF) for each component by multiplying together all of its individual effort multipliers in columns 4 to 18. Actually, we need only multiply together the factors that are different from 1.00 (non-nominal ratings). Thus, for example, we compute the EAF for the I/O component as

$$EAF = (0.94)(0.87)(1.10)(0.91) = 0.82$$

and enter the result in column 19.

Steps 10 and 11. We can now compute an adjusted effort estimate for each component by multiplying its nominal effort estimate (column 20) by its EAF (column 19). Thus, for the I/O component, the result is

$$(MM)_{ADJ} = (0.82)(37 \text{ MM}) = 30 \text{ MM}$$

We enter each of the adjusted estimates in column 21, add up the total adjusted effort estimate for the overall product (77 MM), and enter this in row 11 of column 21.

Step 12. We use the organic-mode development schedule equation (at the bottom of Table 9–1) to estimate the schedule for the project

$$TDEV = 2.5(77)^{0.38} = 13 \text{ months}$$

which we enter in row 12 of column 21.

Step 13. For each component and for the entire product, we compute the estimated productivity in DSI/MM. Examples:

> I/O component: 10,000 DSI/30 MM = 333 DSI/MM
> Product: 22,000 DSI/77 MM = 286 DSI/MM

We enter the results in column 22.

Step 14. For each component, we estimate the average cost per man-month for personnel. This is generally related to the level of capability and experience of the personnel assigned to the component. Thus, the use of high capability analysts and programmers on the OPSYS component leads to an average labor cost of $6000 per MM. The use of nominal capability analysts and programmers on the I/O component leads to an average labor cost of $5000 per MM. We enter these estimates in the upper half of the subsystem's row in column 23.

Steps 15 and 16. We multiply the number of man-months required to develop each component by the corresponding labor cost to obtain the estimated dollar cost of each component. For example:

> OPSYS component: (23 MM)($6000/MM) = $138,000
> I/O component: (30 MM)($5000/MM) = $150,000

We enter these estimates in the lower half of the component's row in column 23. We then add up all of the component costs to determine the development cost estimate for the overall product ($420,000) and enter this in row 11 of column 23.

Step 17. For each component and for the entire product, we compute the estimated cost per instruction in $/DSI. For example:

I/O component: $150,000/10,000 DSI = $15/DSI
Product: $420,000/22,000 DSI = $19/DSI

We enter these results in column 24, completing the estimation process.

9.3 USING THE CLEF WITH ADAPTED SOFTWARE

For the refinery process control job just described, suppose that we could adapt the OPSYS and I/O components from an existing process control system using a similar computer configuration.

The operating system component is fairly close to what we need; our estimate of its adaptation parameters is

$$DM = 15; \quad CM = 30; \quad IM = 60$$

The I/O component will require a good deal of work to accommodate some different sensor data formats and operator terminal displays, but its basic capabilities fit our needs reasonably well. We estimate its adaptation parameters as

$$DM = 30; \quad CM = 60; \quad IM = 80$$

Table 9–2 summarizes our calculation of the adaptation adjustment factor (AAF) and equivalent DSI (EDSI) for these components, using the equations given at the bottom of Table 9–1.

TABLE 9–2 Process Control Software Adaptation Calculations

Component	DM	CM	IM	AAF	ADSI	EDSI
OPSYS	15	30	60	33	5000	1650
I/O	30	60	80	54	10,000	5400

Following the steps in Table 9–1, we enter the quantities EDSI and AAF for the adapted components in columns 2 and 3, and continue the CLEF procedure as before. The results are shown in Fig. 9–2. The major effects of adapting existing OPSYS and I/O software rather than developing it from scratch are:

- The estimated effort is reduced from 77 to 47 man-months. In particular, the effort for OPSYS is reduced from 23 to 7 MM, and the effort for I/O from 30 to 16 MM.
- The estimated cost is reduced from $420K to $254K.
- The estimated schedule is reduced from 13 to 11 months.

| (1) Component | (2) EDSI | (3) AAF | Product | | | Computer | | | | Personnel attrib. | | | | | Project | | | (19) EAF | (20) MM NOM | (21) MM DEV/AM | (22) EDSI/MM ACT | (23) $K | (24) $/EDSI |
			(4) RELY	(5) DATA	(6) CPLX	(7) TIME	(8) STOR	(9) VIRT	(10) TURN	(11) ACAP	(12) AEXP	(13) PCAP	(14) VEXP	(15) LEXP	(16) MODP	(17) TOOL	(18) SCED						
1. PROCESS	7,000	1.0	HI 1.15	LO 0.94	HI 1.15	HI 1.11	N 1.0	N 1.0	LO 0.87	HI 0.86	N 1.0	N 1.0	N 1.0	N 1.0	HI 0.91	N 1.0	N 1.0	0.94	25	24	292	5.5 / 132	19
2. OPSYS	1,650	0.33	HI 1.15	LO 0.94	VHI 1.30	HI 1.11	N 1.0	N 1.0	LO 0.87	HI 0.86	LO 1.13	HI 0.86	LO 1.10	LO 1.07	HI 0.91	N 1.0	N 1.0	1.21	6	7	236	6.0 / 42	25
3. I/O	5,400	0.54	N 1.0	LO 0.94	N 1.0	N 1.0	N 1.0	N 1.0	LO 0.87	N 1.0	N 1.0	N 1.0	LO 1.10	N 1.0	HI 0.91	N 1.0	N 1.0	0.82	20	16	338	5.0 / 80	15
4.																							
5.																							
6.																							
7.																							
8.																							
9.																							
10.																							
11. Total EDSI	14,050																		Totals	47	299	254	18
12. (MM)NOM	51																		Schedule (months)	11			
13. (EDSI/MM)NOM	275																						

Development mode: *Organic*

FIGURE 9-2 Refinery process control estimate: Adapted software

9.4 TRANSACTION PROCESSING SYSTEM (TPS) EXAMPLE: BASIC DEVELOPMENT ESTIMATE

This section describes a transaction processing system (TPS) which will be used as an example throughout Part III of this book. In places, we will need an estimate of the development cost of the operating system (OS) portion of the TPS. We will use Intermediate COCOMO to estimate the development cost in this section. For completeness, we will continue to use this example in the following section to illustrate the use of Intermediate COCOMO to generate a complete life-cycle cost estimate for a project, including component-level maintenance costs and phase distribution of project effort.

TPS Description

The usual distinguishing features of a TPS are:

- Input transactions are generated by users at unspecified (unpredictable) times.
- Input transactions arrive in standard formats. Generally, there are a limited number of such formats.
- The amount of processing per transaction is not large.
- Each transaction must be processed in a short time.

The type of transactions being processed by the TPS might be financial transactions, airline reservations, messages in a store-and-forward digital communications system, or sales transactions in a large department store. The techniques used in this book to analyze the example TPS could apply to any of these types of TPS.

At the point that we enter into discussion of the TPS, we have decided—primarily on the basis of required capacity, cost, growth potential, and backup redundancy—to employ a multiple microprocessor configuration for the central portion of the TPS.

The basic configuration of this portion of the TPS is shown in Fig. 9–3. It consists of a front-end processor, several parallel transaction processors, and a file system. For our application, we will need 25 copies of this configuration, for processing transactions in 25 different geographical locations.

Front-End Processor (FEP) Software Subsystems

Transactions arrive at the front-end processor (FEP) over a number of communications lines. They are brought into the FEP, scanned, categorized, and stored by the communications software component. The task control component assigns each transaction to one of the parallel transaction processors (TP's); another portion of the communications component in the FEP picks up the transaction from storage and sends it to the appropriate TP.

The other software components in the FEP are a status monitoring component, which keeps track of keepalive messages sent by the TP's, and takes appropriate action when one of the TP's goes down or when it is restored to service. The keyboard/display component provides information on the TPS status and performance via the display, and accepts operator commands via the keyboard to modify transaction priori-

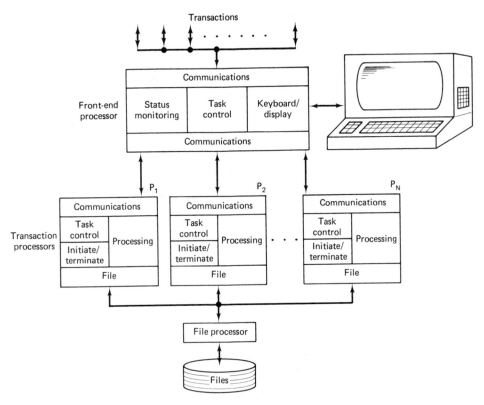

FIGURE 9-3 Transaction processing system: Basic configuration

ties, terminate or reinitiate processing, provide additional information on status or performance, and so on.

Transaction Processor (TP) Software Subsystems

Each TP has an identical copy of the TP software. The operating system portion of this software consists of a communications component to handle incoming transactions sent from the FEP and send back the results; a file component to query and update the transaction system status files whenever necessary; a task control component which monitors and allocates control and resources; and an initiate/terminate component for shutting down and restarting the TP. Each TP also has a processing portion of the software, which performs the actual transaction processing functions (such as financial transactions, airline seat reservations, inventory additions or reductions), and which is also supervised by the task control component.

TPS Operating System Software
Development Estimate

An estimate of the cost of developing a TPS operating system is developed using the Intermediate COCOMO CLEF form in Fig. 9–4. The procedure used to develop the estimate is the same 17-step procedure shown in Table 9–1 and described via

Project: TPS Operating System Development Analyst: J Fernandez Date: 4/1/81

(1) Component	(2) EDSI	(3) AAF	Product			Computer					Personnel attributes					Project			(19) EAF	(20) MM NOM	(21) MM DEV/AM	(22) EDSI/MM ACT	(23) $K	(24) $/EDSI
			(4) RELY	(5) DATA	(6) CPLX	(7) TIME	(8) STOR	(9) VIRT	(10) TURN	(11) ACAP	(12) AEXP	(13) PCAP	(14) VEXP	(15) LEXP	(16) MODP	(17) TOOL	(18) SCED						
Front-end proc. 1. Task Control	1,100	1.0	HI 1.15	LO 0.94	VHI 1.30	HI 1.11	N		LO 0.87	HI 0.86	LO 1.13	HI 0.86	LO 1.10	LO 1.07		LO 1.10		1.47	4.1	6.0	180	5.2 / 31	28
2. Communication	1,300	1.0	1.15	0.94	1.30	1.11			0.87	0.86	1.13	0.86	1.10	1.07		1.10		1.47	4.9	7.2	180	5.2 / 37	28
Status 3. Monitoring	500	1.0	1.15	0.94	1.30	1.11	1.06		0.87	0.86	1.13	0.86	1.10	1.07		1.10		1.47	1.9	2.8	180	5.2 / 15	28
Keyboard / 4. Display	1,200	0.50	N	0.94	HI 1.15	N			0.87	0.86	1.13	N	1.10	1.07		1.10		1.18	4.5	5.3	226	4.5 / 24	20
Transaction Processing 5. Task cont. TP	700	1.0	HI 1.15	0.94	VHI 1.30	HI 1.11	HI 1.06		0.87	0.86	1.13	HI 0.86	1.10	1.07		1.10		1.56	2.6	4.1	171	5.2 / 21	30
6. Comm-TP	400	1.0	1.15	0.94	1.30	1.11	1.06		0.87	0.86	1.13	0.86	1.10	1.07		1.10		1.56	1.5	2.3	171	5.2 / 12	30
7. File	1000	1.0	1.15	N	1.30	1.11	1.06		0.87	0.86	1.13	N	1.10	1.07		1.10		1.93	3.8	7.3	137	4.5 / 33	33
8. Init form	300	1.0	HI 1.15	LO 0.94	HI 1.15	N	1.06		0.87	0.86	1.13	HI 0.86	1.10	1.07		1.10		1.24	1.1	1.4	214	5.2 / 7	23
9.																							
10.																							
11. Total EDSI	6,500																		Totals	364	179	180	28
12. (MM)NOM	24.4																		Schedule (months)	9			
13. (EDSI/MM)NOM	266																						

Development mode: Semidetached

FIGURE 9-4 TPS operating system: Development estimate

example in Section 9.2. The only differences are that, for simplicity and readability, only the down-the-column changes in cost driver ratings are shown in Columns 4 to 18, and the 1.0 multipliers are not entered.

The overall size of the operating system is 6500 EDSI,* and the overall development cost is $180,000, for an average cost per instruction of $28 per EDSI. However, the cost per instruction varies from $20 per EDSI for the relatively simple FEP keyboard/display component to $33 per EDSI for the parallel TP file system software. The total number of man-months required for development is 36.4 MM, for an average productivity rate of $\frac{6500 \text{ EDSI}}{36.4 \text{ MM}} = 179$ EDSI/MM. Again, there is a wide variation in productivity between subsystems, from 137 EDSI/MM for the TP file component to 226 EDSI/MM for the FEP keyboard/display component. The required development schedule is 9 months.

9.5 TPS COMPONENT-LEVEL MAINTENANCE ESTIMATE AND PHASE DISTRIBUTION

The maintenance phase of the TPS operating system is estimated to have the following characteristics:

- A nominal rather than a low rating for the experience cost drivers: applications experience, virtual machine experience, and language experience.
- A low rather than a nominal rating for virtual machine volatility.
- An annual change traffic of 15% for the keyboard/display component, and 10% for the other components.

The CLEF form used in making Intermediate COCOMO software development estimates can also be used for maintenance estimates. Table 9–3 gives the procedural steps for using the CLEF to estimate maintenance costs at the component level. Figure 9–5 shows the results of applying these steps to the TPS maintenance estimate, as explained below.

Step 1. The EAF figures for each component are taken from column 19 of the TPS development CLEF (Fig. 9–4) and entered in the lower half of column 19 of the maintenance CLEF.

Step 2. The high reliability rating for all components other than keyboard/display has its maintenance multiplier changed from 1.15 to 0.98 (Table 8–7). The changed cost driver ratings for AEXP, VEXP, LEXP, and VIRT (noted above) have their corresponding multiplier changes indicated.

---

* The actual size in DSI is 7700 DSI. The 2400-DSI keyboard/display component is to be adapted from existing software, requiring 35% design modification, 60% code modification, and 60% integration modification, with the resulting adaptation adjustment factor (AAF) and equivalent DSI (EDSI):

$$AAF = (0.40)(0.35) + (0.30)(0.60) + (0.30)(0.60) = 0.50$$
$$EDSI = 2400(0.50) = 1200$$

TABLE 9–3 Procedures for Using the CLEF for Software Maintenance Cost Estimation

1. For each component, enter the effort adjustment factor computed for software development in the lower half of column 19.
2. For each component, identify any changes in cost driver effort multipliers between development and maintenance by entering the development multiplier in the lower half of the cost driver column, and the corresponding maintenance multiplier in the upper half of the cost driver column (columns 4 to 18). Effort multipliers will change for any of the following reasons:
   - Non-nominal SCED multipliers for development will be changed to 1.00 for maintenance.
   - Non-nominal RELY and MODP multipliers for development will have different values (RELY: Table 8–7; MODP: Table 8–8).
   - Cost driver ratings may change (for example, experience ratings).
3. For each component, compute its maintenance EAF

$$(EAF)_M = (EAF)_{DEV} \times \frac{\text{Product of maintenance multipliers changed}}{\text{Product of development multipliers changed}}$$

   and enter it in the upper half of column 19.[a]
4. For each component, enter the annual change traffic (ACT) as a fraction (such as 0.10 for 10%) in column 22.
5. If all components have an AAF of 1.0, enter the nominal development man-months $(MM)_{NOM}$ for each component in column 20.
   If not, we need to recompute $(MM)_{NOM}$ based on the size of the product being maintained. For any component whose AAF is not 1.0, compute its actual DSI = EDSI/AAF, and enter this number in column 2. Then
   - Compute a revised total DSI and enter it in row 11, column 2.
   - Compute a revised $(MM)_{NOM}$ for the product, using the revised total DSI and the appropriate nominal effort equation for the given mode (at the bottom of Table 9–1), and enter it in row 12, column 2.
   - Compute a revised nominal project productivity

$$(DSI/MM)_{NOM} = \frac{\text{Total DSI}}{(MM)_{NOM}}$$

   and enter it in row 13, column 2.
   - For each component, compute a revised $(MM)_{NOM} = DSI/(DSI/MM)_{NOM}$ and enter it in column 20.
6. For each component, compute the annual maintenance effort

$$(MM)_{AM} = (EAF)_M (MM)_{NOM}(ACT)$$

   and enter it in column 21.
7. Add up the total maintenance effort for all components and enter it in row 11, column 21.
8. Estimate the average labor cost ($K/MM) for maintaining each component and enter it in column 23 (upper half).
9. Compute the dollar cost for annual maintenance of each component $K = (MM)_{AM} (\$K/MM)$, and enter it in column 23.
10. Add up the total annual maintenance cost for all components and enter it in row 11, column 23.

---

[a] Steps 2 and 3 are a short cut method of computing $(EAF)_M$ when relatively few multipliers change between development and maintenance. If many multipliers change, it may be easier to compute $(EAF)_M$ directly as the product of all the maintenance effort multipliers.

Project: _TPS Operating System Maintenance_ Analyst: _J. Fernandez_ Project Date: _8/1/81_

(1) Component	(2) EDSI	(3) AAF	Product (4) RELY	(5) DATA	(6) CPLX	Computer (7) TIME	(8) STOR	(9) VIRT	(10) TURN	Personnel attributes (11) ACAP	(12) AEXP	(13) PCAP	(14) VEXP	(15) LEXP	Project (16) MODP	(17) TOOL	(18) SCED	(19) EAF	(20) MM NOM	(21) MM DEV/AM	(22) EDSI/MM ACT	(23) $K	(24) $/EDSI
Front end																							
1. Task Control	1,100		0.98					0.87			1.0		1.0	1.0				0.82	4.2	0.34	0.10	5.5	
			1.15					1.0			1.13		1.10	1.07				1.47				1.9	
Communication 2.	1,300		0.98					0.87			1.0		1.0	1.0				0.82	6.0	0.41	0.10	5.5	
			1.15					1.0			1.13		1.10	1.07				1.47				2.3	
Status 3. Monitor	500		0.98					0.87			1.0		1.0	1.0				0.82	1.9	0.16	0.10	5.5	
			1.15					1.0			1.13		1.10	1.07				1.47				0.9	
Keyboard/ 4. Display	2,400	0.50						0.87			1.0		1.0	1.0				0.77	9.2	1.06	0.15	5.5	
								1.0			1.0		1.0	1.07				1.18				5.8	
Transaction processing TP																							
5. Task Control	700		0.98					0.87			1.0		1.0	1.0				0.87	2.7	0.23	0.10	5.5	
			1.15					1.0			1.13		1.10	1.07				1.56				1.3	
Communication 6. TP	400		0.98					0.87			1.0		1.0	1.0				0.87	1.5	0.13	0.10	5.5	
			1.15					1.0			1.13		1.10	1.07				1.56				0.7	
7. File	1,000		0.98					0.87			1.0		1.0	1.0				1.08	3.8	0.41	0.10	5.5	
			1.16					1.0			1.13		1.10	1.07				1.93				2.3	
8. Init/term.	300		0.98					0.87			1.0		1.0	1.0				0.69	1.1	0.08	0.10	5.5	
			1.15					1.0			1.13		1.10	1.07				1.24				0.4	
9.																							
10.																							
11.		Total EDSI 7,700																Totals		2.82		15.6	
12.	29.5	(MM)$_{NOM}$																					
13.	261	(EDSI/MM)$_{NOM}$													Schedule (months)								

Development mode: _Semidetached_

FIGURE 9-5 TPS operating system: Maintenance estimate

158

Step 3. The modified $(EAF)_M$ for maintenance is calculated and entered in the upper half of column 19. For all the components except keyboard/display, the same adjustment factor applies

$$(EAF)_M = (EAF)_{DEV} \times \frac{(0.98)(0.87)(1.00)(1.00)(1.00)}{(1.15)(1.00)(1.13)(1.10)(1.07)} = 0.56 \ (EAF)_{DEV}$$

Step 4. An ACT of 0.15 is entered in column 22 for the keyboard/display component, and an ACT of 0.10 for the others.

Step 5. Since the adaptation adjustment factor (AAF) for the keyboard/display component is not 1.0, we compute its actual DSI (2400 DSI); the revised total DSI (7700 DSI); the revised $(MM)_{NOM} = 29.5$ MM; the revised $(DSI/MM)_{NOM} = 261$ DSI/MM; and a revised $(MM)_{NOM}$ for each component. The resulting $(MM)_{NOM}$ for the keyboard/display component is 9.2 MM.

Steps 6 and 7. The annual maintenance effort for each component is computed and entered in column 23. For example, $(MM)_{AM}$ for the file subsystem is

$$(MM)_{AM} = (1.08)(3.8)(0.10) = 0.41 \ MM$$

The total annual maintenance effort for the TPS is 2.82 MM, or 0.23 FSP.

Steps 8, 9, and 10. Since TPS operating system maintenance is estimated to require less than a quarter-time person (0.23 FSP), we assume that the same person will maintain all components, at a uniform labor cost of $5500 per MM. Thus, the total annual maintenance cost estimate is $15.6K (row 11, column 23).

TPS Phase Distribution of Effort and Schedule

We can use Table 6–8 to determine the phase distribution of effort and schedule for the TPS operating system. We note that the size of the product, 6500 DSI, is three-fourths of the way between the small and intermediate entries in Table 6–8, so we interpolate three-fourths of the way between these entries to find the correspond-

TABLE 9–4 TPS Phase Distribution of Effort and Schedule

Phase	Effort		Schedule		
	Percent	MM	Percent	Months	FSP
Product Design	17	6.2	24.75	2.2	2.8
Programming	61.75	22.5	53	4.8	4.7
Integration and Test	21.25	7.7	22.25	2.0	3.8
Development	100	36.4	100	9.0	
Maintenance		2.8			0.2

ing phase distribution percentages. The resulting estimated distribution of the 36.4 MM of development effort and 9 months of development schedule is given in Table 9–4.

The peak staffing on the project would be between 5 and 6 FSP. Even at this point, the organizational structure will consist of a single project manager leading a relatively small team. Thus, we do not need to go through an exercise to determine how the project's organization chart will vary by phase.

9.6 QUESTIONS

9.1. In the process control example (Fig. 9–1), suppose that the PROCESS and OPSYS components were staffed by personnel with nominal analyst and programmer capability, high applications experience, virtual machine experience, and language experience, and a cost of $6K per MM. How would this affect the total development effort and cost?

9.2. In the TPS example (Figs. 9–4, 9–5), suppose that the project were able to employ a high level of modern programming practices. How many dollars and man-months would this save in development and annual maintenance?

9.3. Compute the annual maintenance effort and dollar cost for the process control project, under the following assumptions:
- Nominal experience levels (applications, virtual machine, language) for all components
- No other changes in development cost drivers
- ACT = 0.05 for OPSYS, 0.10 for PROCESS and I/O
- Labor cost: $5K/MM

9.4. Suppose that the required reliability in the TPS example were nominal for all components. How would this affect the development and annual maintenance effort and dollar cost?

9.5. Figure 9–6 shows the filled out CLEF entries describing a project to take a fairly large ecology simulation program and develop an interactive-graphics version of it. Complete the CLEF process and derive the effort and dollar estimates for the project.

9.6. Figure 9–7 shows the filled out CLEF entries for an integrated management information system for the Montana Mining and Manufacturing Corp. Complete the CLEF process and derive the effort and dollar estimates for the project.

9.7. Estimate the annual maintenance effort and dollar cost involved in the interactive-graphic ecology simulation, under the following assumptions:
- No changes in development cost driver ratings or labor costs
- ACT = 0.15 for ECOSIM, 0.20 for DISP/CONT, 0.05 for FILES

9.8. Use the CLEF to estimate the development and maintenance cost and effort for a project with which you are familiar.

9.9. This example shows the difficulties that can arise from using a *macro* cost-estimation model with averaged cost driver ratings, rather than using a *micro* cost-estimation model with individual cost driver ratings for each component. It is taken from an example and an averaging technique recommended for use with a leading commercial macro software cost-estimation model, in estimating the effect of storage constraints on a software product with several overlays.

The recommended technique:

1. Compute the storage utilization percentage s_i for each component: $i = 1, 2, \ldots n$.

Project: _Interactive Ecology Simulation._ Analyst: _____ Project: _____ Date:

(1) Component	(2) EDSI	(3) AFF	Product (4) RELY	(5) DATA	(6) CPLX	Computer (7) TIME	(8) STOR	(9) VIRT	(10) TURN	Personnel attributes (11) ACAP	(12) AEXP	(13) PCAP	(14) VEXP	(15) LEXP	Project (16) MODP	(17) TOOL	(18) SCED	(19) EAF	(20) MM NOM	(21) MM DEV/AM	(22) EDSI/MM ACT	(23) $K	(24) $/EDSI
1. ECOSIM	8,000	0.40	LO	N	HI	N	N	LO	LO	HI	VHI	HI	N	VHI	HI	HI	N					6.0	
2. DISP/CONT	12,000	1.0	LO	LO	N	N	N	LO	LO	HI	HI	HI	N	HI	HI	N	N					5.0	
3. FILES	6,000	1.0	LO	HI	N	N	N	LO	LO	N	N	N	HI	HI	HI	HI	N					4.5	
4.																							
5.																							
6.																							
7.																							
8.																							
9.																							
10.																							
11. Total EDSI																			Totals				
12. $(MM)_{NOM}$																			Schedule (months)				
13. $(EDSI/MM)_{NOM}$																							

Development mode: _Organic_

FIGURE 9-6 Interactive graphics: Ecology simulation CLEF

Project: _Corporate MIS : Montana M.M._ Analyst: _____ Date: _____

Project: _____

(1) Component	(2) EDSI	(3) AAF	Product (4) RELY	(5) DATA	(6) CPLX	(7) TIME	(8)	Computer (9) VIRT	(10) TURN	Personnel attributes (11) ACAP	(12) AEXP	(13) PCAP	(14) VEXP	(15) LEXP	Project (16) MODP	(17) TOOL	(18) SCED	(19) EAF	(20) MM NOM	(21) MM DEV/AM	(22) EDSI/MM ACT	(23) $K	(24) $/EDSI
1. Finance	24,000	0.60	HI	VHI	LO	N	HI	HI	HI	N	VHI	LO	HI	VHI	LO	N	LO					5.0	
2. Personnel	16,000	0.64	N								VHI											5.0	
3. Production Control	20,000	1.0									N											5.0	
4. Inventory	30,000	1.0									HI											5.0	
5. Order Processing	4,000	0.40			N						HI											5.0	
6. Planning	30,000	1.0									N											5.0	
7. Batch DBMS	10,000	0.20			HI			LO	N		N	N		HI								6.0	
8. Online DBMS	8,000	0.32			VHI			LO	N		LO	N		HI								6.0	
9.																							
10.																							
11. Total EDSI																							
12. (MM)NOM																							
13. (EDSI/MM)NOM																							

Totals

Development mode: _Semidetached_

Schedule (months)

FIGURE 9-7 Montana mining and manufacturing MIS CLEF

2. Compute the average storage utilization percentage $s = (s_1 + s_2 + \ldots + s_n)/n$.

3. Use s to determine an overall storage cost multiplier from the model, by interpolation from the following table:

Percent Storage Utilization	Cost Multiplier
0	1.00
50	1.00
60	1.08
70	1.21
80	1.47
85	1.73
90	2.25
95	3.78
99	6.00

4. Multiply the cost per instruction obtained from the other factors by the overall storage cost multiplier and the product size in words to determine the estimated development cost. The example given is shown below, assuming a 15,000-word machine:

Overlay	Words	% Utilization	
1	1496	10.0	
2	6936	46.2	
3	4593	30.6	
4	4921	32.8	
5	9804	65.4	
6	7325	48.8	
7	9471	63.1	
8	14841	98.9	
9	12396	82.6	
10	12750	85.0	
11	10443	69.0	
12	14281	95.2	
Total:	109257	60.6:	Average

Calculate the estimated cost of the software defined above, assuming a cost per instruction obtained from the other factors of $30/word, and using two methods:

1. The single-component averaging technique defined above;
2. A micro cost-estimation technique based on the Intermediate COCOMO component-level estimation techniques:
   (a) Determine a cost multiplier for each component by computing its storage utilization and using that to interpolate for the cost multiplier in the table above.
   (b) Determine the cost of each component by multiplying the cost per instruction obtained from the other factors (here, $30 per word) by the component's storage cost multiplier and its size in words.
   (c) Sum the costs of all components to determine the estimated overall development cost.

What are the two problems with technique 1 which cause it to produce such sizeable cost underestimates?

```
┌─────────────────────────────────────────────┐
│  I.    INTRODUCTION                          │
│                                              │
│  1.  Case Study 1:  Scientific American      │
│  2.  Case Study 2:  Urban School System      │
│  3.  The goals of software engineering       │
└─────────────────────────────────────────────┘
```

```
┌───────────────────────────────────┐   ┌──────────────────────────────────────────────┐
│ II.  THE SOFTWARE LIFE-CYCLE:      │   │ III.  FUNDAMENTALS OF SOFTWARE               │
│      A QUANTITATIVE MODEL          │   │       ENGINEERING ECONOMICS                  │
│                                    │   │                                              │
│  4.  The software life-cycle:      │   │ III A.   Cost-Effectiveness Analysis         │
│        phases and activities       │   │                                              │
│  5.  The basic COCOMO model        │   │ 10. Performance models and                   │
│  6.  The basic COCOMO model:       │   │       cost-effectiveness models              │
│        development modes           │   │ 11. Production functions: economies of scale │
│  7.  The basic COCOMO model:       │   │ 12. Choosing among alternatives:             │
│        activity distribution       │   │       decision criteria                      │
│  8.  The intermediate COCOMO model:│   │                                              │
│        product level estimates     │   │ III B.   Multiple-Goal Decision Analysis     │
│  9.  Intermediate COCOMO:          │   │                                              │
│        component level estimation  │   │ 13. Net value and marginal analysis          │
│                                    │   │ 14. Present vs. future expenditure and income│
└───────────────────────────────────┘   │ 15. Figures of merit                         │
                                         │ 16. Goals as constraints                     │
                                         │ 17. Systems analysis and constrained optimization │
                                         │ 18. Coping with unreconcilable and unquantifiable │
                                         │       goals                                  │
                                         │                                              │
                                         │ III C.   Dealing with Uncertainties, Risk, and the Value │
                                         │          of Information                      │
                                         │                                              │
                                         │ 19. Coping with uncertainties: risk analysis │
                                         │ 20. Statistical decision theory: the value of information │
                                         └──────────────────────────────────────────────┘
```

```
┌────────────────────────────────────────────────────────────────┐
│ IV.  THE ART OF SOFTWARE COST ESTIMATION                       │
│                                                                │
│ IV A.   Software Cost Estimation Methods and Procedures        │
│                                                                │
│ 21. Seven basic steps in software cost estimation              │
│ 22. Alternative software cost estimation methods               │
│                                                                │
│ IV B.   The Detailed COCOMO Model                              │
│                                                                │
│ 23. Detailed COCOMO: summary and operational description       │
│ 24. Detailed COCOMO cost drivers: product attributes           │
│ 25. Detailed COCOMO cost drivers: computer attributes          │
│ 26. Detailed COCOMO cost drivers: personnel attributes         │
│ 27. Detailed COCOMO cost drivers: project attributes           │
│ 28. Factors not included in COCOMO                             │
│ 29. COCOMO evaluation                                          │
│                                                                │
│ IV C.   Software Cost Estimation and Life-Cycle Management     │
│                                                                │
│ 30. Software maintenance cost estimation                       │
│ 31. Software life-cycle cost estimation                        │
│ 32. Software project planning and control                      │
│ 33. Improving software productivity                            │
└────────────────────────────────────────────────────────────────┘
```

Part III

FUNDAMENTALS OF SOFTWARE ENGINEERING ECONOMICS

INTRODUCTION

In our illustrations of the use of the COCOMO software cost-estimating model throughout Part II, we dealt with a number of case studies and questions which required some basic economic analysis to resolve. These included:

- Make-or-buy analyses comparing in-house software development versus purchased or adapted software products
- Cost benefit analyses of system performance (such as response time) versus software development cost
- Sensitivity analysis of the software cost implications of development assumptions or management options

The techniques we used to handle these issues in Part II represent the first level in a hierarchy of increasingly powerful economic analysis techniques which have been developed over the past several decades. These techniques are used extensively throughout the information processing field as support for both major and minor decisions affecting software development, acquisition, and maintenance. Thus, for practical purposes, it is highly valuable for a software engineer to understand how to use these analysis techniques.

Just as valuable, though, are the overall economic concepts and principles underlying the specific techniques we will address in this part of the book: concepts dealing with cost effectiveness, present value, constrained optimization, identification of objectives and alternatives, risk, utility, and the value of information. These concepts and principles provide us with a frame of reference for identifying what problems we need to solve, what options we have for solving them, and what priorities to put on our various efforts, as we confront the extremely complex situations involved in software engineering.

And, even further, the economics world-view provides a helpful perspective for confronting decision issues in other parts of our lives: buying cars, houses, or stereo sets; deciding how much insurance to carry; or even choosing a graduate school.

SOFTWARE ENGINEERING ECONOMICS

This part of the book provides an introduction to the basic concepts of engineering economics that you are likely to need as a software engineer. The economic concepts covered in Part III deal with the branch of economics called *microeconomics*. The other main branch of economics, called *macroeconomics*, deals with economics on a national and international scale: with problems of inflation, balance of payments, unemployment, and the like. Microeconomics deals with economic decisions on a more personal scale: with make-or-buy decisions, lease-or-purchase decisions, or decisions on how much simulation or how much testing is enough.

Even within the area of microeconomics, we will cover only topics of central interest in software engineering. These include techniques of cost effectiveness analysis, net value analysis, marginal analysis, present value analysis, constrained optimization, risk analysis, and statistical decision theory. Part III will not cover such topics as supply-and-demand analysis and pricing.*

However, Part III does cover several important software engineering issues beyond those usually treated in microeconomics. In keeping with our main GOALS theme of continual reconciliation of the goals of human relations, program engineering, and resource engineering throughout the software life-cycle, we will discuss a number of techniques of multiple goal reconciliation, particularly those dealing with reconciliation between quantitative and nonquantitative goals.

Further, there is a strong emphasis in Part III on economic analysis as an aid to software engineering *decisions,* and on the closely related concepts of the economic value of information in making decisions. Usually, software engineers are *producers* of management information to be consumed by other people, but during the software life-cycle we must also be *consumers* of management information to support our

---

* These topics are of interest, however, in such information processing areas as product marketing and computer center management. See [Sharpe, 1969] for a good treatment of these subjects.

own decisions. As we come to appreciate the factors which make it attractive for us to pay for processed information which helps *us* make better decisions as software engineers, we will get a better appreciation for what our customers and users are looking for in the information processing systems we develop for *them*.

PART IIIA: COST-EFFECTIVENESS ANALYSIS

Part III contains three main components. The first component (Part IIIA) includes Chapters 10, 11, and 12. It deals with the basic concepts of cost-effectiveness analysis and decisionmaking. Chapter 10 provides a bridge from the more familiar computer science domain of computer system performance analysis into the domain of cost-effectiveness analysis. Chapter 11 introduces some highly useful basic microeconomic concepts—production functions, economies and diseconomies of scale—in terms of the cost-effectiveness framework established in Chapter 10. Chapter 12 discusses various cost-effectiveness decision criteria—fixed budget, minimum requirement, maximum effectiveness/cost ratio, and so on—and indicates their advantages and difficulties in various software engineering situations.

PART IIIB: MULTIPLE GOAL DECISION ANALYSIS

Part IIIB (Chapters 13 to 18) is concerned with overall techniques of multiple goal decisionmaking and goal reconciliation. These techniques deal with situations in which decisions must be made with respect to a number of goals which we desire to achieve. Chapter 13 presents the concept of net value (basically, the value of the software product or service minus the cost of providing it), and discusses the related economic techniques of marginal analysis. Chapter 14 shows how to use present value concepts and techniques to reconcile the goals of present benefits versus future benefits. Chapter 15 presents various figures of merit used to reconcile a large number of objectives into a single decision criterion, and discusses their applicability to such decision issues as computer selection and software package selection. Chapter 16 shows how multiple goal situations can often be simplified by treating some of the goals as constraints. Chapter 17 discusses the concepts and techniques of systems analysis within the constrained optimization framework established in Chapter 16. Chapter 18 presents and discusses various techniques for aiding decisionmakers to reconcile quantifiable goals with unquantifiable goals, such as the human relations goals we must consider in software engineering.

PART IIIC: DEALING WITH UNCERTAINTIES AND THE VALUE OF INFORMATION

The techniques discussed in Parts IIIA and IIIB assume that we are able to determine all of our criterion values (such as cost and performance) precisely and with certainty. Particularly with software cost estimation, this is not a fully valid assumption; we are often confronted with uncertainties in the estimated cost and performance of a system about which we must make a decision. Part IIIC deals with techniques for decisionmaking under uncertainty. Chapter 19 discusses techniques of risk analysis and their software engineering implications. Chapter 20 presents a basic introduction to the area of statistical decision theory, and shows how its concepts can be helpful both in software engineering decisionmaking and in establishing the value of processed information in a software engineering application.

Structure of Chapters

Each chapter in Part III (and each section in Chapter 10) contains the following three sections:

1. An example, which shows how each technique works and why it is useful. The example involves both the basic hardware and software aspects of the multi-microprocessor transaction processing system introduced in Chapter 9.
2. A general discussion of the technique presented in the example: its general form, its capabilities and limitations, and its relevance to software engineering.
3. Questions on the material in the section.

Part IIIA

COST-EFFECTIVENESS ANALYSIS

Most significant software engineering decisions involve the assessment of the relative cost and effectiveness of alternative courses of action. Part IIIA covers the basic concepts of cost-effectiveness analysis required for software engineering decisions. These basic concepts serve as a foundation for the more sophisticated methods of economic analysis covered in Parts IIIB and IIIC.

Chapter 10 presents the basic objectives and framework of cost-effectiveness analysis, and introduces the transaction processing systems (TPS) example used to illustrate the economic concepts and techniques presented in Part III.

Chapter 11 introduces some highly useful basic microeconomic concepts—production functions, economies and diseconomies of scale—in terms of the cost-effectiveness framework established in Chapter 10. Chapter 12 discusses various cost-effectiveness decision criteria—fixed budget, minimum requirement, maximum effectiveness/cost ratio, etc.—and indicates their advantages and difficulties in various software engineering situations.

Chapter 10

$\bowtie\!\!\!=\!\!\!=\!\!\bowtie\!\!=\!\!\bowtie\!\!=\!\!\bowtie\!\!=\!\!\bowtie\!\!=\!\!\bowtie\!\!=\!\!\bowtie\!\!=\!\!\bowtie\!\!=\!\!\bowtie\!\!=\!\!\bowtie\!\!=\!\!\bowtie$

Performance Models and Cost-Effectiveness Models

10.1 PERFORMANCE MODELS

Example

The example we will use throughout this chapter (and the remainder of Part III of this book) is a proposed transaction processing system (TPS). It has been described, and some of its software costs analyzed, in Chapter 9. The type of transactions being processed by the TPS might be financial transactions, airline reservations, messages in a store-and-forward digital communications system, or sales transactions in a large department store.

At the point we enter into discussion of the proposed TPS, it has been decided—primarily on the basis of required capacity, cost, growth potential, and backup redundancy—to employ a multiple-microprocessor configuration for the central portion of the TPS. Figure 10–1, reproduced from Chapter 9, shows the basic configuration being considered; 25 of these configurations are needed to service 25 different geographical locations.

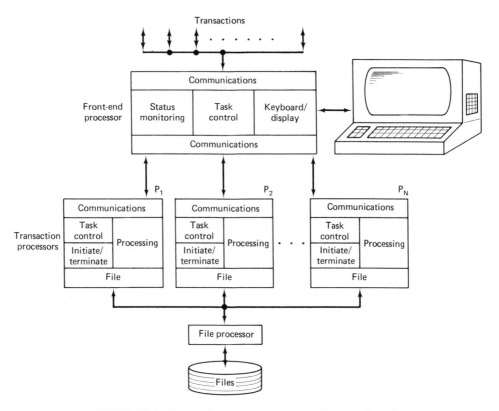

FIGURE 10–1 Transaction processing system: Basic configuration

A particular microprocessor has been determined to be the best match for the TPS functions. It operates at a speed of 1 million operations per second (1000 Kops/sec), and can process transactions at a rate of 20,000 operations per transaction (20 Kops/tr).

Thus, if the control software could be completely transparent, each processor in the TPS could handle 50 transactions per second (50 tr/sec). But the control software is required to perform a number of *overhead* functions, such as scheduling, resource management, dispatching, error checking and handling, and performance monitoring. These functions consume roughly 200 Kops/sec for each processor, reducing the TPS capacity to 40 tr/sec per processor.

On top of this processor overhead, there is also a multiprocessor overhead factor, which covers the added overhead functions of multiple processor scheduling, resource management, and so on, plus the multiple update in each processor of status tables which may be modified during the processing of a transaction. The added multiprocessor overhead in a TPS with N processors is $80(N-1)$ Kops/sec. Thus, if an additional processor is brought into the system, each of the existing processors will have to spend another 80 Kops/sec resolving conflicts between itself and the new processor.

In order to make effective decisions on how many processors to buy for the TPS, we would like to know how the TPS performance, or throughput, varies as a function of the number of processors, N. If we define the following as TPS parameters:

- S, The processor speed in Kops/sec
- P, The processor overhead in Kops/sec
- M, The multiprocessor overhead factor
- T, The number of operations required per transaction in Kops,

we can then derive a formula for the TPS performance, $E(N)$

$$E(N) = \frac{\text{Total number of Kops available for processing}}{\text{Number of Kops required per transaction}}$$

$$E(N) = \frac{N[S - P - M(N - 1)]}{T} \tag{10-1}$$

For our particular TPS situation, with $S = 1000$, $P = 200$, $M = 80$, and $T = 20$, the formula reduces to

$$E(N) = \frac{N[1000 - 200 - 80(N - 1)]}{20}$$

$$= \frac{N(880 - 80\,N)}{20}$$

$$= 4\,N(11 - N)$$

A graph of $E(N)$ for this situation is shown as Fig. 10–2.

From Fig. 10–2, we can see that we would get our best performance of 120 tr/sec from a TPS configuration of 5 or 6 processors. Beyond 6 processors, the performance gets worse and worse, as each additional processor slows down the other processors more than it contributes in additional performance.*

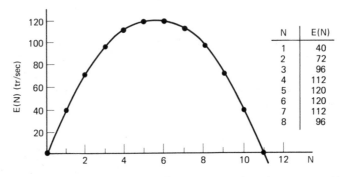

N	E(N)
1	40
2	72
3	96
4	112
5	120
6	120
7	112
8	96

FIGURE 10–2 TPS throughout: $E(N)$ versus number of processors, N

* It should be noted that the type of multiprocessor performance shown in Fig. 10–2 has often been experienced in practice. On one large government multiprocessor system, the maximum performance was achieved with four processors, with virtually no throughput achieved at all when using nine processors. For other analyses of multiprocessor performance exhibiting similar behavior, see [Thurber, 1976] and [Raskin, 1978].

General Discussion

Equation (10–1) is an example of a *performance model.* Performance models consist of a sequence of formulas that determine the estimated performance of a system in terms of a set of variables called *system parameters.* In Eq. (10–1), not only N but also S, P, M, and T are system parameters. Thus, properly, we should refer to $E(N)$ as $E(N,S,P,M,T)$.

The major uses of performance models in software engineering are to provide the following types of information to support development or acquisition decisions:

1. *Optimal Performance Information.* We can analyze performance models to determine which choice of system parameters will yield the maximum performance.
2. *Sensitivity Analysis Information.* We can analyze performance models to determine the sensitivity of system performance to assumptions embedded in the model or in the given values of the system parameters.

These uses are discussed in turn in the following two sections.

10.2 OPTIMAL PERFORMANCE

Example

We can use the performance model in Eq. (10–1) to determine the number of processors, N_{max}, which will give us the best TPS performance, given any set of values of the system parameters. We do this by noticing in Fig. 10–2 that the slope of the curve is zero when $E(N)$ achieves its maximum, and by using the fact that the formula for the slope of the curve is the derivative of $E(N)$ with respect to N, given that the values of the other parameters are fixed.

If we rewrite Eq. (10–1) in the form

$$E(N) = \left(\frac{S-P+M}{T}\right)N - \left(\frac{M}{T}\right)N^2 \qquad (10\text{–}2)$$

we can easily calculate the derivative*

$$\frac{dE(N)}{dN} = \frac{S-P+M}{T} - \left(\frac{2M}{T}\right)N \qquad (10\text{–}3)$$

---

* In this book, only one simple calculus result is used: the formula for the derivative of a polynomial.

If
$$E(x) = a_n x^n + a_{n-1}x^{n-1} + \cdots + a_1 x + a_0$$

then
$$\frac{dE}{dx} = na_n x^{n-1} + (n-1)a_{n-1}x^{n-2} + \cdots + a_1$$

If we have identified N_{max} as the point at which the slope is zero

$$\frac{dE}{dN}(N_{max}) = 0 \tag{10-4}$$

then we can substitute the expression for dE/dN in Eq. (10-3) into Eq. (10-4) and solve for N_{max}

$$\frac{S - P + M}{T} - \left(\frac{2M}{T}\right) N_{max} = 0$$

or

$$N_{max} = \left(\frac{S - P + M}{T}\right)\left(\frac{T}{2M}\right) = \frac{S - P + M}{2M} \tag{10-5}$$

In our TPS example, with $S = 1000$, $P = 200$, and $M = 80$, the optimal number of processors, N_{max}, is

$$N_{max} = \frac{1000 - 200 + 80}{160} = 5.5$$

Since in practice we can't use 5.5 processors, we will have to be satisfied with a choice of either 5 or 6 processors, giving a performance of 120 tr/sec.

One very useful thing about knowing the location of N_{max} is that it allows us to find out just how much of a performance penalty we pay because practical constraints don't allow us to use the absolute optimal solution. Here, from Eq. (10-1)

$$E(5.5) = \frac{5.5[1000 - 200 - 80(4.5)]}{20} = 121$$

and we are reassured that the performance penalty is relatively small.

General Discussion

Using Derivatives to Find Optimum Points. Setting the derivative of a function equal to zero is a necessary but not a sufficient condition for finding the maximum or minimum value of a function, or the *optimal value.* Some of the situations in which the derivative may be zero at points other than the maximum or minimum, or *optimum point,* are the following:

1. Multiple maxima or minima. At the point x_0 in Fig. 10-3, the derivative is equal to zero and the function has a local maximum, but it is not the optimum point or the global maximum of the function. We will encounter this situation frequently. This means that we have to check for multiple solutions when solving for the optimum point.

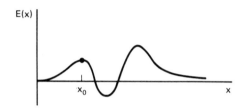

FIGURE 10-3

2. *Points of inflection and saddle points.* In the graph on the left of Fig. 10–4, the point $x = 0$ is an inflection point of the function $E(x) = x^3$. The derivative of the function is $dE/dx = 3x^2$, which is equal to zero at $x = 0$, but the function does not have a minimum or a maximum there.

In the graph on the right, the saddle point is indicated by a black dot. The derivative of the function is zero at the saddle point, but the point is both a maximum if considered from one direction and a minimum if considered from another.

Points of inflection and saddle points are encountered most frequently in the analysis of highly complicated functions. The best way to check for them is to look at the second derivative at the point: If it is zero (and the third derivative is nonzero), the point is an inflection point; if it is positive in some directions and negative in others, the point is a saddle point. If it is negative in all directions, then the point is a maximum; if it is positive in all directions, then the point is a minimum.

All of the above assumes that the derivatives of these functions exist. In software

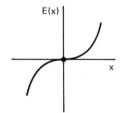

FIGURE 10-4

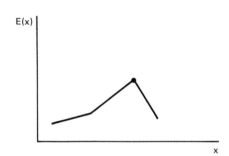

FIGURE 10-5

engineering, this is often not the case. Communications tariff rates and computer usage rates often have discontinuities, and performance of digital systems often yields discrete rather than continuous values. Thus we must also make sure that we don't confine our search for maxima to places where we can compute derivatives. We must also be on the lookout for the type of maximum shown in Fig. 10–5.

Optimal solutions in software engineering. In software engineering, optimal performance solutions are most frequently used in the detailed design and coding phases. In the earlier phases of the software life-cycle, we may often find a nonoptimal performance candidate preferable to the optimal solution.

As we shall see in later chapters, there are a number of considerations—risk, operational constraints, user morale and growth, maintainability—which may lead us to choose a solution other than the one with optimal performance. However, even in these situations, we will generally find it valuable to determine the optimal point and the optimal value, as it allows us to judge how much effort it is worth spending to try to improve a nonoptimal solution.

10.3 SENSITIVITY ANALYSIS

Example

Any decision, in software engineering or elsewhere, is based on a number of assumptions. In the TPS example, a decision to buy five processors in order to process 120 tr/sec would be based on the assumptions that the actual performance of the hardware and software would be quite close to the performance indicated by the system parameters used in the model. One such assumption is that the actual multiprocessor overhead factor M will be close to the given value of 80.

Suppose, however, that this assumption is not borne out in practice. What effect will this have on the TPS performance?

Let us examine a situation in which the value of M is 160, while all of the other system parameters are unchanged. In this case, from Eq. (10–1)

$$E(N) = \frac{N[1000 - 200 - 160(N-1)]}{20}$$

$$= \frac{N(960 - 160N)}{20} = 8N(6 - N)$$

The resulting comparison is shown in Fig. 10–6.

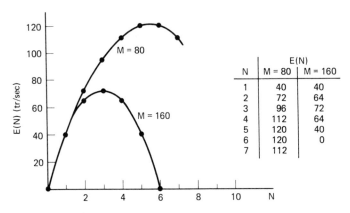

FIGURE 10–6 TPS performance for two multiprocessor overhead factors

Thus, had we proceeded to buy five processors, and then found when we got them running that the multiprocessor overhead factor was $160(N-1)$ Kops/sec rather than $80(N-1)$, we would end up with a five-processor TPS which performed at a rate of 40 tr/sec. This would be no better than a one-processor TPS, and a far cry from the 120 tr/sec performance we expected.

We can get a more complete picture of the sensitivity of $E(N, S, P, M, T)$ to M in this situation by setting $N=5$, leaving $S=1000$, $P=200$, and $T=20$, and studying

$$E(M) = \frac{5[1000 - 200 - M(5-1)]}{20} = \frac{5(800 - 4M)}{20} = 200 - M$$

Figure 10–7 shows the resulting sensitivity curve. In this situation, for the five-processor TPS, any increase in the multiprocessor overhead factor M by x units will result in a decrease of x tr/sec in TPS performance.

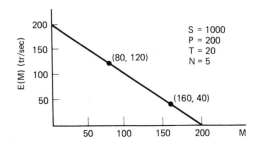

FIGURE 10–7 Five-processor TPS performance sensitivity

General Discussion

In general, if we have a function involving several parameters, $E(a, b, \ldots, z)$, we can determine its sensitivity to one of the parameters, say z, at a given point $(a_0, b_0, \ldots, z_0)$, by computing the partial derivative* of E with respect to z at the point $(a_0, b_0, \ldots, z_0)$

$$\frac{\partial E}{\partial z}(a_0, b_0, \ldots, z_0)$$

In the TPS example, we have from Eq. (10–1)

$$E(N, S, P, M, T) = \frac{N[S - P - M(N-1)]}{T} = \frac{N(S-P)}{T} - M\frac{N(N-1)}{T}$$

Thus, the partial derivative of E with respect to M for the TPS example is

$$\frac{\partial E}{\partial M} = \frac{-N(N-1)}{T} = \frac{-5(4)}{20} = -1$$

which is the slope of the sensitivity curve shown in Fig. 10–7.

In many software engineering situations, it will be difficult to compute the partial derivatives, as the function E may be extremely complicated. Or, it may turn out that it has undefined or discontinuous derivatives. In such cases, the best we can do for a sensitivity analysis is to pick neighboring values of the parameters we wish to investigate, calculate the resulting values of E, and compare them with our nominal results.

Sensitivity analysis is extremely important in two major software engineering activities: feasibility studies during the exploratory and conceptual phases, and risk analyses during the plans and requirements and product design phases. Particularly important areas to investigate are sensitivities of assumptions about operating system overhead, performance under imperfect conditions, performance of resource sharing algorithms, and performance of artificial intelligence applications such as natural language processing, pattern recognition, or heuristic search techniques.

10.4 COST-EFFECTIVENESS MODELS

In the previous sections, we have developed a performance model which allows us to solve the decision problem of optimal performance:

Given a set of system parameters S, P, M, *and* T, *decide how many processors* N *to buy in order to maximize the performance* E(N, S, P, M, T).

---

* The partial derivative of a function of several variables $E(a, b, \ldots, z)$ with respect to one of the variables, say z, is calculated by treating the other variables as constants and computing the regular derivative of the resulting expression with respect to z. Thus, in the previous section, if we had been treating the performance function as $E(N,S,P,M,T)$ rather than as $E(N)$, we would have used the partial derivative $\partial E/\partial N$ instead of the regular derivative dE/dN.

If we had an unlimited supply of processors available, and our only concern was to maximize performance, then this formulation would be fine. However, in most situations, we obtain the processors by using a limited supply of funds, with other competing demands on the use of the funds. Thus, we would prefer to have a model which relates levels of performance or effectiveness to the cost—in dollars or some other scarce resource—it will take us to achieve them. Such a model is called a *cost-effectiveness model.*

Example

In general, it is a fairly straightforward process to extend a performance model into a cost-effectiveness model. For the TPS performance model, we can do so by substituting $N(C)$, the number of processors obtainable for a given cost C, for N, as follows:

$$E(C) = \frac{N(C)[S - P - M(N(C) - 1)]}{T} \tag{10-6}$$

In our TPS system, we have determined that we will need 25 identical copies of the TPS configuration, and that each parallel transaction processor will cost \$400. Thus, each additional processor we add to the configuration will cost 25(\$400) = \$10,000 or \$10K. Thus, if C is measured in \$K, we have $N(C) = C/10$, and

$$E(C) = \frac{\frac{C}{10}\left[S - P - M\left(\frac{C}{10} - 1\right)\right]}{T} \tag{10-7}$$

In this case, we can obtain the cost-effectiveness curve corresponding to Fig. 10–2 simply by rescaling the *x*-axis, as shown in Fig. 10–8.

Looked at in this way, we get a better perspective on whether the choice ($N = 5$ or 6) which maximizes system performance is actually the best in allocation of scarce resources. Clearly, the choice $N = 5$ is better than $N = 6$, but is it better

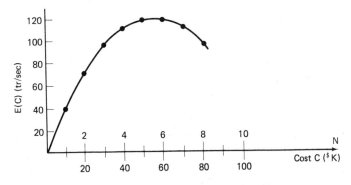

FIGURE 10–8 TPS cost-effectiveness curve at \$10 K per processor

than $N = 4$? It may be hard to justify spending $10K to go from a four-processor system to a five-processor system, when the performance gain is only 8 tr/sec.

Results of improvements in the cost function. One way this situation can be improved is by seeking improvements in the cost function $N(C)$. Suppose, for example, that we are able to negotiate the following (oversimplified) quantity discount schedule with the processor vendor

Price of first 75 processors	$400 each
Price of processors 76+	$240 each

Then the TPS cost-effectiveness curve becomes the one shown in Fig. 10–9. With the quantity discount, the prospect of acquiring a four-processor or five-processor system becomes more attractive.

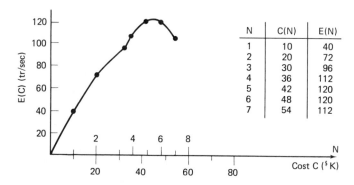

N	C(N)	E(N)
1	10	40
2	20	72
3	30	96
4	36	112
5	42	120
6	48	120
7	54	112

FIGURE 10–9 TPS cost-effectiveness curve using quantity discount

General Discussion

A *cost-effectiveness model* consists of a sequence of formulas which determine the estimated effectiveness of a system as a function of its cost in dollars or some other scarce resource.

Cost-effectiveness models generally take the two-part form exhibited in the examples above:

1. A *cost model* $C = C(F)$ which indicates how much it will cost to acquire a certain set of facilities F.
2. A *performance model* $E = E(F)$ which indicates how much performance will be realized by using the set of facilities F.

This breakdown is primarily for reasons of convenience. It is generally more convenient to think of both the costs and the performance in terms of an intermediate set of facilities (such as the number of processors N in our TPS example), rather than to erase this conceptual link. Also, if the model is viewed as a software product, it is good modularization practice to segment the model in this way, as the functions relating costs to facilities and performance to facilities are most likely to change independently of each other.

Here are some examples of such facilities and their typical price schedules:

- *Computer Hardware.* A typical price schedule for computer hardware is $1000 for units 1 to 4, $850 for units 5 to 14, $750 for units 15 to 49, $650 for units 50 to 199, and $600 for units 200 and up.
- *Computer Time.* A typical charge for a minute of central processing unit (CPU) time on a large general-purpose computer is $5 for rush jobs, $3 for normal (2-hour) turnaround, and $1 for overnight (12-hour) turnaround.
- *Software Products.* A typical price schedule for a software product is $10,000 for use at the first installation in an organization, and $2000 each for use at additional installations.

For an excellent discussion of the price *structures* of computer equipment and services, see [Sharpe, 1969]; the cost data there is out-of-date, however.

Still, getting a good negotiated price does not resolve the decision problem of how many processors to buy. However, the cost-effectiveness model allows us to sharpen the question to the following:

> The cost-effectiveness relationship E(C) *tells us how much performance we can get for a given cost. Now, how much performance are we willing to buy?*

Putting the decision problem in this way helps to clarify the choices and to identify additional issues that should be resolved before making the decision. These include:

1. Suppose we can think of some alternative way to invest our resources in a TPS (for example, to improve the operating system and reduce multiprocessor overhead). How can we determine which is the better alternative? This is the subject of *cost-effectiveness comparisons,* to be discussed in Chapters 11 and 12.
2. What is it worth to us to be able to process a given number of transactions per second? How can we reconcile the various dimensions of cost and worth into a decision criterion which will help us make the right decisions on which alternative to choose and how many processors to buy? This is the subject of *multiple goal decisionmaking,* to be discussed in Chapters 13 to 18.
3. Suppose we feel that we don't know enough about certain sensitive system parameters to make a good decision. How much should we invest in further information and analysis in order to reduce the risk of going down the wrong path? This is the subject of *risk analysis* and *statistical decision theory,* to be discussed in Chapters 19 and 20.

QUESTIONS

10.1. Using Eq. (10–1) as the performance model, draw the graph of *E(N)* for the following set of system parameters: $S = 1000$, $P = 200$, $M = 100$, and $T = 20$.

10.2. Derive a special version of the performance model when only one processor is used.

10.3. Figure 10–2 indicates that the performance of the TPS system would be less than zero if more than 11 processors are used. What do you think would actually happen if, say, 12 processors were used?

10.4. The COCOMO estimation equations can be considered as performance models relating a software project's performance (such as, productivity in DSI/MM) to project parameters (such as, DSI). Using the Basic COCOMO effort equation for embedded-mode software, $MM = 3.6 (KDSI)^{1.20}$, derive a performance model for project productivity in DSI/MM as a function of project size in DSI. Check your answer by evaluating it for standard size projects (2, 8, 32, 128, and 512 KDSI) and comparing your results with those in Table 6–2.

10.5. Derive performance models for expressing the development schedule TDEV for a software product as a function of its size in DSI, using the Basic COCOMO effort and schedule equations, for all three development modes.

10.6. The performance of many computer systems is approximated reasonably well by the simple M/M/1 Markovian single-server queuing system performance model:

$$\bar{t} = \frac{1}{\mu - \lambda}$$

where $\bar{t}$ = The average computer turnaround time between the submission of a job and its completion.

μ = The mean service rate for computer jobs (number of jobs completed per unit of time), assuming an exponential distribution of service times.

λ = The mean arrival rate for computer jobs (number of jobs submitted per unit of time), assuming an exponential distribution of arrival times.

Suppose we are operating a batch-processing computer system in which the mean service rate is $\mu = 0.2$ job/min. The computer system is serving a group of N programmers, each of whom submits a job every 300 min on the average (both service times and arrival times are exponentially distributed), so that $\lambda = N/300$. Compute the average turnaround time, $\bar{t}$, for the system when the number of programmers, N, is 1, 30, 50, 55, and 59. Graph the resulting performance curve. From the standpoint of the computer center manager, which value of N represents the most efficient use of available computer time? From the standpoint of a programmer, which value of N represents the most efficient use of programmer time?

10.7. Suppose that for an investment of $10 per job, we could improve the mean service rate of the computer system in Question 10–6 to 0.3 job/min. What would be the resulting turnaround time for the situation with $N = 59$ programmers? For what value of an hour's reduction in turnaround time does a $10K investment begin to be worthwhile?

10.8. In the TPS example, as the system parameters S, P, M, and T are varied in the ways indicated below, will the optimum number of processors, N_{max}, increase, decrease, or stay the same?

(a) Increase processor speed S
(b) Increase processor overhead P
(c) Decrease multiprocessor overhead factor M
(d) Increase required operations/transaction T

10.9. Determine an equation for the optimal performance of the TPS system $E(N_{max})$ as a function of S, P, M, and T. Check your result by using the values given in the example.

10.10. The effect of compressing or extending the nominal schedule TDEV determined by the SCED multipliers in the Intermediate COCOMO model (Table 8–2) can be approximated by the equation

$$MM = (MM)_{NOM} \left[1 + 4 \left(\frac{T - TDEV}{TDEV} \right)^2 \right]$$

where T is the length of the desired project schedule. Compute the value of T for which $d(MM)/dT = 0$. Is MM maximized or minimized at this value of T?

10.11. The simplified form of the basic schedule equation is

$$TDEV = 2.5 \sqrt[3]{MM}$$

Another way of writing this equation is

$$MM = 0.064(TDEV)^3.$$

Compute the value of TDEV for which $d(MM)/d(TDEV) = 0$. Is MM maximized or minimized at this point?

10.12. The General Appliance Company is planning to develop an inventory control system on their existing computer. They are considering five levels of sophistication of the inventory control program, and have estimated the required software size in DSI and resulting life-cycle savings in reduced inventory costs as follows:

Level	A	B	C	D	E
Program size (KDSI)	20	40	60	80	100
Inventory savings ($K)	600	1100	1500	1800	2000

Assuming an organic-mode software development and a personnel cost of $5000 per MM, determine the level of inventory control program which maximizes the net savings (inventory savings minus software development cost) for General Appliance. Is there a derivative which is equal to zero at this point?

10.13. Precision Products, Inc., is developing a 75–KDSI, embedded-mode, minicomputer-based system to aid in spaceborne pharmaceuticals processing. The project's cost driver ratings are all nominal, except possibly for computer turnaround time (TURN), which is currently under consideration. The effect of the TURN factor in Tables 8–2 and 8–3 can be approximated by the equation

$$MM = (MM)_{NOM} \{.99 + .04 \sqrt{ART}\}$$

where ART is the average computer response time in hours. The performance characteristics of the computer system allow us to use the M/M/1 queuing model of Question 10.6 to determine ART

$$ART = \frac{1}{\mu - \lambda}$$

The mean arrival rate of computer runs during software development is estimated to be $\lambda = 30$ jobs/hr. The mean service rate μ depends on the cost of the computer system purchased

$$C_{HW} = \$10K \, (\mu)$$

Compute the optimal service rate μ_{opt} which minimizes the total development cost

$$C_{DEV} = C_{HW} + C_{SW} = \$10K(\mu) + \$5K(MM)$$

by expressing C_{DEV} in terms of μ, and finding the point μ_{opt} at which $dC_{DEV}/d\mu = 0$. Compute the resulting cost of the system.

10.14. For the Precision Products, Inc., example above, compute the optimal mean service rate μ_{opt} and the resulting system cost if the hardware cost were

$$C_{HW} = \$5K(\mu)$$

10.15. Explain the significance of the endpoints in Fig. 10-7;

$$M = 0, \ E = 200$$
$$M = 200, \ E = 0$$

10.16. Investigate the sensitivity of $E(N,S,P,M,T)$ to processor overhead P by graphing $E(P)$ for $N = 5$, $S = 1000$, $M = 80$, and $T = 20$; and by computing $\partial E/\partial P$ for the above parameter setting.

10.17. In the Precision Products, Inc., spaceborne pharmaceuticals processing software project presented in Question 10.13, we estimated the mean arrival rate of computer runs as $\lambda = 30$ jobs/hr, and computed the resulting optimal mean service rate as $\mu_{opt} = 33$ jobs/hr. Suppose that our estimate of λ were incorrect. Investigate the sensitivity of the development cost

$$C_{DEV} = \$10K(\mu) + \$2250K + \$100(\mu - \lambda)^{-1/2}$$

by computing the partial derivative $\partial C_{DEV}/\partial \lambda$, and evaluating its results for $\mu = 33$ and $\lambda = 30, 32, 32.5,$ and 33.

10.18. For the Precision Products, Inc., example above, suppose we had chosen to purchase a computer system for which $\mu = 40$ jobs/hr rather than $\mu = \mu_{opt} = 33$. Compute the resulting cost and its sensitivity to our estimate of λ for $\lambda = 30, 32, 33,$ and 35. Which do you think is a better choice for Precision Products, Inc., $\mu = 33$ or $\mu = 40$?

10.19. Define the terms performance model, optimum point, optimal value, cost model, cost-effectiveness model.

10.20. Below is another example of a processor price schedule for the TPS.

1–2 processors:	$10 K each
3–4 processors:	9 K each
5–10 processors:	8 K each
11–20 processors:	7 K each

Draw the graph of the cost function $C(N)$. Is there any quantity of processors which is clearly uneconomic to buy?

10.21. Given the performance model in the TPS example and the cost schedule in question 10.20, draw the graph of the resulting cost-effectiveness function $E(C)$.

10.22. Suppose you are developing a nominal 5-KDSI organic-mode software product, using the computer whose price schedule for CPU time is given in the general discussion of this section. The job is estimated to require about 20 hours of computer time for development and test. Using the model given in Question 10.13 for turnaround time effects, graph the project's software development effectiveness (productivity in DSI/MM) as a function of the cost of computer time.

10.23. Suppose that a special test tool package becomes available, at the price schedule for software products given in the general discussion of this section. This package is sufficiently useful to increase the TOOL rating for a class of applications from nominal to high. The current maintenance levels of effort for this class of applications, at five different installations, is

Installation	Maintenance Effort
A	3 FSP
B	0.2 FSP
C	0.1 FSP
D	0.5 FSP
E	1 FSP

At a labor cost of $5000 per MM and a product lifetime of 2 years, for which installations is it worthwhile to purchase the tool?

10.24. Sometimes cost functions are structured to promote the common welfare rather than to maximize profit. One computer center which had a problem with users' disk storage requests used a pricing algorithm which was a straight linear function of the number

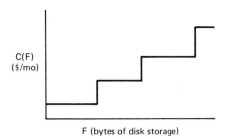

C(F)
($/mo)

F (bytes of disk storage)

FIGURE 10–10

of bytes stored. Rather than discourage users to store information by very high prices or restrictive regulations, the computer center went to a stepwise charging scheme with a few large increments in price as users crossed certain thresholds, as shown in Fig. 10–10.

The result was that users near a threshold would have to treat the problem of storing another block of information as a significant economic decision problem, and would often find several old blocks of information they could discard to keep from crossing the threshold. This pricing policy was very effective in reducing the computer center's disk storage problem.

Can you think of other situations in computing or software engineering in which pricing or reward structures have been (or could be, or should be) used to further the common good. How well do you think the results turned out (would turn out?)

Chapter 11

Production Functions: Economies of Scale

11.1 EXAMPLE

One software engineering decision that is worth considering in our TPS example is the option of developing a better operating system which would reduce the multiprocessor overhead. Suppose, after some analysis, we determine that we can develop an operating system with a multiprocessor overhead factor of $50(N - 1)$, rather than the $80(N - 1)$ factor we obtain if we accept the available vendor-supplied operating system. In Chapter 9, we used Intermediate COCOMO to estimate the development cost of this special operating system at $180K. This compares with a cost of $80K for the vendor-supplied operating system.

Figure 11–1 shows a cost-effectiveness comparison of the option to accept the available operating system (Option A) and the option to build a special-purpose operating system (Option B), assuming a uniform cost of $10K per processor. Note that each curve does not decrease after reaching its peak. This is based on the assumption that we will not want to waste money. If we have $150K to devote to Option A, for example, we will not buy and install a seven-processor system and accept a system

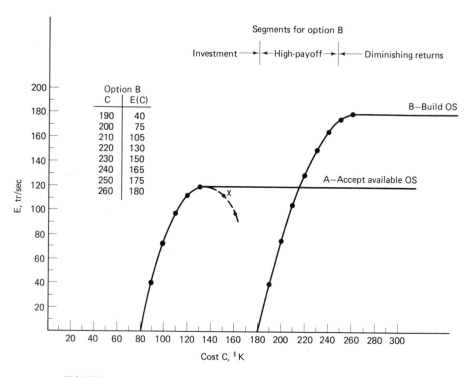

Option B	
C	E(C)
190	40
200	75
210	105
220	130
230	150
240	165
250	175
260	180

FIGURE 11–1 Cost-effectiveness comparison for TPS Options A and B

performance of 112 tr/sec. We would prefer to spend \$130K to buy and install a five-processor system, achieve a system performance of 120 tr/sec, and leave the extra \$20K in reserve for contingencies or other opportunities.

11.2 GENERAL DISCUSSION: DEFINITIONS

In economics, a function of this sort is called a *production function*. A production function relates the achievable output production of a system (here, processed transactions per second) to the level(s) of inputs consumed (here, dollars), under the assumption that only *technologically efficient** combinations of inputs and outputs are used. (In our example, the expenditure of \$150K to achieve a performance of 112 tr/sec —point X in Fig. 11–1—was technologically inefficient.) Based on this assumption, we can assure that the value of a production function will be a *nondecreasing* function of its inputs. Another property of a production function is that it is *nonnegative* since a negative quantity of output is inefficient with respect to the option of doing nothing.

   Typically (but not always), a production function will have three major segments, as in our examples in Fig. 11–1:

   * An input-output combination is technologically efficient if no higher level of output can be obtained using the given level of input.

1. An *investment* segment, in which inputs are consumed without a great deal of resulting output
2. A *high payoff* segment, in which relatively small incremental inputs result in relatively large increments in output
3. A *diminishing returns* segment, in which additional inputs produce relatively little increase in output

11.3 DISCRETE PRODUCTION FUNCTIONS

There are various forms of production functions. One that is encountered frequently in software engineering is the *discrete production function,* in which increases in effectiveness can only be achieved at discrete levels of input. Our TPS example actually has a discrete production function, since we can only achieve increases in effectiveness in increments of $10K in cost, corresponding to the purchase of another processor. Thus, Fig. 11–2 is a more accurate depiction of the production functions for Options A and B.

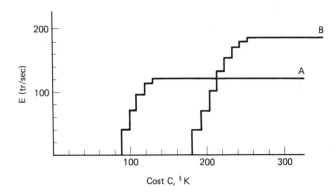

FIGURE 11–2   Discrete production functions for TPS Options A and B

11.4 BASIC PRODUCTION FUNCTIONS
FOR SOFTWARE DEVELOPMENT

The fundamental production function in software engineering is the function relating delivered source instructions as outputs to development man-months as inputs. Figure 11–3 presents the Basic COCOMO versions of these production functions for the three primary modes of software development, as given in Chapter 6.

11.5 ECONOMIES AND DISECONOMIES OF SCALE

The shape of the high end of this and other production functions is the result of a combat between two competing effects. One is the effect of *economies of scale:* factors which make it more efficient to produce large quantities of a product than small

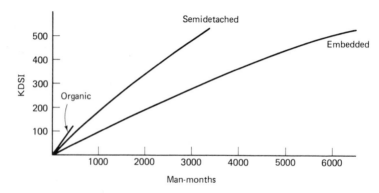

FIGURE 11–3 Nominal software development production functions

quantities. In software production, we can often achieve economies of scale on a large project by investing in special-purpose productivity aids: test tools, diagnostic aids, documentation aids, program library aids, preprocessors, and postprocessors. On a large project, these tools will be used enough to more than repay their cost, thus providing economies of scale unavailable to smaller projects, where the use of the tools would not be enough to repay their cost.

The other competing factor is the effect of *diseconomies of scale*. On software projects, this effect is very similar to the multiprocessor overhead effect in our TPS example: The more individuals that are added to a team, the more of each individual's time is consumed in communication with other team members about updating common information, handling errors, or resolving the use of shared resources. However, group software development also involves some uniquely human diseconomies of scale: The more people on the project, the more opportunities there are that personality conflicts, differences in programming philosophy, and conflicts in work habits between individuals will retard the overall productivity of the team.

11.6 DISECONOMIES OF SCALE ON LARGE SOFTWARE PROJECTS

On a software project with N people, there are $N(N-1)/2$ potential interpersonal communication paths or interactions which can lead to diseconomies of scale. Figure 11–4 gives a feel for how the number of these paths increases with N, by showing the paths for $N = 4$, 6, and 8.

Thus, as a software engineer on a large project, you will be right in the middle of this combat between economies of scale and diseconomies of scale. In practice, there are a number of organizational, technical, and motivational initiatives which you can use to reduce the effects of diseconomies of scale. The major one, of course, is the hierarchical, functionally specialized organizational structure for large software projects discussed in Chapter 7. For example, the number of two-person interactions in the programming phase organization chart in Fig. 7–3 is 144, rather than the $(48)(47)/2$, or 1128, two-person interactions required if all 48 persons had to coordinate with each other to get their job done.

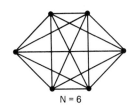 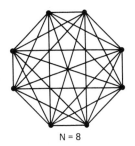

FIGURE 11-4   Potential communication paths between N individuals

11.7   THE BEST WAY TO COMBAT DISECONOMIES OF SCALE

We can't leave this subject before we point out the most powerful technique of all for reducing diseconomies of scale. This is to

> REDUCE THE SCALE

On a software project, there are an unlimited number of temptations to make the product, and the job, bigger and more grandiose. Avoid them. You'll be much better off by reducing the scale via such techniques as prototyping, incremental development, and wish-list pruning.

Avoiding diseconomies of scale: sources of software gold-plating.   For any software product, we can think of a long list of features which will enhance the product in various ways. Some classes of features have turned out to be highly valuable in general. Others have usually ended up as *gold-plating:* features which make the job bigger and disproportionately more expensive, but which turn out to provide little help to the user or maintainer when put into practice.

Below, we present some examples of classes of features which have frequently turned out to be gold-plating in practice; classes of features which usually are not gold-plating, but which are often unfortunately eliminated in an attempt to reduce gold-plating; and classes of features with about an equal potential of going either way.

Classes of features which are frequently gold-plating

- *Instant Response Time.* For some operations and decisions, rapid response time is essential. But many systems have been overloaded with requirements for instant response time on information which is only used on a day-to-day basis. For example, the initial specifications for the ill-fated $216-million Advanced Logistics System [Congress, 1976] required quick response on 90% of the requests; a later review indicated that only 10% of the requests needed quick response.
- *Pinpoint Accuracy.* One organization saved itself $6 million earmarked for an additional supercomputer when it was found that the current computer was spending

most of its time producing results to four-digit accuracy, when users only needed two-digit accuracy.

- *Unbalanced Systems.* An unbalanced system produces in one or more of its parts a high level of performance which is not needed by the rest of the system. One urban emergency service information system, for example, unsuccessfully spent over $1 million trying to automate the generation of geographic coordinates from street addresses to three-digit accuracy, to feed into a travel time calculation accurate to only one significant digit. Finally, a simple manual coordinate-entry system was developed which produced results with adequate accuracy for less than $5000.

- *Artificial Intelligence (AI) Features.* AI is a fascinating research area, and one with high user attractiveness when described in general terms (natural language input, speech understanding, sales trend pattern recognition, and so on). Some AI-type functions, such as complex scheduling, have been successfully developed for software products—and have usually been dropped out of the AI domain as a result. Others have consumed millions of dollars on software products, only to be scrapped in frustration.

- *Interactive Multicolor Vector Graphics.* This is another fascinating research area, with a great deal of potential for improving human-machine system effectiveness, but with a long track record of overspecified gold-plate. One strategic management information system, for example, spent several million dollars producing beautiful test patterns and a number of displays which the top management users found pretty, but confusing and irrelevant to their decisions.

- *"Everything for Everybody" Systems.* In the late 1960s, a number of attempts were made to develop "total management information systems" which combined the corporation's entire information processing needs into one comprehensive integrated system. By the early 1970s, it had become quite clear that these systems were unsuccessful, due primarily to diseconomies of scale and to shortfalls in understanding the corporation's real information processing needs [see, for example, Dearden, 1972; Kanter, 1972].

Classes of features which are usually not gold-plating

- *Humanized Input Preprocessors.* Putting extra effort into features which facilitate simple, reliable data entry for a product which involves a good deal of data entry is not gold-plating. For examples see [Gilb-Weinberg, 1977].

- *Humanized Output Postprocessors.* Putting extra effort into exception reporting capabilities which save users from having to scan huge piles of printout is not gold-plating. Of course, one can go to excesses here and on the input side, as with interactive multicolor vector graphics, for example.

- *Modularity and Information Hiding.* This takes extra front-end effort, but as we have seen from the modern programming practices factor in intermediate COCOMO (Tables 8-2, 8-8) the investment pays off strongly in both development and maintenance.

- *Measurement and Diagnostic Capabilities, Backup and Recovery Capabilities, and so on.* There are a number of software quality enhancing features which are generally not gold-plating, except perhaps on programs which are truly one-shot, short life-span products. See [Boehm and others, 1978; Lipow and others, 1977] for other examples.

Classes of features which are sometimes gold-plating. There are some features which are highly useful in some applications, but highly excessive in others. Some examples:

- Highly generalized control and data structures
- Sophisticated user command languages
- General-purpose utilities and support software
- Automatic trend analysis

How to recognize software gold-plating. The best way to recognize software gold-plating is to use the production function concepts we have been discussing in this chapter. For any candidate software product feature, evaluate its contribution to the information processing system's effectiveness and its contribution to the cost of developing the product. If these contributions place the feature in the diminishing returns segment of the production function for the system (see Fig. 11–5, for example),

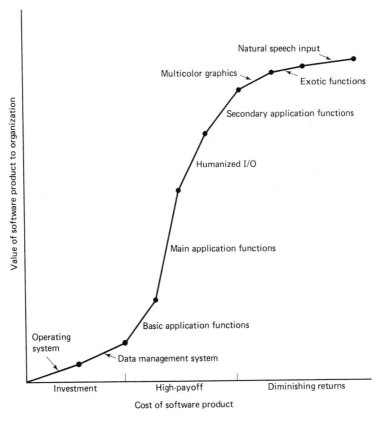

FIGURE 11–5 Typical production function for software product features

it is a gold-plating feature which should be dropped. If the contributions place the feature in the investment or high payoff segment of the production function for the system, it should be included in the software product. However, for the initial development of the product, we should also judge whether its inclusion could be deferred to a later increment of development without compromising the initial viability of the system. Thus, for example, in Fig. 11–5, we might organize the development into an initial increment up to and including the basic application functions, a second increment comprising the main application functions, a third increment comprising the humanized I/O and secondary application functions, and a research project to explore the possibilities of the other features.

In the context of the software development cycle, these evaluations and judgments fall naturally within the goal-review activity performed as Step 5 of the GOALS approach of Table 3–2, and in particular as part of the validation activities performed at the end of the feasibility, plans and requirements, and product design phases.

Some more specific guidelines for judging the value of information processing product features are given in the value-of-information approach presented in Chapter 20.

Avoiding diseconomies of scale in hardware–software products. For a hardware–software information processing product, there are similar opportunities to reduce diseconomies of scale by reducing scale. One very powerful technique in this regard is *functional modularity.*

Suppose we need a TPS which is able to process 180 tr/sec, which by Fig. 11–1 we will barely be able to do with an investment of $260K. However, suppose that

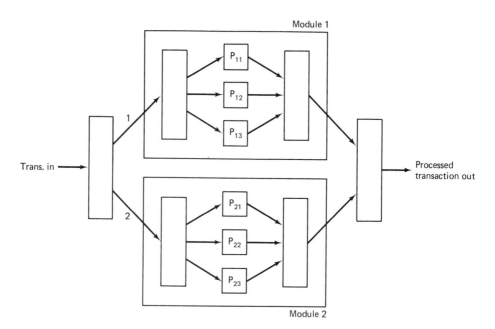

FIGURE 11–6 Modular transaction processing system

we can also find a way to segment the transactions into two different types, which do not require knowledge of each other for satisfactory transaction processing. The relative volume of these two types is relatively equal: 95 tr/sec of Type 1 and 85 tr/sec of Type 2. If this is the case, we can partition the system into two functionally oriented modules, one for Type 1 transactions and one for Type 2 transactions, as shown in Fig. 11–6.

For both Module 1 and Module 2, we have reduced the scale of the multiprocessor down to three processors. Even with the available vendor operating system, this configuration can handle 96 tr/sec per module, which is sufficient to cover the volume of both types of transaction.

The resulting cost is $60K for the processors and $80K for the software,* or a total of $140K. By using functional modularity to reduce the required multiprocessor scale, we have cut the original cost in half, and also left ourselves with much more growth potential.

11.8 QUESTIONS

11.1. Which of the graphs in Fig. 11–7 are production functions?

11.2. Does a production function always have to go through the origin?

11.3. The basic production functions for software development in Fig. 11–3 appear not to have an investment segment. Do you think this is true, or is it just that it is too small to show in the figure? (Consider the following related question: Is it easier to specify, develop, test, and document two typical 10-instruction software products or one typical 20-instruction software product?)

11.4. Suppose that for a cost of $180K, we could develop an operating system with the same multiprocessor overhead factor $M = 80$, but with the single-processor overhead factor reduced to $P = 40$. Graph the production function for this alternative. Does it provide a viable alternative to the A and B alternatives for some range of costs? Do you think it would be a good choice, given the existence of the other alternatives?

11.5. Work out other multiprocessor designs that might combat diseconomies of scale in the TPS, even if all processors require access to a consistent, up-to-date data base.

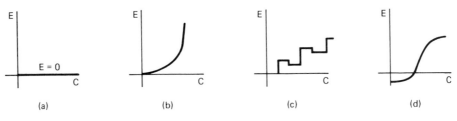

FIGURE 11–7

---

* There would be some added cost to tailor the software to the two separate transaction types, but it would be small relative to the overall savings.

11.6. Give some examples of gold-plating on information system products with which you are familiar.

11.7. Standard University is developing a computer program for student registration and class assignment. The following table represents the estimated number of students the program would be able to serve per hour, as a function of the size of the program in KDSI:

Program size (KDSI)	5	10	15	20	25	30	35	40
Students/hour	40	100	200	800	1100	1200	1250	1260

Graph the production function relating students per hour served, as output, to software development man-months as input, assuming an organic-mode software development. Identify the investment, high payoff, and diminishing returns segments of the production function.

11.8. Standard University's Engineering Computer Center (ECC) has a staff of 15 programmers developing software to support engineering research projects. The typical ECC software product is a 5-KDSI, organic-mode development, having nominal ratings for all cost drivers except TOOL. The ECC uses a minicomputer with very poor tool support, rating a very low on the Intermediate COCOMO TOOL rating scale (Table 8–3).

The MiniTool software house has developed a set of tools which could be used to improve ECC's TOOL rating. MiniTool's price schedule for achieving various levels of tool capability is:

Cost ($K)	0	20	30	50	200
TOOL rating	VL	L	N	H	VH

Determine and graph the production function relating ECC's typical software production in DSI/month for its 15-FSP staff as a function of dollars invested in tools. Identify the investment, high payoff, and diminishing returns segments of the production function. Which TOOL level do you judge would be the best investment for ECC?

11.9. Determine a rough production function relating your grade in one of your courses to the number of hours you devote to the course. Identify other similar production functions you encounter as a student.

Chapter 12

Choosing Among Alternatives: Decision Criteria

12.1 EXAMPLE: MAXIMUM AVAILABLE BUDGET

Suppose that we are not able to partition our transactions and modularize our TPS as discussed in the previous chapter. We are then back to the situation of Fig. 11–2, which is reproduced here as Fig. 12–1 for convenience.

Figure 12–1 confronts us with a difficult decision problem. Which option should we choose, A or B? If one production function F, dominates (is never less than) another production function, G, as in Fig. 12–2, the choice is easy: pick Option F. But in Fig. 12–1, Option A is superior up to an expenditure of $220K, and Option B is superior thereafter.

There are several decision criteria that allow us to resolve the decision issue in various ways, each of which is appropriate for different situations. These are:

1. Maximum Available Budget
2. Minimum Performance Requirement
3. Maximum Effectiveness/Cost Ratio

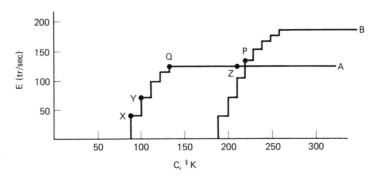

FIGURE 12–1 Production function for TPS Options A and B

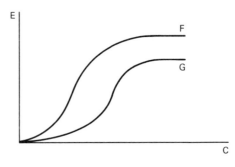

FIGURE 12–2

4. Maximum Effectiveness-Cost Difference
5. Composite Alternatives

We shall discuss each of these in turn.

If we only have $150K available to pay for the TPS, then our decision is clear: choose Option A. However, in some situations this criterion can lead to missed opportunities if an arbitrary budget limit is adhered to too strictly. For example, a budget limit of $90K would lead to a decision to establish a TPS whose performance lies at the low end of the high payoff portion of the curve (point X in Fig. 12–1). Relaxing the budget constraint by about 10%, to $100K, yields a performance improvement of 80% (40 to 72 tr/sec; point Y).

In other cases, the budget limit might lead us to choose the wrong alternative. For example, a budget limit of $210K would force the choice of Option A (point Z), an unfortunate choice if some growth potential beyond 120 tr/sec is needed.

12.2 MINIMUM PERFORMANCE REQUIREMENT

If our application requires a performance of at least 160 tr/sec, then our decision is clearly to go with Option B. Here, similarly, imposing an overly rigorous performance requirement can lead to an unsatisfactory commitment. For example, an arbitrary performance requirement of 125 tr/sec forces a decision to spend $220K (point P in Fig. 12–1). If the application could be handled satisfactorily with a capability of 115 tr/sec, an acceptable system could be provided for $130K (point Q).

12.3 MAXIMUM EFFECTIVENESS/COST RATIO

Another decision criterion involves choosing the situation which yields the maximum payoff per unit of investment, or effectiveness/cost ratio. In Fig. 12–3, all points with a given effectiveness/cost ratio lie on a line through the origin. For example, the line L consists of all points with an effectiveness/cost ratio of 2.

Thus, we want to find the line through the origin with the highest possible slope, that still contains a point on the TPS production function. As seen in Fig. 12–3, this is the line K, with a slope of 0.93, and the point of maximum effectiveness/cost ratio is the point R with a cost of $120K and an effectiveness of 112 tr/sec.

In general, this decision criterion leads to an acceptable solution. However, it does so in a way independent of any budget constraints, performance requirements, or growth considerations. In some situations, these considerations can be very important, and the maximum effectiveness/cost ratio criterion may lead to the wrong decision.

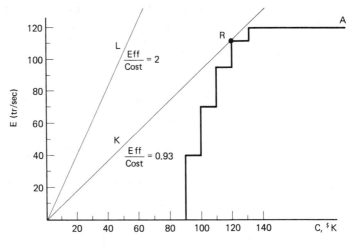

FIGURE 12–3 Maximum effectiveness/cost ratio

12.4 MAXIMUM EFFECTIVENESS-COST DIFFERENCE

Suppose that we can find some way to relate cost and effectiveness on the same scale. For example, if we determined that each transaction per second of processing capability was worth $2500, we could measure effectiveness in terms of dollars, and use the effectiveness-cost difference as the basis of our decision. Figure 12–4 shows the production functions for Options A and B in terms of the dollar effectiveness

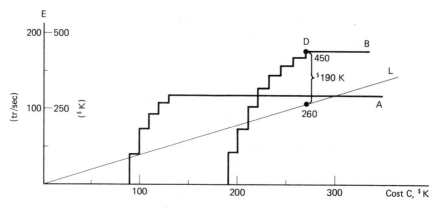

FIGURE 12–4 Maximum effectiveness–cost difference

criterion. It also shows the line *L* representing the points for which effectiveness is equal to cost. Since the effectiveness-cost difference for any point on a production function is equal to the vertical distance between the point and the line *L*, we can determine the point of maximum effectiveness-cost difference by finding the point on a production function that is the highest vertically above the line *L*. In this case, it is the point D with E = $450K, C = $260K, and E–C = $190K.

If we had a different value for the worth of each transaction, we would get a different line *L'*, and often a different location of the point D' with maximum effectiveness-cost difference. Figure 12–5 shows the situation when the value of each transaction per second is $2000 instead of $2500.

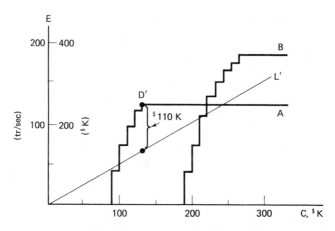

FIGURE 12–5 Maximum E–C difference II

As with the maximum effectiveness/cost ratio criterion, the maximum effectiveness-cost difference criterion generally leads to a good solution, but in a way independent of budget constraints, performance requirements, or growth considerations. We will discuss techniques of dealing with these considerations in Part IIIB.

12.5 COMPOSITE OPTIONS

There is no rule that says we have to pick one alternative and discard all the others. In fact, the best decision is often to choose a composite of the available alternatives. For example, suppose that the $180K cost of TPS Option B includes $30K worth of costs which are common to the $80K cost of Option A; for items such as test support software, common documentation, etc.

Then we can consider the following strategy:

1. Develop and install a system using the available vendor operating system and five processors that will operate at 120 tr/sec and cost $80K.
2. While using this configuration, proceed to invest another $150K in building the special-purpose operating system.
3. When it is ready, install the new operating system on the five-processor system, raising its performance to 150 tr/sec.
4. Add more processors as appropriate.

This strategy leads to the composite production function shown in Fig. 12–6.

Compared to the pure-build Option B, the composite alternative costs another $50K to achieve the same upper levels of effectiveness. However, the $50K allows us to use the system at the 120 tr/sec level while the special-purpose operating system is being developed. This provides a valuable opportunity to phase in the TPS, and to learn some operational lessons while there is still time to feed them into the design of the special-purpose operating system. It also relieves the developers of the operating system from pressures to get the job done as quickly as possible, generally at some cost to the quality of the software product.

The fact that costs and benefits are realized at different times in this option introduces some complications in comparing present and future resources. A dollar available for use today is definitely not the same thing as a dollar which becomes available two years from now. These issues will be covered in Chapter 14.

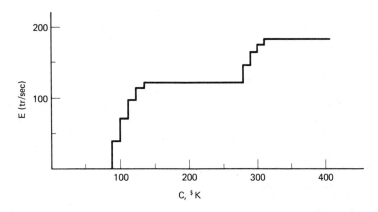

FIGURE 12–6 Production function for TPS composite alternative

12.6 GENERAL DISCUSSION

Decisions made in most software engineering situations are not as simple as the ones presented above. However, these decision criteria are extremely helpful as conceptual aids in formulating and resolving many software life-cycle decision issues. They also provide a foundation for the more sophisticated decision aids to be discussed in the remainder of Part III.

12.7 QUESTIONS

12.1. Some other decision criteria are the following:
(a) Choose the alternative with the maximum effectiveness.
(b) Choose the alternative with the minimum cost.
Can you think of any conditions under which these would be good decision criteria? Under what conditions would they be poor decision criteria?

12.2. Figure 12–7 shows production functions for two alternative designs for an inventory control system for the Montana Mining and Manufacturing Company: a small interactive system and a large batch system. Effectiveness is expressed in terms of average inventory reduction (AIR). Based on these production functions, what decisions would be best for the following criteria:
(a) cost ≤ $1000K
(b) AIR ≥ 120K
(c) maximum effectiveness/cost ratio
(d) maximum effectiveness-cost difference, if each AIR unit is worth $15

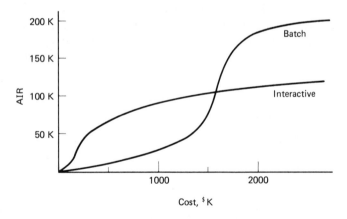

FIGURE 12–7

12.3. Can you develop a composite option that would be attractive to the Montana Mining and Manufacturing Co.?

12.4. In Fig. 12–8, alternative Q is not dominated by either A or B, but it is dominated by the combination of A and B. Is there any reason not to discard alternative Q?

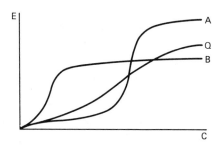

FIGURE 12–8

12.5. Figure 12–9 shows production functions for unit-level error detection (percentage of errors caught) versus cost (percentage of programming effort) for two unit-level verification techniques: inspections [Fagan, 1976] and unit testing. If you could choose only one technique, which would you choose? Why? What additional information would help you make a good decision? Suggest a good composite alternative.

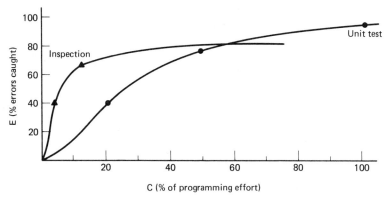

FIGURE 12–9

12.6. Standard University is selecting a system for grading standardized tests and analyzing the test results in various ways (by year, by class, by question, by major, etc.). After polling the faculty to determine desired features of the system and prioritizing the resulting desired capabilities, the evaluation team has identified three alternative systems to acquire.

(a) A small local microprocessor package, which for $1K could provide 10% of the desired capability and for $10K could provide 30%.

(b) An existing commercial software package, which for $12K could provide 90% of the desired capability.

(c) A completely new system, developed by Standard as an organic-mode project with personnel costing $3000 per MM. A 10-KDSI program could provide 60% of the desired capability; a 20-KDSI program could provide 95%.

Using the Basic COCOMO effort equation for alternative (c), determine production functions (percent of desired capability versus cost) for the three alternatives. Which alternative would you recommend for Standard University?

12.7. Several customers approach the Shakespeare Word Processing Company with potential orders for word-processing systems. Indicate via possible system development production functions what problems might be encountered by each customer if Shakespeare were to follow their orders literally?

Customer A: "Build me the best word processor you can for $100K."

Customer B: "Build me a word processor which will correct 95% of my staff's spelling errors."

Customer C: "Build me the cheapest word processor you can."

Customer D: "Build me a word processor which can process more business correspondence per dollar than any other."

Customer E: "Build me the most powerful word processor you can."

Customer F: "Each business letter we currently generate costs our company $10 to prepare. Build me a word processor which maximizes the reduction in my cost of generating business letters, including the cost of your system."

Part IIIB

MULTIPLE GOAL
DECISION ANALYSIS

The essence of the GOALS approach to software engineering presented in Part I is that successful software engineering requires a continuous process of identifying goals, reconciling and making decisions with respect to conflicting goals, and managing with respect to several simultaneous goals. It is very rare to have the luxury of making software engineering decisions with respect to a single decision criterion. And, as we have seen in the case studies in Chapters 1 and 2, it is very dangerous to operate as if multiple goals did not exist. Thus, it is extremely important to have a good understanding of the techniques of goal reconciliation and multiple goal decisionmaking.

The basic techniques that will be covered in Part IIIB are:

1. *Net Value and Marginal Analysis.* Chapter 13 covers techniques for dealing with situations in which all of the significant goals can be expressed in terms of a common unit of *net value.*
2. *Present versus Future Expenditure and Income.* Particularly in an inflationary economy, a dollar spent or received today is worth more than a dollar spent

or received a year from now. Chapter 14 covers *present value* techniques for dealing with such issues.

3. *Figures of Merit.* Chapter 15 covers techniques of compressing several decision criteria into a single *figure of merit* criterion.

4. *Goals as Constraints: Constrained Optimization.* Chapter 16 covers techniques in which the multiple-goal decision process is simplified by treating some goals as constraints.

5. *Systems Analysis and Constrained Optimization.* The techniques covered in Chapter 17 form a part of the more general discipline of systems analysis, which provides the most effective available approach for dealing with decision issues in the feasibility phase of the software life-cycle. This chapter introduces the framework and key concepts of systems analysis in the context of constrained optimization.

6. *Coping with Unreconcilable or Unquantifiable Goals.* Frequently, software engineering decisions must be made with respect to a set of goals—development cost, employee morale, product reliability, ease of use—which are either fundamentally unquantifiable or virtually impossible to express in terms of some universal criterion such as dollars. Chapter 18 introduces some techniques for coping with such situations.

Chapter 13

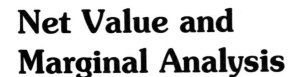

Net Value and Marginal Analysis

13.1 EXAMPLE

Our example here is the same one we discussed under the maximum effectiveness-cost difference decision criterion in Section 12.1. In that section, we showed that if we could determine a way to measure effectiveness in terms of dollars (here called *total value* or *TV*), then we could use the net effectiveness-cost difference as a useful decision criterion. Thus, once we had determined that each transaction per second of processing capability was worth $2500 to us, we could use Fig. 12–4 (reproduced here as Fig. 13–1) to determine the TPS configuration with the largest effectiveness-cost difference as our preferred system to develop. In Fig. 13–1, this is the point D, an eight-processor configuration using a to-be-developed special-purpose operating system, with a cost, $C = \$260K$, a total value, $TV = \$450K$, and a net value, $TV - C = \$190K$.

Another way of representing this situation is to graph the *net value NV = TV − C* of the various options, in which case the point D is simply the maximum point on any net value curve, as shown in Fig. 13–2.

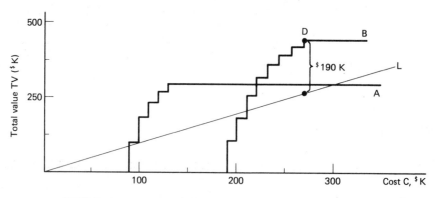

FIGURE 13-1 Maximum effectiveness–cost difference (net value)

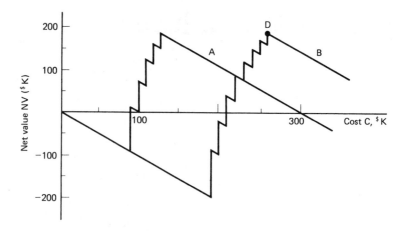

FIGURE 13-2 Net value of TPS alternatives vs. cost

13.2 GENERAL DISCUSSION: MARGINAL ANALYSIS

The total value *TV* of an information processing system is its effectiveness when expressed in the same units used to express the cost *C* of the system. In that case, the net value *NV* is defined as the effectiveness-cost difference, $NV = TV - C$.

Figure 13–2 shows the net value as a function of cost. Since cost often varies with the *activity level** of an alternative (here, the number of processors to be acquired), it is often useful to express the cost, the total value, and the net value as functions of the activity level.

Figures 13–3a and b show typical forms of the cost function *C(x)*, the total value function *TV(x)*, and the net value function $NV(x) = TV(x) - C(x)$, as functions of the activity level *x*.

---

* The activity level of an alternative is a quantity which measures the extent to which the alternative is being employed.

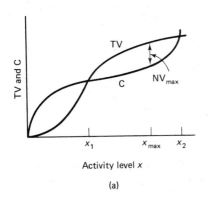

FIGURE 13–3a Cost and total value

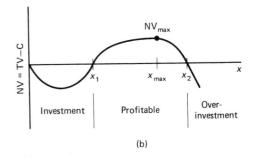

FIGURE 13–3b Net value vs. activity level

We can view the typical net value function as having segments similar to the investment, high payoff, and diminishing returns segments of the total value function (or production function) we discussed in Section 11.2. The net value function similarly begins with an investment segment, which consists of the initial negative portion of the curve, ending at the point x_1. The net value function then enters a profitable segment including the point x_{max}. Beyond this point, the cost function increases faster than the total value function, and by the point x_2, the net value function enters an overinvestment segment in which the total value is again smaller than the cost involved in obtaining it.

Marginal Net Value

At any given activity level x, we can determine the immediate consequences of increasing the activity level by calculating the slope of the net value curve, called the *marginal net value (MNV)*

$$MNV = \frac{d(NV)}{dx}$$

If we are in the profitable segment of the net value curve, we can then formulate the following decision rules for maximizing net value

1. If *MNV* is positive, increase the activity level.
2. If *MNV* is negative, decrease the activity level.
3. If *MNV* is zero, the activity level is optimal (x_{max}).

Thus, we can determine the optimal activity level x_{max} by calculating the marginal net value $MNV = d(NV)/dx$ and solving the equation

$$\frac{d(NV)}{dx} = 0 \tag{13–1}$$

Since $NV = TV - C$, we can also express this equation as

$$\frac{d(NV)}{dx} = \frac{d(TV)}{dx} - \frac{dc}{dx} = 0$$

or

$$\frac{d(TV)}{dx} = \frac{dc}{dx} \qquad (13\text{--}2)$$

The quantities $d(TV)/dx$ and dc/dx are called the *marginal value* and *marginal cost*, respectively. The decision rule above can thus be expressed in terms of marginal value and marginal cost

1. If marginal value is greater than marginal cost, increase the activity level.
2. If marginal value is less than marginal cost, decrease the activity level.
3. If marginal value equals marginal cost, the activity level is optimal (x_{max}).

Again, the use of the rule assumes that we are in the profitable segment of the net value curve.

Figures 13–4a and b show the marginal value and marginal cost functions corresponding to the value and cost functions in Figs. 13–3a and b.

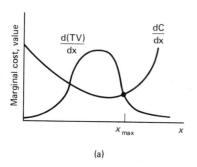

(a)

FIGURE 13–4a Marginal cost and total value

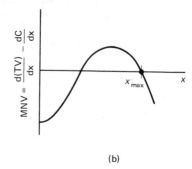

(b)

FIGURE 13–4b Marginal net value

13.3 ILLUSTRATION

Let us see how to put these concepts to work for us in our TPS example. Our earlier analysis (Fig. 13–1) indicated that our net value was maximized by an eight-processor configuration using alternative B. However, this conclusion was based on an estimate of $2500 for the value, V_T, of a transaction per second of processing capability, and we are not sure of the accuracy of this estimate. So, we would like to perform a sensitivity study to determine how the value of N_{max} varies with the value of V_T.

Our activity level variable is N, the number of processors. Our cost function and total value function are

$$C(N) = 180 + 10N$$

$$TV(N) = V_T \frac{N[1000 - 200 - 50(N - 1)]}{20} \qquad \text{(from Eq. 10–1)}$$

$$= V_T (42.5N - 2.5N^2)$$

Then the marginal cost and the marginal value are

$$\frac{dC}{dN} = 10$$

$$\frac{d(TV)}{dN} = V_T (42.5 - 5N)$$

By Eq. (13–2), we can find N_{max} by setting these quantities equal to each other and solving for N_{max}

$$10 = 42.5 V_T - 5 V_T N_{max}$$

$$N_{max} = \frac{42.5 V_T - 10}{5 V_T} = 8.5 - \frac{2}{V_T} \qquad (13–3)$$

The graph of Eq. (13–3) is shown as Fig. 13–5.

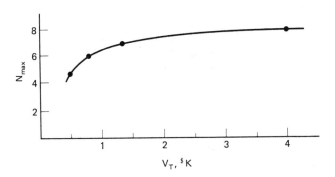

FIGURE 13–5 Optimal number of processors vs. transaction value

We note that the curve is very flat around the region of $V_T = \$2.5K$. Thus we are assured that if we proceed to acquire an eight-processor system on the basis of our earlier analysis, we will not have to worry about the system being poorly matched (having an optimal number of processors significantly different from eight) if our initial estimate of $V_T = \$2.5K$ turns out to be somewhat off the mark.

Net Value and Marginal Analysis

13.4 SOME CAVEATS IN DEALING WITH NET VALUE AND PROFIT

In many economic treatments, "net value" is identified as the profit of a business firm, and a "theory of the firm" is developed, based on the assumption that the firm's overriding objective is to maximize its profit. The use of dollar profit as the only criterion to be used in decisionmaking often leads to decisions with good short-term profit properties, but poor social outcomes for the people involved (and often, as a result, poor long-term profit prospects). The banking example discussed in Question 2.4 is a good illustration of this danger.

The net value approach used in this book assumes that *all* of the relevant components of effectiveness—employees' need-fulfillment, customers' good will, users' information privacy, operators' ease of use—have been translated into dollar values and incorporated as such in the total value function. If this cannot be done quantitatively for some factors, then we must either find some way to treat them as constraints, as discussed in Chapter 16, or we must treat them subjectively as unquantifiable goals, as discussed in Chapter 18.

In this way, it is possible to benefit from the power of the quantitative methods of economics when it is appropriate to use them, and still have room to emphasize the subjective human considerations when they dominate the quantitative factors.

13.5 VALUE OF INFORMATION PROCESSING PRODUCTS

Even in situations in which social implications are relatively minor considerations, it may be difficult to determine as well-defined quantitative function for expressing the value of an information processing product. The value of a certain number of processed transactions per second in our TPS is an example.

In economics, the "value" of an item is the largest price that someone is willing to pay for the item. For an information processing product, this can be a complex function of a good many different factors. Here are a few examples relevant to our TPS system.

- *Time.* A financial transaction which misses the daily deadline loses a day's worth of interest. Large banks process over a billion dollars of financial transactions per day; one day's interest on a billion dollars is roughly $300,000 [DiNardo, 1975].
- *Cost of Alternatives.* If the only alternative is to process transactions by hand, the value of developing a computer-based TPS may be quite high. However, if economical transaction processing services already exist, the value of developing another one may be relatively low.
- *Opportunities Presented by Information.* In a stock market TPS, considerable added value may accrue from the opportunity to observe and capitalize on trends in market activity. A point-of-sale TPS will accrue added value from the opportunity to perform more cost-effective inventory management.

A number of other factors may also be influential, such as the accuracy, reliability, volume, and structure of the information. The effect of information reliability will be discussed in Chapter 20.

In more basic terms, the value of an information processing product depends on two primary factors:

1. *The degree to which the resulting information helps us make critical decisions.* Thus, in an airline reservation TPS, information on numbers and types of seats available and reserved is more valuable than information on numbers and types of aircraft engines. In an aircraft maintenance TPS, on the other hand, the engine information would be more valuable.
2. *The degree to which the information processing product satisfies basic human needs.* Thus, a paycheck has value primarily for the food, entertainment, security, and so on that it makes available, not because the information on it is used for decisionmaking.

Factor 1 will be discussed in more detail in Chapters 19 and 20.

13.6 QUESTIONS

13.1. Define the following terms: value, net value, marginal value, marginal net value.

13.2. State the three decision rules for adjusting activity levels in order to maximize net value. Why was their use restricted to the profitable segment of the net value curve? Is there a less binding restriction that is still satisfactory?

13.3. Consider the TPS example discussed in Section 13.2 with a somewhat different cost function

$$C(N) = 100 + 20N$$

Using this cost function, derive an equation for N_{max} in terms of V_T. Determine N_{max} for $V_T = 2.5$, 1.0, and 0.5.

13.4. Consider the TPS example discussed in Section 13.2 with $V_T = 2$ and $C(N) = 180 + 10N$. For the case $S = 1000$, $P = 200$, and $T = 20$, derive an equation for N_{max} in terms of the multiprocessor overhead factor M. Determine N_{max} for $M = 200$, 100, 50, and 25.

13.5. In the General Appliance Company inventory control system presented in Question 10.10, the value of the inventory savings in dollars, achievable by developing an inventory control program of a given size in KDSI, can be represented by the function

$$\text{Value} = \tfrac{1}{8} [260(\text{KDSI}) - (\text{KDSI})^2]$$

The cost in dollars of developing the given program was determined from Basic COCOMO to be

$$\text{Cost} = 5000 [2.4(\text{KDSI})^{1.05}]$$

Determine the optimal size of the inventory control program by finding the point $KDSI_{max}$ at which the marginal net value of the program is equal to zero.

13.6. What factors influence the value of the following information processing products:
(a) an airlines reservation transaction
(b) a paycheck
(c) a stock market analysis
(d) a table of the first million prime numbers
(e) a spacecraft control signal
(f) a computer-generated portrait

13.7. The book *Small Is Beautiful* [Schumacher, 1973] contrasts the profit-maximizing Western economics with Buddhist economics, in which the prime objective of an enterprise is to provide work which helps people develop character. Do you think that Buddhist economics could be viable in the United States or in Europe? Can you think of a more satisfactory basic objective for an economic system?

13.8. The book *Atlas Shrugged* [Rand, 1957], graphically depicts the downfall of the United States into widespread violence, starvation, and chaos as a result of a number of national directives issued in the name of curbing the profit motive and promoting equality and social welfare, for example:

- setting very low ceilings on the amount of production allowed by any one company
- eliminating the patent system and the copyright system
- freezing people and companies into their existing jobs and income levels

Do you think that such measures could succeed? If not, would they fail more for economic reasons (for example, by eliminating economies of scale) or more for social reasons (for example, by eliminating people's motivation to make things better?)

Chapter 14

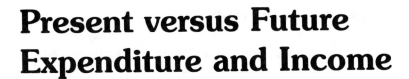

Present versus Future Expenditure and Income

14.1 EXAMPLE: AN OVERSIMPLIFIED COST ANALYSIS

Suppose that, in our TPS example, we decide to use Option A (accept the available operating system) for a period of two years. During this period, we will gain experience with the system, and develop an appropriate follow-on option to be ready at the end of the period.

Another economic decision problem we may face is that of choosing between rental and purchase of our processors. Suppose we have decided to use the five-processor system with Option A, and we have the following options:*

- A1 Rent the processors at a total rental of $1200 per month
- A2 Purchase the processors from an agent who will sell them to us for $50,000 and buy them back after 2 years for $25,000

---

* These options are more characteristic of terms for larger computers than they are for microprocessors.

A simple analysis is the following:

$$\text{Cost of A1} = \$1200/\text{mo} \times 24 \text{ mo} = \$28,800$$
$$\text{Cost of A2} = \$50,000 - \$25,000 = \$25,000$$

This would lead us to the purchase decision, Option A2.

However, this may be the wrong conclusion, because the analysis is based on a faulty assumption: that a dollar available to us 24 months from now is the same as a dollar available to us now. In fact, though, a dollar available now is worth more, if only because we can lend it to a bank for two years and collect added interest.

14.2 INTEREST CALCULATIONS

Suppose that we can find a way to earn interest on our money at a rate of 9% per year or 0.75% per month, compounded monthly. On Option A2, we have $25K tied up for 2 years in the purchase of our processors. Let us see how much this $25K would have been worth to us at the end of 2 years, if at the end of each month its current value were increased by 0.75% (a factor of 1.0075). At the end of the first month, we would have

$$V(25,000, 1) = \$25,000 (1.0075)$$

At the end of the second month, we would have

$$V(25,000, 2) = [\$25,000 (1.0075)] (1.0075) = \$25,000 (1.0075)^2$$

Reasoning similarly, at the end of the 24th month, we would have

$$V(25,000, 24) = \$25,000 (1.0075)^{24} = \$25,000 (1.1964) = \$29,910$$

Thus, we have lost the opportunity to earn almost $5000 by having our $25K tied up in the purchase of processors.

14.3 PRESENT VALUE CALCULATIONS

Another way of evaluating the reduced value of Option A2 is to determine the worth in today's dollars of the $25K we will receive in 2 years when we sell back the processors. We can calculate this by solving for X in the relationship

$$\$25,000 = V(X, 24) = X(1.0075)^{24}$$

or

$$X = \frac{\$25,000}{(1.0075)^{24}} = \frac{\$25,000}{1.1964} = \$20,896$$

This is the *present value* of the $25,000 to be received in 2 years. Therefore the cost of Option A2 in terms of present value is

$$\$50,000 - \$20,896 = \$29,104$$

If we can calculate the present value of Option Al, we can then decide between the two options on a more realistic basis. If we look at the equation above for X, the present value of $25,000 at an interest rate of .0075 per month for 24 months, we have

$$X = PV(\$25,000, .0075, 24) = \frac{\$25,000}{(1.0075)^{24}}$$

In general, since the reasoning we used above would also hold for any cash flow F, any interest rate r per time period, and any number of time periods n, we can express the general formula for present value as

$$PV(F,r,n) = \frac{F}{(1+r)^n} \qquad (14\text{--}1)$$

Often it is more convenient to express the present value in terms of the *discount rate*

$$D = \frac{1}{1+r}$$

$$PV(F,D,n) = FD^n \qquad (14\text{--}2)$$

See Section 14.6 for more information on discounting.

14.4 PRESENT VALUE OF A SERIES OF CASH FLOWS

Using Eq. (14–2), we can calculate the present value of our monthly rental payments in Option A1. Our monthly payments are $1200 each, paid at the beginning of each of the 24 months. After the first payment, we have

$$PV_s(1200,D,1) = PV(1200,D,0) = \$1200$$

After the second payment, we have

$$PV_s(1200,D,2) = \$1200 + PV(1200,D,1) = \$1200 + 1200D$$

where the subscript s (for series) is added to distinguish this quantity from the single-payment present value function. The second term is obtained from Eq. (14–2), since we have a cash flow $F = 1200$ paid after $n = 1$ time periods at a discount rate D.

After the third payment, we have

$$PV_s(1200,D,3) = \$1200 + 1200D + 1200D^2 = \$1200(1 + D + D^2), \cdot$$

again using Eq. (14–2) to obtain the final term.

Reasoning similarly, after the 24th payment, we have*

$$PV_s(1200,D,24) = \$1200 (1 + D + D^2 + D^3 + \cdots + D^{23})$$

$$= \$1200 \frac{1 - D^{24}}{1 - D}$$

In fact, using the same flow of reasoning, we can derive a general formula for the present value of a series of m equal periodic cash flows p, issued at the beginning of each period, using a discount rate D

$$PV_s(p,D,m) = p\left(\frac{1 - D^m}{1 - D}\right) \qquad (14\text{–}3)$$

For our example, the discount rate is

$$D = \frac{1}{1.0075} = .9925558,$$

and the present value of our series of payments is

$$PV_s(1200,.9925558,24) = \$1200 \left(\frac{1 - .9925558^{24}}{1 - .9925558}\right)$$

$$= \$1200 \left(\frac{.16417}{.0074442}\right) = \$26,464$$

14.5 SUMMARY OF RENTAL VERSUS PURCHASE ANALYSIS

The table below summarizes the costs of Options A1 and A2 in terms of our first simple analysis and in terms of present value.

	Simple Analysis	Present Value Analysis
Cost of A1	$28,800	$26,464
Cost of A2	$25,000	$29,104

* For any m, we can demonstrate this identity by multiplying and dividing by $1 - D$:

$$1 + D + D^2 + \cdots + D^{m-1} = \frac{(1 + D + D^2 + \cdots + D^{m-1})(1 - D)}{1 - D}$$

$$= \frac{1 + D + D^2 + \cdots + D^{m-1} - D - D^2 - D^3 - \cdots - D^m}{1 - D} = \frac{1 - D^m}{1 - D}$$

The use of present values leads us to the opposite conclusion from that of our earlier simple analysis. Rental Option A1 gains value, since its deferred payments give us opportunities to do other useful things with our money. The purchase option loses value, since it denies us such opportunities. Therefore, Option A1 is the preferred choice.

14.6 GENERAL DISCUSSION: SUMMARY OF PRESENT VALUE CONCEPTS AND FORMULAS

The *value* of an item is the largest amount of money that someone is willing to pay for the item.

The *present value* of a future amount of money or cash flow is a present amount of money or cash flow of equal value.

Often, the present value can be expressed in terms of a constant *interest rate r* over a given time period. If so, the relation between the future amount of money or cash flow F at the end of the period and the present value of the cash flow $PV(F,r)$ is

$$F = PV(F,r)(1 + r)$$

or

$$PV(F,r) = F\left(\frac{1}{1 + r}\right)$$

The relation is often expressed in terms of the *discount rate*

$$D = \frac{1}{1 + r}$$

$$PV(F,D) = FD$$

The calculation of the present value of future cash flows is called *discounting*.

If the future cash flow F occurs after n periods of time, and the interest is compounded after each period, then the present value of F is

$$PV(F,r,n) = \frac{F}{(1 + r)^n} \tag{14-1}$$

or

$$PV(F,D,n) = FD^n \tag{14-2}$$

If the overall cash flow consists of a *series* of m equal cash flows or payments p at the beginning of each time period, and the discount rate D is constant, then the present value of the series of payments is

$$PV_s(p,D,m) = p\frac{1 - D^m}{1 - D}. \qquad (14\text{–}3)$$

Clearly, these present value concepts and the concepts of net value and marginal analysis discussed in the previous section can be combined, so we can analyze systems in terms of such concepts as net present value, marginal present value, and so on.

14.7 PRESENT VALUE CHARACTERISTICS

The main benefit of the present value concept to decisionmakers is that it provides a consistent framework for reconciling cash flows which occur at different points in time, to a single common scale of units: current dollars. Otherwise, adding or comparing present and future cash flows is about like adding or comparing quantities of apples and oranges.

The preference of present resources over future resources is rooted in two common components of human nature: time preference and risk avoidance. Our time preference for a resource stems from the fact that we have more options for using it if we receive it earlier—or, conversely, we may miss some golden opportunities for using it if it isn't available until later. The risk aversion discount factor stems from the fact that we can't absolutely guarantee the future value of the resource. The value of money may be wiped out by a runaway inflation; the value of goods may be wiped out by a future oversupply. And further, we can't guarantee that we will be around to enjoy the use of the resources in the future.

14.8 SENSITIVITY TO INTEREST RATE OR DISCOUNT RATE

The results of present value comparisons can be very sensitive to the value of the interest rate or discount rate. Our TPS example above provides an illustration. Figure 14–1 shows how the present values of the Options A1 (rental) and A2 (purchase) vary with the magnitude of the interest rate.

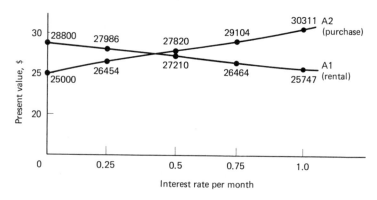

FIGURE 14–1 Present value comparison vs. interest rate

For an interest rate of zero, our original simple analysis is valid, since it means there are no differences between present and future cash flows. For very low interest rates, the purchase option is preferred, up to an interest rate of roughly 0.42% per month, or roughly 5% per year. For interest rates higher than 5% per year, the rental option is preferred.

14.9 APPLICATIONS TO SOFTWARE ENGINEERING

The major application of present value analysis to software engineering is in making life-cycle cost comparisons between alternative systems during the feasibility phase, in order to decide on the most cost-effective concept for development. This type of analysis is similar to the analysis performed in the example above, with the possible addition of other streams of payments for hardware maintenance, operators, and software personnel, and cash flows of resulting revenues from the developed system.

Another software engineering decision which generally involves a present value analysis is that of the timing of the purchase of the target machine for a new system. Buying the machine too early ties up a lot of capital for a resource that will not be used very much until the coding phase. Buying the machine too late will cause software development costs and schedules to increase. Besides interest rates, such decisions also may involve considerations of tax, insurance, operations, and maintenance payments. Often, these factors can be combined into a composite discount rate for analysis.

Another related software engineering consideration is the software life-cycle budget. Often, a software project has gotten into budget trouble during the later stages, because the budgets were put together using constant values for people's salaries, company overhead rates, costs of purchased supplies, and so on. Accounting for escalation in these factors is not exactly a present value analysis—but it is related, and particularly important on long projects budgeted in dollars (as opposed to manmonths).

There are some situations in which a present value analysis is not worth the effort. The major class of such situations is the comparative analysis of systems which have very similar distributions of cash flows versus time. In such cases, the differences due to present value considerations will be in the noise level with respect to other considerations.

14.10 QUESTIONS

14.1. Define the following terms: present value, net present value, discount rate, marginal present value.

14.2. If we are working with an interest rate of 10% per year, compounded annually, what is the present value of a payment of $10,000 which we will receive in 3 years?

14.3. Suppose we agree to pay $30,000 for a software package in 12 equal monthly installments of $2500 at the beginning of each month. Assuming that the monthly interest rate is 1%, what is the present value of the series of payments?

14.4. In the situation described in Question 14.3, will the present value of the series of payments increase, decrease, or stay the same under the following conditions:
- increasing the interest rate
- increasing the discount rate
- paying $5000 in 6 installments at the beginning of each 2-month period

14.5. Suppose in our TPS example that we can resell the processors for $30K after 2 years rather than $25K in Option A2. Which option is then preferable in terms of present value?

14.6. Given the situation in Question 14.5, suppose further that Option A2 requires us to pay $100/mo at the beginning of each month for taxes, insurance, and maintenance service on the processors. Which option would then be preferable?

14.7. Standard University has just completed the design of a student record information system, and now has two choices for developing it:

D1 Total system development, requiring 20 programmers for one year

D2 Incremental development, requiring 10 programmers for two years

Each programmer begins with a salary of $2K per month, paid at the beginning of each month, and receives a 10% raise after one year. The interest rate is 0.75% per month, compounded monthly. Perform a present value analysis of Options D1 and D2, and determine which is preferable on a present value basis.

14.8. [Sharpe, 1969]. A service bureau is considering renting a computer for 24 months at $10,000 per month. The first 11 months will be required to test software for the particular application to be offered by the firm. During each of the remaining 13 months, the service is expected to yield $20,000 in revenue. On a present value basis, is the investment worthwhile if the interest rate is 1% per month, compounded monthly? Is it worthwhile at an interest rate of 1.25% per month? (Assume payments and income flow at the beginning of each month.)

14.9. Derive a formula for the present value of a series of equal cash flows or payments issued at the *end* of each period, using a discount rate *D*.

Chapter 15

Figures of Merit

The previous two chapters introduced the concepts of net value and present value as techniques for combining several different cost and effectiveness functions into a single criterion function: the net present value of an alternative in dollars. Often, though, it is a difficult or controversial process to express performance criteria in terms of dollars. In such cases, we may resort to other techniques of combining several criteria into a single decision criterion. Such single criteria are generally called *figures of merit*.

15.1 EXAMPLE: SOFTWARE PACKAGE SELECTION

At this stage in our discussion of the TPS example, we have decided to use Option A1 (the rental of a number of processors for two years, using the available vendor-supplied operating system). Suppose now that the vendor offers us a choice of two versions of the operating system:

- System A, the standard operating system
- System A Plus, which has the same performance characteristics, but has improved measurement and diagnostic capabilities, and an additional price tag of $5K

Our investigation of these two options yields the information in Table 15–1.

TABLE 15–1 Alternative TPS Operating System Characteristics

	Alternative	
Criterion	System A	System A Plus
1. Added cost	0	$5K
2. Processor overhead	200	200
3. Multiprocessor overhead	80	80
4. Measurement capability	Poor	Good
5. Trace capability	None	Adequate
6. Diagnostics, error messages	Adequate	Good
7. Maintenance support	Marginal	Good
8. Accounting system	Adequate	Very good
9. Usage summaries	None	Good
10. Documentation	Good	Adequate

Again, we have a multiple-goal decision problem. We would like the improved capability at no extra cost, but that option is not available. Thus, we must reconcile our low-cost goal with additional goals involving a number of other performance criteria.

15.2 NET VALUE ANALYSIS

One way to resolve the problem is simply to estimate dollar values for each of the criterion rating levels in Table 15–1, and use them to perform a net value analysis. There are two primary ways we can estimate the dollar values.

1. Perform top-of-the-head estimates for each criterion; that is, a "good" diagnostic capability will be worth $3000 to us over the two years, an "adequate" capability will be worth only $2000. This type of assessment has the advantage of being quick. Its main disadvantages are that significant factors may be neglected in the assessment, and that the assessment may not be easy to rationalize if called into question.

2. Perform an analysis of the number of times the diagnostic capability (and other capabilities) will be needed, the amount of time, availability, and performance saved by improved diagnostic capabilities, and the resulting dollar savings. This has the advantages of providing a stronger assurance that all significant factors have been considered, and of providing a more defensible rationale for the dollar assessments. The main disadvantage is the amount of effort required to make such detailed analyses. The cost difference between

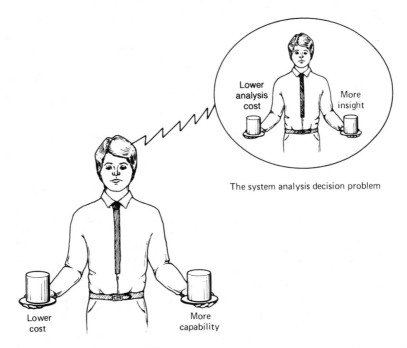

Lower
analysis
cost

More
insight

The system analysis decision problem

Lower
cost

More
capability

The system decision problem

FIGURE 15–1 Levels of decision problems

Systems A and A Plus is only $5K. If we spend more than $5K analyzing which system to choose, we will achieve a false economy indeed.

If we plan to perform a net value analysis, we must choose which of these ways of estimating dollar values to use. This involves us in a mini decision problem of its own. As above, where we needed to decide between a low-cost system and a high-performance system, we would now like both the low-cost analysis and the high-fidelity analysis, but we can't get both. So we must now evaluate in our minds the costs and benefits of the top-of-the-head technique and the detailed analysis technique and decide which analysis technique to use (see Fig. 15–1).

Before doing so, however, we should also consider the possibility of using a figure of merit analysis, as described in the next section.

15.3 FIGURE OF MERIT ANALYSIS

Another technique for resolving the decision problem presented by Table 15–1 is to derive a dimensionless figure of merit for each option, and choose the option with the higher figure of merit.

The most common figure of merit technique is the *weighted sum* technique. To use this technique, we assign a set of weights to the criteria (generally adding up to 100), which reflect the relative importance of each criterion. Then for each option,

TABLE 15-2 TPS Operating System Figure of Merit Calculation

Criterion	Weight	System A			System A Plus		
		Characteristic	Rating	Weighted Rating	Characteristic	Rating	Weighted Rating
1. Added cost	30	$0	10	300	$5K	4	120
2. Processor overhead	10	200	3	30	200	3	30
3. Multiprocessor overhead	15	80	3	45	80	3	45
4. Measurement capability	7	Poor	2	14	Good	8	56
5. Trace capability	8	None	0	0	Adequate	6	48
6. Diagnostics, error messages	10	Adequate	6	60	Good	8	80
7. Maintenance support	10	Marginal	4	40	Good	8	80
8. Accounting system	2	Adequate	6	12	Very good	10	20
9. Usage summaries	3	None	0	0	Good	8	24
10. Documentation	5	Good	8	40	Adequate	4	20
Total	100			541			523

we assign a rating for each criterion (generally on a scale of 0 to 10), which reflects how well the option satisfies the criterion. When we apply this technique to our example, we get the results shown in Table 15–2.

The result of this analysis would lead us to choose System A. We should note, however, that this conclusion is very sensitive to the weights and ratings we assigned. If we assigned a rating of 5 rather than 4 to the cost of System A Plus, it would then win by a score of 553 to 541. Or, if the weights of the processor overhead (10) and accounting system (2) criteria were reversed, as might be the case in some applications, System A Plus would win by a score of 579 to 565.

These are fairly serious concerns. It is hard to get a very secure feeling about choosing one system over another on the basis of this analysis. The best that can be said for the analysis at this point is

- The weighted sum approach provides a clean, objective framework, which allows us to pick out which weights and ratings are most influential, and to discuss and iterate them.
- This particular analysis is trying to do too much within the framework, particularly in trying to incorporate the cost criterion. Perhaps a modified version of the figure of merit would prove more useful.

We will revisit this example with an improved figure of merit at the end of this section, after we discuss a case study on the use of the weighted sum technique in large scale computer system selection.

15.4 GENERAL DISCUSSION: WEIGHTED SUM ANALYSIS FOR HARDWARE AND SOFTWARE SELECTION: A CASE STUDY

The TPS example above is a small sample of the sort of decision problem frequently encountered in computer system or software package selection. In either of these situations, we are required to choose between complex systems with a large number of capabilities and attributes, many of which are difficult to analyze in terms of their added value to an organization in dollars.

The weighted sum technique is a fairly good match for this sort of problem. The CODASYL study, *Selection and Acquisition of Data Base Management Systems* [CODASYL, 76], recommends the use of the weighted sum technique in evaluating the relative merits of alternative data base management systems for a specified application. In particular, it recommends a hierarchical weighted sum technique, called PEGS (Parametric Evaluation of Generalized Systems) [Dowkont and others, 1967] and the MECCA (Multi-Element Component Comparison and Analysis) Method [Gilb, 1969]. In fact, the technique must be considerably older, as it was being used in computer selection activities in the mid-1960s. One such evaluation activity is discussed as a case study below, as it contains a number of useful lessons learned in applying the weighted sum technique. It also gives a good feel for the number and type of criteria used in a large hardware–software selection activity.

15.5 CASE STUDY: ACTIVITY DESCRIPTION

The objective of this activity was to select a more powerful general-purpose computer system to replace an IBM 7040/7044 system. The system's workload included scientific, text-processing, and corporate business applications, but was primarily scientific. About 70% of the workload consisted of FORTRAN programs, about 25% assembly language, with the remainder primarily COBOL and SIMSCRIPT. Roughly 75% of the jobs ran less than 5 min; the average run time for a job was 3.5 min. (A separate system was available for small interactive jobs.) The primary goal for the new computer system was to provide greater problem-solving capabilities for the professional staff via improved software support capabilities and increased computer power. The secondary goal was to significantly increase computer power without significantly increasing costs.

An extensive hierarchy of evaluation criteria was defined. It is shown in Table 15–3, with its associated weighting factors. It is noteworthy that, even in a 1965–66 scientific computing shop, the hardware weighting factor was only 27%, while the software factors made up 63% of the total weight. (The other 10% covered vendor support considerations.) The candidate computer systems evaluated were the IBM 7040/7044 (the existing system), IBM 360/67-TSS, IBM 360/65-OS, Univac 1108, CDC 6400, and GE 635. These were formulated as essentially equal-cost configurations; therefore, cost was not a major evaluation criterion at this point.

TABLE 15–3 Hierarchical Computer Evaluation Criteria (weighting factors at left)

0.27	I.	Hardware	
	0.07	A.	General system modularity
			1. Processor units
			2. Storage units
			3. I/O control units
			4. Peripherals
	0.08	B.	Range of line
		0.10	1. Number in family
		0.34	2. Range of processor speeds
		0.43	3. Range of storage sizes
		0.13	4. Peripherals
	0.20	C.	Processing units
		0.15	1. Number possible
		0.49	2. Speeds
		0.19	3. Instruction set versatility
		0.09	4. Interrupt handling
		0.04	5. Timers and clocks
		0.04	6. Internal checking
	0.14	D.	Primary storage
		0.50	1. Access times
		0.23	2. Word length and word utilization
		0.23	3. Protection features
		0.04	4. Internal checking
	0.03	E.	Time-sharing hardware
			1. Speeds
			2. Addressing capability

TABLE 15–3 (Cont'd)

0.05	F.		Character set
		0.45 1.	Internal
		0.55 2.	External (peripherals)
0.11	G.		I/O control units (channels)
		0.20 1.	Degree of independence
		0.25 2.	Transmission rates
		0.04 3.	Number possible
		0.08 4.	Number of device interfaces possible
		0.05 5.	Buffer sizes (capacity)
		0.18 6.	Priority control and interrupt handling
		0.14 7.	Assignment flexibility
		0.05 8.	Programming considerations
0.05	H.		Device interfaces (control units)
		1.	Number of controllers per interface
		2.	Number of devices per interface
		3.	Transmission rates
		4.	Degree of independence
		5.	Assignment flexibility
		6.	Programming considerations
0.15	I.		Secondary storage devices
		0.05 1.	Very high speed (bulk core)
		0.40 2.	High speed
		0.25 3.	Medium speed
		0.15 4.	Large capacity units
		0.15 5.	Tape units
0.06	J.		I/O devices
		0.18 1.	Card equipment
		0.36 2.	Printers
		0.04 3.	Paper tape equipment
		0.24 4.	Displays
		0.18 5.	Typewriters
0.06	K.		Communications multiplexors
		1.	Line handling and switching capabilities
		2.	Number of devices
		3.	Transmission speeds
		4.	I/O channel interfaces

0.27	II.		Supervisor
	0.58	A.	Functional capability
		0.13 1.	Command interpretation
		0.17 2.	Task scheduling
		0.07 3.	Interrupt handling
		0.16 4.	Storage allocation
		0.08 5.	Multiple processor capabilities
		0.14 6.	Program and data protection
		0.05 7.	Fail-soft mechanism
		0.10 8.	Self-analysis and accounting
		0.05 9.	Debugging
		0.03 10.	System/operator interaction
		0.02 11.	Cold starting and stopping
	0.11	B.	Ease of revision
		0.65 1.	Modularity
		0.35 2.	System editing
	0.12	C.	Reliability

TABLE 15–3   *(Cont'd)*

0.16	D.	Ease of usage
0.40	1.	Command language
0.20	2.	Appropriateness of response
0.40	3.	Virtual memory
0.03	E.	Hardware requirements

0.08   III.   Data management
 0.66   A.   File management
  0.20   1.   File manipulation
  0.13   2.   Reliability and recovery features
  0.20   3.   Data protection
  0.16   4.   Storage utilization
  0.16   5.   File structure
  0.15   6.   Integration with operating system
 0.21   B.   Data manipulation
                1.   Operations available
                2.   Types of elements accessible
 0.13   C.   Physical I/O Operations
0.16   IV.   Language processors
 0.58   A.   FORTRAN
  0.18   1.   Compiler efficiency
  0.27   2.   Object code efficiency
  0.10   3.   Comparison to standards
  0.08   4.   Reliability
  0.08   5.   Debugging features
  0.14   6.   Reenterability
  0.10   7.   Response and diagnostics
  0.05   8.   Intralanguage compatibility
 0.10   B.   PL/I
                (Same considerations as in A, when applicable.)
 0.04   C.   COBOL
                (Same considerations as in A, when applicable.)
 0.15   D.   Assembler
                (Same considerations as in A, when applicable.)
 0.08   E.   SIMSCRIPT
                (Same considerations as in A, when applicable.)
 0.05   F.   Interlanguage compatibility
  0.40   1.   Subprogram linkage
  0.40   2.   Linkage to data
  0.20   3.   Use of same loader
0.02   V.   General programming support
 0.15   A.   Library
                1.   Extensiveness
                2.   Availability to system processors
                3.   Language compatibility
                4.   Reenterability
 0.35   B.   Mathematical/statistical package
                (Same considerations as in A, when applicable.)
 0.45   C.   Applications programs (linear programming, sort/merge, and so on)
                (Same considerations as in A, when applicable.)
 0.05   D.   Utilities
                (Same considerations as in A, when applicable.)
0.12   VI.   Conversion considerations
 0.65   A.   Ability to handle present languages

TABLE 15–3   *(Cont'd)*

	0.70	1.	Machine language/assembly language
	0.20	2.	FORTRAN, degree of compatibility
	0.05	3.	SIMSCRIPT, degree of compatibility
	0.05	4.	Supervisor command language, degree of compatibility
0.15		B.	Data files
		1.	Word length
		2.	Character set and collating sequence
		3.	Physical and logical tape formats
0.20		C.	Vendor-supplied assistance
	0.40	1.	Machine time
	0.40	2.	Personnel
	0.20	3.	Training
0.08		VII.	Vendor reliability and support
	0.20	A.	General reliability and reputation
	0.13	1.	Number of machines installed and on order
	0.19	2.	Delivery record
	0.31	3.	Customer satisfaction
	0.23	4.	Reliability of hardware and software (present state)
	0.14	5.	Length of time in field
	0.10	B.	Technology
	0.60	1.	Newness of line and predicted obsolescence date
	0.20	2.	Predicted additions to line
	0.20	3.	Circuit technology
	0.10	C.	Maintenance procedures
		1.	Hardware
		2.	Software
	0.25	D.	Continuing support
		1.	On-site personnel
		2.	Availability of experts
	0.25	E.	Documentation
	0.80	1.	Quality and readability of manuals
	0.20	2.	Availability of manuals and flowcharts
	0.10	F.	User group effectiveness
	0.40	1.	Information exchange
	0.30	2.	Program exchange
	0.15	3.	Manufacturer's control
	0.15	4.	Manufacturer's responsiveness

Each of these candidate systems was evaluated on a scale of 0 to 10 with respect to each of the criteria in Table 15–3. Several man-months were devoted to detailed study of each vendor's offering, and benchmark jobs were run on each configuration except the 360/67, which was represented by the 360/65 during benchmark testing, as the 360/67's TSS operating system was still under development. Some of the software evaluation results are shown as Table 15–4.

Each of the ratings was then multiplied by its appropriate hierarchical set of weights, and the results summed to give an overall score for each candidate.

Table 15–5 summarizes the results of the weighted sum evaluation. The IBM 360/67-TSS and Univac 1108 systems were clearly highest in scoring. They were subjected to further evaluation, and the IBM 360/67 system was selected and ordered for purchase.

TABLE 15–4 Portion of Weighted Sum Evaluation for Computer Design

CEG Category	Weight Factors	IBM 7040/7044	CDC 6400	GE 635	IBM 360/65	IBM 360/67	UNIVAC 1108
II	.27	3.67	4.91	5.44	4.58	6.80	6.64
A	.58	2.64	4.33	5.35	4.46	7.54	7.42
1	.13	4½	3	4½	6	8	8
2	.17	1	4	5	5	7	8
3	.07	6	5	6	6	6	7
4	.16	1	5	5	4	8½	7½
5	.08	0	0	7	0	8	8
6	.14	3	8	7	5	8	8
7	.05	3	4	3	3	7	8
8	.10	3	3	5	3	7	6
9	.05	3	3	4	6	8	5
10	.03	6	6	6	6	6	6
11	.02	5	8	6	7	7	7
B	.11	5.35	7.30	6.00	6.35	6.00	7.00
1	.65	5	8	6	6	6	7
2	.35	6	6	6	7	6	7
C	.12	8	7	8	5	4	6
D	.16	2.60	3.20	3.20	3.20	7.00	4.00
1	.40	5	5	5	5	8	7
2	.20	3	6	6	6	7	6
3	.40	0	0	0	0	6	0
E	.03	6	8	7	6	5½	7
III	.08	3.02	2.62	3.46	5.43	6.47	6.33
A	.66	2.19	2.22	2.66	4.81	6.08	5.86
1	.20	2	3	2	7	7	5
2	.13	0	0	0	0	2	2
3	.20	2	2	2	4½	8	6½
4	.16	0	0	1	4	5	7
5	.16	4	2	5	7	7	8
6	.15	5	6	6	5	6	6
B	.21	5	3	5	7	8	8
C	.13	4	4	5	6	6	6
IV	.16	3.40	3.23	4.61	4.86	5.22	6.26
A	.58	3.32	3.11	4.20	4.52	5.29	7.42
1	.18	2	6	4	5	5½	9
2	.27	3	3	5	4	4½	8½
3	.10	5½	4	6½	7	7	8
4	.08	9	4	5	5	4	7
5	.08	6	0	6	6	6	6
6	.14	0	0	0	4	7	4
7	.10	4	5	6	4	6	8
8	.05	0	0	0	0	0	6
B	.10	0	0	4½	6	6	2
C	.04	4.17	4.81	4.17	4.89	4.89	5.48
1	.18	6	6	6	6	6	6
2	.26	6	6	6	6	6	6
3	.11	6	7	6	6	6	7

TABLE 15–4 *(Cont'd)*

CEG Category	Weight Factors	IBM 7040/7044	CDC 6400	GE 635	IBM 360/65	IBM 360/67	UNIVAC 1108
4	.09	6	3	6	6	6	7
5	.09	0	4	0	8	8	5
6	.16	0	0	0	0	0	0
7	.11	3	7	3	3	3	9
8	—	—	—	—	—	—	—
D	.15	5.47	4.03	5.25	5.98	7.22	5.85
1	.60	6	5	6	7	8	7
2	—	—	—	—	—	—	—
3	—	—	—	—	—	—	—
4	.11	9	5	7	6	5	7
5	.08	5	0	5	8	6	5
6	.13	0	0	0	0	7	0
7	.08	6	6	6	6	6	6
8	—	—	—	—	—	—	—
E	.08	2.79	4.30	6.34	3.31	0.00	4.30
1	.18	2	6	8	4	0	6
2	.26	2	6	8	4	0	6
3	.11	5	6	8	5	0	6
4	.09	9	5	7	5	0	5
5	.09	0	0	6	0	0	0
6	.16	0	0	0	0	0	0
7	.11	5	5	7	5	0	5
8	—	—	—	—	—	—	—
F	.05	5.20	5.60	5.20	5.60	5.60	6.40
1	.40	5	6	5	5	5	6
2	.40	4	5	4	5	5	6
3	.20	8	6	8	8	8	8

TABLE 15–5 Summary of Scores (Weighted Averages)

Guide Division	IBM 7040/7044	CDC 6400	GE 635	IBM 360/65	IBM 360/67	UNIVAC 1108	Weight
I	3.81	5.79	5.75	6.40	7.08	6.87	0.27
II	3.67	4.91	5.44	4.58	6.80	6.64	0.27
III	3.02	2.62	3.46	5.43	6.47	6.33	0.08
IV	3.40	3.23	4.61	4.86	5.22	6.26	0.16
V	6.58	4.73	5.38	7.55	6.53	7.85	0.02
VI	10.00	2.94	7.51	6.61	5.86	4.00	0.12
VII	6.57	4.69	5.86	6.50	6.30	5.98	0.08
Total	4.66	4.44	5.51	5.64	6.44	6.27	1.00

15.6 CASE STUDY: PROBLEMS WITH THE EVALUATION FUNCTION

A few months later, it was discovered that the 360/67's TSS operating system, the first large production virtual-memory operating system, was plagued by serious overhead problems. Typically, it would only deliver 10 to 15% of the available 360/67 cycles to the user.

Clearly, this made the 360/67 an unacceptable alternative, and plans were made to select and order a different system. The surprising thing was that this new information made almost no perceptible difference in the 360/67's evaluation score when it was fed into the weighted sum evaluation model. There is only one criterion in the evaluation hierarchy which covers this consideration. It is item II.E, Supervisor: Hardware requirements, with a total weight of $(0.27)(0.03) = 0.0081$. Even by assigning a zero as a rating for the criterion, the total score was reduced by less than 1%, and the 360/67-TSS system still achieved the highest score.

Why did this happen, and what could be done to improve the figure of merit analysis? There are two alternative diagnoses of the problem, which lead to two main avenues of improvement.

1. The wrong set of factors and weights were used. If effective throughput was a critical consideration, it should have been a high-level criterion with a large weighting factor in the evaluation.*
2. An additive criterion function was being used to evaluate a factor (operating system overhead) whose effect on system performance was multiplicative, not additive. Low throughput degrades all of the other system capabilities by the same multiplicative factor. Thus, a criterion function with a multiplicative factor reflecting this situation should have been used.

The appropriate remedy for diagnosis 1 is to improve the weighted sum analysis by formulating a more representative set of factors and weights. The appropriate remedy for diagnosis 2 is to modify the weighted sum figure of merit to reflect nonadditive characteristics of the system's performance.

Both of those remedies have some merit. Remedy 1 maintains the advantage of the simplicity of the weighted sum technique. Remedy 2 requires a more complex figure of merit which more closely represents the system's behavior.

After concluding our discussion of the case study, we will present a figure of merit representing Remedy 2, the *delivered system capability* (DSC), followed by a summary discussion comparing it to the weighted sum technique.

---

*Another point made by Gilb is that the weighted sum or MECCA method is most effectively used to evaluate the relative merits of acceptable, competitive alternatives [Gilb, 1979]. This implies that "pathological" alternatives with some extremely high ratings and some totally unacceptable ratings should be dropped from consideration. This is a form of the goals-as-constraints approach to be discussed in the next chapter.

15.7 CASE STUDY: PROBLEMS WITH WEIGHTS AND RATINGS

Other problems in the evaluation concerned the weights for each criterion and the 0–10 scales for rating the candidates. Initially, an attempt was made to determine the weights provided by representatives of various computer usage interests. One problem here was a temptation by some special interest representatives (such as big production jobs which benefited much more from hardware power than from software aids) to give extremely high weights to their particular interest, in order to raise its average weight in the evaluation.

This problem was resolved reasonably well by individual followup with representatives to have them clarify and discuss the rationale behind their weights, and submit revised weights as a result of the discussion.

Another problem was an initial assumption given to the representatives that no in-house software support was planned for the new system. This was unrealistic, and led to even higher weights for the software and vendor support criteria. The assumption was later revised to assume a small (three to five person) in-house software support group, resulting in lower revised weights for the software and vendor support criteria.

The problem with the ratings was a difficulty in obtaining a consistent scale. For some criteria, the ratings tended to look like Fig. 15–2a; for others, they tended to look like Fig. 15–2b. The result is in effect to multiply the weight of criterion A by another factor of two with respect to the weight of criterion B.

This problem was largely resolved by an independent review and iteration of the evaluation scale. Also, sensitivity studies were performed to see whether the conclusions were highly sensitive to certain weights and ratings. The basic dominance of the 360/67 and the 1108 in the ratings was only rarely changed in the sensitivity studies.

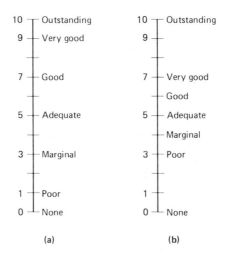

FIGURE 15–2   (a) Criterion A Scale (b) Criterion B Scale

15.8 CASE STUDY: SUMMARY

The problems discussed above should serve as caveats on when to use a weighted sum figure of merit, and how to tailor it to the software decision problem being addressed. They should not be interpreted as reasons never to use a figure of merit technique at all. Particularly for situations with as many component criteria as there tend to be in the selection of a complex hardware–software product, a hierarchical weighted sum technique provides a great deal of help. It provides a readily understandable framework for discussing priorities, for gathering evaluation data, for assessing subjective factors, and for presenting, discussing and iterating the evaluation results.*

Other figures of merit.   Any performance equation can be considered as a figure of merit formula. For example, the formula

$$E(N,S,P,M,T) = \frac{N[S - P - M(N - 1)]}{T} \tag{10-1}$$

is a better figure of merit for the performance of our multiprocessor TPS system than is any formula of the form

$$E(N,S,P,M,T) = a_0 + a_1 N + a_2 S + a_3 P + a_4 M + a_5 T$$

Thus, we should not expect to find a universal figure of merit which covers the full range of software engineering decision problems.† Each figure of merit must be tailored to the application and the evaluation purpose for which it is needed. The next section provides a figure of merit, delivered system capability or DCS, which provides a good match for several classes of computer system evaluations.

15.9 THE DELIVERED SYSTEM CAPABILITY (DSC) FIGURE OF MERIT

Definitions.   The delivered system capability (DSC) figure of merit takes the form

---

* The very useful book *Computer Selection* [Joslin, 1968] comes out strongly in favor of the net value approach (called the cost-value technique in the book), as opposed to the figure of merit approach. The book contains a very good treatment of how to determine dollar values for such criteria as hardware growth potential and performance on benchmark runs. It also contains a good set of procedures and guidelines for conducting a computer selection activity. However, it does not go into much depth in covering the software aspects of computer selection, such as those included in Table 15–3. These software criteria are usually at least as important as the hardware criteria, and much more difficult to evaluate in terms of dollars. Therefore, some technique such as the weighted sum technique is needed to incorporate these criteria into the decision problem.

† The same conclusion has been drawn for other proposed universal figures of merit, such as those for evaluating software quality. See [Boehm and others, 1978].

$$\text{DSC} = (\text{System capability})(\text{Delivered capacity})(\text{Availability})$$

$$= (\text{SC})(\text{DC})(\text{AV}) \tag{15-1}$$

The individual terms are defined as follows:

- *System capability* (SC) is defined as a hierarchical weighted sum of individual criterion ratings

$$\sum_{i=1}^{n} w_i r_i \tag{15-2}$$

where w_i is the weight assigned to the ith criterion and r_i is the rating assigned to the criterion for a given alternative. The weights w_i should add up to 1.0 and the ratings should be assigned on a scale of 0.0 to 1.0.
- *Delivered capacity* (DC) is defined as the actual computer capacity which can be used to provide the desired capabilities. This means that such factors as operating system overhead are deducted from the overall machine capacity to form DC.
- *Availability* (AV) is defined as the fraction of time that the computer system is available to deliver computer capacity to perform the functions. Thus AV excludes time spent on preventive maintenance or system down time.

15.10 PROPERTIES OF THE DSC FIGURE OF MERIT

1. It is basically a dimensionless figure of merit, as there is no physical or economic significance in the weights and ratings comprising the SC component.
2. It is strictly an effectiveness criterion, which must be further reconciled with cost criteria. Including cost in the figure of merit would mean that the DSC portion would have to be expressed in dollars, which is difficult because of its nondimensional nature. Further, this would just make the DSC technique into a net value technique, in which case we might as well use the net value approach directly.
3. The SC component of the DSC obtains the advantages of the hierarchical weighted sum approach where they are needed the most: in the ability to handle large numbers of hard-to-quantify criteria, as in Table 15–3 of our computer selection case study.
4. The DC and AV components of the DSC avoid the weaknesses of the hierarchical weighted sum approach in handling the multiplicative effects of delivered capacity and availability. Also, they allow DC and AV to be calculated in whatever way is most appropriate; such as by using Eq. (10–1) to calculate the delivered capacity for the TPS example. They can also be extended to cover other system components such as personnel, communications, and so on.

15.11 THE TPS EXAMPLE REVISITED

Let us return to the TPS problem of choosing between System A and System A Plus as candidate operating systems, using the DSC figure of merit approach.

First, we consider the cost separately, and in the process we try to estimate the cost impact of any of the changed capabilities provided by System A Plus, based on a two-year maintenance cost at $15K/year (from Section 9.4) of $30K.

	System A	System A Plus
Basic Cost	$130K	$135K
Maintenance Support (10% reduction of $30K maintenance cost)	0	− 3K
Diagnostics and Error Messages (5% reduction of $30K maintenance cost)	0	−1.5K
Documentation (5% increase in $30K maintenance cost)	0	1.5K
Total	$130K	$132K

Next, we consider the delivered capacity and availability separately, and again try to estimate the impact of any of the improved capabilities provided by System A Plus.

Delivered Capacity	System A	System A Plus
(3% improvement from measurement)	180.0	185.4

Availability	System A	System A Plus
(50% decrease in downtime from diagnostics, error messages; trace capabilities)	0.95	0.975

Next, we incorporate those functional capabilities which have not been completely covered elsewhere into the weighted sum system capability component, *including the basic transaction processing functions,* as follows:

Criterion	Weight	System A Rating	System A Weighted Rating	System A Plus Rating	System A Plus Weighted Rating
Basic TP functions	0.95	1.0	0.950	1.0	0.950
Accounting system	0.01	0.6	0.006	1.0	0.010
Usage summaries	0.01	0.0	0.000	0.8	0.008
OS documentation	0.03	0.8	0.024	0.4	0.012
Total	1.00		0.980		0.980

The overall results are summarized in Table 15–6. Based on these results, we would strongly favor System A Plus, with a fairly clear underlying rationale, compared to our previous choice of System A, with the relatively questionable rationale provided in Table 15–2.

TABLE 15–6 TPS Comparison: Delivered System Capability

Criterion	System A	System A Plus
System capability (SC)	0.980	0.980
Delivered capacity (DC)	180.0	185.4
Availability (AV)	0.95	0.975
Delivered system capability (DSC) = (SC)(DC)(AV)	167.6	177.1
Cost	$130K	$132K

15.12 COMPARISON OF WEIGHTED SUM AND DSC FIGURES OF MERIT

The DSC approach clearly gives us a better understanding of our TPS decision problem than did the weighted sum approach given in Table 15–2. Before we conclude that the DSC is necessarily better than the weighted sum approach for this problem, we should recall from our discussion of the computer selection case study that there was an alternate remedy for an inadequate weighted sum analysis: to formulate a more representative set of factors and weights.

In the TPS situation, it turns out that the DSC analysis provides us with a way to identify a more suitable set of factors and weights for a weighted sum analysis. If we use system capability (SC), delivered capacity (DC), and availability (AV) as our factors, with roughly equal weights, we arrive at the weighted sum analysis shown in Table 15–7.

With these factors and weights, the weighted sum technique gives us a roughly equivalent understanding of the TPS decision problem as does the DSC technique. In this case, it is able to do so because the delivered capacity and availability factors

TABLE 15–7 Revised TPS Weighted Sum Analysis

Criterion	Weight	System A			System A Plus		
		Value	Rating	Weighted Rating	Value	Rating	Weighted Rating
System capability (SC)	40	0.980	9	360	0.980	9	360
Delivered capacity (DC)	30	180.0	8	240	185.4	9	270
Availability (AV)	30	0.950	7	210	0.975	9	270
Total	100			810			900

are roughly comparable. If the alternative systems exhibited a wide variation in those factors, the weighted sum technique would have more difficulty.

On the other hand, the weighted sum technique is better at assessing side effects of the delivered capacity and availability factors. In a large bank, for example, with close to a million dollars in daily interest dependent on the availability of the computer system to process its financial transactions, the difference between AV = 1.00 and AV = 0.99 is much greater than a 1% difference in delivered system capability. The weighted sum technique allows the evaluator to reflect this in the weights and ratings.

Table 15–8 summarizes the major comparative strengths of the weighted sum and DSC figure of merit techniques, and provides a basic guideline for deciding which to use.

- If delivered capacity and availability vary widely among the systems being evaluated, use the delivered system capability technique. Otherwise, use the weighted sum technique, but if you find the variation of DC and AV to be wider than you expected, use the DSC technique also as a check.

TABLE 15–8 Comparison of Weighted Sum and DSC Figures of Merit

	Weighted Sum	Delivered System Capability
Relative advantages	Simpler	More representative of many computer systems
	Better for assessing side effects of DC, AV factors	Better for assessing wide variations in DC, AV factors
Recommendation	Use where DC, AV factors will not vary widely	Use where DC, AV factors may vary widely

Some Final Remarks

The weighted sum and DSC figure of merit techniques are of particular utility in situations such as the selection of a computer system or a complex software package, where we must consider a large (≥ 20) number of hard to quantify criteria. However, we should still be prepared to admit that there may be no satisfactory way to combine all of our criteria into a single acceptable figure of merit. In such cases, we have two remaining evaluation approaches:

- To treat some of the factors as constraints. This approach is discussed in Chapters 16 and 17 below.
- To find some appropriate techniques for presenting the unreconcilable criteria to decisionmakers, in ways which will enhance their ability to absorb all of the factors and to make satisfactory decisions based on the information presented. This topic is discussed in Chapter 18 below.

15.13 QUESTIONS

15.1. Define the following terms: figure of merit, weighted sum technique, delivered system capability (DSC), system capability (SC), delivered capacity (DC), availability (AV).

15.2. Suppose the additional price of System A Plus was $10K instead of $5K. How would this affect the calculations in the weighted sum analysis and the DSC analysis? How would it affect the conclusions?

15.3. Suppose the vendor finds major problems in the trace, diagnostic, and error message capabilities of System A Plus, and does not offer them as part of the system, although the price remains the same. How does this affect the calculations and the conclusions of the original weighted sum analysis and the DSC analysis?

15.4. How well do you think the use of the DSC figure of merit would have done in anticipating or highlighting the operating system overhead problem in the computer selection case study?

15.5 Can you think of some additional criteria that should now be used if Table 15–3 was to be used as the basis of a computer selection activity? Which of the existing criteria should be dropped or modified?

15.6. Standard University is considering the acquisition of a multiple-microprocessor energy management system to better regulate and conserve the university's energy expenditures. Three vendors, Energy, Inc., Micro Controls, and Econetics, have proposed systems with roughly the same life-cycle costs for acquisition and basic maintenance. The table below shows the results of an evaluation of their proposed systems with respect to a number of performance criteria.

Criterion	Energy, Inc.	Micro Controls	Econetics
Steady-state energy savings	10%	8%	12%
Controls	Adequate	Very good	Marginal
Ease of operation	Adequate	Good	Adequate
Diagnostics	Adequate	Good	Poor
Availability	0.990	0.995	0.975
Growth/update capability	Adequate	Good	Adequate
Safety features	Very good	Good	Adequate
Accounting system	Good	Good	Very good
Vendor reliability, support	Very good	Good	Adequate
Savings analysis package	Good	None	None

Perform a weighted sum analysis of the three alternatives, and indicate which alternative you would recommend. Do you think a DSC analysis would reach a different conclusion? What additional information would you wish to know to improve your confidence in you analysis?

15.7. The Standard University Psychology Laboratory is acquiring a minicomputer to perform experiment monitoring and data reduction functions. Three minicomputer vendors, Associated Minicomputers, Inc., Amalgamated Minicomputers, Inc., and Consolidated Minicomputers, Inc. have proposed candidate systems, each at a total cost of about $100,000 and a basic hardware speed of 1 million ops/sec. The table following shows the results of the Psychology Lab's evaluation of the proposed systems.

Criterion	Associated	Amalgamated	Consolidated
Hardware features	Very good	Good	Good
Operating systems features	Good	Outstanding	Good
Data management features	Good	Outstanding	Adequate
Language support	Adequate	Good	Good
Programming support	Good	Very good	Good
Ease of conversion	Very good	Adequate	Good
Vendor reliability, support	Good	Good	Very good
Application packages	Adequate	Very good	Good
Operating system overhead	10%	50%	5%
System availability	75%	90%	95%

Perform a weighted sum analysis and a DSC analysis on the three alternatives. Which analysis do you think gives you the better insight on which alternative to choose? What additional information would you wish to know to improve your confidence in your analysis?

15.8. In Section 15.1, it was indicated that if the difference in purchase price between the two systems was less than $5000, then we should not spend more than $5000 evaluating their relative merits. On the other hand, in one situation involving the acquisition of a Structured FORTRAN preprocessor, a very cursory analysis of the relative merits of a $200 preprocessor and a $2000 preprocessor led to the acquisition of the $200 preprocessor. Subsequently, its deficiencies were estimated to have cost the company over $20,000 in wasted programmer effort and computer time. Considering this experience, can you formulate a better guideline for scoping the amount of money or effort which should be spend on a decision analysis?

Chapter 16

Goals as Constraints

16.1 EXAMPLE: TPS OPTION A FAILURE MODES

Let us consider again our TPS example and our choice of Option A1: the rental of a number of processors for two years, using the available vendor-supplied operating system, in its extended System A Plus form. Suppose that in investigating Option A1 further, we find that the operating system software has the unfortunate property that whenever one of the processors fails, the entire system fails, and it takes an average of 30 minutes to get the system working again with the remaining in-service processors. We also find that the reliability of each processor is 99% per hour. That is, for each processor, during any given hour, there is a 0.99 probability that the processor will not fail.

16.2 SYSTEM RELIABILITY AND AVAILABILITY

If we have N processors, the *system reliability* $\text{Rel}(N)$ per hour is defined as the probability that the overall system will not fail in a given hour. Since in this case the system will fail each time one of the processors fails, $Rel(N)$ is equal to the probability that none of the processors fails during a given hour. This probability is equal to the product of the individual processor reliabilities

$$Rel(N) = (0.99)^N \qquad (16\text{--}1)$$

The resulting *system availability* (the fraction of the time that the system is working) can be calculated as

$$AV(N) = 1 - (\text{Fraction of time system down})$$

$$= 1 - \frac{(\text{Prob. of failure per time period}) (\text{Avg. down time per failure})}{\text{Length of time period}}$$

$$= 1 - \frac{(1 - Rel(N)) (30 \text{ min})}{60 \text{ min}}$$

or

$$AV(N) = 1 - 0.5 (1 - 0.99^N) \qquad (16\text{--}2)$$

The resulting graph of the system reliability and system availability as functions of the number of processors is shown in Fig. 16–1, along with a graph of the performance $E(N)$ in tr/sec.

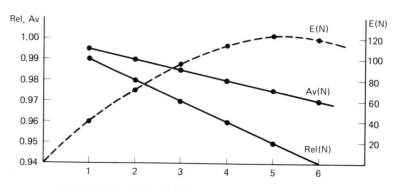

FIGURE 16–1   TPS reliability, availability, and performance

16.3   FIGURE OF MERIT EVALUATION

From Fig. 16–1, we see that performance improves as we buy more processors, but reliability and availability degrade. In order to decide how many processors to buy, we need to reconcile the goals of performance and reliability/availability.

One way to do this is to use the DSC approach developed in the previous section. The transaction processing functions do not vary with the number of processors N, so we will assume that the system capability SC is a constant; we will use SC = 1.0

for convenience. For delivered capacity DC, we will use Eq. (10–1) or Fig. 10–2 for $E(N)$ in tr/sec, and for availability AV we will use Eq. (16–2). Thus, for $N = 3$, we would get

$$DSC(3) = (1.0) [E(3)][AV(3)] = (96) (0.985) = 94.6$$

Figure 16–2 shows the resulting graph of DSC *(N)*.

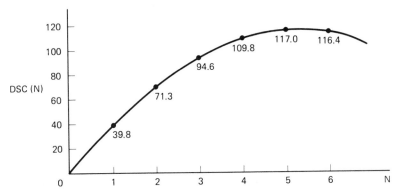

FIGURE 16–2 TPS delivered system capability versus number of processors

Based on the DSC decision criterion, we would still choose $N = 5$ processors as the best system. However, the DSC may not completely capture our concern for high availability in a transaction processing system.

In many cases, the cost of interruptions in service to the TPS user is much greater than just the cost of a reduction in throughput. If the TPS is an airline reservation system, for example, the cost would be much greater due to the loss of repeat customers, good will, and the airline's image of being a reliable organization with whom to trust your fate while traveling. Or, if the TPS is an emergency vehicle dispatching system (police, fire, ambulance), the cost would be some increase in the probability of people losing their lives.

Thus, although the DSC criterion is well suited for general-purpose computer selection, software package selection, and most batch processing applications, its treatment of availability is not wholly satisfactory for many transaction processing systems. For some of these TPS situations, it may be possible to assign a dollar value to the cost to the user (for example, "each interruption in service costs the company $1000 per minute"), and proceed with a net value analysis as before. But in many situations, particularly those involving human life, neither the net value analysis nor the DSC figure of merit will be adequate to cover the range of decision considerations.

16.4 EXPRESSING GOALS AS CONSTRAINTS

Another way to reconcile our availability goal with our cost and performance goals for the TPS is to say

Whatever we do, we can't afford to have a system with an availability of less than 0.98. Let us choose the number of processors, N, which gives us the maximum delivered capacity E(N) subject to the condition that system availability AV(N) be at least 0.98.

In this way, we have expressed the availability goal as a *constraint.* From Fig. 16–1, we can see that our decision would then be to choose $N = 4$ processors for the TPS. This would give us the minimum acceptable availability of 0.98, and a delivered capacity of 112 tr/sec.

Any criterion can be turned into a constraint in this way. For example, we could also have said

Whatever we do, we can't afford to have a system with a delivered capacity of less than 90 tr/sec. Let us choose N to give us the maximum availability such that E(N) $\geq$ 90 tr/sec.

From Fig. 16–1, we can see that this would lead us to the decision to choose $N = 3$ processors, with a delivered capacity of 96 tr/sec and an availability of 0.985.

In software engineering, constraints may be self-imposed, as with the availability and performance constraints above, or they may be imposed by other conditions, particularly equipment and user limitations or external interface conditions. For example, our TPS may be served by a communication system with a maximum capacity of 75 tr/sec. In this case, our original decision problem above would be revised to:

$$\text{Choose } N \text{ to maximize } E(N)$$
$$\text{subject to } AV(N) \geq .98$$
$$\text{and } E(N) \leq 75$$

From Fig. 16–1, we can see that the constraint $E(N) \leq 75$ *dominates* the constraint $AV(N) \geq .98$ (or $N \leq 4$). Our decision here would be to choose $N = 2$, with $E(N) = 72$ and $AV(N) = .99$.

16.5 GOALS AS CONSTRAINTS: FEASIBLE SETS AND COST-VALUE CONTOURS

Actually, the constraint $E(N) \leq 75$ need not imply $N \leq 2$. If it were to our benefit, we could choose a three-processor system and limit it to processing 75 tr/sec rather than the 96 tr/sec it would be capable of. If the value per processed tr/sec is $2K, then this would not be worthwhile, as we would have to pay $10K for the additional processor, and would only receive $6K for the additional 3 tr/sec. If the value per processed tr/sec were $4K, though; the additional 3 tr/sec would be worth $12K, making it worth our while to pay $10K for a third processor.

One way of looking at this situation is shown in Fig. 16–3a and b, which show our decision problem as a function of two decision variables, the number, *N,* of processors to acquire, and the number, *E,* of tr/sec at which to run the system. The set of all possible decision points *(N,E)* is generally called the *decision space.*

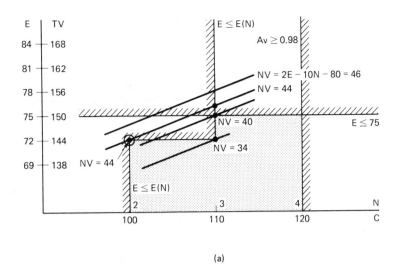

(a)

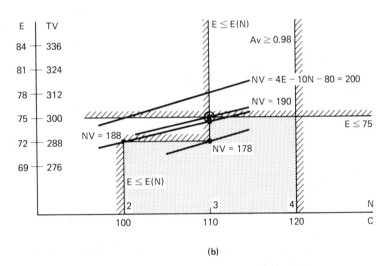

(b)

FIGURE 16–3 (a) TPS constrained decision problem, $V(E) = 2E$
(b) TPS constrained decision problem, $V(E) = 4E$

The constraint $E \leq 75$ then divides the decision space into a set of *feasible points* $E \leq 75$ and a set of *infeasible points* $E > 75$ for the constraint. Similarly, the stair-step performance function $E(N)$ defines another partition of the decision space into feasible points $E \leq E(N)$ and infeasible points $E > E(N)$: points for which the given level of performance E cannot be achieved by the given number of processors N. Finally, the line $N = 4$ separates the decision space into feasible points $AV \geq .98$ and infeasible points $AV < .98$, or $N > 4$.

The set of points which are feasible with respect to all the specified constraints is called the *feasible set*. It is indicated by the shaded areas in Figs. 16–3a and b.

Our decision problem in this case is to find the point $(N,E)_{max}$ in the feasible set which maximizes the net value (total value minus cost)

$$NV(N,E) = TV(E) - C(N)$$

One way to find $(N,E)_{max}$, which is often called the *optimal solution,* is to consider the sets of points (N,E) which have the same net value, or the *contours of constant net value*

$$NV(N,E) = TV(E) - C(N) = \text{constant} \qquad (16\text{--}3)$$

Figures 16–3a and b show some of these contours. Their slope is different in the two figures, because of the difference in the total value function $TV(E)$. In Fig. 16–3a, each tr/sec is worth \$2K, or $TV(E) = 2E$. In Fig. 16–3b, each tr/sec is worth \$4K, or $TV(E) = 4E$.

For the two cases we use Eq. (16–3) to express the contours of constant net value

$$\text{Fig. 16--3a:} \quad NV(N,E) = 2E - (80 + 10N) = \text{constant}$$
$$\text{Fig. 16--3b:} \quad NV(N,E) = 4E - (80 + 10N) = \text{constant}$$

These contours are parallel lines within the space of decision points (N,E). Figures 16–3a and b show some of these contours, including the critical ones for our problem of finding the optimal solution $(N,E)_{max}$.

The key observation in Figs. 16–3a and b is that the optimal solution $(N,E)_{max}$, indicated by the symbol $\odot$, lies on the contour of maximum net value among those contours which have points in the feasible set. Thus, in Fig. 16–3a, the point $(N,E) = (2,72)$ is the optimal solution, because its contour $NV = 44$ is the highest one (the one with the largest value of NV) to intersect the feasible set. In Fig. 16–3b, the point (2,72) is not optimal, because its contour $NV = 188$ is not the highest one to intersect the feasible set.

16.6 GENERAL DISCUSSION: DECISION PROBLEMS WITH CONSTRAINTS

The example above is a special case of the general optimal decision problem with constraints that is illustrated in Fig. 16–4. The mathematical formulation of the problem is

Choose values of the decision variables $x_1, x_2, \ldots, x_n$ *so as to* maximize the objective function $f(x_1, x_2, \ldots, x_n)$ *subject to the* constraints

$$g_1(x_1, x_2, \ldots, x_n) \leq b_1$$
$$g_2(x_1, x_2, \ldots, x_n) \leq b_2$$
$$\vdots$$
$$g_m(x_1, x_2, \ldots, x_n) \leq b_m \qquad (16\text{--}3)$$

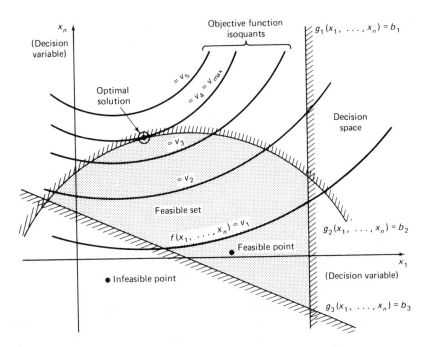

FIGURE 16–4 The constrained optimization problem

In Fig. 16–4, we only use two decision variables, called x_1 and x_n, for simplicity of illustration. Each point $(x_1, x_2, \ldots, x_n)$ is called a *decision point,* and the set of all possible decision points is called the *decision space.* The $m = 3$ *constraint boundaries*

$$g_i(x_1, x_2, \ldots, x_n) = b_i, \quad i = 1, 2, \ldots, m$$

are graphed as functions of the decision variables x_1 and x_n. A decision point outside any of the constraint boundaries is called an *infeasible point.* A decision point within all of the constraint boundaries is called a *feasible point.* The set of all feasible points is called the *feasible set.*

The objective function $f(x_1, x_2, \ldots, x_n)$ can be visualized in terms of a family of contours of constant value of the objective function, or *objective function isoquants*

$$f(x_1, x_2, \ldots, x_n) = v$$

Then, as in our TPS example above, the *optimal solution* $(x_1, x_2, \ldots, x_n)_{max}$ and the optimal value v_{max} for our decision problem are characterized by the following *necessary and sufficient conditions for an optimal solution:*

1. $(x_1, x_2, \ldots, x_n)_{max}$ is a feasible point on the isoquant $f(x_1, x_2, \ldots, x_n) = v_{max}$
2. If $v > v_{max}$, then its isoquant $f(x_1, x_2, \ldots, x_n) = v$ does not contain any feasible points

In some situations, the decision problem is so constrained that there are no feasible points satisfying all of the constraints. Such a situation is called an *infeasible decision problem*. Thus, for example, if we added the constraint

$$f(x_1, x_2, \ldots, x_n) \geq v_5$$

to our decision problem in Fig. 16–4, we would make it into an infeasible decision problem.

16.7   SOFTWARE ENGINEERING APPLICATIONS

Here are some typical software engineering problem areas where mathematical optimization techniques can be helpful.

- *Optimal hardware–software configuration problems* in feasibility studies for information processing systems. In such problems, we wish to choose hardware–software configurations so as to maximize net value subject to constraints on resources, personnel, facilities, and acceptable performance. See [Stone and others, 1978] and [Ferrari, 1978] for examples.
- *Optimal computer networks,* such as allocation of processors, storage devices, and communication channels so as to maximize throughput subject to constraints on resources or response time, to minimize resources subject to constraints on acceptable throughput and response time, and so on. See [Kleinrock, 1976] and [Graham, 1978] for examples.
- *Optimal computing algorithms* for performing various information processing functions such as sorting, searching, storage allocation, and so on so as to minimize execution time subject to constraints on available storage or vice versa. See [Knuth, 1969, 1973, and 1973a] and [Horowitz-Sahni, 1978] for examples.

16.8   MATHEMATICAL OPTIMIZATION TECHNIQUES

The optimal decision problem above is presented as a mathematical problem. For certain classes of problems, there are mathematical algorithms which can be used to determine the optimal solution (or to determine that the problem is infeasible). An example of one of the most common mathematical optimization techniques, linear programming, is given in this section, along with a short discussion of nonlinear programming. There are a large number of books to consult for more detailed information on algorithms, special cases, and extensions of these and other mathematical optimization techniques; [Wagner, 1977] provides a very good balance of theory, practice, and comprehensiveness.

Linear programming.   If the objective function f is a linear function of the decision variables $x_1, x_2, \ldots, x_n$, that is, if

$$f(x_1, x_2, \ldots, x_n) = c_1 x_1 + c_2 x_2 + \cdots + c_n x_n$$

and the constraint functions g_i are also linear functions, then our optimal decision problem is a *linear programming** problem. The linear programming problem has the form

Choose values of the decision variables $x_1, x_2, \ldots, x_n$
so as to maximize $c_1 x_1 + c_2 x_2 + \cdots + c_n x_n$
subject to the constraints $a_{11} x_1 + a_{12} x_2 + \cdots + a_{1n} x_n \leq b_1$
$$a_{21} x_1 + a_{22} x_2 + \cdots + a_{2n} x_n \leq b_2$$
$$\vdots$$
$$a_{m1} x_1 + a_{m2} x_2 + \cdots + a_{mn} x_n \leq b_m$$
$$x_1 \geq 0, \ x_2 \geq 0, \ldots, x_n \geq 0.$$

A linear programming example: Universal Software, Inc. As an example of the use of mathematical optimization techniques, let us formulate a linear programming problem and find its solution. The software house Universal Software, Inc., has a staff of 16 analysts and 24 programmers, and has a computer used for software development which is available 15 hours per day. Universal specializes in the development of highly similar text-processing software systems and process control software systems and has a continuing source of orders for each. Each text-processing project requires 2 analysts, 6 programmers, and 3 hr/day of computer time to develop, and returns a profit of $20,000, or $20K. Each process control system requires 4 analysts, 2 programmers, and 3 hr/day of computer time and returns a profit of $30K.

Universal is currently making its annual business plan for the following year, and would like an answer to the problem

- How many text-processing systems and how many process control systems should Universal develop within its available labor force and computer time constraints, in order to maximize its profit?

Below is a five-step sequence of questions which can guide Universal to the solution to this problem. Note its similarity to the five-step sequence of questions used by *Scientific American* in successfully analyzing their subscription-processing system in Chapter 1.

Step 1. *What objective are we trying to optimize?*
In this simple analysis, Universal's objective is to maximize profit.
Step 2. *What decisions do we control which affect the objective?*
There are some decisions which could affect the objective, but which are not under Universal's control. For example, if each customer decided to pay Universal twice as much money per system developed, this would favorably affect Universal's profit. However, in a competitive equilibrium situation, such

---

* "Linear programming" and "computer programming" derive from the same meaning of the verb "to program": to work out a sequence of operations. The major motivation behind the linear programming technique, formulated by Dantzig in 1947, was to find a way to handle the massive manual programming activities involved in World War II logistics operations [Dantzig, 1963].

a decision is not Universal's to control. Here, the decision variables that Universal does control which affect its profit are:

$$x_1 = \text{the number of text-processing systems it will develop}$$
$$x_2 = \text{the number of process control systems it will develop}$$

Step 3. *What items dictate constraints on the range of choices?*

Universal could make an unlimited profit if it could take on an unlimited number of text-processing or process control jobs. But it only has a limited number of analysts, programmers, and computer hours available. For example, since each text-processing job requires 2 analysts and each process control job requires 4 analysts, and Universal has only 16 analysts available, the constraint on analysts is

$$2x_1 + 4x_2 \leq 16$$

Similarly, the constraints on programmers and computer time are

$$6x_1 + 2x_2 \leq 24$$
$$3x_1 + 3x_2 \leq 15$$

There are two additional constraints which ensure that Universal cannot take on a negative number of text-processing or process control jobs

$$x_1 \geq 0 \qquad x_2 \geq 0$$

Step 4. *How are the values of the objective function related to the values of the decision variables?*

Since Universal makes a $20K profit on each text-processing system, and a $30K profit on each process control system, its total profit, P, can be expressed as

$$P = 20x_1 + 30x_2$$

Step 5. *What decision provides us with the optimal value of the objective function?*

First, we note that when we collect all of the relations above, we have a linear programming problem of the form given in Eq. (16–4)

$$\text{Choose values of the decision variables } x_1, x_2$$
$$\text{so as to maximize} \qquad P = 20x_1 + 30x_2$$
$$\text{subject to the constraints} \qquad 2x_1 + 4x_2 \leq 16$$
$$6x_1 + 2x_2 \leq 24$$
$$3x_1 + 3x_2 \leq 15$$
$$x_1 \geq 0, \qquad x_2 \geq 0$$

There are a number of ways to solve a linear programming problem. The most common algorithm, the simplex algorithm [Dantzig, 1963], involves the use of matrix-vector manipulations similar to those used in matrix inversion and the solution of simultaneous linear equations. Here, we will demonstrate a graphical solution to the problem, using the necessary and sufficient conditions for an optimal solution discussed in Section 16.2.

We do this by graphing the constraint boundaries as functions of the decision variables x_1 and x_2, as shown in Fig. 16-5. This determines the *feasible set* of decision variables satisfying all of the constraints, indicated by the shaded areas in Fig. 16-5 and Fig. 16-6. We then graph the contours of constant profit, or the *objective function isoquants*

$$20x_1 + 30x_2 = \text{constant}$$

as shown with respect to the feasible set in Fig. 16-6.

From Fig. 16-6, we can see that the objective function isoquant

$$20x_1 + 30x_2 = 130$$

is the highest value isoquant containing a point in the feasible set. The point is

$$x_1 = 2, \ x_2 = 3$$

This point satisfies our necessary and sufficient conditions for an optimal solution

1. $(x_1,x_2)_{max} = (2,3)$ is a feasible point on the isoquant $20x_1 + 30x_2 = 130 = v_{max}$
2. If $v > v_{max}$, then its isoquant $20x_1 + 30x_2 = v$ does not contain any feasible points

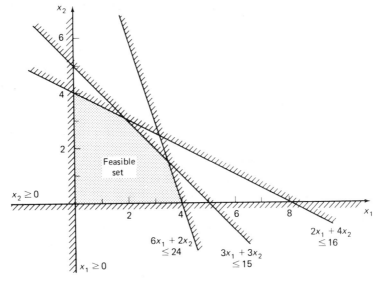

FIGURE 16-5   Linear programming constraints and feasible set

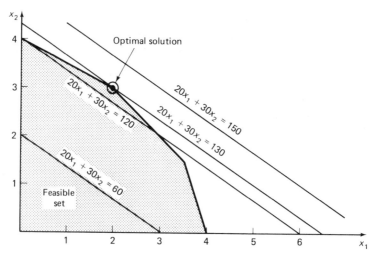

FIGURE 16-6 Linear programming isoquants and optimal solution

Thus, the answer to Universal Software, Inc.'s decision problem is to develop 2 text-processing systems and 3 process control systems, realizing a total profit of $130K.

In pursuing this solution, we made a number of assumptions which may not generally be borne out in practice, such as

- Programmers and analysts are interchangeable from project to project.
- There would be no learning curve effects, or nonlinear economies of scale, resulting from performing several similar jobs.
- Any programmers or analysts not employed in the optimal solution (for $x_1 = 2$, $x_2 = 3$, the number of programmers employed is $6x_1 + 2x_2 = 18$, leaving 6 unemployed programmers) can be immediately relocated to some other productive job.

These and other assumptions are often sufficiently questionable that we should always add two further steps to any linear programming or other mathematical optimization solution

Step 5a. *How sensitive is the optimal decision to assumptions made in the analysis? Are there alternative decisions providing satisfactory results with less sensitivity to these assumptions?*

Step 6. *Does the performance of any of the above steps cause a reconsideration of the previous steps? If so, iterate the previous steps that are affected.*

These concerns will be discussed further in Chapter 17.

Nonlinear programming. In most decision situations, the constraints or the objective function will be sufficiently nonlinear that approximate linear programming solutions will not be useful. Optimal software project scheduling problems may have nonlinear objective functions: the cost of overrunning a schedule may be highly sensitive to such deadlines as end-of-the-year inventory and accounts balancing, or a satellite launch. Optimal network problems often have to deal with nonlinear communications tariffs. Optimal configuration problems may have some highly nonlinear production functions reflecting the investment, high payoff, and diminishing returns segments we discussed in Chapter 11.

Techniques for solving nonlinear programming problems are generally much more complex than techniques for linear programming. There are situations in which nonlinear programming algorithms will not converge to a solution, and other situations in which the solution is not the optimum. This latter problem stems from the fact that nonlinear objective functions can have multiple local maxima (see Fig. 16–7). Nonlinear programming algorithms generally work by determining the local gradient (direction pointing to higher values), and following it to the top of the local maximum. Thus, in Fig. 16–7, if the nonlinear programming algorithm started at the point $\bar{x}$, determined the local gradient, and followed it to the local maximum $g(x) = 30$, there is no way for the algorithm to "know" whether this local maximum is the overall maximum of the objective function (called the *global maximum*), or whether the global maximum is somewhere else. In this case, had the process been started at the point $\bar{x}'$, the algorithm would have proceeded to the global maximum $g(x) = 40$. Thus, nonlinear programming usage often involves trying several starting points determined by some knowledge of the problem domain.

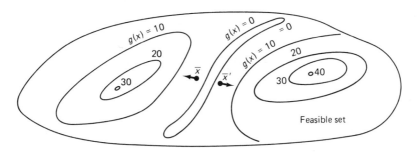

FIGURE 16–7 Nonlinear programming problem with multiple maxima

16.9 CAPABILITIES AND LIMITATIONS OF MATHEMATICAL OPTIMIZATION TECHNIQUES

For the software engineer, there are several practical limitations involved in using mathematical optimization techniques. In formulating practical problems mathematically, we must make assumptions (for example, linearity, neglect of nonquantifiable factors) which are often difficult to justify. For large problems, the determination of optimal solutions may be expensive. Some of the techniques, particularly in nonlinear programming, either may not converge or may converge on a local maximum that is not the global maximum.

Another difficulty is that often we may not want to choose the optimal solution for practical implementation: it may be at the edge of a "cliff" in the objective function (such as, the point $x = 10$ in Fig. 16–8), and we may prefer to settle for a nonoptimal but less risky choice (such as $x = 6$).

However, mathematical optimization techniques offer a number of benefits that often outweigh the difficulties. Even if we choose not to use the mathematically optimal solution, we will have the knowledge of where it is and how much value it would yield if chosen. This knowledge is often very helpful in practical decisionmaking.

Further, most of the mathematical optimization techniques provide valuable information on the sensitivity of the solution to various problem inputs. Or, such sensitivity information may be obtained easily by varying input parameters and rerunning the algorithm.

Finally, the major value of the constrained optimization approach is as a conceptual aid to problem formulation, problem solution, and decisionmaking. It helps to clarify many of the issues (What are we trying to optimize? Which variables are decision variables? Which values are under our control?) involved in software engineering decision problems. An example of this conceptual clarification is provided in the next chapter, which discusses the process of systems analysis in terms of the conceptual model provided by the constrained optimization approach.

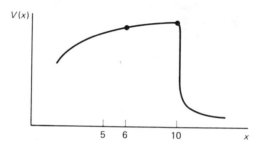

FIGURE 16–8 A risky optimum

16.10 QUESTIONS

16.1. Define the following terms: objective function, decision space, constraint, feasible set, isoquant, optimal solution, infeasible decision problem.

16.2. What are the necessary and sufficient conditions which characterize the optimal solution and the optimal value for a constrained optimization problem?

16.3. In the situation illustrated by Fig. 16–1, what is the optimal solution to the following problems:
   (a) Maximize $E(N)$ subject to $AV(N) \geq .985$
   (b) Maximize $Rel(N)$ subject to $E(N) \geq 50$
   (c) Maximize $AV(N)$ subject to $E(N) \geq 130$
   (d) Maximize $E(N)$ subject to $Rel(N) \geq .984$

16.4. In the situation illustrated by Fig. 16–1, what is the feasible set of values of N for the following sets of constraints:

(a) $E(N) \geq 75$ and $AV(N) \geq .975$

(b) $E(N) \geq 110$ and $Rel(N) \geq .99$

(c) $E(N) \leq 100$ and $AV(N) \geq .95$

(d) $E(N) \geq 80$ and $Rel(N) \geq .995$

16.5. In the situations illustrated by Figs. 16–3a and b, suppose that the value of each tr/ sec is \$3K. Draw the contours of constant net value $NV = 106$, $NV = 116$, and $NV = 124$. In this situation, what is the optimal solution $(N,E)_{max}$?

16.6. In the situations illustrated by Figs. 16–3a and b, suppose that the constraints were changed to $E \leq 100$ and $AV(N) \geq .975$. Draw figures illustrating the new situations [for both $V(E) = 2E$ and $V(E) = 4E$] and determine the new optimal solutions by constructing appropriate new contours of constant net value.

16.7. Which of the following are linear programming problems? Choose $x_1 \geq 0$, $x_2 \geq 0$, $x_3 \geq 0$ to

(a) Maximize $x_1 - x_3^2$ subject to $x_1 + x_2 \leq 2$, $x_2 + x_3 \leq 4$

(b) Maximize $2x_1 + 3x_2$ subject to $x_1 + x_2 + x_3 \leq 4$

(c) Maximize $x_1 + x_2 + 2x_3$ subject to $x_1 + 2x_2 \leq 5$, $x_1 \log x_2 \leq 2$

16.8. In our Universal Software, Inc., linear programming problem, suppose that Universal had only 15 analysts available instead of 16. Graph the resulting revised analyst constraint, and determine the resulting optimal solution and value.

- Given this and the previous solution, what is the value of an additional analyst to Universal in terms of contribution to profit in the neighborhood of the optimal solution?
- Given that this solution does not yield an integer number of jobs to perform, what practical alternative solution should be considered?

16.9. Suppose you are the manager of Galactic Software, Inc., which has 5 analysts, 12 programmers, and access to 16 hr/day of computer time over the next year. You are offered the opportunity to develop a number of similar simulation models and operating system utilities for a large computer vendor. Each model you develop will require 1 analyst, 1 programmer, and 4 hr/day of computer time, and will yield you a profit of \$25K. Each utility you develop will require 1 analyst, 3 programmers, and 2 hr/day of computer time, and will yield a profit of \$15K. Your decision problem (which is a linear programming problem) is to choose the number of models x_1 and the number of utilities x_2 to develop, in order to maximize total profit subject to the constraints imposed by your available number of analysts, programmers, and hr/day of computer time. Graph the constraints and the contours of constant profit

$$25x_1 + 15x_2 = 75, = 90, = 105$$

Determine the optimal solution and optimal value.

16.10. Does the optimal solution to Question 16.9 give all your programmers a job to do? As a manager, what do you think you should do in this situation?

Chapter 17

Systems Analysis and Constrained Optimization

Systems analysis is an approach and a body of techniques for analyzing the likely consequences of alternate decisions within the context of a given system. Systems analysis techniques are used extensively during the feasibility phase of the software life-cycle. In the feasibility phases, the primary goal is to make an appropriate choice of which software system to develop (if any), out of the huge number of possible software systems we might specify.

The systems analysis approach helps to narrow down this huge space of possible candidate systems to a smaller number which should be analyzed in more detail, and then converge on the most appropriate choice among those remaining. The constrained optimization process we studied in the previous chapter provides a good conceptual framework for understanding the systems analysis approach.

17.1 EXAMPLE

The steps in the systems analysis approach are presented below. They are roughly the same steps and questions we followed in the *Scientific American* case study in

Chapter 1, and the linear programming example of the previous chapter. Here, they are considered in a more general context, with illustrations in terms of a particular type of TPS: an airline passenger reservation system.

1. *What objectives are we trying to optimize or satisfy?*

Asking this question helps us to sort out the objectives of the system we want to develop *(system objectives)* from the more general objectives of the organization *(global objectives)* and the objectives of alternative systems *(global alternatives)*.

In our airline reservation TPS example, our *system objectives* are to develop a TPS which will process transactions involving passenger seat reservations, cancellations; flight, passenger, and seat status queries, and so on. Further, we wish the TPS to process transactions quickly, accurately, reliably, and in ways which accommodate and satisfy our customers and employees.

We need to support such *global objectives* as achieving satisfactory levels of profit, customer good will, and future business potential*—but, as our TPS can't do all of this by itself, these are not our direct objectives in developing a TPS.

There are also alternative systems whose objectives support these global objectives, such as a new aircraft inventory control system, or an extensive planning model for forecasting future passenger demand patterns. For such *global alternatives,* we will have to consider their possible interactions with a passenger reservations TPS, but we will not have to consider their objectives as direct objectives of our passenger reservations TPS.

If we consider our original decision space to be the space of all possible systems we might develop, the process of defining the objectives of our particular system helps us to eliminate a large number of candidate systems, and to focus our attention on the subset of passenger reservations TPS's which are our primary concern. This is illustrated in Fig. 17–1.

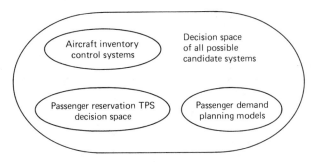

FIGURE 17–1 Sorting out global alternatives

2. *What decisions do we control that affect our objectives?*

---

* Or, in public organizations, satisfactory levels of expenditure versus budget, public welfare, and future organizational capability.

Asking this question helps us to further reduce the size of the decision space by sorting out the following:

- *Systems whose development would involve decisions we don't control.* Thus, we could build a more efficient TPS if we could reorganize the airline's master data base to suit our needs, or if we could change the airline's special-fare policies to simplify the reservation process. In some cases, it may be worthwhile to investigate and press for the authority to make such changes, but in many cases it will be impossible to make such changes within the time frame we need for our system development (such as if the policies are government regulations).
- *System features which won't have much effect on our objectives.* Thus, we could devote a good deal of analysis to the choice of type font to be used on the reservation terminal displays, or to the codes to be used for error messages. But these decisions are not likely to be the primary factors affecting the performance of the system, and can be postponed until later design and development phases.

Thus, this question reduces the decision space of possible *system alternatives* we must consider to just the realistic and significant ones, as illustrated in Fig. 17–2.

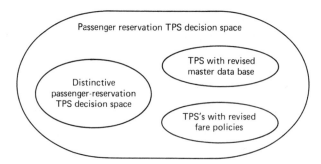

FIGURE 17–2 Sorting out system alternatives

3. *What items dictate constraints on our range of choices?*

This question again reduces the number of alternatives we must evaluate. Typical constraints include:

- *Interface conditions,* such as the limit of 75 tr/sec imposed by communication line capacity
- *Objectives expressed as constraints* as part of the goal-reconciliation process, such as the constraint that system availability be at least 0.98

These constraints reduce the set of candidate systems to an even smaller *feasible set,* as shown in Fig. 17–3.

4. *What criteria should we use to evaluate the remaining alternatives? How are the values of the criterion functions, or objective functions, related to the values of the decision variables that define the alternatives?*

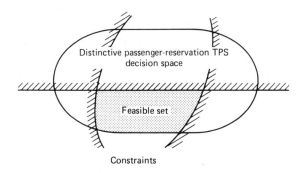

FIGURE 17–3 Sorting out unfeasible alternatives

In systems analysis, the criteria almost always include some measures of cost and effectiveness, and often a combined objective function which attempts to reconcile the cost and effectiveness goals. In our TPS example, we have been using a fairly simply defined net value objective function. In an actual airline passenger reservation system, the objective function(s) would involve such factors as response time, range of transactions to be handled, growth potential, and public image.

As in our TPS example, the objective function can be visualized as a series of isoquants, or contours of constant value of the objective function, as illustrated in Fig. 17–4.

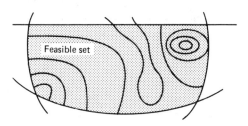

FIGURE 17–4 Evaluating alternatives

5. *What decision provides us with the most satisfactory value of the objective function? How sensitive is the decision to assumptions made during the analysis? Are there alternative decisions providing satisfactory results with less sensitivity to these assumptions?*

In our TPS example, the optimal solution to one of our decision problems (Fig. 16–3a) was to buy two processors and operate at a rate of 72 tr/sec. However, when one processor goes down, and we bring the system back up with only one processor in operation, we will have a processing capacity of only 40 tr/sec.

For many applications, such as a passenger reservation system, this level of degraded performance may be unsatisfactory, particularly if the processor mean-time-to-repair is high. Thus, our solution is highly sensitive to the (unstated) assumption made during the analysis that *any* level of backup performance would be acceptable.

In considering alternative solutions, we might consider the additional alternative of buying a third processor and only using it as a backup. If we do this, our nominal performance will be only 72 tr/sec instead of the 96 tr/sec we would obtain by adding the third processor to the operational system. But our communications constraint only allowed us to operate at a maximum of 75 tr/sec, and an added computer on-line would reduce our reliability from 0.98 to 0.97. Thus, the sensitivity analysis leads us to an alternative which may be preferable to any that we had been previously considering. This is an example of the final component of the systems analysis approach, that of iteration.

6. *Does the performance of any of the above steps cause a reconsideration of the previous steps? If so, iterate the previous steps that are affected.*

17.2 GENERAL DISCUSSION

The mathematical optimization conceptual model helps us to get a perspective on the systems analysis approach, via such concepts as the decision space, the feasible set of alternatives, and the objective function.

Conversely, the systems analysis approach helps us to get a perspective on the mathematical optimization process, by emphasizing that good problem formulation and sensitivity analysis are at least as important as finding the optimal solution.

Figure 17–5 presents a comparison between the mathematical optimization process and the systems analysis approach as formulated in [Quade, 1968]. The similarities are considerable; the major differences are

- The added emphasis in the systems analysis approach on the consideration of subjective, unquantifiable factors
- The ability and the willingness of the systems analysis approach to settle for a feasible but nonoptimal solution.

These two considerations are the primary cautions we should consider when applying mathematical optimization techniques. Most of us in software engineering like to operate in problem solving mode, and it often takes a good deal of self-discipline not to become mesmerized by the pursuit of an absolute mathematical optimum, and to keep in mind that the optimum point may be inferior to alternative points. These alternative solutions may be less sensitive to the assumptions built into the model, better with respect to some of the unquantifiable factors, or more satisfactory with respect to factors which were omitted from the analysis. If we don't exercise such self-discipline, we may end up creating situations such as the following:

- The unused medical support system with optimized response time but an unacceptable user interface
- The major defense system schedule slippage due to an optimized software schedule which could not easily be adapted to the inevitable hardware delays and failures
- The scientific software program with an optimal test sequence which minimized

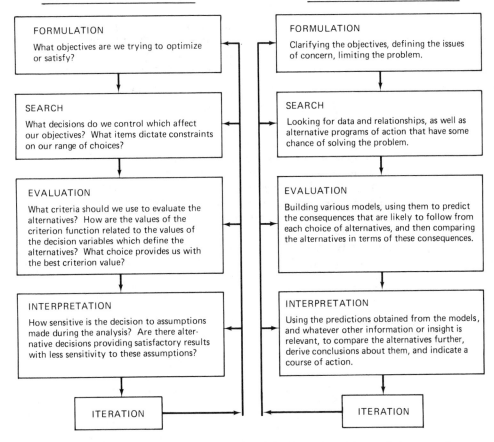

FIGURE 17–5 Comparison of mathematical optimization and systems analysis approaches

the number of test cases required to exercise all the software, but which tripled the amount of effort and time required to generate test inputs and expected outputs

- The urban school attendance system design which optimized throughput, but at the cost of exacerbating a local minority unemployment problem (our case study in Chapter 2).

17.3 QUESTIONS

17.1. Define the following terms: global objectives, global alternatives, system objectives, system alternatives.

17.2. Conduct a series of interviews regarding the development of an improved software-based system for an organization. Analyze the interviews, and identify
    (a) The global objectives that the system should support
    (b) The system objectives that the system should support
    (c) The global alternatives: candidate systems other than this

(d) The system alternatives: candidate schemes for implementing the system

(e) The constraints on the system

17.3. In Step 5 of Section 17.1, we discussed the possibility of buying a third processor and only using it as a backup to the two-processor version of our TPS Option A. Discuss the pros and cons of using this processor to support the development of the special-purpose operating system to be used in TPS Option B.

17.4. Use the systems analysis approach to formulate and analyze the decision problem of selecting which graduate school to attend.

17.5. The *scientific method* commonly used as the basis for scientific endeavor consists of the following basic steps

(a) Develop an understanding of the problem

(b) Formulate candidate solutions to the problem

(c) Develop a testable hypothesis regarding the best solution

(d) Test the hypothesis by experiment or observation

(e) Iterate and refine the hypothesis based on the results of the testing.

To what extent do you think that the scientific method applies to the practice of systems analysis? To what extent do you think that the scientific method applies to the practice of computer science?

Chapter 18

Coping with Unreconcilable
and Unquantifiable Goals

In Chapters 13 through 16, we dealt with quantitative methods of reconciling a number of different goals. In Chapters 13 and 14, we discussed ways of expressing goals in terms of dollars or present dollars. In Chapter 15, we discussed other figure of merit techniques for reconciling a number of goals into a single dimensionless criterion. In Chapter 16, we discussed the practice of expressing goals as quantitative constraints. Throughout these four chapters, and particularly in Chapter 17 on systems analysis, we found that these quantitative methods, although often helpful, were insufficient for dealing with the critical unreconcilable or unquantifiable goals which often confront us in software engineering.

There are two main problems in coping with such unreconcilable goals. They are as follows:

1. Finding techniques for presenting analysis results to decisionmakers in ways which will enhance their ability to absorb all the factors, and to make satisfactory decisions based on the information presented. This topic will be discussed in this chapter.

2. Finding techniques for achieving group consensus on decisions involving un-reconcilable criteria. This topic includes the Delphi technique [Helmer, 1966], organizational development techniques [Fordyce–Weil, 1971], and other techniques outside the scope of this book (such as behaviorial decision analysis [Elbing, 1978]). Chapter 22 discusses Delphi techniques and their use in cost estimation.

18.1 EXAMPLE: TPS OPTION B: SPECIAL-PURPOSE OPERATING SYSTEM DEVELOPMENT

Suppose that we are now preparing to proceed with the Option B portion of the two-step composite approach to the development of our TPS system (discussed in Section 12–1). This portion involves the development of a special-purpose operating system with reduced multiprocessor overhead, which will increase our long range delivered capacity to 180 tr/sec.

Having discovered the unfortunate "one down, all down" reliability characteristic of the existing vendor operating system, we have added further goals of improved system reliability and availability through better switchover and restart capabilities if one or more of the processors fails.

At this point, we have now analyzed our technical approach, and have concluded that, with the added switchover and restart capabilities, we will be able to develop Option B in 12 months for $150K. We have determined also that the added $30K development cost is well worth the added reliability and availability it will provide.

18.2 IN-HOUSE VERSUS VENDOR DEVELOPMENT CONSIDERATIONS

Our hardware vendor, who has been actively following our progress, now comes in with a proposal to develop an Option B operating system for us in 12 months at a cost of $135K, including some of his improved measurement and diagnostic capabilities. We must now evaluate his proposal, not just in terms of cost and performance, but also in terms of a number of other important but largely unquantifiable criteria, such as

- *Availability of key personnel.* If our own systems programmers are overcommitted, the vendor's proposal may look very attractive. If our systems programmers are undercommitted, the proposal will look less attractive.
- *Staff morale and growth.* The Option B assignment presents a stimulating technical challenge. If we let the vendor do the job, our systems programming people may feel frustrated, and they may fall behind the current state of the art in their ability to deal with distributed data processing systems. Again, the extent of these problems depends on the alternative assignments they would be performing otherwise.
- *Controllability.* During the time we are developing Option B, we will be running Option A and learning about things that would make Option B a better operating

system. If we choose to develop Option B in-house, any decision to reorient the development to reflect lessons learned will be entirely under our control. If we contract with the vendor to develop Option B, we will generally find that our control over project reorientation decisions will be complicated by contractual negotiations, vendor personnel constraints, and the vendor's ambitions to develop an operating system he can market elsewhere.
* *Ease of maintenance.* If we opt for in-house development, we will end up with a valuable group of experts for the maintenance portion of the TPS life-cycle. If we opt for vendor development, we will have to either train our own maintenance personnel, or work out a maintenance contract with the vendor.

Expressing considerations such as these in terms of dollars, constraints, or figures of merit will generally not capture all of the subjective concerns and interaction effects involved in making the right decision on vendor versus in-house development. Some alternate methods of presenting these considerations are given below.

18.3 PRESENTATION METHODS

One method is simply to present prose discussions, or *criterion summaries,* of how well each of the alternatives satisfy each of the criteria, as was done in the section above. The decisionmakers can then read each discussion, weight them subjectively, and then make their choice. This is a good practice, as long as the prose discussions are roughly the same length and level of detail as those above on the criteria of availability of key personnel, staff morale and growth, controllability, and ease of maintenance. If they become much longer, the reader will tend to get lost in the detail.

If there are quite a few criteria, a more concise presentation is needed for the decisionmaker to keep all the factors in focus. A good summary technique is the *pros and cons table* or *preference table* shown as Table 18–1. In this table, all the factors leading us to prefer in-house development are in the left column, and the factors favoring vendor development are in the right column.

TABLE 18–1 Preference Table for TPS Alternatives

In-House Development	Vendor Development
Vendor development involves procurement costs and delays	Costs $135K (versus $150K for in-house)
Provides career growth for in-house personnel	Frees in-house personnel for other tasks
Provides expert staff for maintenance	Provides superior measurement and diagnostic capabilities
More control over system development directions	

This kind of table provides a good deal more focus for the decisionmaker. Even here, though, the table may become cumbersome with a large number of alternatives and a large number of criteria. In such a situation, an even more concise summary

RATING SCALE

	CRITERIA	ALTERNATIVES
·	unimportant	unacceptable
*	optional	marginal
**	important	acceptable
***	critical	strong

	Importance	Existing system	In-house development	Vendor development				
COST								
Dollars – acquisition	***		**	**				
Dollars – operation	***		**	**				
Schedule	**		**	*				
Key personnel	**		*	***				
Other:								
EFFECTIVENESS								
Functions:								
Diagnostics	**		**	***				
Performance Measurement	**		**	***				
Accounting System	*		**	***				
Throughput	***		**	**				
Response time	**		**	**				
Accuracy	·							
Ease of use	**		**	**				
Ease of maintenance	***		***	*				
Staff morale and growth	***		***	*				
Sales potential	·							
Reputation	·							
Side effects/Other:								
RISK								
Technology	·							
Availability/Reliability	***		**	**				
Controllability	***		***	*				
Other:								

FIGURE 18–1 Feasibility phase screening matrix

of the alternatives and criteria is provided by rating tables such as the *feasibility phase screening matrix* shown as Fig. 18–1.

This *screening matrix* is a device for screening alternatives during the feasibility phase of the software life-cycle. The rows of the matrix represent criteria of importance in choosing a preferred system concept for development. Some common criteria are provided on the form; others that are specific to the project can be entered in the blank rows. The first column provides a way to indicate the relative importance of each criterion, from unimportant to critical, by placing the appropriate number of stars in the column. The remaining columns provide a way to indicate the relative desirability of each alternative being considered, from unacceptable to strong, again by placing the appropriate number of stars in the row and column.

The number of stars provides a good visual impression of the relative importance of the criterion or the desirability of the alternative, and its precision is about the same as the precision we usually have in making judgements of this nature. Frequently, there will be some difference of opinion in the number of stars that should be awarded to a particular criterion or alternative. Even in such cases, though, the matrix is very helpful as an aid to judging how important it is to settle such a difference. If a criterion is not very important (the accounting system capability, for example), it may not make much difference whether an alternative receives two or three stars in that row. Or, if all of the alternatives receive the same rating on a criterion (response time, for example), it may not make much difference if the criterion receives an importance rating of two or three stars. In general, the screening matrix has proved to be a highly useful device for dealing with relatively large numbers of criteria (5–30) and alternatives (2–10).

With any of these presentation techniques, we would generally find that the choice of in-house development is superior to the vendor development option. However, if we had an extreme shortage of key personnel, and restrictions on hiring more people, we would prefer the vendor development option. It would be difficult to pinpoint the degree of personnel scarcity at which we would begin to feel that the vendor option is superior, as it depends on a complex balance of subjective factors.

18.4 GENERAL DISCUSSION: UNQUANTIFIABLE CRITERIA

Most practical software engineering situations will have some important criteria which are best treated qualitatively. In general, it is good discipline to try to quantify them, but only subject to two limiting considerations

- The cost of the analysis necessary to generate realistic quantitative factors
- The temptation to put a higher evaluation emphasis on the quantitative factors because they are easier to deal with

In general, the effectiveness or benefit criteria are more difficult to quantify than the cost criteria, although some cost criteria are best treated qualitatively (such as the key-personnel criterion in the TPS example above). A good feel for the range of effectiveness/benefit criteria that are associated with information system development is provided by Table 18–2 [King–Schrems, 1978]. The table also gives a good feel for the difficulty of quantifying such benefits (for example, for criteria such as "Improved portability of records" or "Ability to link sites that need search capability through telecommunications.")

TABLE 18–2 Possible Information System Benefits[a b]

Benefits from contributions of calculating and printing tasks
   Reduction in per-unit costs of calculating and printing (CR)
   Improved accuracy in calculating tasks (ER)
   Ability to quickly change variables and values in calculation programs (IF)
   Greatly increased speed in calculating and printing (IS)
Benefits from contributions to record-keeping tasks
   Ability to "automatically" collect and store data for records (CR, IS, ER)
   More complete and systematic keeping of records (CR, ER)
   Increased capacity for recordkeeping in terms of space and cost (CR)
   Standardization of recordkeeping (CR, IS)
   Increase in amount of data that can be stored per record (CR, IS)
   Improved security in records storage (ER, CR, MC)
   Improved portability of records (IF, CR, IS)
Benefits from contributions to record searching tasks
   Faster retrieval of records (IS)
   Improved ability to access records from large databases (IF)
   Improved ability to change records in databases (IF, CR)
   Ability to link sites that need search capability through telecommunications (IF, IS)
   Improved ability to create records of records accessed and by whom (ER, MC)
   Ability to audit and analyze record searching activity (MC, ER)
Benefits from contributions to system restructuring capability
   Ability to simultaneously change entire classes of records (IS, IF, CR)
   Ability to move large files of data about (IS, IF)
   Ability to create new files by merging aspects of other files (IS, IF)
Benefits from contributions of analysis and simulation capability
   Ability to perform complex, simultaneous calculations quickly (IS, IF, ER)
   Ability to create simulations of complex phenomena in order to answer "What if?" questions (MC, IF)
   Ability to aggregate large amounts of data in various ways useful for planning and decisionmaking (MC, IF)
Benefits from contributions to process and resource control
   Reduction of need for manpower in process and resource control (CR)
   Improved ability to fine tune processes such as assembly lines (CR, MC, IS, ER)
   Improved ability to maintain continuous monitoring of processes and available resources (MC, ER, IF)

[a] CR = Cost reduction or avoidance; ER = Error reduction; IF = Increased flexibility; IS = Increased speed of activity; MC = Improvement in management planning or control.
[b] [King–Schrems, 1978].

18.5 PRESENTATION TECHNIQUES FOR UNQUANTIFIABLE CRITERIA

In the TPS example at the beginning of this section we discussed three main techniques for presenting the results of evaluations involving unquantifiable criteria

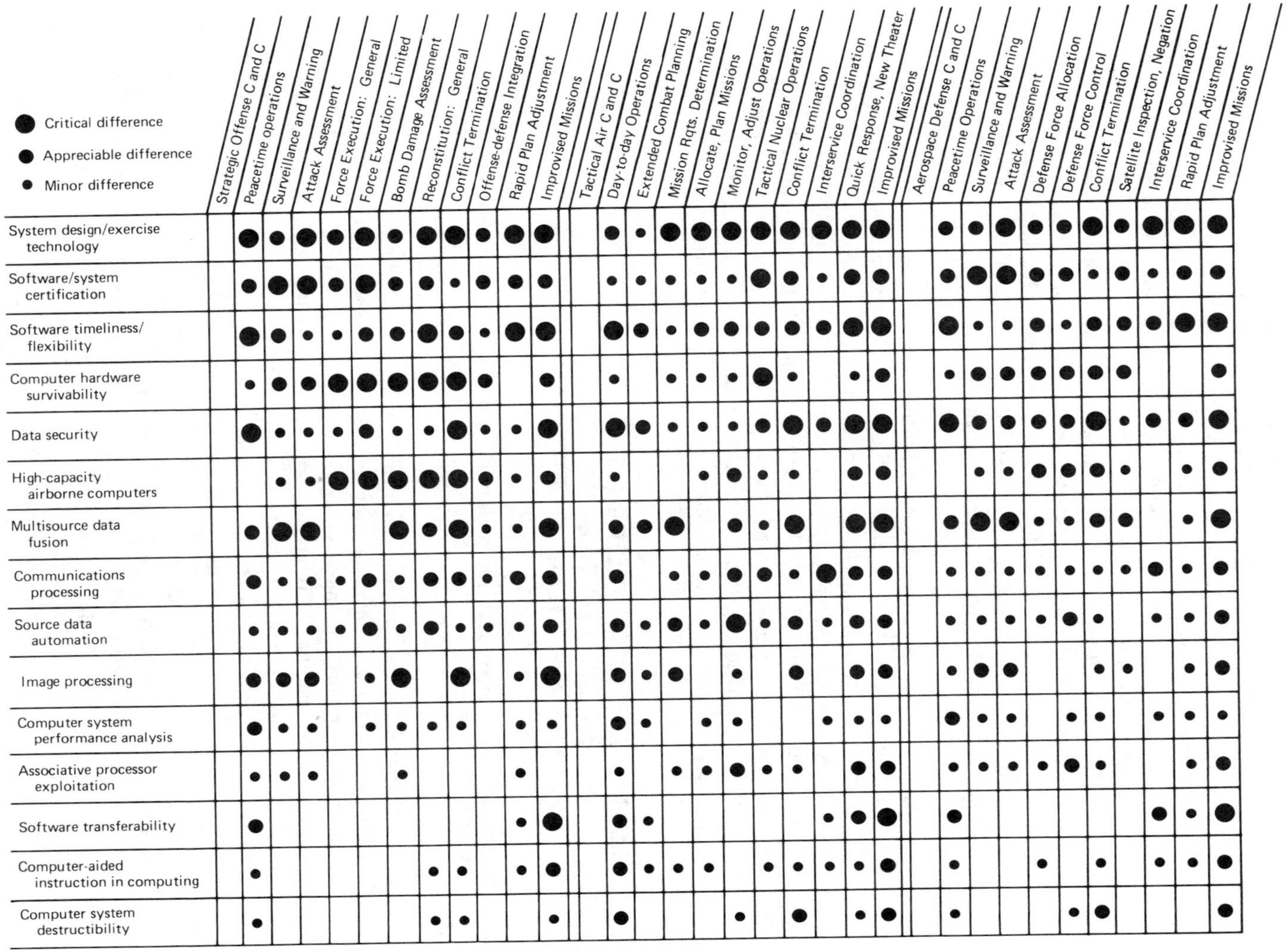

FIGURE 18-2 Information processing research and development screening matrix

271

1. *Criterion summaries.* Individual prose summaries of the alternatives, one summary for each criterion. Good for presenting analysis of a small (2 to 10) number of criteria for a small (2 to 3) number of alternatives.
2. *Preference table.* A table summarizing the major relative strengths of each alternative. Good for presenting analyses of a moderate number of criteria (2 to 20) and alternatives (2 to 5). Key points should have backup information in criterion summary form.
3. *Screening matrix.* A matrix of ratings (0 to 3 stars) of the relative importance of each criterion, and the relative desirability of each alternative with respect to each criterion. Good for presenting analysis of a fairly large number of criteria (5 to 30) and alternatives (2 to 10). Key points should have backup information in criterion summary form.

Situations with more criteria or alternatives than this are hard to deal with by any technique. For example, Fig. 18–2 shows a type of screening matrix generated to evaluate 15 information processing research and development alternatives with respect to 32 defense command and control mission criteria, taken from the CCIP-85 Study [Boehm–Haile, 1972]. The general amount of black space in each row gives a general impression of gross research decision priorities, but the amount of information is too great for decisionmakers to try to make specific research project priority decisions based on a particular set of command and control mission priorities.

18.6 PRESENTATION TECHNIQUES FOR MIXED QUANTIFIABLE AND UNQUANTIFIABLE CRITERIA

Some additional techniques for presenting mixed quantitative and nonquantitative criteria are given below.

Tabular methods. Various tabular methods can be used. Table 18–3 shows one example taken from a study comparing an in-house development option (COCOMO) versus a software package purchase option (SOFTCOST) for acquiring a software cost-estimation capability. This table presents the results with respect to some predetermined desired and acceptable values for each criterion. The table also provides a multiple star rating for each alternative to enhance the visual perception of the results; tables of numbers and ratings are generally hard to assimilate.

Cost versus capability graph. Another mixed-criterion presentation technique is the cost-versus-capability level comparison of the COCOMO and SOFTCOST options shown in Fig. 18–3. Here the values along the vertical axis are successive capability levels (operation of the model for longer time periods, addition of new functional capabilities) which can be purchased with increasing dollar expenditures. The placement of the capability levels along the axis reflects a subjective judgment of the relative value of each capability. With this type of presentation, we can draw on

TABLE 18–3 Tabular Comparison of COCOMO and SOFTCOST Options

Objectives	Desired Value	Acceptable Value	Expected Value COCOMO	Expected Value SOFTCOST	Rating C	Rating S	Rating Imp.
Five-year life-cycle cost	$150K	$325K	$179–284K	$295–430K	***	*	***
Acquisition cost	25K	75K	55K	45K	**	**	***
Five-year O&M cost	125K	250K	124–229K	250–385K	***	*	***
Accuracy	± 20%, 80% of time	± 20%, 66% of time	72%	50–75%	**	*	***
Privacy	In-house control	Proven third party	In-house	Third party	***	*	***
Schedule (months)	3	9	5	1	**	***	**
Maintainability	In-house control	2x in-house cost, response	In-house	2x in-house	***	*	**
Detail	By phase, activity, subsystem, labor-grade, dollars/MM	By phase, sub-system	By phase, activity, subsyst, MM	By phase, dollars, some activity	**	**	**
Staff growth	In-house cost exper-tise	Basic knowledge	Potential expertise	Basic	**	*	**

Acronyms: O&M: Operations and Maintenance   ***: Desired or Better
            MM: Man-months   **: Intermediate
             K: Thousands   *: Acceptable
           Imp: Importance   .: Unacceptable

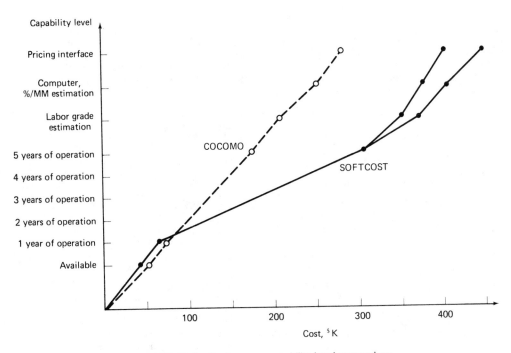

FIGURE 18–3 Cost versus capability level comparison

some of the decision criteria we discussed in Chapter 12 for cost-effectiveness comparisons.

Polar graphs or Kiviat graphs. A third presentation technique for the COCOMO–SOFTCOST comparison is the polar graph or *Kiviat Graph** shown in Fig. 18–4. This chart compares the two alternatives with respect to eight criteria, by using each of the eight radial lines emanating from the center as a measurement axis. In Fig. 18–4, both numerical axes (for cost, schedule, and accuracy) and capability level axes (with a scale of unacceptable, acceptable, intermediate, and desired) are used. In this case, a better candidate is one which fills out more of the circle; in other cases, a better candidate is one which more closely approaches a desired shape, such as a star shape.

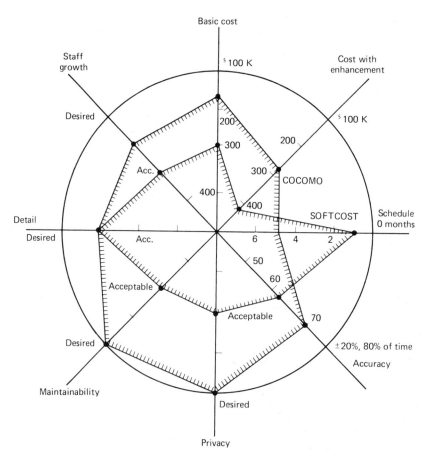

FIGURE 18–4 Polar graph of software cost model evaluation

* Polar graphs were initially used in the medical field for presenting multiparameter patient information [Wolff, 1970]. They have been successfully adapted by Kiviat and others to present the results of computer performance evaluation activities [Bell and others, 1975], in which context they are called Kiviat Graphs. Their use in computer performance evaluation is discussed in [Ferrari, 1978].

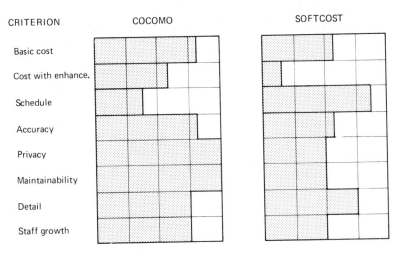

FIGURE 18-5 Bar chart comparison

Bar charts. A similar technique is a bar chart representation of the results, as shown in Fig. 18–5 above for the COCOMO–SOFTCOST data.

The comparative bar chart presentation is not quite as good as the polar graph in visual impact, but it is easier to construct and more flexible. If we want to add another bar to the graph, we don't need to reorganize the whole chart.

18.7   SOME CAUTIONS IN PRESENTING AND INTERPRETING MULTIVARIATE DATA

Choice of scale. One caution in either the visual presentation or interpretation of data is to make sure that the choice of scale does not bias the presentation. As an example, consider the two bar chart presentations in Fig. 18–6 of the same data. In the upper comparison, COCOMO looks better; in the lower one, SOFTCOST looks far better.

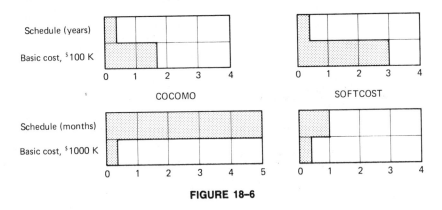

FIGURE 18-6

Another related caution is the choice of starting or ending points of the scale, as illustrated in the comparisons of the same data shown in Fig. 18–7.

Double counting. Another particular caution in presenting multivariate criteria is that of double counting. The visual impact of a difference with respect to a given criterion will be significantly enhanced if it shows up two or three times under different criterion headings. For example, consider the two bar-chart comparisons shown in Fig. 18–8.

By introducing some synonyms for maintainability as additional criteria, we have made the comparison appear to favor COCOMO, where it originally favored SOFTCOST.

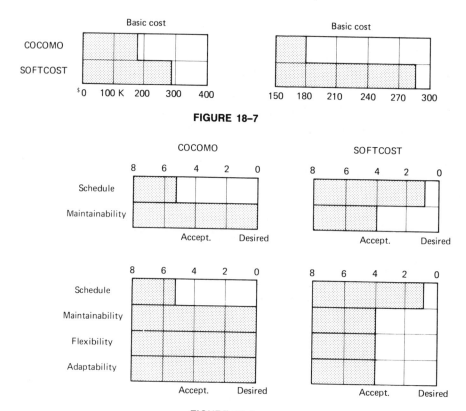

FIGURE 18–7

FIGURE 18–8

18.8 QUESTIONS

18.1. Develop an example of the following presentation techniques:
- preference table
- screening matrix
- cost-versus-capability graph
- polar graph

18.2. Develop a polar graph presentation of the information in the screening matrix given in Fig. 18–1. Use just eight criteria: the seven (***) criteria plus key personnel.

18.3. Below are the results of a more detailed comparison of Option A and Option B of our TPS. Present the results in terms of a preference table, a polar graph, and a bar chart comparison.

Which option would you choose? What considerations might lead you to choose the other option?

Criterion	Option A	Option B
1. Life-cycle cost	$130K	$290K
2. Delivered capacity	112 tr/sec	180 tr/sec
3. Reliability	0.95	0.99
4. Availability	0.975	0.996
5. Development time	6 months	20 months
6. Key personnel	available for other pro-jects	unavailable for other projects
7. Staff growth	little	strong
8. Controllability	via vendor	in-house

18.4. Perform an experiment in your class to see whether people reach the same decision when provided with one or more of the presentations above. What hypothesis will you test? Will the experiment actually test the hypothesis? Do the resulting data support your hypothesis?

18.5. Discuss how you would quantify the benefits presented in Table 18–2, "Possible Information System Benefits."

18.6. The presentation techniques discussed in this section did not provide any good way to present weighted (high priority versus low priority) ratings. Formulate and discuss techniques which might do this.

18.7. *(Research Project)* Most of the research in visual presentation of information has concentrated on support of human decisions in human-machine control systems [Grether and others, 1972; Meister, 1976; and Martin, 1973]. Relatively little is known about how the presentation of information affects the way people make choices between alternatives in nonreal-time situations. Develop and test techniques and hypotheses which add to our understanding of this important issue.

Part IIIC

DEALING WITH
UNCERTAINTIES, RISK,
AND THE VALUE
OF INFORMATION

The decision techniques we discussed in Part IIIB all assume that we have perfect information about the costs and benefits of alternative systems. Unfortunately, we rarely have perfect information in software engineering decision situations. Part IIIC discusses techniques of *risk analysis* (Chapter 19) and *statistical decision theory* (Chapter 20) that can help in situations of *decisionmaking under uncertainty*. In the process, we will also develop a further appreciation of the *value of information:* that basic phenomenon underlying the demand for software and information processing products in general.

Chapter 19

Coping with Uncertainties: Risk Analysis

19.1 EXAMPLE: OPERATING SYSTEM DEVELOPMENT OPTIONS

Suppose that we have decided to implement TPS Option B in-house, and we now find ourselves confronted with an additional decision problem. After analyzing the various technical approaches to developing the operating system, we find that there are two primary candidates

1. The Option B-Conservative (BC) approach, involving the use of standard operating system techniques. Option BC is sure to work, but will only achieve a peak performance of 160 tr/sec with the eight-processor configuration.
2. The Option B-Bold (BB) approach, involving the use of the recently developed *hypermonitor* concept. If Option BB works, it will achieve a peak performance of 190 tr/sec with the eight-processor configuration. If Option BB doesn't work, though, the team will have to reprogram the system using the conserva-

tive techniques, achieving a performance of 160 tr/sec and an added software cost of $60K.

The potential outcomes of these two approaches (and Option A) are summarized in Table 19–1 below, under the assumption that each tr/sec has a value of $4K.

TABLE 19–1 Operating System Development Options

| | Option BB (Bold) | | Option BC (Conservative) | Option A |
	Successful	Not Successful		
Performance (tr/sec)	190	160	160	120
Value ($4K per tr/sec)	760	640	640	480
Basic cost	260	260	260	130
Total cost	260	320	260	130
Net value NV	500	320	380	350
NV relative to Option A	150	−30	30	0

Which option should we choose, based on net value? One thing is clear: the conservative Option BC is better than Option A. But what are we to do about Option BB? If Nature is favorable, and the bold approach succeeds, we will be rewarded handsomely. But if Nature is unfavorable, we will end up worse off by $30K than if we had stayed with Option A.

19.2 DECISION RULES FOR COMPLETE UNCERTAINTY

The problem of choosing between Options BB and BC, when we have no knowledge of the chance of success of Option BB, is called a problem of *decisionmaking under complete uncertainty.*

There are a number of decision rules for this situation, or any other involving a choice among several alternatives, where

- The outcome or payoff depends on which of several *states of nature* may hold.
- Given any state of nature, the payoff for each alternative is known.
- The probability that any given state of nature holds is unknown.

Table 19–2 is a *payoff table* which summarizes the decision problem. For each alternative and state of nature, it indicates our payoff (here, in terms of net value relative to Option A) if we use the alternative when that state of nature is the case.

The decision rules vary according to their optimism or pessimism about the states of nature. The most pessimistic is the

- *Maximin Rule:* Determine the minimum payoff for each alternative. Choose the alternative which maximizes the minimum payoff.

TABLE 19–2 Payoff Matrix for Operating System Decision Problem

Alternative	State of Nature	
	Favorable	Unfavorable
BB (Bold)	150	−30
BC (Conservative)	30	30

In Table 19–2, this means that we determine the minimum payoff of −30 from Option BB and the minimum payoff of 30 from alternative BC, and choose Option BC.

The maximin rule plays it safe. No matter what nature brings, we are guaranteed a net value of $30K greater than Option A. However, the maximin rule is completely blind to the high potential payoff of Option BB if the state of nature is favorable. Even if the payoff matrix looked like this

	Favorable	Unfavorable
BB	1,000,000	29
BC	30	30

the maximin rule would still choose Option BC.

The most optimistic decision rule is the

- *Maximax Rule:* Determine the maximum payoff for each alternative. Choose the alternative which maximizes the maximum payoff.

The maximax rule would choose Option BB in Table 19–2, because its maximum payoff is the highest. Here again, though, the rule does not have much perspective. Even if the payoff matrix looked like this

	Favorable	Unfavorable
BB	31	−1,000,000
BC	30	30

the maximax rule would still choose Option BB.

One rule that does recognize the relative magnitudes of the payoff values is the

- *Laplace or Equal-Probability Rule:* Assume all of the states of nature are equally likely. Determine the expected value for each alternative, and choose the alternative with the maximum expected value.

Under the equal-likelihood assumption, the expected value* for Option BB in Table 19–2 is $(0.5)(150) + (0.5)(-30) = 60$, and the expected value of Option BC is 30. Thus, we would choose Option BB.

This rule is only as good as the assumption of equal probability, which is often not very good. It is also subject to pitfalls, such as duplication of the states of nature. Suppose, for example, that we split the unfavorable state into two states, U_1 and U_2 (say U_1 = performance failure of hypermonitor and U_2 = reliability failure). Then our payoff matrix, and the expected value, would look like this:

	Favorable	U_1	U_2	Expected Value
BB	150	−30	−30	30
BC	30	30	30	30

Although nothing has changed in the real world situation, our relabeling of the states of nature causes a significant change in the expected value and the recommended decision, because of the equal-probability assumption.

There are some other decision rules for the total uncertainty situation, but all of them have pitfalls of one sort or another which make them less than totally satisfactory. The best that can be said for these rules is that they provide a well-defined, consistent framework for decisionmaking under complete uncertainty, whose drawbacks are at least well-understood. The main conclusion we can draw is that complete uncertainty about the states of nature is a very difficult position for good decisionmaking.

19.3 SUBJECTIVE PROBABILITIES

One way to improve on our total ignorance of the states of nature is to have some experts give us their subjective estimates of the probabilities of each state. We can refine these into a group estimate, either by some form of averaging or by using a group consensus technique such as the Delphi method [Helmer, 1966], to be discussed in Chapter 22.

Suppose that, after doing so, we have an estimate of 0.4 as the probability that the state of nature is favorable and that Option BB would succeed. We can then compare the expected values

$$BB: \ 0.4(150) + 0.6(-30) = 42$$
$$BC: \ 0.4(30) + 0.6(30) = 30$$

and decide that Option BB is preferred.

A related technique is *breakeven analysis*. This involves treating the uncertainties as parameters, and calculating the expected value in terms of the parameters, as

---

* If we have an activity with n possible outcomes whose values are $v_1, v_2, \cdots, v_n$, and whose probabilities of occurrence are $p_1, p_2, \cdots, p_n$, the *expected value* EV of the activity is $EV = p_1 v_1 + p_2 v_2 + \cdots + p_n v_n$.

shown in Fig. 19–1. Here, the breakeven point is at Prob(favorable) = 0.333. If we feel that the probability of successfully implementing the hypermonitor concept is greater than 0.333, we should choose Option BB; if less, we should choose Option BC.

Note that the previous decision rules are special cases in Fig. 19–1. The pessimistic maximin rule corresponds to the leftmost point, Prob(favorable) = 0. The optimistic maximax rule corresponds to the rightmost point, Prob(favorable) = 1. The Laplace or equal-probability rule corresponds to the midpoint, Prob(favorable) = 0.5.

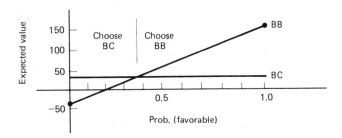

FIGURE 19–1 Breakeven analysis

19.4 GENERAL DISCUSSION: DECISION RULES UNDER COMPLETE UNCERTAINTY

The problem of *decisionmaking under complete uncertainty* involves choosing among a number of *alternatives* (courses of action) under the following conditions:

- The outcome or *payoff* depends on which of several *states of nature* may hold
- Given any state of nature, the payoff for each alternative is known
- The probability that any given state of nature holds is unknown

We have defined and discussed in the previous section the leading decision rules for this situation—the *maximin rule,* the *maximax rule,* and the *Laplace or equal-probability rule*—and illustrated their relative optimism or pessimism, and their strong and weak points.

All of them have serious weak spots. For each rule, there are classes of situations in which the rule counsels a counterintuitive or insensitive decision.*

19.5 THE VALUE OF INFORMATION

It would not be surprising if you finished reading the discussion of these rules with a general feeling of frustration, and thoughts like

* The same is true of the other rules formulated for decisionmaking under complete uncertainty, such as the Hurwicz rule or the Savage minimax regret rule [Luce–Raiffa, 1957].

I can't see myself using a rule like that in a practical software engineering situation. There's got to be a better way

or

I don't feel comfortable in this situation at all. If I'm supposed to make a management decision here, I need to know more about those possible states of nature than I'm given here.

If you felt this way, you were expressing a fundamental human need which provides the main reason for the existence of the software profession: *the need for information which helps people make better decisions.* Virtually all of the models, management information systems, query systems, computer-aided design systems, and automatic test equipment systems developed by the software profession are built because people are willing to pay good money for processed information which will help them make better decisions. In the next chapter, we will focus more on the economic value of information, particularly for making software engineering decisions.

19.6 USE OF SUBJECTIVE PROBABILITIES

One way to buy information to help make software engineering decisions is to acquire information on subjective probabilities, as discussed in Section 19.1. In general, subjective probability information is very useful, and is not very expensive to obtain. It has some practical problems, in that the people most qualified to judge the success probability of an approach on technical grounds are the people closest to the situation, technically or operationally. This closeness often tends to heighten any natural tendencies toward optimism or pessimism they may have, with a resulting bias in their subjective probability estimates. For this reason, the use of group consensus techniques is often valuable.

There are also a number of team-building benefits to be gained by such group-consensus techniques. Further, having the people on the project participate in estimating subjective probabilities gives them a better understanding and feeling of control over their destiny on the project. See Section 22.2 for a discussion of group consensus techniques.

19.7 UTILITY FUNCTIONS

The concept of a *utility function* is often introduced in discussing the use of expected value techniques for decisionmaking. To illustrate the problem they address, suppose you are a manager presented with the following two choices:

- An option which has a guaranteed payoff of $60K
- An option which has a 50% chance of a payoff of $150K, and a 50% chance of a loss of $30K

Which would you prefer?

Although both options have exactly the same expected value, managers will virtually always prefer Option 1. This is largely because the difference in perception

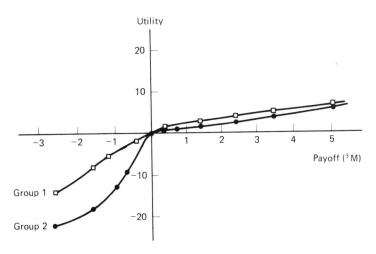

FIGURE 19-2 Utility functions of two groups of managers

between a $60,000 success and a $30,000 failure is much larger than the differences in perception between a $60,000 success and a $150,000 success—and such differences in perception are extremely important to a manager's future career.

Figure 19–2 shows some examples of utility functions which were obtained by asking two groups of managers to express their preferences in various risk situations [Canada, 1971]. A manager in Group 1, for example, has an expected utility of +2 units for the prospect of a $1 million ($1M) gain, and an expected utility of −5 units for the prospect of a $1M loss. Thus, if we presented this manager with a business opportunity which had a 60% chance of earning $1M and a 40% chance of losing $1M, he would refuse it because his expected utility

$$(0.60)(2) + (0.40)(-5) = 1.2 - 2.0 = -0.8$$

is less than zero. His aversion to losses tells him to decline the opportunity even though its expected value is positive

$$(0.60)(\$1M) + (0.40)(-\$1M) = \$0.4M.$$

In order for the manager to accept this business opportunity, he would have to be assured of a positive expected utility, which in this case means a probability of success of at least 5/7 or 71.4%.

19.8 SOFTWARE ENGINEERING IMPLICATIONS

The primary implications of Fig. 19–2 to you as a software engineer are the following:

- You will be dealing largely with managers whose aversion toward losses is much stronger than their desire for gains. Don't expect them to act on an expected value basis in balancing gains and losses.

- On the other hand, managers' utility functions in comparing alternative *positive* payoffs are often reasonably linear, as seen in Fig. 19–2. For such cases, expected value calculations (which are linear) are a reasonable approximation to use in dealing with decisions involving risk.
- Don't assume that everyone has the same or similar utility functions. In Fig. 19–2, the managers in Group 2 have a much stronger aversion toward losses than do the managers in Group 1.
- Don't assume that you can always predict people's utility functions from the type of job they have, although this is often the case. The utility functions in Fig. 19–2 are the results of an experiment to test the hypothesis that research managers (Group 2) have a much smaller aversion to losses than do manufacturing managers (Group 1). To everyone's surprise, the results in Fig. 19–2 show that the opposite was true for the eight managers in this particular study [Canada, 1971].
- Don't assume that people's utility functions are constant. In fact, the utility function is a form of figure of merit which balances a large number of personal variables— needs for money, recognition, security, excitement, belonging, and so on—whose variation with time will cause changes in a person's utility function.

19.9 QUESTIONS

19.1. State the following rules for decisionmaking under complete uncertainty:

- Maximin rule
- Maximax rule
- Laplace or equal-probability rule

19.2. For the following payoff matrix, which alternatives would be chosen by the three decision rules above.

Alternative	State of Nature	
	C	D
A	7	9
B	5	13

19.3. Suppose we are developing software for a spacecraft microprocessor at Precision Products, Inc. (PPI). We wish to decide whether or not to build an emulator of the microprocessor to test the software before the processor is delivered. If we don't develop an emulator, and the processor is delivered on time for testing, PPI will make a profit of $100K. Building the emulator will cost $60K, and will reduce our test costs by $20K if the processor is delivered on time. If the processor is not delivered on time, testing will cost us an additional $20K if the emulator is available, and an added $150K if the emulator is not available.

Set up the payoff matrix for this situation. Determine the best alternative under the maximin rule, the maximax rule, the Laplace rule, and the expected value rule if the probability of on-time processor delivery P(on-time) = 0.8. Compute the breakeven point for P(on-time).

19.4. Consider the utility function shown in Fig. 19–3 for a decisionmaker.

    (a) Based on the payoff matrix of Table 19–2, compute the expected utility of each alternative if the probability of a favorable state of nature is 0.75. Which decision would you make in Table 19–2 if Prob(favorable) >.75? Which if Prob(favorable) <.75?

    (b) Based on the payoff matrix you developed in Question 19.3, compute the expected utility of each alternative if the probability of on-time delivery is 0.8. Which alternative would you choose in this situation?

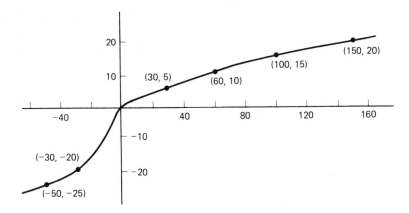

FIGURE 19–3 Possible TPS utility function

19.5. Suppose you have a choice of two software programs to develop for a term project in a class: a relatively hard one and a relatively easy one. The payoff matrix below indicates your course grade as a function of the alternative you pick and the state of nature (unfavorable means that the hard project was too hard to do well).

Alternative	State of Nature	
	Favorable	Unfavorable
Hard	A	C+
Easy	B	B

Determine your best alternative under the maximin rule, the maximax rule, and the Laplace rule, using the following scale to compute expected values:

A	A−	B+	B	B−	C+	C
10	9	8	7	6	5	4

Does this scale adequately reflect your utility function in this situation? If not, what would be a better one?

19.6. Montana Mining and Manufacturing, Inc. has three times at which it can take delivery of some process control equipment and put its process control system into operation: in 2, 4, or 6 months. Suppose also that there are three possible states of nature: that Montana's process control software will be fully checked out and ready to go in 2, 4, or 6 months. The payoff matrix for this situation is as follows (in $K):

State of Nature / Alternative	Software ready in (months)		
	2	4	6
Deliver equipment in (months) 2	100	60	20
4	70	90	50
6	40	60	80

Determine the best alternative under the maximin rule, the maximax rule, and the Laplace rule. Determine the best alternatives under the following probability distributions of the states of nature.

	Software Ready in (months)		
	2	4	6
Distribution 1	0.2	0.6	0.2
Distribution 2	0.2	0.2	0.6

19.7. Many people are willing to pay hundreds of dollars to go to Las Vegas or Atlantic City in order to play games which, for each dollar they bet, they have roughly a 53% chance of losing the dollar and a 47% chance of winning a dollar. Can you construct a utility function which explains this behavior?

Chapter 20

Statistical Decision Theory: The Value of Information

20.1 EXAMPLE: THE PROTOTYPE APPROACH

In the previous chapter, we analyzed a problem in choosing between a bold and a conservative approach in developing the special-purpose operating system for our TPS. We found that it took the form of a decision problem under uncertainty:

Alternative	State of Nature	
	Favorable	Unfavorable
BB (Bold)	150	−30
BC (Conservative)	30	30

We also found that it was difficult to make a good decision in the absence of any information about the probable occurrence of the states of nature. We thus concluded that such information can be of considerable economic value in decision problems under uncertainty.

In this context, let us look at the idea of building a rough prototype of the key portions of the hypermonitor, which is the high-risk element involved in the Bold approach. Suppose that for $10K we can conduct an investigation to build, exercise, and evaluate a prototype which will tell us whether or not the hypermonitor concept will work for our application, and that the prototype can be developed without any compromise in our schedule.

Then, if the state of nature is favorable, our prototype will work, and we can proceed to develop the production version of the operating system using the hypermonitor concept. Our payoff in this case will be $150K minus $10K for the prototype, or $140K. If the state of nature is unfavorable, our prototype will not work, and we will build the operating system using standard techniques. Our payoff in this case will be $30K minus $10K, or $20K. If these two states of nature are equally likely, our expected payoff would be $(0.5) (\$140K) + (0.5) (\$20K) = \$80K$.

20.2 EXPECTED VALUE OF PERFECT INFORMATION

Let us compare the expected value and expected utility of the prototype approach with those of Options BB and BC, using the utility function in Fig. 19–3, and assuming that the states of nature are equally likely. We get the following results:

Approach	Expected Value	Expected Utility
Option BB	$60K	0
Option BC	30K	5
Prototype	80K	11.5

By investing $10K in obtaining information on the actual state of nature, we achieved an expected value which was $20K better than either of the original alternatives. Thus, we could invest up to $30K in obtaining such information and still come out ahead. We can therefore say that the *expected value of having perfect information* on the state of nature is $30K.

20.3 WORKING WITH IMPERFECT INFORMATION

In general, we will not obtain perfect information on the state of nature by developing a prototype, or by other investigations for information to improve our knowledge of the state of nature. There will be two sources of imperfection, which we can express as probabilities

$P(IB|SF)$ Read "the probability of IB given SF"; the probability that the investigation (that is, prototype) would lead us to choose the Bold alternative, in a state of nature in which the Bold option will fail

$P(IB|SS)$ The probability that the investigation would lead us to choose the

Bold alternative, in a state of nature in which the Bold option will succeed

The probability $P(IB|SF)$ will generally not be 0.0 because the prototype may not have adequately covered some key technical issue, or because of problems of scaling up from the rough prototype to the production system. Thus the prototype would succeed, and lead us to choose the Bold alternative, but the Bold option would fail. The probability $P(IB|SS)$ will generally not be 1.0 because the prototype may have been developed with implementation errors which would not be repeated in a full production system. This means that there is some probability that the prototype would fail, causing us to choose the Conservative alternative, in a situation where the Bold option would succeed.

20.4 EXAMPLE

Suppose that the best investigation we can perform involving the development of a $10K prototype has the following sources of imperfection, as defined above

$$P(IB|SF) = 0.20, \qquad P(IB|SS) = 0.90$$

Let us now try to calculate the expected value $EV(IB,IC)$ of using this prototype-based investigation to determine whether to use the Bold or the Conservative alternative. In calculating the expected value, we shall assume as before that the states of nature for success and failure of the Bold alternative are equally likely, that is

$$P(SS) = P(SF) = 0.50$$

The expected value is obtained by multiplying each potential payoff by the probability of its occurrence

$$\begin{aligned} EV(IB,IC) &= P(IB)(\text{Payoff if use Bold alternative}) \\ &\quad + P(IC)(\text{Payoff if use Conservative alternative}) \qquad (20\text{–}1) \\ &= P(IB)[P(SS|IB)(\$150K) + P(SF|IB)(-\$30K)] + P(IC)(\$30K) \end{aligned}$$

This formula calls for a number of probabilities that we do not know directly: $P(IB)$, $P(IC)$, $P(SS|IB)$, and $P(SF|IB)$. The ones that we know from the problem statement are:

$$P(SS) = P(SF) = 0.50, \qquad P(IB|SF) = 0.20, \qquad P(IB|SS) = 0.90$$

20.5 BAYES' FORMULA

Fortunately, given these quantities and their definitions, there is a series of formulas that will give us the values we need to use Eq. (20–1). They are

$$P(IB) = P(IB \mid SS)P(SS) + P(IB \mid SF)P(SF) \qquad (20\text{--}2)$$

$$P(IC) = 1 - P(IB) \qquad (20\text{--}3)$$

$$P(SS \mid IB) = \frac{P(IB \mid SS)P(SS)}{P(IB)} \qquad (20\text{--}4)$$

$$P(SF \mid IB) = 1 - P(SS \mid IB) \qquad (20\text{--}5)$$

Equation (20–2) reflects the fact that there are two different situations in which our prototype investigation will lead us to choose the Bold alternative.

1. Situations in which we choose the Bold approach in a state of nature where the Bold approach will succeed. The probability of doing this is $P(IB \mid SS)P(SS)$.
2. Situations in which we choose the Bold alternative in a state of nature where the Bold approach will fail. The probability of doing this is $P(IB \mid SF)P(SF)$.

Equation (20–2) thus states that the probability of choosing the Bold approach is the sum of the probabilities of these two mutually exclusive situations.

Equation (20–3) complements Eq. (20–2). It covers the two situations in which the prototype investigation will lead us to the Conservative alternative. It is simply one minus the probability of the Bold alternative.

Equation (20–4) indicates that the probability that the Bold option will succeed, given that our prototype investigation led us to choose the Bold option. It is expressed by the ratio

$$P(SS \mid IB) = \frac{\text{Prob (we will choose Bold in a state of nature where it will succeed)}}{\text{Prob (we will choose Bold)}}$$

Equation (20–4), a form of *Bayes' formula,* is the key to our ability to determine the expected value of using the imperfect prototype, which we can then use as a guide to choosing either the Bold or Conservative approach for system development.

We may now substitute our known probabilities into Eqs. (20–2) through (20–5) to determine the probabilities we need in order to use the expected value formula, Eq. (20–1)

$$P(IB) = (0.50)(0.90) + (0.50)(0.20) = 0.55$$

$$P(IC) = 1 - 0.55 = 0.45$$

$$P(SS \mid IB) = \frac{(0.50)(0.90)}{0.55} = 0.82$$

$$P(SF \mid IB) = 1 - 0.82 = 0.18$$

$$EV(IB,IC) = (0.55)[(0.82)(\$150K) + (0.18)(\$-30K)] + (0.45)(\$30K)$$

$$= (0.55)(\$117.6K) + \$13.5K = \$78.2K$$

Since the largest expected value* we could obtain without developing a prototype was $60K, using the Bold option, the expected value of the imperfect information provided by the prototype investigation is $18.2K. Even though the information is imperfect, it is worth more than the $10K we planned to spend on the prototype.

20.6 MAXIMIZING THE NET EXPECTED VALUE OF THE PROTOTYPE

We can use the Bayes' formula approach above to determine the net values of different levels of investment in prototypes, giving different estimated levels of reliability in their predictions of the states of nature. Such a determination is summarized in Table 20–1 and Fig. 20–1. Thus, for example, an investment in a $20K prototype might eliminate some of the sources of imperfection, decreasing the estimated $P(IB|SF)$ to 0.10 and improving the estimated $P(IB|SS)$ to 0.95. The resulting expected value for the $20K prototype approach would be $86.8K, implying an expected value of the prototype's information of $26.8K and a net expected value of $6.8K, or less than that obtained by the $10K prototype.

TABLE 20–1   Net Expected Value of Prototype versus Cost

Cost of Prototype	Estimated P(IB|SF)	P(IB|SS)	Expected Value	Expected Value of Information	Net Expected Value of Prototype
0			$60 K	0	0
$ 5K	0.30	0.80	69.3K	$ 9.3K	$4.3K
10K	0.20	0.90	78.2K	18.2K	8.2K
20K	0.10	0.95	86.8K	26.8K	6.8K
30K	0.00	1.00	90.0K	30.0K	0

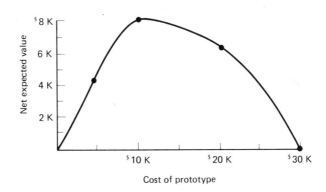

FIGURE 20–1   Net expected value of prototype versus cost

* Strictly speaking, we should be calculating expected utilities rather than expected values here. However, since the form of the equations and the resulting conclusion is the same, we have used expected values to simplify the presentation.

In this situation, the investment of $10K in a prototype is the best decision. Investing less will not produce a sufficient payoff, while investing more will not provide enough of an additional payoff to be worth the additional cost.

20.7 GENERAL DISCUSSION: EXPECTED VALUE OF PERFECT INFORMATION

Definitions. Here is the general form of the problem of *decisionmaking under uncertainty* that we have been discussing

Given a choice between m *alternatives* $A_1, A_2, \ldots, A_m$:

- In a situation involving *n* possible *states of nature* $S_1, S_2, \ldots, S_n$
- Whose probabilities of occurrence are $P(S_1), P(S_2), \ldots, P(S_n)$
- Where the *payoff* value of choosing alternative A_i while in a state of nature S_j is given by the *payoff matrix*

	S_1	S_2	$\cdots$	S_n
A_1	V_{11}	V_{12}	$\cdots$	V_{1n}
A_2	V_{21}	V_{22}	$\cdots$	V_{2n}
$\vdots$	$\vdots$	$\vdots$	$\ddots$	$\vdots$
A_m	V_{m1}	V_{m2}	$\cdots$	V_{mn}

Find the choice of alternative which gives the maximum expected value of the payoff.

In this formulation, the payoff values can be expressed in dollars, figure of merit units, personal utility units, or any other units.

In Chapter 19, we discussed approaches to solving this problem when we had no information about which of the states of nature was actually the case. When we had subjective estimates of the probabilities of the states of nature $P(S_j)$, we used the subjective probability approach: to compute the expected value of choosing each alternative A_i

$$EV(A_i) = P(S_1)V_{i1} + P(S_2)V_{i2} + \cdots + P(S_n)V_{in}$$

and pick the alternative providing the maximum expected value

$$(EV)_{\text{no info}} = \max_{i=1, \ldots, m} [P(S_1)V_{i1} + \cdots + P(S_n)V_{in}] \qquad (10\text{–}6)$$

If we have perfect information on which state of nature will occur, then for each state of nature we will choose the alternative which provides the maximum payoff for that state of nature. In this situation, the expected value is

$$(EV)_{\text{perfect info}} = P(S_1)\left(\max_{i=1, \ldots, m} V_{i1} \right) + \cdots + P(S_n)\left(\max_{i=1, \ldots, m} V_{in} \right) \qquad (20\text{–}7)$$

Then the *expected value of acquiring the perfect information (EVPI)* is

$$EVPI = (EV)_{\text{perfect info}} - (EV)_{\text{no info}}$$

$$= \sum_{j=1}^{n} P(S_j) \left(\max_{i=1, \ldots, m} V_{ij} \right) - \max_{i=1, \ldots, m} \sum_{j=1}^{n} P(S_j) V_{ij} \qquad (20\text{--}8)$$

Illustration. Let us refer back to our TPS example with two alternatives (here called A_1 and A_2) and two states of nature SS (Success) and SF (Failure), with equal probabilities of occurrence:

	$S_1 = SS$	$S_2 = SF$
$A_1 = $ Bold	150	−30
$A_2 = $ Conservative	30	30
$P(S_i)$	0.5	0.5

In this case, we have

$$(EV)_{\text{no info}} = \max\ [(0.5)(150) + (0.5)(-30);\ (0.5)(30) + (0.5)(30)]$$
$$= \max\ [60,30] = 60$$

$$(EV)_{\text{perfect info}} = (0.5)\ \max\ (150,30) + (0.5)\ \max\ (-30,30)$$
$$= (0.5)(150) + (0.5)(30) = 90$$

$$EVPI = 90 - 60 = 30$$

20.8 EXPECTED VALUE OF IMPERFECT INFORMATION

If our investigations produce perfect information on which state of nature holds, we will always be able to recommend the alternative which maximizes the payoff for that state of nature. In such a case, the alternatives we recommend based on our investigations, IA_i, hold the following relationship with the states of nature, S_j:

$$P(IA_i|S_j) = 1.0 \text{ if } A_i \text{ maximizes } V_{ij} \text{ for the state } S_j$$
$$P(IA_i|S_j) = 0.0 \text{ otherwise}$$

Usually, the recommended alternatives IA_i will not be based on perfect information on the actual state of nature. Thus, for each alternative A_i and each state of nature S_j, the probability $P(IA_i|S_j)$ provides a measure of how often our recommendations are likely to deviate from the ideal (0.0 or 1.0) precision above for that combination of A_i and S_j. For each state of nature S_j, the probabilities $P(IA_i|S_j)$ must add up to 1.0, that is

$$\sum_{i=1}^{m} P(IA_i|S_j) = 1.0 \qquad \text{for} \qquad j = 1, \ldots, n \qquad (20\text{--}9)$$

The general expression for the expected value of a decision rule based on recommending alternatives $IA_1, \ldots, IA_m$ is

$$EV(IA_1, \ldots, IA_m) = \sum_{i=1}^{m} P(IA_i) \, EV(\text{payoff using recommendation } IA_i)$$

$$= \sum_{i=1}^{m} P(IA_i) \left[\sum_{j=1}^{n} P(S_j | IA_i) V_{ij} \right] \qquad (20\text{--}10)$$

As in our TPS example (where the IA_i were called IB and IC, and the S_j were called SS and SF), we now need general formulas to calculate $P(IA_i)$ and $P(S_j|IA_i)$ from our known values of $P(S_j)$ and $P(IA_i|S_j)$, in order to calculate $EV(IA_1, \ldots, IA_n)$. These general formulas are the following:

$$P(IA_i) = \sum_{j=1}^{n} P(IA_i|S_j) P(S_j) \qquad (20\text{--}11)$$

$$P(S_j|IA_i) = \frac{P(IA_i|S_j) \, P(S_j)}{P(IA_i)} \qquad (20\text{--}12)$$

Equation (20–12) is the general form of Bayes' formula.

20.9 THE VALUE-OF-INFORMATION PROCEDURE

Given these formulas, we can describe a *value-of-information procedure* for determining what kind of investigation (simple prototype, detailed prototype, simulation, questionnaire, etc.) will give us the best balance between the cost of performing the investigation and the value we receive from the information produced by the investigation.

1. Formulate a set of alternative information system development approaches $A_1, \ldots, A_m$.
2. Determine the states of nature $S_1, \ldots, S_n$ which influence the outcome of using the alternative approaches.
3. Determine the values V_{ij} of the payoff matrix, where V_{ij} represents the payoff of using alternative A_i if nature is in a state S_j.
4. Determine the probabilities $P(S_j)$ that nature is actually in a state S_j.
5. Compute $(EV)_{\text{no info}}$, $(EV)_{\text{perfect info}}$, and EVPI from Eqs (20–6, 7, and 8).
6. If the EVPI is negligible, then it is not worth our time and effort to conduct investigations to determine the actual state of nature. In this case, we would simply choose the development approach which provided the best $(EV)_{\text{no info}}$, and proceed to implement it. Before doing so, though, we might wish to determine the sensitivity of the EVPI to our assumptions about key payoffs and probabilities, which may cause us to reconsider the prospect of conducting an investigation.

7. If the EVPI is not negligible, it provides a rough* upper bound for the amount of effort we should put into an investigation of the states of nature. Within this limit, determine the most promising type(s) of investigation to perform, and their estimated costs C_k.

8. For each type of investigation, estimate the probability $P\,(IA_i|S_j)$ that the investigation will recommend alternative A_i when nature is in a state S_j.

9. Compute the expected value of the information provided by investigation k, EV (I_k), using Eqs (20–10, 11, and 12).

10. Compute the net value of each investigation

$$NV\,(I_k) = EV\,(I_k) - C_k$$

11. Choose a preferred investigation approach based on the following considerations:
   (a) The relative net values of the investigations
   (b) Whether or not any of the net values are positive
   (c) Whether the results of the investigation will be available in time to aid in choosing which alternative to develop
   (d) The relative magnitude of the side benefits derived from performing the investigations

20.10 USE OF THE VALUE-OF-INFORMATION PROCEDURE IN SOFTWARE ENGINEERING

The value-of-information procedure can help us to resolve a number of key software engineering decisions of the form

How much should we invest in further information gathering and analysis investigations before committing ourselves to a course of action?

The four major issues of this nature in software engineering are

1. How much should we invest in feasibility studies (user questionnaires and interviews, scenarios, concept analyses, models, demand predictions, workload characterizations) before committing ourselves to a particular concept for development?

2. How much should we invest in alternative vendor hardware–software product analysis (workload characterization, benchmarking, reference checking, make-or-buy analysis, rental-versus-purchase analysis) before committing ourselves to a particular product?

3. How much should we invest in risk analysis (simulation, prototyping, user

---

* This is because the investigation may produce *side benefits* of training, concept validation, design sensitivity analysis, user and customer involvement, etc., which are not included in the quantitative calculation of net value.

interaction studies, workload characterization, models, sensitivity analyses) before committing ourselves to a baselined requirements specification and a build-to product design specification?

4. How much should we invest in verification and validation (requirements V & V, design V & V, requirements testing, program proving, stress testing, field testing) before committing ourselves to full operational use of the software product?

20.11 VALUE-OF-INFORMATION DECISION GUIDELINES

As the situations above are common in software engineering practice, the value of information procedure is very helpful in providing a stepwise approach for confronting the decision issue, performing the necessary analyses, and communicating our decision rationale to others.

The value-of-information procedure is far from being a cut and dried, cookbook approach. Several steps involve subjective estimates of quantities that are hard to pin down accurately, particularly the payoff values in Step 3, the probabilities of the states of nature in Step 4, and the conditional probabilities $P\,(IA_i|S_j)$ in Step 8. Thus, we may settle for a more informal version of the procedure in most situations.

Even the informal value-of-information approach will be very useful, because it embodies some basic decision guidelines which will help us avoid some serious common pitfalls, some of which are described in the next section.

Here are the basic decision guidelines embodied in the value-of-information approach, on the *conditions under which it makes good sense to decide on investing in more information* before committing ourselves to a particular alternative.

Condition 1. *There exist attractive alternatives whose payoff varies greatly, depending on some critical states of nature.*
If not, we can commit ourselves to one of the attractive alternatives with no risk of significant loss.

Condition 2. *The critical states of nature have an appreciable probability of occurring.*
If not, we can again commit ourselves without major risk. For situations with extremely high variations in payoff, the appreciable probability level is lower than in situations with smaller variations in payoff.

Condition 3. *The investigations have a high probability of accurately identifying the occurrence of the critical states of nature.*
If not, the investigations will not do much to reduce our risk of loss due to making the wrong decision.

Condition 4. *The required cost and schedule of the investigations do not overly curtail their net value.*
It does us little good to obtain results which cost more than they can save us, or which arrive too late to help us make a decision.

Condition 5. *There exist significant side benefits derived from performing the investigations.*

Again, we may be able to justify an investigation solely on the basis of its value in training, team-building, customer relations, or design validation.

20.12 PITFALLS AVOIDED BY USING THE VALUE-OF-INFORMATION APPROACH

The guideline conditions provided by the value-of-information approach provide us with a perspective which helps us avoid some serious software engineering pitfalls. The pitfalls below are expressed in terms of some frequently expressed but faulty pieces of software engineering advice.

Pitfall 1. *Always use a simulation to investigate the feasibility of complex real-time software.* Simulations are often extremely valuable in such situations. However, there have been a good many simulations developed which were largely an expensive waste of effort, frequently under conditions that would have been picked up by the guidelines above. Some have been relatively useless because, once they were built, nobody could tell whether a given set of inputs was realistic or not (picked up by Condition 3). Some have taken so long to develop that they produced their first results the week after the proposal was sent out, or after the key design review was completed (picked up by Condition 4).

Pitfall 2. *Always build the software twice.* The guidelines indicate that the prototype (or build-it-twice) approach is often valuable, but not in all situations. Some prototypes have been built of software whose aspects were all straightforward and familiar, in which case nothing much was learned by building them (picked up by Conditions 1 and 2).

Pitfall 3. *Build the software purely top-down.* When interpreted too literally, the top-down approach does not concern itself with the design of low level modules until the higher levels have been fully developed. If an adverse state of nature makes such a low level module (automatically forecast sales volume, automatically discriminate one type of aircraft from another) impossible to develop, the subsequent redesign will generally require the expensive rework of much of the higher level design and code. Conditions 1 and 2 warn us to temper our top-down approach with a thorough top-to-bottom software risk analysis during the requirements and product design phases.

Pitfall 4. *Every piece of code should be proved correct.* Correctness proving is still an expensive way to get information on the fault-freedom of software, although it strongly satisfies Condition 3 by giving a very high assurance of a program's correctness. Conditions 1 and 2 recommend that proof techniques be used in situations where the operational cost of a software fault is very large, that is, loss of life, compromised national security, major financial losses. But if the operational cost of a software fault is small, the added information on fault-freedom provided by the proof will not be worth the investment (Condition 4).

Pitfall 5. *Nominal-case testing is sufficient.* This pitfall is just the opposite of Pitfall 4. If the operational cost of potential software faults is large, it is highly imprudent not to perform off-nominal testing or more rigorous program verification activities.

20.13 VALUE OF INFORMATION: WRAP-UP

Another useful function provided by the value-of-information approach is a means to answer the question posed in Section 15.1: "How do we determine how much cost-effectiveness analysis is enough?" Again, the guideline conditions provide us with a good way to generate a first-cut answer, and the full value-of-information procedure provides a sequence of steps for determining the appropriate size and scope of a large cost-effectiveness analysis in more detail.

Finally, it is worth re-emphasizing that the value of information for improved decisionmaking is the main reason that people build software and information systems. Thus, we will find that the value-of-information guidelines will be very helpful in analyzing the requirements for software and information systems in terms of the types of operational decisions to be supported by the information processing products.

For example, in scoping our airline-reservations TPS, we might receive a suggestion to include information on passenger profiles. The five value-of-information decision guidelines would help us to structure our evaluation of this suggestion. Condition 1, for example, would require us to identify how this information would make a significant difference in our long-range benefits (allowing us to better predict seasonal passenger loads and thus produce better flight schedules; allowing us to give passengers the type of seat and meal they usually request and thus obtain more satisfied customers and repeat business; and so on). The other conditions would help us to evaluate how much expected benefit the passenger-profile information would actually provide in practice.

20.14 QUESTIONS

20.1. State the general problem of decisionmaking under uncertainty. With respect to this statement, give formulas for $(EV)_{no\ info}$, $(EV)_{perfect\ info}$, and EVPI.

20.2. State the general form of Bayes' formula.

20.3. Consider the TPS example discussed in Section 20.1, with the following changes: $P\ (SS) = 0.4$, $P\ (SF) = 0.6$. For this modified problem, compute $(EV)_{no\ info}$, $(EV)_{perfect\ info}$, EVPI, and the expected value using the \$10K prototype investigation.

20.4. Consider the TPS example in Section 20.1, with a different payoff matrix:

Alternative	State of Nature	
	Favorable	Unfavorable
Bold (BB)	150	−100
Conservative (BC)	30	30

Compute the resulting $(EV)_{no\ info}$, $(EV)_{perfect\ info}$, and EVPI. Develop a counterpart of Table 20–1 for the expected value of various levels of imperfect information.

20.5. Query Systems, Inc. is planning to develop the data base query system for Project Zenith, the community information utility. They have a choice of three data structuring alternatives:
- Alternative A works well if the workload is primarily simple queries
- Alternative B works well if the workload is primarily complex queries
- Alternative C works well if the workload is primarily updates

Below is the payoff matrix in $K for each combination of alternatives and states of nature (actual workload distribution):

Alternative	State of Nature (Primary type of workload)		
	Simple Query	Complex Query	Update
A	1200	600	300
B	800	1000	0
C	400	200	1000
Probability	0.3	0.2	0.5

At this stage, nobody knows which of the states of nature is actually the case.

(a) Compute $(EV)_{no\ info}$, $(EV)_{perfect\ info}$, and EVPI.

(b) Query Systems wishes to determine whether the following type of user survey would be worthwhile. Its cost would be $200K, and it would have the following accuracy $P(IA_i|S_j)$ in determining the actual states of nature:

Alternative	State of Nature		
	Simple	Complex	Update
A	0.8	0.1	0.1
B	0.1	0.8	0.1
C	0.1	0.1	0.8

Calculate the expected value achieved by using the information from the user survey, and determine whether the survey is worthwhile.

20.6. What are the five value-of-information guideline conditions under which an investment in additional decisionmaking information is worthwhile?

20.7. Elaborate the guideline conditions into a set of guidelines for determining how much one should invest in
(a) Developing a simulation as part of a feasibility study
(b) Developing a prototype or other type of analysis of high risk, low level modules before proceeding into top-down development
(c) Program proving or off-nominal testing before committing a product to full-scale operation.

20.8. The value-of-information approach indicates that the value of information for decision-making is a function of two main factors
(a) The magnitude of the risk involved if the wrong decision is made
(b) The accuracy or reliability of the information
What other factors do you believe influence the value of information for decisionmaking? Are these two the most important factors?

20.9. National Motors, Inc., is developing a microprocessor-based carburetor control system for their next series of automobile models. The software for the system contains 5000 DSI of microprocessor assembly code, packaged in each automobile as a Programmable Read Only Memory (PROM) chip and to be installed in about 5,000,000 automobiles.

Currently, National Motors is investigating the possible use of program proof techniques to reduce the risk of an expensive recall should there be a fault in the software installed in the automobiles. National estimates that conventional test techniques will assure an 0.95 probability that there are no faults in the software. National has two main options for handling a fault, once the 5,000,000 automobiles are in use.

Option A: Take no steps other than to retain the capabilities used in the original software development and chip production. If Nature is favorable and no faults occur, this option incurs no additional cost. If not, and a fault occurs, it will cost National an additional $200 million to service the recall.

Option B: Spend $30 million to develop some additional local service kits to handle the fault correction, should it be needed. This option would cost National an additional $30 million, whether or not a fault occurs.

This situation is summarized in the table below:

	$S_1 = SS$ No Software Fault	$S_2 = SF$ Software Fault
IA_1 = No local service kits	0	200
IA_2 = Local service kits	30	30
$P(S_j)$	.95	.05

The expected cost of Option A_1 is

$$(.05)(200) + (.95)(0) = \$10 \text{ million}$$

The expected cost of Option A_2 is

$$(.05)(30) + .95(30) = \$30 \text{ million}$$

Option A, thus, appears better on an expected cost basis, but National is concerned about its high risk should a fault actually be present in the software. Their investigation of program proof techniques as a way of reducing this risk has produced the following estimates:

$P\ (IA_1|SF) = 0.01$ (1% of the time, the proof technique will result in the recommendation: "There are no faults; don't produce local service kits," when a fault still exists)

$P\ (IA_2|SS) = 0.98$ (2% of the time, the proof techniques will result in the recommendation: "This situation is too complex to fully analyze, but the chances of it being in error are high enough that we recommend producing the local service kits," in a situation where no fault exists)

Cost of proof activity = (5000 instr)($200/instr)* = $1,000,000

Calculate the expected cost resulting from the use of the program-proof approach, and determine whether the resulting cost savings are worth the investment in the program-proof activity for National Motors.

---

* [Miller, 1980] estimates the cost of a program proof activity in the range $50–500/instruction.

I. INTRODUCTION

1. Case Study 1: Scientific American
2. Case Study 2: Urban School System
3. The goals of software engineering

II. THE SOFTWARE LIFE-CYCLE:
A QUANTITATIVE MODEL

4. The software life-cycle:
   phases and activities
5. The basic COCOMO model
6. The basic COCOMO model:
   development modes
7. The basic COCOMO model:
   activity distribution
8. The intermediate COCOMO model:
   product level estimates
9. Intermediate COCOMO:
   component level estimation

III. FUNDAMENTALS OF SOFTWARE
ENGINEERING ECONOMICS

III A.   Cost-Effectiveness Analysis

10. Performance models and
    cost-effectiveness models
11. Production functions: economies of scale
12. Choosing among alternatives:
    decision criteria

III B.   Multiple-Goal Decision Analysis

13. Net value and marginal analysis
14. Present vs. future expenditure and income
15. Figures of merit
16. Goals as constraints
17. Systems analysis and constrained optimization
18. Coping with unreconcilable and unquantifiable
    goals

III C.   Dealing with Uncertainties, Risk, and the Value
of Information

19. Coping with uncertainties: risk analysis
20. Statistical decision theory: the value of information

IV. THE ART OF SOFTWARE COST ESTIMATION

IV A.   Software Cost Estimation Methods and Procedures

21. Seven basic steps in software cost estimation
22. Alternative software cost estimation methods

IV B.   The Detailed COCOMO Model

23. Detailed COCOMO: summary and operational description
24. Detailed COCOMO cost drivers: product attributes
25. Detailed COCOMO cost drivers: computer attributes
26. Detailed COCOMO cost drivers: personnel attributes
27. Detailed COCOMO cost drivers: project attributes
28. Factors not included in COCOMO
29. COCOMO evaluation

IV C.   Software Cost Estimation and Life-Cycle Management

30. Software maintenance cost estimation
31. Software life-cycle cost estimation
32. Software project planning and control
33. Improving software productivity

Part IV

THE ART OF SOFTWARE
COST ESTIMATION

Parts I and II of this book discussed the basic goals and structure of the software life-cycle, and presented the Basic COCOMO and Intermediate COCOMO models for estimating the magnitude and distribution of effort required to develop a software product and support it throughout its life-cycle. In Part III, we showed how these techniques could be combined with the general methods of economics to provide a set of software engineering economics techniques for dealing with the major decision issues arising throughout the software life-cycle.

Part IV returns to the subject of software cost estimation. Its main objective is to provide more detailed guidelines and information in the art of software cost estimation. Part IV presents Detailed COCOMO, the most accurate and extensive of the COCOMO hierarchy of models, and the detailed foundation on which the higher levels of the COCOMO model are built. Part IV also provides a framework of methods, techniques, and data essential to practical software cost estimation and control. It further surveys the state of the art in software cost estimation, and identifies topics for further research which would advance our current understanding and ability to perform software cost-estimation activities.

PART IVA: SOFTWARE COST-ESTIMATION METHODS AND PROCEDURES

Part IV contains three main components. Part IVA (Chapters 21 and 22) covers the practical procedural aspects of software cost estimation.

First, in Chapter 21, we present a set of seven basic steps for a software cost-estimation activity. Two of these basic steps focus on the need to use more than one type of estimating method—expert judgment, algorithmic model, ratio estimation, etc.—and to compare and iterate the results from the different methods. The main reasons for this combining of techniques are discussed in Chapter 22, which presents an analysis of available cost-estimation methods, and concludes that there is no single method which is better than the others in all respects. Chapter 22 also presents guidelines for using various expert-consensus techniques for cost estimation, culminating with the effective Wideband Delphi technique.

PART IVB: THE DETAILED COCOMO MODEL

Part IVB (Chapters 23 to 29) covers the Detailed COCOMO model, which differs in two major ways from the Intermediate COCOMO model presented in Part II. One is its ability to describe a software product and its attributes in a more detailed three-level hierarchy. The other is a more detailed set of effort multipliers, which indicate the effect of a cost driver on each *phase* of software development. Chapter 23 presents a set of summary tables and procedures for using the Detailed COCOMO Software Hierarchy Estimating Form (SHEF), and gives a step-by-step example of its use.

Chapters 24 through 27 discuss the COCOMO cost drivers in detail, providing

- Phase-by-phase effort multiplier tables for each cost driver
- Definitions of the cost driver rating levels
- A table relating the cost driver rating levels to the corresponding differences in project activity (effort) levels
- An analysis of the effort multipliers with respect to project actuals in the COCOMO data base
- A discussion of current knowledge about the cost driver's effect, via related observational data and study results
- A set of topics for further research

Chapter 24 covers the software product attributes: required software reliability, data base size, and product complexity. Chapter 25 covers the computer attributes: execution time and main storage constraints, virtual machine volatility, and computer turnaround time. Chapter 26 covers personnel attributes: analyst and programmer capability, and experience with the applications area, the virtual machine, and the programming language. Chapter 27 covers the software project attributes: use of modern programming practices, software tools, and the required development schedule.

Three related issues are also covered in the final two chapters of Part IVB:

- *How positive are we that COCOMO includes all the significant factors needed for software cost estimation?* Chapter 28 presents a set of criteria for evaluating the worth of a software cost model, and discusses the major factors not included in COCOMO with respect to these criteria.
- *How well do COCOMO estimates agree with project experience?* Chapter 29 presents the COCOMO data base of 63 completed projects, summarizes the correlation between COCOMO estimates and project actuals, and discusses the overall CO-COMO model with respect to the evaluation criteria given in Chapter 28.
- *How can we calibrate COCOMO to a particular installation?* COCOMO is most effective if some preliminary effort has been made to calibrate it to an installation's individual circumstances. Chapter 29 also discusses ways to perform this calibration.

PART IVC: SOFTWARE COST ESTIMATION AND LIFE-CYCLE MANAGEMENT

Good software cost estimation is not an end in itself, but rather a means toward more effective software life-cycle management. Part IVC (Chapters 30 to 33) covers several topics of importance in using COCOMO over the software life-cycle. Chapter 30 covers techniques for estimating software maintenance costs, and related guidelines for software maintenance management. Chapter 31 covers techniques for estimating overall software life-cycle costs, including conversion, installation, training, and other software-related costs (computer time, documentation, etc.). Chapter 32 presents techniques for using software cost estimates to improve software project planning and control—and vice versa. Finally, Chapter 33 discusses the problem of improving software productivity from the perspective and insights provided by software cost-estimation technology.

Part IVA

SOFTWARE COST-ESTIMATION METHODS AND PROCEDURES

Having a good software cost model available does not guarantee good software cost estimates. As with other computer-based models, a software cost-estimation model is a "garbage in–garbage out" device: if you put poor sizing and attribute-rating data in on one side, you will receive poor cost estimates out the other side.

This situation has two major implications:

1. We need a methodology for using a software cost-estimation model, which will lead us to generate an appropriate set of cost model inputs with respect to our cost-estimation objectives. Chapter 21 provides a seven-step process for accomplishing this.
2. We need to employ other techniques as a check on our use of algorithmic software cost-estimation models. Chapter 22 presents the major alternative techniques available, and evaluates their comparative strengths and weaknesses.

308

Chapter 21

Seven Basic Steps in Software Cost Estimation

To get a reliable software cost estimate, we need to do much more than just put numbers into a formula and accept the results. This chapter provides a seven-step process for software cost estimation, which shows that a software cost estimation activity is a miniproject and should be planned, reviewed, and followed up accordingly.

The seven basic steps are

1. Establish Objectives
2. Plan for Required Data and Resources
3. Pin Down Software Requirements
4. Work Out as Much Detail as Feasible
5. Use Several Independent Techniques and Sources
6. Compare and Iterate Estimates
7. Followup

Each of these steps is discussed in more detail in Sections 21.1 through 21.7.

21.1 STEP 1: ESTABLISH OBJECTIVES

In software cost estimation, a lot of effort can be wasted in gathering information and making estimates on items that have no relevance to the need for the estimate. For example, in one situation, an extremely detailed conversion estimate was made to support a decision on whether or not to upgrade to a different make of computer. The decision required only a general estimate of conversion costs, and when it was decided not to go to a different make of computer, a great deal of hard work and careful analysis was thrown out. Thus, it is extremely important to establish the objectives of the cost estimate as the first step, and to use these objectives to drive the level of detail and effort required to perform the subsequent steps.

Objectives versus Phase, or Level of Knowledge

The main factor that helps us establish our cost-estimation objectives is our current software life-cycle phase. It largely corresponds with our level of knowledge of the software whose costs we are trying to estimate, and also to the level of commitment we will be making as a result of the cost estimate.

Figure 21–1 illustrates the accuracy within which software cost estimates can be made, as a function of the software life-cycle phase (the horizontal axis), or of the level of knowledge we have of what the software is intended to do. This level of uncertainty is illustrated in Fig. 21–1 with respect to a human-machine interface component of the software.

When we first begin to evaluate alternative concepts for a new software application, the relative range of our software cost estimates is roughly a factor of four on either the high or low side.* This range stems from the wide range of uncertainty we have at this time about the actual nature of the product. For the human-machine interface component, for example, we don't know at this time what classes of people (clerks, computer specialists, middle managers, etc.) or what classes of data (raw or pre-edited, numerical or text, digital or analog) the system will have to support. Until we pin down such uncertainties, a factor of four in either direction is not surprising as a range of estimates.

The above uncertainties are indeed pinned down once we complete the feasibility phase and settle on a particular concept of operation. At this stage, the range of our estimates diminishes to a factor of two in either direction. This range is reasonable because we still have not pinned down such issues as the specific types of user query to be supported, or the specific functions to be performed within the microprocessor in the intelligent terminal. These issues will be resolved by the time we have developed a software requirements specification, at which point, we will be able to estimate the software costs within a factor of 1.5 in either direction.

By the time we complete and validate a product design specification, we will have resolved such issues as the internal data structure of the software product and the specific techniques for handling the buffers between the terminal microprocessor

---

*These ranges have been determined subjectively, and are intended to represent 80% confidence limits, that is, "within a factor of four on either side, 80% of the time."

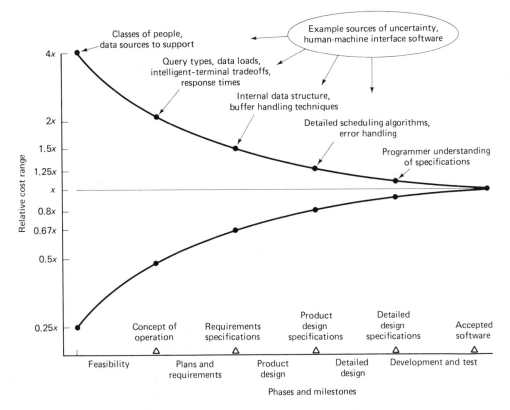

FIGURE 21-1 Software cost estimation accuracy versus phase

and the central processors on one side, and between the microprocessor and the display driver on the other. At this point, our software estimate should be accurate to within a factor of 1.25, the discrepancies being caused by some remaining sources of uncertainty such as the specific algorithms to be used for task scheduling, error handling, abort processing, and the like.* These will be resolved by the end of the detailed design phase, but there will still be a residual uncertainty about 10%, based on how well the programmers really understand the specifications to which they are to code. (This factor also includes such considerations as personnel turnover uncertainties during the development and test phases.)

Estimating Implications

The primary estimating implication of Fig. 21-1 is that we need to be consistent in defining our estimating objectives for the various components of the software product. If our understanding of the human-machine interface is at the concept-of-operation level, for example, it will generally be a waste of effort to define and estimate conversion costs at the detailed-design level. (The exception to this statement is the situation

---

* Within the factor of 1.25 range (80–125%), a good software manager can generally turn a software effort estimate into a self-fulfilling prophecy. See Chapter 32.

in which conversion costs are an order of magnitude larger than the human-machine interface software costs.)

In general, we wish to achieve a *balanced* set of estimating objectives: one in which the absolute magnitude of the uncertainty range for each component is roughly equal. Thus, suppose we have a human-machine interface component of roughly $1,000,000 defined at the requirements-spec level (say, within the range $667,000 to $1,500,000). If we then have a conversion component of roughly $500,000, we can afford to define it at the concept-of-operation level, since the resulting range ($250,000–$1,000,000) is roughly the same magnitude as the range on the human-machine interface component.

Another estimating implication is that *each cost estimate should include an indication of its degree of uncertainty.*

Relative versus Absolute Estimates

In other situations, even a concept-of-operation level conversion estimate may not be necessary. For example, suppose we are making cost estimates to support a make-or-buy decision, and the conversion costs will be roughly the same for each option. Then, for the make-or-buy decision, there is no need to have an estimate of conversion costs at all. Of course, at some subsequent stage, an overall life-cycle cost estimate will be required, including a conversion cost estimate, but at that point, our increased knowledge of the system will make it easier to perform the conversion estimate.

Here, the major concern is to make sure that our estimating objectives are consistent with the needs of the decisionmaker who will use the estimate.* Thus, we are dealing with the same issues—of balancing the cost of obtaining information with the value of the information to a decisionmaker—that we discussed in Chapter 20.

Generous versus Conservative Estimates

Often, in a cost analysis to support a make-or-buy decision or a go/no-go decision on system development, it becomes clear early in the analysis that a particular decision is highly likely to result. In such a situation, we may wish to revise our objectives to try to demonstrate the following:

> Even if we use conservative assumptions for Option A and generous assumptions for Option B, Option A is still the more cost-effective.

This sort of revision has two major benefits. First, it increases our confidence that we are making the right decision. Second, the ability to make generous or conservative assumptions will often simplify our cost-estimation effort. For example, we might assume that a potentially adaptable software component is completely adaptable (generous), or completely unadaptable (conservative), rather than perform an analysis to determine its adaptation adjustment factor (AAF).

From the standpoint of estimation objectives, this means that we should reexamine

---

* For an excellent general treatment of the use of cost information in decisionmaking, see *Cost Considerations in Systems Analysis* [Fisher, 1971].

our objectives as we proceed, and modify them when a change is advantageous (that is, we may begin with a requirements level accuracy objective, but relax it to a generous or conservative concept-of-operation level accuracy objective later in the analysis).

Summary Guidelines

In summary, here are the three major guidelines for establishing the objectives of a cost-estimation activity:

1. *Key the estimating objectives to the needs for decisionmaking information.* (Absolute estimates for labor or resource planning, relative estimates for either/ or decisions, generous or conservative estimates to heighten confidence in the decision.)
2. *Balance the estimating accuracy objectives for the various system components of the cost estimates.* (This means that the absolute magnitude of the uncertainty range for each component should be roughly equal—assuming that such components have equal weight in the decision to be made.)
3. *Re-examine estimating objectives as the process proceeds, and modify them where appropriate.* (A further implication of this guideline is that *budget commitments in the early phases should cover only the next phase.* Once a validated product design is complete, a total development budget may be established without too much risk.)

21.2 STEP 2: PLAN FOR REQUIRED DATA AND RESOURCES

The following scenario is all too common:

> *Rumpled Proposal Manager:* We've got this proposal that has to be signed off by noon so we can get it on the afternoon plane to Washington. Can you work me up a quick software cost estimate for it?
>
> *Software Cost Estimator:* You want it *when???*

Typically, this scenario (and many similar ones) leads to a terribly inaccurate software cost estimate, which becomes cast into an ironclad organizational commitment (usually underpriced) affecting a lot of innocent software people who deserve a much better fate.

If we consider the software cost-estimation activity as a miniproject, then we automatically cover this problem by generating a project plan at an early stage. Table 21–1 shows a simple general form for a project plan which applies quite naturally to the cost-estimating miniproject.

The miniplan doesn't have to be a fancy, detailed document, particularly if your estimating activity is small. But even an informal early set of notes to yourself on the why, what, when, who, where, how, how much, and whereas of your estimating activity will often save your neck, and the necks of all those software people who have to perform to your estimate.

An example software cost-estimation plan to support a feasibility study of a computer-controlled rapid transit system is shown in Fig. 21–2.

TABLE 21–1 Software Cost-Estimating Miniproject Plan

1. *Purpose. Why* is the estimate being made?
2. *Products and Schedules. What* is going to be furnished by *when?*
3. *Responsibilities. Who* is responsible for each product? *Where* are they going to do the job organizationally? geographically?
4. *Procedures. How* is the job going to be done? Which cost-estimation tools and techniques will be used (see Chapter 22)?
5. *Required Resources. How much* data, time, money, effort, etc. is needed to do the job?
6. *Assumptions.* Under what conditions are we promising to deliver the above estimates, given the above resources (availability of key personnel, computer time, user data)?

1. Purpose:
   To help determine the feasibility of a computer-controlled rapid-transit system for the Zenith metropolitan area.

2. Products and Schedules:
   2/1/84 Cost-estimation plan
   2/15/84 First cost model run
   2/22/84 Definitive cost model run
   Expert estimates complete
   2/29/84 Final cost estimate report, incorporating model and expert iterations. Accuracy to within factor of 2.

3. Responsibilities:
   Cost-estimation study: Z.B. Zimmerman
   Cost model support: Application Software Department
   Expert estimators (2): Systems Analysis Department

4. Procedures:
   Project will use SOFTCOST model, with sensitivity analysis on high-leverage cost driver attributes.
   Experts will contact BART personnel in San Francisco and Metro personnel in Washington, D.C. for comparative data.

5. Required Resources:
   Z.B. Zimmerman: 2 man-weeks
   Expert estimators: 3 man-days each
   Computer: $200.

6. Assumptions:
   No major changes to system specification dated 15 January 1984.
   Authors of specification available to answer sizing questions.

FIGURE 21–2 Software cost estimation plan: Zenith rapid transit system

21.3 STEP 3. PIN DOWN SOFTWARE REQUIREMENTS

If we don't know what products we are building, we certainly can't estimate the cost of building them very well. This means that it is important to have a set of software specifications that are as unambiguous as possible (subject to qualifications with respect to our estimating objectives).

The best way to determine to what extent a software specification is *costable* is to determine to what extent it is *testable*.

A specification is testable to the extent that one can define a clear pass/fail test for determining whether or not the developed software will satisfy the specification. In order to be testable, specifications must be specific, unambiguous, and quantitative wherever possible. Below are some examples of specifications which are *not* testable:

- The software shall provide interfaces with the appropriate subsystems.
- The software shall degrade gracefully under stress.
- The software shall be developed in accordance with good development standards.
- The software shall provide the necessary processing under all modes of operation.
- Computer memory utilization shall be optimized to accommodate future growth.
- The software shall provide a 99.9999% assurance of information privacy (or reliability, availability, or human safety, when these terms are undefined).
- The software shall provide accuracy sufficient to support effective flight control.
- The software shall provide real-time response to sales activity queries.

These statements are good as goals and objectives, but they are not precise enough to serve as the basis of a pass-fail acceptance test, or to serve as the basis of an accurate cost estimate. Below are some more testable versions of the last two requirements:

- The software shall compute aircraft position within the following accuracies:
  ±50 feet in the horizontal plane
  ±20 feet in the vertical plane
- The system shall respond to:
  Type A queries in ≤2 sec
  Type B queries in ≤10 sec
  Type C queries in ≤2 min
  where Type A, B, and C queries are defined in detail in the specification.

In many cases, even these versions will not be sufficiently testable without further definition. For example:

- Do the terms "±50 ft" or "≤2 sec" refer to root mean square performance, 90% confidence limits, or never-to-exceed constraints?
- Does "response" time include terminal delays, communications delays, or just the time involved in computer processing?

Thus, it will often require a good deal of added effort to eliminate the vagueness and ambiguity in a specification and make it testable. But such effort is generally well worthwhile, for the following reasons:

- It would have to be done eventually for the test phase anyway.
- Doing it early eliminates a great deal of expense, controversy, and possible bitterness in later stages.
- Doing it early means that we can generate more accurate cost estimates.

In many cases, it will be impossible or infeasible to make sure all of the software requirements are testable (see the discussion in Section 4.3). Or, it may require more effort than we need to satisfy our estimation objectives. In such cases, it is valuable to *document any assumptions* that were made in estimating the cost of developing the software, particularly if they were generous or conservative assumptions as discussed in Step 1.

21.4 STEP 4. WORK OUT AS MUCH DETAIL AS FEASIBLE

"As feasible" here means "as is consistent with our cost-estimating objectives," as discussed in Section 21.1. In general, the more detail to which we carry our estimating activities, the more accurate our estimates will be, for three main reasons

1. The more detail we explore, the better we understand the technical aspects of the software to be developed, as indicated by Fig. 21–1 and its discussion.
2. The more pieces of software we estimate, the more we get the law of large numbers working for us to reduce the variance of the estimate. If we have one large piece of software and overestimate its cost by 20%, we are stuck with a 20% error. If we break the large piece into 10 smaller pieces, we may underestimate on most of the pieces, but overestimate on some, and on balance end up with a considerably smaller estimating error.
3. The more we think through all the functions the software must perform, the less likely we are to miss the costs of some of the more unobtrusive components of the software.

As an example of item 3, Fig. 21–3 shows the results of an experiment in which two teams specified and developed a small (2000-DSI) software product (actually, an interactive early version of the Detailed COCOMO model, performed as a group project in a software engineering class at USC [Boehm, 1980]). The most significant aspect of Fig. 21–3 is that the actual cost model calculations comprised only 2% of the code in one product, and 3% of the code in the other. Much of the remainder of the code was involved with the unobtrusive components of the software, such as help message processing, error processing, and moving data around. These overhead functions are often missed in software sizing and cost estimating. This is one of the

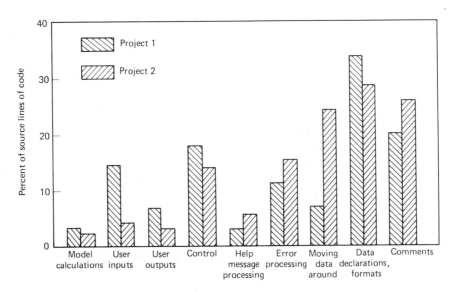

FIGURE 21-3　What does a software product do?

main reasons that software costs are so often underestimated: There is a powerful tendency to focus on the highly visible mainline components of the software, and to underestimate or completely miss the unobtrusive components.

On Software Sizing

It would be convenient if we could provide some software sizing formulas that could say, for example:

If we are developing an operating system which performs the following functions thoroughly, the following functions minimally, and the following functions not at all, then the estimated size of the operating system is 11 ± 2 KDSI.

Unfortunately, quantitative software engineering has not progressed to the point that we can even begin to provide such formulas. And it is not clear that we will ever get very close to such an ideal. Having spent a good deal of time looking at sizing data and the programs they represent, and generally in going around in circles in pursuit of a simplified sizing formula, I would summarize the experience in terms of some analogies.

1. Solving the automatic software sizing problem has a good many of the aspects of solving the automatic programming problem. For example, both require a sufficiently detailed specification of the desired software to assure that some different, undesired neighboring piece of software will not be what is sized or generated. And providing this specification goes a long way toward sizing the software itself.

2. Generating a formula for sizing software has a good many of the aspects of generating a formula for sizing a novel. Both deal with a product capable of virtually unlimited levels of elaboration, and it is difficult to characterize these levels of elaboration in any way related to sizing. Just consider the problem of estimating the number of pages in a novel with

- four characters who influence each others' lives profoundly
- 20 more or less incidental characters
- three different locations
- two years' time span
- five detailed flashbacks

and you begin to get a better appreciation of the software sizing problem. Some further appreciation of this point can be obtained from the sizing data in the [Weinberg-Schulman, 1974] experiment discussed in Chapter 3. In the experiment, six teams were asked to develop the same program (solution of simultaneous linear equations by Gaussian elimination), but were given different objectives to optimize. The resulting programs had a 5:1 variation in size for implementing the same function, as shown below.

Team Objective: Optimize	Program Size (DSI)	Man-Hours	Productivity (DSI/MH)
Program size	33	30	1.1
Memory required	52	74	0.7
Program clarity	90	40	2.2
Execution time	100	50	2.0
Effort to complete	126	28	4.5
Output clarity	166	30	5.5

On the other hand, the software sizing problem doesn't have *all* of the aspects of the automatic programming problem or the novel-sizing problem, so there is some hope of making eventual progress. In the meantime, however, there is no substitute for a detailed understanding of each software component to ensure accurate software sizing.

PERT Sizing

One implication of the discussion above of software sizing is that we should be careful not to make sizing appear easier than it is. One technique which unfortunately does this is the PERT sizing technique discussed in [Putnam–Fitzsimmons, 1979].

The simplest version of this technique involves estimating two quantities

$a =$ The lowest possible* size of the software (say, 22 **KDSI**)
$b =$ The highest possible size of the software (say, 64 **KDSI**)

---

* These formulas are based on the understanding that the low and high estimates a and b represent 3σ (three standard deviation) limits on the probability distribution of the actual software size. For a normal probability distribution, this means that the actual software size would lie between a and b 99.7% of the time.

Then the PERT statistical equations estimate the expected size of the software as

$$E = \frac{a+b}{2} = 43 \text{ KDSI}$$

and the standard deviation of the estimate as*

$$\sigma = \frac{b-a}{6} = 7 \text{ KDSI}$$

This means that 68% of the time, the actual size of the software should fall between 36 and 50 KDSI (and that about 16% of the time each, the actual size should fall between the ranges 22–36 KDSI and 50–64 KDSI).

These formulas are based on the assumption of a normal distribution of sizes between the two extremes a and b. However, anyone familiar with current software practice will recognize that if the upper limit b is 64 KDSI because this is the maximum amount of code that will fit in the machine, there is much more than a 16% chance that the final size of the software will be between 50 KDSI and 64 KDSI.

A somewhat better PERT sizing technique discussed in [Putnam–Fitzsimmons, 1979] is one based on a beta distribution and on the separate estimation of individual software components. Here, three sizing quantities are generated for each component:

a_i = The lowest possible size of the software component
m_i = The most likely size of the component
b_i = The highest possible size of the component

The PERT equations estimate the expected size E_i and standard deviation σ_i of each component as

$$E_i = \frac{a_i + 4m_i + b_i}{6} \qquad \sigma_i = \frac{b_i - a_i}{6}$$

The estimated total software size E and standard deviation σE are then

$$E = \sum_{i=1}^{n} E_i, \qquad \sigma E = \left(\sum_{i=1}^{n} \sigma_i^2 \right)^{1/2}$$

For example, suppose we are estimating the size of the software to be developed for a 64K-word microprocessor point-of-sale terminal. The individual estimates and resulting overall estimates are shown in Table 21–2.

This PERT sizing technique is somewhat better in that it requires more thought to break up the software into components and to estimate most likely sizes for each component as well as upper and lower limits. Again, however, the calculation of

TABLE 21-2 Example of PERT Sizing Technique

Component	a_i	m_i	b_i	E_i	σ_i
SALES	6K	10K	20K	11K	2.33K
DISPLAY	4	7	13	7.5	1.5
INEDIT	8	12	19	12.5	1.83
TABLES	4	8	12	8	1.33
TOTALS	22	37	64	39	$\sigma E = 3.6$

σE is highly misleading, as it assumes that the estimates are unbiased toward either underestimation or overestimation. Current experience, however, indicates that "most likely" estimates tend to cluster more toward the lower limit than the upper limit,* while actual product sizes tend to cluster more toward the upper limit, imparting a significant underestimation bias to PERT results.

In this example, the estimated σE implies that there is a 68% chance that the actual size of the microprocessor point-of-sale software will be between 35.4K and 42.6K words, and that sizes between 49.8K and 64K words would only occur 0.15% of the time. Again, experience to date would lead us to expect these larger sizes to be a much more frequent occurrence than this.

Why Do People Underestimate Software Size?

The software undersizing problem is our most critical road block to accurate software cost estimation. Software cost models, like other computer models, are "garbage in–garbage out" devices: put a too-small sizing estimate in, and you will get a too-small cost estimate out.

Our discussion of sizing formulas above should convince us that there are no magic formulas that we can use to overcome the software undersizing problem. In the absence of any such formula, it is important to understand the major sources of the software undersizing problem, for it is only from understanding them that we will be able to overcome them.

Current experience indicates that there are three main reasons why people underestimate software size. These are:

1. *People are basically optimistic and desire to please.* Everybody would like the software to be small and easy. High estimates lead to confrontation situations, which people generally prefer to avoid. This phenomenon is not limited to software sizing. Figure 21–4, from [Augustine, 1979], displays the estimated completion times versus the actual completion times for about 100 recent

---

* Most people tend to follow a geometric progression in making "most likely" estimates, rather than an arithmetic progression or something even more pessimistic. Thus, given low and high limits of 16K and 64K, people are more likely to choose the geometric mean of 32K as their "most likely" estimate, rather than the arithmetic mean of 40K, and very rarely choose a "most likely" estimate of 48K or higher.

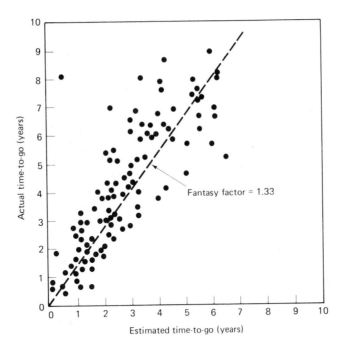

FIGURE 21-4 Accuracy of projecting accomplishment date for major milestones

official schedule estimates within the Department of Defense, showing a fairly consistent "fantasy factor" of about 1.33.

2. *People tend to have incomplete recall of previous experience.* In terms of the distribution of source code by function in Fig. 21-3, for example, people tend to have a strong recollection of the primary application software functions to be developed—the 2 to 3% of the product devoted to model calculations in Fig. 21-3—and a much weaker recollection of the large amount of user-interface and housekeeping software that must also be developed.*

3. *People are generally not familiar with the entire software job.* This factor tends to interact with the incomplete-recall factor to produce underestimates of the more obscure software products to be developed as well as of the more obscure portions of each product. A major example is a strong tendency to underestimate the size of support software, which for large operational systems is generally three to five times as large as the operational software. Some typical comparative sizes for large operational systems are given in Table 21-3. Although the sizing is in different units between projects and even displays a variability between two summaries of the same project (Safeguard), the general pattern of the results is fairly consistent. As indicated in the final column, a typical very large (500 KDSI) operational system will contain

* A similar underestimating phenomenon holds for estimating software development activity; see Section 22.7.

TABLE 21-3 The Preponderance of Support Software on Very Large Systems

System Type of Software	Safeguard [Asch and others, 1975] K words	Safeguard [Stephenson, 1976] KDSI	BMD-STP [Distaso and others, 1979] KDEMI	TSQ-73 [Asch and others, 1975] KDEMI	AWACS [Asch and others, 1975] KDEMI	SAGE [Sackman, 1967] KDEMI	Typical Very Large System KDSI
Operational	653	789	276	20	280	200	100
On-site support (maintenance and diagnostics)	630 (.96)	100+ (.13+)		30 (1.50)			100 (1.0)
Development support (compilers, tools, utilities)	913 (1.40)	532 (.67)	525 (1.90)	40 (2.00)	1190 (4.24)	430 (2.15)	150 (1.5)
Off-site support (simulation, data reduction, training)	835 (1.28)	840 (1.06)	751 (2.72)	5 (.25)	244 (.87)	430 (2.15)	150 (1.5)
Total Nonoperational	2378 (3.64)	1472+ (1.87+)	1276+ (4.62+)	75 (3.75)	1434 (5.12)	860+ (4.30+)	400 (4.0)
TOTAL	3031	2261+	1552+	95	1747	1060+	500

NOTE: (x): size is x times size of operational software.
 y+: size is at least as large as y.
KDEMI: thousands of delivered, executable machine instructions.

322

only about 100 KDSI of mission-oriented operational software, with another 100 KDSI of hardware and system-related maintenance and diagnostic software, 150 KDSI of development support software (compilers, tools, utilities, etc.), and a final 150 KDSI of mission-oriented support software (simulation, data reduction, and training software).

In summary, then, there is no royal road to software sizing. There is no substitute for a thorough understanding of the software job to be done; a thorough understanding of our basic tendencies to underestimate software size; and a thoughtful, realistic application of this understanding to our software sizing activities.

21.5 STEP 5: USE SEVERAL INDEPENDENT TECHNIQUES AND SOURCES

Chapter 22 will discuss the major classes of techniques available for software cost estimating. They are

1. Algorithmic Models
2. Expert Judgment
3. Analogy
4. Parkinson
5. Price-to-Win
6. Top-Down
7. Bottom-Up

The main conclusions of Chapter 22 are

- None of the alternatives is better than the others from all aspects
- Their strengths and weaknesses are complementary

Therefore, it is important to use a combination of techniques, in order to avoid the weaknesses of any single method and to capitalize on their joint strengths. An excellent example of practical experience in surveying and using a combination of software cost estimation techniques on a large contract software procurement is given in [Lasher, 1979].

21.6 STEP 6: COMPARE AND ITERATE ESTIMATES

The most valuable aspect of using several independent cost-estimation techniques is the opportunity to investigate why they give different estimates. Thus, if a bottom-up technique estimated a software cost of $4 million, and a top-down technique estimated at $7 million, we could probe into the reasons for the difference by identifying the components of the cost in each and pinning down the differences in detail.

For example, we might find that the bottom-up technique had overlooked system level activities such as integration, configuration management, and quality assurance, while the top-down technique had included these but overlooked some postprocessing software components included in the bottom-up estimate. An iteration of the two estimates may converge to a more realistic estimate of $8 million rather than some arbitrary compromise between $4 million and $7 million. Thus, it is important not just to perform independent estimates, but also to investigate why they produce different results.[a]

The Optimist/Pessimist Phenomenon

There are two other major reasons to iterate a cost estimate: the optimist/pessimist phenomenon, and the "tall pole in the tent" phenomenon.

In multicomponent estimates, one often finds very similar components with strikingly different cost-per-instruction estimates. This is often because personal differences cause some people to be highly optimistic about estimates and others to be highly pessimistic. Often, also, the differences are due to the person's role and incentives. A proposal manager, who is rewarded for winning the job, is more likely to be optimistic. A project or line manager, who is rewarded for performing the job within budget, is more likely to be pessimistic.

Because of this phenomenon, it is valuable to include some overlap in the software components estimated by different people, and to calibrate the relative optimism and pessimism of different estimators.

The Tall Pole in the Tent Phenomenon

In most multicomponent estimates, there are one or two components whose costs stand out as tall poles in the tent, often containing the majority of the software costs.[b] In such cases, it is particularly important to examine and iterate these components in greater detail than the others.

These components tend to be the larger ones in size, and are frequently overestimated with respect to complexity. First, there is a tendency for people to equate size with complexity, whereas most cost models (including COCOMO) define complexity as an inherent attribute of the code which is independent of size. Second, there is a tendency for people to rate the complexity of a component as the complexity of the hardest part in it. Large components often have a great deal of simple housekeeping code included, which easily becomes overestimated with respect to its complexity. Both of these tendencies should be checked as part of the review and iteration of the cost estimate.

[a] The need to investigate differences between estimates is the main reason why it is so important for an algorithmic cost model to be *constructive*. A constructive estimate makes it easy and clear to reviewers why the model gave the results it did. Otherwise, there is no way to compare algorithmic cost model estimates with other types of estimates. Constructiveness has been a paramount objective for the COCOMO model.

[b] Often, the estimates follow "Pareto's Law," which in this context is expressed as "80% of the cost is contained in 20% of the components."

Some Useful Review Questions

In reviewing a software cost estimate upon which a development budget will be based, it is important that we obtain a clear understanding of the estimate's soundness and degree of optimism. With respect to the estimation accuracy versus phase graph in Fig. 21–1, if we accept an estimate as a relatively sound requirements specification level estimate (within a factor of 1.5) when it is actually only an early feasibility estimate (within a factor of four), we are likely to encounter some unpleasant surprises and budget renegotiations later on. We are likely to encounter similar surprises if we accept an optimistic estimate (near the lower boundary curve in Fig. 21–1) as our budgetary estimate for the project.

Here are some review questions whose answers help us to judge the relative soundness of a software cost estimate (that is, how far to the right or left in Fig. 21–1).

1. How would the estimated cost change if
   (a) there was a big change in the (human-machine, data communications, inventory system, etc.) interface?
   (b) we had to supply a more extensive (data base query, maintenance and diagnostic, trend analysis, etc.) capability?
   (c) our workload estimates were off by a factor of two?
   (d) We had to do the job on a (smaller, different, distributed, etc.) computer configuration?
2. Suppose our budget were 20% (less, greater). How would this affect the product?
3. How does the cost of the (user interface, data base management, process control, etc.) subsystem break down by component?

If the answers to such questions are vague and general ("Oh, that wouldn't impact the cost much") or are unaccompanied by any rationale ("Adding that capability would cost you $200,000"), then we need to treat the estimates as very preliminary, early figures which may change a great deal as we proceed to define the software in more detail.

Here are some review questions whose answers help us judge the relative *optimism* of a software cost estimate (that is, how far up or down in Fig. 21–1).

1. How do the following compare with our past experience
   (a) sizing of subsystems?
   (b) cost driver attribute ratings?
   (c) cost per instruction?
   (d) assumptions about adaptation, vendor software, key personnel, etc.?
2. Has a cost–risk analysis been performed? If so, what are the high risk items, and how well are they covered?
3. Suppose we had enough money to really do this job right. How much would we need?

21.7 STEP 7: FOLLOWUP

Once a software project is started, it is essential to gather data on its actual costs and progress and compare these to the estimates. Here are a number of reasons why this is essential.

1. Software estimating inputs are imperfect (sizing estimates, cost driver ratings). If a project finds a difference between estimated and actual costs which can be explained by improved knowledge of the cost drivers, it is important for the project manager to update the cost estimate with the new knowledge, providing a more realistic basis for continuing to manage the project.
2. Software estimating techniques are imperfect. For long-range improvements, we need to compare estimates to actuals and use the results to improve the estimating techniques.
3. Some projects do not exactly fit the estimating model (for example, in time-phasing the costs of incremental development). Both near-term project-management feedback and long-term model-improvement feedback of any estimates-versus-actuals differences are important here.
4. Software projects tend to be volatile: components are added, split up, rescoped, or combined in unforeseeable ways as the project progresses. Again, the project manager needs to identify these changes and generate a more realistic update of the estimated upcoming costs.
5. Software is an evolving field. Estimating techniques are all calibrated on previous projects, which may not have featured structured programming, automated aids, specification languages, microprocessors, or distributed data processing. For both short- and long-term purposes, it is important to sense differences due to these trends and incorporate them into improved project estimates and improved estimating techniques.

A detailed treatment of software project planning and control followup techniques is given in Chapter 32. Techniques for ongoing project data collection and analysis are given in Appendix A. A simple followup technique, the cost-schedule-milestone chart, is illustrated below.

The Cost-Schedule-Milestone Chart

A simple but highly useful technique for comparing estimates to actuals is the cost-schedule-milestone chart. An example is shown in Fig. 21–5, using a basic, embedded-mode, 32-KDSI software project as an example. It shows the estimated number of months and man-months required to achieve four major project milestones

SRR Software requirements review (4.5 months, 18 MM)
PDR Product design review (9.3 months, 60 MM)
UTC Unit test completion (15.9 months, 184 MM)
SAR Software acceptance review (18.5 months, 248 MM)

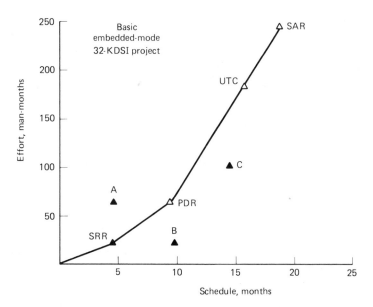

FIGURE 21-5 Cost-schedule-milestone chart

Starting with these estimates, the project manager can plot the actual cost and schedule associated with the achievement of these milestones. If there is a significant difference between the estimates and the actuals, there is a basis for investigating and taking corrective action.

For example, three possible points *A, B,* and *C* are shown in Fig. 21-5, representing projects whose achievement of a product design review (PDR) occurs at significantly different cost-schedule points than the 9.3 months and 60 man-months estimated.

Project A has taken about the right amount of effort, but has reached PDR considerably ahead of schedule. Its personnel loading is considerably higher than usual for such projects. This may be because the product is easy to segment into a number of pieces which can be usefully worked by a larger number of analysts than the usual product. In this case, the project manager can revise the estimates by simply advancing the project schedule. On the other hand, the project may have succumbed to the temptation to bring a lot of people on-board early, and the PDR milestone may not be as thoroughly satisfied as it should have been.* This is one possibility that the project manager needs to investigate before proceeding much further.

Project B has taken about the right amount of time to reach PDR, but has not used the estimated amount of labor. This may be because the job has been redefined in scope to be a simpler job (less work to define, but more time consumed in renegotiation), in which case the project manager can re-estimate a lower cost to complete. Or, it may mean that the project has experienced problems in staffing up, and has not fully achieved PDR, which again the project manager needs to investigate as a possibility.

* See Table 4–1 for a summary of what a software project needs to complete by PDR.

Project C has taken considerably more schedule *and* labor to achieve **PDR**. This may be for any of the five reasons discussed at the beginning of this section. Here again, the project manager needs to find out which of these reasons have caused the discrepancy before an appropriate course can be charted for the remainder of the project.

21.8 QUESTIONS

21.1. Consider a project which cost $4 million to develop. What was the range of uncertainty of its estimated cost at SRR (requirements specification available)? At **PDR** (product design specification available)?

21.2. What are the three major guidelines for establishing the objectives of a software cost-estimation activity? What are the seven basic steps in software cost estimation?

21.3. Suppose we have defined a $2 million electric power distribution software component to the product design level. For an overall project cost proposal, we need an estimate of the diagnostic and support software, which is roughly in the $500,000 cost range. Based on Fig. 21–1, to what level do we need to define the diagnostic and support software to achieve a balanced overall estimate of the total product cost?

21.4. Prepare a miniproject plan for estimating the costs of developing a compiler, data base management system, or some other software product with which you are familiar.

21.5. Suppose you were the project manager on the project illustrated in Fig. 21–5, and you reach your PDR milestone with an expended schedule of 6 months and an expended effort of 30 MM. What possibilities should you investigate to explain the difference between the actual and estimated schedule and budget, and what steps should you take as a project manager if a given possibility was true?

21.6. Work Question 21.5 given that the actual schedule to PDR was 9.5 months and the actual effort 110 MM.

21.7. *(Research Project)* Test the hypothesis that the distribution of source code by function in Fig. 21–3 is the same for all software products, by compiling comparable distributions for other products. If the hypothesis is false, prepare and test an improved hypothesis.

21.8. *(Research Project)* Develop and investigate improved methods of software product sizing. *Note:* Such investigations are more likely to be productive if restricted to a particular application domain: for example, compilers, payroll systems, software tools (refer to Table 27–9).

Chapter 22

Alternative Software Cost-Estimation Methods

A number of methods have been used to estimate software costs. They include

1. *Algorithmic Models.* These methods provide one or more algorithms which produce a software cost estimate as a function of a number of variables which are considered to be the major cost drivers. COCOMO is an example of an algorithmic model.
2. *Expert Judgment.* This method involves consulting one or more experts, perhaps with the aid of an expert-consensus mechanism such as the Delphi technique.
3. *Analogy.* This method involves reasoning by analogy with one or more completed projects to relate their actual costs to an estimate of the cost of a similar new project.
4. *Parkinson.* A Parkinson principle ("Work expands to fill the available volume") is invoked to equate the cost estimate to the available resources.
5. *Price to Win.* The cost estimate developed by this method is equated to the

price believed necessary to win the job (or the schedule believed necessary to be first in the market with a new product, etc.).

6. *Top-Down.* An overall cost estimate for the project is derived from global properties of the software product. The total cost is then split up among the various components.

7. *Bottom-Up.* Each component of the software job is separately estimated, and the results aggregated to produce an estimate for the overall job.

The strengths and weaknesses of each of these techniques are discussed in the sections below. The chapter ends with a set of conclusions regarding the use of these techniques.

22.1 ALGORITHMIC MODELS

Algorithmic models provide one or more mathematical algorithms which produce a software cost estimate as a function of a number of variables considered to be the major cost drivers. The most common forms of algorithms to be used for software cost estimation are

- Linear models
- Multiplicative models
- Analytic models
- Tabular models
- Composite models

Each of these types is discussed in turn, followed by a summary of the general strengths and weaknesses of algorithmic models.*

Linear Models

A linear cost estimating model has the form

$$\text{Effort} = a_0 + a_1 x_1 + \cdots + a_n x_n$$

where $x_1, \ldots, x_n$ are the cost driver variables, and $a_0, \ldots, a_n$ are a set of coefficients chosen to provide the best fit to a set of observed data points. The development cost is generally obtained by multiplying the *effort* quantity by a constant cost for labor.

This is the type of model used in the large, pioneering software cost-estimation study performed by System Development Corporation in the mid-1960s [Nelson, 1966]. This study investigated over 100 candidate cost drivers, using 169 project data points, a larger sample than any other set of data points available today. The best linear model obtained from the data was a 13-variable model with a mean estimate of 40 man-months and a standard deviation of 62 man-months; not a very accurate

---

* A discussion of individual cost models is given in Section 29.7.

predictor. The best conclusion we can draw from this result is that there are too many nonlinear interactions in software development for a linear model to work very well.

Multiplicative Models

A multiplicative cost-estimating model has the form

$$\text{Effort} = a_0 a_1^{x_1} a_2^{x_2} \dots a_n^{x_n}$$

where $x_1, \dots, x_n$ are again the cost driver variables, and $a_0, \dots, a_n$ are a set of coefficients chosen to best fit the observational data.

This is the type of model used in the IBM Walston–Felix analysis [Walston–Felix, 1977], in which the cost driver variables were constrained to the values -1, 0, and 1; and in the Doty model [Herd and others, 1977], in which the cost driver variables can assume only the values 0 and 1.

The multiplicative form of the model appears to work reasonably well if the variables chosen are reasonably independent (otherwise, one has problems with double counting of costs and interaction effects). The constraint that variables assume only values such as -1, 0, and 1 makes for somewhat unstable models; the cost estimates can change only in large steps. For example, the Doty estimate is multiplied by $1.83^1 = 1.83$ if there is concurrent development of computer hardware, and by $1.83^0 = 1.0$ if not; there are no intermediate multipliers.

Analytic Models

An analytic model takes the more general mathematical form

$$\text{Effort} = f(x_1, \dots, x_n)$$

where $x_1, \dots, x_n$ are again the cost driver variables, and f is some mathematical function other than linear or multiplicative.

For example, the Halstead model [Halstead, 1977] takes the form

$$\text{Effort} = \frac{\eta_1 N_2 N \log_2 \eta}{2 S \eta_2}$$

where η_1 is the number of distinct operators in the program; η_2 is the number of distinct operands; $\eta = \eta_1 + \eta_2$; N_2 is the total usage of all operands in program; N is the total usage of all operators and operands; and $S = 18$, approximately.

As another example, the [Putnam, 1978] model takes the form

$$S_s = C_k K^{1/3} t_d^{4/3}$$

where S_s is the software product size, C_k is a constant, K is the development effort in man-years, and t_d is the development time in years.

To date, the analytic models which have been developed contain only a small number of variables. Thus they are insensitive to a number of factors (for example, hardware constraints) which are often critical determinants of software cost.

Tabular Models

Tabular models contain a number of tables which relate the values of cost driver variables either to portions of the software development effort, or to multipliers used to adjust the effort estimate. The Aron model [Aron, 1969] consists of a simple 3×3 table relating development effort to project duration and project difficulty. The Wolverton model [Wolverton, 1974] estimates development effort as a tabular function of type of software, difficulty, and novelty. The Boeing model [Black and others, 1977] estimates a basic productivity rate as a tabular function of the type of software, and modifies the productivity rate by multipliers obtained as tabular functions of other cost drivers such as language, project size, novelty, etc.

Tabular models are generally easy to understand and implement, and are also easy to modify based on new cost driver insights. They may run into some difficulties based on the number of cost driver variables used in the tables. If only a small number of variables is used, the model will be insensitive to some important cost drivers. If a large number of variables is used, the model will have an even larger number of table values to calibrate, requiring a large data base for thorough model calibration and validation.

Composite Models

Composite models incorporate a combination of linear, multiplicative, analytic, and tabular functions to estimate software effort as a function of cost driver variables. Two commercially available software cost models, the RCA PRICE S model [Freiman–Park, 1979] and the Putnam SLIM model [Putnam–Fitzsimmons, 1979] are evidently composite models, although most of their internal details have not been published (some of the details of the SLIM model have been described in [Putnam, 1978]). The TRW SCEP model [Boehm–Wolverton, 1978] and the COCOMO model are also composite models.

Composite models have the advantage of using the most appropriate functional form for each component of the cost estimate. Their main difficulties are that they are more complicated to learn and to use by hand (this is the main reason that COCOMO provides simpler Basic and Intermediate versions as well as a Detailed version) and that they require more data and effort to calibrate and validate.

General Strengths and Weaknesses
of Algorithmic Models

Compared to other estimation methods, algorithmic models have a number of strengths. They are objective, and not influenced by such factors as a desire to win, desire to please, or distaste for the project. They are repeatable; you can ask them the same question a week later and get the same answer. They are efficient and able to support a family of estimates or a sensitivity analysis. And they are objectively calibrated to previous experience.

On the other hand, algorithmic models have several weaknesses. Since they are calibrated to previous projects, it is always an open question to what extent these projects are representative of future projects using new techniques, using new computer system architectures, dealing with new application areas, etc. They are unable to deal with exceptional conditions, particularly exceptional personnel, exceptional project teamwork, or exceptional matches (or mismatches) between the project personnel and the job to be done. And, like any other model, there is no way the model can compensate for poor sizing inputs and inaccurate cost driver ratings.

22.2 EXPERT JUDGMENT

Expert judgment techniques involve consulting with one or more experts, who use their experience and understanding of the proposed project to arrive at an estimate of its cost. The strengths and weaknesses of these methods are highly complementary to the strengths and weaknesses of algorithmic models.

On the strong side, an expert's judgment is able to factor in the differences between past project experiences and the new techniques, architectures, or applications involved in the future project. The expert can also factor in exceptional personnel characteristics and interactions, or other unique project considerations.

On the weak side, expert judgment is no better than the expertise and objectivity of the estimator, who may be biased, optimistic, pessimistic, or unfamiliar with key aspects of the project. It is difficult to strike a balance between the quick response expert estimate (timely, efficient, but hard to calibrate and rationalize), and the thorough, well-documented group-consensus estimate (soundly based and analyzable, but highly time consuming—and difficult to do all over again the following week when the specifications have changed somewhat).

Group Consensus Techniques: Delphi

Because of the many possible causes of bias in individual experts (optimist, pessimist, desire to win, desire to please, political), it is preferable to obtain estimates from more than one expert.

If estimates are obtained from a number of experts, there are a number of ways to combine them into a single estimate. One is simply to compute the mean or median estimate of all the individual estimates. This method is quick, but subject to adverse bias by one or two extreme estimates.

Another method is to hold a group meeting for as long as is necessary to get the experts to converge on, or at least agree to, a single estimate. This method has the advantage of filtering out uninformed estimates in general, but it has two main drawbacks. One is that group members may be overly influenced by the more glib and assertive members. The other is that group members may be overly influenced by figures of authority or political considerations.

One technique that has been used to avoid the drawbacks of the group meeting is the Delphi technique [Helmer, 1966]. This technique was originated at The Rand Corporation in 1948 as a means of predicting future occurrences (hence the name, which comes from the location of the ancient Greek oracle), and has since been used as an expert-consensus method in various other applications such as corporate planning and cost estimation. Table 22–1 shows the steps involved in the standard Delphi technique. It has been used in various software cost-estimating activities, including estimation of factors influencing software costs [Scott–Simmons, 1974].

TABLE 22–1 Standard Delphi Technique for Cost Estimation

1. Coordinator presents each expert with a specification and a form upon which to record estimates.
2. Experts fill out forms anonymously. They may ask questions of the coordinator, but should not discuss the situation with each other.
3. Coordinator prepares a summary of the experts' responses on a form requesting another iteration of the experts' estimate, and the rationale behind the estimate (see Fig. 22–1).
4. Experts fill out forms, again anonymously, and the process is iterated for as many rounds as appropriate.
5. No group discussion is to take place during the entire process.

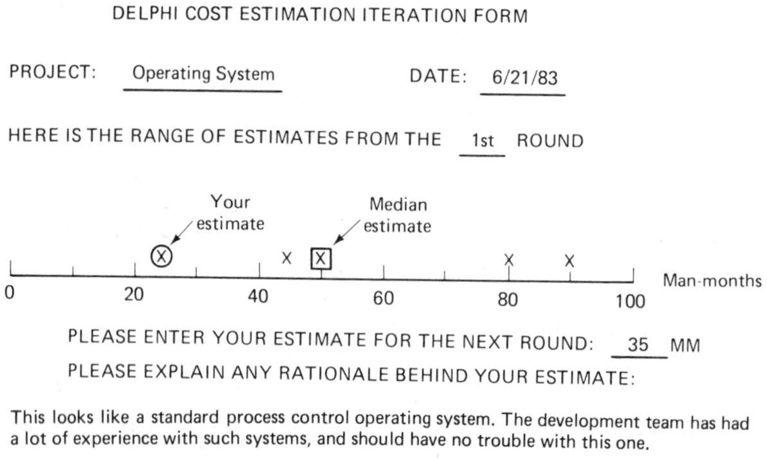
DELPHI COST ESTIMATION ITERATION FORM
PROJECT: Operating System
DATE: 6/21/83
HERE IS THE RANGE OF ESTIMATES FROM THE 1st ROUND
Your estimate
Median estimate
0
20
40
60
80
100
Man-months
PLEASE ENTER YOUR ESTIMATE FOR THE NEXT ROUND: 35 MM
PLEASE EXPLAIN ANY RATIONALE BEHIND YOUR ESTIMATE:
This looks like a standard process control operating system. The development team has had a lot of experience with such systems, and should have no trouble with this one.

FIGURE 22–1 Typical Delphi iteration form

A Delphi/Group Meeting Software Cost-Estimation Experiment

In 1970, an experiment was performed at The Rand Corporation to determine the relative merits of Delphi and group meeting techniques for estimating software costs [Farquhar, 1970]. Four groups were given the same software specification (for a large Air Force information system), which had taken 489 man-months to develop. Two groups used the standard Delphi technique, and two groups used a standard half-day group meeting to arrive at a joint estimate. The Delphi groups did achieve an impressive convergence of some initially diverse estimates, but their results were considerably less accurate than the group meeting results as shown below:

	Delphi	Group
Experiment A	217	485
Experiment B	1090	656
Actual:		489

The extremely accurate estimate produced by the group meeting in Experiment A is an example of a group doing all the wrong things and still coming out extremely well (perhaps by coincidence). The group was dominated by a fairly assertive individual who proposed a Parkinsonian (see Section 22.4) solution: "Since there were 20 people available, they were all used full-time, and they must have finished in two years, because projects either finish in two years or they don't finish at all." This led the group to a very close estimate of 485 man-months in this instance, but subsequent attempts to apply such a method have been quite inaccurate.

The Wideband Delphi Technique

In reviewing the results of this experiment, Farquhar and I concluded that the written feedback in the standard Delphi technique did not provide a sufficiently broad communications bandwidth for the participants to exchange the volume of information necessary to calibrate their estimates with those of the other participants. This led to the formulation of an alternative method, which we called the Wideband Delphi technique, and which is summarized in Table 22–2.

TABLE 22–2 Wideband Delphi Technique

1. Coordinator presents each expert with a specification and an estimation form.
2. Coordinator calls a group meeting in which the experts discuss estimation issues with the coordinator and each other.
3. Experts fill out forms anonymously.
4. Coordinator prepares and distributes a summary of the estimates on an iteration form (similar to Fig. 22–1, but excluding the written rationale).
5. Coordinator calls a group meeting, specifically focusing on having the experts discuss points where their estimates varied widely.
6. Experts fill out forms, again anonymously, and Steps 4 to 6 are iterated for as many rounds as appropriate.

The Wideband Delphi technique has subsequently been used in a number of studies and cost estimation activities, for example, [Boehm and others, 1974]. It has been highly successful in combining the free discussion advantages of the group meeting technique and the advantages of anonymous estimation of the standard Delphi technique.

22.3 ESTIMATION BY ANALOGY

Estimation by analogy involves reasoning by analogy with one or more completed projects to relate their actual costs to an estimate of the cost of a similar new project. It is equivalent to the similarities and differences estimating technique discussed in [Wolverton, 1974].

As an example, one might say, "This environmental impact report generator for Oregon is similar to the one we developed for Florida last year for $1,200,000. The Oregon system has about 30% more types of reports than the Florida system had, so we'll add $360,000 to cover them. On the other hand, we'll be using many of the same people, so we can reduce the estimate by about 20%, or $240,000, to account for the time we spent getting up the learning curve on the Florida project. Also, we can save probably another 20% by reusing some of the low level report generation modules and most of the pollution model software, for another reduction of $240,000. Thus, our cost will probably be around

$$\$1,200K + \$360K - \$240K - \$240K = \$1,080K."$$

Estimating by analogy can be done either at the total project level or at a subsystem level. The total project level has the advantage that all components of the system cost will be considered (such as including the costs of integrating the subsystems), while the subsystem level has the advantage of providing a more detailed assessment of the similarities and differences between the new project and the completed projects.

The main strength of estimation by analogy is that the estimate is based on actual experience on a project. This experience can be studied to determine specific differences from the new project, and their likely cost impact. The main weakness of estimation by analogy is that it is not clear to what degree the previous project is actually representative of the constraints, techniques, personnel, and functions to be performed by the software on the new project.

22.4 PARKINSONIAN ESTIMATION

Parkinson's Law [Parkinson, 1957] says, "Work expands to fill the available volume." A Parkinsonian estimate takes the form

This flight control software must fit on a 65,536-word machine; therefore, its size will be roughly 65,000 words. It must be done in 18 months, and there are 10 people available to work on it, so the job will take roughly 180 man-months.

In some cases, a Parkinsonian estimate has turned out to be remarkably accurate. These have generally been cases in which the estimate left a good deal of extra time and money to continue adding marginally useful "bells and whistles" to the software until the budget ran out, at which point the software was declared complete. Even in these cases, it is not clear that this final embellishment phase made the best use of the people involved on the project.

There have been other cases in which the Parkinsonian estimate has been grossly inaccurate. An example is the flight control software estimate above; by the time the project was finished, it had added another 65,536-word on-board computer to accommodate the 127,000 words of software actually developed, and it required a total of 32 months and 550 man-months.

Parkinsonian estimation is not recommended. Besides not being particularly accurate, it tends to reinforce poor software development practice.

22.5 PRICE-TO-WIN ESTIMATING

Here are some examples of price-to-win estimating:

> *I know the cost model estimated $2 million for this job, and none of our experts believe we can do it for less than a million and a half. But I also know that the customer has only $1 million budgeted for this software contract, so that's what we're gonna bid. Now go and fix up the cost estimate and make it look credible.*

> *We absolutely have to announce this product at the National Computer Conference next June, and here it is September already. That means we've got 9 months to get the software ready.*

The price-to-win technique has won a large number of software contracts for a large number of software companies. Almost all of them are out of business today. The inevitable result is that the money or schedule runs out before the job is done, everybody gets mad at each other, a lot of compromises are made about the software to be delivered, and a lot of programmers work long hours just trying to keep the job from becoming a complete disaster.

The main reason that the price-to-win technique continues to be used is because the technology of software cost estimation has not provided powerful enough techniques to enable software customers or software developers to convincingly differentiate between a legitimate estimate and a price-to-win estimate. One of the primary objectives of the COCOMO model is to begin to provide a way for people to make these differentiations. It is possible to make the COCOMO model give you a lower cost estimate, but *only by changing some objectively defined cost driver rating*, whose validity can be checked by someone other than the estimator.

22.6 TOP-DOWN ESTIMATING

In top-down estimating, an overall cost estimate for the project is derived from the global properties of the software product. The total cost is then split up among the various components.

Top-down (and bottom-up) estimating can be done in conjunction with any of the methods discussed above. The examples given for analogy, Parkinsonian, and price-to-win estimating are also examples of top-down estimating.

The major advantage of top-down estimating is its system level focus. To the extent that the estimate is based on previous experience on entire completed projects, it will not miss the costs of system level functions such as integration, users' manuals, configuration management, etc.

The major disadvantages of top-down estimating are that it often does not identify difficult low level technical problems that are likely to escalate costs; that it sometimes misses components of the software to be developed; that it provides no detailed basis for cost justification and iteration; and that it is less stable than a multicomponent estimate, in which estimation errors in the components have a chance to balance out [Wolverton, 1974].

22.7 BOTTOM-UP ESTIMATING

In the usual bottom-up estimate, the cost of each software component is estimated by an individual, often the person who will be responsible for developing the component. These costs are then summed to arrive at an estimated cost for the overall product.

Bottom-up estimating is complementary to top-down estimating, in that its weaknesses tend to be top-down's strengths, and vice versa. Thus, the bottom-up estimate tends to cover just the costs associated with developing individual components, and to overlook many of the system level costs (integration, configuration management, quality assurance, project management) associated with software development. Bottom-up estimates are often underestimated as a result.

A bottom-up estimate also requires more effort than does a top-down estimate, but in many respects this is an advantage. In particular, having each part of the job costed by the person responsible for its success will be very helpful in two main ways.

1. Each estimate will be based on a more detailed understanding of the job to be done.
2. Each estimate will be backed up by the personal commitment of the individual responsible for the job.

Further, a bottom-up estimate tends to be more stable, in that the estimation errors in the various components have a chance to balance out.

The most effective way to ensure that system level costs are included in a bottom-up estimate is to organize the software job into a work breakdown structure (WBS) which includes not only the product hierarchy of software product components but also the activity hierarchy of project jobs to be done (see Chapter 4, Figs. 4–6a and b). This ensures that the costs of such activities as integration and configuration management are included. However, unless their estimates can be delayed until the estimates for the product components are established, they may be inaccurate; for example, it is difficult to estimate integration costs without a good idea of the size and nature of the components to be integrated.

The Task-Unit Approach to Software Cost Estimation

The traditional approach to software cost estimation, and the one used most frequently for bottom-up estimation, is the task-unit approach. In this approach, the job of developing a software component is broken up into task units. The effort required for each task unit is estimated, generally by the component developer, and the resulting estimates summed to produce the overall effort estimate for the software component. An example is given in Fig. 22–2.

The major advantages of the task-unit approach are those of bottom-up estimating; it promotes a deeper understanding of the job to be done, and it allows the individual developers to plan their own jobs, ensuring their personal commitment to the resulting estimate, and giving them more control over their own project destinies. In addition, the task estimates provide a sound basis for overall project planning and control, as will be discussed in Chapter 32.

The main difficulties with the task-unit approach are those of overlooking system

FIGURE 22–2 Sample task unit planning sheet

COMPONENT: Inventory Update   DEVELOPER: W. Ward   Date: 2/8/82

Phase	Task Unit	Man-days	Totals
Plans and requirements	Component requirements	5	
	Development plan	1	6
Product design	Product design	6	
	Draft users' manual	3	
	Test plan	1	10
Detailed design	Detailed PDL	4	
	Data definitions	4	
	Test data and procedures	2	
	Full users' manual	2	12
Code and unit test	Code	6	
	Unit test results	10	16
Integration and test	As-built documentation	4	
	Integration support	5	9
Grand Total			53

level costs, and those of overlooking two significant additional sources of software cost. These are

1. *Incidental project activities,* which may add another 30 to 50% to the amount of effort spent on producing the items enumerated on the Task Planning Sheet in Fig. 22–2. Figure 22–3 shows the distribution of effort by activity for the two small application software projects discussed in [Boehm, 1980]; it shows that such activities as reading, reviewing, meeting, and fixing consumed roughly 40% of the development effort for both projects.

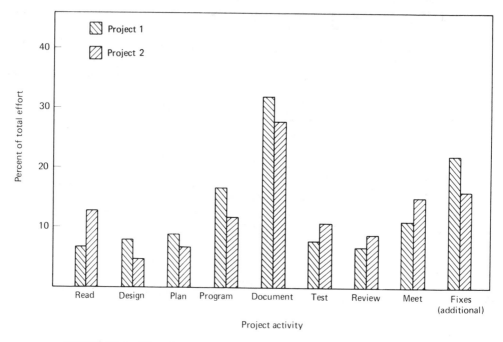

FIGURE 22–3 What does a software project do? Distribution of project effort by activity

2. *Incidental nonproject activities,* which may add still another 30 to 50% to the amount of effort devoted to all the project activities. Figure 22–4 shows the results of a Bell Laboratories time and motion study of 70 programmers [Bairdain, 1964], indicating that roughly 30% of the programmer's workday is devoted to nonproject activities: training, personal business, nonproject communication, etc.

These difficulties should not be considered as fundamental drawbacks to the task-unit approach, but more as considerations to be covered in reviewing task-unit estimates for completeness. On balance, the task-unit method is an extremely valuable one, and the most appropriate approach to software cost estimation for very small (less than 2000 DSI) software projects.

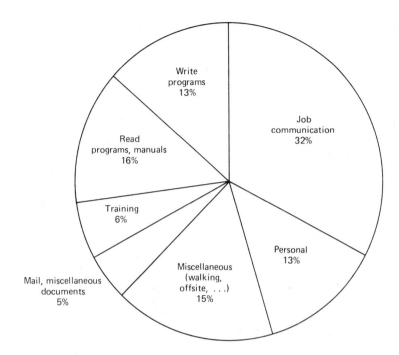

ACTIVITY	List, Cards, Worksheet	Business	Personal	Meeting	Training	Mail/Misc. Documents	Technical Manuals	Oper. Proc. Misc.	Program Test	Totals
Talk or listen	4%	17%	7%	3%				1%		32%
Talk with manager		1								1%
Telephone		2	1							3%
Read	14					2	2			18%
Write/recording	13					1				14%
Away or out		4	1	4	6					15%
Walking	2	2	1			1				6%
Miscellaneous	2	3	3			1		1	1	11%
Totals	35%	29%	13%	7%	6%	5%	2%	2%	1%	100%

FIGURE 22–4 What do programmers do?

22.8 SUMMARY COMPARISON OF METHODS

Table 22–3 summarizes the relative strengths and weaknesses of the software cost-estimation methods discussed in this chapter. The main conclusions that we can draw are

- None of the alternatives is better than the others from all aspects.
- The Parkinson and price-to-win methods are unacceptable and do not produce sound cost estimates.
- The strengths and weaknesses of the other techniques are complementary (particularly the algorithmic model versus expert judgment and top-down versus bottom-up).

TABLE 22-3 Strengths and Weaknesses of Software Cost-Estimation Methods

Method	Strengths	Weaknesses
Algorithmic model	• Objective, repeatable, analyzable formula • Efficient, good for sensitivity analysis • Objectively calibrated to experience	• Subjective inputs • Assessment of exceptional circumstances • Calibrated to past, not future
Expert judgment	• Assessment of representativeness, interactions, exceptional circumstances	• No better than participants • Biases, incomplete recall
Analogy	• Based on representative experience	• Representativeness of experience
Parkinson Price to win	• Correlates with some experience • Often gets the contract	• Reinforces poor practice • Generally produces large overruns
Top-down	• System level focus • Efficient	• Less detailed basis • Less stable
Bottom-up	• More detailed basis • More stable • Fosters individual commitment	• May overlook system level costs • Requires more effort

Thus, as we discussed in Sections 21.5 and 21.6, it is important to use a combination of techniques, and to compare and iterate the estimates obtained from each. The particular combination we choose will depend on our cost-estimation objectives (for example, more top-down for rough early estimates; more bottom-up for detailed planning estimates). In general, however, an effective combination is the following:

• A top-down estimate using the judgment of more than one expert, using analogy estimation where a comparable previous project is available.
• Bottom-up estimation using an algorithmic model, with inputs and component-level estimates provided by future performers.
• Comparison and iteration of both estimates.

The component level Intermediate COCOMO model presented in Chapters 8 and 9 can be used to support bottom-up algorithmic model estimates, but often a more detailed model with more hierarchical levels will be more effective. The next chapter presents the Detailed COCOMO model, which can provide this level of support.

22.9 QUESTIONS

22.1. Define the seven methods of software cost estimation discussed in this chapter.

22.2. Perform a Delphi exercise to estimate the size of the operating system on your main computer, and compare the results with its actual size. Did the range of estimates in the successive Delphi rounds decrease? Did the median estimate converge more closely to the actual size?

22.3. Can you think of other possible software cost-estimation techniques which do not fall within the categories discussed in this chapter? What would be their relative strengths and weaknesses?

22.4. *(Research Project)* Perform a comparative study of the standard Delphi technique and the Wideband Delphi technique on a software cost-estimation activity.

22.5. *(Research Project)* Perform comparative studies of the relative effectiveness of different algorithmic models over a range of software cost-estimation situations.

22.6. Suppose you were the president of Query Systems, Inc., a commercial software house. Your company has prepared a proposal to develop a data base management system and an interactive query system for a hardware vendor with a new minicomputer. Your performers have given you an estimate of $1200K to do the job, and your marketing expert tells you that the price to win is $800K. What should you do?

Part IVB

THE DETAILED COCOMO MODEL

The Intermediate COCOMO model presented in Chapters 8 and 9 is a highly effective model for most software cost-estimation purposes. However, it has two primary limitations which may become significant, particularly in detailed cost estimates for large software projects.

- Its estimated distribution of effort by phase may be inaccurate.
- It can be very cumbersome to use on a product with many components.

The Detailed COCOMO model presented in Chapters 23 to 27 provides two main capabilities which address the limitations of Intermediate COCOMO.

1. Phase-Sensitive Effort Multipliers. In Intermediate COCOMO, the phase distribution of effort is determined solely by the size of the product. In practice, factors such as required reliability, applications experience, and interactive software development affect some phases much more than others. Detailed COCOMO provides a set of phase-sensitive effort multipliers for each cost

driver attribute. These multipliers are used to determine the amount of effort required to complete each phase.

2. Three-Level Product Hierarchy. In Intermediate COCOMO, separate cost driver ratings can be furnished for different product components. This process can be very tedious and is unnecessarily repetitive if a number of components are grouped into a subsystem with practically all the same cost driver ratings. Detailed COCOMO avoids this problem by providing a three-level product hierarchy, for which:

- Some effects, which tend to vary with each bottom level module, are treated at the *module level.*
- Some effects, which vary less frequently, are treated at the *subsystem level.*
- Some effects, such as the effect of total product size, are treated at the *system level.*

In addition, Detailed COCOMO has some other capabilities, such as a procedure for adjusting the phase distribution of the development schedule. For some capabilities, such as the estimation of overall development schedule and the estimation of effort distribution by activity, Detailed COCOMO uses the same techniques that are used in Intermediate COCOMO and Basic COCOMO.

Chapter 23 presents a set of summary tables and procedures for using the Detailed COCOMO Software Hierarchy Estimating Form (SHEF), and gives a step by step example of its use.

Chapters 24 through 27 discuss each of the fifteen COCOMO cost driver attributes in detail, presenting detailed effort multipliers, rating definitions, calibration data, and state of the art assessments for each cost driver attribute. The chapters are organized as follows:

* For a given software product, the underlying virtual machine is the complex of hardware and software (OS, DBMS, etc.) it calls upon to accomplish its tasks.

Chapter 27: *Project Attributes*

Chapter 28 discusses the major possible cost driver attributes that were not included in COCOMO. This is accomplished with respect to a set of criteria used to evaluate the worth of a software cost model. Finally, Chapter 29 summarizes the comparison between the estimates produced by the Basic, Intermediate, and Detailed COCOMO models and the project actuals in the COCOMO data base. Chapter 29 also provides a comparative discussion of software cost models other than CO-COMO, and presents techniques for calibrating COCOMO to a particular installation's experience and special circumstances.

Chapter 23

Detailed COCOMO: Summary and Operational Description

23.1 INTRODUCTION

In Chapters 21 and 22, we discussed the point that the more detail we provide as input to a cost estimate, the more accurate our resulting estimate is likely to be. The Detailed COCOMO model provides a way to prepare estimates in considerable detail, and yet specify and process them with reasonable efficiency.

The Module–Subsystem–System Hierarchy

The way this is done is by employing a three level hierarchical decomposition of the software product whose cost is to be estimated. The lowest level, the *module* level, is described by the number of delivered source instructions (DSI) in the module and by those cost drivers which tend to vary at the lowest level: the module's complexity and adaptation from existing software; and the module programmers' capability level and experience with the language and the virtual machine on which the software will be built.

The second level, the *subsystem* level, is described by the remainder of the cost drivers (time and storage constraint, analyst capability, tools, schedule, etc.), which tend to vary from subsystem to subsystem, but which tend to be the same for all the modules within a subsystem.

The top level, the *system* level, is used to apply major overall project relations such as the nominal effort and schedule equations, and to apply the nominal project effort and schedule breakdowns by phase.

Phase Sensitive Effort Multipliers

The three level hierarchy is one of the two main differences between Intermediate COCOMO and Detailed COCOMO. The other is the use of phase sensitive effort multipliers, in order to accurately reflect the effect of the cost drivers on the phase distribution of effort. For example, a low level of applications experience will mean additional effort in the early phases; by the later phases, the team will have become familiar with the application, and will not spend as much additional effort in false starts, errors, or background learning activities. On the other hand, a high (that is, slow) computer response time will have relatively little effect on the requirements and design phases, but will certainly consume more of the team's time during the code and test phases.

For each cost driver attribute, Detailed COCOMO has a set of tables which show, for each cost driver rating, a separate effort multiplier accounting for its effect on each major development phase. Each of these tables is explained further in Chapters 24 to 27, which include tables showing which project activities account for the size of the effort multiplier in each phase.

Detailed COCOMO Procedures

The rest of this chapter presents an operational description of Detailed COCOMO in terms of the forms, tables, and procedures used to generate a Detailed COCOMO cost estimate. Section 23.2 presents the two-part Software Hierarchy Estimation Form (SHEF) used in making Detailed COCOMO estimates. Section 23.3 presents the step by step procedures for using the SHEF, including a summary of the Detailed COCOMO effort multiplier tables. Section 23.4 provides an example of the use of the SHEF and the procedures in estimating the cost of a student job information system software project.

23.2 THE SOFTWARE HIERARCHY ESTIMATING FORM (SHEF)

Figures 23–1 and 23–2 show the subsystem level and the module level portions of the Software Hierarchy Estimating Form (SHEF) used in making Detailed COCOMO estimates. The use of this form is illustrated with respect to a student job information system (STUJOB), that consists of three subsystems.

1. A QUERY subsystem by which students or employers can query the data base of available jobs or available students to find out whether there are any job–student matches of interest to them. QUERY consists of a query input and edit module, QEDIT; a file search module, SEARCH; and a module for reporting the results of the query, OUTPUT.

2. An UPDATE subsystem by which entries in the data base of available jobs and available students can be added, deleted, or changed. UPDATE consists of an update input and edit module, UPEDIT; and a file modification module, MODIFY.

3. A UTILITIES subsystem consisting of various useful associated software components: a file backup capability, a file load or reload capability, some simple integrity-checking capabilities, and some associated statistical analysis and reporting capabilities.

After we present the SHEF procedures and Detailed COCOMO tables in the next section, we will show how the procedures, when applied to the STUJOB example, produce the estimates shown in Figs. 23–1 and 23–2.

23.3 THE SOFTWARE HIERARCHY ESTIMATING FORM (SHEF) PROCEDURES

Table 23–1 presents a set of procedures for using the SHEF to produce Detailed COCOMO cost estimates. The procedures have been organized to make manual cost estimation at this detailed level as simple and straightforward as possible. Still, the procedures are rather lengthy, and the user may wish to consider embodying them in a computer program—an option which is quite straightforward to implement.

The procedures involve a set of phase sensitive effort multiplier tables that show, for each cost driver attribute rating, what the effect of that rating is for each major software development phase. The effort multipliers for the module level cost driver attributes are given in Table 23–2; the effort multipliers for the subsystem level attributes are given in Table 23–3. Again, the nature and derivation of these tables will be explained in Chapters 24 to 27.

23.4 DETAILED COCOMO EXAMPLE: STUDENT JOB INFORMATION SYSTEM

Project Overview

The Student Job Information System (STUJOB) is planned to be implemented on a medium size, largely batch-oriented, general-purpose computer. The computer hardware, operating system, compiler, and basic file handling and report generation capabilities to be used by STUJOB are all quite stable, and the system has a large number of helpful tools to aid in software development. The application does not

Project: STUDB   Analyst: T. J. Murphy   Date: 7/12/81

(1) SS NO.	(2) Subsystem	(8) EDSI	Product (21) RELY	(22) DATA	Computer Attributes (23) TIME	(24) STOR	(25) VIRT	(26) TURN	Personnel (27) ACAP	(28) AEXP	Project (29) MODP	(30) TOOL	(31) SCED	(32) EAF SS	(20) MM MOD	(33) MM EST	(34) $K/MM	(35) $K	(36) TOTALS AVGS
1	QUERY	3700	1.0	1.0	1.0	1.0	0.95	1.0	0.75	0.75	1.0	0.95	1.0	0.52	2.0	1.0	6.0	6.0	6.8
PD							0.90		0.90	0.90	0.95	0.95		0.58	3.2	1.9	5.0	9.5	35.5
DD							0.95		0.90	0.85	0.90	0.90		0.53	5.5	2.9	5.0	14.5	5.44
CUT							0.90		0.85	0.95	0.83	0.95		0.41	2.5	1.0	5.5	5.5	10
2	UPDATE	2600					0.95		0.75	0.75		0.98		0.52	1.4	0.7	6.0	4.2	5.1
PD							0.90		0.90	0.90	0.95	0.95		0.58	2.4	1.4	5.0	7.0	26.6
DD							0.95		0.90	0.85	0.90	0.90		0.53	4.1	2.2	5.0	11.0	5.10
CUT							0.90		0.85	0.85	0.83	0.85		0.41	1.9	0.8	5.5	4.4	10
3	UTILITIES	1700					0.95		1.0	1.0		0.98		0.93	0.7	0.7	5.0	3.5	4.2
PD							0.90				0.95	0.95		0.81	1.4	1.1	5.0	5.5	22.2
DD							0.95				0.90	0.90		0.69	2.5	1.7	5.5	9.4	405
CUT							0.80				0.83	0.85		0.56	1.2	0.7	5.5	3.8	13

(9) Total EDSI: 8000
(10) (MM)$_{NOM}$: 28.4
(11) (EDSI/MM)$_{NOM}$: 282

Mode: Organic

(12) Phase Fraction	
PD	0.16
DD	0.25
CUT	0.40
IT	0.19

	(33) MM EST	(35) $K
PD	2.4	13.7
DD	4.4	22.0
CUT	6.8	34.9
IT	2.5	13.7
Total	16.1	84.3 $K

MM: 7.2 Sched

$$\frac{\$K}{MM} = \frac{\$K}{EDSI}$$

FIGURE 23-1 Software Hierarchy Estimating Form (SHEF): Subsystem Level

350

Project: STUJOB Analyst: T. J. Murphy Date: 7/12/81

	(3) SS NO.	(4) MOD NO.	(5) Module	(6) EDSI	(7) AAF	(14) CPLX	(15) PCAP	(16) VEXP	(17) LEXP	(18) EAF M	(13) MM NOM	(19) MM MOD	(37) MM EST	Percent %
PD DD CUT IT	1	1	QEDIT	1800	100	1.0	1.0	1.0	1.0	1.0 1.0 1.0 1.0	1.0 1.6 2.6 1.2	1.0 1.6 2.6 1.2	0.5 0.9 1.4 0.5	15 27 42 15
	1	2	SEARCH	700	100		0.83 0.83 0.83	0.90 0.90 0.90 0.90	0.98 0.92 0.92	0.90 0.73 0.69 0.69	0.4 0.6 1.0 0.5	0.4 0.4 0.7 0.3	0.2 0.2 0.4 0.1	22 22 45 12
	1	3	OUTPUT	1200	100	0.85 0.85 0.85 0.85	1.20 1.20 1.20	1.05 1.05 1.15 1.15	1.05 1.10 1.10	0.89 1.12 1.29 1.29	0.7 1.1 1.7 0.8	0.6 1.2 2.2 1.0	0.3 0.7 1.2 0.4	12 27 46 15
	1	TOT		3700								2.0 3.2 5.5 2.5	1.0 1.8 3.0 1.0	15 26 44 15
	2	1	UPEDIT	1700	100					1.0 1.0 1.0 1.0	1.0 1.5 2.4 1.1	1.0 1.5 2.4 1.1	0.5 0.9 1.3 0.5	16 28 40 16
	2	2	MODIFY	900	100	0.85 0.85 0.85 0.85	1.20 1.20 1.20	1.05 1.05 1.15 1.15	1.05 1.10 1.10	0.89 1.12 1.29 1.29	0.5 0.8 1.3 0.6	0.4 0.9 1.7 0.8	0.2 0.5 0.9 0.3	11 26 47 16
	2	TOT		2600								1.4 2.4 4.1 1.9	0.7 1.4 2.2 0.8	14 27 43 16
	3	1 TOT	UTILS	1700	34	0.70 0.70 0.70 0.70	1.20 1.20 1.20	1.05 1.05 1.15 1.15	1.05 1.10 1.10	0.74 0.93 1.06 1.06	1.0 1.5 2.4 1.1	0.7 1.4 2.5 1.2	0.7 1.1 1.7 0.7	17 26 40 17

FIGURE 23–2 Software Hierarchy Estimating Form (SHEF): Module Level

TABLE 23-1 Software Hierarchy Estimating Form (SHEF) Procedures

1. On the Subsystem (SS) Form, for each subsystem within the software system, enter the subsystem number in column 1 and the subsystem identification in column 2.
2. On the Module (M) form, for each subsystem identified in Step 1 and each module within the subsystem, enter the subsystem number in column 3, the module number within the subsystem in column 4, and the module identification number in column 5. After entering all of the modules in a subsystem, establish an additional row to accumulate subsystem totals (not necessary if the subsystem has only one module). More than one M Form (or SS Form) may be used if necessary.
3. On the M Form, enter the size of each module in equivalent delivered source instructions (EDSI) in column 6. If a module is to be adapted from existing software, compute its adaptation adjustment factor (AAF), using the equations at the end of this table, and enter it in column 7. Add up the total EDSI for each subsystem and enter it in its subsystem total row.
4. On the SS Form, enter the subsystem EDSI totals in column 8. Add up the total EDSI for the system and enter it as item 9.
5. On the SS Form, identify the development mode for the system, and compute the nominal effort $(MM)_{NOM}$ required to develop the system from the appropriate nominal effort equation at the end of this table. Enter this as item 10.
6. On the SS Form, compute the nominal productivity $(EDSI/MM)_{NOM} = EDSI/(MM)_{NOM}$ and enter it as item 11.
7. On the SS Form, obtain the phase distribution of effort, $(FRAC)_P$, as a function of total system size in DSI from Table 23–4. Split up the programming phase into a detailed design (DD) phase and a code and unit test (CUT) phase. Enter the $(FRAC)_P$ values in area 12.
8. On the M Form, compute the nominal phase distribution of effort for each module as $(MM)_{NOM.P} = [(EDSI)(FRAC)_P] \div [(EDSI/MM)_{NOM}]$, obtaining EDSI from column 6, $(FRAC)_P$ from area 12, and $(EDSI/MM)_{NOM}$ from item 11. Enter the results in column 13.
9. On the M Form, for each module, determine cost driver attribute ratings for the attributes CPLX, PCAP, VEXP, and LEXP. Use the ratings to determine the phase effort multipliers for the attribute (from Table 23–2), and enter them in columns 14 to 17 as appropriate. Nominal effort multipliers (1.00) can be left blank.
10. On the M Form, multiply the effort multipliers in columns 14 to 17 of each row together to obtain a module effort adjustment factor $(EAF)_M$ for each phase. Enter the result in column 18.
11. On the M Form, for each module and each phase, multiply the nominal phase effort for the module $(MM)_{NOM.P}$ (column 13) by the corresponding $(EAF)_M$ (column 18), to obtain the module level adjusted phase effort for the module $(MM)_{MOD.P}$. Enter the result in column 19.
12. On the M Form, for each subsystem and each phase, add up the $(MM)_{MOD.P}$ effort estimates for all of the modules in the subsystem, and place the results in its subsystem total row in column 19.
13. On the SS Form, enter the $(MM)_{MOD.P}$ phase effort totals for each subsystem in column 20.
14. On the SS Form, for each subsystem, determine cost driver attribute ratings for the attributes shown in columns 21 to 31. Use the ratings to determine the phase effort multipliers for the attribute (from Table 22–3), and enter them in the appropriate column. Nominal effort multipliers (1.00) can be left blank.
15. On the SS Form, multiply the effort multipliers in columns 21 to 31 of each row together to obtain a subsystem effort adjustment factor $(EAF)_{SS}$ for each phase. Enter the result in column 32.
16. On the SS Form, for each subsystem and each phase, multiply the module adjusted effort estimates $(MM)_{MOD.P}$ (column 20) by the corresponding $(EAF)_{SS}$, to obtain the fully adjusted phase effort estimate for each subsystem, $(MM)_{EST.P}$. Enter the result in column 33.
17. On the SS Form, for each phase, add up the phase effort estimates $(MM)_{EST.P}$ for all of the subsystems to produce the phase effort estimates for the overall system. Then add up the system phase effort estimates to produce the effort estimate for the overall system. Enter these five estimates at the bottom of column 33.
18. On the SS Form, compute the estimated development schedule for the system, using the appropri-

TABLE 23-1 *(Cont'd)*

ate development schedule equation at the end of this table. Enter the result at the bottom of column 34.

19. On the SS Form, for each subsystem and phase, enter the estimated labor cost ($K/MM) in column 34. Multiply this cost by the corresponding effort estimate in column 33 to produce a dollar cost estimate for each subsystem and phase. Enter the result in column 35.

20. On the SS Form, for each phase, add up the phase cost estimates for all of the subsystems (column 35) to produce the phase cost estimates for the overall system. Then add up the system phase cost estimates to produce the cost estimate for the overall system. Enter these five estimates at the bottom of column 35.

21. On the SS Form, for each subsystem, add up the man-month estimates for each phase (column 33) and enter the resulting total man-month estimate for the subsystem in the top (MM) component of the subsystem's row in column 36. Similarly, compute the total dollar estimate for the subsystem from the phase cost estimates (column 35), and enter the result in the second ($K) component of the subsystem's row in column 36.

22. On the SS Form, for each subsystem, compute the estimated productivity in EDSI/MM (from column 8 and column 36, MM component), and enter it in the EDSI/MM component of column 36. Similarly, compute the cost per instruction (from column 36, $K component and column 8), and enter it in the $/EDSI component of column 36.

23. On the SS Form, for the entire system, compute the estimated productivity in EDSI/MM (from item 9 and the bottom entry in column 33), and enter it in the bottom EDSI/MM component of column 36. Similarly, compute the system cost per instruction (from the bottom entry in column 35 and item 9), and enter it in the bottom $/EDSI component of column 36.

24. On the M Form, for each module and each phase, multiply the module level adjusted phase effort $(MM)_{MOD.P}$ (column 19) by the corresponding subsystem effort adjustment factor $(EAF)_{SS}$ (column 32, on the SS Form) to obtain the estimated effort $(MM)_{EST.P}$ by phase for each module. Enter the results in column 37.

25. On the M Form, for each subsystem and each phase, add up the $(MM)_{EST.P}$ estimates (column 37) for all of the modules in the subsystem, and place the results in its subsystem total row in column 37. Compare these results with the $(MM)_{EST.P}$ estimates for the subsystem entered in column 33. They should be equal, with perhaps some slight differences in the last digit due to roundoff effects. If not, there is a computational error which needs to be found and fixed.

Adaptation Equations (COCOMO Eq. 8-1, 8-2)

$$AAF = 0.4 \text{ (Percent design modified)}$$
$$+ 0.3 \text{ (Percent code modified)}$$
$$+ 0.3 \text{ (Percent integration modified)}$$
$$EDSI = \text{(Adapted DSI) (AAF)}/100$$

Nominal Effort and Schedule Equations (COCOMO Table 8-1)

Development Mode	Nominal Effort	Schedule
Organic	$(MM)_{NOM} = 3.2(KEDSI)^{1.05}$	$TDEV = 2.5(MM)_{DEV}^{0.38}$
Semidetached	$(MM)_{NOM} = 3.0(KEDSI)^{1.12}$	$TDEV = 2.5(MM)_{DEV}^{0.35}$
Embedded	$(MM)_{NOM} = 2.8(KEDSI)^{1.20}$	$TDEV = 2.5(MM)_{DEV}^{0.32}$

strain the available execution time and core memory at all, and does not require an especially high level of reliability. The data base of job and student information is not particularly large.

The project is currently beginning its plans and requirements phase, and is using Detailed COCOMO, along with some independent expert estimates, to arrive at an

TABLE 23-2 Module Level Effort Multipliers

Attribute	Rating	RPD	DD	CUT	IT
CPLX	Very low	.70	.70	.70	.70
	Low	.85	.85	.85	.85
	Nominal	1.00	1.00	1.00	1.00
	High	1.15	1.15	1.15	1.15
	Very high	1.30	1.30	1.30	1.30
	Extra high	1.65	1.65	1.65	1.65
PCAP	Very low	1.00	1.50	1.50	1.50
	Low	1.00	1.20	1.20	1.20
	Nominal	1.00	1.00	1.00	1.00
	High	1.00	.83	.83	.83
	Very high	1.00	.65	.65	.65
VEXP	Very low	1.10	1.10	1.30	1.30
	Low	1.05	1.05	1.15	1.15
	Nominal	1.00	1.00	1.00	1.00
	High	.90	.90	.90	.90
LEXP	Very low	1.02	1.10	1.20	1.20
	Low	1.00	1.05	1.10	1.10
	Nominal	1.00	1.00	1.00	1.00
	High	1.00	.98	.92	.92

TABLE 23-3 Subsystem Level Effort Multipliers

Attribute	Rating	RPD	DD	CUT	IT
Product					
RELY	Very low	.80	.80	.80	.60
	Low	.90	.90	.90	.80
	Nominal	1.00	1.00	1.00	1.00
	High	1.10	1.10	1.10	1.30
	Very high	1.30	1.30	1.30	1.70
DATA	Low	.95	.95	.95	.90
	Nominal	1.00	1.00	1.00	1.00
	High	1.10	1.05	1.05	1.15
	Very high	1.20	1.10	1.10	1.30
Computer					
TIME	Nominal	1.00	1.00	1.00	1.00
	High	1.10	1.10	1.10	1.15
	Very high	1.30	1.25	1.25	1.40
	Extra high	1.65	1.55	1.55	1.95

TABLE 23–3 *(Cont'd)*

Attribute	Rating	RPD	DD	CUT	IT
STOR	Nominal	1.00	1.00	1.00	1.00
	High	1.05	1.05	1.05	1.10
	Very high	1.20	1.15	1.15	1.35
	Extra high	1.55	1.45	1.45	1.85
VIRT	Low	.95	.90	.85	.80
	Nominal	1.00	1.00	1.00	1.00
	High	1.10	1.12	1.15	1.20
	Very high	1.20	1.25	1.30	1.40
TURN	Low	.98	.95	.70	.90
	Nominal	1.00	1.00	1.00	1.00
	High	1.00	1.00	1.10	1.15
	Very high	1.02	1.05	1.20	1.30
Personnel					
ACAP	Very low	1.80	1.35	1.35	1.50
	Low	1.35	1.15	1.15	1.20
	Nominal	1.00	1.00	1.00	1.00
	High	.75	.90	.90	.85
	Very high	.55	.75	.75	.70
AEXP	Very low	1.40	1.30	1.25	1.25
	Low	1.20	1.15	1.10	1.10
	Nominal	1.00	1.00	1.00	1.00
	High	.87	.90	.92	.92
	Very high	.75	.80	.85	.85
Project					
MODP	Very low	1.05	1.10	1.25	1.50
	Low	1.00	1.05	1.10	1.20
	Nominal	1.00	1.00	1.00	1.00
	High	1.00	.95	.90	.83
	Very high	1.00	.90	.80	.65
TOOL	Very low	1.02	1.05	1.35	1.45
	Low	1.00	1.02	1.15	1.20
	Nominal	1.00	1.00	1.00	1.00
	High	.98	.95	.90	.85
	Very high	.95	.90	.80	.70
SCED	Very low	1.10	1.25	1.25	1.25
	Low	1.00	1.15	1.15	1.10
	Nominal	1.00	1.00	1.00	1.00
	High	1.10	1.10	1.00	1.00
	Very high	1.15	1.15	1.05	1.05

TABLE 23-4 Phase Distribution of Effort and Schedule: All Modes

Mode	Effort distribution / Phase	Small 2 KDSI	Inter-mediate 8 KDSI	Medium 32 KDSI	Large 128 KDSI	Very large 512 KDSI
Organic	Plans and requirements (%)	6	6	6	6	
	Product design	16	16	16	16	
	Programming	68	65	62	59	
	Detailed design	26	25	24	23	
	Code and unit test	42	40	38	36	
	Integration and test	16	19	22	25	
Semidetached	Plans and requirements (%)	7	7	7	7	
	Product design	17	17	17	17	17
	Programming	64	61	58	55	52
	Detailed design	27	26	25	24	2:
	Code and unit test	37	35	33	31	2!
	Integration and test	19	22	25	28	31
Embedded	Plans and requirements (%)	8	8	8	8	:
	Product design	18	18	18	18	18
	Programming	60	57	54	51	48
	Detailed design	28	27	26	25	2.
	Code and unit test	32	30	28	26	2.
	Integration and test	22	25	28	31	34

Mode	Schedule distribution	2 KDSI	8 KDSI	32 KDSI	128 KDSI	512 KDSI
Organic	Plans and requirements (%)	10	11	12	13	
	Product design	19	19	19	19	
	Programming	63	59	55	51	
	Integration and test	18	22	26	30	
Semidetached	Plans and requirements (%)	16	18	20	22	2.
	Product design	24	25	26	27	28
	Programming	56	52	48	44	40
	Integration and test	20	23	26	29	32
Embedded	Plans and requirements (%)	24	28	32	36	4
	Product design	30	32	34	36	38
	Programming	48	44	40	36	32
	Integration and test	22	24	26	28	30

estimate of the effort and schedules required for development. The project manager does not plan to depart significantly from the estimated schedule.

The project manager plans to operate in a "democratic Chief Programmer" mode, performing the early analysis herself, and working with the other programmers in the analysis and design of the modules they will be programming. She plans to program the SEARCH module herself—this is the smallest module, but the one requiring the deepest understanding of the underlying operating system and data management software—and to be primarily responsible for software integration and test. One of her programmers on the project is reasonably capable and experienced;

he will be working on the QEDIT and UPEDIT modules. The other three modules—OUTPUT, MODIFY, and UTILITIES—are less complex. Some new programmer trainees have recently joined the group, and one or two of them will work on these modules.

Estimation Steps

Below is a discussion of the steps involved in using the SHEF forms (Figs. 23–1 and 23–2) to estimate the cost, effort, and schedule involved in developing the STUJOB software.

Steps 1 and 2. The subsystems and modules are identified on the Subsystem (SS) and Module (M) Forms. Added subsystem total rows (TOT) are established on the M Form after entering all the modules in each subsystem (except for the UTILITIES subsystem, which contains only one module).

Step 3. The size of each module is entered in column 6, and the sizes of each subsystem are calculated (QUERY: 3700 EDSI; UPDATE: 2600 EDSI; UTILITIES: 1700 EDSI). The UTILITIES are being adapted from 5000 DSI of existing software, with 25% design modified, 50% code modified, and 30% integration modified, yielding

$$AAF = 0.4(25) + 0.3(50) + 0.3(30) = 34$$

$$EDSI = (5000)(34)/100 = 1700$$

Step 4. The subsystem sizes are transferred to column 7 on the SS Form. The total size of the STUJOB product is calculated to be 8000 EDSI.

Steps 5 and 6. The nominal effort is $3.2(8)^{1.05} = 28.4$ MM, and the nominal productivity is $8000/28.4 = 282$ EDSI/MM.

Step 7. Conveniently, we do not have to interpolate in Table 23–4 to determine the phase distribution percentages.

Step 8. As an example, we will calculate $(MM)_{NOM.P}$ for the UPEDIT module for the four phases

$$PD: \quad (MM)_{NOM.PD} = \frac{(1700 \text{ EDSI})(0.16)}{282 \text{ EDSI/MM}} = 1.0 \text{ MM}$$

$$DD: \quad (MM)_{NOM.DD} = \frac{(1700 \text{ EDSI})(0.25)}{282 \text{ EDSI/MM}} = 1.5 \text{ MM}$$

$$CUT: \quad (MM)_{NOM.CUT} = \frac{(1700 \text{ EDSI})(0.40)}{282 \text{ EDSI/MM}} = 2.4 \text{ MM}$$

$$IT: \quad (MM)_{NOM.IT} = \frac{(1700 \text{ EDSI})(0.19)}{282 \text{ EDSI/MM}} = 1.1 \text{ MM}$$

Step 9. The QEDIT module has nominal ratings for all the module level cost drivers. The SEARCH model, being programmed by the project leader, receives smaller effort multipliers, as her capability and experience should reduce the nominal amount of effort required to develop the SEARCH module. Note that the effect of her programming language experience is to reduce the effort in the code and unit test phase and the integration and test phase, with virtually no effect on the earlier phases.

Step 10. The module level EAFs for the QEDIT module are equal to 1.00 for each phase, since all the QEDIT ratings were nominal. The module level EAF for the last phase of the SEARCH module, integration and test, as an example, is (0.83)(0.90)(0.92) = 0.69.

Step 11. The module level adjusted phase effort for the QEDIT module is the same as the nominal phase effort. For the SEARCH module integration and test phase, the effect of the project leader's capability and experience is to reduce the estimated effort required for this phase from 0.5 MM to (0.69)(0.5MM) = 0.3 MM.

Note that both UPEDIT and UTILS have the same nominal effort distribution for the four phases: (1.0, 1.5, 2.4, 1.1). UPEDIT, having no non-nominal module level ratings, retains the same phase distribution in this step. For UTILS, the lower programmer capability and experience ratings tend to shift the effort distribution more to the later phases: (0.7, 1.4, 2.5, 1.2).

Step 12. The total effort estimated at this step for the product design phase for the QUERY subsystem is 1.0 + 0.4 + 0.6 = 2.0 MM. For the detailed design phase, it is 1.6 + 0.4 + 1.2 = 3.2 MM. No addition of module totals is needed for the UTILITIES subsystem, since it contains only one module.

Step 13. The subsystem phase effort totals are transferred from the M Form to the SS Form (column 20, between columns 32 and 33).

Step 14. The three subsystems of the STUJOB product are very similar with respect to their subsystem level attributes. Most of the ratings are nominal, with some cost reduction effects resulting from the stable virtual machine base (VIRT is rated low) and the high use of tools and modern programming practices. The UTILITIES subsystem has nominal ratings on analyst capability and applications experience, while the QUERY and UPDATE subsystems have high ratings for these cost drivers. These reflect the project manager's judgment that her capability and experience will be the major factor in the analysis and development of the QUERY and UPDATE subsystems, but not for the UTILITIES subsystem. Actually, since the analysis and development for each subsystem will be done jointly by people of mixed capabilities, some interpolated values for these effort multipliers would be appropriate.

Step 15. The overall subsystem effort adjustment factors (EAFs) are the same for the QUERY and UPDATE subsystems. Note that their cumulative effect is to reduce the estimated effort required to roughly 50% of the nominal estimate, with the biggest reduction in effort occurring in the integration and test phase.

Step 16. The final effort estimates are obtained by multiplying the module level adjusted estimates (such as 2.0 MM for the QUERY subsystem PD phase) by the corresponding subsystem EAFs (such as by 0.52 for the QUERY subsystem PD phase, to obtain the final estimate of 1.0 MM).

Step 17. The overall estimate for the STUJOB project is 16.1 MM, slightly over half of the nominal effort estimate of 28.4 MM. The phase distribution has also been modified by the phase dependent effort multipliers, as follows:

Phase	Original FRAC	Adjusted FRAC
PD	0.16	2.4/16.1 = 0.15
DD	0.25	4.4/16.1 = 0.27
CUT	0.40	6.8/16.1 = 0.42
IT	0.19	2.5/16.1 = 0.16

Step 18. The resulting estimated schedule is

$$2.5(16.1)^{0.38} = 7.2 \text{ months}$$

Step 19. The estimated labor costs for the QUERY and UPDATE subsystems are higher for the PD phase because of the major participation by the more highly paid project leader. They are higher for the IT phase because of expected salary increases. The cost estimates include a roughly 100% overhead rate, which is typical for software organizations [Phister, 1979].

Step 20. The estimated overall labor cost to develop the STUJOB system is $84,300. The cost distribution by phase (0.16, 0.26, 0.41, 0.16) is slightly closer to the nominal phase distribution than was the effort distribution.

Steps 21 and 22. For the QUERY subsystem, the estimated development effort is 6.8 MM, the estimated development cost is $35,500, the estimated productivity is 3700 EDSI/6.8 MM = 544 EDSI/MM, and the estimated cost per instruction is $35,500/3700 EDSI = $10/EDSI.

Step 23. The estimated productivity for the entire STUJOB project is 8000 EDSI/16.1 MM = 497 EDSI/MM. The estimated cost per instruction is $84,300/8000 EDSI = $11/EDSI.

Step 24. For the QEDIT module, the estimated development effort by phase is

$$\text{PD:} \quad (0.52)(1.0 \text{ MM}) = 0.5 \text{ MM}$$

$$\text{DD:} \quad (0.58)(1.6 \text{ MM}) = 0.9 \text{ MM}$$

$$\text{CUT:} \quad (0.53)(2.6 \text{ MM}) = 1.4 \text{ MM}$$

$$\text{IT:} \quad (0.41)(1.2 \text{ MM}) = 0.5 \text{ MM}$$

Step 25. For the QUERY subsystem, the module totals by phase add up to (1.0, 1.8, 3.0, 1.0) MM, as compared to the subsystem level calculation in column 33 of (1.0, 1.9, 2.9, 1.0) MM. These figures check to within the accuracy expected, given roundoff effects.

For this example, a final column has been added to the right, showing the resulting phase distribution of effort for each module and subsystem. Note that the SEARCH module, being developed by the project leader, has a higher fraction of effort (22%) devoted to product design, and a lower fraction of effort (11%) devoted to integration and test.

23.5 SCHEDULE ADJUSTMENT CALCULATIONS

As we saw in the example in the previous section, the phase-dependent effort multipliers change the phase distribution of effort to something different from the nominal distribution. Clearly, this change should be reflected by a change from the nominal phase distribution of the project schedule. This is accomplished by the schedule adjustment calculations described below, which basically employ proportionality factors to arrive at the revised schedule estimate.

Schedule Adjustment Procedure

Step 1. Determine the nominal fraction of project schedule devoted to the PD, PG, and IT phases by interpolation in Table 23–4. Call these functions $(F_{PD})_{NOM}$, $(F_{PG})_{NOM}$, and $(F_{IT})_{NOM}$. [The corresponding nominal fractions of project effort, $(E_{PD})_{NOM}$, $(E_{DD})_{NOM}$, $(E_{CUT})_{NOM}$, and $(E_{IT})_{NOM}$ have already been determined in area 12 of the SHEF SS Form.]

Step 2. Determine the adjusted fraction of project effort devoted to PD, DD, CUT, and IT phases from the estimated effort figures at the bottom of column 33 of the SS Form. Call these fractions E_{PD}, E_{DD}, E_{CUT}, and E_{IT}.

Step 3. Determine the proportional changes in project schedule distribution relative to the corresponding changes in project effort distribution, by computing a set of adjusted schedule distribution fractions

$$F_{PD} = (F_{PD})_{NOM} \cdot (E_{PD})/(E_{PD})_{NOM}$$

$$F_{PG} = (F_{PG})_{NOM} \cdot \frac{E_{DD} + E_{CUT}}{(E_{DD})_{NOM} + (E_{CUT})_{NOM}}$$

$$F_{IT} = (F_{IT})_{NOM} \cdot (E_{IT})/(E_{IT})_{NOM}$$

Step 4. As the adjusted schedule distributed fractions may not add up to 1.0, compute a normalization factor

$$F_N = F_{PD} + F_{PG} + F_{IT}$$

Step 5. Take the adjusted total development schedule T_D (from the bottom of column 34 on the SS Form) and divide it among the phases according to the normalized adjusted fractions:

$$T_{PD} = (T_D)(F_{PD})/F_N$$

$$T_{PG} = (T_D)(F_{PG})/F_N$$

$$T_{IT} = (T_D)(F_{IT})/F_N$$

Example

Here is how the schedule adjustment procedure is applied to the student job information system example.

Steps 1 and 2. From Table 23–4 the nominal schedule distribution fractions are

$$(F_{PD})_{NOM} = 0.19$$

$$(F_{PG})_{NOM} = 0.59$$

$$(F_{IT})_{NOM} = 0.22$$

The nominal and adjusted effort distribution fractions are

$$(E_{PD})_{NOM} = 0.16 \qquad E_{PD} = 2.4/16.1 = 0.15$$

$$(E_{DD})_{NOM} = 0.25 \qquad E_{DD} = 4.4/16.1 = 0.27$$

$$(E_{CUT})_{NOM} = 0.40 \qquad E_{CUT} = 6.8/16.1 = 0.42$$

$$(E_{IT})_{NOM} = 0.19 \qquad E_{IT} = 2.5/16.1 = 0.16$$

Steps 3 and 4. The proportional changes in project schedule distribution, and the resulting normalization factor, are

$$F_{PD} = (0.19)(0.15)/(0.16) = 0.18$$

$$F_{PG} = (0.59)\frac{0.27 + 0.42}{0.25 + 0.40} = 0.63$$

$$F_{IT} = (0.22)(0.16)/(0.19) = 0.19$$

$$F_N = 1.00$$

Step 5. The adjusted development schedule estimate is $T_D = 7.2$ months. The resulting adjusted schedule estimates for the phases are

$$T_{PD} = (7.2)(0.18)/1.00 = 1.3 \text{ months}$$

$$T_{PG} = (7.2)(0.63)/1.00 = 4.5 \text{ months}$$

$$T_{IT} = (7.2)(0.19)/1.00 = 1.4 \text{ months}$$

As a check, the sum of the phase schedules adds up to 7.2 months.

23.6 DISCUSSION

Phase Distribution of Effort

The main contribution Detailed COCOMO provides beyond Basic and Intermediate COCOMO is a better basis for detailed project personnel planning with respect to the level of staff required to successfully complete each software development phase. Projects with very high reliability requirements or hardware constraints will take more effort to integrate and test; projects whose personnel have very little applications experience will take more effort to develop a product design.

Thus, rather than to assume a single phase distribution of effort, based only on product size and development mode (as in Intermediate COCOMO) or to assume a single family of Rayleigh-distribution personnel-level curves, Detailed COCOMO reflects the observed differences in phase distribution due to other cost drivers. Chapters 24 to 27 contain tables, one for each cost driver attribute, which indicate the differences in project activities resulting from higher or lower project ratings with respect to the cost driver attribute. These tables are part of the attempt in COCOMO to provide a constructive cost model, which explains in project terms why the model gives the answers it does.

The correlation of Detailed COCOMO estimates to actual project data from the COCOMO data base will be presented in Chapter 29. The results there show that the phase-sensitive multipliers generally produce phase distributions of effort which are considerably closer to the project actuals than are the nominal phase distributions of effort.

Phase Distribution: An Extreme Example

As an extreme example of the phase sensitivity of Detailed COCOMO, Figs. 23–3 and 23–4 show the Detailed COCOMO calculations for a hypothetical project whose cost driver ratings were chosen to provide the highest possible fraction of project effort devoted to the integration and test phase. The ratings are

RELY	Required reliability	Very high
DATA	Data base size	Very high
TIME	Execution time constraint	Extra high
STOR	Main storage constraint	Extra high
VIRT	Virtual machine volatility	Very high
TURN	Computer turnaround time	Very high
ACAP	Analyst capability	Very low
AEXP	Applications experience	Very high
MODP	Modern programming practices	Very low
TOOL	Use of software tools	Very low
SCED	Required development schedule	Very low
CPLX	Project complexity	Nominal
PCAP	Programmer capability	Very low
VEXP	Virtual machine experience	Very low
LEXP	Programming language experience	Very low

The likelihood of a project being organized in such a way is also "very low," but the example is instructive in giving us an upper bound on the effect of the Detailed COCOMO phase multipliers.

Project: High Integration and Test   Analyst: _____   Date: _____

(1) SS NO.	(2) Subsystem	(8) EDSI		(21) RELY	(22) DATA	(23) TIME	(24) STOR	(25) VIRT	(26) TURN	(27) ACAP	(28) AEXP	(29) MODP	(30) TOOL	(31) SCED	(32) EAF SS	(20) MM MOD	(33) MM EST	(34) $K/MM	(35) $K	(36) TOTALS AVGS
						Product		Computer Attributes				Personnel		Project						
1	Subsys	32,000	PD	1.30	1.20	1.65	1.55	1.20	1.02	1.80	0.75	1.05	1.02	1.10	5.01	36	180			
			DD	1.30	1.10	1.55	1.45	1.25	1.05	1.35	0.90	1.10	1.05	1.25	6.58	86	566			
			CUT	1.30	1.10	1.55	1.45	1.30	1.20	1.35	0.85	1.25	1.35	1.25	12.1	117	1420			
			IT	1.70	1.30	1.95	1.85	1.40	1.30	1.50	0.85	1.50	1.45	1.25	50.3	117	5885			

(9) Total EDSI 32,000
(10) $(MM)_{NOM}$ 179
(11) $(EDSI/MM)_{NOM}$ 179

Mode: Embedded

(12) Phase Fraction: PD 18, DD 26, CUT 28, IT 28

	MM MOD	MM EST	$K/MM
PD	36	180	2%
DD	86	566	7%
CUT	117	1420	18%
IT	117	5885	73%
Total		8051	

MM $K   Sched

FIGURE 23-3 Software Hierarchy Estimation Form (SHEF): Subsystem Level: High I&T

Project: High Integration and Test   Analyst: _____   Date: _____

	SS NO. (3)	MOD NO. (4)	Module (5)	EDSI (6)	AAF (7)	CPLX (14)	PCAP (15)	VEXP (16)	LEXP (17)	EAF M (18)	MM NOM (13)	MM MOD (19)	MM EST (37)
PD	1	1	Module	32,000	100	1.0	1.0	1.10	1.02	1.12	32	36	
DD							1.50	1.10	1.10	1.82	47	86	
UT							1.50	1.30	1.20	2.34	50	117	
IT							1.50	1.30	1.20	2.34	50	117	

FIGURE 23-4 Software Hierarchy Estimation Form (SHEF): Module Level: High I&T

The example project is a medium-size, 32-KDSI embedded-mode job, whose nominal phase distribution of effort is

Product design: 18%

Detailed design: 26%

Code and unit test 28%

Integration and test: 28%

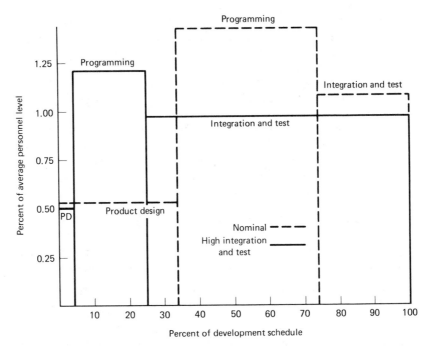

FIGURE 23–5 Detailed COCOMO: Comparison of nominal and extreme phase distribution

After the estimated effort required for each phase has been modified by the extreme effects of the cost driver ratings, the resulting Detailed COCOMO estimated phase distribution of effort is

    Product design: 2%

    Detailed design: 7%

    Code and unit test: 18%

    Integration and test: 73%

If we perform the resulting schedule adjustment calculations and graph the resulting relative personnel levels in comparison with the nominal phase distribution, we obtain the result shown in Fig. 23–5, with the great bulk of both time and effort going into the integration and test phase for the extreme case.

    Again, this is an artificially extreme example. One would not try to organize a project in this way (although some projects have come disconcertingly close). An added advantage of Detailed COCOMO is that it helps point out to us why we shouldn't do so.

Other Components of Detailed COCOMO

Two other components of Detailed COCOMO are the same as in Intermediate COCOMO

- *Maintenance Effort.* Calculated as a function of the development effort determined by Detailed COCOMO, the annual change traffic, and the Intermediate COCOMO cost driver multipliers for maintenance effort (Section 8.5). The modified MODP multipliers (Table 8–8) again apply to the size of the entire project.
- *Activity Distribution.* Calculated as a function of project size and development mode, using the Basic COCOMO activity distribution tables (Section 7.2).

Detailed COCOMO also differs from Intermediate COCOMO with respect to the estimation of the effort required for the plans and requirements phase. Detailed COCOMO uses the product design phase effort multipliers to calculate adjustments to the nominal plans-and-requirements phase effort percentages derived from Table 23–4, in the same way as they are used for the product design phase.

Summary of COCOMO Hierarchy of Models

Table 23–5 summarizes the similarities and differences among the three levels (Basic, Intermediate, and Detailed) of the COCOMO hierarchy of models. It also

TABLE 23–5   Summary of COCOMO Hierarchy of Models

Estimate	COCOMO Level		
	Basic	Intermediate	Detailed
Development effort, MM_{DEV}	f(mode, KDSI) Table 6–1	$f\begin{pmatrix}\text{mode, KDSI,} \\ \text{15 cost drivers}\end{pmatrix}$ Tables 8–1, 8–2	$f\begin{pmatrix}\text{mode, KDSI,} \\ \text{15 cost drivers}\end{pmatrix}$ Tables 8–1, 23–2, 23–3
Development schedule	f(mode, MM_{DEV}) Table 6–1	Same as for Basic level	Same as for Basic level
Maintenance effort	f(MM_{DEV}, ACT) Eq. 5–6	$f\begin{pmatrix}MM_{DEV}\text{, ACT,} \\ \text{15 cost drivers}\end{pmatrix}$ Eq. 5–6 Tables 8–2, 8–7, 8–8	Same as for Intermediate level
Product hierarchy	Entire system	System/components CLEF form and procedures Table 9–1	System/subsystem/ module SHEF form and procedures Table 23–1
Phase distribution of effort	f(mode, KDSI) Table 6–8	Same as for Basic level	$f\begin{pmatrix}\text{mode, KDSI,} \\ \text{15 cost drivers}\end{pmatrix}$ Tables 6–8, 23–2, 23–3
Phase distribution of schedule	f(mode, KDSI) Table 6–8	Same as for Basic level	$f\begin{pmatrix}\text{Basic schedule distribution} \\ \text{Detailed effort distribution}\end{pmatrix}$ Table 6–8, Section 23.5
Activity distribution	f(mode, KDSI) Tables 7–1, 7–2, 7–3	Same as for Basic level	Same as for Basic level
Requirements phase effort percentage	f(mode, KDSI) Table 6–8	Same as for Basic level	$f\begin{pmatrix}\text{mode, KDSI,} \\ \text{15 cost drivers}\end{pmatrix}$ Tables 6–8, 23–2, 23–3

shows which particular tables and equations are used at each level of the model hierarchy to calculate each estimate (development effort and schedule, maintenance effort, phase distribution of effort and schedule, activity distribution).

23.7 QUESTIONS

23.1. Which Detailed COCOMO cost driver attributes can have a separate rating for each module, and which can only have a separate rating for each subsystem?

23.2. Which Detailed COCOMO cost driver attribute does not change the phase distribution of effort for any of its ratings? Which cost driver attribute does not change the phase distribution of effort for one of its non-nominal ratings? Which cost driver attribute rating produces the largest decrease in code-and-unit-test phase effort relative to the other phases?

23.3. The percentage phase distribution of effort for a nominal, 128-KDSI, organic-mode project is
Product design: 16%
Detailed design: 23%
Code and unit test: 36%
Integration and test: 25%
How do the following individual changes in cost driver attributes change the percentage phase distribution of effort?
Very low analyst capability?
Very high analyst capability?
Very low use of modern programming practices?
Very high use of modern programming practices?
Very low required reliability?
Very high required reliability?
Low computer response time?
Extra high module complexity?

23.4. Work out the Detailed COCOMO estimates for the Refinery Process Control system used as an example for Intermediate COCOMO in Fig. 9–1, and compare the Intermediate COCOMO and Detailed COCOMO results.

23.5. Work out the Detailed COCOMO estimates for the Transaction Processing System (TPS) operating system used as an example for Intermediate COCOMO in Fig. 9–4, and compare the Intermediate COCOMO and Detailed COCOMO results.

23.6. Work out the Intermediate COCOMO estimates for the high-rated integration and test project used as an example for Detailed COCOMO in Figs. 23–3 and 23–4, and compare the Intermediate COCOMO and Detailed COCOMO results. Why do you think there is a large difference in the overall estimated development effort between the two models' estimates?

23.7. Compute the adjusted schedule distribution for the high-rated integration and test example presented in Figs. 23–3 and 23–4.

23.8. Determine the Detailed COCOMO cost driver attribute ratings which will produce the highest possible percentage of estimated effort in the product design phase. Develop a Detailed COCOMO estimate for a 32-KDSI, embedded-mode project using these cost driver attribute ratings.

23.9. Compute the adjusted schedule distribution for the high-rated product design example of Question 23.8.

23.10. The Shakespeare Word Processing Company has obtained capital funding to develop an experimental prototype of a limited (800-word basic English) voice-driven typewriter. The major components of the software for this prototype are shown in Fig. 23–6.

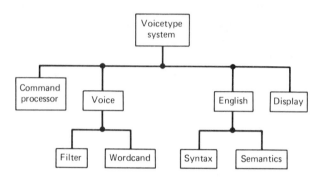

FIGURE 23–6   Voice typewriter system

- The *Command Processor* subsystem handles log on and log off, mode management (compose, edit, file, retrieve, etc.), hardcopy options, etc.
- The *Voice* subsystem accepts speaker utterances and produces candidate word streams. It includes a *Filter* module, which analyzes the voice pressure waves to identify basic speech elements or phonemes, and a *Word Candidate* module which analyzes the phoneme combinations and voice stress patterns to produce candidate streams of basic English words.
- The *English* subsystem analyzes candidate word streams and produces candidate combinations of English sentences and voice-typewriter commands. This subsystem includes *Syntax* and *Semantics* modules which analyze the likely sentence structure and attempt to resolve ambiguities by analyzing the sentences' context.
- The *Display* subsystem shows the speaker the system's interpretation of his or her utterance, for verification or editing.
- Figures 23–7 and 23–8 show the Detailed COCOMO SHEF subsystem and module forms describing the subsystems and modules of the voice-typewriter software system. Estimate the phase distribution of cost and effort required to develop the system by completing the forms.

23.11. Develop a Detailed COCOMO estimate of the phase distribution of effort and schedule for a project with which you are familiar.

Project: Voice-Typewriter Prototype   Analyst: J. Shakespeare   Date: 1/25/85

(1) SS NO.	(2) Subsystem	Phase	(8) EDSI	(21) RELY	(22) DATA	(23) TIME	(24) STOR	(25) VIRT	(26) TURN	(27) ACAP	(28) AEXP	(29) MODP	(30) TOOL	(31) SCED	(32) EAF SS	(20) MM MOD	(33) MM EST	(34) $K/MM	(35) $K	(36) TOTALS AVGS
1	Command	PD	8,000	0.80	1.0	1.0	1.05	1.0	0.98	0.75	0.75	1.0	0.98	1.0				7		
		DD		0.80			1.05		0.95	0.90	0.80	0.95	0.95					7		
		CUT		0.80			1.05		0.70	0.90	0.85	0.90	0.90					7		
		IT		0.60			1.10		0.90	0.85	0.85	0.83	0.85							
2	Voice	PD	20,000	0.80		1.10	1.05		0.98	0.55	0.75	1.0	0.98					8		
		DD		0.80		1.10	1.05		0.95	0.75	0.80	0.90	0.95					8		
		CUT		0.80		1.10	1.05		0.70	0.75	0.85	0.90	0.90					8		
		IT		0.60		1.15	1.10		0.90	0.70	0.85	0.83	0.85					8		
3	English	PD	45,000	0.80		1.10	1.05		0.98	0.55	0.75	1.0	0.98					8		
		DD		0.80		1.10	1.05		0.95	0.75	0.80	0.95	0.95					8		
		CUT		0.80		1.10	1.05		0.70	0.75	0.85	0.90	0.90					8		
		IT		0.60		1.15	1.10		0.90	0.70	0.85	0.83	0.85					8		
4	Display	PD	7,000	0.80		1.0	1.05		0.98	0.75	0.75	1.0	0.98					7		
		DD		0.80			1.05		0.95	0.90	0.80	0.95	0.95					7		
		CUT		0.80			1.05		0.70	0.90	0.90	0.90	0.90					7		
		IT		0.60			1.10		0.90	0.85	0.85	0.83	0.85					7		

Column labels at far left: PD, DD, CUT, IT

Mode: (9) Semi-detached   (10)   (11)

Total EDSI
(MM)_NOM
(EDSI/MM)_NOM

(12) Phase Fraction: PD, DD, CUT, IT

PD
DD
CUT
IT
Total

MM   Sched $K

FIGURE 23-7 Software Hierarchy Estimation Form (SHEF): Subsystem Level: Voice Typewriter

369

	SS NO. (3)	MOD NO. (4)	Module (5)	EDSI (6)	AAF (7)	CPLX (14)	PCAP (15)	VEXP (16)	LEXP (17)	EAF M (18)	MM NOM (13)	MM MOD (19)	MM EST (37)
PD DD CUT IT	1	1 TOT	COMMAND	8,000	100	1.0	1.0 0.83 0.83 0.83	0.90 0.90 0.90 0.90	1.0 0.98 0.92 0.92				
	2	1	FILTER	5,000	50	1.30 1.30 1.30 1.30	1.0 0.65 0.65 0.65	0.90 0.90 0.90 0.90	1.0 0.98 0.92 0.92				
	2	2	WORDCAND	15,000	50	1.65 1.65 1.65 1.65	1.0 0.65 0.65 0.65	0.90 0.90 0.90 0.90	1.0 0.98 0.92 0.92				
	2	TOT		20,000									
	3	1	SYNTAX	20,000	100	1.30 1.30 1.30 1.30	1.0 0.65 0.65 0.65	0.90 0.90 0.90 0.90	1.0 0.98 0.92 0.92				
	3	2	SEMANTICS	25,000	100	1.65 1.65 1.65 1.65	1.0 0.65 0.65 0.65	0.90 0.90 0.90 0.90	1.0 0.98 0.92 0.92				
	3	TOT		45,000									
	4	1 TOT	DISPLAY	7000	35	1.0	1.0 0.83 0.83 0.83	0.90 0.90 0.90 0.90	1.0 0.98 0.92 0.92				

FIGURE 23–8   Software Hierarchy Estimation Form (SHEF): Module Level: Voice Typewriter

Chapter 24

Detailed COCOMO Cost Drivers: Product Attributes

This chapter covers the COCOMO software product attributes. The sections are

24.1 RELY Required software reliability
24.2 DATA Data base size
24.3 CPLX Software product complexity

Each section presents one of the COCOMO cost drivers and provides both the basic information relating to the use of the cost driver in the COCOMO model, and related constructive information indicating why the COCOMO model gives the results it does for the various cost driver ratings. Specifically, each section

- Presents an effort multiplier table for the cost driver, and a related graph showing how much the cost of each software development phase is affected by the cost driver attribute
- Provides definitions of the cost driver rating levels

- Presents a table relating the cost driver rating levels to the corresponding differences in project activity (effort) levels
- Compares the effort multipliers for the cost driver with the results from the 63 projects in the COCOMO data base
- Discusses related observational data and study results
- Provides questions and topics for further research on the material presented

24.1 RELY: REQUIRED SOFTWARE RELIABILITY

As defined in Chapter 8, a software product possesses reliability to the extent that it can be expected to perform its intended functions satisfactorily. Quantitatively, we can define software reliability as a probability:

$$R = \text{Prob} \begin{bmatrix} \text{the software performs its intended} \\ \text{functions satisfactorily over its} \\ \text{next run or its next quantum of} \\ \text{execution time} \end{bmatrix}$$

In principle, we can calculate R if we have the following information:

- The software's *operational profile:* the probability distribution over the space of possible inputs or input sequences to the software, representing the probability that each input or input sequence will be selected for the next run or quantum of execution time
- A precise definition of what it means for the software to "perform its intended functions satisfactorily"

Given this information, we can obtain a minimum variance unbiased estimator of R by performing the following steps [Brown–Lipow, 75]:

- Choose N inputs or input sequences randomly from the operational profile distribution
- Use the inputs to exercise the software for N runs or execution time quanta
- Use the success criterion to determine how many runs or quanta resulted in satisfactory outcomes (call this number M)
- Calculate the estimator $R = M/N$

Figure 24–1 illustrates this process.

If we could perform the above steps easily in practice, we could calculate values of R for software products and use R as the cost driver attribute for Detailed COCOMO. Unfortunately, the above steps are not easy, for the following major reasons:

- The input space is incredibly large
- Characterizing the operational profile is a superset of the workload-characterization problem, already a very difficult problem

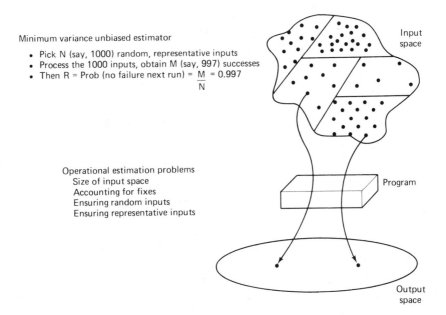

Minimum variance unbiased estimator

- Pick N (say, 1000) random, representative inputs
- Process the 1000 inputs, obtain M (say, 997) successes
- Then R = Prob (no failure next run) = $\frac{M}{N}$ = 0.997

Input space

Operational estimation problems
  Size of input space
  Accounting for fixes
  Ensuring random inputs
  Ensuring representative inputs

Program

Output space

FIGURE 24-1 Input space sampling provides a basis for software reliability measurement

- Ensuring random, representative trial inputs is extremely difficult, as anyone encountering the usual surprises in field testing software products can testify
- In general, one result of finding a software failure is to generate a fix, which to some unknown extent invalidates any results based on the unfixed software.

Most attempts to estimate R to date have been based on software test data. Their generally poor results to date (for example, [Sukert, 1978]) are due largely to the fact that the testing process is not a good approximation to the "random selection from an operational profile" process identified above [Thayer and others, 1978]. The best results to date [Musa, 1975; Musa, 1980] have come from error data obtained from the operation of production real-time and timesharing systems, in which the sequence of inputs is a good approximation to random selection from an operational profile.

As a practical result, for Detailed COCOMO, we find that we must be satisfied with more qualitative cost driver ratings for required software reliability, and with indirect rather than direct data to use as a basis for estimating the tradeoff relationships between increased software reliability and increased software cost.

Ratings and Effort Multipliers

Table 24-1 presents the Detailed COCOMO software development effort multipliers as a function of the degree of reliability required for a software subsystem. This degree may vary from subsystem to subsystem in Detailed COCOMO, reflecting situations in which some subsystems (such as an operating system or key applications

TABLE 24–1 Required Software Reliability (RELY) Effort Multipliers

RELY Rating	Phase Requirements and Product Design	Detailed Design	Code and Unit Test	Integration and Test	Overall
Very low	0.80	0.80	0.80	0.60	0.75
Low	0.90	0.90	0.90	0.80	0.88
Nominal	1.00	1.00	1.00	1.00	1.00
High	1.10	1.10	1.10	1.30	1.15
Very high	1.30	1.30	1.30	1.70	1.40

subsystem) may require a higher degree of reliability than others (such as a support-software or postprocessor subsystem). However, the degree of required reliability will generally not vary from module to module within a subsystem.

The overall effort multipliers in Table 24–1 are calculated from the phase multipliers using the phase weights: product design, 15%; detailed design, 30%; code and unit test, 30%; integration and test, 25%. They are the effort multipliers used for the RELY factor in Intermediate COCOMO.

The rating scale for RELY is as follows:

Very low   The effect of a software failure is simply the inconvenience incumbent on the developers to fix the fault. Typical examples are a demonstration prototype of a voice typewriter or an early feasibility-phase software simulation model.

Low   The effect of a software failure is a low level, easily-recoverable loss to users. Typical examples are a long-range planning model or a climate forecasting model.

Nominal   The effect of a software failure is a moderate loss to users, but a situation from which one can recover without extreme penalty. Typical examples are management information systems or inventory control systems.

High   The effect of a software failure can be a major financial loss or a massive human inconvenience. Typical examples are banking systems and electric power distribution systems.

Very high   The effect of a software failure can be the loss of human life. Examples are military command and control systems or nuclear reactor control systems.

The operational significance of the rating scales for RELY were discussed in some detail in the presentation of Intermediate COCOMO in Chapter 8. The main difference between the treatment of the RELY attribute in Intermediate COCOMO and in Detailed COCOMO is in the phase by phase variation of the effort multipliers. As seen in Table 24–1, the added effort required to achieve high levels of reliability (or the decreased effort required for lower levels) is about the same for the first three phases, and considerably higher (lower) for the integration and test phase. The magnitude of these effects is shown graphically in Fig. 24–2.

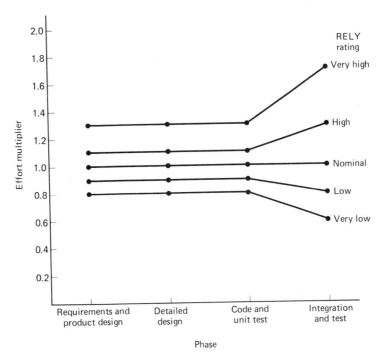

FIGURE 24-2 Effort multipliers by phase: Required software reliability

Project Activity Differences Corresponding to RELY Ratings

Some of the reasons behind the Detailed COCOMO effort multipliers are given in Table 24–2. This table indicates the differences in project activities which will result from having a higher or lower required reliability, and which in turn result in the higher or lower costs experienced on the project.

Thus, for example, a very high level of required reliability will result in 30% additional effort in the plans and requirements phase and the product design phase. This additional effort will be devoted to detailed requirements and product design verification, and more detailed levels of quality assurance (QA)* and configuration management (CM) planning, product standards definition, product design review (PDR) activities, and product documentation. In addition, the project may have to spend further effort communicating with an independent verification and validation (IV & V) organization, and will generate more detailed test plans and procedures.

A very high level of required reliability will also result in a 70% additional effort in the integration and test phase. In this phase, beside the additional care required for QA, CM, and the like, there will be a great deal of additional effort in stress testing, off-nominal testing, and perhaps mathematical verification of the soft-

---

* Several acronyms are used to save space in the tables. Definitions of these and other terms and acronyms are given in Appendix C.

TABLE 24-2 Project Activity Differences Due to Required Software Reliability[a]

Rating	Rqts. and Product Design	Detailed Design	Code and Unit Test	Integration and Test
Very low	Little detail Many TBDs Little verification Minimal QA, CM, draft user manual, test plans Minimal PDR	Basic design information Minimal QA, CM, draft user manual, test plans Informal design inspections	No test procedures Minimal path test, standards check Minimal QA, CM Minimal I/O and off-nominal tests Minimal user manual	No test procedures Many requirements untested Minimal QA, CM Minimal stress, off-nominal tests Minimal as-built documentation
Low	Basic information, verification Frequent TBDs Basic QA, CM, standards, draft user manual, test plans	Moderate detail Basic QA, CM, draft user manual, test plans	Minimal test procedures Partial path test, standards check Basic QA, CM, user manual Partial I/O and off-nominal tests	Minimal test procedures Frequent requirements untested Basic QA, CM, user manual Partial stress, off-nominal tests
Nominal	Nominal project V & V			
High	Detailed verification, QA, CM, standards, PDR, documentation Detailed test plans, procedures	Detailed verification, QA, CM, standards, CDR, documentation Detailed test plans, procedures	Detailed test procedures, QA, CM, documentation Extensive off-nominal tests	Detailed test procedures, QA, CM, documentation Extensive stress, off-nominal tests
Very high	Detailed verification, QA, CM, standards, PDR, documentation IV & V interface Very detailed test plans, procedures	Detailed verification, QA, CM, standards, CDR, documentation Very thorough design inspections Very detailed test plans, procedures IV & V interface	Detailed test procedures, QA, CM, documentation Very thorough code inspections Very extensive off-nominal tests IV & V interface	Very detailed test procedures, QA, CM, documentation Very extensive stress, off-nominal tests IV & V interface

[a] Acronyms are explained in Appendix C.

ware. The added effort in stress testing might include, for example: extreme levels of input volume to process, off-nominal input distributions (such as singularities and extreme points), extreme levels of input error rates, violations of operating assumptions (for example, user protocols), induced or simulated hardware faults, use by inexperienced personnel, or use by expert personnel.

Comparison with Project Results

The simplest way for us to analyze the correlation between the COCOMO effort multipliers and the actual data from software projects is to examine project productivity in DSI/MM as a function of the project's rating level for a given cost driver attribute.* This correlation is shown for the RELY attribute in Fig. 24–3, using the Intermediate COCOMO overall effort multipliers for simplicity.

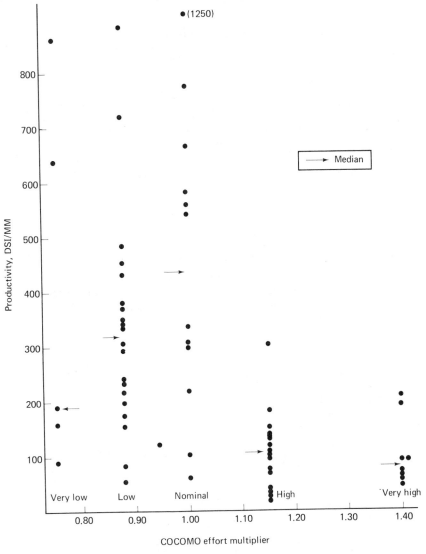

FIGURE 24–3 Correlation of project productivity with required reliability 377

The results are fairly inconclusive. The correlation between the very high and high levels of required reliability and lower values of project productivity is clear, but the trend does not continue throughout the lower RELY ratings. This is evident from the trend in the median productivity values for the various ratings (the arrows in Fig. 24–3). The main reason for the lack of full correlation is that the effects of other cost drivers are mixed in with the RELY effects in complex ways. For example, some of the projects in the COCOMO data base with very low required reliability had relatively low productivity because they were performed with very low-rated analysts and programmers, and with very low use of modern programming practices. (The detailed project data are given in Table 29–1.)

In order to get a clearer picture of the contribution of required reliability to development productivity, we need to eliminate the contaminating effects of the other cost driver attributes as well as possible. The best way we have found to normalize out these other effects is to compute a quantity called the *ideal effort multiplier* for the project/cost-driver combination. It is defined as follows, again using the overall Intermediate COCOMO effort multipliers for simplicity:

> *For the given project* P, *compute the estimated development effort using the standard Intermediate COCOMO procedure, with one exception: do not include the effort multiplier for the cost driver attribute (CDA) being analyzed. Call this estimate MM*(P,CDA). *Then the* ideal effort multiplier, *IEM*(P,CDA), *for this project/cost-driver combination is defined as the multiplier which, if used in Intermediate COCOMO, would make the estimated development effort for the project equal to its actual development effort MM*(P,actual). *That is*

$$IEM(P,CDA) = \frac{MM(P,\text{actual})}{MM(P,CDA)} \qquad (24\text{--}1)$$

As an example, the first project in the COCOMO project data base (Project 1, Table 29–1) required an actual development effort MM(1,actual) = 2040 man-months. If its Intermediate COCOMO estimate of 2218 man-months were to exclude the 0.88 effort multiplier resulting from its low required reliability rating, the result would be

$$MM(1,RELY) = \frac{2218 \text{ MM}}{0.88} = 2520 \text{ MM}$$

Then the ideal effort multiplier for the project/cost-driver combination is

$$IEM(1,RELY) = \frac{MM(1,\text{actual})}{MM(1,RELY)} = \frac{2040 \text{ MM}}{2520 \text{ MM}} = 0.81$$

---

*This is the primary type of analysis performed on the IBM project data base in [Walston–Felix, 1977].

a quantity not too distant from the Intermediate COCOMO cost driver of 0.88.

Using the ideal effort multiplier, we can thus get a clearer assessment of a cost driver's effect on a project, and a comparison of that effort with the COCOMO multiplier for the cost driver. The results for the RELY cost driver attribute are shown in Fig. 24–4. Unlike the inconclusive results obtained in Fig. 24–3, the results here show a strong correlation between the COCOMO effort multipliers (the circles

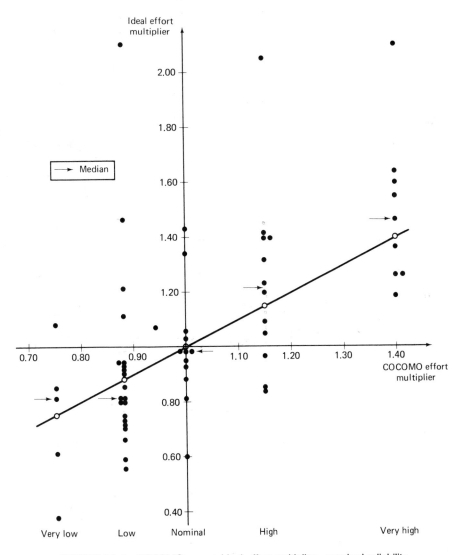

FIGURE 24–4 COCOMO versus ideal effort multiplier—required reliability

in Fig. 24–4) and the project's ideal effort multipliers for the RELY attribute, as is evidenced by the median values of the project data (the arrows in Fig. 24–4) for each RELY rating. The correlation is not perfect, but it gives us reasonable confidence that the COCOMO effort multipliers for RELY are approximately the right magnitude and going in the right direction as a function of cost driver attribute rating. (If the model were perfect, the ideal effort multiplier for each project would be equal to the corresponding COCOMO effort multiplier. That is, all the data points would lie within the circles in Fig. 24–4.)

Discussion

Somewhat surprisingly, very few of the existing software cost-estimation models have incorporated a required reliability factor. The two which have are proprietary: the TRW SCEP model [Boehm–Wolverton, 1978] and the RCA PRICE S model [Freiman–Park, 1979], which has a "Platform" variable which is somewhat correlated with required reliability. Some experimentation with PRICE S indicated a productivity range (ratio of the highest to lowest overall project effort multipliers for the cost driver attribute) of about 6 to 9 for the "Platform" variable (see Fig. 29–13). This is considerably higher than the COCOMO productivity range of 1.87 (1.40 overall multiplier for very high divided by 0.75 overall multiplier for very low; from Table 24–1). The difference is most likely due to the other factors included in the PRICE S "Platform" variable, whose ratings go from Production Center-Internal to Manned Space software.

Some corroborative data on the overall magnitude and phase distribution of the COCOMO effort multipliers is found in the discussions of Independent Verification and Validation (IV & V) in [Hartwick, 1977] and [Reifer, 1978]. IV & V is an activity in which a separate contractor or agency independently performs V & V activities on software being developed by another contractor or agency. It is generally used only to guarantee levels of reliability higher than the nominal level.

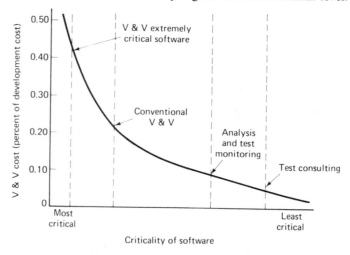

FIGURE 24–5 Spectrum of V&V levels

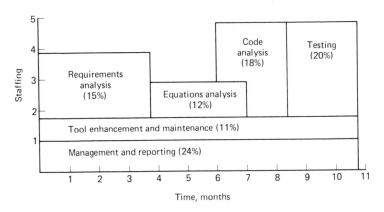

FIGURE 24-6 Sample V&V case-activity allocation

Figure 24-5, taken from [Hartwick, 1977], shows that the overall trend in IV & V costs is comparable to the trend in the COCOMO effort multipliers. Actually, the COCOMO very high required reliability rating corresponds to the Conventional V & V point in Fig. 24-5,* which has an effort multiplier of only 1.20 compared to the COCOMO overall effort multiplier of 1.40. The difference is explained primarily by the facts that the IV & V agent does not have to fix the faults found, and that the developers also increase their own level of fault detection and associated activities.

Figure 24-6, also from [Hartwick, 1977], shows the phase distribution of IV & V effort for a Conventional V & V level activity. It shows a rough match to the COCOMO phase distribution, except for a lower level in the integration and test phases. Again, the difference is largely explained by the added effort required by the developer to fix detected faults, which is greatest in the integration and test phase (see Fig. 24-2).

The Software Reliability Production Function

Ideally, we would like to have a production function of the form shown in Fig. 24-7, relating desired values of software reliability R to the cost or effort required to achieve them.

Although the ultimate ideal is going to be extremely difficult to achieve, a number of contributions have been made recently which give us a good deal of insight into the nature of this production function (and into the complexities of achieving the ultimate ideal).

The Software Error Introduction and Removal Model. The best conceptual model currently available for understanding the nature of the software reliability production function is the software error introduction and removal model shown in Fig. 24-8.* It shows that the software development process can be viewed as introducing a

---

* The *extremely critical* V & V level is used for software performing functions such as nuclear missile control. It represents an exceptional level of required reliability beyond that modeled by COCOMO.

* This model is analogous to the "tank and pipe" model introduced in [Jones, 1975], in which errors conceptually flow into a holding tank through various error-source pipes, and are drained off through various error-elimination pipes.

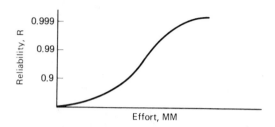

FIGURE 24-7 Software reliability production function

certain number of errors into each software product artifact (requirements spec, design, code, documentation), and subsequently performing a number of error removal activities (automated requirements aids, independent requirements V & V, simulation, etc.), each of which has a characteristic production function relating its level of error removal to the level of cost or effort devoted to its use. In principle, then, we can select levels of investment in each of these error removal activities and determine the resulting level of residual software errors left at the end of the last error removal activity.

One thing we know from our earlier cost-to-fix versus phase curve in Fig. 4–2 is that the relative cost of error elimination activities increases in the later software development phases, as we accumulate a larger inventory of items to fix per error eliminated. In addition, there have been a number of useful studies of the relative magnitudes of some of the error flows in Fig. 24–8, and of the nature of some of the individual error removal production functions.

Table 24–3 shows the results of three fairly comparable studies [Jones, 1978;

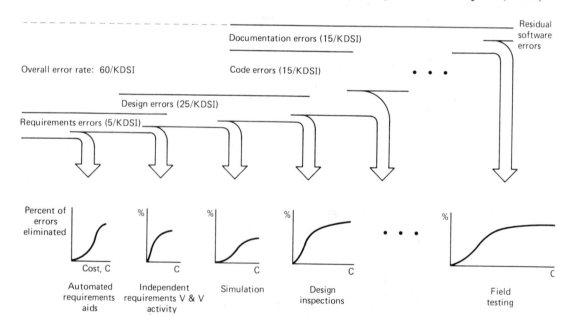

FIGURE 24-8 Software error introduction/removal model

TABLE 24-3 Error Introduction and Removal During Software Development

	[Jones, 1978]			[Thayer and others, 1978]	[Boehm, 1980]
Errors introduced					
Overall rate	30–35/KDSI			40–80/KDSI[a]	65–85/KDSI
Percentage by component					
Requirements				10%	8–10%
Functional design	15%			} 55	15–20
Logical design	20				25–35
Coding	30			35	25
Documentation, etc.	35				17–20
Errors removed	Function	Logic	Coding		
Automated requirements aids				63[b]	
Functional specifications review	50				45–60
Simulation				21	
Design language				32	
Design standards				29	
Logic specifications review	40	50			50–60
Module logic inspection	60	70		58	
Module code inspection	65	75	70	63	
Code standards auditor				20	
Set/use analyzer				14	
Unit test	10	10	25	} 73	
Function test	20	25	55		
Component test	15	20	65	} 46	50
Subsystem test	15	15	55		
System test	10	10	40	46	50

[a] Equivalent figure. Reported rate (10–20/KDSI) covered only post-integration test errors discovered.
[b] From [Bell–Thayer, 1976].

Thayer and others, 1978; and Boehm, 1980] of the relative magnitudes of the error introduction and removal flows during software development. The Thayer data are the result of a retrospective analysis of several thousand software problem reports on large TRW software projects; the Jones data cover a wide variety of IBM projects; the Boehm data cover two small (2-KDSI) products developed to the same overall specification.

The error removal data in Table 24–3 indicate only the overall potential error removal percentage for full application of each technique or activity; they do not provide any indication of the relative cost of the techniques or of the shapes of their production functions. Much less is known about the individual error removal production functions; perhaps the best characterizations have been the code inspection and unit test production functions shown as Fig. 24–9.

The data in Fig. 24–9 are corroborated fairly well by other studies which provide single points on error-removal functions, primarily for code inspection and unit test activities. Table 24–4 summarizes the results of these studies, including the results in Fig. 24–9 indentified as Project A. (Project A had a programming rate of roughly 4 DSI/MH. Thus, the unit test rate of 5 DSI/MH in Table 24–4 corresponds with the 80% of programming effort point in Fig. 24–9, etc.)

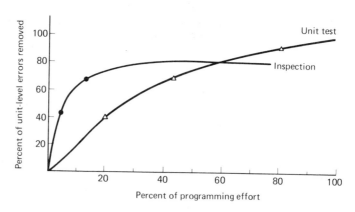

FIGURE 24-9 Code inspection and unit test production functions

TABLE 24-4 Error Removal Cost and Effectiveness

Activity	Source	Effort	Error Removal
Code inspection	[Jones, 1977]	10–48 DSI/MH[a]	70%
	[Myers, 1978]	10 DSI/MH	38%
	[Boehm, 1980]	20 DSI/MH	89%
	Project A	120 DSI/MH	41%
		30 DSI/MH	64%
	[Crossman, 1979]	25 DSI/MH	50–60%
Unit test	[Jones, 1977]	18–40 DSI/MH	20% after inspection
	[Myers, 1978]	24 DSI/MH	36%
	Project A	20 DSI/MH	40%
		10 DSI/MH	68%
		5 DSI/MH	89%
	[Crossman, 1979]	10 DSI/MH	50–60%
Program proving	[Miller, 1980]	$50–500/DSI	Very high, but not 100%

[a] DSI/MH = Delivered source instructions processed per man-hour.

Completing the Software Reliability Production Function Picture. In principle, we should be able to construct similar production functions for other error-avoidance and error-removal activities, and thus complete the picture established in Fig. 24–8; one which allows us to select desired levels of investment in the various activities and determine the resulting residual software error level in errors/KDSI. From this quantity, there are reliability estimation techniques such as those discussed in [Musa, 1980] or [Duvall, 1979] for converting an estimate of residual error level into an estimate of software reliability R, under an appropriate set of assumptions. Or, we can use a simpler reliability metric, such as (errors discovered)/(KDSI-year), and simply spread the residual errors across the anticipated software product lifetime, as is done in [Remus–Zilles, 1979].

Difficulties in Completing the Picture. In practice, however, completing the picture will not be so easy. The process of combining the production functions is complicated by the fact that each error-removal activity is highly effective against some classes of errors, and much less effective against others, Thus, we cannot superimpose the effects of individual production functions to obtain a composite production function unless we know their relative overlap in removing errors of the same class.

An example of such a complication is given by the [Myers, 1978] experience on code inspections given in Table 24–4. The required effort there of 1 man-hour of inspection effort per 10 DSI with a resulting error-removal yield of 38% is much less cost-effective than the other code inspection experiences in Table 24–4. The difference is most likely explained by the fact that Myers' sample program contained a number of considerably more subtle errors than are found in most applications software (for example, 6 of the 15 errors in the program had gone undetected when a version of the program was generated using correctness-proof techniques [Naur, 1969; Goodenough–Gerhart, 1975]).

As another example, the process of combining the inspection and unit test production function in Fig. 24–9 will encounter the following overlap-assessment issues:

Technique	Inspections	Unit Test
Strengths	• Simple programming blunders, logic errors • Developer blind spots • Interface errors • Missing portions • Specification errors	• Simple programming blunders, logic errors • Numerical approximations • Program dynamics errors
Weaknesses	• Numerical approximations • Program dynamics errors	• Developer blind spots • Interface errors • Missing portions • Specification errors

The two activities are fairly complementary in addressing different classes of errors, but overlap strongly in the most common class: simple programming blunders and logic errors. Thus, developing a composite production function will not be easy, as higher levels of investment in both techniques will encounter more and more errors detectable by both techniques.

Another complicating factor is the relative seriousness of errors, which must be considered in any error-removal investment strategy. For example [Rubey and others, 1975] has shown that documentation errors are much less severe on the average than other classes of errors, over a sample of several hundred errors classified according to type and severity.

In closing, however, even though the characterization of software cost–reliability tradeoffs is a complex issue, there are a number of useful studies and data sources available to help us understand the situation. [Thayer and others, 1978] contains several analyses of error data indicating the relative effectiveness of different error-removal techniques in removing various classes of errors. [Boehm, 1979] contains a relative assessment of software requirements and design V & V techniques and their cost-effectiveness in removing different classes of errors. [Rubey and others, 1975], [Endres, 1975], [Weiss, 1979], [Christensen, 1980], [Howden, 1978], the RADC Data Analysis Center for Software [Nelson, 1978], and the NASA Goddard/Univ. of Maryland Software Engineering Laboratory [Basili and others, 1977] contain valuable data on the relative frequency of software errors of different classes, their relative severity, and the relative effectiveness of various techniques in eliminating them.

A great deal of important work remains to be done in this area in order to obtain a thorough understanding of the relations between software cost and software reliability. Some of the most significant candidates are discussed at the end of this chapter as topics for further research.

24.2   DATA: DATA BASE SIZE

The amount of effort required to develop a software product clearly is influenced by the size and complexity of the data base. However, the specific attributes of a software product data base which influence the product's cost have been extremely difficult to characterize. To date, most of the work on software complexity metrics has concentrated on program complexity rather than data complexity, and many software cost-estimation models exclude data base effects completely by using only executable instructions as a size parameter.

Further, software practitioners have not evolved a common vocabulary for expressing data base size effects well. For example, one software cost data collection survey included the quantity, "Number of classes of items in the data base." The answers received from several projects with very similar data base characteristics ranged from 3 to 1,000,000. The survey followup reconciled some of the differences in interpretation, but still left so many cloudy issues unresolved that the quantity was dropped as a candidate cost driver attribute.

Reflecting this general situation, the COCOMO approach to characterizing data base effects is still somewhat ad hoc and piecemeal. Data base cost driver effects are covered in three ways.

1. The total amount of data to be assembled for the data base is characterized by the DATA cost driver attribute presented in this section.
2. The structure of the data base is characterized by its contribution to the number of delivered source instructions (DSI) in the software product.*
3. The complexity of data handling activities is characterized by the *data management operations* scale in the complexity (CPLX) cost driver attribute discussed in the following section.

This approach has been a clear improvement over some of the earlier false starts toward incorporating data base considerations into COCOMO. It may turn out to be a highly appropriate approach in the long run. But a great deal of additional research, data collection, and analysis will be needed to establish this definitively.

---

* Even here, an additional wrinkle has been necessary: for COBOL programs, the COCOMO DSI count weights the nonexecutable source lines of code by a factor of $\frac{1}{3}$.

Ratings and Effort Multipliers

Table 24–5 presents the Detailed COCOMO software development effort multipliers as a function of the relative size of the data base to be developed. The ratings are defined in terms of the following ratio

$$D/P = \frac{\text{Data base size in bytes or characters}}{\text{Program size in DSI}}$$

where data base size refers to the amount of data to be assembled and stored in nonmain storage (that is, tapes, disks, drums, bubble memories, etc.) by the time of software acceptance. The magnitude and phase distribution of the data base size effects are shown graphically in Fig. 24–10.

TABLE 24–5 Data Base Size Effort Multipliers

DATA Rating	Phase	Requirements and Product Design	Detailed Design	Code and Unit Test	Integration and Test	Overall
Low (D/P < 10)		.95	.95	.95	.90	.94
Nominal (10 ≤ D/P < 100)		1.00	1.00	1.00	1.00	1.00
High (100 ≤ D/P < 1000)		1.10	1.05	1.05	1.15	1.08
Very high (D/P ≥ 1000)		1.20	1.10	1.10	1.30	1.16

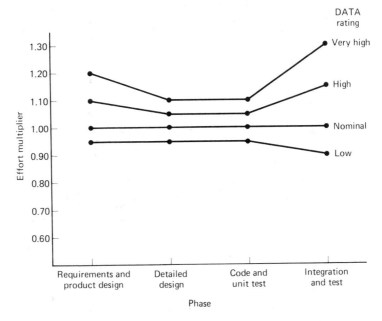

FIGURE 24–10 Effort multipliers by phase: Data base size

TABLE 24-6 Project Activity Differences Due to Data Base Size

Rating	Requirements and Product Design	Detailed Design	Code and Unit Test	Integration and Test
Low (D/P < 10)	Easy data base design and validation Easy HW/SW storage interface Easier test plans Minimal data base CM, documentation	Easy data base design and validation Less data checking in program Easier test plans Minimal data base CM, documentation	Easy data base development Less data checking in program Less data assembly Minimal data base CM, documentation	Less data base testing, data base acceptance activity Easy code and data base integration Less data assembly Minimal data base CM, documentation
Nominal (10 ≤ D/P < 100)	No change	No change	No change	No change
High (100 ≤ D/P < 1000)	Complex data base design and validation Complex HW/SW storage interface More test planning More data base CM, documentation Data base administrator functions	Complex data base design and validation More data checking in program More test planning More data base CM, documentation	Harder data base development More data checking in program More data assembly More data base CM, documentation	More data base testing, data base acceptance activity Difficult code/data base integration More data assembly More data base CM, documentation
Very high (D/P ≥ 1000)	More of above	More of above	More of above	More of above

Table 24–6 indicates the project activity differences resulting from the differing levels of data base size. The differences in data base planning, code/data base integration, and verification tend to be the main reasons why the first and last phases have a wider effort variation than the two middle phases.

Comparison with Project Results

Based on our analysis in Section 24.1 of the comparison between COCOMO RELY effort multipliers and the project results in the COCOMO project data base, we will use the ideal effort multiplier defined there (Eq. 24–1) as the basis for our comparison for the DATA attribute. Recall that the ideal effort multiplier

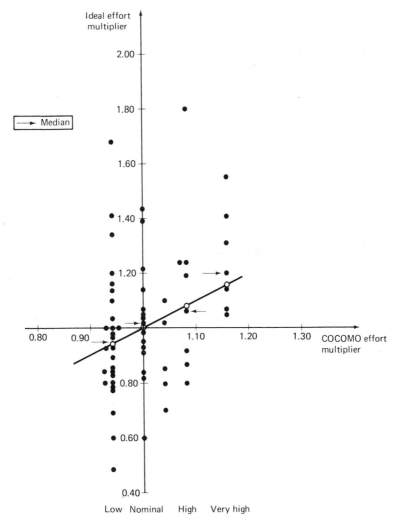

FIGURE 24–11 COCOMO versus ideal effort multiplier—Data base size

IEM(*P*,DATA) for each project *P* is the value of the DATA effort multiplier which would make the Intermediate COCOMO estimated man-months for the project exactly equal to the actual man-months required for the project, assuming that all the other Intermediate COCOMO effort multipliers retained the values determined by their attribute ratings.

Figure 24–11 shows the values of IEM(*P*,DATA) for the projects in the CO-COMO project data base, as compared to the values of the overall (Intermediate COCOMO) effort multipliers for the four DATA attribute ratings. As with the RELY attribute, we see a good correlation between the COCOMO multipliers (the circles in Fig. 24–11) and the project data, particularly with respect to the median values of IEM(*P*,DATA) for each DATA rating (the arrows in Fig. 24–11).

Discussion

Table 24–5 is meant to account simply for the overall size of the data base to be designed, assembled, and validated prior to acceptance. Considerations of the complexity of data structures are accommodated in COCOMO via the inclusion of data statements as source instructions and via the data management operations scale in the complexity factor (Section 24.3).

Relatively little has been determined about the effect of this factor. The Doty study [Herd and others, 1977] indicated it had a "minor" effect, but no quantitative data were given. The Air Force-Industry Software Cost Estimation Workshop [Air Force, 1974] considered it an important factor, but provided no estimates on the magnitude of its effect. The IBM [Walston–Felix, 1977] study indicates a productivity range of 1.73 for the factor, "Number of classes of items in the data base per 1000 lines of code." The COCOMO productivity range is 1.16/.94 or 1.23.

24.3 CPLX: SOFTWARE PRODUCT COMPLEXITY

Ratings and Effort Multipliers

Table 24–7 presents the Detailed COCOMO software development effort multipliers as a function of the level of complexity of the module to be developed. The ratings are given in Table 24–8 as a function of the type of operations to be primarily

TABLE 24–7 Module Complexity Effort Multipliers

CPLX Rating	Phase Requirements and Product Design	Detailed Design	Code and Unit Test	Integration and Test	Overall
Very low	.70	.70	.70	.70	.70
Low	.85	.85	.85	.85	.85
Nominal	1.00	1.00	1.00	1.00	1.00
High	1.15	1.15	1.15	1.15	1.15
Very high	1.30	1.30	1.30	1.30	1.30
Extra high	1.65	1.65	1.65	1.65	1.65

TABLE 24–8 Module Complexity Ratings versus Type of Module

Rating	Control Operations	Computational Operations	Device-Dependent Operations	Data Management Operations
Very low	Straightline code with a few non-nested SP operators: DOs, CASEs, IFTHEN-ELSEs. Simple predicates	Evaluation of simple expressions: for example, $A = B+C*(D-E)$	Simple read, write statements with simple formats	Simple arrays in main memory
Low	Straight forward nesting of SP operators. Mostly simple predicates	Evaluation of moderate level expressions, for example, $D = SQRT$ $(B**2-4.*A*C)$	No cognizance needed of particular processor or I/O device characteristics. I/O done at GET/ PUT level. No cognizance of overlap	Single file subsetting with no data structure changes, no edits, no intermediate files
Nominal	Mostly simple nesting. Some intermodule control. Decision tables	Use of standard math and statistical routines. Basic matrix and vector operations	I/O processing includes device selection, status checking and error processing	Multifile input and single file output. Simple structural changes, simple edits
High	Highly nested SP operators with many compound predicates. Queue and stack control. Considerable intermodule control	Basic numerical analysis: multivariate interpolation, ordinary differential equations. Basic truncation, roundoff concerns	Operations at physical I/O level (physical storage address translations; seeks, reads, etc). Optimized I/O overlap	Special purpose subroutines activated by data stream contents. Complex data restructuring at record level
Very high	Reentrant and recursive coding. Fixed-priority interrupt handling	Difficult but structured NA: near-singular matrix equations, partial differential equations	Routines for interrupt diagnosis, servicing, masking. Communication line handling	A generalized, parameter-driven file structuring routine. File building, command processing, search optimization
Extra high	Multiple resource scheduling with dynamically changing priorities. Microcode-level control	Difficult and unstructured NA: highly accurate analysis of noisy, stochastic data	Device timing-dependent coding, microprogrammed operations	Highly coupled, dynamic relational structures. Natural language data management

performed by the module: control, computation, device-dependent, or data management operations. For each type of module, Table 24–8 provides a scale of increasingly complex operations which correspond to the module complexity ratings of very low, low, nominal, high, very high, and extra high.

Thus, for example, a computational module consisting purely of simple expressions such as $A = B + C*(D\text{-}E)$ would be given a very low rating. If the module contained somewhat more involved expressions such as $D = \text{SQRT}(B**2\text{--}4.*A*C)$, it would be given a low rating.

No counterpart is given for the usual table indicating project activity differences due to differing rating levels. The effect of increased complexity tends to be more of a uniform increase in all project activities. This effect is manifested in the uniform phase distribution of the CPLX effort multipliers, shown graphically in Fig. 24–12.

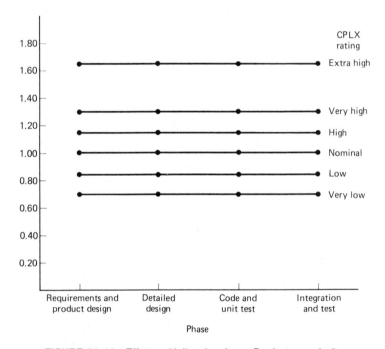

FIGURE 24–12 Effort multipliers by phase: Product complexity

Comparison with Project Results

As in our comparisons above between the COCOMO effort multipliers and project results, we will use the ideal effort multiplier IEM(P,CPLX) for each project P in the COCOMO project data base as the basis of project comparisons.

Figure 24–13 shows the values of IEM(P,CPLX) for the projects in the COCOMO data base, as compared to the values of the COCOMO effort multipliers for the six CPLX attribute ratings (the circles in Fig. 24–13). The correlation between the COCOMO effort multipliers and the median values of IEM(P,CPLX)—the arrows in Fig. 24–13—is again fairly good, except for the extra high rating, which has only

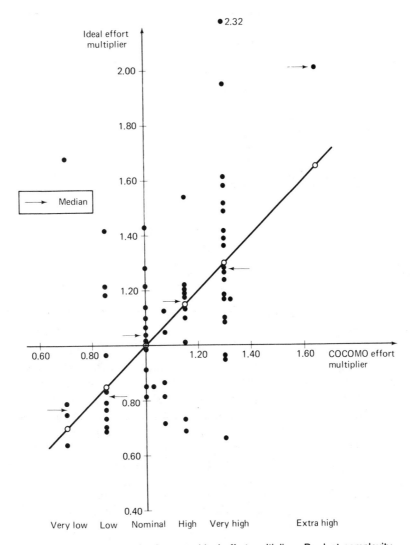

FIGURE 24-13 COCOMO versus ideal effort multiplier—Product complexity

one data point. Without additional extra high complexity data points, it is premature to suggest any upward revision of the extra high effort multiplier.

Discussion

Some of the earliest software cost models had only one effort multiplier, which was associated with the overall complexity or difficulty of the job to be done. Perhaps the best of these early models was the one based on the 1964–66 System Development Corporation (SDC) study [Nelson, 1966] of 169 software projects. Figure 24–14 shows the cumulative distribution of project productivity or programming rate for these 169 projects. To use Fig. 24–14 for estimation, one would initially rate one's project

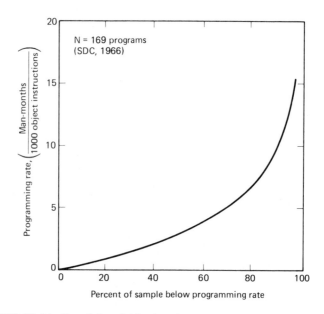

N = 169 programs
(SDC, 1966)

Percent of sample below programming rate

FIGURE 24-14 Cumulative distribution of programming rates, 169 programs

as, say, more complex than 80% of the projects in the SDC sample. Figure 24–14 would then indicate that the new project would take 7 man-months to produce 1000 object instructions, or 143 instructions/MM. A 60% rating would indicate a programming rate of 4 MM/1000 instructions, or 250 instructions/MM.

The major practical difficulty of such a model is that the ratings are based on pure subjective opinion. Thus if one estimator rates a project at the 80% complexity level and another at the 60% level, there is no way for a third party to decide which rating is more accurate—although they will produce cost estimates which differ by almost a factor of two.

COCOMO follows the TRW SCEP model [Boehm–Wolverton, 1978] in attempting to bound the subjective variability due to the complexity factor in the following ways:

- Making the complexity rating a module-level rather than a subsystem- or system-level rating
- Factoring as many sources of variance in productivity as possible into separate cost drivers independent of the complexity cost driver (for example, execution time and main storage constraints, required reliability, etc.)
- Providing the rating scales in Table 24–8 in order to make each complexity rating as objective as possible

The resulting COCOMO productivity range due to complexity is 2.36. This is considerably less than the productivity ranges of 4 to 6.67 in the [Aron, 1969] model and 6 to 7 in the RCA PRICE S model [Freiman–Park, 1979]. The later [Aron,

1974] model has productivity ranges of 2 to 4 for assembly language and 4 to 6 for higher order languages, depending on the type of function being developed. The [Wolverton, 1974] model had a relatively small productivity range due to complexity of 1.42 to 1.53; this was most likely due to its being based on a highly uniform project sample. The NARDAC model [Williamson, 1979] has a productivity range due to complexity of 12, but as it is a module level rating, its range of variability across an entire product is less pronounced. The [Scott–Simmons, 1974] Delphi survey of productivity determinants surprisingly gave "Complexity of Application" a slight *positive* correlation with increased productivity (+1 on a scale of −7 to +7). The [Daly, 1979] model has productivity ranges of 1.5 for intra-module complexity and 1.2 for inter-module complexity. The [Griffin, 1980] model has a productivity range of 1.5 for complexity.

Complexity metrics. A number of metrics have been formulated to characterize software complexity, for example, [Weissman, 1974; McCabe, 1976; Halstead, 1977; and Dunsmore–Gannon, 1979]. These metrics have provided a number of valuable insights, but have not yet produced a sufficient base of general familiarity and correlation with productivity to be used as a production cost model attribute. (This point will be discussed further in Chapter 28.)

Some early exploratory work indicates that the correlation between these metrics and the complexity scales in Table 24–8 is positive, but not extremely strong. The metrics seem somewhat insensitive to the relative amount of analytic effort involved in formulating and programming modules with higher or lower ratings on the CO-COMO scale. Obtaining more definitive results on this and related questions are some of the main topics for further research identified below.

24.4 QUESTIONS

24.1. What activities account for the 10% added effort in the detailed design phase of a software project which must produce a software product with high reliability?

24.2. What activities account for the 40% less effort in the integration and test phase of a software project which is to produce software with very low reliability?

24.3. The nominal phase distribution of effort for a large (128-KDSI) embedded-mode software project is

Product design: 18%
Detailed design: 25%
Code and unit test: 26%
Integration and test: 31%

What would the phase distribution of effort be for such a project if it required very high reliability?

24.4. What would the phase distribution of effort be for the above project if it required very low reliability?

24.5. What would the phase distribution of effort be for the above project if it consisted of 64 KDSI of high reliability mission software and 64 KDSI of very low reliability support software?

24.6. Suppose you are planning the inspection and unit test activities for a 5000-DSI software product. How many man-hours would you allocate for each?

24.7. What activities account for the 10% added effort in the code and unit test phase of a software project with a very high data base size?

24.8. A nominal 32-KDSI organic-mode management information system requires a development effort of 122 man-months and has a nominal phase distribution of effort by percentage of (16,24,38,22) for the four development phases. What will be the total effort and phase distribution if the system requires the development of a data base with 10,000,000 bytes? A data base with 100,000,000 bytes?

24.9. Suppose the management information system of Question 24.8 required the development of a data base with 20,000,000 bytes. Work out an interpolation scheme for using the DATA effort multiplier tables which supports the comparison of project effort for the 10-, 20-, and 100-megabyte jobs.

24.10. Suppose you are performing an independent cost estimate for Standard University to help evaluate vendor proposals for Standard's multimicroprocessor campus energy management system. How would you rate the complexity of the modules performing the following functions:
(a) Determining required heat output for a room by interpolation from a two-dimensional table versus temperature deficiency and room volume?
(b) Creating and deleting entries in the master building file?
(c) Microcode level fault-tolerance switchover logic?
(d) Preparing messages for selected console displays, using standard display routines?
(e) Handling high-priority emergency interrupts?
(f) Computing average daily temperatures for management reports?
(g) Parsing operator console commands?

24.11. For the Standard University energy management system, suppose you had a choice between two ways of implementing the procedure to compute expected monthly temperatures

- A 50-DSI procedure using a simple FOR loop to cover each month
- A 30-DSI procedure using some complex recursive formulas to perform computations

Which approach would require less effort to develop?

24.12. Provide COCOMO complexity ratings for the major components of a compiler.

24.13. The SDC curve in Fig. 24–14 can be used as the basis of a cost-estimation model which calibrates perfectly to past experience, in that any completed project can be given a complexity rating exactly corresponding to its experienced productivity. From this complexity rating and the product's size, the SDC curve will predict exactly the number of man-months that were used by the project. What is the major deficiency in using this model for practical cost estimation? What does it tell us about using calibration to past projects as a single sufficient condition for the goodness of a cost-estimation model?

24.5 TOPICS FOR FURTHER RESEARCH

24.A. Perform experiments and observations to test the hypotheses that the RELY effort multipliers
- are of the same magnitudes used in COCOMO
- vary by phase as in Detailed COCOMO
- are independent of project size, type, or mode
- interact multiplicatively with the other COCOMO cost driver attributes (such as TURN, PCAP, MODP)

24.B. Perform experiments to test the hypothesis that the RELY rating scales are sufficiently objective to assure reasonably uniform cost driver ratings.

24.C. Project A, the source of the error removal production functions for code inspection and unit test in Fig. 24–9, was a large real-time aerospace software project. Test the hypothesis that these production functions are independent of project type by gathering similar data for other projects and comparing the results. Extend the results by classifying the errors by type and severity. Develop a composite production function for the two techniques based on the extended results. See [Christensen, 1980] for some related results.

24.D. Perform observations and experiments to determine the error-removal production functions for
- Requirements reviews
- Design reviews
- Program proving techniques
- Simulation, use of checklists, prototyping, and other requirements and design V & V techniques analyzed in [Boehm, 1979]
- Path testing, symbolic testing, and other test techniques analyzed in [Howden, 1978]
- Code auditors, set-use analyzers, and other automated aids analyzed in [Reifer–Trattner, 1977; Reifer, 1978]
- Dual code, data base inspection, and other techniques analyzed in [Gilb, 1977]

24.E. Perform experiments and observations to validate the error introduction rates and component distributions given in Table 24–3.

24.F. Reports to date on the amount of effort on a software project devoted to defect removal show a good deal of variance. [Jones, 1977], Figure 3, indicates that defect removal consumes about 1 MM/KDSI or about 50% of a 2-KDSI project's effort, growing to 22 MM/KDSI or about 73% of a 2048-KDSI project's effort. The data on two 2-KDSI projects in [Boehm, 1980] indicated that defect removal consumed about 0.6 MM/KDSI or about 17 to 22% of the project's effort. The carefully-prepared A-7 requirements specification experienced a very low error-removal effort [Basili-Weiss, 1981]. Perform experiments and observations to clarify the issue.

24.G. Develop a relationship between the amount of calendar time or execution time used to test a software product and the amount of effort spent in testing. Use this relationship to develop production functions for testing error removal based on the data on error removal versus calendar time and execution time in [Thayer and others, 1978], [Musa, 1979], and the RADC Data Analysis Center for Software [Nelson, 1978].

24.H. One necessary step toward a quantitative basis for software cost–reliability decision-making is an appropriate metric reflecting the relative severity of software errors.

The most effective treatment of this subject to date has been the *normalized error time* metric used by the European Space Agency as the basis of contract incentive payments for a software maintenance team [Formica, 1978]. Each software failure encountered was characterized by its duration D_i and its severity W_i, rated on the following scale:

$W_i = 10,000$ for failures affecting all supported spacecraft
    $= 1,000$ for failures affecting only one spacecraft
    $= 100$ for failures affecting experiment data analysis
    $= 10$ for minor failures (such as incorrect printout)
    $= 1$ for trivial failures (such as typo in text).

The normalized error time T for a given period was then calculated as

$$T = \sum_{i=1}^{n} W_i D_i$$

This metric was highly successful as an incentive for reliable maintenance of the software. (It was effectively used as a basis for awarding incentive payments to software maintainers.)

Develop and experiment with more general metrics for accommodating the relative severity of errors into software reliability analyses and production functions.

24.I. Perform experiments and observations to test the hypothesis that the DATA effort multipliers
- are of the same magnitude used in COCOMO
- vary by phase as in Detailed COCOMO
- are independent of project size, type, or mode
- interact multiplicatively with the other COCOMO cost driver attributes (such as STOR, TURN)

24.J. Formulate improved metrics for data base size and complexity. Investigate their applicability across a wide variety of software applications, including distributed data base applications. Perform experiments and observations with respect to their correlation with software or data base development effort.

24.K. Collect and analyze data on the distribution of effort among the various data base activities on a software project (for example, the activities in Table 24–6).

24.L. Collect and analyze data on the activities involved in adapting an existing data base to a new application. Formulate extensions to the COCOMO adaptation adjustment factor (AAF) to cover data base adaptation effects, and evaulate them with respect to the collected data.

24.M. Perform experiments and observations to test the hypotheses that the CPLX effort multipliers
- are of the same magnitudes used in COCOMO
- are independent of project size, type, or mode
- do not vary by phase
- interact multiplicatively with the other COCOMO cost driver attributes (for example, ACAP, PCAP, AEXP, LEXP, MODP)

24.N. Perform experiments to test the hypothesis that the CPLX rating scales are sufficiently objective to assure reasonably uniform cost driver ratings.

24.O. Formulate and calibrate complexity rating scales for other types of software modules, such as text processing and display processing.

24.P. Perform experiments similar to those discussed in [Curtis and others, 1979a, 1979b; Sunohara and others, 1981] testing hypotheses on the correlation between software development productivity and complexity metrics such as those in [Weissman, 1974; McCabe, 1976; Halstead, 1977; and Dunsmore–Gannon, 1979], for example:

- The complexity metrics correlate well with software productivity on (large, small, systems, applications) software projects
- The complexity metrics correlate well with the COCOMO CPLX rating scales
- The complexity metrics are a better productivity estimator than the COCOMO CPLX rating scales

[Curtis, 1979] provides an excellent survey of software complexity issues.

24.Q. Perform similar experiments on the correlation of the above metrics to software reliability and maintenance productivity.

24.R. Formulate improved software complexity metrics and test their improved correlation with software development productivity, maintenance productivity, or reliability.

Chapter 25

━━━

Detailed COCOMO
Cost Drivers:
Computer Attributes

This chapter discusses the Computer attributes used as software cost drivers in the Intermediate and Detailed COCOMO models. These are

25.1 TIME Execution time constraint
25.2 STOR Main storage constraint
25.3 VIRT Virtual machine volatility
25.4 TURN Computer turnaround time

25.1 TIME: EXECUTION TIME CONSTRAINT

Ratings and Effort Multipliers

Table 25–1 presents the Detailed COCOMO software development effort multipliers as a function of the degree of execution time constraint imposed upon a software

TABLE 25–1 Execution Time Constraint Effort Multipliers

TIME Rating \ Phase	Requirements and Product Design	Detailed Design	Code and Unit Test	Integration and Test	Overall
Nominal ($\leq 50\%$)	1.00	1.00	1.00	1.00	1.00
High (70%)	1.10	1.10	1.10	1.15	1.11
Very high (85%)	1.30	1.25	1.25	1.40	1.30
Extra high (95%)	1.65	1.55	1.55	1.90	1.66

subsystem. The rating is expressed in terms of the percentage of available execution time expected to be used by the subsystem and any other subsystems consuming the execution time resource. The tables do not cover situations in which over 95% of the available execution time is to be used. The magnitude and phase distribution of the execution time constraint effects is shown graphically in Fig. 25–1.

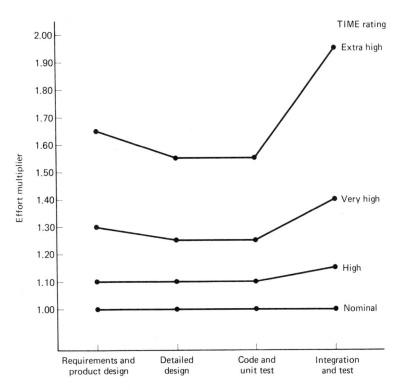

FIGURE 25–1 Effort multipliers versus phase: Execution time constraint

Table 25–2 indicates the project activity differences resulting from the differing levels of execution time constraint. The higher escalation in integration and test phase cost stems primarily from the higher cost of error detection and fixes caused by the execution time constraints.

TABLE 25-2 Project Activity Differences Due to Execution Time Constraint

Rating	Requirements and Product Design	Detailed Design	Code and Unit Test	Integration and Test
Nominal (<50%)	No change	No change	No change	No change
High (70%)	Added analysis, simulation, prototyping, validation	Added analysis, simulation, prototyping, validation	Added analysis Code and data trickier to program and debug	More complex test procedures Harder to debug, fix, fix correctly Added performance measurement functions Tight execution time budget control
	Complex resource management requirements to design More complex test plans, procedures	Complex resource management requirements to design More complex test plans, procedures	Complex resource management routines to develop Tight execution time budget control	
Very high (85%)	More of above	More of above	More of above	More of above
Extra high (95%)	Much more of above	Much more of above	Much more of above	Much more of above

Comparison with Project Results

Based on our earlier analysis in Section 24.1 of the comparison between COCOMO Reliability (RELY) effort multipliers and project results, we will use the ideal effort multipliers defined there (in Eq. 24–1) as the basis for our comparison for the computer attributes discussed in this chapter. For the TIME attribute, the ideal effort multiplier, IEM (P,TIME), for each project P is the value of the Time effort multiplier which would make the Intermediate COCOMO estimated man-months for the project exactly equal to the actual man-months required for the project, assuming that all the other Intermediate COCOMO effort multipliers retained the values determined by their attribute ratings.

Figure 25–2 shows the values of IEM (P,TIME) for the projects in the COCOMO

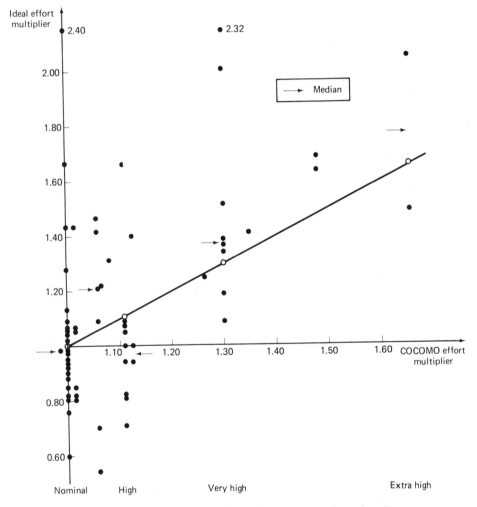

FIGURE 25–2 COCOMO versus ideal effort multiplier—Execution time constraint

project data base, as compared to the values of the effort multipliers determined by the TIME attribute rating for the project. Here again, there is a reasonably good correlation between the COCOMO multipliers (the circles in Fig. 25–2) and the medians of the project data for each rating level (the arrows in Fig. 25–2). The median IEM for the high rating falls considerably below the actual COCOMO multiplier for the high rating, but if the projects with near-high mixed ratings are included in the high group, the resulting median IEM is quite close to the corresponding COCOMO multipliers.

Discussion

This section will discuss both the execution time constraint factor (TIME) and the next factor that will be covered, main storage constraint (STOR), as they are closely interlinked. The initial results on the effects of those cost driver attributes were obtained in an analysis of 34 avionics software projects at Rockwell-Autonetics. The data for these projects are shown in Fig. 25–3 [Williman, 1969]. From these data [Williman–O'Donnell, 1970] hypothesized the curve shown in Fig. 25–4 relating software cost per instruction to the level of hardware speed and storage constraints. In 1971, an additional nine data points on highly hardware constrained software projects were obtained during the U.S. Air Force CCIP-85 study [Boehm–Haile, 1972]. As shown in Fig. 25–4, these data points tend to corroborate the curve given in the figure.

Subsequently, other studies and cost modeling activities have found similar results,

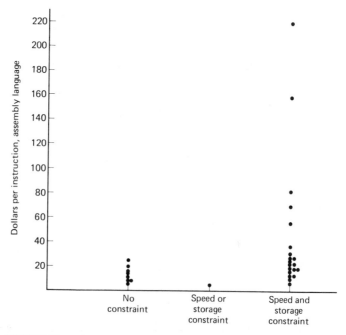

FIGURE 25–3 Rockwell-autonetics data on hardware constraint effects

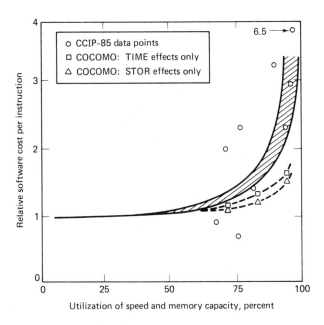

FIGURE 25-4 Effect of hardware constraints on software cost

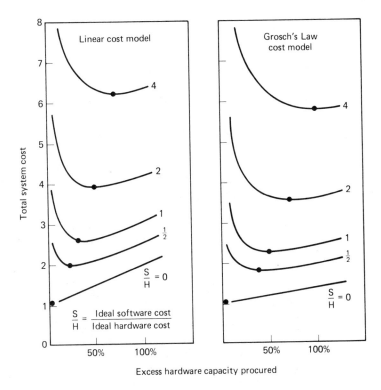

FIGURE 25-5 Hardware-software system costs

for example [Schluter, 1977] and [Freiman–Park, 1979]. The latter refers to the RCA PRICE S software cost-estimation model, which uses a curve very similar to Fig. 25–4 for estimating hardware constraint effects (given as Fig. 29–12).

Separate influence factors for time constraint alone and storage constraint alone have been reported recently. Table 25–3 shows the main results.

TABLE 25–3 Hardware Constraint Productivity Ranges

Source	Time Constraint Productivity Range	Storage Constraint Productivity Range
TRW, 1972 [Wolverton, 1974]	3.00	—
Boeing, 1977 [Black and others, 1977]	3.33–6.67	—
Doty, 1977 [Herd and others, 1977]	1.33–1.77	1.43
GRC, 1979 [Carriere–Thibodeau, 1979]	1.60	7.00
GTE, 1979 [Daly, 1979]	1.25	1.25
IBM, 1977 [Walston–Felix, 1977]	1.37–1.77	2.03
RCA, 1979 [Freiman–Park, 1979]	combined (see Fig. 29–12)	
COCOMO	1.66	1.56

The GRC productivity range is difficult to interpret. The tables in [Carriere–Thibodeau, 1979] begin with a 0.0 multiplier for unconstrained software, implying that unconstrained software can be built for zero cost. In Table 25–3, we assume that the tables were intended to begin with a 1.0 multiplier.

Productivity Ranges in the IBM-FSD Data Base

The productivity ranges in the IBM Federal Systems Division (IBM-FSD) data base given in [Walston–Felix, 1977] are also somewhat difficult to interpret. It is important to understand them well, though, as they are based on a very careful and thorough data collection effort and a good deal of analysis.* In the IBM-FSD data base, time and storage constraints for 60 projects are characterized as either minimal, average, or severe. The average project productivity in DSL/MM† for each group of projects with a given rating is shown below.

Program Design Constraints on:	Mean Productivity (DSL/MM)		
	Minimal	Average	Severe
Main storage	391	277	193
Timing	303	317	171

* Only fragmentary information is available about the details of the IBM-FSD data base. Understandably, competitive software houses are reluctant to disclose too much of their cost data.

† The IBM-FSD cost–productivity definitions are similar to those of COCOMO except that IBM's DSL (Delivered source lines) counts include an unknown fraction of comment cards.

Thus, the full productivity range for these attributes may be underestimated because the projects with the most severe hardware constraints are averaged into a general Severe category. On the other hand, the productivity ranges may be overestimated because the time and storage constraints are lumped with all of the other cost driver effects. It is thus difficult to separate out how much of the productivity range is due to time and storage constraint effects, and how much is due to other cost driver effects which tend to be correlated with hardware constraints on IBM-FSD projects.

Table 25–4 shows another view of the IBM-FSD data base [Brustman, 1978], which indicates that decreased productivity is associated both with severe timing constraints (here, rated on a scale of 1 to 3) and with larger project and product size. Thus, for example, it is hard to tell how much of the low (66 DSL/MM) average productivity for "large most stringent requirements" projects is due to timing-constraint effects and how much is due to size effects.

Another glimpse of the IBM-FSD data base given in [Brustman, 1978], shown as Table 25–5, indicates that the situation is reasonably complex. For some types of applications given in Table 25–5, such as special-purpose operating systems and real-time, interactive command and control, low productivity and large size are strongly correlated. On the other hand, process control systems have relatively low productivity and small size, indicating that other cost drivers such as hardware constraints exert a significant effect on productivity independent of size effects.

We will encounter similar difficulties in separating out the effects of correlated factors as we discuss the IBM-FSD productivity ranges in relation to other COCOMO cost driver attributes, such as use of modern programming practices. For reference, the entire set of IBM-FSD productivity ranges in [Walston–Felix, 1977] is given here as Table 25–6.

TABLE 25–4 IBM-FSD Software Project Averages by Size and Timing Constraint

	Number of Samples	Effort (MM)	Duration (months)	Peak Manning	Code (KDSL)	Timing Constraints	Productivity (DSL/MM)
Small, less stringent requirements	9	26	8	5	15	1.1	576
Medium, less stringent requirements	24	84	12	8	30	1.7	357
Medium, more stringent requirements	19	312	16	23	80	2.6	256
Large, most stringent requirements	8	2486	43	71	165	2.9	66
Total or average	60	468	17	21	62	2.0	132

Recently, some additional analysis of the IBM-FSD data base intercorrelation was reported in [Brooks, 1980]. It yielded execution time constraint productivity ranges of 2.4 for large projects and 1.4 for unstructured projects; and nonsignificant productivity ranges for small projects and structured projects.

TABLE 25–5 IBM-FSD Software Project Averages by Application Type

	Number of Samples	Average Delivered KDSL	Average Effort (MM)	Average Duration (months)	Average Number of People	Average Productivity DSL/MM
Batch applications	13	27	69	10	8	391
Models and simulators	9	77	214	19	14	359
Interactive information retrieval	13	78	232	13	19	336
Process control	6	9	49	7	9	190
Special-purpose operating systems	13	58	568	25	28	101
Real-time, interactive command and control	6	143	2420	31	65	59

TABLE 25–6 Productivity Ranges in the IBM–FSD Data Base [Walston–Felix, 1977]

Question or Variable	Response Group Mean Productivity (DSL/MM)			Productivity Change (DSL/MM)
Customer interface complexity	< Normal 500	> Normal 295	> Normal 124	376
User participation in the definition of requirements	None 491	Some 267	Much 205	286
Customer originated program design changes	Few 297		Many 196	101
Customer experience with the application area of the project	None 318	Some 340	Much 206	112
Overall personnel experience and qualifications	Low 132	Average 257	High 410	278
Percentage of programmers doing development who participated in design of functional specifications	< 25% 153	25–50% 242	< 50% 391	238
Previous experience with operational computer	Minimal 146	Average 270	Extensive 312	166
Previous experience with programming languages	Minimal 122	Average 225	Extensive 385	263
Previous experience with application of similar or greater size and complexity	Minimal 146	Average 221	Extensive 410	264

TABLE 25–6 (cont.) Productivity Ranges in the IBM-FSD Data Base

Question or Variable	Response Group Mean Productivity (DSL/MM)			Productivity Change (DSL/MM)
Ratio of average staff size	< 0.5	0.5–0.9	> 0.9	
to duration (people/month)	305	310	173	132
Hardware under concurrent	No		Yes	
development	297		177	120
Development computer	0%	1–25%	> 25%	
access, open under special	226	274	357	131
request				
Development computer	0–10%	11–85%	> 85%	
access, closed	303	251	170	133
Classified security	No		Yes	
environment for computer	289		156	133
and 25% of programs and				
data				
Structured programming	0–33%	34–66%	66%	
	169	—	310	141
Design and code inspections	0–33%	34–66%	> 66%	
	220	300	339	119
Top-down development	0–33%	34–66%	> 66%	
	196	237	321	125
Chief programmer team usage	0–33%	34–66%	> 66%	
	219	—	408	189
Overall complexity of code	< Average		> Average	
developed	314		185	129
Complexity of application	< Average	Average	> Average	
processing	349	345	168	181
Complexity of program flow	< Average	Average	> Average	
	289	299	209	80
Overall constraints on	Minimal	Average	Severe	
program design	293	286	166	127
Program design constraints on	Minimal	Average	Severe	
main storage	391	277	193	198
Program design constraints	Minimal	Average	Severe	
on timing	303	317	171	132
Code for real-time or inter-	< 10%	10–40%	> 40%	
active operation or executing	279	337	203	76
under severe timing constraint				
Percentage of code for	0–90%	91–99%	100%	
delivery	159	327	265	106
Code classified as nonmathemati-	0–33%	34–66%	67–100%	
cal application and I/O format-	188	311	267	79
ting programs				
Number of classes of items in	0–15	16–80	> 80	
the data base per 1000	334	243	193	141
lines of code				
Number of pages of delivered	0–32	33–88	> 88	
documentation per 1000	320	252	195	125
lines of delivered code				

25.2 STOR: MAIN STORAGE CONSTRAINT

Ratings and Effort Multipliers

Table 25–7 presents software development effort multipliers as a function of the degree of main storage constraint imposed on a software subsystem. Main storage refers to direct random access storage such as core, integrated-circuit, or plated-wire storage; it excludes such devices as drums, disks, tapes, or bubble storage.

The rating is expressed in terms of the percentage of main storage expected to be used by the subsystem and any other subsystems consuming the main storage resources. The tables do not cover situations in which over 95% of the available main storage is to be used.

TABLE 25–7 Main Storage Constraint Effort Multipliers

STOR Rating	Phase Requirements and Product Design	Detailed Design	Code and Unit Test	Integration and Test	Over- all
Nominal (≤50%)	1.00	1.00	1.00	1.00	1.00
High (70%)	1.05	1.05	1.05	1.10	1.06
Very high (85%)	1.20	1.15	1.15	1.35	1.21
Extra high (95%)	1.55	1.45	1.45	1.85	1.56

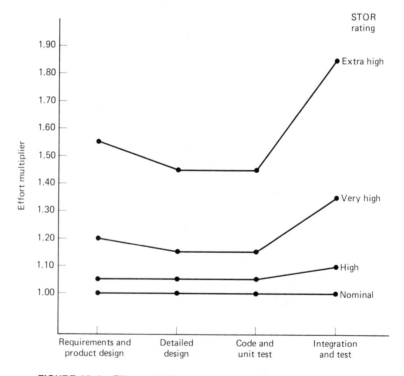

FIGURE 25–6 Effort multipliers versus phase: Main storage constraint

TABLE 25-8 Project Activity Differences Due to Main Storage Constraint

Rating	Requirements and Product Design	Detailed Design	Code and Unit Test	Integration and Test
Low (≤50%)	No change	No change	No change	No change
High (70%)	Added analysis, simulation, prototyping, validation	Added analysis, simulation, prototyping, validation	Added analysis Code and data trickier to program and debug Tight core control	Added analysis Code and data trickier to program and debug Tight core control Harder test drivers, measurement, diagnostics
Very high (85%)	More of above	More of above	More of above	More of above
Extra high (95%)	Much more of above	Much more of above	Much more of above	Much more of above

The magnitude and phase distribution of the storage constraint effects is shown graphically in Fig. 25–6.

Table 25–8 indicates the project activity differences resulting from the differing levels of main storage constraint. The higher escalation in integration and test phase cost is due primarily to the higher cost of testing (for example, getting the code and the test drivers in the main memory at the same time) and error correction.

Comparison with Project Results

As before, we will use the ideal effort multiplier, IEM(P,STOR), for each project P in the COCOMO project data base as the basis of project comparisons.

Figure 25–7 shows the values of IEM(P,STOR) for the projects in the COCOMO

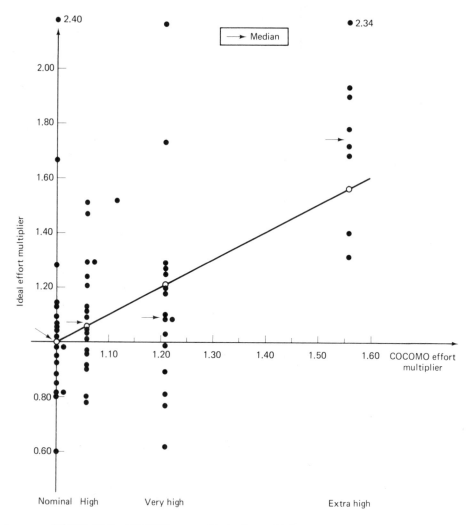

FIGURE 25–7 COCOMO versus ideal effort multiplier—Main storage constraint

data base, as compared to the values of the overall COCOMO effort multipliers for the four STOR attribute ratings (the circles in Fig. 25–7). The correlation between the COCOMO effort multipliers and the median values of IEM(P,STOR)—the arrows in Fig. 25–7—is not as good as experienced with most of the other COCOMO cost driver attributes. The project data indicate that perhaps lower values for the very high STOR effort multipliers and higher values for the extra high STOR effort multipliers would be appropriate. However, the differences are not extreme, and the existing STOR multipliers have been retained for the present in the interests of model stability.

Discussion of Related Data and Studies

This discussion is contained under the previous section on execution time constraint (TIME) effects.

25.3 VIRT: VIRTUAL MACHINE VOLATILITY

Ratings and Effort Multipliers

Table 25–9 presents software development effort multipliers as a function of the level of volatility of the virtual machine underlying the subsystem to be developed. For a given software subsystem, the underlying virtual machine is the complex of hardware and software that the subsystem calls upon to accomplish its tasks. For example:

- If the subsystem to be developed is an operating system, the underlying virtual machine is the computer hardware.
- If the subsystem to be developed is a data base management system (DBMS), the underlying virtual machine generally consists of the computer hardware plus an operating system.
- If the subsystem to be developed is a data base oriented user-application subsystem, the underlying virtual machine often consists of the computer hardware, an operating system, and a DBMS.

TABLE 25–9 Virtual Machine Volatility Effort Multipliers

| VIRT Rating | Change Frequency | | Phase | | | | |
	Major	Minor	Requirements and Product Design	Detailed Design	Code and Unit Test	Integration and Test	Overall
Low	12 months	1 month	.95	.90	.85	.80	.87
Nominal	6 months	2 weeks	1.00	1.00	1.00	1.00	1.00
High	2 months	1 week	1.10	1.12	1.15	1.20	1.15
Very high	2 weeks	2 days	1.20	1.25	1.30	1.40	1.30

- In addition, the underlying virtual machine includes any compilers or assemblers supporting the languages in which the software subsystem is written.

Clearly, the development of any of these subsystems will take more effort if its underlying virtual machine is concurrently undergoing change.

The ratings are defined in terms of the relative frequency of major changes and minor changes to the underlying virtual machine. These are defined as follows:

- Major change: significantly affects roughly 10% of routines under development
- Minor change: significantly affects roughly 1% of routines under development

The magnitude and phase distribution of the virtual machine volatility effects is shown graphically in Fig. 25–8.

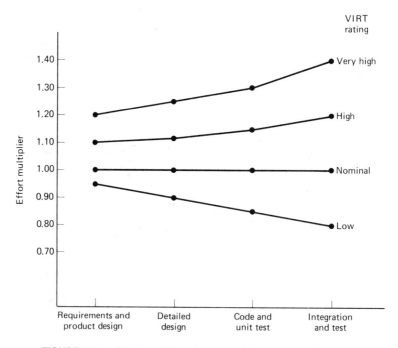

FIGURE 25–8   Effort multipliers by phase: Virtual machine volatility

Table 25–10 indicates the project activity differences resulting from the differing levels of virtual machine volatility. The higher escalation in integration and test phase costs stems primarily from the higher cost of making changes and error fixes in later phases.

Comparison with Project Results

Figure 25–9 shows the values of the ideal effort multiplier, IEM(P,VIRT), for the projects in the COCOMO data base, as compared to the values of the overall

Phase Rating	Requirements and Product Design	Detailed Design	Code and Unit Test	Integration and Test
Low	Less HW/SW analysis, validation ⟶ Fewer interface changes, errors, ⟶ configuration management ⟶ Less rework of test plans ⟶ Fewer TBDs to design around ⟶			Fewer volatile compo- nents to integrate
Nominal	No change ⟶			

High	More HW/SW analysis, validation ⟶
	More interface changes, errors, con-
	    figuration management ⟶
	More rework of test plans ⟶
	More TBDs to design around ⟶
	Possible development and use of
	    hardware emulator ⟶
				More volatile compo-
				nents to integrate

Very high	More of above ⟶ Second order problems from multiple changes ⟶			

COCOMO effort multipliers for the four VIRT attribute ratings (the circles in Fig. 25–9). The correlation between the COCOMO effort multipliers and the median values of IEM(P,VIRT)—the arrows in Fig. 25–9—is excellent.

Discussion

The overall productivity range due to virtual machine volatility in Table 25–9 is 1.49. The IBM [Walston–Felix, 1977] study indicated a productivity range of 1.62 for the factor, "Hardware under concurrent development" (again, possibly including the effects of correlated factors). The Doty model [Herd and others, 1977] has a productivity range of 1.82 for the factor "first software developed on CPU." The RCA PRICE S model [Freiman–Park, 1979] has a complexity adjustment factor of +0.3 for the attribute "hardware developed in parallel," which generally corresponds to a productivity range of about 1.4. None of the other published models and studies include a virtual machine volatility factor.

25.4 TURN: COMPUTER TURNAROUND TIME

Ratings and Effort Multipliers

Table 25–11 presents software development effort multipliers as a function of the level of computer response time experienced by the project team developing the subsystem. The ratings are defined in terms of average response time (ART) in hours (the time from when a developer submits a job to be run until the results are back

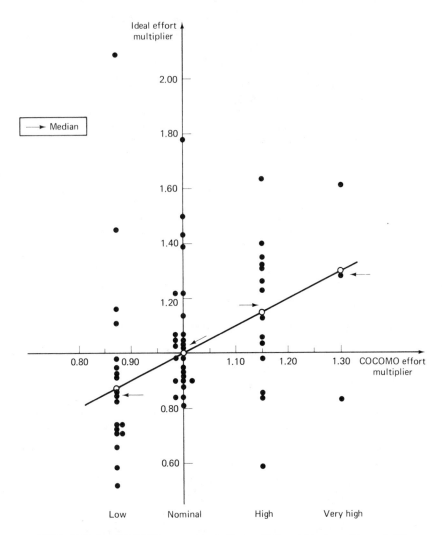

FIGURE 25–9 COCOMO versus ideal effort multiplier—Virtual machine volatility

in the developer's hands). One exception is a rating for on-line interactive development, in which software development can be done in a conversational mode from individual developer terminals, with response time for simple operations in the range of 0 to 5 sec.

The magnitude and phase distribution of the computer turnaround time effects is shown graphically in Fig. 25–10.

Table 25–12 indicates the project activity differences resulting from the differing levels of computer response time. The larger reduction in effort due to interactive operation in the code and unit test phase stems primarily from the predominance of source-code editing and unit-level debugging performed during that phase.*

* It is likely that current and future interactive systems employing integrated word-processing capabilities will produce larger effort reductions in the requirements and design phases.

TABLE 25-11   Computer Turnaround Time Effort Multipliers

TURN Rating	Phase	Requirements and Product Design	Detailed Design	Code and Unit Test	Integration and Test	Overall
Low (Interactive)		.98	.95	.70	.90	.87
Nominal (ART < 4 hr)		1.00	1.00	1.00	1.00	1.00
High (4 hr ≤ ART < 12 hr)		1.00	1.00	1.10	1.15	1.07
Very high (ART ≥ 12 hr)		1.02	1.05	1.20	1.30	1.15

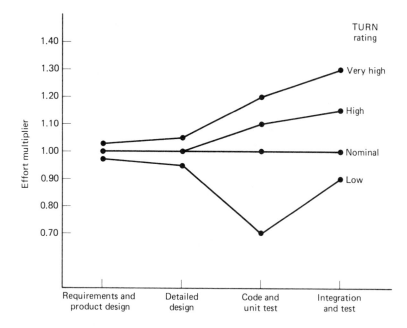

FIGURE 25-10   Effort multipliers by phase: Computer turnaround time

Comparison with Project Results

Figure 25-11 shows the values of the ideal effort multiplier, IEM(P,TURN), for the projects in the COCOMO data base, as compared to the values of the overall COCOMO effort multipliers for the four TURN attribute ratings (the circles in Fig. 25-11). The correlation between the COCOMO effort multipliers and the median values of IEM(P,TURN)—the arrows in Fig. 25-11—is not as good as one might like. For example, the median value of the ideal effort multipliers for the 21 projects using interactive software development (low ratings for TURN) is 0.93 rather than the 0.87 used as the COCOMO overall effort multiplier. One is tempted to increase the values of the low-rating COCOMO effort multipliers for TURN (they were higher in an earlier version of the model), but the existing multipliers are retained here in the interest of model stability and agreement with other experience discussed below.

TABLE 25–12 Project Activity Differences Due to Computer Turnaround Time

Rating	Requirements and Product Design	Detailed Design	Code and Unit Test	Integration and Test
Low (Interactive)	Faster text editing Interactive simulation, prototyping	Faster text editing Interactive simulation, prototyping	Faster text editing Interactive debugging	Faster text editing Interactive debugging
Nominal (Batch, < 4 hr)	No change	No change	No change	No change
High (Batch, 4–12 hr)	Slower simulation, prototyping	Slower simulation, PDL	Slower compile, test, debug, tool use	Slower compile, test, debug, tool use
Very High (Batch, > 12 hr)	More of above	More of above	More of above	More of above

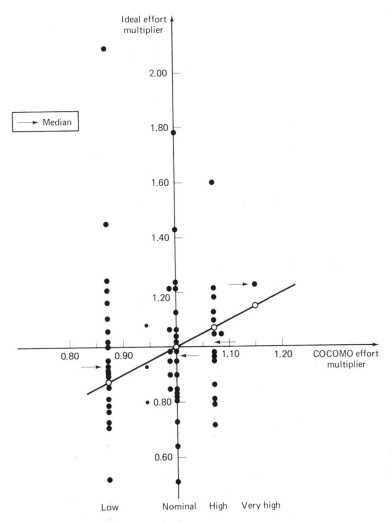

FIGURE 25–11 COCOMO versus ideal effort multipliers—Computer turnaround time

Discussion

The effect of interactive programming on software productivity has been the subject of considerable study. Early studies summarized in [Sackman, 1970] indicated an average of 20% improvement in productivity in code and unit test tasks. Since 1970, improved interactive systems have been developed which provide a more powerful range of conversational programming capabilities. Several more recent controlled studies have been summarized in [Jones–Nelson, 1976]. The equivalent effort multipliers determined, generally for code and unit test tasks, are

U.S. Army	0.47
Royal Globe	0.50
Rolls Royce	0.56
AT&T	0.62

Several difficulties arise in evaluating the meaning of the above figures. For the later studies, the TURN effects are mixed in with effects of improved TOOL capabilities. Also, it is difficult to tell how much of the programmer time used in waiting for batch results (about 16% in the U.S. Army Study [Reaser–Carrow, 1975]) could be productively used on other tasks, such as documentation or work on other portions of the code, particularly on larger projects. Further, there are a number of nonprogrammer activities (management, integration and test planning, and quality assurance) going on during even the code and unit test phase which are not strongly affected by interactive programming. Thus, it is not too surprising that current cost-estimation models incorporate smaller effort multipliers for interactive programming effects than those summarized above. Below is a summary of effort multipliers used in current models.

	Effort Multipliers	
Model	Code and Unit Test	Overall Project
Boeing [Black and others, 1977]	.54	.875
Doty [Herd and others, 1977]		.83
GTE [Daly, 1979]		.80
NARDAC [Williamson, 1979]		.75
COCOMO	.70	.87

Studies on the effect of longer response times are scarce. The IBM [Walston–Felix, 1977] study reports effort multipliers in the range of 1.58 to 1.78 for two factors reflecting restrictions in computer access. The Doty model contains three multiplicative factors covering related effects

- Developer using computer at another facility   1.43
- Development at operational site   1.39
- Development computer different from target computer   1.25
- Combined effect of all three factors   2.48

The combined effect of these factors appears extremely high.

The NARDAC model [Williamson, 1979] contained the following effort multipliers for batch turnaround times

More than one per day	0.8
One per day	1.0
Less than one per day	1.2

The [Daly, 1979] model has an effort multiplier of 1.1 for batch turnaround greater than four hours. The [Griffin, 1980] model has a productivity range of 1.46 between instant turnaround and 12–24 hour turnaround.

On the other hand, some studies have indicated that easy access to the computer does not assure improved productivity, as it can stimulate trial-and-error approaches to programming and concentration on the tactics rather than the strategy of software development. For example, the [Gayle, 1971] summary of the Eudy software productivity study reported a negative correlation between productivity and the distance between the programmer and computer measured in feet. The [Boehm and others, 1971] experiment on interactive programming and problem solving showed that subjects with unrestricted interactive computer access obtained poorer results than subjects whose terminal keyboards were locked for a short period of time after being presented with the results of their current run. A typical lockout subject's comment was, "I didn't much like the lockout, but it did *give* me time to think" (italics added). Other similar results are discussed in [Shneiderman, 1980].

These results do not imply that interactive software development and quick response time should be discouraged, but only that their use should be accompanied by other good programming practices. This is certainly the direction in which interactive software development systems are going today, evolving toward a coalescence of interactive access, use of extensive software tools, and support of modern programming practices. This will make it more difficult in the future to separate the effects of the COCOMO TURN, MODP, and TOOL factors, but easier to achieve enhanced software productivity. Another likely future trend is that the COCOMO effort multipliers for interactive software development will probably decrease for the requirements and design phases, as more interactive systems integrate programming support and word-processing support, allowing more efficient performance of requirements and design documentation, review, and iteration activities.

25.5 QUESTIONS

25.1. What activities account for the 10% added effort in the detailed design phase of a software project with a 70% execution time constraint?

25.2. Suppose you are designing the new microprocessor-based point-of-sale terminal for Colonel Mac's fast-food chain. With the current 1-sec response time required for transaction processing, the best available microprocessors will require 90% of the available execution time to process the workload, resulting in a 10-year software life-cycle cost of $4,000,000. By how much would the software life-cycle cost be reduced if the response time requirement were reduced to 1.5 seconds? To 2 seconds?

25.3. Figure 25–5 (on p. 405), from [Boehm, 1973], shows how the software cost versus hardware capacity constraint curve in Fig. 25–4 can be used to determine how much excess hardware capacity to procure in order to minimize total system (hardware plus software) acquisition cost. The total system cost curves are given in terms of the ratio

$$\frac{S}{H} = \frac{\text{Ideal software cost}}{\text{Ideal hardware cost}}$$

where the ideal software cost excludes any extra costs due to hardware constraints, and the ideal hardware cost excludes any extra costs for acquiring excess hardware capacity over the minimal capacity required to support the application. Two sets of curves are given, one for a linear hardware cost model in which hardware cost increases linearly with hardware capacity, and one for a "Grosch's Law" model in which hardware cost increases as the square root of hardware capacity. For a project with an ideal software cost of $1,000,000, what is the optimum percentage of excess capacity to procure if the ideal hardware costs and cost/capacity models are

(a) $500,000, linear model
(b) $500,000, Grosch's Law model
(c) $4,000,000, linear model
(d) $4,000,000, Grosch's Law model

25.4. Recent analyses in [Phister, 1979] indicate that the current hardware cost/capacity model (or production function)

$$\text{Cost} = a(\text{Capacity})^b$$

has an economy-of-scale factor b in the range of 0.67 to 0.90 (for the linear model, $b = 1.0$, and for Grosch's Law, $b = 0.5$). Construct a set of curves similar to those in Fig. 25–4, using the model

$$\text{Cost} = a(\text{Capacity})^{0.8}$$

Determine the optimum percentage of excess capacity to procure for a project with an ideal software cost of $2,500,000 and an ideal hardware cost of $5,000,000, using this cost versus capacity model.

25.5. What activities account for the 85% added effort in the integration and test phase of a software project with a 95% main storage constraint?

25.6. The nominal phase distribution of effort for an intermediate (8-KDSI) semidetached-mode software project is:
Product design: 17%
Detailed design: 26%
Code and unit test: 35%
Integration and test: 22%
What would the phase distribution of effort for such a project be if it had extra high execution time and main storage constraints?

25.7. Suppose, as in Question 25.2, you are designing the new microprocessor-based point-of-sale terminal for Colonel Mac's fast-food chain. You have determined the 10-year life-cycle cost for the software to be $3,000,000, without considering any storage constraint effects, and have a firm estimate of the software size to be 60K microprocessor words. You need to buy 20,000 microprocessors for the entire Colonel Mac's fast-food chain; their 10-year life-cycle cost is a function of the amount of main storage you purchase, as indicated below:

Main Storage (16-bit words)	Hardware Life-Cycle Cost
64K	$4,000,000
72K	$4,200,000
80K	$4,400,000
88K	$4,600,000
96K	$4,800,000

Considering the total hardware software life-cycle costs, including the effects of storage constraints on software costs, what amount of main storage produces the minimum-cost solution for Colonel Mac's? Is there any reason why this solution might not be preferred?

25.8. What activities account for the 15% reduction of effort in the code and unit test phase of a project with low virtual machine volatility?

25.9. Query Systems, Inc., originally estimated a cost of $120,000 to develop an interactive real-estate query system based on a data base management system (DBMS) assumed to be very stable (major changes every 12 months, minor changes every month). However, in practice, the DBMS has turned out to be highly volatile, with major changes every month, and minor changes every three days. What is the likely effect on Query Systems' cost to develop the real-estate system?

25.10. Precision Products, Inc., is developing a 32-KDSI, embedded-mode, microprocessor-based life support system for a future manned spacecraft. Two space-qualified microprocessors are available
  - An older product, which is very stable (low volatility), but which would require 75% of the processor's execution time to process the workload.
  - A new processor, which would process the workload in 40% of its available execution time, but which will have a high volatility level during the software development period.

Assuming that the other cost driver attribute ratings are nominal, how do the estimated man-months for software development and their distribution by phase, compare for these two alternatives?

25.11. What activities account for the 30% reduction in effort in the code and unit test phase of a project with low-rated (interactive) computer turnaround time? Can you think of other contributing activities not mentioned in the text?

25.12. Project Zenith is a 512-KDSI, embedded-mode project to develop the software for a prototype community information utility for the residents of the city of Zenith. By how many full-time software personnel (FSP) will the project be reduced in the code and unit test phase if it uses interactive software development rather than two-hour turnaround batch processing?

25.13. In Question 10.13, we presented an approximation to the batch turnaround time portion of the TURN overall effort multipliers

$$MM = (MM)_{NOM}\{.99 + 0.4\sqrt{ART}\}$$

where ART is the average computer response time in hours. Using this equation, compute the reduction in total effort required to develop the Project Zenith software as a result of the following possible one-hour reductions in ART
- Reducing ART from 2 to 1
- Reducing ART from 8 to 7

25.14. In one recent 8-KDSI semidetached-mode microcomputer software development, a group of five programmers shared a single microprocessor development system (MDS) in one-hour shifts, making their project's TURN rating high rather than low or interactive. An investment of $12K in two more MDS stations would have allowed the programmers to operate interactively nearly all the time, changing the project's TURN rating to low. At a burdened cost of $5000 per MM for programmers, would the investment have been worthwhile?

25.6 TOPICS FOR FURTHER RESEARCH

25.A. Perform experiments and observations to test the hypotheses that the TIME effort multipliers
- are of the same magnitudes used in COCOMO
- vary by phase as in Detailed COCOMO
- are independent of project size, type, or mode
- interact multiplicatively with the other COCOMO cost driver attributes (for example, TURN, MODP)

25.B. Collect and analyze data on the effect of execution time constraints on the individual software project activities itemized in Table 25–2.

25.C. Various attempts have been made to characterize the value of computer-processed information in terms of its timeliness, for example, [Gregory–Atwater, 1957; Miller, 1968; Doherty, 1970; Emery, 1971; and Kleijnen, 1980]. Starting from these studies and the results in this section, develop techniques for evaluating the tradeoffs between total hardware–software system costs and the value of rapidly processed (or fresh) information for a particular type of application. Evaluate the techniques by applying them to an application of this type.

25.D. Software development on microprocessors has many potential problems with respect to time and storage constraints. Formulate, and analyze the cost effectiveness of, strategies for developing microprocessor software on a large host machine, and then downloading it onto a target microprocessor. Evaluate the strategies and cost-effectiveness relations by analyzing how well they work on an actual application.

25.E. Perform experiments and observations to test the hypotheses that the STOR effort multipliers
- are of the same magnitudes used in COCOMO
- vary by phase as in Detailed COCOMO
- are independent of project size, type, or mode
- interact multiplicatively with the other COCOMO cost driver attributes (for example, DATA, TURN, MODP)

25.F. Collect and analyze data on the effect of main storage constraints on the individual software project activities itemized in Table 25–8.

25.G. Virtual memory systems allow a software developer to act as if there was no main storage constraint, but often at a cost of added concern for hardware efficiency. Investigate the tradeoff relations between hardware constraints and software costs for virtual memory systems, as functions of their degree of multiprogramming and page fault rate [Ferrari, 1978].

25.H. Perform experiments and observations to test the hypotheses that the VIRT effort multipliers
- are of the same magnitudes used in COCOMO
- vary by phase as in Detailed COCOMO
- are independent of project size, type, or mode
- interact multiplicatively with the other COCOMO cost driver attributes (for example, RELY, TURN, SCED)

25.I. Perform experiments to test the hypothesis that the VIRT rating scale is sufficiently objective to assure reasonably uniform cost driver ratings.

25.J. Collect and analyze data on the effect of virtual machine volatility on the individual project activities itemized in Table 25–10.

25.K. The modularization and information hiding techniques given in [Parnas, 1979] provide ways to minimize the adverse effects of virtual machine volatility by identifying in advance the virtual machine characteristics most likely to change, and hiding information about them in a single module. Then, when they change, only this module needs revision. Perform experiments to determine the extent to which these techniques reduce the usual added costs due to virtual machine volatility.

25.L. As discussed in [Shneiderman, 1979], the older batch versus interactive studies need to be redone to reflect changes in hardware and software capabilities. Perform experiments and observations to test the hypotheses that the COCOMO TURN effort multipliers
- are of the same magnitudes used in COCOMO
- vary by phase as in Detailed COCOMO
- are independent of project size, type, or mode
- interact multiplicatively with the other COCOMO cost driver attributes (for example, RELY, VIRT, MODP, TOOL, SCED)

25.M. Collect and analyze data on the effect of computer turnaround time on the individual project activities itemized in Table 25–12; for example see the [Boies–Spiegel, 1973] study of interactive debugging.

25.N. The early batch versus interactive studies also determined that the support of interactive software development required considerably (40 to 50%) more computer resources than with batch-oriented development. Perform experiments and observations to determine whether this is still the case.

25.O. In Question 10.13, we investigated the hardware–software cost tradeoffs involved in providing and using fast turnaround computer capabilities, using a simple M/M/1 queuing model for hardware performance and an oversimplified model of hardware costs. Provide more accurate tradeoff relationships based on improved hardware–software cost and performance relationships (for example, [Phister, 1979; Ferrari, 1978; Doherty-Kelisky, 1979]).

Chapter 26

━━━━━━━━━━━━━━━━━━━━━━━━━━━━━━━━

Detailed COCOMO
Cost Drivers:
Personnel Attributes

This chapter discusses the personnel attributes that are significant cost drivers. They are

26.1   ACAP Analyst capability
26.2   AEXP Applications experience
26.3   PCAP Programmer capability
26.4   VEXP Virtual machine experience
26.5   LEXP Language experience

As these personnel attributes are highly interdependent, we will cover some portions of this chapter jointly, concluding with a general discussion of issues involved in the measurement and evaluation of software personnel attributes.

26.1 ACAP: ANALYST CAPABILITY

Ratings and Effort Multipliers

Table 26–1 indicates five ratings for the level of capability of the analysts working on a software subsystem. For each rating, a set of multipliers indicates by how much the nominal level of effort in each phase is to be multiplied to account for the difference in the capability of the analysts, with respect to the nominal level of analyst capability.

TABLE 26–1 Analyst Capability (ACAP) Effort Multipliers

ACAP Rating \ Phase	Requirements and Product Design	Detailed Design	Code and Unit Test	Integration and Test	Overall
Very low (15%)	1.80	1.35	1.35	1.50	1.46
Low (35%)	1.35	1.15	1.15	1.20	1.19
Nominal (55%)	1.00	1.00	1.00	1.00	1.00
High (75%)	.75	.90	.90	.85	.86
Very high (90%)	.55	.75	.75	.70	.71

Example

Suppose that the effort distribution on a subsystem employing a nominal-rated team of analysts is estimated to be 10 man-months for each major phase. Suppose that a decision is then made to replace the nominal-rated analysts on the subsystem with a team of high-rated analysts. Using the effort multipliers in Table 26–1, the resulting estimated effort to develop this subsystem would be 7.5 man-months for requirements and system design; 9.0 man-months for detailed design; 9.0 man-months for code and unit test; and 8.5 man-months for integration and test.

The main reasons for the decrease in man-months are given in Table 26–2, which shows the main differences in the activities to be carried out during each phase as a function of the level of analysts involved in performing them. Thus, the 25% reduction in requirements and system design effort for the subsystem is due to the fact that the high-rated team of analysts will work more efficiently, spend less time resolving interface and communication problems, and spend less time in false starts and error correction than would a nominal team of analysts.

The model assumes the following pattern of activity by the analyst team during the development cycle

- All of the development and validation of the requirements and preliminary design specifications, and associated test plans
- A consultant level of effort during the detailed design and code-and-unit-test phases, to clarify the specifications for the programming group and iterate them where necessary
- Major participation in the integration and test phase

TABLE 26-2 Project Activity Differences Due to Analyst Capability

Phase / Rating	Requirements and Product Design	Detailed Design	Code and Unit Test	Integration and Test
Very low (15%)	More interface and communication problems — Less efficient activity — More errors, false starts	More requirements and systems design reworks, errors in reworks — Less effective response to programmer questions		More problems on test plans
Low (35%)	Intermediate level of above effects			
Nominal (55%)	No change in activities			
High (75%)	Fewer interface and communication problems — More efficient activity — Fewer errors, false starts	Fewer requirements and systems design reworks, errors in reworks — More effective response to programmer questions		Fewer problems on test plans
Very high (90%)	Higher level of above effects			

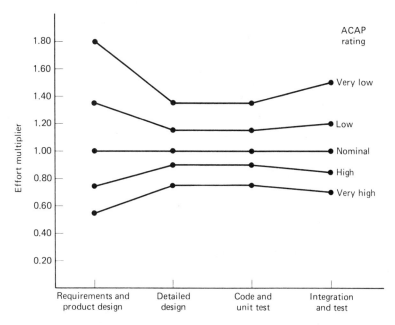

FIGURE 26–1 Effort multipliers by phase: Analyst capability

However, the model also covers situations in which the analysts also work as programmers on the project.

The ratings for analyst capability level in are expressed in Table 26–1, in terms of percentiles with respect to the overall population of software analysts. The major attributes which should be considered in the rating are

- Analysis ability
- Efficiency and thoroughness
- Ability to communicate and cooperate

These attributes should be roughly equally weighted in the evaluation. The evaluation *should not* consider the level of experience of the analysts; experience effects are covered by other factors. The evaluation should be based on the capability of the analysts as a *team* rather than as individuals.

As with the nominal project productivity versus size tables, intermediate values may be specified, yielding intermediate-value effort multipliers via interpolation. The magnitude and phase distribution of the analyst capability effects is shown graphically in Fig. 26–1.

Comparison with Project Results

Figure 26–2 shows the values of the ideal effort multiplier, IEM(P,ACAP)—defined in Eq. (24–1)—for the projects in the COCOMO data base, as compared to the values of the overall COCOMO effort multipliers for the five ACAP attribute

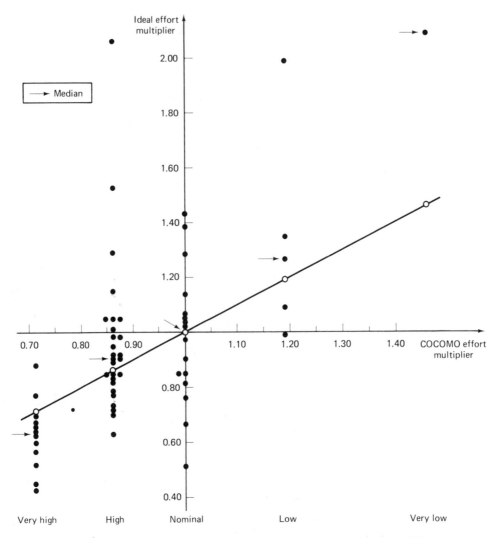

FIGURE 26-2 COCOMO versus ideal effort multipliers—Analyst capability

ratings (the circles in Fig. 26–2). The correlation between the COCOMO effort multipliers and the median values of IEM(P,ACAP) for each rating—the arrows in Fig. 26–2—is quite good. The single IEM data point for very low analyst capability is much higher than the corresponding COCOMO multiplier (2.09 versus 1.46), but without additional data points, there is not enough evidence to warrant revising the COCOMO multiplier.

Discussion

The overall COCOMO productivity range across a project due to Analyst Capability (between the very low and very high ratings) amounts to a factor of 2.06. This may seem rather low in light of the following observational findings:

- A productivity range of 26 between experienced programmers participating in the Sackman–Grant batch versus timesharing experiments [Sackman, 1970]
- A productivity range of 3.11 between IBM projects characterized as low versus high with respect to overall personnel experience and qualifications [Walston–Felix, 1977]
- A typical productivity range of 5.0 due to personnel reported at the U.S. Air Force–Industry Software Costing Workshop [Air Force, 1974]

However, COCOMO has other cost drivers which help account for variations in personnel

- The programmer capability factor has a productivity range of 2.03. Together with the analyst capability factor, this yields an overall personnel capability productivity range of 4.18.
- There are three personnel experience factors in COCOMO. They are, with their productivity ranges in parentheses, applications experience (1.57), virtual machine experience (1.34), and language experience (1.20). Together, these yield an overall personnel experience productivity range of 2.52.
- The overall personnel capability and personnel experience ranges combine to yield a (4.18) $\times$ (2.52) or 10.53 productivity range. This means that a project staffed with uniformly very low rated personnel on all the capability and experience factors would require 10.53 times as much effort to complete the project as would a project team with the highest rating in all the above factors.
- Further, the COCOMO productivity ranges are not intended to cover the absolute extremes in human performance. The ACAP ratings and effort multipliers above do not cover analysts who perform below the 15th percentile or above the 90th percentile. Thus, for example, projects with exceptional personnel such as the F. T. Baker Chief Programmer Team, which averaged over 600 DSI/MM on the 83,000 DSI New York Times project [Baker, 1972] will be somewhat overestimated by COCOMO.

26.2 AEXP: APPLICATIONS EXPERIENCE

Ratings and Effort Multipliers

Table 26–3 presents software development effort multipliers as a function of the level of applications experience of the project team developing the software subsystem. The ratings are defined in terms of the project team's equivalent level of experience with this type of application.

Very low:	≤ 4 months average experience
Low:	1 year average experience
Nominal:	3 years average experience
High:	6 years average experience

TABLE 26–3 Applications Experience Effort Multipliers

AEXP Rating \ Phase	Requirements and Product Design	Detailed Design	Code and Unit Test	Integration and Test	Overall
Very low (≤4 months)	1.40	1.30	1.25	1.25	1.29
Low (1 year)	1.20	1.15	1.10	1.10	1.13
Nominal (3 years)	1.00	1.00	1.00	1.00	1.00
High (6 years)	.87	.90	.92	.92	.91
Very high (≥12 years)	.75	.80	.85	.85	.82

Very high: ≥ 12 years average experience, or reimplementation of subsystem

The magnitude and phase distribution of the applications experience effects are shown graphically in Fig. 26–3.

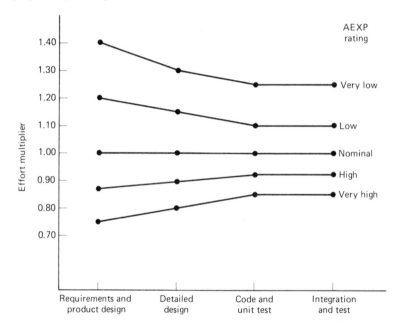

FIGURE 26–3 Effort multipliers by phase: Applications experience

Table 26–4 indicates the project activity differences resulting from the differing levels of applications experience. It indicates that the wider variation in effort in the earlier phases is due to larger learning-curve effects at the beginning of the project.

Comparison with Project Results

Figure 26–4 shows the values of the ideal effort multiplier, IEM(P,AEXP), for the projects in the COCOMO data base, as compared to the values of the overall COCOMO effort multipliers for the five AEXP attribute ratings (the circles in Fig.

TABLE 26–4 Project Activity Differences due to Applications Experience

Rating	Requirements and Product Design	Detailed Design	Code and Unit Test	Integration and Test
Very low (≤ 4 months)	More test planning More learning, data gathering More analysis More false starts More errors, requirements fixes	More test planning Somewhat more learning, data gathering, false starts, errors More requirements, preliminary design fixes	More test planning Somewhat more learning, data gathering, false starts, errors More requirements and design fixes	Somewhat more test plan, procedures rework More requirements and design fixes
Low (1 year)		Intermediate level of above effects		
Nominal (3 years)	No change	No change	No change	No change
High (6 years)	Less test planning Less learning, data gathering, analysis, false starts, errors Less requirements fixes	Less test planning Somewhat less learning, data gathering, false starts, errors Less requirements, preliminary design fixes	Less test planning Somewhat less learning, data gathering, false starts, errors Less requirements, design fixes	Somewhat less test plan, procedures rework Less requirements, design fixes
Very high (≥ 12 years)		Higher level of above effects		

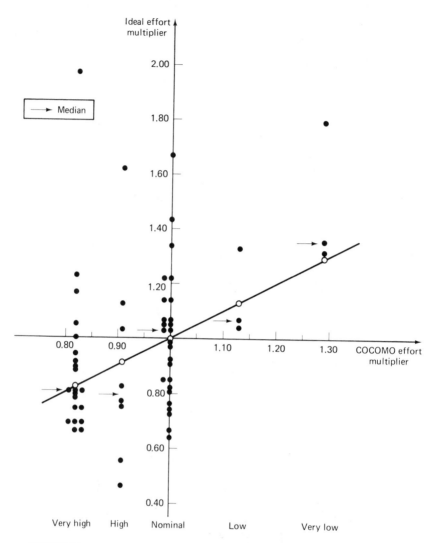

FIGURE 26–4 COCOMO versus ideal effort multiplier—Applications experience

26–4). The correlation between the COCOMO effort multipliers and the median values of IEM(P,AEXP)—the arrows in Fig. 26–4—is generally quite good. The median value for the high rating is rather low, but a change in only one of the high-rated projects would bring the median value into line with the COCOMO multiplier value.

Discussion

The table below is a summary of applications experience productivity ranges reported in recent software cost-estimation studies and models.

Source	Applications Experience Productivity Range
TRW, 1972 [Wolverton, 1974]	1.46–1.65
Boeing, 1977 [Black and others, 1977]	2.05
NARDAC [Williamson, 1979]	3.00
IBM, 1977 [Walston–Felix, 1977]	2.81
RCA PRICE S [Freiman–Park, 1979]	1.70
GTE, 1979 [Daly, 1979]	1.20
COCOMO	1.57

It should be noted again that the productivity ranges for factors in the IBM Walston–Felix study are not generally independent. Thus, they tend to be larger than the other ranges, since they often include the effects of other correlated factors, as discussed in Section 25.1. In the [Scott–Simmons, 1974] Delphi survey, the factor for "Programmer experience in functional area" was one of the highest-ranked correlates of programmer productivity, being rated +5 on a scale of [−7 to +7]. On the other hand, the [Jeffery–Lawrence, 1979] study found very little correlation between experience and productivity.

26.3 PCAP: PROGRAMMER CAPABILITY

Ratings and Effort Multipliers

Table 26–5 presents software development effort multipliers as a function of the level of capability of the programmers who will be working on the software module. The ratings are expressed in terms of percentiles with respect to the overall population of programmers. The major factors which should be considered in the rating are

- Programmer ability
- Efficiency and thoroughness
- Ability to communicate and cooperate

These attributes should be roughly equally weighted in the evaluation. The evaluation *should not* consider the level of experience of the programmers; experience effects

TABLE 26–5 Programmer Capability (PCAP) Effort Multipliers

PCAP Rating	Phase Requirements and Product Design	Detailed Design	Code and Unit Test	Integration and Test	Overall
Very low (15%)	1.00	1.50	1.50	1.50	1.42
Low (35%)	1.00	1.20	1.20	1.20	1.17
Nominal (55%)	1.00	1.00	1.00	1.00	1.00
High (75%)	1.00	.83	.83	.83	.86
Very high (90%)	1.00	.65	.65	.65	.70

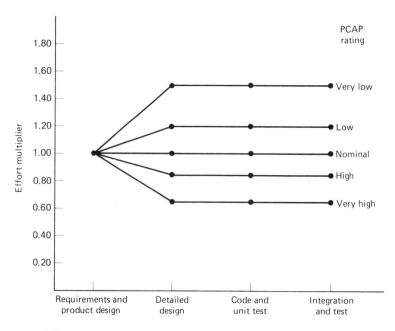

FIGURE 26-5 Effort multipliers by phase: Programmer capability

are covered by other factors. The evaluation should be based on the capability of the programmers as a *team* rather than as individuals. The magnitude and phase distribution of the programmer capability effects are shown graphically in Fig. 26–5. Table 26–6 indicates the project activity differences resulting from the differing levels of programmer capability. It shows, for example, that no changes in activities or costs are experienced during the requirements and product design phases due to differences in programmer capability, as programming activities do not significantly begin until the detailed design phase.

Comparison with Project Results

Figure 26–6 shows the values of the ideal effort multiplier, IEM(P,PCAP), for the projects in the COCOMO data base, as compared to the values of the overall COCOMO effort multipliers for the five PCAP attribute ratings (the circles in Fig. 26–6). The correlation between the COCOMO effort multipliers and the median values of IEM(P,PCAP)—the arrows in Fig. 26–6—is quite good, with the possible exception of the very low programmer capability rating (1.42 in COCOMO versus 1.62 project median). But with only three project data points at this rating, a change in the COCOMO multipliers does not appear warranted.

TABLE 26-6 Project Activity Differences due to Programmer Capability

Phase / Rating	Requirements and Product Design	Detailed Design	Code and Unit Test	Integration and Test
Very low (15%)	No change	More problems in interaction with analysts ———————————————→		
		Less efficient activity More errors, false starts ———————————————→		
			More detailed design reworks, errors in reworks ——————→	
				More code and documentation reworks, errors in reworks
Low (35%)	No change	Intermediate level of above effects ————————————————→		
Nominal (55%)	No change			
High (75%)	No change	Fewer problems in interaction with analysts ——————————→		
		More efficient activity Fewer errors, false starts ——————————→		
			Fewer detailed design reworks, errors in reworks ——————→	
				Fewer code and documentation reworks, errors in reworks
Very high (90%)	No change	Higher level of above effects ————————————————→		

Discussion

The discussion of the productivity range due to programmer capability was covered in the discussion of analyst capability earlier (Table 25–1). The effects of analyst capability and programmer capability are complementary with respect to phase. The major difference due to analyst capability occurs in the requirements and system design phase, with a smaller continuing effect across the latter three phases, while the differences in programmer capability occur strongly, and almost exclusively, in the latter three phases.

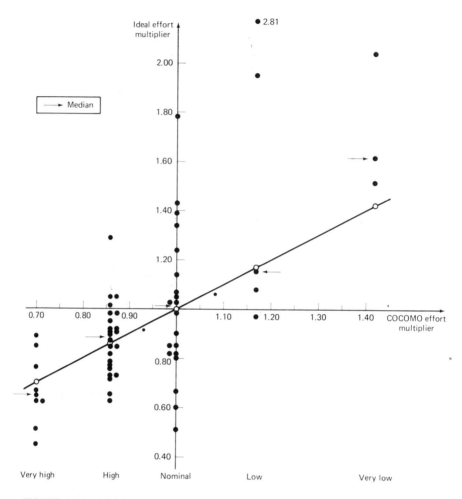

FIGURE 26-6 COCOMO versus ideal effort multiplier—Programmer capability

On a project, a set of good analysts can largely compensate for a set of poor programmers, and vice versa, while if both the analysts and the programmers are good or poor, the project effects will be highly magnified. It is instructive to observe how these effects are modeled by the COCOMO multiplicative model.

Capability Rating		Combined Effort Multiplier				
Analyst	Programmer	Requirements and Product Design	Detailed Design	Code and Unit Test	Integration and Test	Overall
Very low	Very low	1.80	2.02	2.02	2.25	2.04
Very low	Very high	1.80	.88	.88	.98	1.04
Very high	Very low	.55	1.12	1.12	1.05	1.02
Very high	Very high	.55	.49	.49	.46	.49

26.4 VEXP: VIRTUAL MACHINE EXPERIENCE

Ratings and Effort Multipliers

Table 26–7 presents software development effort multipliers as a function of the level of virtual machine experience of the project team developing the software module. The underlying virtual machine for an application is defined as in Section 25–3: the complex of hardware and software (computer, operating system, and/or data base management system) that the module calls upon to accomplish its tasks. In this case, the programming language is not considered part of the virtual machine; it will be covered separately in Section 26.5.

TABLE 26–7 Virtual Machine Experience (VEXP) Effort Multipliers

VEXP Phase Rating	Requirements and Product Design	Detailed Design	Code and Unit Test	Integration and Test	Overall
Very low (≤ 1 month)	1.10	1.10	1.30	1.30	1.21
Low (4 months)	1.05	1.05	1.15	1.15	1.10
Nominal (1 year)	1.00	1.00	1.00	1.00	1.00
High (≥ 3 years)	.90	.90	.90	.90	.90

The ratings are defined in terms of the project team's equivalent duration of experience with the virtual machine to be used

Very low:	≤ 1 month average experience
Low:	4 months average experience
Nominal:	1 year average experience
High:	≥ 3 years average experience

The magnitude and phase distribution of the virtual machine experience effects are shown graphically in Fig. 26–7.

Table 26–8 indicates the project activity differences resulting from the differing levels of virtual machine experience.

Comparison with Project Results

Figure 26–8 shows the values of the ideal effort multiplier, IEM(P,VEXP), for the projects in the COCOMO data base, as compared to the values of the overall COCOMO effort multipliers for the four VEXP attribute ratings (the circles in Fig. 26–8). The correlation between the COCOMO effort multipliers and the median values of IEM(P,VEXP)—the arrows in Fig. 26–8—is again quite good. The median IEM for the very low rating is somewhat high, but the sample of three data points does not provide a sufficiently strong case to change the COCOMO multipliers.

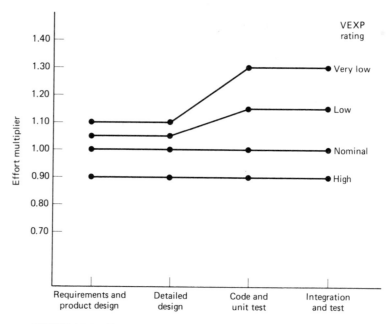

FIGURE 26–7   Effort multipliers by phase: Virtual machine experience

TABLE 26–8   Project Activity Differences Due to Virtual Machine (VM) Experience

Phase Rating	Requirements and Product Design	Detailed Design	Code and Unit Test	Integration and Test
Very low (≤ 1 month)	More VM and application interface analysis, er- rors ——————————————————————————→			
	VM training ——————————————————————————————————→			
		More reworks, errors in reworks ————————————————————————→		
	Tool conversion planning			More tuning for efficiency
		Tool conversion ——————————————————→		
		More documentation effort ————————————————————————→		
Low (4 months)	Intermediate level of above effects ——————————————————————————————→			
Nominal (1 year)	No change ——————————————————————————————————————→			
High (≥ 3 years)	Less VM and application interface analysis, er- rors ——————————————————————————————————→			
		Fewer reworks, errors in reworks ————————————————————————→		
		Less documentation effort ————————————————————————→		
				Less tuning for efficiency

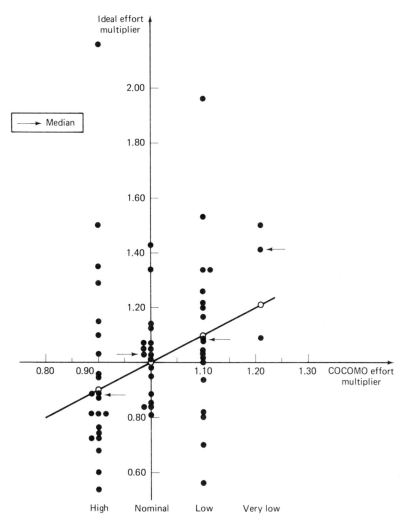

FIGURE 26-8 COCOMO versus ideal effort multiplier—Virtual machine experience

Discussion

Many models do not have a factor for virtual machine experience. The Doty model [Herd and others, 1977] gives a productivity range of 1.92 (the highest of all the factors in the model) for the factor, "first software developed on CPU." The IBM [Walston–Felix, 1977] study gives a productivity range of 2.14 for the factor, "previous experience with operational computer;" again, this may be partly the effect of other correlated factors. The RCA PRICE S Model [Freiman–Park, 1979] assigns a complexity adjustment factor of +0.1 to the item "new hardware," producing a corresponding effort multiplier of roughly 1.2. The COCOMO productivity range is 1.34.

26.5 LEXP: PROGRAMMING LANGUAGE EXPERIENCE

Ratings and Effort Multipliers

Table 26–9 presents software development effort multipliers as a function of the level of programming language experience of the project team developing the software module. The ratings are defined in terms of the project team's equivalent duration of experience with the programming language to be used.

Very Low: ≤ 1 month average experience

Low: 4 months average experience

Nominal: 1 year average experience

High: ≥ 3 years average experience

TABLE 26–9 Programming Language Experience (LEXP) Effort Multipliers

LEXP Rating	Phase Requirements and Product Design	Detailed Design	Code and Unit Test	Integration and Test	Overall
Very low (≤ 1 month)	1.02	1.10	1.20	1.20	1.14
Low (4 months)	1.00	1.05	1.10	1.10	1.07
Nominal (1 year)	1.00	1.00	1.00	1.00	1.00
High (≥ 3 years)	1.00	.98	.92	.92	.95

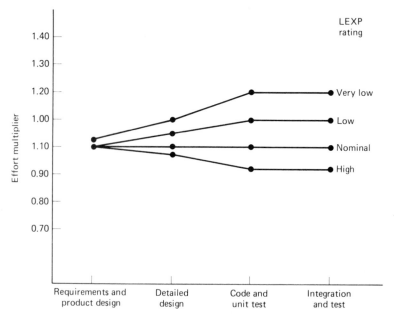

FIGURE 26–9 Effort multipliers by phase: Language experience

TABLE 26–10 Project Activity Differences Due to Programming Language Experience

Rating \ Phase	Requirements and Product Design	Detailed Design	Code and Unit Test	Integration and Test
Very low (≤ 1 month)	Language training ⟶		More learning, errors, false starts	More errors to fix
		Design versus language mismatches to rework ⟶		
	Tool conversion planning ⟶			
		Tool conversion More documentation effort ⟶		
Low (4 months)	Intermediate level of above effects ⟶			
Nominal (1 year)	No change ⟶			
High (≥ 3 years)		Fewer design versus language mismatches to rework ⟶		
		Less documentation effort ⟶		
			Fewer errors, false starts	Fewer errors to fix

The magnitude and phase distribution of the language experience effects are shown graphically in Fig. 26–9.

Table 26–10 indicates the project activity differences resulting from the differing levels of programming language experience.

Comparison with Project Results

Figure 26–10 shows the values of the ideal effort multiplier, IEM(P,LEXP), for the projects in the COCOMO data base, as compared to the values of the overall COCOMO effort multipliers for the four LEXP attribute ratings (the circles in Fig. 26–10). The correlation between the COCOMO effort multipliers and the median values of IEM(P,LEXP)—the arrows in Fig. 26–10—is again quite good. As with the PCAP and VEXP attributes, the median IEM for the very low rating is somewhat high, but the sample of three data points (actually, the same three projects as for VEXP) does not provide a sufficiently strong case to change the COCOMO multipliers.

Discussion

Although some studies indicate that language experience is a significant cost driver, most models do not include it as a factor. The IBM [Walston–Felix, 1977] study gives the factor a productivity range of 3.14; again, this is likely to be partly the effect of other correlated factors, as discussed in Section 25.1. The RCA PRICE S

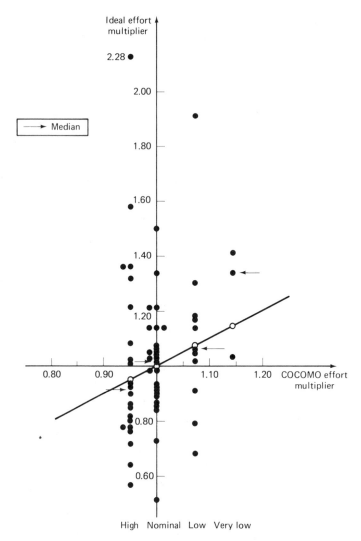

FIGURE 26-10 COCOMO versus ideal effort multiplier—Language experience

model [Freiman–Park, 1979] assigns a complexity adjustment factor of +0.1 to the item "New language," producing a corresponding effort multiplier of roughly 1.2. The COCOMO productivity range for the LEXP factor is 1.20.

26.6 GENERAL DISCUSSION OF PERSONNEL ATTRIBUTES

Quantitative estimation of human performance has traditionally been more accurate in situations in which we require the person doing the job to act more or less like a machine (such as a drill press operator, automobile assembler, or keypuncher).

Since we don't want to stimulate software engineers to act like machines, this means that we must be prepared to season our quantitative estimation activities with a great deal of human sensitivity and judgment, in order to make the estimation process realistic and helpful. This section discusses three key factors in evaluating personnel attributes and assessing their effects on software productivity

1. *Attribute Ratings.* These are not as simple as they may have seemed from the rating scales given earlier in this chapter.
2. *Related Studies on Software Personnel Attributes.* These provide some added insight into software cost-estimation and productivity issues.
3. *Data Collection and Analysis Considerations.* In pursuing the topics for further research in this chapter and elsewhere in this book, it is important to be aware of the main principles and pitfalls accumulated from previous psychological studies of software engineering.

Attribute Ratings: Personnel Capability

The COCOMO rating scales for analyst and programmer capabilities are given in terms of some hypothetical percentile distribution with respect to the overall population of software analysts and programmers. Actually

- There is no such one-dimensional scale. Analyst and programmer capability are highly multidimensional attributes, and ratings must be made with respect to the particular combination of skills needed for the job. An indication of the complexity of the situation is given by the AFIPS Programmer Job Description Survey [AFIPS, 1973].
- There are no objective measurement instruments whose results correlate reliably with analyst or programmer capability. Instruments such as the IBM Programmer Aptitude Test (PAT) or the Test on Sequential Instructions (TSI) for measuring programming ability and the Strong Vocational Interest Blank (SVIB) for measuring interest or motivation level have at best produced very weak correlations with analyst capability or programmer capability. See [Mayer–Stalnaker, 1968; Weinberg, 1971; and Shneiderman, 1980].
- The important attribute to rate is not averaged individual analyst or programmer capability, but the effective analyst or programmer *team* capability. This means including factors such as the team's cohesiveness, communication ability, and motivation toward group versus individual achievement. [Weinberg, 1971] is a goldmine of good examples and principles on effective versus ineffective software team performance.

Underlying the evaluation of a software team's basic capability (programming expertise, communication skills, and so on) is the need to evaluate the strength of the team's motivation. Here again, there is no good rating scale on which to evaluate motivation level, but it is extremely important to factor team motivation into the capability ratings used to predict productivity. Further discussion of programmer motivation factors is provided in Chapter 33.

When using COCOMO in practical software engineering situations, it is valuable to consider the ACAP and PCAP rating scales as *relative* scales which can be used to calibrate a particular installation's level and range of analyst and programmer capabilities to the effort estimates produced by COCOMO. Developing an installation-specific counterpart to the COCOMO rating scales is generally more meaningful to the installation. It would also be less demotivating than an implicit assertion that, say, a given programming team is only 15th-percentile material. Methods of calibrating and tailoring COCOMO to a particular installation's experience are given in Section 29.9.

Attribute Ratings: Personnel Experience

The COCOMO rating scales for applications experience, virtual machine experience, and language experience are given in terms of calendar months or years of experience. Again, it is important to temper the pure time-in-service length of experience with personal judgment as to the contribution of that experience to the job being estimated. Two main considerations are of importance here.

1. Experience with the aspects of the applications, virtual machine, or language relevant to the job being estimated. For example, three years of batch business programming on an IBM OS/VS system does not help much if the next job involves the detailed use of OS/VS teleprocessing and networking features.
2. Amount learned from experience. Some people who have been programming for 10 years have 10 years of accumulated experience; others have one year of accumulated experience repeated 10 times.

Here again, the important attribute to rate is the effective *team* experience. For example, if only two or three people on the team are to deal with the exotic aspects of network protocols, their level of experience in that area is all that need be considered in the experience rating.

Related Studies on Software Personnel Attributes

The potential range of human variability in software development is best illustrated by the results shown in Fig. 26–11 summarizing the [Grant–Sackman, 1966] study of batch versus time-sharing programming effectiveness. In this study, Grant and Sackman attempted to eliminate sources of human variability from the batch versus timesharing comparison by using only experienced subjects having from 2 to 11 years of programming experience. Even so, the batch versus timesharing comparisons were eclipsed by the wide range of individual performance variability shown in Fig. 26–11. The combined ranges of coding man-hours (18:1) and debugging man-hours (28:1) yielded a composite productivity range of 26:1 between the best and worst performances in the experiment. Additionally, on one of the problems in the experiment, the best and worst performances were achieved by the two programmers with the greatest (11 years) length of experience. A similar productivity range of 16:1 was observed in [Sackman, 1969] on a study of batch versus timesharing operation

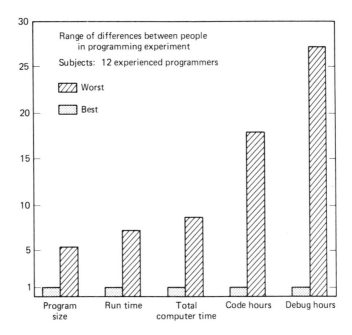

FIGURE 26-11 Influence of personnel on software productivity

for student instruction. In both of these studies, however, the wide productivity ranges were due to a small number of extreme performances, with productivity ranges of 3:1 to 5:1 better characterizing the COCOMO 15th to 90th percentile range of software personnel.

Some useful information on the correlation between applications experience, language experience, and general programming experience was obtained in the [Chrysler, 1978] study of software productivity determinants in a batch COBOL business data processing installation. In this installation, the correlation between months of business applications experience and months of COBOL experience was 0.977, and the correlation between total programming experience and business applications experience was 0.963. If these correlations were typical of all software installations, there would be no need for separate COCOMO AEXP, VEXP, and LEXP attributes. As can be seen by scanning or analyzing the project ratings in the COCOMO project data base, the correlation between various experience attributes is reasonably high, but not sufficiently high to warrant eliminating the separate COCOMO experience ratings. However, the Chrysler data indicate that individual installations can take advantage of such correlations existing in their environment to tailor a simplified COCOMO model to their situation, as discussed in Section 29.9.

Data Collection and Analysis Considerations

The topics for further research presented in this chapter, as well as those presented in other chapters in Part IV, often imply the design and implementation of an experiment or observation program involving software personnel. In performing such activities, it is important to be aware of the main principles and common pitfalls accumulated from previous psychological studies of software engineering. A good list of common pitfalls to avoid is given in [Weinberg, 1971]

1. Using introspection without validation
2. Using observations on an overly narrow base
3. Observing the wrong variables, or failing to observe the right ones
4. Interfering with the observed phenomenon
5. Generating too much data and not enough information
6. Overly constraining experiments
7. Depending excessively on trainees as subjects
8. Failing to study group effects and group behavior
9. Measuring what is simple to measure
10. Using unjustified precision
11. Transferring borrowed results to inapplicable situations

A good set of guidelines for psychological experimentation is [Chapanis, 1959]. Other valuable insights relative to their use in software engineering experiments and observations are given in [Sackman, 1970; Weinberg, 1971; Shneiderman, 1980, and Moher-Schneider, 1981].

26.7 QUESTIONS

26.1. What project activities account for
(a) The 80% added effort in the product design phase for a project team with very low analyst capability?
(b) The 13% less effort in the product design phase for a project team with high applications experience?
(c) The 20% added effort in the code and unit test phase for a project team with low programmer capability?
(d) The 10% added effort in the detailed design phase for a project team with very low virtual machine experience?
(e) The 8% less effort in the integration and test phase for a project team with high language experience?

26.2. Develop a set of combined effort multipliers (by phase and overall) for Overall Programming Experience, assuming equal levels of applications, virtual machine, and language experience. Use the experience levels ≤ 1 month, 4 months, 1 year, 3 years, 6 years, and ≥ 12 years.

26.3. The phase distribution of effort for a nominal, organic-mode software project is
Product design: 16%
Detailed design: 25%
Code and unit test: 40%
Integration and test: 19%
What would be the phase distribution effort under the following conditions:
(a) Very low analyst capability?

(b) Very low analyst capability and programmer capability?

(c) Very high applications experience?

26.4. The Standard University Environmental Studies Laboratory is developing a new, 20-KDSI, organic-mode environmental impact model for coastal water quality. Two staffing choices are available: computer center personnel and graduate students. The personnel attribute ratings for each candidate team are given below.

Attribute	Computer Center Personnel	Graduate Students
ACAP	Nominal	High
AEXP	Nominal	Nominal
PCAP	Nominal	High
VEXP	High	Very low
LEXP	High	Very low

Based on the estimated man-months required for software development, which group is the better choice? Are there other criteria which might make the choice go the other way?

26.5. Colonel Mac's fast-food chain has an opening for a senior analyst-programmer for its inventory control system. The choice has narrowed down to Sally Sharpe and Herbert Hack, whose capability ratings, experience ratings, and desired salaries are given below. On a cost–productivity basis, which candidate should Colonel Mac's hire?

Attribute	Sally Sharpe	Herbert Hack
ACAP	90%	35%
AEXP	3 yr	12 yr
PCAP	90%	35%
VEXP	4 mo	12 yr
LEXP	6 yr	12 yr
Desired Salary	$40,000	$28,000

26.8 TOPICS FOR FURTHER RESEARCH

26.A. Perform experiments and observations to test the hypotheses that the effort multipliers for one or more of the COCOMO personnel attributes (ACAP, AEXP, PCAP, VEXP, LEXP):

- are of the same magnitudes used in COCOMO
- vary by phase as in Detailed COCOMO
- are independent of project size, type, or mode
- interact multiplicatively with each other
- interact multiplicatively with the other COCOMO cost driver attributes (for example, RELY, CPLX, MODP, SCED)

26.B. One of the weakest spots in the COCOMO multiplicative model is the assumption that a very high-capability programmer would be as strongly affected by a lack of language experience or virtual machine experience as would be a very low capability programmer. Perform experiments or observations to test this assumption.

26.C. Collect and analyze data on the effect of the various personnel attributes on the individual project activities itemized in Tables 26–2, 26–4, 26–6, 26–8, and 26–10.

26.D. Test the hypothesis that the personnel attribute rating scales used in COCOMO are sufficiently objective to assure reasonably uniform cost driver ratings, for one or more of the attributes: ACAP, AEXP, PCAP, VEXP, LEXP.

26.E. Expand the basic capability rating criteria given in this chapter (analysis or programming ability, efficiency and thoroughness, ability to communicate and cooperate) into a multi-attribute rating scheme for developing COCOMO analyst or programmer capability ratings. One candidate is the typical set of criteria used for programmer salary reviews, for example, quality, quantity, and complexity of work performed, versatility, dependability, cooperation, communication, attitude, technical potential, leadership potential. Test the rating scheme by comparing its results with actual or supervisor-estimated productivity ratings.

26.F. For a given installation, develop COCOMO personnel attribute ratings for each analyst or programmer's contribution to group capability or experience. Compute the resulting COCOMO effort multipliers for each individual and compare the results with the individual's salary level. Explain any difference in the order or range of variation between the two.

26.G. Develop metrics to measure the relative "egolessness" of a software team [Weinberg, 1971]. Investigate the correlation of this metric with software team productivity.

26.H. Perform experiments similar to those in [Weinberg-Schulman, 1974] discussed in Section 3.6, comparing team performance with respect to such criteria as productivity, program efficiency, program reliability, or program modifiability, when each team is given a different criterion to optimize.

26.I. Some significant studies of the factors which motivate software personnel have recently been reported in [Couger–Zawacki, 1978] and [Fitz–Enz, 1978]. These factors include achievement, recognition, work content, responsibility, advancement, salary, growth status, and various work environment and interpersonal relations factors. Perform experiments and observations to determine the effect of these motivational factors on software productivity.

Chapter 27

Detailed COCOMO
Cost Drivers:
Project Attributes

This chapter discusses those project attributes that are significant software cost drivers. They are

27.1 MODP Use of modern programming practices
27.2 TOOL Use of software tools
27.3 SCED Development schedule constraint

27.1 MODP: USE OF MODERN PROGRAMMING PRACTICES

Ratings and Multipliers

Table 27–1 presents software development effort multipliers as a function of the degree to which modern programming practices (MPPs) are used in developing software. The specific practices included here are

1. *Top-Down Requirements Analysis and Design.* Developing the software requirements and design as a sequence of hierarchical elaborations of the users' information processing needs and objectives. This practice is extended to include the appropriate use of incremental development, prototyping, and anticipatory documentation as discussed in Chapter 4.

2. *Structured Design Notation.* Use of a modular, hierarchical design notation (program design language, structure charts, HIPO) consistent with the structured code constructs in item 5.

3. *Top-Down Incremental Development.* Performing detailed design, code, and integration as a sequence of hierarchical elaborations of the software structure.

4. *Design and Code Walkthroughs or Inspections.* Performing preplanned peer reviews of the detailed design and of the code of each software unit.

5. *Structured Code.* Use of modular, hierarchical control structures based on a small number of elementary control structures, each having only one flow of control in and out.

6. *Program Librarian.* A project participant responsible for operating an organized repository and control system for software components.

These concepts are described in detail in a number of books and articles, for example, [Mills, 1970; Yourdon, 1975; and Infotech, 1978]. One practice often associated with the practices above—not included here, but included under the TOOL attribute—is that of the Program Support Library. Another practice not included here is the Chief Programmer Team. This practice has had highly mixed results; with a first class chief programmer, productivity can be very high; with a poor chief programmer, productivity can be very low.

The ratings are defined in terms of the range of MPPs used in developing the subsystem, and the relative experience of the project team in using the MPPs

Very low:	No use of MPPs
Low:	Beginning, experimental use of some MPPs
Nominal:	Reasonably experienced in use of some MPPs
High:	Reasonably experienced in use of most MPPs
Very high:	Routine use of all MPPs

The magnitude and phase distribution of MODP effects are shown graphically in Fig. 27–1.

TABLE 27–1 Modern Programming Practices (MODP) Effort Multipliers

MODP Rating	Requirements and Product Design	Detailed Design	Code and Unit Test	Integration and Test	Overall
Very low	1.05	1.10	1.25	1.50	1.24
Low	1.00	1.05	1.10	1.20	1.10
Nominal	1.00	1.00	1.00	1.00	1.00
High	1.00	.95	.90	.83	.91
Very high	1.00	.90	.80	.65	.82

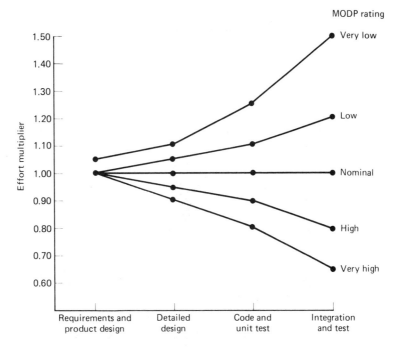

FIGURE 27–1 Effort multipliers by phase: Modern programming practices

Table 27–2 indicates the project activity differences resulting from the differing levels of use of MPPs. It shows, for example, why most of the savings from using MPPs come in the Integration and Test phase: with MPPs, errors are avoided or discovered earlier, when they are much less expensive to fix.

Comparison with Project Results

Figure 27–2 shows the values of the ideal effort multiplier, IEM(P,MODP), defined in Eq. 24–1, for the projects in the COCOMO data base, as compared to the values of the overall COCOMO effort multipliers for the five MODP attribute ratings (the circles in Fig. 27–2). The correlation between the COCOMO effort multipliers and the median values of IEM(P,MODP)—the arrows in Fig. 27–2—is extremely good. Thus, as all of the other COCOMO attributes are normalized out of this comparison, this correlation implies that the COCOMO effort multipliers are a good predictor of the effect of modern programming practices on software development productivity, at least for the sample of 63 projects in the COCOMO data base.

Discussion

There have been quite a number of papers written which cite impressive productivity gains due to the adoption of modern programming practices. Even more so than with the other factors, it has been difficult to distinguish the gains due to MPPs from the effects of possibly correlated factors: use of better people, better software

TABLE 27–2 Project Activity Difference Due to the Use of Modern Programming Practices

MODP Rating	Phase / Requirements and Product Design	Detailed Design	Code and Unit Test	Integration and Test
Very low	More requirements errors to fix			
	Less requirements and system analysis and validation	More product design errors to fix		
	Less front-end documentation	Design harder to fix and modify; errors in fixes		
		Less design walk-through effort	More detailed design, code errors to fix	
			More tests to rerun	
			More test scaffolding	
			More documentation rework, CM	
			Less code walk-through effort	Many more system-level errors to fix
			Fewer stubs to develop	
Low	Intermediate level of above effects			
Nominal	No change			
High	Fewer requirements errors to fix			
	More requirements, product design V&V effort	Fewer product design errors to fix; fewer errors in fixes		
	More front-end documentation	More design walk-through effort	Fewer detailed design, code errors to fix; fewer errors in fixes	
			Fewer tests to rerun	
			Less test scaffolding	
			Less documentation rework, CM	
			More code walk-through effort	Fewer system-level errors to fix
			More stubs to develop	
Very high	Higher level of above effects			

454

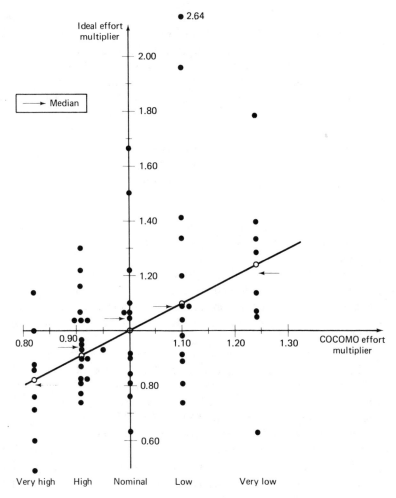

FIGURE 27-2 COCOMO versus ideal effort multiplier—Modern programming practices

tools, higher management visibility, concurrent improvements in management, etc. The table below shows the results from a workshop in which a reasonably thorough (but far from exhaustive) attempt was made to relate several sets of collected data within a consistent framework [Boehm and others, 1975].

Company	Application Area	Number of Projects	Average DSI	Average Improvement in Productivity
IBM	Many	> 20	2K–500K	1.67
Hughes	Real-time	2	10K	2.00
McAuto 73	Business	2	3K	.69
McAuto 74	Business	4	6K	1.25

The negative impact of McAuto 73 was due to inadequate preparation and misuse of some of the MPPs. The COCOMO improvement factor of 1.51 assumes that appropriate training, preparation, and incremental introduction of the MPPs is being applied.

Subsequently, a more extensive analysis of the IBM data base was performed in the [Walston–Felix, 1977] study. Their productivity ranges below represent the ranges between projects using an MPP $< 66\%$ of the time and projects using an MPP $< 33\%$ of the time.

Structured programming	1.78
Design and code inspections	1.54
Top-down development	1.64
Chief programmer terms	1.86

Again, these figures may include the effects of correlated factors*, and certainly include a high degree of correlation between the individual factors above. That is, the ranges above largely represent the joint effect of the four MPPs, since they were usually used together. The larger productivity range for the use of Chief Programmer Teams may also be due to another correlation effect: Chief Programmer Teams tend to be more commonly used on smaller projects than on larger projects, and smaller projects were more productive in the IBM sample, as shown in Table 25–4 [Brustman, 1978].

More recently, an MPP productivity improvement factor of 1.44 has been cited at the Bank of Montreal [Comper, 1979], a factor of 1.48 at SNETCo [Pitchell, 1979], and a factor of 1.58 in a French software organization [Galinier, 1978]. Brown's study of the use of MPPs on a large TRW project [Brown, 1977] provides a great deal of information on the impact of various MPPs on a number of software project characteristics (morale, product control, maintainability, etc.), but no quantitative estimates of productivity improvements. A similar study of the use of MPPs at Boeing [Black and others, 1977] cites productivity improvement factors (actual productivity/estimated productivity) of 1.08, 1.18, 2.31, 5.05, and 6.41 on five projects, but it is not clear to what extent these results are due to deficiencies in the cost-estimation model used.

The GUIDE Survey of MPP Usage

Of particular interest are the results of a recent survey by GUIDE (the commercial IBM users group) of about 800 user installations on their use and evaluation of MPPs [GUIDE, 1979]. Table 27–3 shows the installations' use of various MPPs, indicating that structured programming and top-down design have the most acceptance (roughly 50% of the installations using them; less than 10% rejecting them), while

---

* A more recent intercorrelation analysis [Brooks, 1980] of the IBM-FSD data base indicates that the use of MPPs was correlated with improved productivity for both small and large projects, with significantly larger improvements on large projects. Further, the analysis indicated that the use of MPPs reduced the negative effect of other cost drivers such as complexity and hardware constraints.

TABLE 27–3 Guide Survey of MPP Usage: Use of Individual Techniques

	What Is Your Current Use of New Programming Technologies?			Total Responding
	Rejected	Considering	Using	
Chief programming teams	134	307	224	665
Walkthrough	51	288	307	646
Top-down design	43	329	332	704
Structured programming	37	351	412	800
HIPO	139	278	188	605
Librarian function	109	286	237	632
Interactive programming	86	320	280	686

Chief Programmer Team and HIPO have the least acceptance (roughly 33% of the installations using them; over 20% rejecting them).

Table 27–4 shows the installations' estimates of the effects of MPP usage on various software product and life-cycle characteristics. It indicates that the areas of greatest improvement have been in code quality and early error detection. The effects on programmer productivity and maintenance cost are strongly positive, with about 50% of the installations reporting "improved some" and about 30% reporting "improved greatly."

TABLE 27–4 GUIDE Survey of MPP Usage: Effect on Software Product and Life-Cycle

Consider only the new programming technologies you entered in the "using" column. What has been the effect on each of the following?

	Improved Greatly	Improved Some	No Effect	Negative Improvement	Total Responding
Project estimating or control	63	294	206	8	571
Communication with users	89	227	252	3	571
Organizational stability	47	193	303	10	553
Accuracy of design	166	297	107	3	573
Code quality	206	287	94	2	589
Early error detection	213	276	87	4	580
Programmer productivity	165	350	80	6	601
Maintenance time or cost	178	272	108	11	569
Programmer or analyst morale	108	292	160	20	580

The productivity improvements in Table 27–4 represent only part of the potential MPP improvement achievable at the installation, as indicated in Table 27–5. This table shows the installations' response to the question: "How much further productivity improvement would you expect from using your current MPPs as extensively as practical?" The results indicate that about 40% of the installations could realize an additional 10 to 25% productivity gain, and about 12% could realize an additional 25 to 50% productivity gain.

In summary, the GUIDE results appear consistent with the 51% total potential productivity gain established by the COCOMO model and its corroboration via the 63 projects in the COCOMO data base.

TABLE 27–5 GUIDE Survey of MPP Usage: *Further* Productivity Improvement Potential

Consider only the new programming technologies you checked in the "using" column. If they were to be used as extensively as practical in your installation and your current number of development people were to continue doing the same kind of work, the level (amount) of application development would be:

8	Decrease from current level	
132	The same as the current level	
153	0 to 10% increase over current level	Total
264	10 to 25% increase over current level	Responding
82	25 to 50% increase over current level	658
18	50 to 100% increase over current level	
1	More than 100% increase over current level	

MPPs and Software Routinization

The results in Table 27–4 on the effects of MPPs on programmer or analyst morale (19% improved greatly, 50% improved some, 28% no effect, 3% negative improvement) should be a pleasant surprise to a number of people who predicted the opposite result. For example, *Programmers and Managers* [Kraft, 1977] developed the thesis—based on a good deal of opinion and relatively little data—that the MPP movement was a management attempt to routinize the programmers' jobs and to stifle their creativity. Certainly, there have been a number of cases of management insensitivity in imposing MPPs on programmers, and there is still need for concern in this direction. But such [Kraft, 1977] comments as

The centerpiece of management efforts to de-skill programmers is structured programming, . . .

and

It is hard to anticipate a happy future for the majority of software workers, . . .

do not seem to be borne out by either the GUIDE data (even discounting for the fact that many of the responses were prepared or reviewed by managers), or by current trends in the software personnel marketplace.

27.2 TOOL: USE OF SOFTWARE TOOLS

Ratings and Effort Multipliers

Table 27–6 and Figure 27–3 present software development effort multipliers as a function of the degree to which software tools are used in developing the software subsystem. Five levels of tool support are identified

Very low	Basic microprocessor tools
Low	Basic minicomputer tools
Nominal	Strong minicomputer or basic maxicomputer tools
High	Strong maxicomputer tools
Very high	Advanced maxicomputer tools

TABLE 27–6 Software Tools (TOOL) Effort Multipliers

TOOL Rating	Requirements and Product Design	Detailed Design	Code and Unit Test	Test and Integration	Overall
Very low	1.02	1.05	1.35	1.45	1.24
Low	1.00	1.02	1.15	1.20	1.10
Nominal	1.00	1.00	1.00	1.00	1.00
High	.98	.95	.90	.85	.91
Very high	.95	.90	.80	.70	.83

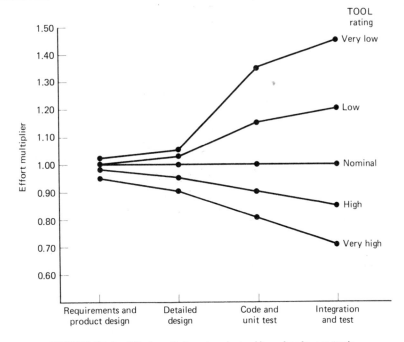

FIGURE 27–3 Effort multipliers by phase: Use of software tools

TABLE 27-7 Software Tools Rating Scale

Rating	Typical Tools
Very low (Basic microprocessor tools)	Assembler Basic linker Basic monitor Batch debug aids
Low (Basic mini)	HOL compiler Macro assembler Simple overlay linker Language independent monitor Batch source editor Basic library aids Basic data base aids
Nominal (Strong mini, Basic maxi)	Real-time or timesharing operating system Data base management system Extended overlay linker Interactive debug aids Simple programming support library Interactive source editor
High (Strong maxi, Stoneman MAPSE)	Virtual memory operating system Data base design aid Simple program design language Performance measurement and analysis aids Programming support library with basic CM aids Set-use analyzer Program flow and test case analyzer Basic text editor and manager

Very high (Advanced maxi, Stoneman APSE)	Full programming support library with CM aids
	Full, integrated documentation system
	Project control system
	Requirements specification language and analyzer
	Extended design tools
	Automated verification system
	Special-purpose tools:
	  Crosscompilers, instruction set simulators,
	  display formatters, communications
	  processing tools, data entry control
	  tools, conversion aids, etc.

Table 27-7 provides a categorization of the typical set of tools available at each level. In rating any particular tool environment, which may have a mixture of tools at different levels, a certain amount of judgment is necessary to determine an equivalent level of tool support. Also, a judgment of the quality and degree of integration of the tool support environment is important in making an appropriate TOOL rating.

Table 27–8 indicates the project activity differences resulting from the differing levels of software tool use. The larger reduction in effort due to tool use in the later phases is due partly to the earlier elimination of errors via tools, and partly to the greater number and maturity of tools to aid in the later phases.

Comparison with Project Results

Figure 27–4 shows the values of the ideal effort multiplier, IEM(P,TOOL), for the projects in the COCOMO data base, as compared to the values of the overall COCOMO effort multipliers for the five TOOL attribute ratings (the circles in Fig. 27–4). The correlation between the COCOMO effort multipliers and the median values of IEM(P,TOOL)—the arrows in Fig. 27–4—is quite good for the intermediate rating levels. There are some differences evident for the outer (very high and very low) rating levels, but these are based on too few data points to warrant changing the COCOMO effort multipliers at this time.

Discussion

Aside from the above analysis of the projects in the COCOMO data base, there has been relatively little assessment of the impact of tools on software cost and productivity. The [Scott–Simmons, 1974] Delphi survey gave a high rating to the factor, Availability of programming tools, as a contributor to software productivity: +5 on a scale of [−7 to +7]. The [Boehm and others, 1974] phase-by-phase Delphi analysis of the potential cost savings of using the National Software Works [Millstein and others, 1976] tool capability on a very large business data processing project yielded median estimated savings of 17% in development and 22% in maintenance (with group estimate ranges of 11 to 24% in development and 10 to 31% in maintenance). Various software development teams recently coming from well-tooled maxi-computer environments onto poorly-tooled microprocessor software projects have estimated typical productivity losses of 33% as a result.

A curve relating software productivity to percentage of support software available was developed by System Development Corporation (SDC) for the U.S. Army Military Computer Family studies [Stone, 1978 and Stone–Coleman, 1979]. The curve has a productivity range of 1.93 between its 30th and 70th percentiles, and a range of 2.66 between its 20th and 80th percentiles. This curve was used in [Stone, 1978] as the basis of assessing the hardware–software life-cycle cost aspects of several candidate Military Computer Family architectures. Each candidate architecture's available software tool base was assessed on a percentile basis with respect to the tool capabilities shown in Table 27–9 (organized along the lines of the COCOMO rating levels), and its tool contributions to the software life-cycle cost determined by use of the SDC curve.

TABLE 27–8 Project Activity Differences Due to Use of Software Tools

Phase / Rating	Requirements and Product Design	Detailed Design	Code and Unit Test	Integration and Test
Very low (basic micro)	More effort for simulation, prototyping ——————————————————————→	More requirements and design errors; harder to find and fix ——————→	More code, data base errors; harder to find and fix ——————→	
			More effort for CM, QA, documentation, testing ———→	More effort in linking, exercising subsystems
Low (basic mini)	Intermediate level of above effects ——→			
Nominal (basic maxi)	No change ——→			
High (strong maxi)	Less text processing effort ——→			
	Easier simulation, prototyping ——→			
		Fewer requirements, and design errors; easier to find and fix ——→	Fewer code, data base errors; easier to find and fix ——→	
		Reduced design effort (PDL)	Less effort for CM, QA, testing ———→	Less effort in linking, exercising subsystems
Very high (advanced maxi)	Higher level of above effects ——→			
	Less requirements, design specification effort	Less requirements, design update effort ————————————————————————→		
	Reduced management effort; faster management problem resolution	Easier implementation of special-purpose functions ————————————→		

A Software Tooling Production Function

Table 27–9 is also of interest for the purposes of sizing and costing of support software, as it shows the typical cost (in 1978 dollars) of providing a production-engineered version of each tool. This information can also be used to determine a rough production function relating levels of software productivity improvement (from the COCOMO effort multipliers) to levels of investment in software tool support for a new computer (from the cumulative cost column in Table 27–9, enhanced by

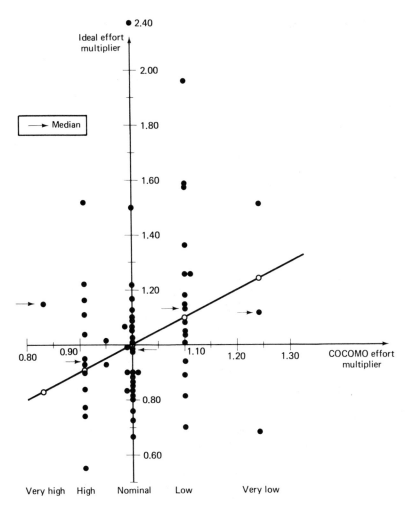

FIGURE 27-4 COCOMO versus ideal effort multiplier—Use of software tools

estimates of the cost of the tools not included at the higher levels). Such a production function is shown in Fig. 27–5.

Further Categories of Software Tools

The production function in Fig. 27–5 covers several categories of software tools besides the basic support tools covered in the [Stone, 1978] study and listed in Table 27–9. These include

- Tools supporting the software development process, such as CM aids, requirements traceability tools, and management tools. Good summaries of such tools are given in [Reifer–Trattner, 1977] and [Reifer, 1978].

TABLE 27-9 Software Tools in Military Computer Family Study

COCOMO Level	Software Tool	Cost (1978$K)	Level Cost (1978$K)	Cumu- lative Cost (1978$K)
Very low (Basic micro)	Assembler	$ 135K		
	Basic linker	130		
	Batch debug aids	50		
	Language dependent monitor	50	$ 365K	$ 365K
Low (Basic mini)	Macro assembler	800		
	Simple overlay linker	210		
	HOL compiler	1000		
	Batch source editor	100		
	Language independent moni- tor	210		
	Integrated library	100	2420	2785
Nominal (Basic maxi)	Extended overlay linker	500		
	Interactive debug aids	500		
	Interactive source editor	130		
	Real-time/timeshare operat- ing system	3500		
	Data base management sys- tem	4200		
	Reformatter	100	8930	11715
High (Strong maxi)	Data base design aid	1150		
	Real-time, time sharing, or vir- tual memory operating sys- tem	2800		
	Automatic software produc- tion and test	1000		
	Standards enforcer	90		
	Test case design advisor	400		
	Test case instrumentation and analysis	280		
	Test data auditor	140		
	Test data generator	350		
	Text-processing system	630	6840	18565
Very high (Advanced maxi)	Computer system simulator	420		
	Instruction simulator	350		
	General-purpose system sim- ulator	700	1470	20035

- Tools extending operating system services or providing special-purpose support, such as decision table processors, display formatters, data management aids, or communications processing support tools. A good catalog of such aids for IBM systems is [IBM, 1977].
- Tools to perform or aid in many of the common programming functions, such as the text processing functions of filtering data streams, filing, sorting, pattern

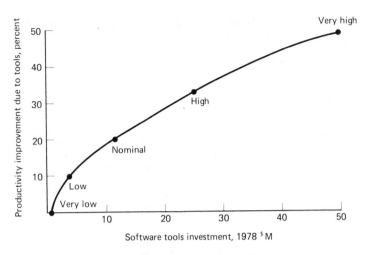

FIGURE 27-5 Software tooling production function

detection, editing and formatting. An excellent compendium of such tools is [Kernighan–Plauger, 1976].

These sources of tools have contributed to the recent major U.S. Department of Defense "Stoneman" effort [Buxton, 1980] to define a programming support environment for the Ada programming language. Stoneman is based on the concept of a unified data base which acts as the repository for all information associated with a software project, and the associated tool linkages supporting creation, modification, analysis, transformation, display, linking, execution, and maintenance of objects in the project's data base.

The Stoneman Ada Programming Support Environment (APSE) is organized into a number of levels

Level 0   The underlying hardware and host software

Level 1   A Kernel APSE, or KAPSE, which provides data base, communication, and run time support for Ada program execution and APSE tool usage, and which serves as a virtual machine interface for the higher level tools

Level 2   A Minimum APSE, or MAPSE, which provides the basic tools deemed necessary for all Ada software development

Level 3   A number of project specific APSE's, which extend the MAPSE to cover special project tool needs.

The tools included in the MAPSE and a typical APSE are listed in Table 27–10. They correspond reasonably well to the high and very high levels of tool support used in COCOMO (Table 27–7).

As a final caution, it is important to re-emphasize that the quality and conceptual integrity of a set of tools is at least as important as the number of tools in the set.

TABLE 27–10 Ada Programming Support Environment (APSE) Tools

Level	Tools
Minimal APSE (MAPSE) (similar to high rating in COCOMO)	Text editor Prettyprinter Translator Linkers Loaders Set-Use static analyzer Control flow static analyzer Dynamic analysis tool Terminal interface routines File administrator Command interpreter Configuration manager
Full APSE (similar to very high rating in CO-COMO)	Ada program editor Documentation system Project control system Configuration control system Performance measurement Fault report system Requirement specification tools Design tools Program verification tools (as available) Translators Command interpreters

Particularly good examples of well-integrated tool environments are the Bell Laboratories Unix-Programmers' Workbench [Dolotta and others, 1978], the Xerox Alto system [Thacker and others, 1979], and the ETH Lilith system [Wirth, 1981].

27.3 SCED: SCHEDULE CONSTRAINT

Ratings and Effort Multipliers

Table 27–11 presents software development effort multipliers as a function of the level of schedule constraint imposed on the project team developing a software subsystem. The ratings are defined in terms of the percentage of schedule stretchout or acceleration with respect to a nominal schedule for a project requiring a given amount of effort. The nominal schedule for a project is given by the Basic COCOMO schedule equations

$$\text{Organic mode} \qquad \text{TDEV} = 2.5(\text{MM}_{\text{DEV}})^{0.38}$$

$$\text{Semidetached mode} \qquad \text{TDEV} = 2.5(\text{MM}_{\text{DEV}})^{0.35}$$

$$\text{Embedded mode} \qquad \text{TDEV} = 2.5(\text{MM}_{\text{DEV}})^{0.32}$$

where MM_{DEV} is the number of man-months required to go from the beginning of the product design phase to the end of the integration and test phase, and TDEV

TABLE 27-11 Development Schedule Constraint (SCED) Effort Multiplier

SCED Rating \ Phase	Requirements and Product Design	Detailed Design	Code and Unit Test	Integration and Test	Overall
Very low [Severe acceleration (75%)]	1.10	1.25	1.25	1.25	1.23
Low [Moderate acceleration (85%)]	1.00	1.10	1.10	1.10	1.08
Nominal (100%)	1.00	1.00	1.00	1.00	1.00
High [Moderate stretchout (130%)]	1.10	1.10	1.00	1.00	1.04
Very high [Severe stretchout (≥160%)]	1.15	1.15	1.05	1.05	1.10

is the corresponding number of months between these endpoints. A schedule acceleration below 75% of nominal is considered impossible by COCOMO.

The magnitude and phase distribution of the schedule constraint effects are shown graphically in Fig. 27–6.

Table 27–12 indicates the project activity differences resulting from the differing levels of schedule constraint. The accelerated-schedule situations (very low and low ratings) tend to produce more effort in the later phases, primarily because more issues are left to be determined (TBD) in the later phases due to lack of time to resolve them earlier. The schedule-stretchout situations (high and very high ratings) tend to produce more effort in the earlier phases, as there is more time for thorough planning, specification, and validation.

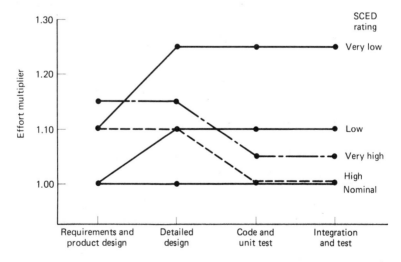

FIGURE 27–6 Effort multipliers versus phase: Required development schedule

TABLE 27-12 Project Activity Differences Due to Schedule Constraints

Phase Rating	Requirements and Product Design	Detailed Design	Code and Unit Test	Integration and Test

Very low
[Severe
acceleration
(75%)]
	Shorter period for level
	  of effort activities
	  (management), etc. ———————————————————————————————→			

	More interface prob-
	  lems (more people ——————————————————————————————————→
	  in parallel)			

	More TBDs in specs,
	  plans
		More work resolving
		  earlier TBD's ———————————————————————→		

	Shortened SRR, PDR
	More advance staffing
	  and training
		Shortened CDR	More test overlap and ——————→
			  redundancy	

		More specification er-
		  rors to fix, errors in ————————————————————→
		  fixes, CM		

	More clerical support ——————————————————————————————————————→			
Low [Moder- ate accel- eration (85%)]	Intermediate level of above effects ————————————————————————→			
Nominal (100%)	No change ———→			

High [Moder-
ate
stretchout
(130%)]
	Longer period for level
	  of effort compo- ——————————————————————————————————————→
	  nents (manage-
	  ment, etc.)			

	Higher likelihood of
	  reinterpreting ———————————————————————————————————————→
	  specs			

	More thorough plan-
	  ning, specs, valida- —————————————————————→
	  tion
			Fewer errors to fix, er-
			  rors in fixes, less ————→
			  CM	

Very high [Severe stretchout (≥160%)]	Higher level of above effects ———————————————————————————→			

Comparison with Project Results

Figure 27–7 shows the values of the ideal effort multiplier, IEM(P,SCED), for the projects in the COCOMO data base, as compared to the values of the overall COCOMO effort multipliers for the five SCED attribute ratings (the circles in Fig. 27–7). The correlation between the COCOMO effort multipliers and the median values of IEM(P,SCED) is not as good as one might like. There appears to be a strong indication that the COCOMO SCED multipliers should be higher.

However, without further or stronger evidence in this direction, it is difficult to justify raising the effort multipliers higher in the light of other software project phenomenology. The current value (1.23) of the overall effort multiplier for the very low (75% of nominal) schedule implies that the average personnel level on the accelerated project is being increased by a factor of

$$\frac{1.23}{0.75} = 1.64$$

Assigning a higher effort multiplier to the very low SCED rating is equivalent to expecting a project to accommodate an even higher average personnel level than 1.64 times nominal. This would strain the project's ability to coordinate its various parts to an extreme degree.

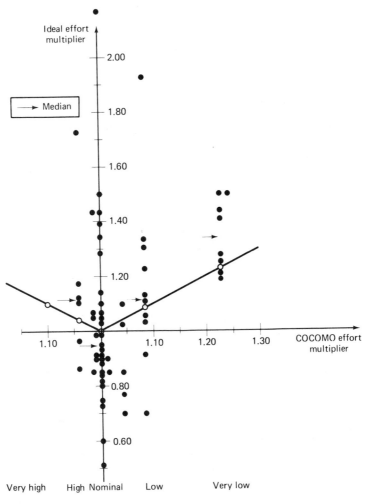

FIGURE 27-7 COCOMO versus ideal effort multiplier—Required development schedule

Discussion

The tables assume that the project manager knows about any required schedule acceleration or stretchout in advance, and is able to plan and control the project in the most cost-effective way with respect to an off-nominal schedule. For a stretchout, this primarily implies spending a longer time with a smaller front-end team to thoroughly develop and validate the software requirements and design specifications, test plans, and draft users' manuals.

For a schedule acceleration, there are a number of ways that the manager can buy some schedule reduction at an increased cost in effort or dollars:*

- Providing extra advance training for programmers and test personnel on the application area, the computer, and support software
- Buying added computer hardware resources (terminals, computers) to support faster coding, checkout, and testing
- Providing extra clerical personnel
- Acquiring automated aids, and training personnel in their use
- Developing extra-detailed unit level and interface design specifications for maximum parallel programmer effort
- Deferring all nonessential documentation and testing

However, there is a limit beyond which a software project cannot reduce its schedule by buying more personnel and equipment. This limit occurs at roughly 75% of the nominal schedule.

Related Data and Studies

The correlation of the COCOMO basic schedule equations with project data and other schedule estimation equations was discussed in Section 6.4.

[Putnam, 1978] gives the following relationship for the minimum development time T_d of a stand-alone software project

$$K = cT_d^3$$

where K is total effort in man-years, T_d is measured in years, and c is in the range of 14 to 15. Converting to months and using $c = 14.5$ yields

$$T_d = 2.15(MM)^{1/3}$$

Relative to the 2.5 coefficient in the COCOMO formula, this represents a typical minimum compression of about 86% compared to the 75% used by COCOMO.

Analysis of other project data bases appears to corroborate the figure of 75% as a schedule compression limit (see Fig. 27–8). Of Putnam's 19 project data points [Putnam, 1978], only one falls below the 75% limit, and that one has a compression of 68.4%. Of the 37 data points in [Belady–Lehman, 1979] (which appears to be a

---

* This is only true at the beginning of the project. Projects attempting to compress schedule by adding more people in the middle of the project will run afoul of Brooks' Law [Brooks, 1975]: "Adding manpower to a late software project makes it later."

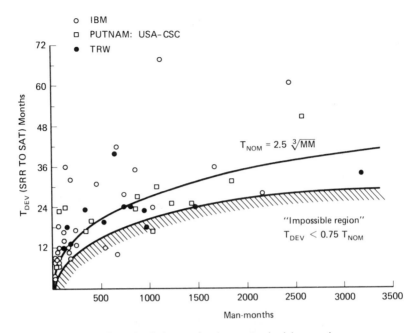

FIGURE 27–8 Software development schedule experience

subset of the IBM data analyzed by Walston and Felix), only two clearly show a compression below 75%; these two have compression factors of 59% and 46%. One would like to know more about how those projects achieved such impressive schedule compressions.

Figure 27–9 shows the schedule compression or expansion factor for the projects in the COCOMO data base. Only four of the 63 projects have schedule compression factors below 75%. The main distinguishing characteristic of these projects is their small total effort: 6, 7, 8, and 15 man-months. Other distinguishing features appear to be low required reliability, high personnel capability, and use of modern programming practices.

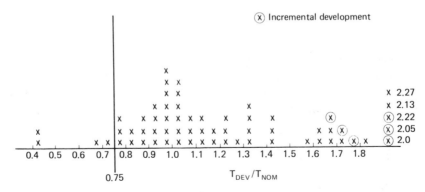

FIGURE 27–9 Schedule compression or expension in COCOMO data base projects

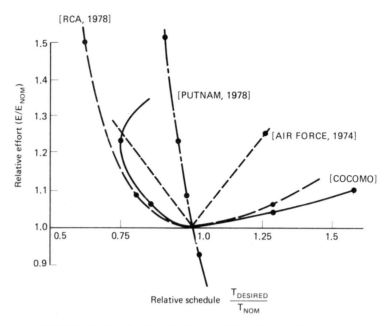

FIGURE 27-10 Relative effort required for off-nominal schedule

The cost effect of a schedule compression or stretchout has been represented in a variety of functional forms, as indicated in Fig. 27–10. The [Air Force, 1974] workshop indicated that an X% compression or stretchout produced an X% increase in cost. The COCOMO relationship is flatter around the nominal schedule and in the stretchout direction, and reaches a maximum of 23% added effort to achieve the maximum schedule compression of 75% of nominal. The RCA PRICE S relationship [RCA, 1978] is similar to COCOMO, except that an unlimited amount of schedule compression is allowed, leading to extremely high personnel levels for highly compressed schedules. The [Putnam, 1978] effort-schedule tradeoff equation

$$\text{Effort} = c/T_d^4$$

produces an extremely steep penalty for compression and an extremely steep effort reduction for a stretchout: by the equation, for example, doubling the schedule of a nominal 100 man-month project would reduce the required effort to $100/2^4 = 6.25$ man-months. Although the data in Fig 27–7 indicate that relative effort may be somewhat more sensitive to relative schedule constraint than in the current COCOMO SCED multipliers, they do not at all support the extreme schedule sensitivity indicated in the [Putnam, 1978] model.

27.4 QUESTIONS

27.1. What project activities account for:
   (a) The 10% added effort in the detailed design phase of a project using a very low level of modern programming practices?

(b) The 15% less effort in the integration and test phase of a project with high use of software tools?

(c) The 25% added effort in the code and unit test phase of a project with a very low schedule constraint (severe acceleration)?

27.2. Develop a set of combined effort multipliers (by phase and overall) for use of modern software technology, assuming equal levels of use of modern programming practices and software tools.

27.3. The Hunt National Bank has 100 people performing software development. The software department manager proposes a training program in modern programming practices which will require an investment of 200 man-months of software personnel time, and is expected to raise each future project's MODP rating from low to high. Assuming that the MODP benefits begin to be realized immediately after the training activity, how long will it take to repay the bank's training investment from the savings in project effort due to use of MPPs?

27.4. The Standard University Kinesiology Department is developing a microprocessor-based, 8-KDSI, organic-mode system for analyzing track and field performance data. The project has the choice of two microprocessors:

(a) A $3500 system with very low tool support.

(b) A $7000 system with low tool support.

If all of the other attribute ratings are nominal, and the system will be developed by graduate students whose burdened cost is $1500 per man-month, which microprocessor represents the better buy in total hardware–software costs?

27.5. The oil rich country of Petro is developing its own computer system, the Petro-1. It plans to install the Petro-1 in all of the country's computer centers, which employ a total of 200 software personnel at a total burdened cost of $10 million per year. Based on the production function in Figure 27–5, how much money should Petro invest in Petro-1 software tools to minimize the country's five-year software costs (tool costs plus five years of software development costs).

27.6. Onageristic Software, Inc., is just completing the negotiation of a fixed-price, 260-MM inventory control software job for a large textile company. The negotiated price is $1,300,000, plus a 10% fee, with delivery of the software system on a nominal 16 months schedule. Suddenly the Onageristic marketing manager bursts in with the announcement, "I've just gotten the customer to double our fee if we deliver the system in 12 months rather than 16. Here's the signed contract!" Has he made a good deal for Onageristic?

27.7. Suppose the Onageristic marketing manager had renegotiated the contract to triple the fee, with guaranteed delivery in 10 months. What should the president of Onageristic do in this situation?

27.5 TOPICS FOR FURTHER RESEARCH

27.A. Perform experiments and observations to test the hypotheses that the effort multipliers for one or more of the COCOMO project attributes (MODP, TOOL, SCED)
- are of the same magnitude used in COCOMO
- vary by phase as in Detailed COCOMO

- are independent of project size, type, or mode (for example, [Brooks, 1980] indicates that MODP effects may vary with project size during development as well as maintenance)
- interact multiplicatively with each other
- interact multiplicatively with the other COCOMO cost driver attributes (for example, RELY, TURN, ACAP, AEXP, PCAP); see [Brooks, 1980].

27.B. Collect and analyze data on the effect of one or more of the project attributes on the individual project activities itemized in Tables 27–2, 27–8, and 27–12. See, for example, [Basili-Reiter, 1979; Basili-Weiss, 1981; Sheppard and others, 1981; Paster, 1981].

27.C. Test the hypotheses that the MODP and TOOL rating scales are sufficiently objective to assure reasonably uniform cost driver ratings.

27.D. Develop a more detailed rating scale for MODP, and test its objectivity and utility by applying it in software cost estimation activities. See [Bailey-Basili, 1981].

27.E. Analyze the effect of individual MPPs or groups of MPPs on software productivity and other quantities, such as software reliability and team morale (see, for example [Fagan, 1976] and [Myers, 1978] on inspections; [Milliman-Curtis, 1980] on overall MPPs; [Chen-Zelkowitz, 1981] on methodology signatures versus error rates; [Woodfield and others, 1981] on modularization versus understanding).

27.F. Analyze the effect of Chief Programmer Teams on software productivity and other quantities, such as software reliability and team morale. Make sure to define terms carefully.

27.G. Define an extra high rating for MODP including such techniques as information hiding, formal specifications, abstract interfaces, cooperating sequential processes, process synchronization routines, resource monitors [Heninger and others, 1978], unit development folders [Ingrassia, 1977], or others which appear significant. Determine appropriate effort multipliers for the extra high rating by experimentation and observation.

27.H. Refine the software tools production function in Figure 27–5 by determining updated or newly estimated costs for each of the software tools enumerated in Table 27–7.

27.I. Analyze the effect of individual tools on software productivity and other quantities, such as software reliability (for example, [Thayer and others, 1978]).

27.J. The COCOMO SCED effort multipliers indicate that, up to a point, one can reduce development schedule by adding more people, if this result is recognized and planned from the beginning. Brooks' Law [Brooks, 1975] indicates that this cannot be done once the project is well underway. Analyze this apparent dichotomy in more detail (see, for example, [Gordon–Lamb, 1977]).

27.K. Perform a detailed analysis of the schedule–effort tradeoff relations in COCOMO, those in RCA PRICE S [RCA, 1978] and in [Putnam, 1978], and those in other models such as [Esterling, 1980].

Chapter 28

Factors Not Included in COCOMO

This chapter discusses a number of possible software cost driver attributes which have not been included in COCOMO. They are

1. Type of application
2. Language level
3. Other size measures: complexity, entities, and specifications
4. Requirements volatility
5. Personnel continuity
6. Management quality
7. Customer interface quality
8. Amount of documentation
9. Hardware configuration
10. Security and privacy restrictions

In order to see why these factors have not been included in COCOMO, we will first present a set of criteria useful in evaluating software cost models and their attributes.

Criteria for Evaluating a Software Cost Model

We have found the following criteria most helpful in evaluating the utility of a software cost model for practical estimation purposes

1. *Definition.* Has the model clearly defined the costs it is estimating, and the costs it is excluding?
2. *Fidelity.* Are the estimates close to the actual costs expended on the projects?
3. *Objectivity.* Does the model avoid allocating most of the software cost variance to poorly calibrated subjective factors (such as complexity)? That is, is it hard to jigger the model to obtain any result you want?
4. *Constructiveness.* Can a user tell why the model gives the estimates it does? Does it help the user understand the software job to be done?
5. *Detail.* Does the model easily accommodate the estimation of a software system consisting of a number of subsystems and units? Does it give (accurate) phase and activity breakdowns?
6. *Stability.* Do small differences in inputs produce small differences in output cost estimates?
7. *Scope.* Does the model cover the class of software projects whose costs you need to estimate?
8. *Ease of Use.* Are the model inputs and options easy to understand and specify?
9. *Prospectiveness.* Does the model avoid the use of information which will not be well known until the project is complete?*
10. *Parsimony.* Does the model avoid the use of highly redundant factors, or factors which make no appreciable contribution to the results?

For the most part, the significance of each of these criteria is reasonably self-evident. A more detailed discussion of their significance is given in Section 29.8, as well as in [Boehm–Wolverton, 1978].

The parsimony criterion meant excluding some factors from COCOMO, even though they occasionally play a significant role in determining a project's costs. For such factors (as also for the case of extraordinary values of the existing factors), the decision was made to keep COCOMO simple and not to try to account for extraordinary situations in the model. In general, if you find yourself in such a situation, you will be better off to rely more on further analysis of the project specifics and less on the ability of a general-purpose model to explain your special situation.

28.1 TYPE OF APPLICATION

Many software cost-estimation models use some categorization of application types as a cost driver. Examples are

---

* Clearly, this criterion is specific to the objective of cost *prediction.* For other objectives, such as technology impact assessment, a retrospective model could be appropriate.

- Control, input/output, pre/postprocessors, algorithm, data management, time critical [Wolverton, 1974].
- Mathematical, Report, Logic, Signal, Real-Time [Black and others, 1977].

An attempt was made to incorporate such a cost driver into the COCOMO model, but it was not considered successful for the following reasons

- Difficulties in providing precise definitions of the types (for example, virtually all mathematical or algorithmic routines or applications include some control, logical, or data management activity; see Fig. 21–3).
- Overlaps with other COCOMO factors (such as complexity, execution time constraint, and data base) made it harder to justify using a multiplicative model without double counting.
- Difficulties in achieving any consensus among experienced personnel on the relative order of difficulty of the application types (some people considered algorithmic software very easy; others considered it very difficult).

For these main reasons, the separate "type" factor was dropped, although an aspect of it is retained in the four type-dependent complexity rating scales given in Table 24–8.

Comparison with Project Results

Figure 28–1 shows the values of the ideal effort multiplier, IEM(P, TYPE), for the six types of projects catalogued in the COCOMO data base: business, control, human-machine, scientific, support, and system software projects.

One might conclude from the median values of IEM(P, TYPE)—the arrows in Fig. 28–1—that the COCOMO model slightly overestimates on business and support software, and slightly underestimates on control and human-machine software. But the differences from unity, compared to the variation among projects of each type, is so small as to reject the prospect of adding a TYPE multiplier to COCOMO on the grounds of model parsimony.

28.2 LANGUAGE LEVEL

An earlier version of COCOMO used *deliverable, executable machine instructions* (DEMI) as its basic size parameter. This version uses *Delivered Source Instructions* (DSI) as its basic size parameter for the following major reasons

- It was found (and corroborated by [Walston–Felix, 1977] and [Nelson, 1978]) that DSI correlated more closely with total effort, and that the amount of effort per source statement was highly independent of language level. (This point is discussed further in Section 33.4.)
- A large majority of people now find it more natural to estimate the size of software components in DSI rather than DEMI. Given the wide variation in the expansion

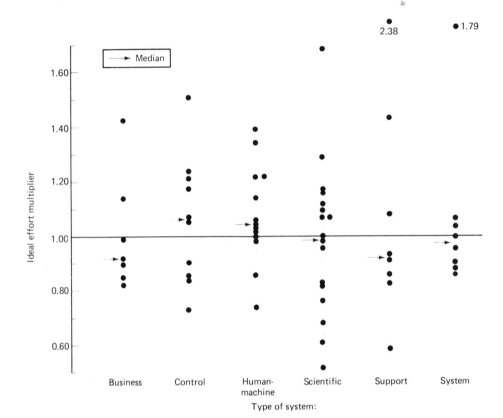

FIGURE 28-1 Ideal effort multipliers by type of system

ratio (number of DEMI's per DSI) between languages, computers, and applications, it is better to use DSI directly rather than to introduce an additional source of variation by estimating in executable DSI and using some assumed expansion ratio to determine the number of DEMI to be used in the model. Table 28-1 shows some typical values and ranges of variation for DEMI/executable DSI expansion

TABLE 28-1 Object/Source Instruction Expansion Ratios (DEMI/Executable DSI)

Language	IBM [Climis, 1979] (Average)	TRW (Range)	PRICE S [RCA, 1978]
FORTRAN	6–7:1	4–6:1	4–8:1
COBOL	5:1	4–6:1	2.5–3.5:1
PL/I	5:1	—	7.5–13:1
Pascal	8:1	5–7:1	3–5:1
APL	12:1	—	15:1
PL/S	2.5:1	—	—
JOVIAL	—	3–5:1	3–5:1
C	—	—	3:1
CMS-2	—	—	2.5–3.5:1

ratios. The difference between the IBM and TRW data probably reflects the fact that the TRW software includes more products on machines with larger than 32-bit word lengths and more powerful individual machine instructions. As we evolve toward HOL software for minicomputers and microcomputers, we should probably see the average expansion ratio increase from the IBM ratios.*

- Using *executable machine* instructions makes it difficult to account for the relative effort required for data declarations, format statements and other nonexecutable portions of the program. Using *total machine* words used by the program makes it difficult to distinguish between programs with large, simple data regions and programs with more complex data and instruction regions. Using *total source* instructions as a basis leads to fewer anomalies in correlating the program size measure to the amount of intellectual and administrative effort required to develop the program.

Comparison with Project Results

Figure 28–2 shows the values of the ideal effort multiplier, IEM(*P*,LANG), for the projects in the COCOMO data base, for the seven types of programming language cataloged in the data base: assembly, FORTRAN, COBOL, JOVIAL, PL/I, Pascal, and Other Higher Order Languages.

One might conclude from the median values of IEM(*P*,LANG)—the arrows in Figure 28–2—that COCOMO slightly overestimates on assembly and COBOL software, but the effects are not strong enough to modify the model.

An earlier analysis of this nature did identify a significant pattern of overestimation on COBOL programs. This anomaly was traced to the high COBOL source instruction counts generated by including large numbers of often redundant nonexecutable source statements. This anomaly is currently rectified in COCOMO by the rather pragmatic procedure of weighting nonexecutable COBOL source statements by a factor of 1/3.

28.3 OTHER SIZE MEASURES: COMPLEXITY, ENTITIES, SPECIFICATIONS

Many people have criticized the use of any kind of instruction count as the basic program size parameter to be used in estimating software costs. They argue that this is about like trying to estimate the cost of an automobile by its gross weight, or by the total number of parts in it. One approach to counter this insensitivity problem is to incorporate a number of sensitivity factors which help to rate the relative difficulty of developing different kinds of instructions or groups of instructions (modules): storage-constrained modules, complex computational modules, etc. This weighted-instruction approach is the approach taken by COCOMO.

Another main approach is to use some measure other than number of instructions as the basic size parameter. Several such parameters have been tried, but generally

---

* Further, the entire concept of DEMI becomes clouded as the concepts of direct or interpretive execution of HOL programs become more prevalent.

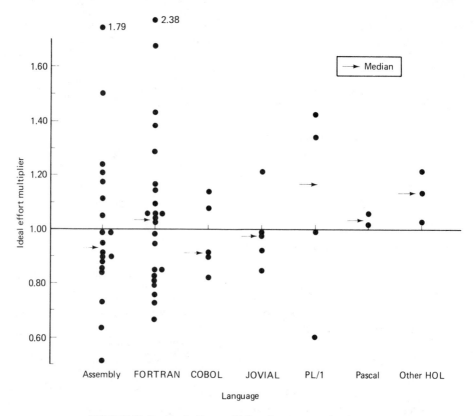

FIGURE 28–2   Ideal effort multipliers by programming language

they run into even more difficult insensitivity problems than does the number of instructions parameter. Several examples are given below.

Complexity Measures

These measures are attempts to determine some more fundamental characteristic of a computer program which will serve as a predictor of the cost required to develop the program. The two primary candidates at present are

1. Halstead's program volume measure [Halstead, 1977], defined as

$$V = (N_1 + N_2) \log_2(\eta_1 + \eta_2)$$

where

$\eta_1 =$ number of unique operators in the program
$\eta_2 =$ number of unique operands in the program
$N_1 =$ total number of operator occurrences in the program
$N_2 =$ total number of operand occurrences in the program

Halstead's resulting effort equation is

$$\text{Effort} = \frac{\eta_1 \, N_2 \, V}{36\eta_2}$$

2. McCabe's cyclomatic complexity measure [McCabe, 1976], defined as

$$V = e - n + 2p$$

where e, n, and p are properties of the program's control graph

e = number of edges (links)
n = number of vertices (nodes)
p = number of connected components

Some work has been done to correlate these measures with the amount of programming effort required to produce or maintain a program [Halstead, 1978; Curtis and others, 1978, 1979a, 1979b; Elshoff, 1978; Milliman-Curtis, 1980; Sunohara and others, 1981]. In general, the results have shown (for both measures, but more extensively for Halstead's volume measure) that

- There is a reasonable correlation between each measure and the amount of programming effort.
- There is a comparable correlation between each measure and the number of instructions in the program.
- No results have shown either measure to be a significantly better predictor of software development effort for large programs (over 1000 DSI) than is the number of instructions.*

In addition, both measures are insensitive to such factors as personnel experience, hardware constraints, and the use of tools and modern programming practices, all of which have been seen above to have a significant effect upon required software development effort. Further, these measures are less familiar to people who must do program sizing estimates, and in general, they involve knowledge of program attributes which are not well known until the code has been completed. Thus, in consideration of three of the major criteria for goodness of a software cost-estimation model—parsimony, ease of use, and prospectiveness—COCOMO has chosen to use the number of instructions rather than any of these complexity measures.

Number of Program Entities: Routines, Reports, Inputs, Outputs, Files

Some attempts have been made to use the number of program entities (routines, reports, inputs, outputs, or files) as sizing parameters in software cost estimation.

---

* However, some recent studies have shown that the Halstead and McCabe metrics correlate considerably better than DSI with the amount of terminal time (excluding non-terminal think time) required to program small (10–40 DSI) programs [Sheppard and others, 1980].

None of the attempts has been very successful, primarily because of definition and normalization problems, such as

- There is no attempt to distinguish between small versus large or simple versus complex instances of a routine, report, etc.
- There have been no good, precise definitions of what constitutes an instance of a routine, report, etc.

In practice, therefore, any of these entities (say, routines) may be broken up into several entities (or any group of routines may be redefined as a single routine) in a way which significantly changes the value of the sizing parameter without having made any real difference in the software development job to be done. Therefore, with respect to the goodness criteria of definition and objectivity, these quantities are less than satisfactory as sizing parameters for cost estimation.

However, particularly in installations with a fairly uniform product line, these quantities can provide some useful insight on early estimation of software development effort. The best work to date is the [Albrecht, 1979] approach, based on the "function point" metric, a linear combination of number of inputs, outputs, inquiries, and master files.

Number of Specification Elements

Some work has been done to correlate the amount of software development effort to the number of specification elements, such as

- Number of paragraphs in the software requirements specification
- Number of instances of the word "shall" in the software requirements specification
- Number of lines of program design language in the software design specification
- Number of structure-chart or HIPO-chart elements in the software design specification

These attempts have run into the same sort of definition and normalization problems as have the "number of routines, reports, etc." quantities discussed above. They have therefore not been used in COCOMO because of the same basic type of problems with definition and objectivity.

Use of Source Instructions for Sizing: The RADC Data Base

Further justification for the use of source instructions as the primary size parameter for software cost estimation is given in Fig. 28–3, which shows the strong correlation between *delivered source lines of code* (DSLOC) and total man-months for software development ($R = 0.85$) over the sample of over 400 project data points in the RADC data base [Nelson, 1978]. Although the definitions of such quantities as DSLOC and total man-months display a wide variation among the projects in the RADC Data Base, the size of the sample gives us much more confidence in the use of

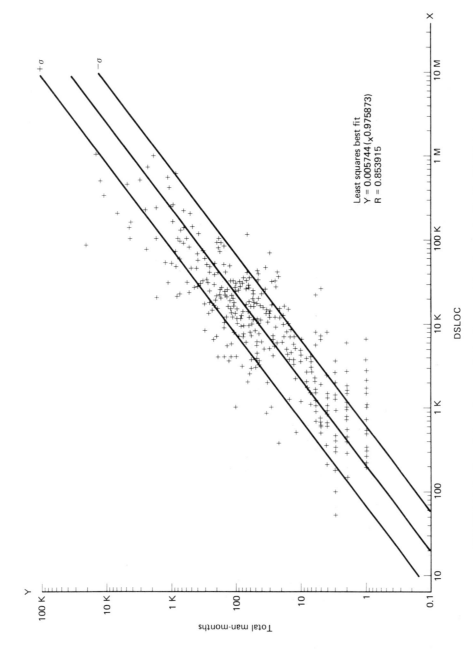

FIGURE 28-3 Correlation of source instructions and development effort in RADC data base

483

DSLOC or DSI as a sizing parameter in software cost estimation than can be generated for any alternative sizing parameter.

Of course, we need to be careful in defining developers' objectives in ways that induce them not to produce more lines of code than the application warrants. In general, the overall urge to get the job done, plus such practices as core budgeting and peer code review, tend to minimize any intentional padding of code with extra instructions in order to appear productive. However, the wide spread of lines of code versus assigned objective in the [Weinberg–Schulman, 1974] experiment cited in Section 21.4 indicates the ease with which lines of code per function can grow.

28.4 REQUIREMENTS VOLATILITY

Requirements volatility, or the amount of change in the software requirements between the beginning and end of a software development project, is clearly a significant factor affecting the cost of the software. For example, on one highly ambitious radar software application [Schluter, 1977], software costs escalated by a factor of four because of software *breakage:* software which had to be rebuilt because of changes in requirements. In this example, the software that was developed before the radar was accurately characterized had a breakage factor of 318% (33K instructions delivered, 105K instructions discarded), because of changes in radar interface and processing requirements.

An earlier version of the COCOMO model included a requirements volatility factor to account for the effects of software breakage. However, it made the resulting estimates extremely sensitive to a highly subjective, imprecisely defined parameter whose value would not be known until the completion of the project. The factor was therefore eliminated from the COCOMO estimation model because of the difficulties with the criteria of objectiveness, definition, and prospectiveness. Thus, a CO-COMO estimate predicts the number of man-months required to develop the software defined by the current requirements specification. As requirements change, both the specification and the cost estimate can and should be updated.*

Comparison with Project Results

The calibration version of COCOMO still retains a requirements volatility factor to normalize projects which have experienced high or low degrees of change in requirements throughout the development period.

The effort multipliers used to account for requirements volatility in calibrating completed projects are given in Table 28–2. They do not vary by phase.

Figure 28–4 shows the values of the ideal effort multiplier, IEM(*P*,RQTV), for the projects in the COCOMO data base, as compared to the values of the COCOMO effort multipliers (the circles in Fig. 28–4). The correlation between the COCOMO

* Some requirements volatility is generally unavoidable. For example, IBM's Santa Teresa Laboratory has found, on a sample of roughly 1,000,000 instructions of software produced per year to IBM-determined requirements, that the average project experiences a 25% change in requirements during the period of its development [Climis, 1979].

TABLE 28-2 Requirements Volatility Effort Multipliers

Rating	Project Rework Due to Requirements Changes	Effort Multiplier
Low	Essentially none	0.91
Nominal	Small, noncritical redirections	1.00
High	Occasional moderate redirections	1.19
Very high	Frequent moderate or occasional major redirections	1.38
Extra high	Frequent major redirections	1.62

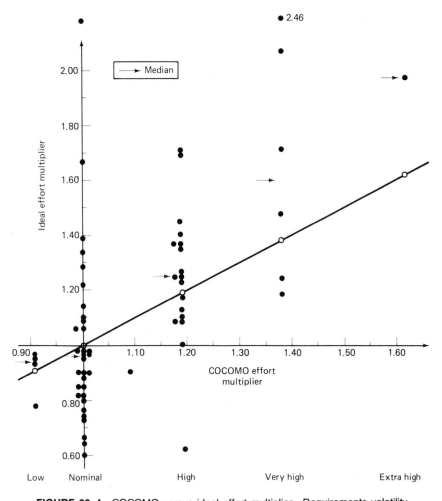

FIGURE 28-4 COCOMO versus ideal effort multiplier—Requirements volatility

effort multipliers and the median values of IEM(P,RQTV)—the arrows in Fig. 28–4—is reasonably good, although there is some indication that the COCOMO effort multipliers may be somewhat low.

28.5 PERSONNEL CONTINUITY

Personnel continuity was originally considered as a candidate for inclusion in the COCOMO model. However, it was eventually not included for the following main reasons

- It is difficult to define precisely, considering that many projects have a built-in degree of personnel turnover due to phasing, use of specialists, use of part-time personnel, etc.
- It has roughly the same prospectiveness problems as does the requirements volatility factor, since critical personnel turnover problems are not easy to predict in advance.

- Surprisingly, a large majority of the COCOMO project data points indicated an *average* level of personnel turnover, making it very difficult to ascertain the factor's influence on software cost.

Thus, COCOMO estimates assume that a project (like most projects) will have an average level of personnel turnover, and that any extraordinary project will provide its own subjective adjustment to the COCOMO estimate. One way that this can be done is via the ACAP and PCAP ratings, which should reflect effective team capability.

Comparison with Project Results

Figure 28–5 shows the values of the ideal effort multiplier, IEM(P,PCON), for the projects in the COCOMO data base, for the low, nominal, and high ratings for personnel continuity. The median values of IEM(P,PCON)—the arrows in Fig. 28–5—show much less deviation from 1.0 than one would expect. The main explanation is that many of the personnel continuity effects were considered in the assignment of ACAP and PCAP ratings on the projects in the COCOMO data base. This makes it difficult to conclude anything about personnel continuity effects from Fig. 28–5. Certainly, general project experience indicates that it is a much more critical factor than is suggested by Fig. 28–5.

28.6 MANAGEMENT QUALITY

Poor management can increase software costs more rapidly than any other factor. Each of the following mismanagement actions has often been responsible for *doubling* software development costs

- Assigning the wrong (combination of) people to project jobs

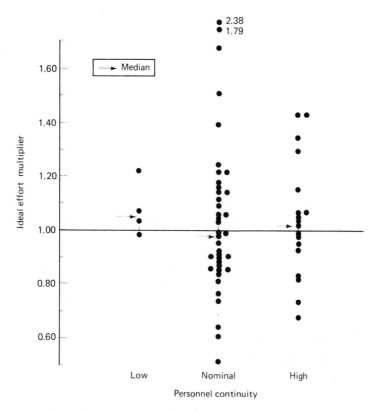

FIGURE 28-5 Ideal effort multipliers: Personnel continuity

- Creating task overlaps and underlaps through poor organization, delegation, and task monitoring
- Demotivating people by unnecessarily poor working conditions and failure to reward good performance
- Bringing large numbers of people onto the project before there is a clear understanding of their responsibilities
- Failing to prepare needed resources: computer time, terminals, communications, test data, support software
- Failing to validate software requirements and design specifications, and to identify and resolve high-risk elements early

Despite this cost variation,* COCOMO does not include a factor for management quality, but instead provides estimates which assume that the project will be well managed. This is done for the following main reasons

- Management quality ratings are not easy to define.

---

* To date, there have been no studies establishing a well-defined productivity range for management quality. One reason for this is that poorly-managed projects rarely collect much data on their experiences.

- Management quality is hard to predict in advance. If the candidate project manager is known to be a poor manager, another candidate should be found.
- It is bad management practice to reward poor managers by giving them more resources to do a job than a good manager would be given.
- Most importantly, both management quality prophecies and cost prophecies can be self-fulfilling. COCOMO assumes that the project will be managed well, and provides both a tool and a standard of excellence to help the project manager exercise good management and realize the COCOMO estimate (see Chapter 32).

This is not to say that a project should not have a management reserve to take care of contingencies. For a well-managed project, the COCOMO estimate does include some management reserve, as the model is calibrated to reasonably well-managed projects, in general, but not to ideally managed projects.

28.7 CUSTOMER INTERFACE QUALITY

Poor management by software customers, or poor customer–developer communications, can also lead to large increases in software costs. Each of the following customer-related actions has often been responsible for *doubling* software costs

- Imposition of impossibly short target schedules (see Chapter 27) which force large personnel commitments before the job is understood.
- Reluctance to define software requirements early, or growth of customer–developer misunderstandings which cause the wrong product to be developed.
- Frequent redirection of project effort by stipulating changes in requirements, interfaces, facilities, or personnel.

Despite these cost variations, COCOMO does not include a customer interface quality factor, for the same basic reason as for the management quality factor: it would lead to negative self-fulfilling prophecies and reward poor performance.

28.8 AMOUNT OF DOCUMENTATION

Documentation, in all its forms, accounts for a large fraction of total software costs. An analysis in Section 31.6 indicates that roughly 51 to 54% of a project's activity results in a document as its immediate end product, and only 34% of the project's activity results in code as its immediate end product. However, it is very difficult to define a cost estimation factor for the amount of documentation, for the following reasons

- Many project documents, such as good specifications and test plans, actually lead to project savings.
- Automated aids (cross-reference generators, flow charters, report generators) can produce large amounts of documentation with little required effort.

- Large amounts of poor quality documentation can be produced more cheaply than smaller amounts of good quality documentation.
- Documentation is not really an add-on, but is integral to good software development practice.

For these reasons, COCOMO does not include an amount-of-documentation factor. However, the following related effects are incorporated into COCOMO.

- *Anticipatory documentation* (early development of project plans, specifications, and manuals as a means of project definition and control) is included within the basic software life-cycle (see Section 4.4), and provided for in the COCOMO early-phase effort estimates.
- The activity distributions in Tables 7–1, 7–2, and 7–3 estimate the effort required for developing users', operations, and maintenance manuals.

Section 31.6 provides further discussion of such topics as documentation sizing.

28.9 HARDWARE CONFIGURATION

The effects of this factor are largely covered by other factors

- Effects of poor software support for mini- and microcomputers are covered in the TOOL factor (Tables 27–6 and 27–7).
- Effects of unstable or unreliable underlying hardware—software configurations are covered in the VIRT factor (Table 25–9).
- Effects due to the added complexity of distributed processing systems are covered in the CPLX factor (Tables 24–7 and 24–8).

Comparison with Project Results

Figure 28–6 shows the values of the ideal effort multiplier, IEM(P,COMP), for the projects in the COCOMO data base, for the four computer types catalogued in the data base: micro, mini, midi, and maxi. Except for the small sample of microcomputer projects, the median values of IEM(P,COMP) are sufficiently close to 1.0 to eliminate hardware configuration as an additional COCOMO parameter.

28.10 SECURITY AND PRIVACY RESTRICTIONS

Information system security or privacy restrictions may impose additional constraints on software development, which lead to added costs. Some of these effects are already incorporated in existing COCOMO factors

- Effects of restricted computer access are included in the TURN factor (Table 25–11)

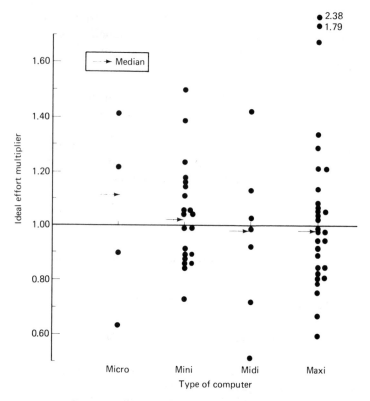

FIGURE 28–6 Ideal effort multipliers by type of computer

- Effects of increased requirements for reliable software are covered in the RELY factor (Table 24–1)

  Some other effects are not included in the standard COCOMO factors

- Added product features (security markings, operational controls)
- Reduced access to documentation and added documentation control

Since these requirements in their stringent form are relatively rare, and even then generally add only 10% to project costs, COCOMO does not include this as an added factor on the grounds of model parsimony. Those exceptional projects with stringent security or privacy restrictions should add a factor of roughly 5 to 10% to cover the above effects.

28.11 TOPICS FOR FURTHER RESEARCH

28.A. One recent experiment [Boehm, 1980], involving two project teams using FORTRAN and Pascal to develop a small applications software product, concluded that the choice of programming language had only a minor influence on the overall project results.

Conduct similar experiments to check the validity of this conclusion for small applications software projects, or to determine its applicability in other software development contexts.

28.B. After many years and hundreds of millions of compiler runs, the subject of source/object code expansion ratios is still a topic of considerable mystery. Perform an analysis of expansion ratios and determine their range of variability by

- Programming language
- Type of compiler
- Computer characteristics (word size, instruction set, registers)
- Type of application
- HOL statement mix
- Other significant characteristics

28.C. Formulate improved measures of software size or complexity, and investigate their utility in software cost estimation (see, for example, the software complexity-metric investigations in Research Topics 24.P, Q, and R).

28.D. Perform experiments to test the hypothesis that the requirements volatility rating scale in Table 28–2 is sufficiently objective to assure reasonably uniform cost driver ratings.

28.E. Collect and analyze data on the effect of requirements volatility on individual software project activities. Determine the effectiveness of the information-hiding techniques in [Parnas, 1979] in reducing the effects of requirements volatility.

28.F. Investigate the effects of personnel continuity on overall software project productivity and on individual project activities.

28.G. Investigate the effects of the management and customer interface deficiencies listed in Sections 28.6 and 28.7 on software project productivity and other project characteristics. *Warning:* These subjects are highly sensitive, and must be approached with considerable care.

28.H. Investigate the effects of distributed data processing configurations on software project productivity and related characteristics.

28.I. Identify or formulate other candidate software cost driver attributes, and investigate their effects on software project productivity and related characteristics (see, for example, the extensive lists of candidate cost driver attributes in [Nelson, 1966] and [Walston–Felix, 1977]).

28.J. Investigate the tradeoff relations between software project productivity and other software metrics or quality attributes (see, for example, [Gilb, 1977], [Boehm and others, 1978]).

Chapter 29

COCOMO Evaluation

29.1 INTRODUCTION

This chapter presents an overall evaluation of COCOMO with respect to the criteria given in Chapter 28 for the goodness of a software cost model. It also provides techniques for tailoring COCOMO to a particular installation. For evaluating the accuracy of COCOMO estimates, we will use the COCOMO data base of 63 completed software projects, comparing the estimates on these projects given by the Basic CO-COMO, Intermediate COCOMO, and Detailed COCOMO models with the actual efforts, schedules, phase distributions, and activity distributions experienced by the projects. Since Intermediate COCOMO and Detailed COCOMO each have 17 variables (size, mode, and 15 cost driver attributes), the 63 data points represent a reasonable test of the model's fidelity. However, since each variable is represented by several parameters (the effort multipliers for the different ratings) and since many of the data points have been used to help calibrate the model, it is important to provide some background information on the sequence of activities employed to calibrate and evaluate COCOMO with respect to the project data, in order to place the evaluation in perspective.

COCOMO Calibration/Evaluation Sequence

The initial version of COCOMO was based on a review of existing cost models, a two-round Delphi exercise involving 10 experienced software managers in estimating effort multipliers for various cost driver attributes, and experience with several software cost-estimation models at TRW. The initial COCOMO model, which had only a single development mode, was calibrated using 12 completed projects. The resulting model was then evaluated with respect to a fairly uniform sample of 36 projects, primarily aerospace applications, producing fairly good agreement between estimates and actuals.

However, an expansion of the project data base to 50 and then 56 projects, from a wider variety of environments, indicated that a single development mode was not sufficient to explain the variation between projects. The three-mode model was then developed and calibrated to the 56 projects, resulting in additional, relatively small, corrections to the effort multipliers as well. Subsequently, seven more projects (dated 1979) were added to the data base. The COCOMO estimates of the final seven projects have been fairly close to the project actuals.

Statistical Analysis

The calibration and evaluation of COCOMO has not relied heavily on advanced statistical techniques. After trying to apply advanced statistical techniques to software cost estimation, and after observing similar efforts by others, I have become convinced that the software field is currently too primitive, and software cost driver interactions too complex, for standard statistical techniques to make much headway; and that more initial progress could be made by trying to formulate empirically the nature of the interactions between cost drivers, using functional forms which reflected the best available perspectives and data on software life-cycle phenomenology.

An example may be instructive here. In analyzing a set of 88 modules in a TRW software product during the CCIP-85 study in 1971, we attempted to correlate productivity in DSI/MM with the project managers' estimates of module complexity and programmer capability. We expected a significant negative correlation between productivity and complexity, and a significant positive correlation between productivity and capability rating, but were surprised to find an essentially zero correlation for both.

On investigating further, we found that the main reason was that the managers had assigned the most capable personnel to the most complex modules, and vice versa. After recognizing this, we defined a concept of *weighted instructions* (number of instructions multiplied by relative complexity rating) and a corresponding concept of weighted productivity, and obtained an excellent correlation between weighted productivity and capability rating. From this simple concept of weighted productivity, it is a relatively straightforward conceptual step to the concept of weighted productivity embodied in the COCOMO ideal effort multiplier defined in Section 24.1.

Thus, the statistical analyses presented here go as far as to present means, medians, and a few standard deviations, but nothing more advanced statistically. However, at this point, the COCOMO model and data base present attractive subjects for more advanced statistical analyses, as suggested at the end of the chapter in the topics for further research.

Chapter Preview

Section 29.2 presents the characteristics of the 63 completed projects used to calibrate and evaluate COCOMO. Sections 29.3 through 29.6 then discuss the comparison of COCOMO estimates to project actuals for development effort, development schedule, phase distribution, and activity distribution.

Section 29.7 summarizes the current state of the art in software cost modeling by describing some of the other leading cost models available. Section 29.8 then evaluates COCOMO with respect to the set of criteria given in Chapter 28 for the goodness of a software cost model, in terms of the current state of the art.

One of the conclusions of this evaluation is that a given installation can often develop a specially calibrated and tailored version of COCOMO which will be more accurate and easy to use within the context of the particular installation. Techniques for performing such calibration and tailoring activities are given in Section 29.9.

Finally, Section 29.10 identifies a number of topics for further research, including a number of investigations into the quantitative characteristics of software projects based on the data in the COCOMO data base.

29.2   THE COCOMO PROJECT DATA BASE

Table 29–1 summarizes the project data and related COCOMO estimates for the 63 projects in the COCOMO Data Base. A definition of each of the quantities in Table 29–1 is given in Table 29–2.

Considerable effort has been devoted to ensuring that the data in the COCOMO data base is consistent with respect to cost driver attritute ratings, and that the definitions of such quantities as development, man-month, project, and DSI agree with the COCOMO assumptions in Section 5.2, the phase definitions in Table 4–1, and the work breakdown structure components in Fig. 4–6. In some cases, adjustment factors have been included, based on the best information available, to normalize project quantities with respect to use of comment cards, exclusion of project design activities, exclusion of management effort, and the like.

Also, considerable care has been taken to avoid inclusion of distinguishing features of the projects in the data base, in order to preserve the anonymity of some of the projects.

29.3 COCOMO ESTIMATES VERSUS ACTUALS: DEVELOPMENT EFFORT

Figures 29–1, 29–3, and 29–5 show the development effort estimates versus project actuals for Basic COCOMO (reproduced from Fig. 6–4), Intermediate COCOMO (reproduced from Fig. 8–3), and Detailed COCOMO. It is generally clear from these results that

- Intermediate COCOMO and Detailed COCOMO are significantly more accurate than Basic COCOMO
- Detailed COCOMO is not noticeably better than Intermediate COCOMO for estimating overall development effort (However, we will see in Section 29.5 that Detailed COCOMO yields better phase distribution estimates.)

These results can be seen more clearly from Figs. 29–2, 29–4, and 29–6, which present histograms of the percentage of relative error

$$\text{Percentage of relative error} = \frac{(MM)_{EST} - (MM)_{ACT}}{(MM)_{ACT}}$$

between estimates and project actuals for Basic COCOMO, Intermediate COCOMO, and Detailed COCOMO, respectively. The relative error distribution for Basic CO-COMO shows an extreme degree of variation, while the relative error distributions for Intermediate COCOMO and Detailed COCOMO are considerably improved and quite similar.

The data points in Figs. 29–2, 29–4, and 29–6 are also coded by development mode. No significant bias can be detected for any of the development modes in the Intermediate COCOMO or Detailed COCOMO estimates, but a bias toward underestimation can be seen in the Basic COCOMO estimates of embedded-mode projects.

In terms of our criterion of being able to estimate within 20% of project actuals, Basic COCOMO accomplishes this only 25% of the time, Intermediate COCOMO 68% of the time, and Detailed COCOMO 70% of the time.

29.4 COCOMO ESTIMATES VERSUS ACTUALS: DEVELOPMENT SCHEDULE

Figure 29–7 shows the COCOMO development schedule estimates versus actuals for the projects in the COCOMO data base (reproduced from Fig. 6–6). This figure indicates that the COCOMO estimates are reasonably accurate for traditional, single increment software developments, but considerably below the actuals for incremental development projects.

TABLE 29–1 The COCOMO Software Project Data Base

			Product Attributes				Computer Attributes					Personnel Attributes					
PN	Type	Year	LANG	RELY	DATA	CPLX	AAF	TIME	STOR	VIRT	TURN	TYPE	ACAP	AEXP	PCAP	VEXP	LEXP	CONT
1	BUS	72	COB	.88	1.16	.70	1.0	1.0	1.06	1.15	1.07	MAX	1.19	1.13	1.17	1.10	1.0	NOM
2	BUS	76	COB	.88	1.16	.85	.85	1.0	1.06	1.0	1.07	MAX	1.0	.91	1.0	.90	.95	NOM
3	BUS	77	PLI	1.0	1.16	.85	1.0	1.0	1.0	.87	.94	MID	.86	.82	.86	.90	.95	NOM
4	BUS	79	COB	.75	1.16	.70	.76	1.0	1.0	.87	1.0	MID	1.19	.91	1.42	1.0	.95	NOM
5	BUS	69	FTN	.88	.94	1.0	1.0	1.0	1.0	.87	1.0	MAX	1.0	1.0	.86	.90	.95	NOM
6	BUS	74	PLI	.75	1.0	.85	1.0	1.0	1.21	1.0	1.0	MID	1.46	1.0	1.42	.90	.95	HI
7	BUS	79	COB	.75	1.0	1.0	1.0	1.0	1.0	.87	.87	MAX	1.0	1.0	1.0	.90	.95	HI
8	CTL	73	MOL	1.15	.94	1.30	1.0	1.66	1.56	1.30	1.0	MIN	.71	.91	1.0	1.21	1.14	NOM
9	CTL	78	FTN	1.15	.94	1.30	1.0	1.30	1.21	1.15	1.0	MIN	.86	1.0	.86	1.10	1.07	NOM
10	CTL	75	MOL	1.40	.94	1.30	.63	1.11	1.56	1.0	1.07	MIN	.86	.82	.86	.90	1.0	NOM
11	CTL	76	MOL	1.40	.94	1.30	.63	1.11	1.56	1.0	1.07	MIN	.86	.82	.86	.90	1.0	NOM
12	CTL	78	JOV	1.15	.94	1.30	1.0	1.11	1.06	1.0	1.0	MIN	86	.82	.86	1.0	.95	NOM
13	CTL	78	FTN	1.15	.94	1.30	.96	1.11	1.06	1.15	1.0	MID	.71	1.0	.70	1.10	1.0	HI
14	CTL	77	MOL	1.15	.94	1.65	1.0	1.30	1.56	1.15	1.0	MIC	.86	1.0	.70	1.10	1.07	NOM
15	CTL	76	MOL	1.40	.94	1.30	1.0	1.30	1.06	1.15	.87	MIN	.86	1.13	.86	1.21	1.14	NOM
16	CTL	75	MOL	1.40	1.0	1.30	.60	1.30	1.56	1.0	.87	MIN	.86	1.0	.86	1.0	1.0	NOM
17	CTL	77	MOL	1.40	1.0	1.30	.53	1.30	1.56	1.0	.87	MIN	.86	.82	.86	1.0	1.0	NOM
18	HMI	70	FTN	1.15	1.16	1.15	1.0	1.30	1.21	1.0	1.07	MAX	.86	1.0	1.0	1.0	1.0	LO
19	HMI	78	FTN	1.15	1.08	1.0	.84	1.11	1.21	.87	.94	MAX	.71	.91	1.0	1.0	1.0	NOM
20	HMI	74	JOV	1.40	1.08	1.30	.96	1.11	1.21	1.15	1.07	MAX	.71	.82	1.08	1.10	1.07	NOM
21	HMI	77	PLI	1.0	1.16	1.15	1.0	1.06	1.14	.87	.87	MAX	.86	1.0	1.0	1.0	1.0	HI
22	HMI	76	JOV	1.15	1.0	1.0	.92	1.27	1.06	1.0	1.0	MAX	.86	.82	.86	.90	1.0	HI
23	HMI	78	HOL	1.15	1.0	1.0	.98	1.08	1.06	1.0	1.0	MAX	.86	.82	.86	.90	1.0	LO
24	HMI	79	FTN	.88	1.0	.85	1.0	1.06	1.06	1.0	.87	MIN	1.0	1.29	1.0	1.10	.95	NOM
25	HMI	78	JOV	1.15	1.16	1.30	1.0	1.15	1.06	1.0	.87	MAX	.86	1.0	.86	1.10	1.0	NOM
26	HMI	77	HOL	.94	1.0	.85	1.0	1.07	1.06	1.15	1.07	MAX	.86	1.0	.86	1.10	1.0	NOM
27	HMI	77	FTN	1.15	.94	1.15	1.0	1.35	1.21	1.0	.87	MIN	1.0	1.0	1.0	1.0	1.0	HI
28	HMI	72	MOL	1.15	1.08	1.30	1.0	1.11	1.21	1.15	1.07	MIN	.86	1.0	.86	1.10	1.07	NOM
29	HMI	79	FTN	.88	1.0	1.0	1.0	1.0	1.0	1.0	1.0	MAX	1.10	1.29	.86	1.0	1.0	HI
30	HMI	79	PSC	.88	1.0	1.0	1.0	1.0	1.0	1.0	1.0	MAX	1.0	1.29	.86	1.0	1.0	HI
31	SCI	75	MOL	1.40	1.08	1.0	.81	1.48	1.56	1.15	1.07	MIN	.86	.82	.86	1.10	1.07	NOM
32	SCI	72	FTN	.88	1.08	.85	.67	1.0	1.0	1.0	1.0	MAX	.71	.82	1.0	1.0	1.0	NOM
33	SCI	76	FTN	1.40	1.08	1.30	.96	1.48	1.56	1.15	.94	MIN	.86	.82	.86	.90	1.0	HI
34	SCI	77	FTN	1.15	1.08	1.0	.96	1.06	1.0		.87	MIN	1.0	1.0	1.0	1.0	1.0	NOM
35	SCI	68	MOL	.75	.94	1.30	1.0	1.06	1.21	1.15	1.0	MID	1.0	.91	1.0	1.10	1.0	NOM
36	SCI	79	FTN	.88	1.08	.85	.81	1.0	1.0	.87	.87	MAX	1.19	1.0	1.17	.90	.95	NOM
37	SCI	78	FTN	.88	.94	.70	.56	1.0	1.06	1.0	1.0	MIN	.86	.82	.86	1.0	1.0	NOM
38	SCI	77	PLI	1.0	1.0	1.15	1.0	1.0	1.0	.87	.87	MAX	.71	.91	1.0	.90	.95	NOM
39	SCI	64	FTN	1.0	1.0	1.15	1.0	1.0	1.0	.87	1.0	MAX	.71	.82	.70	1.0	.95	HI
40	SCI	74	MOL	1.0	.94	1.30	.83	1.0	1.0	1.0	.87	MIN	.86	.82	1.17	1.0	1.0	NOM
41	SCI	76	FTN	.88	.94	1.0	1.0	1.0	1.0	.87	.87	MAX	1.0	.82	.70	.90	.95	HI
42	SCI	78	FTN	.88	1.04	1.07	.43	1.0	1.06	.87	1.07	MAX	.86	1.0	.93	.90	.95	HI
43	SCI	78	FTN	1.00	1.04	1.07	.98	1.0	1.21	.87	1.07	MAX	.86	1.0	1.0	.90	.95	HI
44	SCI	78	FTN	.88	1.04	1.07	.98	1.06	1.21	.87	1.07	MAX	1.0	1.0	1.0	.90	.95	HI
45	SCI	77	FTN	.88	1.04	1.07	.91	1.0	1.06	.87	1.07	MAX	1.0	1.0	1.0	.90	.95	HI
46	SCI	78	FTN	.88	1.04	1.07	.78	1.0	1.06	.87	1.07	MAX	1.0	1.0	.86	.90	.95	NOM
47	SCI	78	FTN	.75	.94	1.30	1.0	1.0	1.0	.87	.87	MAX	.71	.82	.70	1.10	1.07	NOM
48	SUP	76	FTN	.88	.94	.85	.67	1.0	1.0	.87	1.0	MAX	1.19	.91	1.17	.90	.95	NOM
49	SUP	76	JOV	1.0	1.0	.85	1.0	1.0	1.0	1.0	.87	MID	.71	1.0	.70	1.10	1.0	HI
50	SUP	76	MOL	1.15	1.0	1.0	1.0	1.30	1.21	1.0	.87	MIN	.86	1.0	.86	1.10	1.0	NOM
51	SUP	70	COB	.88	1.0	1.0	1.0	1.0	1.0	1.0	1.15	MAX	1.19	1.0	1.42	1.0	.95	LO
52	SUP	71	MOL	.88	.94	.85	1.0	1.0	1.06	1.15	1.0	MIN	1.0	1.0	1.0	1.10	1.07	NOM
53	SUP	78	MOL	.88	.94	1.15	1.0	1.11	1.21	1.30	1.0	MIC	.71	1.0	.70	1.10	1.07	NOM
54	SUP	78	FTN	1.0	.94	1.0	1.0	1.0	1.06	1.15	.87	MIC	1.0	.82	1.0	1.0	.95	HI
55	SUP	72	FTN	.88	.94	.70	1.0	1.0	1.0	.87	.87	MAX	.86	.82	1.17	.90	.95	NOM
56	SYS	71	MOL	1.15	.94	1.30	1.0	1.30	1.21	1.0	1.0	MAX	.86	.91	1.0	1.10	1.07	NOM
57	SYS	74	MOL	1.0	.94	1.15	.87	1.11	1.21	1.30	1.0	MIN	1.0	1.0	1.0	1.10	1.07	LO
58	SYS	76	MOL	1.40	.94	1.30	1.0	1.66	1.21	1.0	1.0	MIN	.71	.82	.70	.90	.95	NOM
59	SYS	77	HOL	1.15	.94	1.15	.90	1.06	1.06	1.0	.87	MAX	1.0	1.0	1.0	1.0	1.0	NOM
60	SYS	73	MOL	1.15	.94	1.30	1.0	1.11	1.06	1.0	1.0	MAX	.86	1.13	.86	1.10	1.07	NOM
61	SYS	78	PSC	1.0	.94	1.15	1.0	1.0	1.0	.87	.87	MAX	.86	1.0	.86	.90	1.0	HI
62	SYS	78	MOL	.88	.94	1.30	1.0	1.11	1.21	1.15	1.0	MIC	.78	.82	.70	1.21	1.14	NOM
63	SYS	79	MOL	1.0	.94	1.15	1.0	1.0	1.0	1.0	.87	MIN	.71	.82	.86	1.0	1.0	NOM

PN	Project Attributes				Π	MODE	TOT KDSI	ADJ KDSI	Man-Months				Prod	Months			Detailed COCOMO			Basic COCOMO		Doc'n	
	MODP	TOOL	SCED	RVOL					NOM	EST	ACT	E-A/A	ADSI MM	EST	ACT	E-A/A	EST	E-A/A	MM/Π	EST	E/A	KPP	PP/TKDSI
1	1.24	1.10	1.04	1.19	2.72	E	113	113	814	2218	2040	9	55	29	48	-40	2286	12	750	1047	.51	2.0	18
2	1.10	1.0	1.0	1.0	.84	E	293	249	2102	1770	1600	11	156	27	36	-25	1760	10	1905	2702	1.69	11.5	39
3	.91	.91	1.0	1.0	.34	SD	132	132	711	245	243	1	543	17	15	13	248	2	715	711	2.93	10.4	79
4	1.24	1.0	1.04	1.19	1.17	ORG	60	46	178	212	240	-12	192	20	36*	-44	207	-14	205	134	.56	0.8	13
5	1.24	1.0	1.0	1.19	.66	ORG	16	16	59	39	33	18	485	9.4	9	4	38	15	50	44	1.34	0.15	9
6	1.24	1.10	1.0	1.19	2.22	ORG	4.0	4.0	13.7	30	43	-30	93	10.4	12	-13	30	-30	19	10.3	.24	—	—
7	.91	.91	1.0	1.0	.40	ORG	6.9	6.9	24	9.8	8	22	862	5.5	4	38	10.2	28	20	18	2.28	0.5	72
8	1.10	1.10	1.08	1.38	7.62	E	22	22	114	869	1075	-19	20	23	30	-23	994	-8	141	147	.14	—	—
9	.91	1.0	1.0	1.19	2.39	E	30	30	166	397	423	-6	71	17	18	-6	395	-7	177	213	.50	1.1	37
10	1.0	1.0	1.0	1.38	2.38	E	29	18	90	214	321	-33	56	16	30	-47	218	-32	135	115	.36	7.0	241
11	1.0	1.0	1.0	1.38	2.38	E	32	20	102	243	218	11	92	14	24	-42	248	14	91	131	.60	5.2	162
12	.91	1.0	1.08	1.12	1.12	E	37	37	213	238	201	18	184	14	12	17	237	18	179	274	1.36	4.0	108
13	.82	1.0	1.0	1.0	.85	E	25	24	127	108	79	37	304	10.1	10	1	106	34	93	163	2.07	1.1	44
14	1.10	1.24	1.23	1.19	5.86	SD	3.0	3.0	10.3	60	73	-18	41	11.2	12	-7	64	-12	12	10.3	.14	0.05	17
15	.91	1.0	1.23	1.19	3.63	E	3.9	3.9	14.3	52	61	-15	64	9.3	15	-38	51	-16	17	18	.30	0.7	179
16	.91	1.0	1.0	1.19	2.81	E	6.1	3.7	13.5	38	40	-5	92	8.1	10	-19	39	-2	14	17	.43	0.5	82
17	1.0	1.0	1.0	.91	1.78	E	3.6	1.9	6.0	10.7	9	19	211	5.1	6	-15	10.9	21	5.1	7.8	.86	0.3	83
18	1.24	1.10	1.08	1.19	3.89	E	320	320	2840	11056	11400	-3	28	50	72	-31	12380	9	2931	3652	.32	10.0	31
19	.91	.91	1.0	1.0	.73	E	1150	966	10694	7764	6600	18	146	42	40	5	7699	17	9041	13749	2.08	31.4	27
20	1.24	1.0	1.08	1.19	3.85	SD	299	287	1698	6536	6400	2	45	54	51	6	7571	18	1662	1698	.27	18.0	60
21	.91	.91	1.0	1.0	.86	E	252	252	2132	1836	2455	-25	103	30	60*	-50	1864	-24	2855	2741	1.12	3.0	12
22	.91	1.0	1.23	1.0	.94	E	118	109	780	733	724	1	151	21	16	31	728	1	770	1003	1.39	19.5	165
23	1.0	1.0	1.23	1.0	.89	E	77	75	498	443	539	-18	139	19	16	19	445	-17	606	640	1.19	14.9	194
24	.82	.83	1.0	1.0	.70	SD	90	90	463	326	453	-28	199	21	28	-25	337	-26	647	463	1.02	1.5	17
25	.82	.91	1.08	1.62	1.95	E	38	38	220	430	523	-18	73	19	39*	-51	433	-17	268	283	.54	4.7	124
26	.91	1.10	1.08	1.19	1.16	E	48	48	292	339	387	-12	124	17	19	-11	341	-12	334	375	.97	4.0	83
27	.82	1.10	1.08	1.19	2.04	E	9.4	9.4	41	89	88	-5	107	10.5	12	-12	82	-7	43	53	.60	—	—
28	1.10	1.10	1.0	1.0	2.81	ORG	13	13	47	133	98	36	133	14	20	-30	143	46	35	35	.36	—	—
29	.91	.91	1.23	.91	1.00	SD	2.14	2.14	7.0	7.0	7.3	-4	293	5.0	2	150	7.0	-4	7.3	7.0	.96	.14	65
30	.91	.91	1.23	.91	.91	SD	1.98	1.98	6.4	5.8	5.9	-2	336	4.7	2	135	5.9	0	6.5	6.4	1.08	.13	66
31	1.0	1.0	1.0	1.0	3.14	E	62	50	306	962	1063	-10	47	23	24	-4	1057	-1	339	394	.37	2.0	32
32	1.10	1.10	1.0	1.0	.57	SD	390	261	1527	869	702	24	372	25	24	4	868	24	1232	1527	2.18	3.5	9
33	.91	1.0	1.0	1.0	2.26	E	42	40	234	529	605	-13	66	19	24	-21	543	-10	268	301	.50	3.0	71
34	.91	1.10	1.23	1.19	1.76	E	23	22	114	201	230	-14	96	14	12	17	201	-14	131	147	.64	6.7	291
35	1.24	1.24	1.0	1.19	2.63	E	13	13	61	161	82	96	159	10.2	10	2	162	98	31	78	.95	0.1	8
36	1.0	.91	1.04	1.0	.68	SD	15	12	49	33	55	-40	218	10.2	12	-15	34	-38	81	49	.89	0.3	20
37	1.0	1.0	1.0	.91	.34	ORG	60	34	130	44	47	-6	723	10.8	24*	-55	44	-6	138	97	2.07	1.4	23
38	.82	.91	1.0	1.0	.35	ORG	15	15	55	20	12	67	1250	6.4	5	28	20	67	34	41	3.43	—	—
39	.91	1.10	1.0	1.0	.39	ORG	6.2	6.2	22	8.4	8	5	775	5.5	9*	-39	8.3	4	21	16	2.04	0.5	81
40	1.10	1.0	1.0	1.0	.96	ORG	3.0	2.5	8.4	8.1	8	1	312	5.5	9	-39	8.0	0	8.3	6.3	.79	—	—
41	.91	.91	1.0	1.0	.25	ORG	5.3	5.3	18.4	4.7	6	-22	883	4.9	5	2	4.9	-18	24	14	2.30	—	—
42	.95	.95	1.04	1.0	.63	ORG	45.5	19.5	72	46	45	2	433	10.6	8.1	31	46	2	71	54	1.21	1.4	31
43	1.0	1.0	1.04	1.0	.96	ORG	28.6	28	106	102	83	23	337	13.4	14.1	-5	102	23	86	79	.96	1.7	59
44	1.10	1.0	1.04	1.0	1.14	ORG	30.6	30	114	130	87	49	345	13.6	13.9	-2	128	47	76	85	.98	1.8	59
45	1.0	.95	1.04	1.0	.82	ORG	35	32	122	100	106	-6	302	14.7	12.3	20	100	-6	129	91	.86	1.25	36
46	1.0	1.0	1.04	1.0	.74	ORG	73	67	223	166	126	32	452	15.7	16.1	-2	164	30	170	167	1.33	2.6	36
47	1.10	1.0	1.04	1.0	.38	ORG	23	23	86	33	36	-8	639	9.8	22.2	-56	32	-11	95	65	1.79	—	—
48	1.10	1.0	1.04	1.09	.83	SD	464	311	1858	1542	1272	21	244	31	44	-30	1519	19	1533	1858	1.46	10.0	22
49	.82	.91	1.0	1.19	.36	SD	91	91	469	168	156	8	583	15	18	-17	170	8	433	469	3.01	5.5	60
50	1.0	1.0	1.0	1.19	1.52	E	24	24	127	193	176	10	136	13	12	8	194	10	116	163	.93	1.1	46
51	1.24	1.10	1.04	1.38	3.18	ORG	10	10	36	114	122	-7	82	16	34	-53	115	-6	38	27	.22	—	—
52	1.24	1.10	1.0	1.38	1.90	ORG	8.2	8.2	29	55	41	17	174	10.8	14	-23	56	19	25	22	.47	—	—
53	1.0	1.10	1.08	1.0	1.15	SD	5.3	5.3	19.4	22	14	57	379	6.3	6	-5	22	57	12	19.4	1.39	0.03	6
54	.91	1.10	1.0	1.19	.93	ORG	4.4	4.4	15	14	20	-30	220	7.8	7	11	14	-30	22	11.4	.57	0.08	18
55	1.10	1.0	1.0	1.0	.34	ORG	6.3	6.3	22	7.5	18	-58	350	7.5	12	-38	7.4	-59	53	16.6	.92	—	—
56	1.10	1.10	1.08	1.38	3.68	E	27	27	146	537	958	-44	28	22	24	-8	570	-41	260	188	.20	1.5	56
57	1.10	1.10	1.23	1.0	3.32	E	17	15	72	239	237	1	63	14	24*	-42	247	4	71	93	.39	—	—
58	.91	1.0	1.0	1.09	1.09	E	25	25	133	145	130	12	192	11.9	12	-1	143	10	119	171	1.32	3.0	120
59	.91	1.0	1.0	.91	.87	ORG	23	21	78	68	70	-3	300	13	16	-19	68	-3	80	59	.84	—	—
60	1.10	1.0	1.08	1.19	2.53	ORG	6.7	6.7	23.6	60	57	5	118	11.6	12	-3	61	7	23	18	.31	0.1	15
61	.82	1.0	1.0	1.0	.45	ORG	28	28	106	47	50	-6	560	11.1	10	11	48	-4	111	79	1.59	0.4	14
62	.91	1.24	1.0	1.0	1.15	SD	9.1	9.1	36	42	38	11	239	8.9	14	-36	41	8	33	36	.95	0.2	22
63	.82	1.0	1.0	1.0	.39	E	10	10	44	17	15	13	667	5.9	4	48	17	13	38	57	3.80	0.3	30

* incremental development

TABLE 29–2. Quantities in the COCOMO Project Data Base

1.	*PN.*	Sequential project number
2.	*TYPE.*	Type of project
		BUS Business application
		CTL Process control
		HMI Human-machine interaction
		SCI Scientific application
		SUP Support software (tools, utilities, etc.)
		SYS Systems software (operating systems, compilers, etc.)
3.	*YEAR.*	Last two digits of calendar year in which development was completed.
4.	*LANG.*	Primary programming language used on project.
5–7, 9–12, 14–18, 20–23.	*RELY–RVOL.*	The Intermediate COCOMO effort multiplier corresponding to the cost driver attribute rating for the project, as defined in Tables 8–2 and 8–3 (Table 28–2 for RVOL). In some cases, interpolated or averaged values for the effort multipliers have been calculated.
8.	*AAF.*	COCOMO adaptation adjustment factor, as defined in Section 8.8.
13.	*TYPE.*	Type of computer used for development
		MAX Maxicomputer. Equivalent to IBM 370/155 and up
		MID Midicomputer. Equivalent to IBM 370/135 and up
		MIN Minicomputer
		MIC Microcomputer or microprocessor
19.	*CONT.*	Personnel continuity on project
		LO Less that 10% turnover
		NOM 10–30% turnover
		HI Greater than 30% turnover
24.	II.	The product of the effort multipliers for the project
25.	*MODE.*	Software development mode
		E Embedded
		SD Semidetached
		ORG Organic
26.	*TOT KDSI.*	Total delivered source instructions in thousands, as defined in Section 5.2
27.	*ADJ KDSI.*	Adjusted KDSI = (TOT KDSI) (AAF); see Section 8.8
28.	*MM NOM.*	Nominal man-months, computed from adjusted KDSI by the nominal effort equation for the project's development mode (Table 8–1 or 23–1).
29.	*MM EST.*	Intermediate COCOMO estimated man-months for project: MM EST = (MM NOM) (II)
30.	*MM ACT.*	Actual man-months required for the project.
31.	*MM: (E–A/A).*	Percentage estimation error = (100)[(MM EST) − (MM ACT)]/ (MM ACT)
32.	*PROD.*	Project productivity = (Adjusted KDSI)/(MM ACT).
33.	*MO EST.*	Estimated development time in months, computed from MM ACT by the basic schedule equation for the project's development mode.
34.	*MO ACT.*	Actual development time for the project in months.

TABLE 29-2 (Cont'd)

35.	*MO: (E–A)/A.*	Percentage estimation error = (100)[(MO EST) − (MO ACT)]/ (MO ACT)
36.	*DC EST.*	Detailed COCOMO estimated man-months for the project, using the same cost driver attribute ratings as those used for Intermediate COCOMO.
37.	*DC: (E–A)/A.*	Percentage estimation error = (100)[(DC EST) = (MM ACT)]/ (MM ACT)
38.	*MM/*Π.	Normalized effort parameter (MM ACT)/Π. See Fig. 8–4.
39.	*BC EST.*	Basic COCOMO estimated man-months for the project, computed from adjusted KDSI by the Basic Effort Equation for the project's development mode (Table 6–1).
40.	*BC:E/A.*	Basic COCOMO estimation error ratio = (BC EST)/(MM ACT).
41.	*DOC KPP.*	Thousands of pages of project documentation, excluding code listings.
42.	*PP/KDSI.*	Pages of documentation per thousand source instructions = 1000 (DOC KPP)/TOT KDSI.

These conclusions can be seen more clearly in the histogram of percentage of relative error shown in Fig. 29–8. The main conclusions that can be drawn from this distribution are

1. The schedule equations clearly underestimate the time required for a project using incremental development.
2. The estimates are reasonably accurate for nonincremental development (within 20% of the actuals 58% of the time).
3. Although a number of projects were completed on a more relaxed schedule than the nominal estimated schedule, only 4 of the 63 projects were able to compress their schedules below the 75% compression limit discussed in Section 27.3.

To date, the best approach to schedule estimation for an incremental development project is

1. Estimate the total schedule and phase distribution of schedule for the entire project. Use the estimated schedule required to complete the Product Design phase as the initial portion of the schedule estimate.
2. For each increment, estimate the total schedule and phase distribution of schedule as a function of the size of the increment. For all but the final increment, add the duration of the programming phase to the project schedule estimate. For the final increment, add the duration of the programming phase

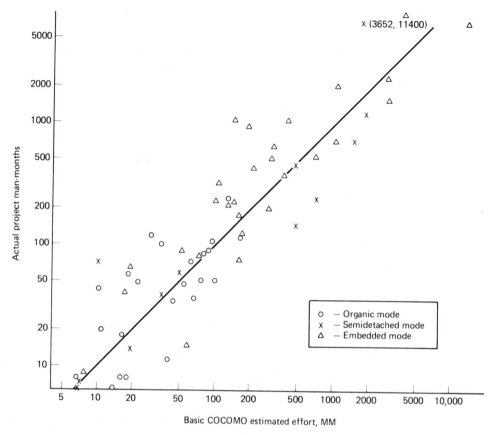

FIGURE 29–1 Basic COCOMO effort estimates versus actuals

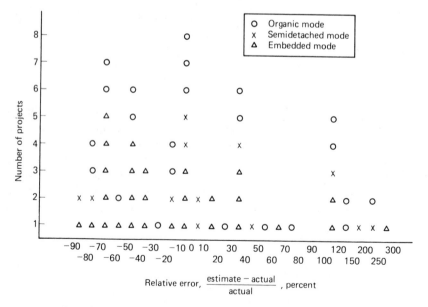

FIGURE 29–2 Relative error distribution, basic COCOMO effort estimates

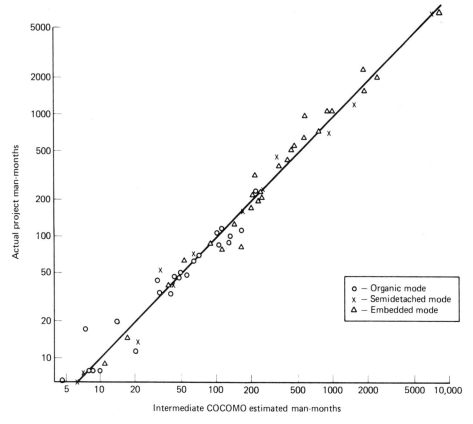

FIGURE 29-3 Intermediate COCOMO estimates versus project actuals

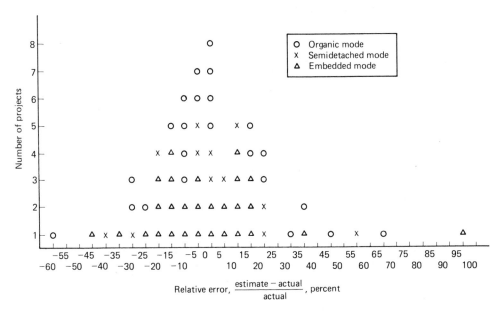

FIGURE 29-4 Relative error distribution, intermediate COCOMO effort estimates

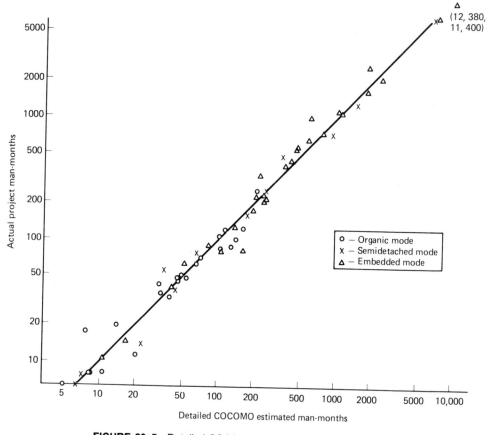

FIGURE 29-5 Detailed COCOMO estimates versus project actuals

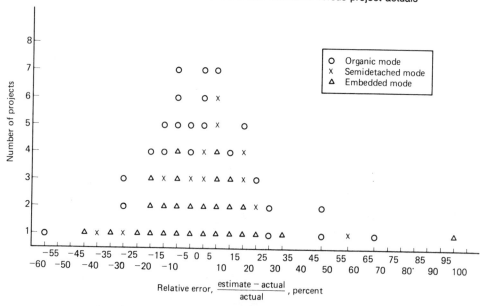

FIGURE 29-6 Relative error distribution, detailed COCOMO effort estimates

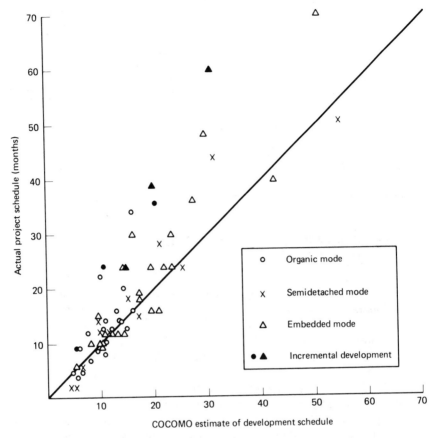

FIGURE 29–7 COCOMO development schedule estimates versus actuals

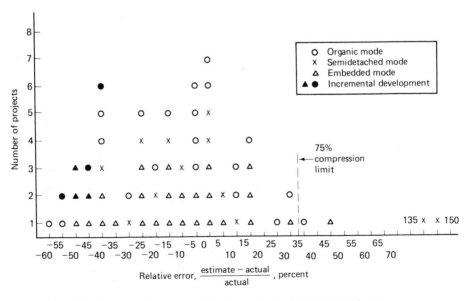

FIGURE 29–8 Relative error distribution, COCOMO schedule estimates

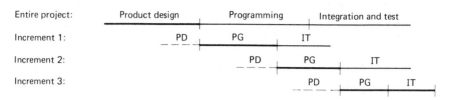

FIGURE 29-9 Incremental development schedule estimation

and that of the integration and test phase for the increment to determine the overall project schedule.

The heavy lines in Fig. 29–9 show the portions of the project schedule thus included.

29.5 COCOMO ESTIMATES VERSUS ACTUALS: PHASE DISTRIBUTION

The amount of project data available to support the evaluation of the COCOMO estimating relationships for phase distribution of effort is considerably less than that available to evaluate the overall project estimates. Only five combinations of project size and development mode have at least two projects for which phase distribution data are available. These are summarized in Table 29–3, which shows for each project

- Its development mode and size category
- Its COCOMO data base project number
- For each of the major development phases, the percentage of effort estimated by Intermediate COCOMO and Detailed COCOMO, and the corresponding actual percentage of effort experienced by the project

A better graphic visualization of the results in Table 29–3 is provided in Fig. 29–10, which shows for each project and each phase, the following quantities:

    ⊙ (the bullseye)—the actual percentage of effort in the phase
    □ (the ballpark estimate)—the Intermediate COCOMO estimate
    x (the refined estimate)—the Detailed COCOMO estimate

The following main properties can be seen from Fig. 29–10:

1. The overall variations in phase percentage by size and mode (for example, the trend in percentages in the integration and test phase), are basically the same for the Detailed COCOMO estimates and the project actuals.
2. The variations in phase percentage caused by off-nominal cost driver attributes are reasonably well tracked by Detailed COCOMO [in Fig. 29–10, when the ballpark is far from the bullseye, the refined (x) Detailed COCOMO estimate is usually much closer].
3. There are still considerable differences between estimates and actuals on some projects. Some of this is due to definition problems that are very hard to

TABLE 29-3 COCOMO Estimates versus Actuals: Phase Distribution

Mode and Size	Project Number	Product Design			Detailed Design			Code and Unit Test			Integration and Test		
		Intermediate COCOMO Estimate	Detailed COCOMO Estimate	Actual	Intermediate COCOMO Estimate	Detailed COCOMO Estimate	Actual	Intermediate COCOMO Estimate	Detailed COCOMO Estimate	Actual	Intermediate COCOMO Estimate	Detailed COCOMO Estimate	Actual
Embedded, very large	18	18	8	5	25.5	14	15	25	20	25	32.5	58	55
	19	18	17	15	24	26	25	24	19	20	34	38	40
	21	18	23	18	25.5	28	23	25	18	22	32.5	31	37
Embedded, medium	8	18	6	8	26	15	25	29	27	17	27	52	50
	9	18	16	18	26	21	20	28	29	26	28	34	38
	50	18	18	15	26	24	20	29	21	30	27	37	35
Semidetached, small	29	17	23	19	27	29	29	37	34	33	19	14	19
	30	17	23	23	27	29	28	37	35	31	19	13	18
Organic, medium	59	16	21	15	24	27	30	39	32	25	21	20	25
	61	16	25	24	24	30	34	38	30	24	22	15	18
Organic, small	39	16	19	25	25	25	30	41	41	30	18	15	15
	40	16	13	10	26	29	24	42	39	42	16	19	24

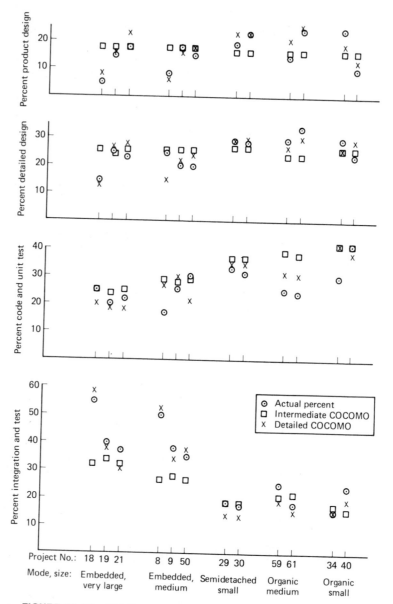

FIGURE 29–10 COCOMO estimates versus actuals: phase distribution

resolve (for example, the exact boundaries between phases, particularly between detailed design and code-and-unit-test). In at least one case (the consistent Detailed COCOMO underestimates of integration and test effort for small, organic-mode projects), the model could be improved; subsequent investigation indicates that the amount of documentation activity during the integration and test phase for these projects makes their overall effort for that phase somewhat higher than currently predicted by COCOMO.

TABLE 29–4 Distribution of Effort by Phase, Various Projects

Mode and Size	Project	Reference	Plans and Requirements	Product Design	Detailed Design	Code and Unit Test	Integration and Test
Embedded, very large	SAGE	[Boehm, 1970]		39		14	47
	NTDS	"		30		20	50
	OS/360	[Brooks, 1975]		33		17	50
	Safeguard	[Stephenson, 1976]		25		21	54
	ALCM	[Bloodworth and others, 1979]		45		15	40
	3 projects	COCOMO data base		13	21	22	44
Embedded, medium large	A	[Wolverton, 1974]	12	18	16	20	34
	GTE	[Daly, 1977]	28		43		29
	3 projects	COCOMO data base		14	22	24	41
Organic, medium	Informatics	[Wolverton, 1974]		43		19	38
	Raytheon	"		44		28	28
	TRW	"		44		26	30
	PARMIS data base	[Gehring, 1976]	7	38		37	18
	NASA-Goddard	[McGarry, 1979]		21		50	29
	2 projects	COCOMO data base		20	32	24	22
Organic, small	PARMIS data base	[Gehring, 1976]	12	34		34	20
	2 projects	COCOMO data base		17	27	36	20

Another check on the COCOMO phase distributions is provided in Table 29–4, which summarizes some of the phase distribution data from other sources in comparison to the COCOMO estimates and actuals. Again, the agreement is reasonably good, but far from perfect.

29.6   COCOMO ESTIMATES VERSUS ACTUALS: ACTIVITY DISTRIBUTION

If the problem of evaluating cost-estimating relationships for phase distribution is plagued by a lack of reliable data and by definition problems, the corresponding problem for estimating activity distributions is even more so. Only two combinations of project size and development mode have at least two projects for which reasonably reliable activity distribution data are available. These are summarized in Table 29–5, which compares activity distribution estimates (from Table 7–1) versus project actuals (from Projects 19 and 21 in the COCOMO data base) for very large, embedded-mode projects; and Table 29–6, which provides a similar comparison for the small,

TABLE 29-5 Activity Distribution Estimates versus Actuals: Very Large, Embedded-Mode Projects

Phase	Plans and Requirements			Product Design			Programming			Integration and Test		
Estimate/Project Numbers	Estimate	P19	P21	Estimate	P19	P21	Estimate	P19	P21	Estimate	P19	P21
Overall phase percentage				20	15	18	45	45	45	35	40	37
Activity percentage												
Requirements analysis				10	16	12	3	3	7	2	2	4
Product design				42	33	43	6	7	12	4	3	7
Programming				14	12	10	55	42	35	48	40	35
Test planning				8	8	5	8	11	8	5	8	4
Verification and validation				10	13	10	12	15	14	20	25	23
Project office				7	6	11	5	7	9	6	5	10
CM/QA				2	3	3	6	7	5	8	9	7
Manuals				7	9	6	5	8	10	7	8	10

Table 29-6 Activity Distribution Estimates versus Actuals: Small, Semidetached-Mode Projects

Phase	Plans and Requirements			Product Design			Programming			Integration and Test		
Estimate/Project numbers	Estimate	P29	P30	Estimate	P29	P30	Estimate	P29	P30	Estimate	P29	P30
Overall phase percentage				23	19	23	63	62	59	14	19	18
Activity percentage												
Requirements analysis	48	40	50	12.5	22	10	4	5	8	2.5	3	1
Product design	16	26	13	41	35	46	8	16	12	5	6	3
Programming	2.5	1	0	12	10	4	51.5	48	46	33	24	36
Test planning	2.5	2	4	4.5	2	2	4	2	3	2.5	0	0
Verification and validation	6	7	3	6	9	10	7	10	8	32	35	32
Project office	15.5	13	17	13	11	14	7.5	7	9	8.5	10	10
CM/QA	3.5	2	3	3	0	1	7	2	3	8.5	3	3
Manuals	6	8	10	8	11	13	9	11	8	8	19	15

semidetached-mode Projects 29 and 30 in the COCOMO data base versus the estimates in Table 7–2.

The main conclusions to be drawn from Tables 29–5 and 29–6 are similar to those for phase distribution

1. The variations in activity distribution by size and mode (for example, in the integration and test phase) are highly similar for both the COCOMO estimates and the project actuals.
2. There are still considerable differences between estimates and actuals. Some of these are again due to definition problems or project idiosyncracies, but a number of them are due also to the fact that the activity distribution estimates are not adjusted as a function of the project's type or cost driver attributes. The high percentages for requirements analysis and manuals are due partly to the fact that all four projects are human-machine interactive applications; the low programming percentages for Projects 19 and 21 are due partly to their use of interactive programming; and the higher V&V percentages for Project 19 are due partly to its high reliability requirement.

From conclusion 2, it would appear that project activity distributions should also be modified as a function of cost driver attributes, but the current level of understanding and reliable data does not support such an analysis at this time.

Some other data and estimators of project activity distributions are given in [Wolverton, 1974; Gehring, 1976; and Jones, 1977]. The COCOMO estimates are in substantial agreement with their results, but not with the activity distributions in [Griffin, 1980], which have an extremely small effort in design activities and a very large amount of effort in test activities.

29.7 OTHER SOFTWARE COST-ESTIMATION MODELS

Section 29.8 will evaluate COCOMO with respect to our set of criteria for the goodness of a software cost-estimation model, in terms of the current state of the art in software cost estimation. In order to do this, it will be helpful to summarize the other main software cost-estimation models available or documented in the literature.

The models summarized in this section are

- The 1965 SDC Model [Nelson, 1966]
- The TRW Wolverton Model [Wolverton, 1974]
- The Putnam SLIM Model [Putnam, 1978; Putnam–Fitzsimmons, 1979]
- The Doty Model [Herd and others, 1977]
- The RCA PRICE S Model [Freiman–Park, 1979]
- The IBM-FSD Model [Walston–Felix, 1977]
- The 1977 Boeing Model [Black and others, 1977]
- The 1979 GRC Model [Carriére–Thibodeau, 1979]
- The Bailey-Basili Meta-Model [Bailey–Basili, 1981]

An overall summary of these models and the COCOMO model is given in Table 29–7, showing which size, program, computer, personnel, and project attributes are used by each model to determine software costs.

TABLE 29-7 Factors Used in Various Cost Models

Group	Factor	SDC, 1965	TRW, 1972	Putnam, SLIM	Doty	RCA, PRICE S	IBM	BOEING, 1977	GRC, 1979	COCOMO
Size attributes	Source instructions	×		×	×	×	×	×		×
	Object instructions	×	×		×	×				
	Number of routines									
	Number of data items						×			×
	Number of output formats								×	
	Documentation				×		×			
	Number of personnel						×	×		
Program attributes	Type	×	×	×	×	×	×	×		×
	Complexity		×			×	×			×
	Language	×		×		×		×	×	×
	Reuse			×		×		×	×	×
	Required reliability			×		×		×	×	×
Computer attributes	Time constraint		×	×	×	×	×	×	×	×
	Storage constraint			×	×	×	×		×	×
	Hardware configuration	×				×				
	Concurrent hardware development	×			×	×	×			×
Personnel attributes	Personnel capability	×		×	×	×	×	×	×	×
	Personnel continuity						×			
	Hardware experience		×	×		×	×	×	×	×
	Applications experience		×	×		×	×	×	×	×
	Language experience			×		×	×		×	×
Project attributes	Tools and techniques	×		×		×	×	×		×
	Customer interface	×					×			
	Requirements definition	×			×		×		×	
	Requirements volatility	×			×		×			
	Schedule			×		×				×
	Security				×	×	×			×
	Computer access			×	×	×		×		×
	Travel/rehosting	×			×	×				×

511

The 1965 SDC Model [Nelson, 1966]

This model is based on the extensive analysis of 104 attributes of 169 software projects studied by System Development Corporation (SDC) in the mid-1960's. The best possible linear estimation model for this sample was produced by statistical techniques. It is

$$
\begin{aligned}
MM = -33.63 \\
+\ 9.15 \ \text{(Lack of Requirements)} \quad (0–2) \\
+10.73 \ \text{(Stability of Design)} \quad (0–3) \\
+\ 0.51 \ \text{(Percent Math Instructions)} \\
+\ 0.46 \ \text{(Percent Storage/Retrieval Instructions)} \\
+\ 0.40 \ \text{(Number of Subprograms)} \\
+\ 7.28 \ \text{(Programming Language)} \quad (0–1) \\
-21.45 \ \text{(Business Application)} \quad (0–1) \\
+13.53 \ \text{(Stand-Alone Program)} \quad (0–1) \\
+12.35 \ \text{(First Program on Computer)} \quad (0–1) \\
+58.82 \ \text{(Concurrent Hardware Development)} \quad (0–1) \\
+30.61 \ \text{(Random Access Device Used)} \quad (0–1) \\
+29.55 \ \text{(Different Host, Target Hardware)} \quad (0–1) \\
+\ 0.54 \ \text{(Number of Personnel Trips)} \\
-25.20 \ \text{(Developed by Military Organization)} \quad (0–1)
\end{aligned}
$$

The numbers in parentheses refer to ratings to be made by the estimator.

When applied to its data base of 169 projects, this model produced a mean estimate of 40 MM and a standard deviation of 62 MM: not a very accurate predictor. Further, the application of the model is counterintuitive: a project with all zero ratings is estimated at minus 33 MM; changing language from a higher-order language to assembly language adds 7 MM, independent of project size. The most conclusive result from the SDC study was that there are too many nonlinear aspects of software development for a linear cost-estimation model to work very well.

Still, the SDC effort provided a valuable base of information and insight for cost estimation and future models. Its cumulative distribution of productivity in Figure 24–14 has been a valuable aid for producing or checking cost estimates. The estimation rules of thumb for various phases and activities have been very helpful, and the data have been a major foundation for the Doty model and the RADC [Nelson, 1978] software cost and productivity analyses.

The TRW Wolverton Model [Wolverton, 1974]

The essence of the TRW Wolverton model is shown in Fig. 29–11, which shows a number of curves of software cost per object instruction as a function of relative degree of difficulty (0 to 100), novelty of the application (new or old), and type of project. The best use of the model involves breaking the software into components and estimating their cost individually. Thus, a 1000 object instruction module of

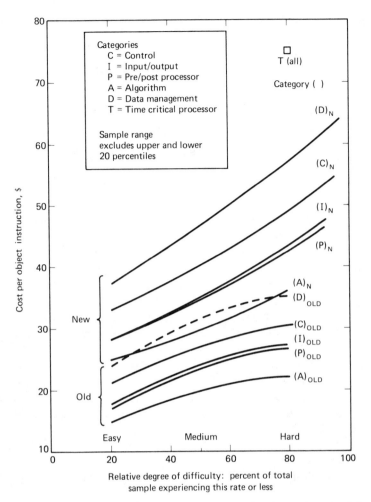

FIGURE 29-11 TRW Wolverton model: cost per object instruction vs. relative degree of difficulty

new data management software of medium (50%) difficulty would be costed at $46/ instruction, or $46,000.

This model is well-calibrated to a class of near-real-time government command and control projects, but is less accurate for some other classes of projects. In addition, the model provides a good breakdown of project effort by phase and activity.

The Putnam SLIM Model [Putnam, 1978; Putnam–Fitzsimmons, 1979]

The Putnam SLIM Model is a commercially available software product based on Putnam's analysis of the software life-cycle in terms of the Rayleigh distribution of project personnel level versus time. The basic effort macro-estimation model used in SLIM is

$$S_s = C_k K^{1/3} t_d^{4/3} \qquad (29\text{--}1)$$

where

S_s = number of delivered source instructions
K = life-cycle effort in man-years
t_d = development time in years
C_k = a "technology constant"

Typical values of C_k are $C_k = 4984$ for 1973-style development and $C_k = 10,040$ for 1978-style development. The current version of SLIM allows one to calibrate C_k to past projects or to estimate it as a function of a project's use of modern programming practices, hardware constraints, personnel experience, interactive development, and other factors. The required development effort, DE, is estimated as 40% of the life-cycle effort, that is, DE $= 0.4K$.

The Rayleigh-curve orientation of SLIM provides a framework for investigating effort–schedule tradeoffs, but it gives rather radical tradeoff relationships, as discussed in Section 27.3. As a method of estimating personnel distribution over time, the Rayleigh distribution is good for some projects but not for others, particularly those employing incremental development; see Sections 4.4, 5.6, and 6.5.

The SLIM model also includes a number of associated estimation capabilities, such as estimation of computer costs and the PERT sizing technique discussed is Section 21.4.

The Doty Model [Herd and others, 1977]

This model is the result of an extensive data analysis activity, including many of the data points from the SDC sample. A number of models of similar form were developed for different application areas. As an example, the model for general application is

$$\text{MM} = 5.288 \ (\text{KDSI})^{1.047}, \text{ for KDSI} \geq 10$$

$$\text{MM} = 2.060 \ (\text{KDSI})^{1.047} \left(\prod_{j=1}^{14} f_j \right), \text{ for KDSI} < 10 \qquad (29\text{--}2)$$

The effort multipliers f_j are shown in Table 29–8. This model has some problems with stability, as it exhibits a discontinuity at KDSI $= 10$, and produces widely varying estimates via the f_j factors (answering "yes" to "First software developed on CPU" adds 92% to the estimated cost).

TABLE 29-8 Doty Model for Small Programs[a]

$$MM = 2.060 \, I^{1.047} \prod_{j=1}^{j=14} f_j$$

Factor	f_j	Yes	No
Special display	f_1	1.11	1.00
Detailed definition of operational requirements	f_2	1.00	1.11
Change to operational requirements	f_3	1.05	1.00
Real-time operation	f_4	1.33	1.00
CPU memory constraint	f_5	1.43	1.00
CPU time constraint	f_6	1.33	1.00
First software developed on CPU	f_7	1.92	1.00
Concurrent development of ADP hardware	f_8	1.82	1.00
Timeshare versus batch processing, in development	f_9	0.83	1.00
Developer using computer at another facility	f_{10}	1.43	1.00
Development at operational site	f_{11}	1.39	1.00
Development computer different than target computer	f_{12}	1.25	1.00
Development at more than one site	f_{13}	1.25	1.00
Programmer access to computer	f_{14}	Limited 1.00 Unlimited 0.90	

[a] Less than 10,000 source instructions

The RCA PRICE S Model [Freiman–Park, 1979]

PRICE S is a commercially available macro cost-estimation model developed primarily for aerospace applications. It has improved steadily with experience; earlier versions with a widely varying subjective complexity factor have been replaced by versions in which a number of computer, personnel, and project attributes are used to modulate the complexity rating.

PRICE S uses many cost-estimating relationships similar to those in COCOMO, such as the hardware constraint function shown in Fig. 29–12 [Wolverton, 1980]. Figure 29–13, also from the [Wolverton, 1980] discussion of PRICE S, shows the range of cost variation in PRICE S as a function of complexity and a Platform parameter, whose typical values are

> Platform = 1.0 Ground system software
> 1.2 MIL-spec ground system
> 1.4 Military mobile
> 1.6 Commercial avionics
> 1.8 MIL-spec avionics
> 2.0 Unmanned space
> 2.5 Manned space

PRICE S also provides a wide range of useful outputs on gross phase and activity distributions, sensitivity analyses, and monthly project cost-schedule-expected progress forecasts.

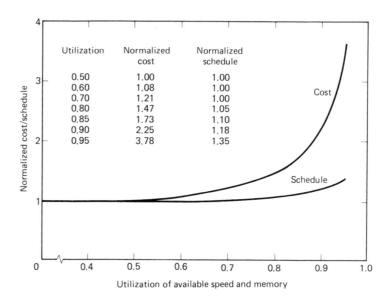

Utilization	Normalized cost	Normalized schedule
0.50	1.00	1.00
0.60	1.08	1.00
0.70	1.21	1.00
0.80	1.47	1.05
0.85	1.73	1.10
0.90	2.25	1.18
0.95	3.78	1.35

FIGURE 29-12 RCA PRICE S model: effect of hardware constraints

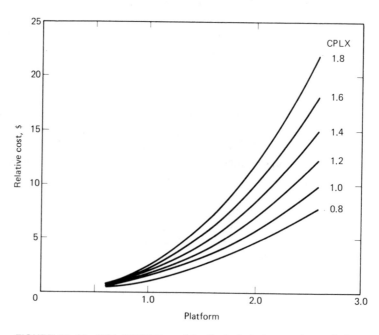

FIGURE 29-13 RCA PRICE S model: effect of platform and complexity

The IBM-FSD Model [Walston–Felix, 1977]

Only parts of the IBM-FSD model have been described in the literature. It is based on the extensive, well-defined data base of IBM-FSD projects described in Section 25.1. A version of the model is used by calculating a productivity index based on the 29 cost driver attributes in Table 25–6

$$I = \sum_{i=1}^{29} W_i X_i$$

The weights W_i are defined as

$$W_i = 0.5 \log_{10} (PC)_i$$

where $(PC)_i$ is the productivity change between a low and high rating for the ith cost driver attribute in Table 25–6 [for example, $(PC)_i = 376$ DSI/MM for the first attribute, Customer Interface Complexity]. The rating X_i is either -1, 0, or $+1$, depending on whether the project rates low, average, or high (or their equivalent) with respect on the ith cost driver attribute.

The main difficulty with this model, as discussed in Section 25.1, is in separating out how much of the ith productivity change is due to the effects of other correlated factors, or in double counting by using four factors to account for the use of modern programming practices. However, the information on cost driver attributes, and related results in [Walston–Felix, 1977] on estimation of schedule, computer costs, and documentation have been highly valuable.

The 1977 Boeing Model [Black and others, 1977]

The 1977 Boeing model is similar to COCOMO in several ways. It produces a nominal man-month estimate as a function of size in DSI, using the following basic productivity rates:

- Mathematical   6 man-months/1000 statements
- Report   8 man-months/1000 statements
- Logic   12 man-months/1000 statements
- Signal   20 man-months/1000 statements
- Real time   40 man-months/1000 statements

It then divides up the nominal man-month estimate by phase, using the following distribution:

Task	Percent of Total Cost
• Requirements definition	5
• Design and specification	25
• Code preparation	10
• Code checkout	25
• Integration and test	25
• System test	10

Next, it applies the effort multipliers shown in Table 29–9 to the nominal effort estimates for each phase to produce an adjusted effort estimate for each phase. These are then summed to produce an overall effort estimate.

TABLE 29–9 Labor Estimate Adjustment Factors: 1977 Boeing Model

		Require-ments Definition	Design and Specifi-cation	Code Prepa-ration	Code Check-out	Integra-tion and test	System Test
1. Reimplementation of existing software		0.2	0.2	0.8		0.8	
2. Follow-on contract with current cus-tomer		0.7					0.9
3. Number of pro-grammers:	1–2	0.2	0.5	0.8		0.2	
(interpolate be-tween values if needed)	6–10	1.0	1.0	1.0		1.0	1.0
	more than 20	6.0	3.3	1.2		3.0	3.0
4. Higher-order lan-guage (seasoned compiler)			0.3	0.3	0.2		
5. Macrolanguage in coding forms for document			0.9	0.9	0.9		
			0.8			0.8	
6. On-line code/data entry				0.9	0.9		
7. On-line debugging					0.6		
8. Poor (or no) de-bug tools except dumps					1.4	1.4	
9. Programming ex-perience with en-gineering/techni-cal discipline of application:	Entry level	2.0	3.0	1.5			1.5
	Moderate	1.0	1.0	1.0			1.0
	High	0.6	0.5	0.8			0.7

Note: In table positions having no entry, the assumed multiplier is 1.0.

Rather surprisingly, this cost model appeared in a report [Black and others, 1977] which was trying to show what a poor estimation model it was. (The report was trying to quantify the benefits of employing modern programming practices.) It overestimated the costs of some Boeing projects by factors of five and six; part of the overestimate may have been due to use of MPPs, but part must also be due to the very large effort multipliers for many-programmer projects and the lack of HOL multipliers to reduce test-phase costs. Its use was once recommended by a U.S. Government guidebook, but subsequently it has fallen out of use.

The 1979 GRC Model [Carriere–Thibodeau, 1979]

This model has a large number of different estimating relationships which are difficult to summarize. It has a number of good features, including a thorough definition of the quantities being estimated and a set of relationships for estimating such quantities as training and installation costs and labor-grade distributions. Some drawbacks, however, include the use of "number of output formats" as the basic size parameter and some evident typos or mistakes in the 0.0 values given in the effort multiplier tables.

The Bailey-Basili Meta-Model [Bailey-Basili, 1981]

The Bailey-Basili meta-model involves a rigorous statistical process similar to the more heuristic process used to determine the COCOMO scaling equations and effort multipliers:

1. Use one's overall project size and effort data to determine the best possible background scaling equation of the form

$$\text{Effort} = a \, (\text{Size})^b + c$$

2. Use other project attributes to determine effort multipliers which account for as much as possible of the error in the background scaling equation.

The Bailey-Basili model developed composite ratings for total methodology (METH), cumulative complexity (CMPLX), and cumulative experience, to be used in determining an Error Ratio (ER) of the form:

$$\text{Effort} = \text{ER} \, [a \, (\text{Size})^b + c]$$
$$\text{ER} = d \, (\text{METH}) + e \, (\text{CMPLX}) + f$$

When used on the well-defined data from 18 fairly uniform projects in the NASA-Goddard Software Engineering Laboratory, the resulting equations were:

$$\text{MM}_{\text{DEV}} = \text{ER} \, [0.73 + (\text{EDSI})^{1.16} + 3.5]$$
$$\text{ER} = -0.035 \, (\text{METH}) + 0.98, \text{ or}$$
$$= -0.036 \, (\text{METH}) + 0.009 \, (\text{CMPLX}) + 0.80$$

The first equation for ER reduced the multiplicative standard error of the estimate from 1.25 to 1.16. The addition of the CMPLX term reduced it further to only 1.15.

29.8 COCOMO EVALUATION WITH RESPECT TO MODEL CRITERIA

This section evaluates COCOMO with respect to the criteria for the goodness of a software cost-estimation model presented at the beginning of Chapter 28, in terms of the current state of the art in software cost estimation as exemplified by the models presented in the previous section. The model criteria are reproduced for convenience below.

1. *Definition.* Has the model clearly defined which costs it is estimating, and which costs it is excluding?
2. *Fidelity.* Are the estimates close to the actual costs expended on the projects?
3. *Objectivity.* Does the model avoid allocating most of the software cost variance to poorly calibrated subjective factors (such as complexity)? That is, is it hard to jigger the model to obtain any result you want?
4. *Constructiveness.* Can a user tell why the model gives the estimates it does? Does it help the user understand the software job to be done?
5. *Detail.* Does the model easily accommodate the estimation of a software system consisting of a number of subsystems and units? Does it give (accurate) phase and activity breakdowns?
6. *Stability.* Do small differences in inputs produce small differences in output cost estimates?
7. *Scope.* Does the model cover the class of software projects whose costs you need to estimate?
8. *Ease of Use.* Are the model inputs and options easy to understand and specify?
9. *Prospectiveness.* Does the model avoid the use of information which will not be well known until the project is complete?
10. *Parsimony.* Does the model avoid the use of highly redundant factors, or factors which make no appreciable contribution to the results?

1. Definition. As soon as a software cost estimate begins to be allocated as a budget commitment, to pay for the accomplishment of specific tasks by specific groups of people, a number of questions begin to arise: "Does this estimate include the cost of management? Requirements analysis? Training? Computer operations?"; "What activities are included in integration and test? Configuration management? Maintenance?" A similar set of questions also begins to arise as to the definition of inputs: "delivered," "instructions," "complexity," etc.

Some models, such as the IBM-FSD model, the Bailey-Basili model, and the 1979 GRC model, provide fairly thorough definitions of their inputs and outputs. But, surprisingly, the documentation for a number of other models does not satisfactorily answer such questions.

For COCOMO, we have provided as thorough as possible a definition of the activities and quantities associated with the model, without overly constraining either the model's generality or a project's flexibility. These definitions include the phase, activity, and work breakdown structure definitions in Sections 4.5 and 4.6, the model definitions and assumptions in Section 5.2, and the detailed rating scales for the cost driver attributes in Chapters 24 through 27.

2. Fidelity. As discussed in Section 29.3, the COCOMO estimates come within 20% of the actual development figures for the projects in the COCOMO data base 68% of the time for Intermediate COCOMO and 70% of the time for Detailed COCOMO. This translates to a standard deviation of the residuals of roughly 20% of the actuals. Relatively few other models have published standard deviations of their estimates with respect to a data base of project actuals. The 1965 SDC model had a standard deviation which was larger than the mean estimate. The analysis of the IBM-FSD model in [Walston–Felix, 1977] reported a standard deviation of a factor of 1.71 (mean of 274 DSL/MM; range about the mean of 160–470 DSL/ MM). The [Bailey-Basili, 1981] model reported a standard deviation of a factor of 1.15 for a fairly uniform set of 18 projects at NASA-Goddard.

The fidelity of the COCOMO model with respect to the COCOMO data base is probably somewhat better than with respect to the population of software projects at large, since a large portion of the data base was also used to calibrate the model's parameters. Similarly, we should not be too surprised to find that COCOMO estimates come closer to the actuals in the COCOMO data base than do the estimates of other models, as has been the case in some initial analyses. The critical test will be its ability to predict accurately on future projects (as yet, no projects estimated by COCOMO have been completed except for two small projects whose results came quite close to the estimates).

The fidelity of the COCOMO phase and activity distributions is more difficult to judge, due to the small sample size of project actuals. On balance, however, these and other COCOMO estimates appear to be at least as accurate as those available from other software cost-estimation models, and to be superior to other models in accounting for the influence of cost driver attributes on a project's phase distribution of effort.

3. Objectivity. In Question 24.13, we discussed "the perfect cost model." It has a single cost driver attribute, complexity, and each completed project is given a complexity rating exactly corresponding to its observed productivity. Thus, the model calibrates perfectly to past experience.

However, since the complexity rating is entirely subjective, there is no way to determine whether an estimator's complexity rating for a future project is appropriate. As has been found on a number of models of this nature, this makes it entirely too easy for an estimator to jigger the model to fit a price-to-win estimate, a punitively high estimate, or the like.

COCOMO attempts to bound the subjective variability due to the complexity factor in the following ways:

- Making the complexity rating a module-level rather than a subsystem- or system-level rating.
- Factoring as many sources of variation in productivity as possible into separate cost drivers independent of the complexity cost driver (for example, execution time and main storage constraints, required reliability, etc.).
- Providing the rating scales in Table 24–8 in order to make each complexity rating as objective as possible.

Some progress has also been made with other cost models, such as SLIM and PRICE S, in expanding a single complexity factor into a number of constituent elements.

4. Constructiveness. As discussed in Chapters 21 and 22, it is important in practical cost estimation to balance algorithmic model estimates with expert judgment and individual performer estimates.

Inevitably, this leads to differences between the various estimates, and a need to understand why one was higher or lower than the other. Similarly, project personnel want to know *in project terms* why different factor ratings give them different cost estimates.

To help answer these questions, and to promote accurate factor ratings by users, we have provided, in Chapters 24 through 27, a table for each of the factors in the COCOMO model indicating the impact on project activities of the various factors and their ratings. In general, we have found that such tables do help the users of a cost model better understand the software job for which they are preparing.

More fundamentally, though, this increased understanding is an end in itself, and not just a means to put an accurate price tag on a software project. The primary objective of COCOMO (and the reason for its name) has been to provide an opportunity to better understand the complexities of the software life-cycle process through the medium of a software cost-estimation model.

5. Detail. As discussed in Section 21.4, software cost-estimation models requiring greater detail tend to produce more accurate estimates, mainly because

1. The gathering of greater detail tends to increase people's understanding of the job to be done.
2. If the added detail results in the overall estimate being the sum of some smaller individual estimates, the law of large numbers tends to work to decrease the variance in the estimate.

For this reason, COCOMO is organized into a hierarchy of models, with a simple macro model for rough early estimates in Basic COCOMO, and more detailed micro models for more accurate and definitive estimation in Intermediate and Detailed COCOMO. The TRW–Wolverton model has served as an effective micro model, and has also been effective in providing considerable detail in its phase and activity breakdowns, as has the 1979 GRC model.

6. Stability. Some models, such as the Doty model, exhibit discontinuities at model boundaries or due to the binary nature of some of their inputs [Boehm–Wolverton, 1978]. COCOMO avoids this problem, as do most of the cost-estimation models, by providing a number of rating levels for cost driver attributes and allowing interpolation between them.

7. Scope. Some models have been developed for and calibrated to a particular domain of software practice—very large projects, aerospace projects, business applications, etc.—and may not be as accurate outside that domain. Others, such as the IBM-FSD model, have been calibrated to a particularly wide variety of projects and applications. COCOMO has been similarly calibrated across a variety of business, process control, human-machine interactive, scientific, support, and systems software projects; its main deficiency in scope is in the area of very small projects below 2000 DSI, where algorithmic cost models have a difficult time in general.

8. Ease of use. A cost model will be less useful in general to the extent that it relies on inputs that are difficult to understand and obtain, or to the extent that the model makes it difficult for the user to perform common cost-estimation functions such as the combination of the estimates of several subsystems into an estimate for the overall system. Aside from this latter difficulty, the commercial macro-estimation models, SLIM and PRICE S, are well user-engineered for ease of use and understanding. The hierarchical macro-to-micro organization of COCOMO makes project subsetting a relatively easy and straightforward activity.

9. Prospectiveness. One current problem with the practical use of the [Halstead, 1977] model is that it relies on knowing detailed properties of the code to estimate such model inputs as program volume. These properties (that is, number of operators and operands) are generally unknown at the time the cost estimate is needed.

In general, most current models, including COCOMO, deal with quantities which can be determined reasonably well at the beginning of a project—with the notable partial exception of the sizing problem, as discussed in Section 21.4.

10. Parsimony. A model will be less useful to the extent that it requires a number of inputs where one would suffice. An example is the [Walston–Felix, 1977] model, which has separate entries for the use of different modern programming practices (MPPs) such as top-down development, structured code, and use of inspections. For the original research purpose of the Walston–Felix model, it was important to distinguish these entries, but for practical estimation of projects using modern management guidelines, a single "use of MPPs" factor would suffice.

For COCOMO, the parsimony concerns have been primarily met by the following considerations:

- Each of the existing cost driver attributes was shown to have a nontrivial effect on software productivity by the Ideal Effort Multiplier analyses in Chapters 24 through 27.
- A number of other candidate factors were explicitly considered and rejected for reasons of parsimony, as discussed in Chapter 28.

However, it may be that the full COCOMO model may have more cost driver attributes than are needed for a particular installation. For example, the installation's staff may have a high correlation between its members' application, language, and virtual machine experience, and the installation may be able to employ a single unified personnel-experience cost driver attribute instead of three separate attributes. Such tailoring considerations are covered in the next section.

29.9 TAILORING COCOMO TO A PARTICULAR INSTALLATION

In general, the COCOMO model presented here will be a reasonable model for most software cost-estimation situations. Often, though, a given installation can develop a specially calibrated and tailored version of COCOMO which will be more accurate and easy to use within the context of the particular installation.

The major opportunities for calibration and tailoring are

- Calibrating the COCOMO nominal effort equations to the installation's experience
- Consolidating or eliminating redundant cost driver attributes within the model
- Adding further cost driver attributes which may be significant at this installation, but not in general (for example, security or privacy restrictions).

Each of these considerations is discussed in more detail below.

Calibrating the COCOMO Nominal Effort Equations

For various reasons, the nominal effort equations for the three standard CO-COMO development modes may not provide the best fit for a particular installation. The main reasons for this are

- An installation may consistently judge the COCOMO cost driver attribute ratings by different standards than were used in calibrating COCOMO. The most common areas where this occurs are required reliability, analyst and programmer capability, and use of modern programming practices. This situation can be accommodated by recalibrating the rating scales, but is often accomplished in an easier fashion by recalibrating the constant term in the nominal effort equation for the installation's development modes.
- An installation may employ consistently different definitions of "delivered," "source instructions," "development," or "man-months" than those used in COCOMO. Here again, the simplest solution would be to recalibrate the constant terms in the COCOMO nominal effort equations.
- An installation's usual development mode may be somewhere in between the standard COCOMO development modes, in which case a special nominal effort equation can be calibrated to the installation's experience.

Techniques for each of these situations are given below, and illustrated by an example.

Calibrating the Constant Term

The simplest and most stable way to calibrate COCOMO to an installation's experience is to establish the most appropriate development mode for the installation, and to use a least-squares approximation technique to calibrate the constant term for the development mode's nominal effort equation to the installation's project data.

To be specific, suppose that the organic mode best represents the development mode of a given installation. Then, we wish to determine the most appropriate constant, c, for the organic-mode nominal effort equation in the COCOMO estimating relationship

$$MM = c(KDSI)^{1.05}\Pi(EM) \qquad (29\text{--}3)$$

where $\Pi(EM)$ represents the overall product of the effort multipliers resulting from a project's cost driver attribute ratings, or, more concisely, its effort adjustment factor, Π.

Suppose that the installation has completed a number of projects $p_1, \ldots, p_n$; whose sizes were $KDSI_1, \ldots, KDSI_n$; whose overall effort adjustment factors were $\Pi_1, \ldots, \Pi_n$; and whose actual development efforts were $MM_1, \ldots, MM_n$. Then, we wish to solve for the value of c in the system of linear equations

$$MM_1 = c(KDSI_1)^{1.05}\Pi_1$$
$$MM_2 = c(KDSI_2)^{1.05}\Pi_2$$
$$\vdots \qquad\qquad (29\text{--}4)$$
$$MM_n = c(KDSI_n)^{1.05}\Pi_n$$

which minimizes the sum of the squares of the residual errors

$$S = \sum_{i=1}^{n} [c(KDSI_i)^{1.05}\Pi_i - MM_i]^2 \qquad (29\text{--}5)$$

or, setting $(KDSI_i)^{1.05}\Pi_i = Q_i$ for simplicity

$$S = \sum_{i=1}^{n} [cQ_i - MM_i]^2$$

As in our earlier optimal value calculations in Part III, we can determine the optimal coefficient $\bar{c}$ by setting the derivative dS/dc equal to zero and solving for $\bar{c}$.

$$0 = \frac{dS}{dc} = 2\sum_{i=1}^{n} [\bar{c}Q_i - MM_i]Q_i$$

or

$$0 = \sum_{i=1}^{n} \bar{c}Q_i^2 - MM_iQ_i$$

or

$$\bar{c} = \frac{\sum\limits_{i=1}^{n} \mathrm{MM}_i Q_i}{\sum\limits_{i=1}^{n} Q_i^2} \tag{29-6}$$

Similar calibration formulas can be generated for the COCOMO embedded or semidetached-mode constant terms, with the exponents 1.20 or 1.12, respectively, replacing the exponent 1.05 in Eq. (29-5) and the expression for Q_i.

Example

Suppose that an organic-mode installation had completed and collected data on five projects, whose sizes KDSI_i, effort adjustment factors Π_i, and development efforts MM_i were those given in Table 29-10, along with the estimates produced by the standard organic-mode estimator $(\mathrm{MM})_{\mathrm{est}} = 3.2\,(\mathrm{KDSI})^{1.05}(\Pi)$. The project actuals are generally somewhat higher than the standard COCOMO estimates, so we would expect the optimal coefficient $\bar{c}$ for the installation to be somewhat higher than the standard coefficient $c = 3.2$.

TABLE 29-10 Calibrating the COCOMO Constant Term to Project Data

Project Number (i)	KDSI$_i$	Π_i	MM$_{\mathrm{est}}$	MM$_i$	Q_i	MM$_i Q_i$	Q_i^2
1	5	0.75	13	15	4	60	16
2	10	1.0	36	44	11	484	121
3	20	0.80	59	60	19	1140	361
4	30	1.0	114	140	36	5040	1296
5	40	0.70	108	133	34	4522	1156
Σ						11,246	2950

And, in fact, we have from Table 29-10

$$\bar{c} = \frac{\sum\limits_{i=1}^{5} \mathrm{MM}_i Q_i}{\sum\limits_{i=1}^{5} Q_i^2} = \frac{11,246}{2950} = 3.81$$

Thus, the tailored effort equation for the installation is

$$\mathrm{MM} = 3.81\,(\mathrm{KDSI})^{1.05}\Pi(\mathrm{EM})$$

Calibrating the Software Development Mode

A similar least-squares technique may be used to calibrate both the coefficient term c and the scale factor b in the COCOMO effort equation

$$MM = c(\text{KDSI})^b \Pi(\text{EM}), \qquad (29\text{–}7)$$

corresponding to the definition of a new COCOMO software development mode tailored to the practice of the particular installation.

Our first step is to rearrange Eq. (29–7), and then to linearize it by taking logarithms of both sides (base-10 is used here, but natural logarithms may be used as well).

$$c(\text{KDSI})^b = MM/\Pi$$

$$\log c + b \log \text{KDSI} = \log (MM/\Pi) \qquad (29\text{–}8)$$

Thus, if an installation has completed a number of projects $P_1, \ldots, P_n$ with sizes $\text{KDSI}_1, \ldots, \text{KDSI}_n$, with overall effort adjustment factors $\Pi_1, \ldots, \Pi_n$, and with actual development efforts $MM_1, \ldots, MM_n$; we now wish to solve for the optimal values of $\log c$ and b in the system of equations

$$\log c + b \log(\text{KDSI})_1 = \log (MM/\Pi)_1$$

$$\log c + b \log(\text{KDSI})_2 = \log (MM/\Pi)_2$$

$$\vdots \qquad\qquad\qquad (29\text{–}9)$$

$$\log c + b \log(\text{KDSI})_n = \log (MM/\Pi)_n$$

which minimize the sum of the squares of the residual errors in Eq. (29–9).

It is a fairly straightforward exercise in numerical analysis to determine that the optimal values $\log \bar{c}$ and $\bar{b}$ may be determined by solving the equations:

$$a_0 \log \bar{c} + a_1 \bar{b} = d_0$$

$$a_1 \log \bar{c} + a_2 \bar{b} = d_1 \qquad (29\text{–}10)$$

where the quantities a_0, a_1, a_2, d_0, and d_1 are calculated as

$$a_0 = n$$

$$a_1 = \sum_{i=1}^{n} \log (\text{KDSI})_i$$

$$a_2 = \sum_{i=1}^{n} [\log (\text{KDSI})_i]^2$$

$$d_0 = \sum_{i=1}^{n} \log (MM/\Pi)_i$$

$$d_1 = \sum_{i=1}^{n} \log (MM/\Pi)_i \log (\text{KDSI})_i$$

The resulting solutions for $\log \bar{c}$ and $\bar{b}$ are given by the equations

$$\log \bar{c} = \frac{a_2 d_0 - a_1 d_1}{a_0 a_2 - a_1^2}$$

$$\bar{b} = \frac{a_0 d_1 - a_1 d_0}{a_0 a_2 - a_1^2}$$

Example

Table 29–11 shows the quantities involved in calculating $\log \bar{c}$ and $\bar{b}$ from the project data given in the previous example.

TABLE 29–11 Calibrating the Nominal Effort Equation to Project Data

Project Number	KDSI	Π	MM	log KDSI	(log KDSI)²	log(MM/Π)	log (MM/Π)log (KDSI)
1	5	0.75	15	0.70	0.49	1.30	0.91
2	10	1.0	44	1.00	1.00	1.64	1.64
3	20	0.80	60	1.30	1.69	1.88	2.44
4	30	1.0	140	1.48	2.18	2.15	3.18
5	40	0.70	133	1.60	2.56	2.28	3.65
Σ				$a_1 = 6.08$	$a_2 = 7.92$	$d_0 = 9.25$	$d_1 = 11.82$

The resulting values of $\log \bar{c}, \bar{c},$ and $\bar{b}$ are then

$$\log \bar{c} = \frac{(7.92)(9.25) - (6.08)(11.82)}{(5)(7.92) - (6.08)^2} = 0.53$$

$$\bar{c} = 3.39$$

$$\bar{b} = \frac{(5)(11.82) - (6.08)(9.25)}{(5)(7.92) - (6.08)^2} = 1.09$$

Thus, the new COCOMO software development mode tailored to the practice of this particular installation would have the effort equation

$$MM = 3.39(KDSI)^{1.09}\Pi(EM)$$

Some Cautions in Recalibrating the Software Development Mode

An installation must be extremely careful in recalibrating a COCOMO software development mode to a group of its projects, particularly if the set of projects is fairly small in number, as above. For sample sizes on the order of five projects, the optimal values of $\bar{c}$ and $\bar{b}$ are very sensitive to relatively small variations in project data. For example, if the number of man-months for Project 1 in Table 29–11 were 18 instead of 15, the tailored development mode equation would change to

$$MM = 4.3(KDSI)^{1.02}\Pi(EM)$$

If the number of man-months were 12, the equation would change to

$$MM = 2.46(KDSI)^{1.19}\Pi(EM).$$

The constant-term calibration process is much more stable. There, if the man-months in Project 1 were changed to 18 or to 12, the resulting optimal coefficient c would only change from 3.81 to 3.82 or remain at 3.81.

Here are some resulting cautions which should therefore be observed in recalibrating COCOMO, and particularly in recalibrating the development mode.

1. Make sure the project data are as consistent as possible.
2. If the project data represent different modes, perform a separate recalibration for each mode.
3. If the sample size of project data is less than 10 projects, pick a standard COCOMO development mode and recalibrate its constant term, rather than recalibrating an overall development mode.
4. Make sure that the projects used for calibration are representative of the projects whose costs will be estimated with the recalibrated model.

Consolidating, Eliminating, or Adding Cost Driver Attributes

Many installations have a highly uniform operation with respect to such features as type of application, computer configuration or virtual machine used, and programming language used on projects. As a result, the three separate cost driver attributes AEXP, VEXP, and LEXP will practically always have the same rating (see, for example, [Chrysler, 1978]). In such a situation, an installation may wish to consolidate these three attributes into a single attribute of personnel experience, using a combined set of effort multipliers as illustrated in Table 29–12. Similar consolidation may also be appropriate for other attributes, such as MODP and TOOL. An example of a model similar to COCOMO using such consolidated attributes is given in [Bailey–Basili, 1981].

Eliminating a cost driver attribute from the model can be done in situations in which all the projects in an installation have the same ratings. This might be the case within a computer center which provides the same level of virtual machine volatility, computer turnaround time, and software tool support for all projects. In such a case, the overall effort multipliers for these levels of service may be incorporated into the coefficient terms of the nominal estimating equations for the three development modes, and the phase distributions adjusted accordingly. For example, if an installation provided low (interactive) turnaround, nominal virtual machine volatility, and a high

TABLE 29–12 Combined Effort Multipliers for Personnel Experience (PEXP)

Amount of Experience	AEXP	VEXP	LEXP	PEXP
1 month	1.29	1.21	1.14	1.78
4 months	1.29	1.10	1.07	1.52
1 year	1.13	1.00	1.00	1.13
3 years	1.00	.90	.95	.86
6 years	.91	.90	.95	.78
12 years	.82	.90	.95	.70

level of tool support for all projects, the corresponding coefficient for the revised organic-mode nominal effort equation would be

$$(3.2)(0.87)(1.00)(0.91) = 2.53$$

Addition of a new cost driver attribute, such as one for security or privacy restrictions, involves the determination of a set of cost driver attribute ratings, and calibration of these ratings through an approach such as the ideal effort multiplier technique. Examples of its use are given for the existing attributes in Chapters 24 to 27 and for some of the other candidate attributes in Chapter 28.

29.10 TOPICS FOR FURTHER RESEARCH

29.A. Determine more detailed error statistics, significance levels, and confidence intervals for the COCOMO estimates with respect to the project actuals in the COCOMO data base.

29.B. Perform an analysis of the correlations between rating levels of different cost driver attributes in the COCOMO data base (for example, between project Applications, Virtual Machine, and Language Experience; between Use of Tools and Modern Programming Practices; between Time and Storage Constraints; between Complexity, Analyst Capability, and Programmer Capability).

29.C. Perform a cluster analysis with respect to the project cost driver attribute rating levels in the COCOMO data base, to determine common project profiles.

29.D. Test the hypothesis that the differences between the organic, semidetached, and embedded modes can be distinguished in terms of characteristic groupings of cost driver attribute ratings.

29.E. Perform analyses similar to those of Topic 29.D for characteristic groupings of cost driver attribute ratings for the different COCOMO project types (business, process control, etc.) for HOL versus MOL projects, for maxi versus minicomputer projects, etc.

29.F. Test hypotheses on the correlation of documentation rate in PP/KDSI and software productivity (or weighted productivity) for the projects in the COCOMO data base.

29.G. Determine the correlation between the degree of effort under- or overestimation and schedule under- or overestimation by COCOMO.

29.H. Collect and analyze additional data on the distribution of effort by phase and activity and compare the results with COCOMO estimates. Document and analyze any differences between the definitions and assumptions underlying your data and the COCOMO data.

29.I. Collect and analyze data on the time distribution of software project effort and compare it with the Rayleigh curve [Putnam, 1978] and other suggested models such as [Parr, 1980]. See, for example, [Basili–Zelkowitz, 1978] and [Basili–Beane, 1980].

29.J. Develop and test hypotheses on the influence of various cost driver attributes (for example, TYPE, RELY, TURN, MODP) on the distribution of project effort by activity. The activity tables in Chapters 24 to 27 provide a good starting point.

29.K. Evaluate other software cost-estimation models with respect to the COCOMO data base. Document and analyze any differences between the definitions and assumptions underlying the model and the COCOMO data.

Part IVC

━━━

SOFTWARE COST ESTIMATION AND LIFE-CYCLE MANAGEMENT

Good software cost estimation is not an end in itself, but rather a means toward more effective software life-cycle management. Part IVC (Chapters 30 through 33) covers several important topics in using COCOMO over the software life-cycle. Chapter 30 covers techniques for estimating software maintenance costs. Chapter 31 covers techniques for estimating overall software life-cycle costs, including conversion, installation, training, and other software-related costs (computer, documentation, etc.). Chapter 32 presents techniques for using software cost estimates to improve software project planning and control, and vice versa. Finally, Chapter 33 discusses the problem of improving software productivity from the perspective and insights provided by software cost-estimation technology.

Chapter 30

Software Maintenance Cost Estimation

30.1 INTRODUCTION

The great majority of software cost-estimation material (in this book and elsewhere) covers the cost of software development; that is, the amount of effort required to go from a software requirements specification to a successful software acceptance test. However, the majority of software costs are incurred during the period after the developed software is accepted. These costs are primarily due to software maintenance, which here refers both to activities to preserve the software's existing functionality and performance, and activities to increase its functionality and improve its performance throughout the life-cycle.

Estimates of the magnitude of software maintenance costs range from slightly over 50% to 75% of overall software life-cycle costs. Figure 30–1, from [Boehm, 1976], shows maintenance percentages of 10-year life-cycle costs ranging from 60% for General Telephone and Electronics [Daly, 1977] to 75% for General Motors [Elshoff, 1976]. Figure 30–2, based on data from 487 business data processing installa-

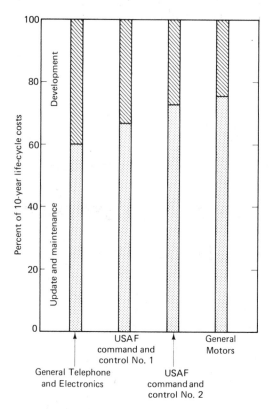

FIGURE 30-1   Software development and maintenance costs in large organizations

tions analyzed in [Lientz–Swanson, 1980], indicates that the average development to maintenance ratio among installations surveyed was 47 to 53.*

For an activity which consumes so much of the total software life-cycle dollar, relatively little is known about the software maintenance process and the factors which influence its cost. This chapter summarizes our current knowledge of software maintenance costs in the context of the COCOMO maintenance model.

30.2   THE COCOMO SOFTWARE MAINTENANCE MODEL

Definitions

Software maintenance is defined as the process of modifying existing operational software while leaving its primary functions intact. This definition *excludes* the following types of activity from the category of software maintenance:

* Not all software programs have high maintenance costs. In fact, the [Kendall–Lamb, 1977] study found that the median application program had a size of 400 DSI and a life expectancy of 14 months.

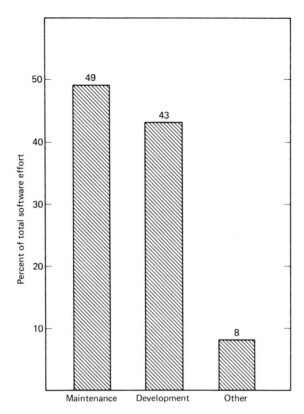

FIGURE 30–2 Software development and maintenance costs in 487 business organizations

- Major redesign and redevelopment (more than 50% new code) of a new software product performing substantially the same functions
- Design and development of a sizable (more than 20% of the source instructions comprising the existing product) interfacing software package which requires relatively little redesign of the existing product
- Data processing system operations, data entry, and modification of values in the data base

The definition *includes* the following types of activity within the category of software maintenance:

- Redesign and redevelopment of small* portions of an existing software product
- Design and development of small interfacing software packages which require some redesign of the existing software product
- Modification of the software product's code, documentation, or data base structure

* Small here means smaller than the size indicated in the exclusions above.

Software maintenance can be classified into two main categories

1. Software *update,* which results in a changed functional specification for the software product
2. Software *repair,* which leaves the functional specification intact

In turn, software repair can be classified into three main subcategories [Swanson, 1976]

2a. Corrective maintenance (of processing, performance, or implementation failures)
2b. Adaptive maintenance (to changes in the processing or data environment)
2c. Perfective maintenance (for enhancing performance or maintainability)

All of these categories of effort are included in the estimates produced by the COCOMO maintenance model. In addition, all of the assumptions made for the COCOMO development model in Section 5.2 also apply to the maintenance model, with one exception: The maintenance cost estimates include the costs of requirements analysis activities performed during maintenance. Thus, with respect to the work breakdown structure activity hierarchy in Fig. 30–3 (reproduced from Fig. 4–6b), the Maintenance activity costed by COCOMO includes WBS elements SX71–74 (but not SX75, Data base administration), and each of WBS elements SX71–74 covers all of the SX1–SX5 activities pursued during software maintenance.

Software Maintenance Effort Estimation

The basic assumption underlying the COCOMO maintenance model is that software maintenance costs are determined by substantially the same cost driver attributes that determine software development costs. The quantity used to determine the equivalent of product size for software maintenance is the *Annual Change Traffic* (ACT), that fraction of the software product's source instructions which undergo change during a (typical) year, either through addition or modification.

If all of the cost driver attribute effort multipliers for maintenance are the same as those for development, the resulting annual maintenance effort estimate is

$$(MM)_{AM} = (1.0)(ACT)(MM)_{DEV} \qquad (30\text{--}1)$$

However, in Intermediate COCOMO and Detailed COCOMO, this estimate may be modified for two reasons

1. The cost driver attribute ratings may be different for maintenance than for development (for example, due to learning effects, personnel changes, etc.).
2. Two of the cost driver attributes, RELY and MODP, have different effort multipliers for maintenance (Tables 30–1 and 30–2) than for development.

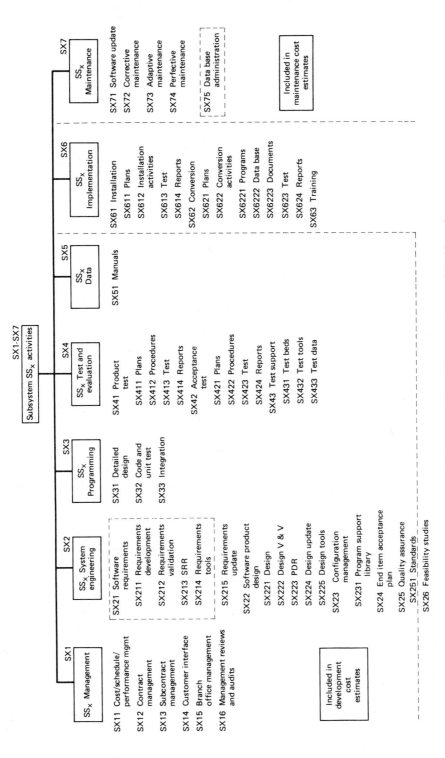

FIGURE 30–3 Software work breakdown structure: activity hierarchy

TABLE 30–1 RELY Maintenance Effort Multipliers

Very Low	Low	Nominal	High	Very High
1.35	1.15	1.00	0.98	1.10

TABLE 30–2 MODP Maintenance Effort Multipliers

Product Size(DSI)	Rating				
	Very Low	Low	Nominal	High	Very High
2K	1.25	1.12	1.00	0.90	0.81
8K	1.30	1.14	1.00	0.88	0.77
32K	1.35	1.16	1.00	0.86	0.74
128K	1.40	1.18	1.00	0.85	0.72
512K	1.45	1.20	1.00	0.84	0.70

In such cases, the modified multipliers are substituted for the original development multipliers, and a maintenance effort adjustment factor $(EAF)_M$ computed as the product of the effort multipliers. The annual maintenance effort is then calculated as

$$(MM)_{AM} = (1.0)(ACT)(MM)_{NOM}(EAF)_M \qquad (30\text{--}2)$$

where $(MM)_{NOM}$ is calculated from the nominal effort equations as a function of the total* number of KDSI in the software product

$$
\begin{aligned}
(MM)_{NOM} &= 3.2\ (KDSI)^{1.05} \quad \text{(Organic mode)} \\
&= 3.0\ (KDSI)^{1.12} \quad \text{(Semidetached mode)} \\
&= 2.8\ (KDSI)^{1.20} \quad \text{(Embedded mode)}
\end{aligned}
$$

The ACT may be the same for the entire system, or it may vary by component (or subsystem or module), in which case Eq. 30–2 is applied to each of the N components and the results summed to determine the overall maintenance estimate

$$(MM_{AM})_i = (ACT)_i\ (MM_{NOM})_i\ (EAF)_i$$

$$(MM)_{AM} = \sum_{i=1}^{N} (MM_{AM})_i \qquad (30\text{--}3)$$

Examples of the application of the COCOMO maintenance estimation relations are given in Section 5.8 for Basic COCOMO and Section 9.5 for Intermediate CO-

---

* Remember that this quantity may be different than the Equivalent KDSI used to calculate development costs, which may have included a discount factor for adapted software.

COMO. The procedures for Detailed COCOMO follow the same pattern as those for Intermediate COCOMO.

Modified Effort Multipliers

The modified effort multipliers for RELY and MODP are given in Tables 30–1 and 30–2. They reflect the facts that increased investment in software reliability and use of modern programming practices during software development have a strong payoff during maintenance. Further discussion of these effort multipliers is given in Section 8.5.

30.3 COMPARISON WITH PROJECT RESULTS

Figure 30–4 shows the comparison between the estimated annual maintenance effort (using Intermediate COCOMO) and the actual effort for the 24 maintenance projects in the COCOMO data base. These include 14 projects from the primary COCOMO project data base, for which cost driver attribute ratings are available for both development and maintenance (the dots in Fig. 30–4), and 10 projects for which the cost driver attribute ratings were unknown. For these 10 projects (the squares in Fig.

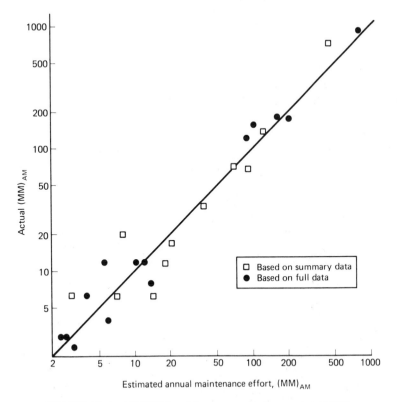

FIGURE 30–4 COCOMO maintenance estimates versus actuals

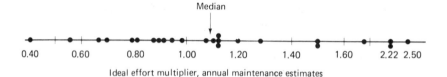

FIGURE 30-5 Distribution of ideal effort multipliers for maintenance model

30-4), an annual maintenance estimate was made under the assumption that the effort multipliers for maintenance were the same as those for development.

The results in Figure 30-4 show a reasonably good agreement between estimates and actuals. The agreement is not as good for small maintenance activities as for large ones, and not as good for the projects assuming equal effort multipliers (the squares) as for the projects based on full data.

Figure 30-5 shows the ideal effort multipliers for each project; the values which, if used instead of the multiplier 1.0 in the equation

$$(MM)_{AM} = (1.0) \ (ACT) \ (MM)_{NOM} \ (EAF)_M \qquad (30\text{-}2)$$

would have made the estimated $(MM)_{AM}$ equal to the actual value for the project. As can be seen from the median value (the arrow in Fig. 30-5), a value of 1.09 would be somewhat better for the model than 1.0, but the difference is so small compared to the spread in the data points that 1.0 is retained for simplicity.

30.4 OTHER SOFTWARE MAINTENANCE COST-ESTIMATION MODELS

Other software maintenance cost-estimation models have largely been based on simple linear ratios. Three primary bases have been used for these ratios: development cost, product size, and number of instructions changed.

The Maintenance/Development Cost Ratio

The maintenance/development cost ratio M/D is used to estimate the overall life-cycle maintenance cost $(MM)_M$, from acceptance test through phaseout, as a function of actual or estimated development cost $(MM)_{DEVEL}$

$$(MM)_M = (M/D) \ (MM)_{DEVEL} \qquad (30\text{-}4)$$

Thus, for example, a 32-KDSI product requiring 100 MM to develop, with an M/D ratio of 2.0 (67% maintenance) would require an estimated (2.0)(100MM) = 200 MM for maintenance.

The Putnam SLIM model [Putnam–Fitzsimmons, 1979] uses a value of 1.5 for the ratio M/D (corresponding to a 60% maintenance, 40% development life-cycle), and calculates the distribution of maintenance effort using the tail of the Rayleigh distribution. Other cited values of M/D range from 0.67 (or 40% maintenance) in [Brooks, 1975] to 4.5 (or 82% maintenance), used for application software in [Stone–Coleman, 1979].

The Cards-per-Person Ratio

This ratio stems from early software folklore often expressed in the form, "Each maintenance person can maintain four boxes of cards." (A box of cards held 2000 cards, or roughly 2000 source instructions in those days of few comment cards.) The number four in the saying would occasionally be replaced by three, or seven, or some number in that general region, and the result served as a handy way to get a rough estimate of maintenance staffing needs.

Currently, the ratio is usually expressed in terms of $(KDSI/FSP)_M$, thousands of source instructions maintained per full-time software person, and the number of maintenance personnel $(FSP)_M$ required to support a product of size $(KDSI)_{DEVEL}$ estimated as

$$(FSP)_M = \frac{(KDSI)_{DEVEL}}{(KDSI/FSP)_M} \qquad (30\text{–}5)$$

The annual maintenance effort $(MM)_{AM}$ is then simply

$$(MM)_{AM} = 12 \ (FSP)_M$$

Thus, a 32-KDSI product with a cards-per-person ratio of $(KDSI/FSP)_M = 16$ would require an estimated $32/16 = 2$ person staff for maintenance, or an annual maintenance effort of $12(2) = 24MM$. Table 30–3 shows the wide range of values that has been presented for the cards-per-person ratio $(KDSI/FSP)_M$. Their variation appears to be primarily a function of application type.

TABLE 30–3 Software Maintenance Cards-per-Person Ratios

Source	Application Type	$(KDSI/FSP)_M$
COCOMO, lowest		3
[Wolverton, 1980]	Aerospace	8
[Ferens–Harris, 1979]	Aerospace	10
COCOMO, 25th percentile		10
[Daly, 1977]	Real-time	10–30
[Griffin, 1980]	Real-time	12
[Elliott, 1977]	Business	20
[Graver and others, 1977]	Business, HOL	20
[Graver and others, 1977]	Business, MOL	22
COCOMO, median		25
[Lientz–Swanson, 1980]	Business, 487 installations	32
COCOMO, 75th percentile		36
[Daly, 1977]	Support software	30–120
COCOMO, highest		132

Another highly significant aspect of Table 30–3 is the comparison from [Graver and others, 1977] between maintenance of higher-order language (HOL) software and maintenance of machine-oriented language (MOL) software. The fact that their $(KDSI/FSP)_M$ ratios are roughly the same *per source instruction* means that there is a large benefit in maintenance costs per object instruction to be gained by programming in a HOL. The HOL program typically compiles into a much larger number of assembly language instructions (ranging from 2.5 to 15; see Table 28–1) which would have to be individually maintained if the job had been written in MOL. The comparative results per object instruction from [Graver and others, 1977] are shown in Fig. 30–6.

The Maintenance Productivity Ratio

The maintenance productivity ratio $(DSI/MM)_{MOD}$ is the average number of instructions which can be modified per man-month of maintenance effort. It can be used to estimate the annual maintenance effort required for a product of size $(DSI)_{DEVEL}$ by means of the annual change traffic parameter ACT

$$(DSI)_{MOD/YR} = (ACT)\,(DSI)_{DEVEL}$$

$$(MM)_{AM} = \frac{(DSI)_{MOD/YR}}{(DSI/MM)_{MOD}} \tag{30–6}$$

Thus, a 32-KDSI product with an ACT of 10% and a maintenance productivity of $(DSI/MM)_{MOD} = 200$ would have $(DSI)_{MOD/YR} = (0.10)(32,000) = 3200$ and an annual maintenance effort of $(MM)_{AM} = 3200/200 = 16$ MM. The quantity $(DSI/MM)_{MOD}$ can also be used to support a task-unit approach to maintenance estimation, in which

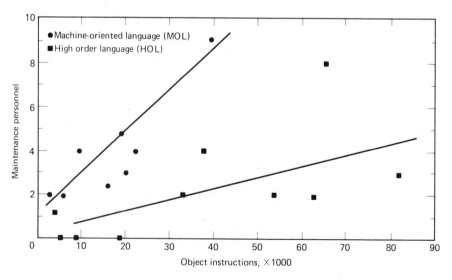

FIGURE 30–6 Effect of language on update and maintenance costs

each maintenance task is sized in terms of the number of instructions to be modified $(DSI)_{MOD}$.

The average values of annual change traffic (ACT) and $(DSI/MM)_{MOD}$ over the 487 business data processing installations surveyed in [Lientz–Swanson, 1980] are obtained from the data as follows:

Average Size:	48.0 KDSI
Average Change/Year:	4.4 KDSI
Average ACT:	4.4/48.0 = 0.092
Average $(FSP)_M$:	1.52
Average $(KDSI/FSP)_M$:	48/1.52 = 32
Average $(DSI/MM)_{MOD}$:	4400/(12 × 1.52) = 241

Another set of values for ACT and $(DSI/MM)_{MOD}$ are given in [Boeing, 1979], in terms of a categorization of software maintenance into easy, medium, and hard ratings. Those values are summarized in Table 30–4.

The estimator can then determine how much of the software product is easy, medium, or hard, and apply Eqs. (30–6) with the appropriate values of ACT and $(DSI/MM)_{MOD}$ to obtain the overall annual maintenance estimates $(MM)_{AM}$.

Comparison with COCOMO Data

The ratios discussed above are useful for rough early estimates of software maintenance costs, but the range of variability of the ratios (because of their insensitivity to other significant cost drivers) makes them unsuitable for life-cycle planning in which fixed, detailed budget commitments may be involved.

The range of variability of these parameters within the COCOMO maintenance data base is summarized in Table 30–5, which shows the highest, lowest, median, and quartile values of the cards-per-person ratio $(KDSI/FSP)_M$, the maintenance productivity ratio $(DSI/MM)_{MOD}$, and the annual change traffic (ACT).

The median values of $(KDSI/FSP)_M$, $(DSI/MM)_{MOD}$, and ACT in the COCOMO data base are lower than their counterpart averages in the [Lientz–Swanson, 1980] data base of business software maintenance. This is most likely due to differences in the maintenance characteristics between business software and other types of software: the five business software data points in the COCOMO data base have generally

TABLE 30–4 Maintenance Productivity Ratios [Boeing, 1979]

Rating	Types of Software	Typical $(DSI/MM)_{MOD}$	Typical ACT
Easy	Nonreal-time input/output	500	0.15
Medium	Mathematical and logical operations, signal processing	250	0.05
Hard	File, data base manipulation, real-time control, input/output	100	0.01

TABLE 30–5 Range of Software Maintenance Parameters in COCOMO Data Base

Parameter	Lowest	25th Percentile	Median	75th Percentile	Highest
Cards per person $(KDSI/FSP)_M$	3.2	10	25	36	132
Maintenance productivity $(DSI/MM)_{MOD}$	36	88	164	250	1238
Annual change traffic (ACT)	.01	.05	.08	.20	.40

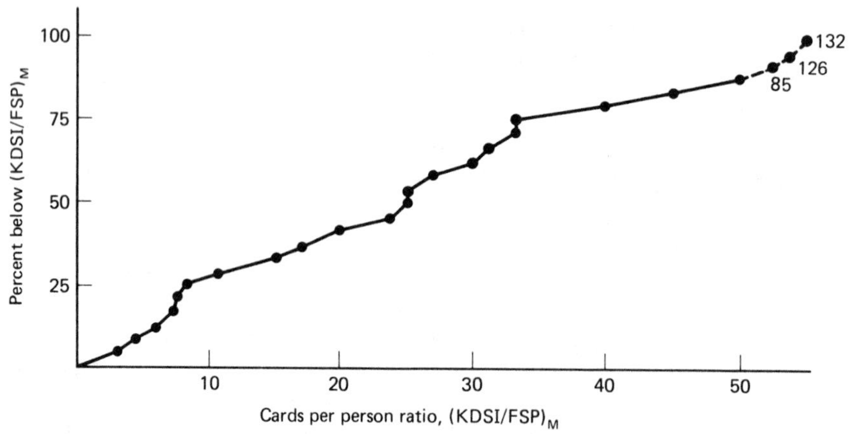

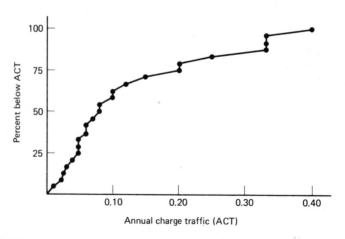

FIGURE 30–7 Cumulative distribution of cards-per-person ratio $(KDSI/FSP)_M$

FIGURE 30–8 Cumulative distribution of annual change traffic parameter (ACT)

higher values for these parameters (except ACT) also; see the COCOMO maintenance data in Table 30–6.

Another use of the parameter ranges in Table 30–5 is as a validity check on an estimated or derived software maintenance parameter. If you assume or calculate that each maintenance person can maintain an average of 50 KDSI, it is well to know that you are well into the upper quartile among maintenance projects. For added help in this direction, Figs. 30–7 and 30–8 show the actual cumulative distributions from the COCOMO data base for the cards-per-person ratio $(KDSI/FSP)_M$ and the annual change traffic. Figure 30–8 indicates that a figure of 50 $(KDSI/FSP)_M$ is at the 85th percentile of the projects in the COCOMO data base.

30.5 SOFTWARE MAINTENANCE PHENOMENOLOGY

The Software Maintenance Production Function

Software maintenance is usually performed as a level-of-effort activity, with the appropriate level of effort being determined from a cost-benefit, point-of-diminishing-returns judgment similar to the situation for software development discussed in Section 11.2.

A typical software maintenance cost-benefit production function is shown in Fig. 30–9. The investment segment consists of those maintenance activities which must be performed if the program is not to deteriorate in value: emergency program fixes, accommodation of changes to the program's environment (hardware, operating system, master data base, input data), and mandated enhancements (for example, new income tax reporting requirements).

The high-payoff segment of the curve consists of primary-priority enhancements for users; primary improvements in program efficiency, reliability, and documentation; and a set of secondary user improvements which provide a lower, but still positive excess of benefits over costs.*

The diminishing-returns segment of the curve consists, as it did in Fig. 11–5 for development, of the software maintenance organization's usual infinite backlog of "nice-to-have" features (limited-demand reports, pie-chart displays, rewriting the poorly-structured but stable inventory module, etc.). All of these features would provide some benefit to the organization, but not as much in relation to their costs as the activities already underway or higher on the priority list.

Dynamics of Software Maintenance

The question of how much maintenance effort should be put into a particular software product can only be resolved by the judgment of each organization as to the nature of its benefit scale and the appropriate breakpoint between the high-payoff and the diminishing-returns segments of the maintenance production function. The

---

* Of course, this characterization is an oversimplified representation of a more complex real-life situation; see Topics for Further Research 30.I.

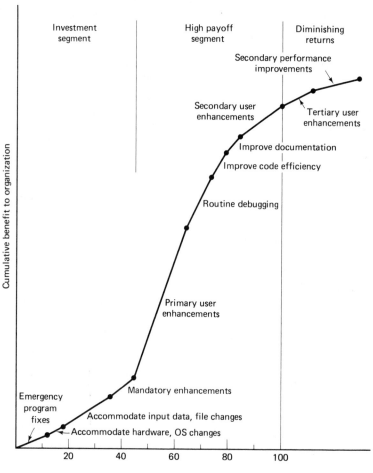

FIGURE 30-9 The software maintenance production function

quantitative and qualitative economic analysis techniques provided in Part III can clarify the issues, but they cannot be used as a substitute for human judgment.

Once an organization has determined its desired level of maintenance for a software product, particularly a large product, the organization's social, economic, and political inertias will generally make it difficult to make significant changes in the level of effort or mode of operation. In some situations, major increases in demand from the investment segment (such as conversion) or significant increases or redirections in demand due to an expanding or changing market for a software-based product may cause instabilities or reorientations. But in most cases, the maintenance activity will settle into a fairly predictable equilibrium.

The Belady–Lehman studies of software maintenance evolution dynamics [Lehman, 1978; Belady–Lehman, 1979] have led to the formulation of a set of "laws of large-program evolution" which provide a useful characterization of the usual software maintenance process. These are [Lehman, 1978]:

1. *Continuing Change.* A large program that is used undergoes continuing change or becomes progressively less useful. (In terms of Fig. 30–9, this is equivalent to saying that "all large programs have a nontrivial investment segment.")

2. *Increasing Complexity.* As a large program is continuously changed, its complexity increases, unless work is done to maintain it. (Figure 30–10, from [Belady–Lehman, 1979], is a good example of this; it shows how successive releases of OS/360 were required to modify more and more modules each time to accommodate more and more side effects.)

3. *The Fundamental Law of Large Program Evolution.* There exists a dynamics of large program evolution which causes measures of global project and system attributes to be cyclically self regulating.

4. *Invariant Work Rate.* The global activity rate in a large programming project is statistically invariant. (Here, there may be exceptions as noted above due to large changes in demand, or to mission discontinuities such as for periodic major launches in the manned space program.)

5. *Conservation of Familiarity.* For reliable, planned evolution, a large program undergoing change must be periodically released at intervals determined by a safe maximum release content (and, presumably, a safe minimum inter-release duration; see the discussion of virtual machine volatility in Section 25.3).

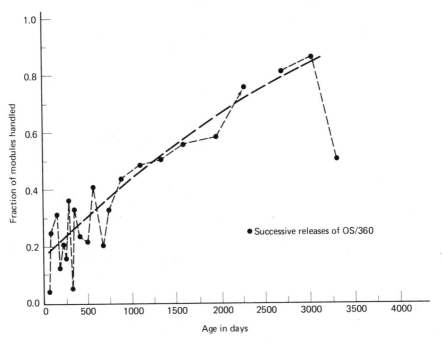

FIGURE 30–10 Fraction of modules handled per release: OS/360 [Belady-Lehman, 1979]

Distribution of Software Maintenance Effort by Activity

Although the benefits part of the software maintenance production function in Fig. 30–9 cannot be generally quantified, some aspects of the cost part can be quantified reasonably well. Thanks to the recent survey [Lientz–Swanson, 1978] of 487 business data processing installations, we now have a clearer picture of some of the gross cost-distribution characteristics of software maintenance. The surveyed installations are mainly business-oriented; the most strongly represented sectors were insurance (10.1%), government (9.9%), primary fabricated metal (8.2%), and banking/credit (7.8%). The relative sizes of the installations had a fairly representative distribution. The graphs and data below indicate some of the major results of the survey.

Figure 30–11 shows how the software maintenance effort is typically distributed among the major categories of update and repair. Corrective maintenance (emergency program fixes and routine debugging), generally the major portion of the hardware maintenance budget, tends to consume only a relatively small (21.7%) portion of

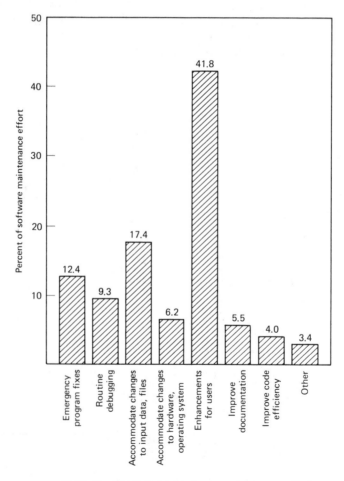

FIGURE 30–11   Distribution of software maintenance effort

the software maintenance activity as defined here. Thus, achieving error free software development does not eliminate the need for a significant budget level for software maintenance.

The major portion (41.8%) of the software maintenance effort is devoted to software updates (enhancements for users). Figure 30–12 shows how the software update effort is typically distributed, in terms of the reports produced by the software system. It becomes clear from this distribution that (at least for business data processing) flexible data structures and report generation capabilities play an important part in improving software maintenance efficiency.

The distribution of effort by activity in Fig. 30–11 is the key to quantifying the cost (or percent of maintenance budget) portion of the software maintenance production function in Fig. 30–9, in that the cumulative activity percentages in Fig. 30–9 are derived from the corresponding activity percentages in Fig. 30–11 (12.4% for Emergency program fixes in the investment segment of Fig. 30–9, etc.).

The most significant feature of the resulting production function in Fig. 30–9

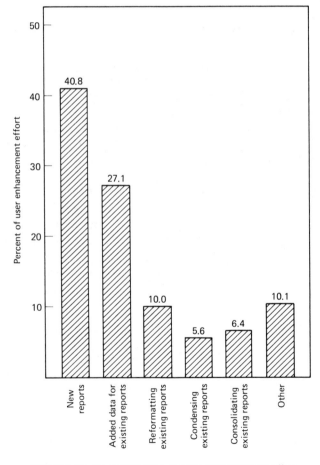

FIGURE 30–12 Distribution of user-enhancement effort

is the very high fraction of maintenance effort (40 to 50%) consumed by the investment segment. This represents an ever-present monkey on the maintenance staff's back: a load of nondiscretionary work which has to be performed just to keep the system's value at roughly its current level. Clearly, this is an area in which the use of modern programming practices to reduce the need for emergency fixing and to minimize the side effects of environmental changes can have a powerful effect on the morale and effectiveness of the maintenance staff, and on the organization's mission in general.

From a life-cycle planning aspect, the main lesson for us in the maintenance production function is that *software maintenance is not optional.* For each dollar spent on software development, another dollar needs to be budgeted just to keep the software viable over its life-cycle; after that another optional dollar can be spent on desirable enhancements over the life-cycle. A project to develop a long-life software product, which allocates significantly less budget for maintenance than for development, "because software doesn't wear out and doesn't have to be maintained," is a project with some painful surprises ahead.* Some good sources of practical software maintenance techniques are [Parikh, 1980] and [Glass-Noiseux, 1981].

30.6 SOFTWARE MAINTENANCE PROJECT DATA

Table 30–6 presents the software project data used to validate the COCOMO maintenance model. It consists of 14 projects from the COCOMO data base of fully described projects (Table 29–1), and 10 additional projects for which only summary development and maintenance data were known.

The 14 fully-described projects are specified and their annual maintenance effort estimated using a variant of the COCOMO CLEF form as described in Section 9.5. The differences from the standard CLEF form are

Column 1 Contains the project number from the COCOMO data base (Table 29–1), the type, year developed, and language for the product

Column 3 Used to eliminate the requirements volatility (RVOL) factor during maintenance; its effects are covered during maintenance by the annual change traffic (ACT) parameter

Column 21 The annual change traffic (ACT) for the project

Column 22 The estimated annual maintenance effort $(MM)_{AM,E}$

Column 23 The actual annual maintenance effort $(MM)_{AM,A}$

Column 24 The relative error $[(MM)_{AM,E} - (MM)_{AM,A}]/(MM)_{AM,A}$, in percent.

The 10 summary projects contain the project development effort in Column 20. Their estimated annual maintenance effort is calculated as

$$(MM)_{AM,E} = (MM)_{DEV} (ACT)$$

* Again, this conclusion refers to larger, long-life products. As indicated in the [Kendall–Lamb, 1977] study, which found a median application program size of 400 DSI and a median program lifetime of 14 months, there are many small, short-lived programs which require less maintenance planning and budget.

Project: *Maintenance Estimates verses Actuals: I* Analyst: _____ Project: _____ Date: _____

PROJ. NO.	TYPE	YR	LANG	KDSI	(2) Mode	(3) RVOL	(4) RELY	(5) DATA	(6) CPLX	(7) TIME	(8) STOR	(9) VIRT	(10) TURN	(11) ACAP	(12) AEXP	(13) PCAP	(14) VEXP	(15) LEXP	(16) MODP	(17) TOOL	(18) SCED	(19) EAF	(20) MM NOM	(21) ACT	(22) MM EST	(23) MM ACT	(24) E−A/A
1	BUS	72	COB	113	E	1.0 / 1.19	1.15 / 0.88							1.0	1.0 / 1.13	1.0	1.0	1.0	1.39 / 1.24		1.0 / 1.04	2.59 / 2.72	814	0.05	105	156	−33
3	BUS	77	PLI	132	SD									1.0 / 0.86		1.0 / 0.86			0.85 / 0.91			0.43 / 0.34	711	0.04	12.2	12	2
14	CTL	77	MOL	3.0	SD	1.0 / 1.19	0.98 / 1.15					1.0 / 1.15					1.0 / 1.10	1.0 / 1.07	1.12 / 1.10		1.0 / 1.23	2.57 / 5.86	10.3	0.15	4.0	6	−33
22	HMI	76	JOV	118	E														0.85		1.0 / 1.23	0.71 / 0.94	858	0.33	201	180	12
23	HMI	78	HOL	77	E														0.91		1.0 / 1.23	0.72 / 0.89	514	0.25	93	120	−22
28	HMI	72	MOL	13	ORG							1.0 / 1.15							1.14 / 1.10			2.53 / 2.81	47	0.12	14	8	75
32	SCI	72	FTN	390	SD									1.0 / 0.71			0.90 / 1.0	0.95 / 1.0	1.19 / 1.10	1.0 / 1.10		0.88 / 0.57	2394	0.08	169	186	−10
38	SCI	77	PLI	15	ORG														0.76 / 0.82			0.32 / 0.35	55	0.33	5.8	4	45
39	SCI	64	FTN	6.2	ORG										0.91 / 1.0		0.90 / 1.0		0.89 / 0.91			0.34 / 0.39	22	0.40	3.0	24	25
51	SUP	70	COB	10	ORG	1.0 / 1.38	1.15 / 0.88								1.0 / 1.0		0.90 / 1.0		1.30 / 1.24		1.0 / 1.04	2.48 / 3.18	36	0.03	2.7	3	−10

TABLE 30–6 Software Maintenance Project Data—I

551

Project: _Maintenance Estimates versus Actuals: II_ Analyst: _____ Date: _____

PROJ. NO.	TYPE	YR	LANG.	(2) KDSI	Mode	(3) RVOL	(4) RELY	(5) DATA	(6) CPLX	(7) TIME	(8) STOR	(9) VIRT	(10) TURN	(11) ACAP	(12) AEXP	(13) PCAP	(14) VEXP	(15) LEXP	(16) MODP	(17) TOOL	(18) SCED	(19) EAF	(20) NOM	(21) ACT	(22) MM EST	(23) MM ACT	(24) E-A/A
52	SUP	71	MOL	82	ORG	1.0	1.15					1.0				1.17			1.30	1.0		1.74	29	0.05	2.5	3	−17
						1.38	0.88									1.0			1.24	1.10		1.90					
56	SYS	71	MOL	27	E	1.0	0.98					0.87			0.82		1.0	1.0	1.16	1.16	1.0	1.47	146	0.025	5.4	12	−55
						1.38	1.15					1.0			0.91		1.10	1.07	1.10	1.10	1.08	3.68					
58	SYS	76	MOL	25	E		1.10							1.0	1.0	1.0	1.0	1.0	0.86			1.63	133	0.05	10.8	12	−10
							1.40							0.71		0.70			0.91			1.09					
18	HMI	70	FTN	320	E	1.0	0.98					1.0			0.91	1.17	0.90	0.95	1.43	1.0	1.0	2.86	2840	0.010	812	900	−10
						1.19	1.15							0.86	1.0	1.0	1.0	1.0	1.24	1.10	1.08	3.89					

SUMMARY DATA ONLY

MM DEV

PROJ. NO.	TYPE	YR	LANG.	(2) KDSI																		(19) EAF	(20) NOM	(21) ACT	(22) MM EST	(23) MM ACT	(24) E-A/A
M1	BUS	76	COB	50																			300	0.06	18	12	50
M2	BUS	77	COB	100																			480	0.008	38	36	6
M3	BUS	77	COB	63																			273	0.01	2.7	6	−55
M4	CTL	75	MOL	26																			288	0.007	20	18	11
M5	HMI	74	FTN	204																			2250	0.20	450	156	−40
M6	SCI	76	FTN	12																			46	0.33	15	6	150
M7	SCI	77	FTN	42																			281	0.024	6.7	59	14
M8	SCI	77	FTN	176																			877	0.10	88	70	26
M9	SCI	78	FTN	25																			40	0.020	8	20	−60
M10	SYS	76	MOL	65																			1115	0.06	67	72	−7

TABLE 30-6 Software Maintenance Project Data—II

This calculation assumes that the cost driver attribute ratings during maintenance are the same as those for development. Since this is not generally true, as can be seen from the 14 fully described projects, we would expect that the summary data projects would exhibit a wider range of variation between estimates and actuals than the fully described project. This is indeed the case; two of the summary data projects are off by factors of 2.5, for example. Still, as was seen in Fig. 30–4, the range of variation is not unreasonable.

30.7 QUESTIONS

30.1. What types of project activity are included in and excluded from the COCOMO definition of software maintenance?

30.2. Define the following terms: software maintenance, software update, software repair, annual change traffic, cards-per-person ratio, corrective maintenance, adaptive maintenance, perfective maintenance.

30.3. The Standard University Kinesiology Department has budgeted $100K to develop the software for its microcomputer-based track-and-field performance data analysis system, but has not budgeted any funds for software life-cycle maintenance. How much additional money is the University likely to need to cover maintenance of this software?

30.4. The Hunt National Bank is developing a life-cycle plan for its large electronic fund transfer system, whose development is estimated to require 3000 man-months. The planning group estimates that the maintenance cost driver attributes ratings will be very similar to the development ratings, and that the annual change traffic will be at about the 25th percentile with respect to the COCOMO data base of software maintenance projects. How many people should Hunt National Bank plan for to support maintenance of the EFT software?

30.5. State the five "laws of large program evolution." How do they fit your experience on large programs? How do they fit your experience on small programs? Can you think of other laws which might be equally valid and important?

30.6. The Standard University Computer Center has three candidate activities which are near the high-payoff–diminishing-returns borderline of the Computer Center's software maintenance production function (Fig. 30–9).

- Acquiring a program development library capability
- Developing a computer-aided instruction and "help" capability for computer center users
- Reworking the university personnel data base and associated programs using data-abstraction techniques to improve its maintainability

Each activity has a similar cost, and the Computer Center has funds to support only one of the three. Using the evaluation techniques presented in Part III, determine which activity should be supported. What additional information might you need to make a sound decision?

30.7. If all three of the above activities have considerable merit, develop a rationale, based on the techniques presented in Part III, which might convince Standard University to support all three activities.

30.8. The Hunt National Bank currently employs 400 people to maintain a large body of software developed with poor software reliability practices. Assuming that the level of the bank's corrective maintenance activities is equal to that given in Fig. 30–10, use the distribution of errors by phase in Fig. 24–8 and the curve of relative cost-to-fix errors by phase in Fig. 4–2 to determine how many of the 400 people could have been saved for more useful and stimulating activities if all of the errors had been fixed during the phase in which they were committed.

30.8 TOPICS FOR FURTHER RESEARCH

30.A. Practically all of the topics for further research into the quantitative aspects of software development identified in Chapters 24 through 28 provide counterpart research opportunities for software maintenance: characterizing the influence and interplay of cost driver attributes, investigating the effect of cost drivers on individual activities, developing simplified or more accurate relationships which apply in limited contexts, etc. Identify an appropriate research topic given for software development and pursue its maintenance counterpart.

30.B. Perform experiments and observations to test the hypotheses that the maintenance RELY and MODP effort multipliers in Tables 30–1 and 30–2

- are of the same magnitudes used in COCOMO
- are independent of project type or mode
- vary by size (MODP) as in COCOMO
- interact multiplicatively with the other COCOMO cost driver attributes

30.C. Collect and analyze data on the effect of using modern programming practices on the individual activities involved in software maintenance (see, for example, [Curtis and others, 1979a]).

30.D. Investigate the effect of other factors on software maintenance

- Programming language (see, for example, [Graver and others, 1977], [Dunsmore–Gannon, 1979])
- Quality and quantity of documentation (see, for example, [Shneiderman and others, 1977])
- Release frequency (see, for example, [Adams, 1980])
- Concepts of evolution dynamics (see, for example, [Woodside, 1980])
- User familiarity with data processing (see, for example, [Lientz–Swanson, 1980])
- Other factors identified as significant in [Lientz–Swanson, 1980]

30.E. Analyze the projects in the COCOMO maintenance data base (Table 30–6) for such phenomena as

- regularities in the data with respect to project type or size
- characteristics which tend to vary most between development and maintenance
- other possible estimating relationships

30.F. The simple ratio models discussed in Section 30.4 sometimes work reasonably well for a highly homogeneous software maintenance activity. Determine the range of variability of these ratios for a particular installation, and evaluate their estimation utility for the installation.

30.G. An earlier definition of annual change traffic also included a contributing factor for amount of code deleted. It was dropped because its effect was relatively insignificant in most cases and difficult to characterize in others. Investigate the effect of code deletion on maintenance effort.

30.H. A software maintenance activity is actually a mini-development cycle in which the existing software might be considered as a large piece of off-the-shelf software to be adapted to form the new product. Investigate this approach to software maintenance cost estimation with respect to the COCOMO model for software adaptation in Section 8.8.

30.I. The software maintenance production function in Fig. 30–9 is a somewhat gross approximation, in that the individual activities comprising software maintenance are distributed along the curve (each with its own investment, high payoff, and diminishing returns segments) rather than being lumped into categories as in Fig. 30–9. Develop a more accurate software maintenance production function for a particular installation in terms of its objectives and activities.

30.J. Most large software installations attain a development–maintenance equilibrium, in which the level of software maintenance is determined by the balance of newly developed products entering the software maintenance inventory and old products being phased out. Based on the data in [Lientz–Swanson, 1980], p. 41, or other data available from a particular installation, develop a Markovian birth/death model which explains the level of maintenance activity and distribution of product lifetimes over the sample of data analyzed.

30.K. Generalize the results in Question 30.8 into a life-cycle model of the relative costs of error elimination in software development versus maintenance.

Chapter 31

K⊐K⊐K⊐K⊐K⊐K⊐K⊐K⊐K⊐K⊐K⊐X

Software Life-Cycle
Cost Estimation

31.1 INTRODUCTION

The primary software life-cycle cost components we have covered so far have been the labor costs of software development, maintenance, and adaptation of existing software. There are a number of other cost components which may be important in a software life-cycle cost analysis, such as conversion, installation, training, computer costs, publications, travel, etc. For these quantities, even less information is available to support estimation of their costs. This chapter summarizes the data and estimating relationships which are available, and concludes with an overall software life-cycle cost-benefit analysis example to show how the techniques are applied.

Estimation of software conversion costs is covered in Section 31.2, which presents a set of basic definitions and cost-estimating relationships (CERs) for conversion, and in Section 31.3, which compares the CERs with project data and other conversion CERs. Section 31.4 discusses CERs for software installation and training; Section 31.5 covers computer costs; Section 31.6 covers publications costs, and Section 31.7 covers other software-related life-cycle costs. Finally, Section 31.8 shows how these

556

techniques are used in a software life-cycle cost-benefit analysis for the development of a software system for equipment management and inventory control.

31.2 SOFTWARE CONVERSION COST-ESTIMATING RELATIONSHIPS

Software conversion costs can be a highly significant component of software life-cycle costs. The U.S. General Accounting Office estimated in 1977 that the annual cost of software conversion activities in the U.S. Government was about $450 million per year [GAO, 1977a]. Particularly when a software life-cycle cost analysis involves the evolution of a large inventory of software to one of several possible new computer configurations, the relative conversion costs can be the critical decision item upon which the best choice of alternatives will depend.

Definitions

The conversion costs covered by COCOMO estimates include the following major activities identified in the software work breakdown structure activity hierarchy of Fig. 4–6b: conversion of programs, data bases, and documentation; validation testing and acceptance testing of the converted software; and preparation of conversion summary reports. The estimated conversion costs do not cover costs of installation, operational demonstrations, or training; nor does conversion cover the costs of continuing adaptive maintenance of a software product to new operating system versions, evolutionary changes in the master data base, or changes in the number of tape drives or on-line terminals in the hardware configuration.

The particular tasks accounting for conversion costs are the following [Oliver, 1979]:

1. *Feasibility Analysis.* Analyzing the inventory of current systems, documenting the conversion aspects of existing systems, determining the best conversion approach.
2. *Conversion Planning.* Reorganizing the system to be converted around the new computer configuration, scheduling conversion tasks, developing conversion acceptance criteria, test standards, and test plans.
3. *Conversion Preparation.* Generating and verifying test data, preparation of conversion aids (scanners, translators, comparators, file conversion programs, etc.), assembling conversion material and backups.
4. *Conversion.* Conversion of programs, data, and documentation; associated configuration management and quality assurance activities.
5. *Integration and Test.* Unit, subsystem, software system and acceptance test.

Further description of the nature of these tasks is given in [Oliver, 1979].

Conversion Cost-Estimating Relationships

Software conversion costs are estimated in COCOMO by considering conversion as an instance of adaptation of existing software for a new application. The effects of adapted software are handled in COCOMO by calculating an equivalent number of delivered source instructions (EDSI), which are used in place of DSI in the other COCOMO estimating relationships. The quantity EDSI is calculated from the following estimated adaptation quantities:

ADSI   *Adapted DSI.* The number of delivered source instructions adapted from existing software to form the new product.

DM   *Percent Design Modified.* The percentage of the adapted software's design which is modified in order to adapt it to the new objectives and environment. (This is necessarily a subjective quantity.)

CM   *Percent Code Modified.* The percentage of the adapted software's code which is modified in order to adapt it to the new objectives and environment.

IM   *Percent of Integration Required for Modified Software.* The percentage of effort required to integrate the adapted software into an overall product, as compared to the normal amount of integration effort for software of comparable size.

The equations for calculating EDSI involve an intermediate quantity, the adaptation adjustment factor (AAF), which is calculated as follows:

$$AAF = 0.40(DM) + 0.30(CM) + 0.30(IM) \tag{8-1}$$

$$EDSI = (ADSI)\frac{AAF}{100} \tag{8-2}$$

For conversion effort estimation, the adaptation adjustment factor (AAF) is increased by an additional *conversion planning increment* (CPI) to cover the added costs of feasibility analysis and planning not included in the adaptation effort estimates. The rating for the CPI is

CPI	Level of Conversion Analysis and Planning
0	None
1	Simple conversion schedule, acceptance plan
2	Detailed conversion schedule, test and acceptance plans
3	Add basic analysis of existing inventory of code and data
4	Add detailed inventory, basic documentation of existing system
5	Add detailed inventory, detailed documentation of existing system

The modified equations for calculating EDSI via the conversion adjustment factor (CAF) are then

$$CAF = AAF + CPI \tag{31-1}$$

$$EDSI = (ADSI)\frac{CAF}{100} \tag{31-2}$$

The quantity EDSI can then be used to calculate a simple conversion estimate using the appropriate Basic COCOMO effort equation, or EDSI can be used in concert with a set of cost driver attribute ratings to calculate an Intermediate COCOMO or Detailed COCOMO estimate. In these latter situations, the maintenance versions of the RELY and MODP effort multiplier tables, (Tables 30–1 and 30–2) should be used, as they better reflect the difficulties of converting unreliable, poorly-structured, poorly-documented software.

Example

As an example, let us perform a more detailed conversion estimate for the example in Section 8.8, involving the conversion of a 50–KDSI organic-mode FORTRAN electronic circuit analysis program from a Univac 1110 computer to an IBM 3033. In this example, we will again suppose that the overlay structure of the electronic circuit analysis program and the change from a 36-bit Univac 1110 word size to a 32-bit IBM 3033 word size require some redesign of the program for efficiency and accuracy considerations. Typically, for this situation, we would have

DM = 15   (some changes in overlay structure, numerical algorithms, and related logic)

CM = 30   (in this range, code changes often run about twice the rate of design changes)

IM = 10   (largely to accommodate overlay changes)

We also estimate a conversion planning increment CPI = 3 for this level of conversion. The resulting estimate of EDSI for conversion would be

$$AAF = 0.40(15) + 0.30(30) + 0.30(10) = 18$$

$$CAF = 18 + 3 = 21$$

$$EDSI = (50,000)\frac{21}{100} = 10,500$$

The conversion effort for the program, using the Intermediate COCOMO Component Level Estimating Form (CLEF), is shown in Fig. 31–1. The estimate is based on nominal ratings for most cost drivers, high ratings for the attributes RELY, CPLX, STOR, VEXP, and LEXP, and a very high rating for applications experience AEXP.

Project: Circuit Analysis Prog Conversion   Analyst: C. Page   Date: 1/1/84

			Product			Computer																	
(1)	(2)	(3)	(4)	(5)	(6)	(7)	(8)	(9)	(10)	(11)	(12)	(13)	(14)	(15)	(16)	(17)	(18)	(19)	(20)	(21)	(22)	(23)	(24)
Component	EDSI	AAF	RELY	DATA	CPLX	TIME	STOR	VIRT.	TURN	ACAP	AEXP	PCAP	VEXP	LEXP	MODP	TODL	SCED	EAF	MM NOM	MM DEV/AM	EDSI/MM ACT	$K	$/EDSI
1. ECAP	10.5	21	HI 0.98	–	HI 1.15	–	HI 1.06	–	–	–	VHI 0.82	–	HI 0.90	HI 0.90	–	–	–	0.84	38	32			
2.																							
3.																							
4.																							
5.																							
6.																							
7.																							
8.																							
9.																							
10.																							
11. Total EDSI	10.5																	Totals		32			
12. (MM)NOM	38																	Schedule (months)					
13. (EDSI/MM)NOM	276																						

Development mode: Organic

FIGURE 31-1 Electronic circuit analysis program conversion estimate

The resulting conversion effort estimate of 32 MM is somewhat higher, but still in the same range as the earlier rough estimate of 26 MM.

31.3 SOFTWARE CONVERSION ESTIMATES VERSUS ACTUALS

Figure 31–2 compares the COCOMO conversion estimates versus data from nine conversion activities. The estimates are reasonably close to the actuals, but the sample size is relatively small and uniform: eight of the nine data points are from a single installation.

The data from the nine projects are given in Table 31–1, a variant of the Intermediate COCOMO CLEF form used to perform the conversion estimates. The differences from the standard CLEF form are

Column 1   Contains a conversion project number, the type, computer size, and programming language for the conversion project ($X \rightarrow Y$ signifies a conversion from language or computer X to language or computer Y)

Column 2   The total KDSI and computed equivalent KDSI for the conversion

Column 3   The conversion planning increment (CPI) and the conversion adjustment factor (CAF) for the project

Column 21   The estimated conversion effort $(MM)_{C,E}$

Column 22   The actual conversion effort $(MM)_{C,A}$

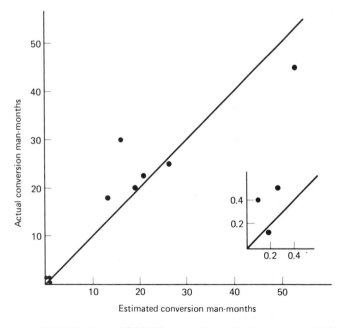

FIGURE 31–2 COCOMO conversion estimates versus actuals

TABLE 31-1 Software Conversion Estimates and Project Data

Project Number	(1) Type	Completely	Language	(2) TDT KDSI / EDSI	(3) CPI / CAF	Product Attributes (4) RELY	(5) DATA	(6) CPLX	Computer Attributes (7) TIME	(8) STOR	(9) VIRT	(10) TURN	Personnel Attribution (11) ACAP	(12) AEXP	(13) PCAP	(14) VEXP	(15) LEXP	Project Attributes (16) MODP	(17) TOOL	(18) SCED	(19) EAF	(20) MM NOM	(21) MM EST	(22) MM ACT	(23) (E−A)/A	(24) DM CM IM
C1	BUS	MAX	COB	25 / 3	5 / 11.5	LO 1.15	VHI 1.16	N	N	HI 1.06	HI 1.15	HI 1.07	N	VHI 0.82	N	N	HI 0.95	LO 1.10	LO 1.10	N	1.64	10	16	30	−47	5 10 5
C2	CTL	MIN	MOL →FN	8.4 / 5.3	3 / 63	LO 1.15		HI 1.15	HI 1.11	HI 1.06			HI 0.86	VHI 0.82	HI 0.86		HI 0.95	LO 1.08	LO 1.10		1.07	18	19	20	−5	0 100 100
C3	SCI	MAX	FN	55 / 4.4	2 / 8	LO 1.15		HI 1.15		VHI 1.21			HI 0.86	HI 0.91		LO 1.10	HI 0.95	LO 1.14	LO 1.10		1.42	15	21	23	−9	0 15 5
C4	SCI	MAX →MID	FN	0.6 / 0.04	6.5 / 2	VLO 1.35							HI 0.86	VHI 0.82	HI 0.86		HI 0.95				0.74	0.11	0.08	0.40	−80	0 10 5
C5	SCI	MAX	FN	58 / 2.3	2 / 4					HI 1.06		VHI 1.15	HI 0.86	HI 0.91	LO 1.17		HI 0.95	LO 1.14	LO 1.10		1.63	8	13	18	−28	0 5 2
C6	SCI	MAX	FN	4 / 0.12	1 / 3			HI 1.15					HI 0.86	HI 0.82	HI 0.86		HI 0.95	VHI 0.92	VHI 0.83		0.51	.35	.18	0.13	38	0 5 2
C7	SUP	MAX	FN	4 / 0.16	2 / 4			HI 1.15					HI 0.86	VHI 0.82	HI 0.86		HI 0.95		HI 0.91		0.54	.47	.25	0.50	−50	0 5 2
C8	SYS	MAX	HOL	100 / 14.5	3 / 14.5	LO 0.94	LO 0.94	HI 1.15					HI 0.86	HI 0.91	LO 1.17						0.99	53	52	45	16	10 15 10
C9	SYS	MAX	HOL	100 / 11	3 / 11	LO 0.94	LO 0.94	HI 1.15					HI 0.86	VHI 0.82		HI 0.90	HI 0.95				0.65	40	26	25	4	5 15 5

Key to rating: VLO = very low; LO = low; N = nominal (value of 1.0); HI = high; VHI = very high

Column 23   The relative error $[(MM)_{C,E} - (MM)_{C,A}]/(MM)_{C,A}$, in percent

Column 24   The adaptation parameters DM, CM, and IM for the conversion project

Other Software Conversion Data and Models

Very little is available in the way of data and models to support software conversion cost estimation. A very good treatment of the subject is [Oliver, 1979], which provides a partial task-unit model for estimating the various components of software conversion cost, backed up by a thorough set of definitions and a fairly sizable sample of conversion cost data.

The overall cost-estimating relationships provided by [Oliver, 1979] are shown in Table 31–2, along with some derived quantities and comparable COCOMO estimates.

The Oliver DSI/MM figure for conversion is based on a figure of $3100 per MM derived from the labor cost data in [Oliver, 1979]. The COCOMO CAF is obtained by taking the midpoint of the Oliver "percent manually converted" range and adding a CPI increment of 2.5 to 3%. The COCOMO DSI/MM figures are then based on assuming a typical development productivity of

$$(DSI/MM)_{DEV} = 300$$

and using the relationship

$$\frac{CAF}{100} = \frac{(MM)_{CONV}}{(MM)_{DEV}} = \frac{(DSI/MM)_{DEV}}{(DSI/MM)_{CONV}}$$

or

$$(DSI/MM)_{CONV} = \frac{300}{(CAF/100)} = \frac{30,000}{CAF}$$

The agreement between COCOMO and the [Oliver, 1979] estimates is not strong, but it is within the range of variation of the inputs. The main advantage of the COCOMO approach is that its effort estimates are a more consistent function of the amount of code to be converted.

TABLE 31–2 Conversion Cost Estimating Relationships

| Percent of Code Manually Converted | [Oliver, 1979] | | | COCOMO | |
	Sample Size	$/DSI	DSI/MM	DSI/MM	COCOMO CAF
0–10%	30	$1.70	1823	3750	8
10–25%	15	2.83	1095	1500	20
25–50%	9	3.12	993	750	40

Other useful conversion cost distribution information in [Oliver, 1979] includes

Labor Grade Distribution:	7%	Management
(percent of effort)	76%	Technical
	7%	Support
	10%	Clerical
Cost Distribution:	60%	Labor
(percent of cost)	25%	Computer
	15%	Miscellaneous
Activity Distribution:	25%	Preparation
	15%	Translation
	50%	Testing
	10%	Installation

Another approach to estimation of conversion (and other maintenance effort) costs is given in [Dittman, 1980]. This approach categorizes a number of software transfer situations (new hardware, new OS, inadequate documentation, reliability, etc.), and provides functional forms for estimating the cost of performing the transfer, using parameter values obtained from a survey of software installations in government and industry. The formulas for software conversion are expressed in terms of the number of DSI to be converted, the percentages of effort required by systems analysts, senior programmers, and junior programmers for various types of conversion jobs, and the unit productivity for software modification by type of performer. Table 31–3 summarizes the unit productivity figures obtained in the survey, in terms of mean values and 90% confidence limits. The figures are given in DSI/MM.

Recently, a landmark study of software conversion cost estimation techniques has been completed by the U.S. Federal Conversion Support Center (FCSC) [Houtz-Buschbach, 1981]. The study provides a thorough categorization, summary, and comparative analysis of a number of conversion cost estimating techniques. It also presents a well-balanced (partly algorithmic, partly task-unit) software conversion cost estimation model developed by FCSC. Although the FCSC model has not been fully calibrated and validated, its estimates appear to be reasonable and consistent. It has a number of highly attractive features, including a careful definition of terms, a program conversion formula similar to the COCOMO adaptation-adjustment-factor approach,

TABLE 31–3 Software Modification Code Rates

Position	Software Modification Productivity in DSI/MM Mean Value (90% Confidence Limits)		
	Applications	Operating Systems	Compilers
Systems analyst	1460 (1090–1810)	940 (670–1230)	550 (290–820)
Senior programmer	1520 (1200–1840)	940 (650–1250)	590 (360–820)
Junior programmer	1140 (880–1400)	—	—

and a great deal more capability in estimating other conversion tasks such as data base conversion, redocumentation, and site preparation.

31.4 SOFTWARE INSTALLATION AND TRAINING COST ESTIMATION

Definitions

Software installation costs include the costs of software activities associated with the integration of the accepted software into the complex of facilities, equipment, personnel, and procedures constituting the users' operational system. They do not include costs of installing computer hardware (which, incidentally, are typically charged at about 3% of the hardware purchase cost). They do include the costs of installation planning, activities, testing, and reports as indicated in the software work breakdown structure in Fig. 4–6b. Installation activities include the following:

- User management orientation
- Accommodation of user-site idiosyncracies: computer model, operating system version, DBMS version, job control language, type and number of peripherals, communications interfaces, system interfaces, etc.
- Preparation of operational data base
- Trial of software capabilities in the user's operational environment, and associated error fixing, documentation update, and consulting
- Post-installation audit

A good detailed checklist of installation tasks is given in [Hice and others, 1974].

Software training costs include the training of users, operations personnel, and data preparation personnel; and the training of software maintenance personnel if they are different from the development personnel. Training costs for software development personnel are included in the effort multipliers for personnel experience (applications, virtual machine, language).

Installation and training project costs as defined above do not include the costs of user participation in installation and training activities (for example, the labor costs of operators being trained). This is appropriate for software project cost estimation, but for software product cost-benefit analyses, the user costs should also be estimated and included.

Installation and Training Cost Data and Models

Data on software installation and training costs are fairly scarce and scattered. Table 31–4 summarizes the COCOMO data base information on installation and training costs, categorized by type of installation activity, in terms of the percentage of software development effort required for installation and training.

TABLE 31-4 Software Installation and Training Costs: COCOMO Data Base

Type of Installation Activity	Number of Projects	Percent of Development Effort	
		Installation	Training
Application program on existing general-purpose computer	4	0, 0, 0.2, 0.6	0, 10, 1.2, 3
Application program on different general-purpose computer	3	0.2, 0.5, 1.8	2, 0, 2.7
Process Control, new computer	3	3, 3, 4	1.3, 1.3, 1.9
Human-machine system, several installations			
3 installations, similar	1	8	6
5 installations, similar	1	6	3
16 installations, similar	1	18	7
3 installations, many differences	1	20	6
8 installations, some differences	1	14	8

Other data in installation costs include a total of 2.3% of development costs from the U.S. Air Force PARMIS data base [Gehring, 1976]: 1.8% for operational test and approval, 0.3% for user review and coordination, and 0.2% for preparing the system for release. The 1979 GRC model [Carriere–Thibodeau, 1979] estimates installation costs as 0.075 times the number of output formats; this works out to an installation cost estimate of 2.5–7.5% of development costs, based on the GRC model's relationships between output formats and development effort.

Recommended Estimation Procedures

Since installation and training costs are so variable and application-specific, the recommended approach to cost estimation is to use the task-unit approach: Break up the installation and training functions into individual tasks and estimate the cost of each (remembering to include such project-wide activities as management and support tasks). The data above may then be used as a rough crosscheck on the task-unit estimates.

31.5 COMPUTER COST ESTIMATION FOR SOFTWARE DEVELOPMENT

The amount of computer time used during software development is highly variable, depending on a number of factors such as the relative scarcity of hardware and software resources. The strongest example of this that I can recall occurred on my first day as a computer programmer, in 1955. My supervisor took me around the computer mainframe, which occupied most of a large room, and told me:

"Now listen. We're paying this computer six hundred dollars an hour, and we're paying you two dollars an hour, and I want you to act accordingly."

Although this initial conditioning was valuable to me in impressing good habits of desk checking, test planning, and analyzing before coding, it also created some bad habits—a preoccupation with saving microseconds, patching object code, etc.—which took me years to unlearn after the balance of hardware and software costs began to tip the other way.

The wide variation in the computer usage data given below reflects this type of concern. It also reflects a number of other phenomena such as the use of timesharing, automated aids, and modern programming practices. As a result, it is very difficult to formulate a set of computer-time estimating relationships which cover all of the various situations which may arise in software development.

Existing Data and Estimating Relationships

Data and estimating relationships for the cost of computer time during software development have centered around three ratios

CHR/KDSI	Number of computer hours per thousand DSI
CHR/MM$_{DEV}$	Number of computer hours per development man-month
$C/$MM	Computer costs as a fraction of development labor costs

Table 31–5 summarizes the results of a number of studies which have included data or estimating relationships for computer time and costs. It is difficult to find a strong consensus among these sources, except to say that there tends to be some clustering around the areas of 15 to 20 CHR/KDSI and 3 to 4 CHR/MM$_{DEV}$, and that all of the data fall within the ranges of the [Jones, 1977] estimates.

Computer Time Data in the COCOMO Data Base

The COCOMO data base contains computer time data for only 17 of the 63 projects. As seen in Table 31–6, the data again appear to be highly variable, although there may be some patterns and trends. These are emphasized (perhaps overly so) by the order in which the data are presented, and also by Figs. 31–3 and 31–4, which show histograms of CHR/KDSI and CHR/MM$_{DEV}$, coded by the type of computer used for development (X = Maxi, D = Midi, N = Mini, C = Micro). The main trends which can be seen are

- Computer time per KDSI or MM is considerably higher on the smaller computers
- Computer time per KDSI or MM is higher on delivered real-time hardware–software systems than on general computer center applications
- CHR/MM$_{DEV}$ tends to vary less than CHR/KDSI

TABLE 31–5 Computer Time and Cost Ratios

Source	Application Type	Size	$\dfrac{\text{CHR}}{\text{KDSI}}$	$\dfrac{\text{CHR}}{\text{MM}_{\text{DEV}}}$	$\dfrac{\$C}{\$MM}$
[Farr and others, 1965]	General	Medium-large	17		
[Wolverton, 1974]	Human-machine	Large	20–30	2–3	20–25%
[Aron–Arthur, 1975]	Familiar	All		6	
	Unfamiliar	All		8	
	Real-time	All		12	
[ADPESO, 1976]	Systems, maxi	Intermediate	1	1	
	Systems, mini	Intermediate	14	14	
[Black and others, 1977]	General	All		3	
[Daly, 1977]	Real-time, no simulation	All	100		
	Real-time, with simulation	All	40		
[Graver and others, 1977]	General	All	20	4	
[Herd and others, 1977]	General	All		4–5	6%
[Jones, 1977]	General	Small	0.2–2	0.15–1.5	
		Intermediate	0.5–4	0.25–2	
		Medium	1–10	0.3–3	
		Large	5–100	0.8–16	
		Very large	10–200	1–20	
[Walston–Felix, 1977]	General	All			10–34%
[Carriere–Thibodeau, 1979]	General	All		2–4	

Recommended Estimating Procedures

Based primarily on the patterns in the COCOMO data, a set of computer time estimating relationships is presented in Table 31–7, in terms of the ratio $\text{CHR}/\text{MM}_{\text{DEV}}$ and a basic characterization of projects in terms of size and the nature of the delivered products.

In using Table 31–7, we would

1. Identify the type of development computer and nature of our software product (such as a minicomputer-based hardware–software process control system).
2. Determine the resulting $\text{CHR}/\text{MM}_{\text{DEV}}$ from Table 31–7 (here, 9 CHR/MM_{DEV}).
3. Determine MM_{DEV} via the appropriate COCOMO model (say, 150 MM).
4. Compute $\text{CHR} = (\text{MM}_{\text{DEV}})(\text{CHR}/\text{MM}_{\text{DEV}})$ (here, $150 \times 9 = 1350$ computer hours).

TABLE 31–6 Computer Time Ratios in COCOMO Data Base

Computer Type	TIME Rating	TURN Rating	Application Type	COCOMO Project Number	KDSI	MM_{DEV}	CHR	$\dfrac{CHR}{KDSI}$	$\dfrac{CHR}{MM_{DEV}}$
Maxi	Nominal	Low	BUS	7	6.9	8	2	0.3	0.25
Maxi	Nominal	Low	SCI	38	15	12	2.3	0.15	0.2
Maxi	Nominal	Low	SYS	61	28	50	12	0.4	0.2
Maxi	Nominal	Nominal	BUS	5	16	33	92	6	2.8
Maxi	Nominal	Nominal	SCI	39	6.2	8	30	4.8	3.8
Maxi	Nominal	Nominal	SUP	48	311	1272	2758	8.9	2.2
Maxi	Nominal	High	BUS	2	249	1600	10000	40	6.7
Maxi	High	Low-nominal	HMI	19	966	6600	14000	14	2.1
Midi	Nominal	Nominal	BUS	6	4	43	107	27	2.5
Mini	Nominal	Low	SCI	40	2.5	8	8	3.2	1.0
Mini	Nominal-high	Low	HMI	24	90	453	2400	27	5.3
Mini	High	Nominal	CTL	12	37	201	2000	54	10.0
Mini	High	Nominal	SYS	57	15	237	1500	100	6.3
Mini	Very high	Low	SUP	50	24	176	330	14	1.9
Mini	Very high	Nominal	CTL	9	30	423	3500	117	8.3
Mini	Extra high	Nominal	SYS	58	25	130	1600	64	12.3
Micro	High	Nominal	SYS	62	9.1	38	800	88	21.0

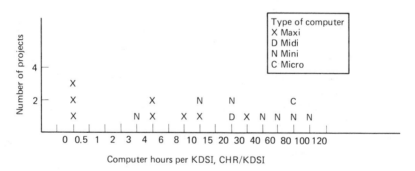

FIGURE 31–3 Histogram of computer hours/KDSI, COCOMO data base

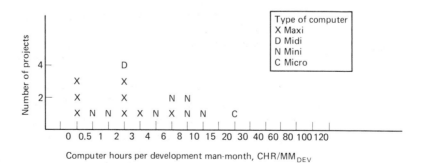

FIGURE 31–4 Histogram of computer hours/MM, COCOMO data base

TABLE 31-7 Computer Time Estimating Relationships

Project Characteristics	$\dfrac{\text{CHR}}{\text{MM}_{\text{DEV}}}$
Small-medium timeshare application	
Maxi	0.2
Midi	0.6
Mini	1.5
Large-very large or batch application	3.0
Real-time hardware–software product	
Maxi	3.0
Midi	6.0
Mini	9.0
Micro	18.0

5. Use the value of CHR to determine the most appropriate set of computer resources to obtain (rental, purchase of one or several computers, etc.), and to determine the resulting costs (here, most likely, the most appropriate approach would be early purchase of the minicomputer to be delivered as part of the process control product).

6. Determine the peak computer utilization during the test phase (typically, the most heavily loaded phase, with a peak computer time demand of about 2.2 times the project average; see Fig. 31–5), to see whether the resources obtained will adequately support the project [here, we have $2.2 \times (1350)/(15) = 198$ CHR/month, which is slightly over one full shift of operation. In this case, acquisition of a second minicomputer for backup or special circumstances is preferable to reliance on second-shift or weekend usage of a single computer].

7. Compare the results with other sources of experience, and iterate as appropriate. The ratios in Table 31–7 are based on a small set of data. They are basically consistent with the other ratios in Table 31–5, but they are still far from definitive.

Computer Time Distribution

The distribution of computer time requirements across the software development cycle still follows the basic shape of the curve given in [Pietrasanta, 1970]. The distribution curve shown in Fig. 31–5 has two small differences from the earlier Pietrasanta curve

1. A flatter overall distribution, reflecting the more even spread of test activities across the development cycle with the use of more top-down test approaches

2. A nonzero computer usage at the beginning of the development cycle, reflecting the use of computer aids to planning and design

A phased incremental development will produce an even further flattening of the computer time distribution.

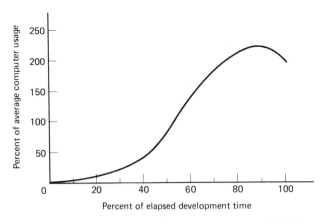

FIGURE 31-5 Software development computer time distribution

31.6 AMOUNT OF SOFTWARE DOCUMENTATION

The cost of software documentation is included in COCOMO estimates as an integral part of software development, rather than as an add-on. This is consistent with the anticipatory-documentation approach to software development discussed in Section 4.4, in which documentation is used as a means of defining the product and project in advance, rather than being produced as an add-on at the end of the project. Still, it is worth discussing the estimated size of a software product's documentation as a guide to detailed project planning.

Documentation Rates

The amount of documentation produced for a software product has been found to be roughly proportional to the product's size in DSI. Table 31–8 compares observed documentation rates from several studies in terms of delivered pages of documentation per thousand DSI (PP/KDSI) in the delivered software product. Some comments on these documentation rates are given below.

1. There is a wide range of variation between the definitions of delivered pages of documentation. The [Walston–Felix, 1977] data include program listings. The [Nelson, 1978] data include a wide variety of definitions. The COCOMO, [Boehm, 1980], and [Freburger–Basili, 1979] data exclude program listings and machine-generated flow charts.
2. The various documentation rates are basically consistent. The [Jones, 1979] rates are somewhat lower, and the [Farr and others, 1965] rates are considerably higher, but the other sources of data exhibit a strong overlap.
3. Documentation rates are widely variable between projects. The [Walston–Felix, 1977], [Nelson, 1978], and COCOMO data exhibit factors of 4 to 6 in differences between their 25th percentile and 75th percentile documentation rates.

TABLE 31–8. Observed Documentation Rates

Source	Attribute	PP/KDSI Specifications	Manuals	Plans, etc.	Total	Man-hours/PP
[Walston–Felix, 1977]	25th percentile				27[a]	
	50th "				69[a]	
	75th "				167[a]	
[Nelson, 1978]	25th "				24	
	50th "				54	
	75th "				127	
COCOMO data base	25th "				19	
	50th "				39	
	75th "				80	
[Freburger–Basili, 1979]	5 organic-mode projects				30–60	
[Jones, 1979]	2–KDSI	6				
	8–KDSI	10				
	32–KDSI	18				
	128–KDSI	20				
	512–KDSI	18				
	Specs, plans					3.2–5
	Manuals					1.8–2.2
[Boehm, 1980]	Two 2–KDSI	34	13	17	64	1.5
	projects	40	10	14	64	1.7
[Farr and others, 1965] summarized in [Morin, 1973]	Draft					1.6–2.7
	Review					0.4
	Edit					0.2
	Revise					0.8
	Total Writing				100–350	3.0–4.1
	Typing					0.4–0.5
	Illustrations					4

[a] Including source code listings

Figures 31–6, 31–7, and 31–8 explore the nature of these differences further with respect to the COCOMO data base. Figure 31–6 shows the overall cumulative distribution of documentation rates, indicating a considerably wider range of variation at the extremes (for example, a range of 12 to 162 PP/KDSI between the 10th and 90th percentiles).

Figure 31–7 shows that a good deal of the variation in documentation rate is due to the type of software. It shows separate histograms of the documentation rates for each of the six types of software (B: Business; C: Control; etc.) in the COCOMO data base, and a combined histogram at the bottom. In general, the business, support, and systems software products have relatively low documentation rates, and the control and human-machine software products tend to have high documentation rates. However, there is still a wide range of variation within each type of software.

Figure 31–8 shows that a good deal of this variation is associated with the software product's Required Reliability rating. It is clear from Fig. 31–8 that products

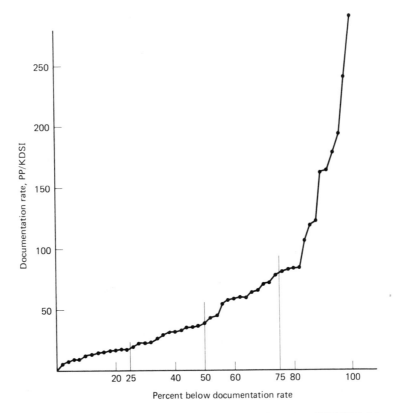

FIGURE 31-6 Cumulative distribution of documentation rates, COCOMO data base

with higher Required Reliability ratings generally have higher documentation rates. Some of this correlation is no doubt a cause and effect relationship (that is, high-reliability products require development of more detailed specifications and test plans), but some of the correlation is no doubt due to both factors being effects of a further cause (for example, a good many of the high-reliability products were Government projects with extensive documentation requirements).

Thus, the problem of estimating the amount of documentation required for a software product exhibits some of the same complexities as estimating the amount of effort required. This is a fruitful area of further study of the COCOMO data base and other sources of data.

Documentation Effort

Table 31-8 also contains some useful data on the amount of effort required to produce a typical page of documentation for a software product. Although the exact boundary is difficult to define, the figures in each case refer just to the effort required to write, review, and complete the specs, plans, etc., and not to the creative design

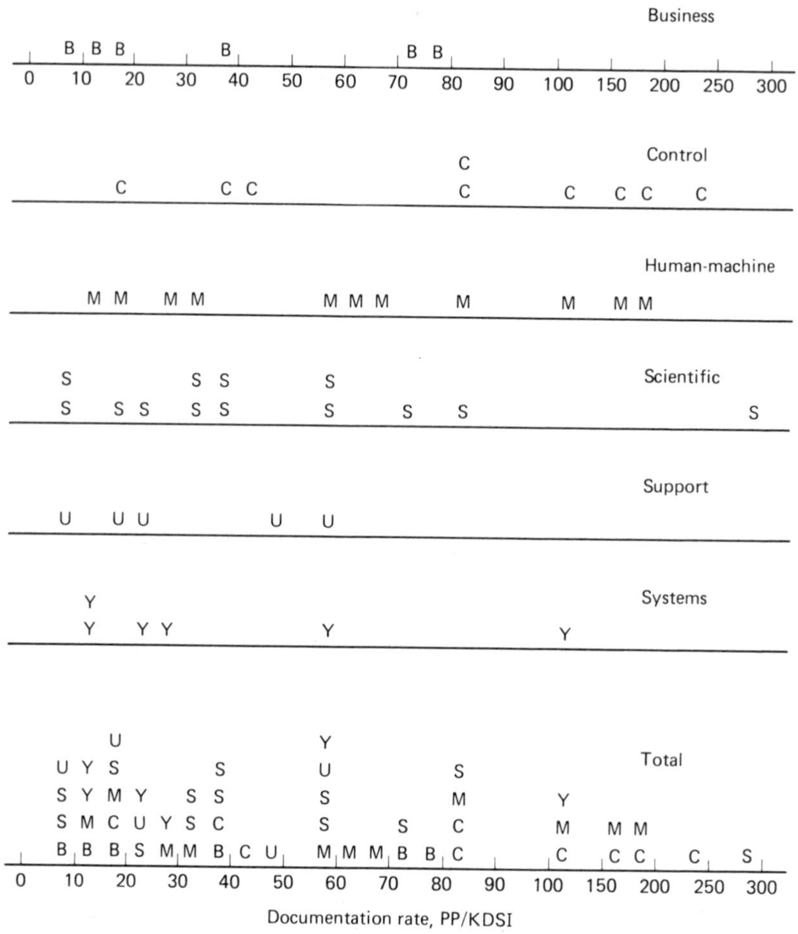

Business

```
      B B B        B              B  B
  |___|_|_|___|___|___|___|___|_|_|___|___|___|___|___|
  0  10  20  30  40  50  60  70  80  90 100 150 200 250 300
```

Control

```
                                  C
        C          C  C           C       C   C C    C
  _____
```

Human-machine

```
        M M    M M        M M M        M      M   M M
  _____
```

Scientific

```
    S          S  S        S
    S    S S   S  S        S     S    S                      S
  _____
```

Support

```
    U    U U              U    U
  _____
```

Systems

```
    Y                                        
    Y    Y Y              Y              Y
  _____
```

Total

```
         U                    Y
    U  Y S           S        U            S
    S  Y M Y    S  S          S         M       Y
    S  M C U  Y S  C          S     S   C       M     M M
    B  B B S M M  B C U       M M M B   B C         C  C C     C     S
  |___|_|_|___|___|___|___|___|___|___|___|___|___|___|
  0  10  20  30  40  50  60  70  80  90 100 150 200 250 300
            Documentation rate, PP/KDSI
```

FIGURE 31-7 Documentation rate distribution by type, COCOMO data base

or planning efforts preceding the writing process. There is some spread in the data in Table 31-8, but the following rates provide reasonable summary estimators:

Small projects, large-project manuals	2 manhours/PP
Large-project specs and plans	4 manhours/PP

Thus, a rough estimate of typical documentation effort on a project might be about 50 PP/KDSI of documentation times 3 manhours/PP of documentation effort, or

$$(3 \text{ MH/PP})(50 \text{ PP/KDSI}) = 150 \text{ MH/KDSI}$$

or about 1 man-month per 1000 DSI in the software product.

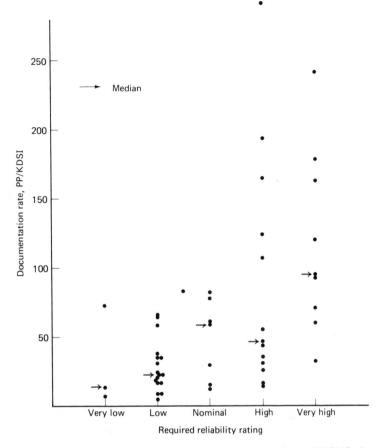

FIGURE 31–8 Documentation rate versus required reliability, COCOMO data base

Another useful insight into documentation effort is obtained by comparing the fraction of a project's effort which primarily produces documentation as its end product, as compared to the fraction which primarily produces code. This can be done using the effort distributions by activity in Tables 7–1, 7–2, and 7–3 for the three COCOMO software development modes. Table 31–9 shows the results for typical medium-size (32-KDSI) organic- and embedded-mode software products, along with the definitions used to calculate the results. It is striking to note that over half of a software project's effort produces documentation as its primary result, while only about one-third of the effort primarily produces code. (If the remainder of the effort is pro-rated across documentation and code, we obtain that 60–61% of the effort covers documentation, and 39–40% covers code.) Among other things, this provides a good rationale for the value of word-processing capabilities as aids to software development.

TABLE 31-9 Relative Project Effort Producing Documentation and Code

Primary Product	Activities	Percent of Project Effort	
		Organic Mode	Embedded Mode
Documentation	Requirements Analysis, Product Design, RA and PD V&V, test plans, Manuals, Half of programming	54	51
Code	Half of programming, full V&V of programming, Integration and test	34	34
Both	Project office, CM/QA	12	15

31.7 OTHER SOFTWARE RELATED LIFE-CYCLE COSTS

Besides the software related life cycle costs covered so far (development, maintenance, conversion, installation, training, computer, publications), there are a number of other costs which may be significant over the software life-cycle. The most significant of these other costs are clerical costs which, when they are charged directly to the project, typically run about 3 to 4% in addition to the dollar costs estimated by COCOMO. A COCOMO estimate covers professional personnel and paraprofessionals such as program librarians, but does not cover clerical effort. One reason for this is that clerical effort is often not charged to the project directly, but absorbed in the organization's overhead rate. Another reason is that the COCOMO phase and activity distributions become much more complex, as the clerical and professional mix must be considered in each of the phase and activity combinations.

Also, the cost per man-month for the two categories is significantly different. Typically, average clerical salaries are about 40% of average professional salaries. Since the typical project has roughly 7 to 10% additional clerical personnel, this implies a 2.8 to 4% additional cost for clerical personnel.

The other software-related costs typically average only about 0.5% of the total cost during software development, but it is important to consider them for two main reasons

1. They may be much higher on a given project (for example, travel, relocation, and telecommunications costs on a project with wide geographical dispersion).
2. They may cause critical-path slippages if not anticipated and ordered in advance (for example, modems, disks, software products).

A checklist of other sources of software-related life-cycle costs, based largely on [Cortada, 1980], is given below. Each of the entries in the list should be considered as an additional source of expenditure or schedule complication. In general, their costs can be determined in terms of quantity times unit price, where quantity is determined by project considerations and unit price can be determined from vendors or product catalogs.

1. *Clerical Costs.*
2. *Related Personnel Costs.* Overtime, benefits, hiring, termination, relocation, education; personnel costs for product acquisition: contracts, legal, receiving inspection, etc.
3. *Related Computer Costs.* Installation, maintenance, insurance, special equipment: terminals, control units, data entry devices, etc.
4. *Office Equipment Costs.* Typewriters, telephones, copiers, file cabinets, desks, chairs, word processing equipment, etc.
5. *Software Product Costs.* Purchase, rental, licensing, maintenance of software components, utilities, tools, etc.
6. *Supplies Costs.* Tapes, disks, forms, cards, paper, print ribbons, office supplies, etc.
7. *Telecommunication Costs.* Line charges, special equipment: modems, multiplexers, cables, connectors, etc.
8. *Facility Costs.* Office rental, electricity, air conditioning, heating, water, taxes, depreciation, cleaning, repairs, insurance, security, fire protection, etc.
9. *Other Costs.* Travel, postage, printing, consulting fees, books, periodicals, conventions, messenger services, equipment relocation, etc.

31.8 AN EXAMPLE SOFTWARE LIFE-CYCLE COST-BENEFIT ANALYSIS

This section provides an example of the use of the various software-related cost-estimation techniques, as applied to a life-cycle cost-benefit analysis for the development of a software system for equipment management and inventory control. The analysis provides an example not only of how the techniques are used but also at what level they are used, since a cost-benefit analysis generally does not require the same level of detail required for a budget-preparation analysis. It also shows the results of a cost-benefit risk analysis, an essential component of any decision-oriented cost analysis. Throughout the section, we will also use the cost-element experience ranges presented in this chapter and the preceding chapter as a basis for verifying that our cost estimates are reasonable.

The PPI, Inc., Equipment Management System

Precision Products, Inc. (PPI), began as a small aerospace electronics firm in 1951. It has rapidly grown into a large diversified corporation with a 1981 annual sales volume of $1.9 billion and 26,300 employees. Its product line centers around its original speciality, sensor-based control systems. PPI has successfully developed versions of these control systems to serve in the fields of medicine, energy, and environmental controls.

In 1972, PPI established a Central Equipment Management Operation (CEMO) to obtain better utilization, maintenance, and calibration of its growing inventory of special project support equipment: microscopes, oscilloscopes, digital voltmeters, temperature controllers, power supplies, test equipment, etc. The CEMO serves the following major functions:

- A unified procurement function, enabling PPI to capitalize on quantity discounts, uniform equipment acceptance procedures, and a continuing corporate memory on vendor products
- A rental library function, using the monthly rental for equipment both to cover costs and to discourage user "squirreling" of unused equipment
- An equipment maintenance and calibration function, providing projects with an assurance of timely repairs, and providing PPI management with an assurance of accurately calibrated equipment

At the end of 1981, the CEMO had an inventory of 75,000 items, valued at about $50,000,000. The inventory is currently growing at about 15% per year. The average number of transactions affecting the equipment inventory is about 7000 transactions per week, currently growing at a rate of 20% per year.

Problems with the Existing Software System

In 1972–73, the PPI Management Systems Software Department developed a set of simple batch COBOL programs to help CEMO keep track of its equipment. These programs were not well-coordinated to begin with, and by 1981 they had evolved into an unwieldy software conglomeration with a large number of patches, arbitrary constraints, and performance problems. They were unable to keep up with PPI's expanding business. After a number of user complaints, an audit of the system was conducted in June 1981. It indicated that the system had

- A 23% discrepancy rate between equipment computer records and actual equipment status
- A 37% delinquency rate in recalling equipment for periodic calibration and preventive maintenance
- A large number (roughly 8 to 12) of clerical personnel performing excessive data preparation, translation, and post-processing to compensate for deficiencies in the software

Replacing the Existing System: Feasibility Study

The audit report recommended that a feasibility study for replacing the existing software system be given a high priority. Such a feasibility study was initiated in September 1981, and by December 1981 had concluded that

- No external software package satisfied PPI's CEMO requirements sufficiently well to serve as a replacement system

- Any newly developed system should be based on a commercial data base management system (DBMS)
- A newly developed system would most likely be highly cost-effective, but further analysis would be necessary to determine this definitively

Based on these conclusions, PPI's management commissioned the analysis team to develop a detailed architecture, concept of operation, life-cycle plan, and life-cycle cost-benefit analysis for a newly developed system based on a commercial DBMS, and to target the start of the system for May 1982 if the cost-benefit analysis was favorable. This study, completed in March 1982, indicated that the CEMO concept of operation with the new system would not differ significantly from the current concept of operation, except that the new system would not need as many clerical people, who could then be reassigned to other jobs. The next sections summarize the architecture of the proposed system, its life-cycle cost analysis and cost-risk analysis, its life-cycle benefit analysis, and the resulting cost-benefit comparisons.

The Proposed Central Equipment Management and Inventory Control System (CEMICS)

The overall architecture of the proposed CEMICS software is shown in Fig. 31–9. It is a batch-oriented system, consisting of a number of stand-alone programs run at different intervals: daily (D), weekly (W), or monthly (M). These programs, some of which are grouped into system components (indicated by the dotted lines) communicate with each other via the master equipment data base or through auxiliary files created from information in the master equipment data base. The functions performed by each of the programs in Fig. 31–9, and their estimated size based on experience with the existing system, are summarized below.

1. *EDIT.* The EDIT program begins by accepting and processing updates to the Edit Tables (such as, changing the limits on an equipment attribute such as its dollar value or its lease period, or changing the set of acceptable codes for such attributes as equipment location, equipment status, or ownership status). It then accepts input data on equipment status changes, equipment additions or deletions, etc., checks their validity versus the Edit Tables, and produces a file and report of erroneous transactions and a valid-transaction file for processing by the UPDATE program. Both the EDIT program and the UPDATE program are run daily (D). Based on experience with the previous system, the size of the EDIT program is estimated at $10,000 \pm 3000$ DSI.*

2. *UPDATE.* The UPDATE program uses the valid-transaction file produced by the EDIT program to update the CEMICS master equipment data base of equipment attributes and status history. It also produces a journal tape for backup and recovery contingencies. Its size is estimated at 6000 ± 2000 DSI.

* For each program, the DSI count represents COBOL source statements, with the Data Division statements weighted by a factor of 1/3, and the "$\pm$" represents a three standard-deviation (99.7%) range.

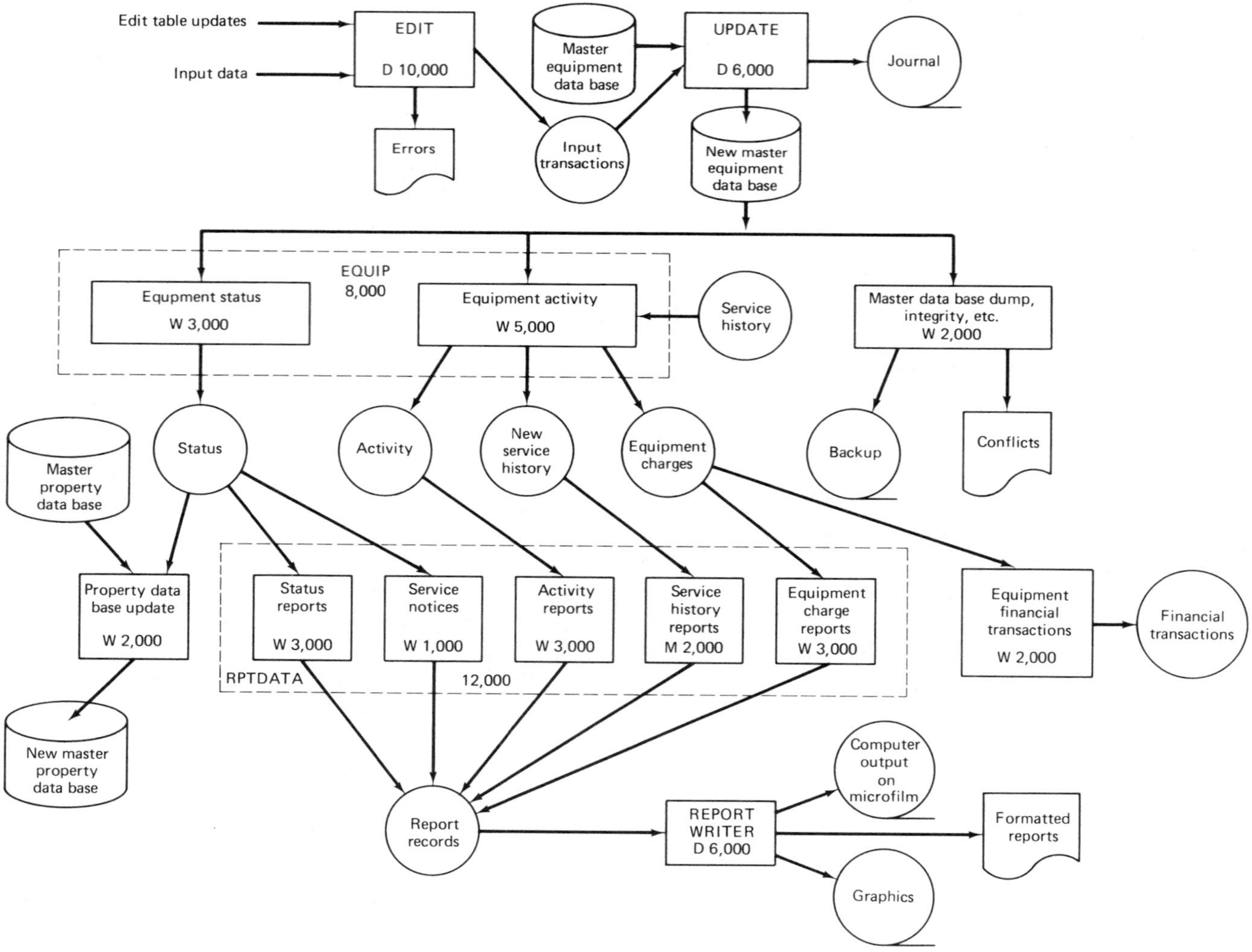

FIGURE 31-9 CEMICS software architecture

3. *EQUIP.* The EQUIP component consists of two programs which operate on the CEMICS master equipment data base to produce intermediate files for use by subsequent CEMICS programs. The EQUIPMENT STATUS program obtains equipment status information from the master equipment data base, verifies it for consistency and completeness, and produces a status file for use in various status reports and in updating the PPI master property data base. The size of this program is estimated at 3000 DSI. The EQUIP-MENT ACTIVITY program obtains equipment activity information from the master equipment data base, verifies it, and uses it to update the service history file and to create intermediate equipment activity and equipment charges files for use in generating reports and billings for equipment used by PPI organizations. Its size is estimated at 5000 DSI. The overall size of the EQUIP component is estimated at 8000 ± 2000 DSI.

4. *RPTDATA.* This component consists of five programs which read the intermediate files produced by EQUIP and generate report records to be formatted and output by the REPORT program: the STATUS REPORTS program (3000 DSI); the SERVICE NOTICES program (1000 DSI), which prepares notices to custodians of equipment whose periodic servicing dates are upcoming; the ACTIVITY REPORTS program (3000 DSI); the SERVICE HISTORY REPORTS program (2000 DSI), which also identifies trouble-prone equipment for further investigation; and the EQUIPMENT CHARGE REPORTS Program (3000 DSI), which also produces various financial summaries. Each of these programs produces both general summary reports and a number of exception reports. The overall size of the RPTDATA component is estimated at 12,000 ± 4000 DSI.

5. *REPORTS.* The REPORTS program formats the report records produced by the RPTDATA programs and outputs them on the desired medium: line printer, computer output on microfilm (COM) device, or graphics plotter. Its size is estimated at 6000 ± 1000 DSI.

6. *Miscellaneous (MISC).* This component includes three miscellaneous programs. The EQUIPMENT DATA BASE DUMP routine (2000 DSI) performs various data base integrity checks, indicates any conflicts, and creates a weekly backup for the data base. The PROPERTY DATA BASE UPDATE program (2000 DSI), uses information on additions, changes, or deletions within the CEMO equipment pool to update PPI's master property data base on all property owned by PPI. The EQUIPMENT FINANCIAL TRANSACTIONS program (2000 DSI) passes the weekly information on CEMO equipment charges to the PPI Financial Information Processing System via an appropriately structured intermediate file. The overall size of the MISC programs is estimated at 6000 ± 3000 DSI.

CEMICS Life-Cycle Cost Analysis

The CEMICS cost-benefit analysis requires a reasonable amount of detail, but not a very detailed estimation of cost by phase, activity, and module. Thus, the Intermediate COCOMO model is sufficient for estimating software development and maintenance costs, using the forms and procedures presented in Sections 9.2 and 9.5.

Figure 31–10 shows the COCOMO Component Level Estimating Form used to estimate CEMICS software development costs. Most of the cost driver attribute ratings for the CEMICS components are nominal; the non-nominal ratings are explained below.

> *DATA*. The CEMICS data base contains an average of 2000 bytes for each of the 75,000 equipment inventory items, for a total of 150,000,000 bytes. Since this is more than 1000 times the estimated program size of 48,000 DSI, a very high rating applies.
>
> *CPLX*. The EDIT routine is quite straightforward. The other components have some more complex features which make their average rating nominal.
>
> *TURN*. CEMICS will be developed in batch mode, and test runs will often have to wait several hours until large production runs are completed.
>
> *ACAP, AEXP*. The project manager and the lead analyst will design all of the components except EDIT, which will be given to an experienced but less capable analyst.
>
> *PCAP, VEXP, LEXP*. The lead analyst will program the key portions of the UPDATE and EQUIP components; the other components will be programmed by newer personnel. All the programmers are experienced in COBOL.
>
> *MODP*. The PPI Business Software Department is well experienced in the use of most modern programming practices.

The resulting Intermediate COCOMO estimates for CEMICS software development are 144 man-months, $792,000, and 16½ months. As an independent Wideband-Delphi expert-opinion cost estimate arrived at a comparable median cost estimate of $750,000, we will accept the COCOMO estimates for the cost-benefit analysis.

The other CEMICS development and implementation costs are estimated as follows.

Computer costs. Based on the estimating guidelines for batch application projects in Table 31–7, computer usage is estimated at 3 hours per development man-month. This is reasonably consistent with the data in Table 31–5. The resulting estimated computer cost is

$$144 \text{ MM} \times 3 \frac{\text{CHR}}{\text{MM}} \times \frac{\$200}{\text{CHR}} = \$86,400$$

which is roughly 11% of the development labor cost.

Implementation. The most likely cutover strategy for the new CEMICS system is a 6-week parallel operation in which the new reports are used as well as the old and the old data entry procedures are phased out. Usually, the best way to estimate in this situation is to apply an average level of effort over the time period. Here,

CEMICS   Analyst: F. Fox   Date: 2/20/82

(1) Component	(2) EDSI	(3) AAF	Product (4) RELY	(5) DATA	(6) CPLX	Computer (7) TIME	(8) STOR	(9) VIRT.	(10) TURN	Personnel attributes (11) ACAP	(12) AEXP	(13) PCAP	(14) VEXP	(15) LEXP	Project (16) MODP	(17) TOOL	(18) SCED	(19) EAF	(20) MM NOM	(21) MM DEV/AM	(22) EDSI/MM ACT	(23) $K	(24) $/EDSI
			N 1.0	VHI 1.16	LO 0.85	N 1.0	N 1.0	N 1.0	HI 1.07	N 1.0	HI 0.91	N 1.0	N 1.0	HI 0.95	HI 0.91	N 1.0	N 1.0	0.83					
1. EDIT	10,000																		39	32	312	5.0 / 160	16
2. UPDATE	6,000				N 1.0					HI 0.86	HI 0.91	HI 0.86	HI 0.90					0.65	23	15	400	6.0 / 90	15
3. EQUIP	8,000									HI 0.86		HI 0.86	HI 0.90					0.65	31	20	400	6.0 / 120	15
4. RPTDATA	12,000									N 1.0		N 1.0	N 1.0					0.84	47	39	308	5.5 / 214	18
5. REPORTS	6,000																	0.84	23	19	315	5.5 / 104	18
6. MISC	6,000																	0.84	23	19	315	5.5 / 104	18
7.																							
8.																							
9.																							
10.																							
11.	48,000 Total EDSI																Totals			144	333	792	16
12.	186 (MM)NOM																Schedule (months)			16.5			
13.	258 (EDSI/MM)NOM																						

Development mode: Organic

FIGURE 31-10 CEMICS software development cost estimate

we assure that four software developers will be required on the average to support the cutover activity

Labor: 4 FSP $\times$ 1.5 month $\times$ \$5.5K per MM   = \$33K
Computer: 50 CHR/month $\times$ 1.5 month $\times$ \$200/CHR = $\underline{\text{15K}}$
                                               \$48K

or about 5% of the development costs. This is higher than the range of installation costs shown in Table 31–4, as implementation here covers a much larger activity.

Training. The project's training-related costs are best estimated on a task-unit basis. Here 2 MM are estimated for preparing the training material, and another 1MM for actually performing the training, for a total of 3MM $\times$ \$5K per MM = \$15K. About 20 clerical personnel will go through a 1-week training course, at a cost of

$$20 \text{ clerks} \times \frac{1 \text{ man-week}}{\text{clerk}} \times \frac{1 \text{ MM}}{4 \text{ man-week}} \times \frac{\$2K}{MM} = \$10K$$

for total training cost of \$25K. The project's training-related cost of \$15K is about 2% of the overall development labor cost. This is consistent with the range of training costs for similar systems given in Table 31–4.

Conversion. No program conversion is contemplated. The cost of data base conversion is included in the development cost via the very high DATA rating.

User Costs. The CEMO estimates that it will require an average of about one full-time CEMO person over the 18-month development and implementation period to work with the developers to ensure a user-responsive system. The resulting cost is

$$1 \text{ FSP} \times 18 \text{ months} \times \$6K/MM = \$108K$$

Other Costs. None of the other cost contributors itemized in Table 31–8 contribute a significant amount to the cost of CEMICS development. One could add another 0.5 to 1% to cover them, but as this would not affect the results of the analysis, it is better not to do so on the grounds of simplicity (PPI's clerical costs are included in its overhead rate).

The total development and implementation costs are thus estimated to be

Development: Labor	\$ 792K
Development: Computer	86K
Implementation	48K
Training	25K
User Labor	108K
Total	\$1059K

The annual software maintenance labor costs for CEMICS are estimated in Fig. 31–11. The only changes in effort multipliers come from the added benefit of a high level of MPP usage, the increased computer system experience of the programmers, and the use of an average-capability analyst on the RPTDATA, REPORTS, and MISC components. The annual personnel effort is estimated 26.7 MM, or approximately 2.2 FSP, and $147,000. This compares to a current staff of 4 FSP for less effective maintenance of the old system. The cards-per-person ratio for maintenance is 48 KDSI/2.2 FSP = 22 KDSI/FSP, a reasonable level for HOL business applications as compared to the experience summarized in Table 30–3.

CEMICS Life-Cycle Benefit Analysis

The benefits of a system such as CEMICS can be categorized into tangible benefits—direct cost savings or increases in revenue—and intangible benefits, which tend to be less-quantifiable and indirect benefits such as improved quality of service, improved morale, etc. If there are no serious intangible problems created and a good many intangible benefits expected, we should try to justify the development of a software system on the basis of its tangible benefits alone, as this yields a less controversial decision situation. In any case, though, it is important to identify and scope the intangible benefits, if only to ensure that there are no significant indirect problems (such as, a significant loss of information privacy or security) likely to result from the system. Further, it is important to perform a cost-benefit risk analysis to test the sensitivity of the results to the assumptions underlying the analysis, and to indicate the level of risk we will incur if a key assumption is unjustified. The following sections cover the CEMICS tangible and intangible benefits, and a cost-benefit risk analysis.

Further, it is usually a good idea to perform the initial benefits analysis using some conservative simplifying assumptions. These make the initial analysis easier and, if it turns out that the benefits outweigh the costs even with the conservative assumptions, then we can avoid the complications (both to ourselves and to the decisionmakers using the analysis results) of a more involved analysis. The CEMICS cost and benefit analyses make the simplifying assumption that all costs, personnel levels, and inventory levels remain constant at their current 1982 levels. This assumption is conservative because of the CEMO's strong growth rate to date in personnel, inventory size, and inventory value. It further eliminates the need to perform present value analyses by assuming that decreases in future cost savings due to present value discounting are roughly balanced by increases in cost savings due to inflation.

CEMICS Tangible Benefits

The major tangible CEMICS benefits are summarized below in terms of their direct cost savings per year.

Reduced Inventory. Surveys of CEMO users have indicated that the increased accuracy and timeliness of CEMICS information will conservatively reduce the amount of new equipment purchased by 5% due to increased utilization of equipment, reduced user squirreling of equipment, and reduced need for backup inventory. The value

Project: CEMICS MAINTENANCE   Analyst: F. Fox   Date: 2/22/82

(1) Component	(2) EDSI	(3) AAF	Product (4) RELY	(5) DATA	(6) CPLX	Computer (7) TIME	(8) STOR	(9) VIRT.	(10) TURN	Personnel attributes (11) ACAP	(12) AEXP	(13) PCAP	(14) VEXP	(15) LEXP	Project (16) MODP	(17) TOOL	(18) SCED	(19) EAF	(20) MM NOM	(21) MM DEV/AM	(22) EDSI/MM ACT	(23) $K	(24) $/EDSI
1. EDIT	10,000												0.90 1.0		0.86 0.91			0.71 0.83	39	6.9	25	5.5 38	
2. UPDATE	6,000														0.86 0.91			0.61 0.65	23	1.4	10	6.0 8	
3. EQUIP	8,000														0.86 0.91			0.61 0.65	31	1.9	10	6.0 11	
4. RPTDATA	12,000									1.0 0.86			0.90 1.0		0.86 0.91			0.83 0.84	47	9.8	25	5.5 54	
5. REPORTS	6,000									1.0 0.86			0.90 1.0		0.86 0.91			0.83 0.84	23	1.9	10	5.5 10	
6. MISC	6,000									1.0 0.86			0.90 1.0		0.86 0.91			0.83 0.84	23	4.8	25	5.5 26	
7.																							
8.																							
9.																							
10.																							
11.	48,000	Total EDSI																	Totals	26.7		147	
12.		$(MM)_{NOM}$																	Schedule (months)				
13.		$(EDSI/MM)_{NOM}$																					

Development mode: Organic

FIGURE 31–11 CEMICS software maintenance cost estimate

of CEMO's new purchases per year is about 30% of the current $50,000,000 inventory value, or about $15,000,000 (depreciation and phaseout reduce the net growth rate of inventory value to 15%). A 5% reduction in this annual purchase cost represents an annual cost savings of $750,000. In addition, PPI will save an additional 25% otherwise required for inventory carrying costs—financial and administrative costs associated with ownership—for an additional annual savings of $187,500.

Reduced Clerical Staff. As a conservative estimate based on the audit results, CEMICS will require only 18 clerical personnel as compared to 26 for the existing system, for an annual savings of $200,000.

Reduced Software Maintenance. As indicated in the life-cycle cost analysis, CEMICS software maintenance costs will be $147K per yr, as compared to the current staff of four people at a cost of about $60K per man-year, or $240K. This represents an annual cost savings of $93K.

Reduced Computer Costs. As indicated in the life-cycle cost analysis, computer costs will be reduced from $96K per yr to $72K per yr, for an annual cost savings of $24K.

The resulting total annual tangible cost savings due to development and operation of CEMICS is estimated to be

Reduced equipment inventory	$ 750K/yr
Reduced carrying costs	188K/yr
Reduced clerical staff	200K/yr
Reduced software maintenance	93K/yr
Reduced computer costs	24K/yr
Total	$1255K/yr

CEMICS Intangible Benefits

Development and use of CEMICS would provide a higher quality of service to PPI equipment users and managers. More timely calibration and preventive maintenance would increase equipment lifetimes, reduce unexpected work stoppages, and reduce the number of invalid product tests. Better user information would reduce delays in locating equipment and enable users to obtain special reports to aid in fault trend analysis, vendor selection, etc. More accurate and timely equipment status and trend information would aid managers in financial planning, facility planning, and project planning.

These benefits are difficult to quantify directly. By making a number of additional assumptions, we can often provide a rough approximation of the benefits, but the assumptions and analysis may not be easy to defend. Still, in some situations in which the magnitude of an intangible benefit is critical to a decision, it is worth making the effort.

One frequently used proxy for quantifying improved quality of service is to calculate how many more people it would take to provide an equivalent quality of service with the old system (for example, providing a CEMICS-level quality of service with the old system would require 50 clerks instead of 26, an equivalent savings of 24 $\times$ $25K per yr = $600K per yr). Such an estimate provides some level of perspective, but unless the organization is seriously thinking of higher staff levels as a real alternative, it will be generally considered as a somewhat soft and unrealistic savings estimate.

Some other intangible benefits are even more difficult to reconcile with the dollar benefits, such as the improved morale of equipment users, CEMO clerks, and maintenance programmers; or such as the system's growth capability. Here again, it is better not to spend too much time quantifying or reconciling these benefits unless they become decision-critical, in which case Chapter 18 has a number of techniques and guidelines which can aid in the analysis.

CEMICS Cost-Benefit Comparison and Risk Analysis

Fortunately, the magnitude of the estimated CEMICS tangible benefits alone ($1255K per yr) is so large that PPI's estimated development and implementation costs ($1059K) would be recouped after the first year of operation. Further, no significant intangible problems appear to accompany the introduction of CEMICS. This means that PPI's decision is already clear without having to introduce and reconcile intangible benefits, or having to introduce more sophisticated financial return analyses such as present-value analysis, yield analysis or return-on-investment analysis (see [Cortada, 1980]).

However, even with such a clear preference, it is advisable to perform a cost-benefit risk analysis, in order to ensure that PPI will not find itself in a deep hole if one of the study's assumptions is invalid.

On the cost-risk side, the major risks are that CEMICS will be larger and more difficult to develop than indicated by the component sizes and ratings in Fig. 31–5. Given the "±" ranges on the sizing estimates, the most conservative estimate we can make is that all of the components are at the maximum size in the range:* 13,000 DSI for EDIT, 8,000 for UPDATE, etc. This would give us a total CEMICS size of 63,000 DSI instead of 48,000. On the attribute ratings, most have been estimated conservatively, but there is some risk that the high capability programmer-analysts will become unavailable, requiring their jobs to be done by nominal level personnel.

If we carry out the Intermediate COCOMO calculations corresponding to these conservative sizings and ratings, we obtain an estimate of 222 MM and $1228K development labor cost. At this point, we should also account for the risk that the Intermediate COCOMO model is underestimating the project costs. By Fig. 29–5, we can see that in 59 of 63 projects (94% of the time), the project actuals have been less than 40% higher than the COCOMO estimates. Thus, increasing the CO-COMO estimate by 40% gives us a highly conservative cost estimate reflecting the COCOMO estimating uncertainty. This increases our conservative estimates to 311

---

* This is a considerably more conservative estimate than the PERT size-risk estimates discussed in Section 21.4, which use a root mean square formula based on the assumption that sizing overestimates will be balanced by underestimates. Given current practice in undersizing software, the PERT sizing assumption is neither very conservative nor very realistic.

MM and $1719K for CEMICS software development, or about 117% higher than our original $792K estimate.

We could similarly recalculate all of the other costs using conservative assumptions, but if the other costs are relatively small and roughly proportional to the development labor cost (as is the case here), we can obtain a good, simple conservative estimate by applying the development labor cost increase across the overall development and implementation cost estimate. Here, by increasing the overall cost by 117%, we obtain a conservative cost estimate for CEMICS of $2299K instead of $1059K, a cost risk of $1240K. The revised development schedule estimate is 22 months rather than 16.5 months, indicating a schedule risk of 5.5 months.

On the benefit-risk side, a very conservative assumption would be that each of the benefits has been overestimated by a factor of two: that reductions in new inventory will be only 2.5% instead of 5%, that the clerical savings will be four people rather than eight, that the savings in software maintenance manpower will be $46K per yr rather than $93K per yr, and that computer cost savings will be $12K per yr rather than $24K per yr. If we reduce the total annual cost savings of $1255K per yr by a factor of two, we have a conservative estimate of tangible benefits of $627K per yr.

Figure 31–12 shows the results of the cost-benefit risk analysis from a payback standpoint. Even with the conservative estimates, although the payback period starts 6 months later, the breakeven point is reached at about $3\frac{1}{2}$ years after the beginning of CEMICS operation, an acceptable payback period (typically 3 to 5 years is considered an acceptable payback period for an information system). Thus, PPI's management decided on the basis of this analysis that the risks are acceptable, and that the CEMICS development should proceed. In the following chapter on planning

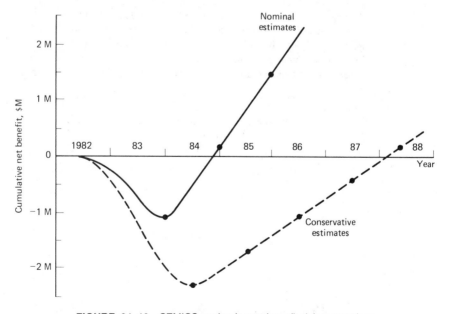

FIGURE 31–12 CEMICS payback cost-benefit risk comparison

and control, we will use the CEMICS example to show how to use the cost estimates developed here as a basis of allocating, monitoring, and controlling project budgets and expenditures versus project progress.

31.9 TOPICS FOR FURTHER RESEARCH

31.A. Perform experiments and observations to test the hypothesis that the COCOMO software adaptation cost model provides accurate conversion cost estimates. Compare the COCOMO results to those given by the [Oliver, 1979] estimating guidelines, and develop appropriate refinements of each.

31.B. Investigate the effect of other factors on software conversion costs, or on COCOMO adaptation factors.

- programming language
- quality and quantity of documentation
- similarity of computer configurations involved in conversion

31.C. Formulate and validate a model for estimating the costs of data base conversion.

31.D. Collect and analyze further data on software installation and training costs, and determine the major factors influencing the costs.

31.E. Formulate and validate a model for estimating the computer time and cost required for software development.

31.F. Collect and analyze data to test the hypothesis that the time distribution of computer costs given in Fig. 31–5 is independent of the type of application, type of computer configuration, required reliability, etc.

31.G. Analyze the documentation data given in the COCOMO data base to determine the primary factors influencing a project's documentation rate—type of application, required reliability, use of MPPs, etc.—and the relative magnitude of the influence factor. Develop an exploratory model for estimating the amount of documentation required for a software product, and perform additional experiments and observations to validate it.

31.H. Collect and analyze data to characterize the magnitude of the other software-related costs itemized in the checklist on p. 577, and to determine the factors primarily influencing the magnitude of their costs.

Chapter **32**

Software Project
Planning and Control

32.1 INTRODUCTION

The Software Cost Estimate as Self-fulfilling Prophecy

A most remarkable property of a software development cost estimate is this

If a software development cost estimate is within 20% of the "ideal" cost estimate for the job, a good manager can turn it into a self-fulfilling prophecy.

The degrees of freedom which allow the project manager to do this are the common slack components of the software person's typical work week. As we discussed in connection with Fig. 22–4 (reproduced here as Fig. 32–1), these slack components—training, personal activities, general professional activities—comprise about 30% of the software person's time on the job.

The primary way that the project manager can stimulate the project team mem-

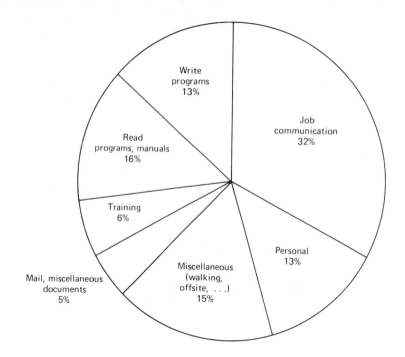

ACTIVITY	List, Cards, Worksheet	Business	Personal	Meeting	Training	Mail/Misc. Documents	Technical Manuals	Oper. Proc. Misc.	Program Test	Totals
Talk or listen	4%	17%	7%	3%				1%		32%
Talk with manager		1								1%
Telephone		2	1							3%
Read	14					2	2			18%
Write/recording	13					1				14%
Away or out		4	1	4	6					15%
Walking	2	2	1			1				6%
Miscellaneous	2	3	3			1		1	1	11%
Totals	35%	29%	13%	7%	6%	5%	2%	2%	1%	100%

FIGURE 32–1 What do programmers do?

bers to appropriately reallocate their slack time is to establish intermediate project milestones whose associated budgets and schedules are based on the cost and schedule estimates for achieving these milestones. Given these milestones, schedules, and budgets, there are two main phenomena which act to modulate people's slack time to meet them and to cumulatively realize the self-fulfilling prophecy. The first of these is

> Parkinson's Law [*Parkinson, 1957*]: *"Work expands to fill the available volume."*

Thus, if the software cost or schedule estimate for meeting a milestone is higher than the ideal, Parkinson's Law indicates that people will use the extra time for training, personal activities, catching up on the mail, etc., so that the actual expenditure for completing the project milestone activity will be (about) equal to the estimated budget for the activity.

The second of these phenomena is to some extent the converse of Parkinson's Law. It is the

> Deadline Effect: *"The amount of energy and effort devoted to an activity is strongly accelerated as one approaches the deadline for completing the activity."*

The Deadline Effect has been observed informally in many situations. Figure 32–2 shows some measured data on two small projects with three major milestones: a plans and requirements review (PRR); a product design review (PDR), and an acceptance test [Boehm, 1980]. It is clear from the data that the Deadline Effect held strongly for both projects, generally producing peak efforts about twice as high as those of the previous week. Here again, the Deadline Effect acts to reallocate people's slack time so that the original budget and schedule estimates for each milestone activity become self-fulfilling prophecies.

Thus, with an appropriate set of project milestones and a good set of project planning and control techniques, a capable software project manager can bring in a reasonably well-estimated project on schedule and within budget. However, if the estimates are too far off (especially on the low side), the project manager will run out of available slack, and a major overrun will result. Also, if an organization attempts to eliminate people's slack activities by consistently underestimating budgets and schedules, and by imposing more and more deadlines, it will encounter serious long-range problems through decreased morale, decreased long-range technical skills, and increased personnel turnover.

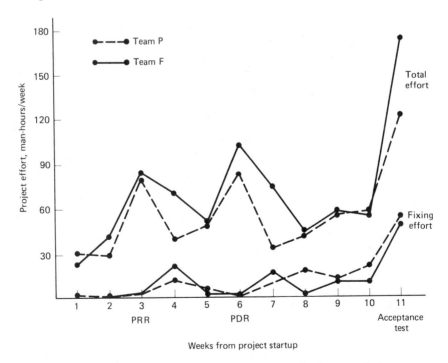

FIGURE 32–2 The deadline effect on two small software projects

The Synergy Between Software Cost Estimation and Software Project Management

The self-fulfilling prophecy effect described above is one example of the synergy available by combining effective software cost-estimation techniques and effective software planning and control techniques. Two further areas of synergy between the two disciplines are the following:

- An effective planning and control capability provides data on the time, effort, and cost distribution for present software projects. These data help to recalibrate the software cost-estimation model to the evolving characteristics of the installation and its projects.
- An effective cost-estimation capability reinforces better project management by specifying enough resources to do the job right (for example, enough time and enough effort in the early phases to do the requirements analysis and design right), and by providing a sound "should-cost" baseline for each project phase and activity to serve as a basis for planning and control.

Chapter Preview

This chapter explains how we can use the COCOMO software cost and schedule estimates as the basis for planning and controlling a software development project. Section 32.2 presents the overall framework of an integrated cost-performance planning and control system, and explains how the various pieces fit together. Some of these pieces have been described in earlier chapters, such as the work breakdown structure in Chapter 4 and the cost-schedule-milestone chart in Chapter 21. The other components are explained in the subsequent sections of this chapter.

Section 32.3 covers project scheduling techniques, such as PERT charts, critical path calculations, and Gantt charts. Section 32.4 discusses the Unit Development Folder and its associated cover sheet as an effective means of detailed software project planning and control. Section 32.5 presents the Earned Value System, which provides a way to use the detailed milestone information from the Unit Development Folder to develop an overall measure of the project's progress with respect to its expenditures.

Section 32.6 then shows how all of these techniques are applied to a typical project, using the Central Equipment Management and Inventory Control System (CEMICS) system presented in Chapter 31 as an example. Section 32.7 summarizes how the data collected during a software project planning and control activity can be organized into a software cost data base for future improvement and calibration of the COCOMO cost model to the installation's experience. Finally, Section 32.8 summarizes the major points of the chapter.

32.2 A SOFTWARE PROJECT PLANNING AND CONTROL FRAMEWORK

Figure 32–3 shows an overall framework of software project planning and control techniques which provide us with the essential capabilities we need to monitor and

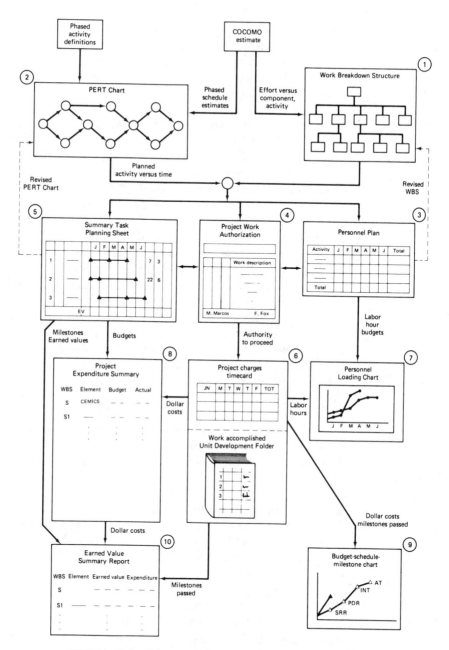

FIGURE 32-3 Software project planning and control framework

control the project's progress and expenditures. Each of the numbered steps in Fig. 32-3 is summarized below.

①　The first thing we need is an organizational structure for keeping track of project expenditures in a way which relates to our estimates of project cost by phase and activity. This capability is provided by the *work breakdown structure* (WBS), which we originally defined and discussed in Section 4.7 as part of our definition of the costs covered by a COCOMO cost estimate. The COCOMO estimates of project cost by software component and activity are used to provide "should-cost" targets for each WBS element.

② The COCOMO estimates of required project calendar time by phase provide a starting point for establishing a hierarchy of *PERT charts,* or activity networks. The PERT chart technique allows us to express the time dependencies of project tasks, to analyze such aspects as the project's critical path between start and finish, and to monitor the actual progress of the project with respect to the milestones in the PERT chart. PERT charts and related techniques will be covered in more detail in Section 32.3.

③ Once we have defined the cost, effort, and schedule required for each major project task, we can establish the other three primary components of the project's resource plan. The first is the project's *personnel plan,* which indicates how many people will be required to work on each project WBS element during each month of the project (the time unit might be a week for small projects, or three months for very large projects). The use of the personnel plan will be illustrated by example in Section 32.6.

④ Another component of the project's resource plan is a set of *project work authorizations (PWAs).* For each separately identified work package of WBS elements, the PWA records the mutual commitment of the responsible individuals in the work package's sponsor organization and performer organization as to

- What work is to be performed
- When the major work package milestones will be completed
- What resources will be provided by the sponsor to the performer to accomplish the work

The PWA will be illustrated by example in Section 32.6.

⑤ The final component of a project's resource plan is a set of *summary task planning sheets (STPSs),* which provide a set of low level schedules and milestones for the project's individual activities, and which serve as a basis for the Earned Value System described in item ⑩. The STPS will be discussed in Section 32.5.

⑥ Once work on the project begins, we need two basic capabilities for tracking progress. The first, generally implemented via a *time card* or its equivalent, records how much of a project member's time has been devoted to the project's various WBS elements, each of which is typically identified by a unique accounting-system job number. (Similar instruments such as purchase orders cover expenditure of other resources.) The second capability records how much progress has been made toward the project member's objectives; one effective milestone-oriented technique for monitoring software work accomplished is the *Unit Development Folder (UDF),* which will be discussed in Section 32.4.

(7) The personnel plan developed as item ③ provides a target personnel distribution versus time. The actual man-hours charged to project activities via the time card can be used to generate an actual personnel distribution versus time which can be used as a basis of controlling the project's desired personnel levels. An example *personnel loading chart* will be illustrated in Section 32.6.

(8) The dollars expended by the various project activities can be similarly compared to the planned expenditure levels via reports such as a *project expenditure summary* provided by a *Job Accounting System*. The use of such a system, and selected exception reporting guidelines, will be illustrated in Section 32.6.

(9) The reports in items ⑦ and ⑧ may indicate that a project is underspending, but they provide no indication whether this is a good or a bad thing. To make such judgments, we need a project tracking mechanism which integrates expenditure information and progress information. One simple example of such a capability, based on a project's major milestones (PRR, PDR, etc.) is the *cost-schedule-milestone (CSM) chart* presented in Section 21.7.

(10) The CSM chart may be adequate for relating expenditures to progress on a small project, but it is inadequate for a large, complex project. An effective technique for large projects is an *Earned Value (EV) System,* which compares project expenditures to a project's current earned value, obtained by allocating individual earned values to a project's intermediate milestones, and calculating the accumulated earned value achieved by the project as it passes its various milestones. Earned value systems will be explained further in Section 32.5.

Of course, Fig. 32–3 is somewhat idealistic in that it portrays an eternally fixed set of budgets, WBS elements, PERT charts, and PWA agreements. In practice, these will inevitably change. To meet this need for change, the techniques presented here have been formulated in ways which accommodate change relatively smoothly; they are also relatively straightforward to automate.

32.3 PROJECT SCHEDULING TECHNIQUES

PERT Charts

A PERT chart is a network or graph* whose nodes represent project activities and their associated durations, and whose links represent precedence relations between pairs of activities. That is, if there is a link (arrow) from node *A* to node *B*, then activity *A* must be completed before activity *B* can start.

---

* In computer science terms, a PERT chart is an acyclic directed graph. A *directed graph* consists of a set of nodes (or vertices) and directed links connecting pairs of nodes (or edges: ordered pairs of vertices). An *acyclic directed graph* is a directed graph in which no sequence of links emanating from a node ever returns to that node.

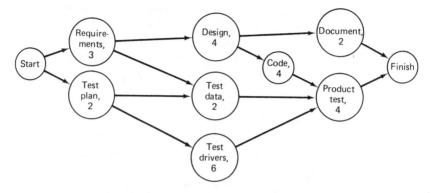

FIGURE 32-4 Simple software development PERT chart

Figure 32–4 is an example of a PERT chart representing an overall set of software development project activities. It shows, for example, that the test data activity has a duration of 2 months, must be completed before the product test activity begins, and cannot itself begin until the requirements and test plan activities are completed.

The term PERT is an acronym for Program Evaluation and Review Technique. PERT charts were developed and first used successfully by Lockheed Corporation and the U.S. Navy for the management of the Polaris missile program in the late 1950s. They are also sometimes called activity networks or precedence diagrams. They have been used effectively for a wide variety of project scheduling activities from building houses through software development to organizing the Olympic Games.

Constructing a PERT Chart

Most people find it easiest to construct a PERT chart by starting at the finishing end and working primarily backward. Here we present an informal procedure for doing so, illustrated with respect to the software development PERT chart shown in completed form in Fig. 32–4.

Step 1. Draw a node called Finish.

Step 2. Identify the activities whose completion, in your best estimate, constitute completion of the project. Add these activities and their durations as predecessor nodes to Finish. For example, we might identify completion of the code and document activities as constituting completion of the project, yielding Fig. 32–5a below.

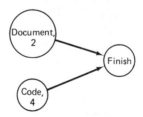

FIGURE 32-5a PERT chart development steps 1 and 2

Step 3. For the existing set of activities, determine whether any further activities are needed to ensure that the existing activities are indeed complete. If so, add these activities as successor nodes to the appropriate set of existing activities. For example, we might realize at this point that a product test activity is needed to ensure that the code will be ready for use, leading to Fig. 32–5b.

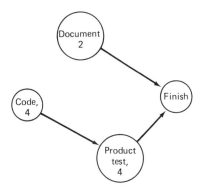

FIGURE 32–5b PERT chart development step 3

Step 4. For the existing set of activities, determine whether any additional activities are needed as prerequisites to the existing activities. If so, add these as predecessor nodes to the appropriate set of existing activities. For example, we might identify design, test data, and test driver development as prerequisite activities, yielding Fig. 32–5c.

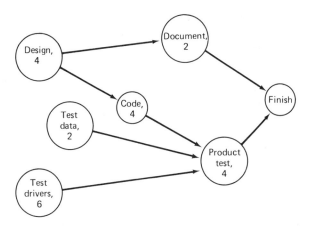

FIGURE 32–5c PERT chart development step 4

Step 5. If some predecessor nodes were added in Step 4, return to Step 3. Otherwise, proceed to Step 6. In this example, we would return to Step 3, in which we would add no successor nodes. In Step 4, though, we would add requirements and test plan as predecessor nodes, so that our next visit to Step 5 would result in a return to Step 3. In this iteration, though, we would find no further nodes to add, so that our third visit to Step 5 would result in our proceeding to Step 6 with our PERT chart in the state shown in Fig. 32–5d.

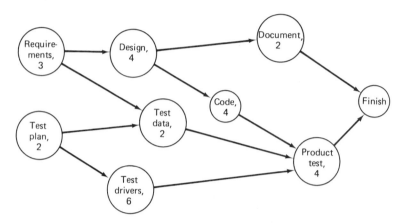

FIGURE 32–5d PERT chart development steps 5, 3, 4, 5, 3, 4, 5

Step 6. Draw a node called Start and connect it as a predecessor node to all existing nodes without predecessor nodes. In our example, these nodes are requirements and test plan. The result of Step 6 is the completed PERT chart as was shown in Fig. 32–4.

It is worth pointing out that, as with practically all mathematical representations of real world processes, a PERT chart model is not exact. For example, full as-built documentation cannot be completed until the code is developed; thus, there is a continuing code versus documentation reconciliation activity going on which is not represented in the PERT chart. In general, though, the PERT chart is a useful approximation to the software development process for project planning and control purposes.

Critical Path Analysis

Given a PERT chart for a software project such as the one in Fig. 32–4, we would like to know

- What is the minimum time it will take to complete the project?
- What activities are critical to our being able to complete the project in the minimum time?

It turns out that the critical activities lie on a path (or set of paths) between the Start node and the Finish node, called the *critical path* (or paths). The critical path is the longest path through the network in terms of total duration of activities.

Determining the Critical Path

Table 32–1 gives a simple procedure for determining the critical path for a PERT chart. It involves labeling each node i on the chart with an ordered pair of numbers (S_i, F_i) representing the earliest times that activity i can be started and finished, as illustrated in Fig. 32–6a.

TABLE 32-1 Critical Path Procedure

1. Label the Start node (0,0).
2. For all unlabeled nodes N whose predecessors are all labeled nodes, compute the earliest possible start time as the latest finishing time of all its predecessor nodes

$$S_N = \max_{i \in P(N)} [F_i] \qquad (32\text{–}1)$$

where $P(N)$ is the set of predecessor nodes of N.
Compute the corresponding finish time $F_N = S_N + D_N$, where D_N is the duration of activity N. Label the node N as (S_N, F_N).
3. Repeat Step 2 until no unlabeled nodes remain.

Thus, in the first iteration of this procedure, we would first label the Start node (0,0) as Step 1. In Step 2, we would find that only the requirements and test plan nodes had all their predecessor nodes labeled, as Start is the only node labeled at this point. The starting time for these two nodes is 0, since their set of predecessor nodes $P(N)$ in Eq. (32–1) consists only of the Start node, whose finishing time is 0. Their finishing times are therefore just their individual durations, so we label the requirements node (0,3) and the test plan node (0,2).

In Step 3, there are still some remaining unlabeled nodes, so we proceed to a second iteration of Step 2. This time, the design, test data, and test drivers nodes have all their predecessor nodes labeled. For the test data node, the set of predecessor nodes $P(N)$ consists of both the requirements and test plan nodes, so by Eq. (32–1), the earliest the test data activity can start is the later of the two finish times for

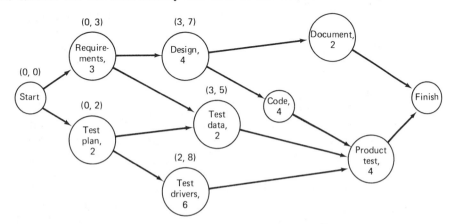

FIGURE 32-6a Critical path determination after two iterations

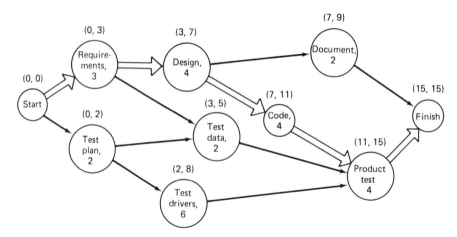

FIGURE 32–6b Critical path determination after five iterations

requirements and test plan, or 3 months. The corresponding earliest finish time for test data is 5 months, as illustrated in Fig. 32–6a, which shows the full state of events after this second iteration of Step 2.

In Step 3, there are still some remaining unlabeled nodes, so we continue to iterate until all of the nodes are labeled, yielding the result shown in Fig. 32–6b, with the critical path shown as double-lined arrows. The resulting minimum completion time for the project is determined to be 15 months.

Determining Late-Start and Slack Times

Given that we have completed the critical-path determination shown in Fig. 32–6b, there are two additional questions we would like to answer

- What is the *latest* time that we can start each activity without delaying the overall project finish time?
- How much *slack* is there in the completion time for each activity? That is, if we start the activity as soon as possible, by how much can we lengthen the duration of the activity without delaying the overall project finish time?

We can determine the answers to these questions by using a similar labeling procedure to our critical-path procedure. It starts with the completed results of the critical-path procedure, as in Fig. 32–6b, and involves underlabeling each node i with an ordered pair of numbers (S_i^l, F_i^l) representing the latest times that activity i can be started and finished. The latest-start procedure, given in Table 32–2, begins with the Finish node and works backwards.

The results of applying the latest-start procedure are shown in Fig. 32–7. From the figure, we can see another property of a critical-path activity: its early-start and early-finish times are the same as its late-start and late-finish times. Or, put another way, the slack time of a critical-path activity is zero. (Actually, this is how an automated algorithm would identify the critical path.)

TABLE 32–2 Latest-Start Procedure

1. Underlabel the Finish node F with its start and finish times as determined from the critical-path procedure, that is

$$(S_F^t, F_F^t) = (S_F, F_F).$$

2. For all non-underlabeled nodes N whose successors are all underlabeled nodes, compute the latest possible finish time as the earliest starting time of all its successor nodes

$$F_N^t = \min_{i \in S(N)} [S_i^t] \qquad (32–2)$$

where $S(N)$ is the set of successor nodes of N.
Compute the corresponding latest-start time $S_N^t = F_N^t - D_N$, where D_N is the duration of activity N. Underlabel the node as (S_N^t, F_N^t). Compute the slack time for the activity as

$$L_N = S_N^t - S_N \text{ (or } L_N = F_N^t - F_N)$$

3. Repeat Step 2 until no non-underlabeled nodes remain.

Planning and Control Implications

The critical-path and slack-time information associated with a **PERT** chart contains a number of significant project planning and control implications, illustrated below with respect to our software development project example.

1. *We can use the slack time associated with an activity either to delay its start time or to lengthen its duration (or both).* For example, in Fig. 32–7, we might choose to perform the test drivers activity from month-end 2 to month-end 8, and the test data activity from month-end 8 to month-end 10, in order to give both jobs to the same person. Or, as another example, we might choose to perform the documentation activity at a reduced level of effort over 6 months from month-end 7 to month-end 13, either to meet a personnel

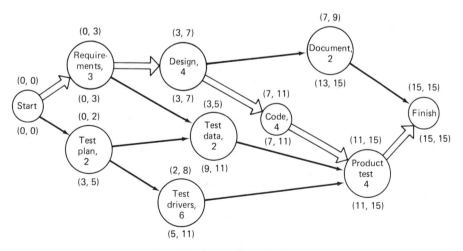

FIGURE 32–7 Determination of late-start times

constraint or to take advantage of coding information in completing the documentation.

2. *If we lengthen the duration of any critical path activity by X time units, we lengthen the project's completion time by X time units.* For example, if the design activity takes 6 months rather than 4 months, the project's completion time becomes 17 months rather than 15 months.

3. *If only a single critical path exists, we can shorten the project's overall duration by shortening the duration of a critical path activity.* Here, though, we can only shorten the project's duration up to a point at which another path becomes a critical path. Thus, as shown in Fig. 32–8, we could shorten the project's duration from 15 to 12 months by reducing the design time from 4 to 3 months and the code time from 4 to 2 months. However, at this point, we could not further shorten the project's duration by shortening the design time, because another path involving test plan and test drivers has also become a critical path.

If multiple critical paths exist, the problem of shortening the project's overall duration becomes more complex. In general, we can shorten the project's duration by shortening an activity common to all critical paths (such as the product test activity in Fig. 32–8). Otherwise, we can only shorten the project's duration by shortening activities on all independent critical-path segments (such as shortening both the design and test drivers activities in Fig. 32–8).

Of course, we must still remember our earlier discussions in Section 27.3 about the realities of compressing software project schedules. If the Design activity takes 6 months rather than 4 months, we can *in principle* maintain our existing 15-month project schedule by reducing the code time from 4 months to 2 months. But, in practice, attempting to do this by adding more people in the middle of the project will just lead to further delays.

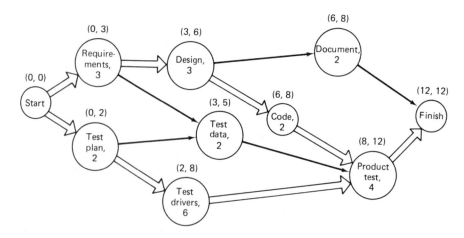

FIGURE 32–8 Shortening the critical path

PERT Charts: Variations and Extensions

There is another common form of the PERT chart, in which the arrowed links represent the activities and the nodes represent the completion of milestone events. This representation has some intuitive advantages, but has the disadvantage of requiring the use and explanation of dummy activities, which are not necessary in the activity-on-node network used here.

A number of more powerful (and more complex) extensions of the PERT chart have been developed to handle such situations as probabilistic estimates of activity durations, cost–schedule tradeoffs, and more complex node-branching operations (such as starting a new activity when m out of n predecessor activities have been completed). A good discussion of the nature, capabilities, and limitations of these techniques is given in [Wiest–Levy, 1977].

The PERT chart data structure and algorithms are examples of a wide class of graph-oriented data structures and algorithms encountered in computer science, such as topological sorting algorithms, shortest path algorithms, tree structures, etc. Good treatments of these related data structures and algorithms are given in [Horowitz–Sahni, 1976] and [Horowitz–Sahni, 1978].

Another useful variation for project management is the activity-responsibility network shown in Fig. 32–9. This representation has the advantage of showing both the activity dependencies and the management responsibilities for each of the activities on the project. It also has the advantage of injecting an additional dimension of reality into project planning. When we have to determine, "What is the V & V manager responsible for in preparing test data?" or, "Who is responsible for what items which the V & V manager will need in order to prepare the test data?" we begin to confront the planning issues with a sharper focus. For example, if we put

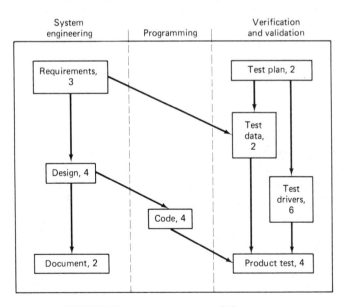

FIGURE 32–9 Activity—responsibility network

ourselves in the V & V manager's place, we may find that we will need a good deal of design information (for example, on data base structures, I/O blocking, etc.) in order to get an effective start in preparing test data.

Gantt Charts

Another very useful scheduling technique is the Gantt chart, which represents project activities as lines on a calendar-oriented chart, with triangles to indicate major milestones associated with the activity. Progress is indicated on the Gantt chart by filling in a triangle on the chart when its associated milestone has been passed.

Figure 32–10 shows a Gantt-chart version of our software project PERT chart, with some initial milestones indicated as complete. If we were to review this Gantt chart on March 15, 1984, everything would look fine: the requirements milestone has been passed two weeks early, and the design activity has begun with a two-week head start. However, if we were to review this Gantt chart on April 15, 1984, we would be a good deal more concerned about some of the activities which are the responsibility of the V & V group: the test plan is two weeks behind schedule, and the test drivers activity is two weeks late getting started.

Comparison of Gantt Charts and PERT Charts

The main difficulty with Gantt charts as compared with PERT charts is that they provide no insight into the dependency relations between the various activities. There is no way that we can tell from the Gantt chart whether the test plan schedule slippage on April 15 is a critical path slippage or not. We need the PERT chart to be able to conclude that the slippage in the test plan activity can be accommodated by overlapping the test drivers and test data activities and finding an additional person to carry out the test data activity.

Because of this ambiguity about dependency relations, Gantt charts can be a source of considerable trouble. For example, if we find that we can compensate for a test plan slippage by overlapping the test drivers and test data activities, we may

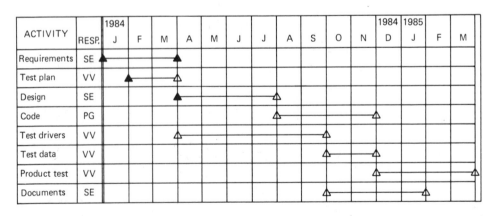

FIGURE 32–10 Gantt chart of software project plan

conclude that there can be a similar compensation for a requirements schedule slippage by overlapping the design and code activities. Only later, when it turns out that there is major breakage on code that was developed before the design was completed and verified, will we realize that the decision to overlap the design and code activities overlooked a strong precedence relationship between the two activities.

For similar reasons, the PERT chart stimulates more thorough planning than the Gantt chart, as the planners need to think through the dependency relations as well as the time durations of the various activities. On the other hand, the PERT chart relations sometimes require the planner to somewhat misrepresent dependency relations between activities, which are often more subtle than the simple yes or no options represented by the PERT chart (for example, the relations between documentation, design, and code).

The Gantt chart has some complementary advantages with respect to the PERT chart. It is simpler, easier to develop, and easier to update. It conveys project status information and calendar-oriented information that are not included in the standard PERT chart (extensions of the PERT chart which do convey status and calendar information exist, but they are more complicated to use). In general, the Gantt chart is preferable to use in simple scheduling situations in which the dependencies are intuitively clear, and the PERT chart is preferable for those parts of projects with complex dependency relations.

32.4 DETAILED SOFTWARE PLANNING AND CONTROL: THE UNIT DEVELOPMENT FOLDER

The 90% Syndrome

Often, software projects have had effective macro-level planning and control capabilities, but have come to grief because of a lack of visibility into project dynamics at the micro level. One frequent difficulty stems from an over-reliance on individual percent-complete estimates as indicators of project progress at the micro level.

Figure 32-11 shows the typical pattern of percent-complete estimates on a software project which ran into such problems several years ago. The percent-complete figures are taken from a series of weekly progress reports submitted by a programmer working on a software component which eventually took 12 weeks to complete. By the end of week 5, the programmer estimated in his weekly progress report that the component was 90% complete (typically, this meant that the basic code had been developed and successfully compiled, and that there were just a couple of small bugs to find and one or two small additional features to incorporate before the program was ready).

Frequently, the manager of such a programmer would note the 90%-complete estimate, proceed to negotiate an assignment on a new project for the programmer after the following week, and schedule the routine to be passed on to the integration team at that time. This meant that a week later, when the job was not done and was now estimated at 95% complete, the manager had to go back to the project manager expecting the programmer and renegotiate the transfer for a week later,

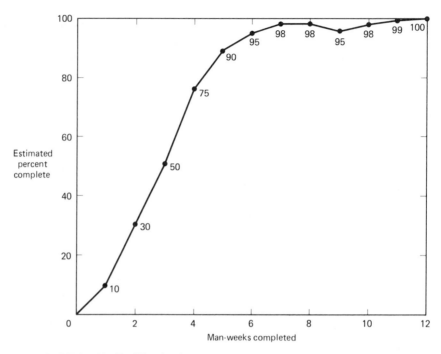

FIGURE 32-11 Traditional software progress measures don't provide visibility

and similarly with the manager of the integration activity. After a few more such weekly negotiations, people get bitter and don't trust each other, and the entire project control process begins to disintegrate. Further, the blight often spreads to other projects through the uncertainties of interface integration and the delays due to performers who do not show up on time.

The Unit Development Folder (UDF)

The Unit Development Folder (UDF) is a formalized programmer's notebook which has been used to successfully overcome the 90% syndrome on many software projects [Williams, 1975; Ingrassia, 1978]. The UDF serves the following primary software development and management purposes:

1. Provides an orderly and consistent approach in the development of each of a software product's units
2. Provides a uniform and visible collection point for all unit documentation and code
3. Aids individual discipline in the establishment and attainment of unit level development milestones
4. Provides improved management visibility and control over the unit level development process

Figure 32–12 shows the nature of the UDF, the content of its various sections, and the relation of the UDF and its sections to the steps and products of the software

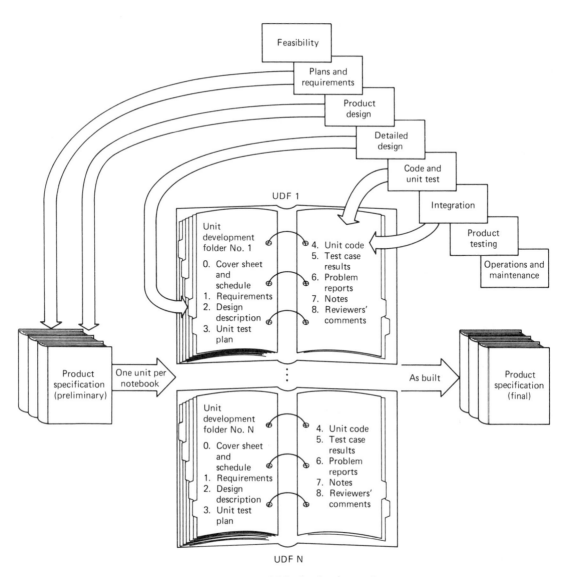

FIGURE 32–12 The UDF in the development process

life-cycle process. Typically, each UDF is established at the end of the product design phase; one of the major functions of product design is to divide the software product into units* and to establish an overall development plan for the units. At this time,

* The size criterion for a unit varies somewhat with the size and type of software product to be developed. A smaller organic-mode project with experienced developers can use large (1000-DSI) units, while a larger embedded-mode project with a good many less experienced developers will require smaller (100–300-DSI) units. Other criteria for defining units are that each unit should

- Perform a specific, well-defined function which is traceable to the software requirements
- Require only one person for its development
- Be conveniently testable by the unit developer

each UDF is furnished with those requirements specifications (Section 1) and overall (preliminary) design specifications (Section 2) from the preliminary product specification which serve to define the unit.

The UDF is then given to a programmer-analyst who serves as its developer and custodian throughout the detailed design, code, unit test, and integration phases. The developer proceeds to develop the detailed design for the unit (a refinement of the preliminary design in Section 2), the unit test plan (Section 3), and the unit code (Section 4). Once the unit testing has been satisfactorily completed, a summary of the test results are placed in Section 5 (a separate binder is generally necessary for the complete unit test results, which may be rather bulky). The final step in the unit development process is to complete the as-built requirements and design specifications in Sections 1 and 2, so that they can be merged with their counterparts from other UDF's into an overall final product specification, as shown in Fig. 32–12.

The remaining sections of the UDF provide convenient repositories for further information concerning the unit. Section 6 contains a copy of all problem reports affecting the unit, including those issued during integration and product test. Section 7 contains any memos, reports, and notes which affect or expand on the contents of the unit. Section 8 contains a record of reviewers' comments and any for-the-record comments resulting from inspections or walkthroughs.

The UDF Cover Sheet

The organization and contents of the UDF thus provide the project with an orderly and consistent means of developing and controlling the documentation and code components of the software product. The objectives of providing micro-level management visibility of the software development process and of avoiding the 90% syndrome are primarily provided by the UDF Cover Sheet.

Figure 32–13 shows an example UDF Cover Sheet for the Increment 1 EDIT unit of the Central Equipment Management and Inventory Control System (CEMICS) presented in Chapter 31. It would usually be employed as follows:

1. The unit developer, Bill Jones, and his supervisor, Fred Fox, negotiate a mutually agreeable overall schedule for the development. Generally, this means that they agree to the date on which Bill will receive the unit requirements and preliminary design specifications and start work (Oct. 1, 1982 in Fig. 32–13), the date on which he will provide the test results indicating that the unit performs as specified (Jan. 1, 1983 in Fig. 32–13), and the date on which he will provide the as-built documentation for the unit (April 1, 1983 in Fig. 32–13).
2. Bill then schedules the intermediate milestone dates himself, based on his assessment of the required development activity, his vacation plans, etc. Thus, in Fig. 32–13, Bill has scheduled completion of his code-to design specification by Nov. 1, 1982; his unit test plan by Nov. 15, 1982; and his unit code by Dec. 1, 1982. This self-scheduling and negotiation gives Bill more of a feeling of control over his destiny, and more of a feeling of commitment to a set of

UNIT DEVELOPMENT FOLDER COVER SHEET

PROJECT: CEMICS

UNIT: EDIT (Increment 1)   CUSTODIAN: W.P. Jones

ROUTINES INCLUDED: EDIN, EDSCAN, EDTAS, EDADD, EDDEL, EDMOD, EDERR

Section	Description		Due date	Date complete	Originator	Reviewer
1	Unit requirements		10/1/82	10/1/82	W.P. Jones *W.P.J.*	R.E. Lee *R.E.L*
2	Unit design	2a. Prelim	10/1/82	10/1/82	*W.P.J.*	*R.E.L*
		2b. Code-to	11/1/82	10/29/82	*W.P.J.*	*R.E.L. 11/1*
		2c. As-built	4/1/83			
3	Test plan		11/15/82	11/18/82	*W.P.J.*	*R.E.L. 11/19*
4	Unit code		12/1/82	11/29/82	*W.P.J.*	*R.E.L. 12/2*
5	Test results		1/1/83			
6	Problem reports					
7	Notes					
8	Reviewers' comments					

FIGURE 32-13 Unit development folder cover sheet: CEMICS EDIT program

milestones he has determined himself, rather than having them imposed on him arbitrarily.

3. As Bill passes each of the milestones, he inserts the milestone product into the UDF, and enters the date and his initials on the cover sheet. The responsible reviewer then reviews the milestone product and enters the date and his initials if the review product is satisfactory.* (Otherwise, he meets with Bill to discuss the actions required to make the product satisfactory). In the example in Fig. 32-13, Bill has completed his code-to design specification a few days early, his test plan a few days late, and his unit code a few days early.

These indicators of progress on the UDF cover sheet are much more effective than the percent-complete indicator of progress. If Bill, for example, had been faced with the possibility of missing his test plan deadline by more than a few days, several things would have been likely to happen to correct the situation

---

* The review process for the code-to design and the unit code should involve some type of inspection or structured walkthrough [Fagan, 1976; Yourdon, 1979a].

- Bill might simply have fallen behind in his work, and might put in an extra effort on the test plan to get back on schedule (the Deadline Effect)
- Bill might find himself stymied by someone else (for example, the V & V group in providing him with test data definitions), and go to his supervisor, Fred Fox, for help—generally, much earlier than if the UDF milestone had not been established
- Bill might not realize the importance of his completing his unit on time, in which case Fred will detect this early, while there is still time to correct the situation

In summary, the UDF provides the micro-level visibility necessary for effective software project level planning and control, particularly for large projects. Further, it creates a set of lower level project milestones upon which an improved cost–progress tracking system can be established, as we will discuss in the following section.

32.5 MONITORING PROJECT EXPENDITURES VERSUS PROGRESS: THE EARNED VALUE SYSTEM

Problems in Overall Project Status Monitoring and Control

Software project status assessment and control would be a fairly straightforward process if everything on the project progressed according to plan. However, particularly on large projects, a great many deviations from the original plan are all happening at the same time. Some parts of the project are completed in fewer man-months than predicted; others turn out to be harder than anticipated and take a good deal more effort than planned. Necessary revisions to the system requirements are introduced, requiring people to reallocate their efforts and reset their priorities. Key people get sick, get promoted, or leave. Some teams are slow in staffing up, while others appear to be staffing too quickly. External events sometimes cause delays (for example, equipment availability, user approvals), and sometimes also provide windfalls (for example, discovering an applicable piece of existing software).

Faced with this welter of incremental deviations from the basic plan, the customer and project manager often have a difficult time assessing the overall progress of the project and, in particular, in estimating the likely cost to complete the job. Here are two typical questions that often need to be answered.

- Is the project overspending because in general the design was easier than expected, and large-scale programming was able to start earlier, implying that the project will require fewer months and dollars to complete?
- Or, is the project overspending because in general the design was harder than expected, and the project absorbed a large number of programmers prematurely, implying that the job will require considerably more months and dollars to complete?

In the middle of a large project, particularly one involving the overlapping incremental development of a series of increasing product capabilities, questions of this sort can be very hard to answer.

Earned Value Concepts and the Summary Task Planning Sheet

The best technique currently available for assessing the status and likely cost to complete of a large, complex software project is the *earned value* concept [U.S. Air Force, 1978]. In an Earned Value (EV) System, we assign earned values for the completion of all the individual component tasks making up a project. Then, as the tasks are completed, we accumulate an overall project earned value which we can compare with our project expenditures to determine how well the project is progressing with respect to its plans. We can also use the ratio of project expenditures to earned value as a basis of estimating the project's cost to complete.

Figure 32–14 shows a typical *summary task planning sheet* (STPS) used in the EV approach, again, using the CEMICS programming activity of Chapter 31 as an example. Table 32–3 explains each of the entries on the STPS. The STPS shown in Fig. 32–14 covers the programming and integration of three CEMICS programs: EDIT, UPDATE, and EQUIP. These are being developed and integrated in phased increments: EDIT in three increments; UPDATE and EQUIP in two increments each.

Task 1 in Fig. 32–14 covers the development and integration of Increment 1 of the EDIT program, which was used in Fig. 32–13 as the subject of our discussion of the UDF cover sheet of Section 32.4. The *D, C,* and *T* milestone triangles in the Gantt chart portion of the Task 1 line in Fig. 32–14 correspond to the code-to design (Nov. 1, 1982), unit code (Dec. 1, 1982), and test results (Jan. 1, 1983) milestones on the UDF Cover Sheet for the Increment 1 EDIT program in Fig. 32–13. The *I* milestone triangle represents the successful integration of the EDIT program into Increment 1 of the CEMICS software product.

The numbers above the milestone triangles in Fig. 32–14 indicate the project's assignment of earned value for the completion of the milestone. The budgeted cost for developing and integrating the entire EDIT program is $73,000 ($73K), broken down into $7K for Increment 1, $22K for Increment 2, and $44K for Increment 3. Here, these budgeted costs are assigned as the earned values for completing each of the increments (column ⑭ in Fig. 32–14). The $7K for development and integration of Increment 1 of the EDIT program is then allocated as $2K for completing the code-to design milestone, $1K for unit code, $2K for test results, and $2K for completing the integration of EDIT into Increment 1.

Suppose that both Figs. 32–13 and 32–14 represent the project status as of January 1, 1983. At this time, Increment 1 of the EDIT program has completed its design and code milestones, and has accumulated a total earned value of $3K, as shown in column ⑮ of Fig. 32–14. Also at this time, Increment 2 has completed its design milestone, and has accumulated a total earned value of $6K. Thus, at this point, the overall work breakdown structure element, EDIT Programming, has accumulated

Summary Task Planning Sheet

Sheet 1 of 3

(1) Project number: B142	(2) Project: CEMICS	(3) Component:
(5) WBS element: S3A, S3B, S3C	(6) Responsible organization: BSD	(7) Manager: F. Fox
		Programming
		(4) Date: 1/1/83
		(8) PWA number: B142-022

(9) Task number	(10) WBS element	(11) Task description	(12) EV type	(13) Year / Month (1982	1983)														(14) Earned value — Total	(15) To date	(16) WBS to date	(17) Expenditure
				O	N	D	J	F	M	A	M	J	J	A	S	O	N	D				
1	S3A	EDIT programming, incr 1	MS		2 D	2 C	2 T												7.0	3.0		
2	S3A	EDIT programming, incr 2	MS			6 D	6 C	5 T	5 C	6 I									22.0	6.0		
3	S3A	EDIT programming, incr 3	MS					5 T	12 D	12 C	10 I	10 T							44.0	0.0	9.0	13.1
4	S3B	UPDATE programming, incr 1	MS		6 D	6 C	5 T	5 C	6 I										22.0	16.0		
5	S3B	UPDATE programming, incr 2	MS				3 D	3 C	2 T	3 I									11.0	3.0	19.0	16.2
6	S3C	EQUIP programming, incr 1	MS		5 D	5 C	5 T		5 I										20.0	15.0		
7	S3C	EQUIP programming, incr 2	MS					5 T	4 C	5 D	6 I								20.0	0.0	15.0	20.3
8																						
9																						
																			(20) 146.0		(21) 43.0	(22) 49.6

Totals:
(18) Earned value: 13.0 11.0 19.0
(19) Expenditures: 14.8 12.2 17.6

FIGURE 32-14 Summary task planning sheet: CEMICS programming

614

TABLE 32-3 Summary Task Planning Sheet (STPS) Entries

1. *Project Number*. A number uniquely identifying this project.
2. *Project*. A short title for the project.
3. *Component*. The portion of the project covered by this STPS.
4. *Date*. The date the STPS was established.
5. *WBS Elements*. The work breakdown structure elements covered by this STPS.
6. *Responsible Organization*. The organization responsible for performing the work covered in the STPS.
7. *Manager*. The individual responsible for work performance.
8. *PWA Number*. The number of the project work authorization covering the work indicated by the STPS.
9. *Task Number*. A sequence number for the tasks in this STPS.
10. *WBS Element*. The WBS element covering the indicated task.
11. *Task Description*. A short title identifying the task.
12. *EV Type*. The type of earned value allocation used for this task:
      MS Earned value accumulated only at specific task milestones.
      LM Earned values associated with major project milestones; task accumulates earned value equal to its expenditure during the phase, up to the total EV for the task during the phase.
13. *Schedule*. A Gantt chart indicating the milestones for each task, and their associated earned values.
14. *EV-Total*. Total earned value allocated to the task.
15. *EV-To Date*. Earned value accumulated to date for the task.
16. *EV-WBS To Date*. Earned value accumulated to date for the WBS element.
17. *Expenditures*. Expenditures to date for the WBS element.
18. *Totals-Earned Value*. Monthly and summary totals of earned value for the tasks on the STPS.
19. *Totals-Expenditures*. Monthly and summary totals of expenditures for the tasks on the STPS.
20. Total earned value allocated to the tasks on the STPS.
21. Total earned value accumulated to date for the tasks on this STPS.
22. Total expenditures to date for the tasks on this STPS.

$9K of earned value (column ⑯) as compared to its expenditure to date of $13.1K.* The shortfall in earned value is due partly ($2K) to missing the Increment 1 test results milestone, and partly ($2.1K) to a higher than expected rate of expenditure.

Similarly, we can see in Fig. 32-14 the relative progress of the two increments of the UPDATE and EQUIP programs, and their overall earned values as compared to their expenditures to date. An overall accumulation of earned values and expenditures for all three programs is given in rows ⑱ and ⑲, both by month and then by totals to date in entries ㉑ and ㉒. At this point, the progress of these three programs appears to be going reasonably according to plan; the 15% overexpenditure is not enough to trigger a revision of the cost-to-complete estimate, but it is enough to warrant an investigation into the causes of the overexpenditure.

An Earned Value Summary Report

One difficulty of the summary task planning sheet is that of accumulating earned value and expenditure totals across a large number of STPS's. A better instrument

* Usually, the lowest level of tracking project expenditures is the entire work breakdown structure (WBS) element, so no record of expenditures by increment is available.

Earned Value Summary Report

PROJECT: CEMICS
BUDGET: $941,000

PROJECT NUMBER: B142
FROM: 7/1/82 TO 12/31/83

DATE: 1/1/83
MANAGER: M. Marcos

WBS Number	Job Number	WBS Element	EV Type	Last Mo $K		To Date $K				TOT EV$K	Percent of total EV			
				EV	Actual	EV	Actual	$\frac{A-E}{E}$	E20	EV$K	EV	Actual	Diff.	E10
S		CEMICS		51.2	61.8	269.0	272.4	1		941.0	29	29	0	
S1	B14201	Mangement	LM	6.2	6.2	38.5	37.1	-4		116.0	33	32	-1	
S2		System engr.		9.6	9.6	107.7	91.7	-15		155.0	69	59	-10	*
S21	B14202	Requirements	LM	2.5	2.5	32.4	24.1	-26	*	47.0	69	51	-18	*
S22	B14203	Product design	LM	7.1	7.1	75.3	67.6	-10		108.0	70	63	-7	
S3		Programming		28.0	34.0	89.0	92.7	4		427.0	21	22	1	
S3A	B14204	EDIT	MS	6.0	4.8	9.0	13.1	46	**	73.0	12	18	6	
S3B	B14205	UPDATE	MS	5.0	5.7	19.0	16.2	-15		33.0	58	49	-9	
S3C	B14206	EQUIP	MS	6.0	7.1	15.0	20.3	35	*	40.0	38	51	13	*
S3D	B14207	RPTDATA	MS	6.0	6.0	16.0	12.2	-24	*	80.0	20	15	-5	
S3E	B14208	Reports	MS	3.0	4.6	12.0	10.6	-12		37.0	32	29	-3	
S3F	B14209	MISC	MS	2.0	5.8	2.0	5.8	190	***	32.0	6	18	12	
S33	B14210	Integration	MS	0.0	0.0	19.0	13.5	-29	*	132.0	14	10	-4	
S4		test		5.0	9.6	19.0	37.0	95	***	157.0	12	24	12	
S41	B14211	Test plan	MS	5.0	9.6	10.0	29.7	197	***	33.0	30	90	60	***
S42	B14212	V&V	MS	0.0	0.0	9.0	7.3	-19		124.0	7	6	-1	
S5	B14213	Documentation	LM	2.4	2.4	14.8	13.9	-6		46.0	32	30	-2	
S6	B14214	Implementation	LM	0.0	0.0	0.0	0.0	-		40.0	0	0	0	

FIGURE 32-15 CEMICS earned value summary report

for this purpose is the earned value summary report, illustrated in Fig. 32–15. This report summarizes the earned value status of each work breakdown structure (WBS) element of the project, showing the comparison of earned value to expenditure for the previous month, for the WBS element to date, and for the WBS element as a percentage of its total earned value. As seen in Fig. 32–15, the overall earned value for the project ($269K) is reasonably close to the expenditures to date ($272.4K).

However, there are portions of the project whose earned values to date are significantly above or below their expenditures to date. These are conveniently identified by the exception reporting capabilities (columns E20 and E10) included in the earned value summary report. The E20 column in the to-date $K region identifies WBS elements with large underexpenditures (minus sign) or overexpenditures relative to their earned value to date, in increments of 20% (*:20 to 40%; **:40 to 60%; ***:over 60%). This column tends to highlight those WBS elements which are getting off to a slow or fast start with respect to earned value. Thus, for example, the EDIT programming effort rates a two-star overexpenditure rate in the to date E20 column, but its small $4.1K overexpenditure relative to its total earned value does not rate even a one-star exception report in the total-EV E10 column.

The total-EV E10 column identifies WBS elements with large underexpenditures (minus sign) or overexpenditures relative to their total earned value, in increments of 10% (*:10 to 20%; **:20 to 30%; ***:over 30%). It tends to highlight WBS elements with potential problems or advantages with respect to balancing their total expenditures and earned values. Thus, for example, the requirements activity has a strong chance of completing all its project tasks with significantly less expenditure than earned value; it has currently achieved 69% of its total earned value with an expenditure of only 51% of its total earned value. (In this case, the project manager has set the total earned value of each WBS element equal to its total budget; this is generally, but not necessarily done.)

If a WBS element has serious overexpenditures in both the to-date and total-EV exception reports, it should be the subject of a major management review, followed by appropriate corrective action. In Fig. 32–15, the most serious problem is in the test planning area, which has spent 90% of its budget and accumulated only 30% of its earned value.

Discussion

At any given reporting time, a project's expenditures are likely to be a few percent higher than the earned value, because there will usually be some milestone activities whose durations overlap the reporting time, accumulating some expenditures but not yet qualifying for the earned value credit awarded on completion of the milestone activity. For example, in Fig. 32–14, the design of Increment 2 of the EQUIP program (task 7) extends from Dec. 1, 1982 to Feb. 1, 1983. On Jan. 1, 1983, the project has probably spent about $3K on this design, but there is no way for the project to obtain partial credit for the $6K worth of earned value due on completion of the design.

A number of alternative methods of earned value calculation have been advanced to counter this difficulty, such as awarding half of the earned value at the beginning of each milestone activity and half at the end, or spreading the earned value uniformly across the period of performance. However, each of these alternatives creates its own biases in some situations and adds further complication to the Earned Value System. Thus, it appears preferable to use the system in its simplest form.

On smaller, straightforward projects with very little change during the development period, the Earned Value System is easy to operate, but its incremental contribution to project visibility is relatively small. On a large, complex project with frequent changes, the Earned Value System provides an irreplaceable contribution to project visibility and management, but it requires much more work to operate. This implies the need for automating an Earned Value System for use on large projects.

For small projects, it is generally best to set up an Earned Value System, even a manual one, since it is hard to tell in advance how much change and elaboration the project will encounter in the future. Furthermore, as with other planning and control techniques such as PERT charts, one strong and irrevocable benefit we will gain is the amount of project understanding and organization we will derive by thinking through the various project activities and determining how much they are worth, and how they fit together.

32.6 SOFTWARE PROJECT PLANNING AND CONTROL EXAMPLE

In this section, we show how the planning and control techniques above are applied to a software project in a coordinated way, using the Central Equipment Management and Inventory Control System (CEMICS) presented in Section 31.8 as an example. In doing so, we will use the overall framework of planning and control techniques outlined in Section 32.2 and shown in Fig. 32–3, which is reproduced here for convenience as Fig. 32–16.

Step 1. The Work Breakdown Structure (WBS)

We begin by developing an initial WBS for the CEMICS software development project, and by using the WBS as a basis for allocating the COCOMO estimates of CEMICS software development costs to specific task budgets associated with specific task responsibilities. Strictly speaking, we should use the Detailed COCOMO model to develop a more extensive estimate of the phase and module cost breakdowns of the CEMICS development costs, rather than the Intermediate COCOMO estimates given in Section 31–6. However, to keep things simple and consistent with Chapter 31 (and since the phase distributions would not be much different, as CEMICS is a reasonably nominal organic-mode project with respect to its cost driver attributes), we will use the Intermediate COCOMO cost estimates developed in Section 31.6 as the overall estimates of CEMICS development cost. To allocate the overall development cost to WBS elements, we will then use the nominal organic-mode activity distributions given in Table 7–3, and the distribution of CEMICS costs by component in the Intermediate COCOMO estimate given in Fig. 31–5.

Figure 32–17 shows the initial WBS for CEMICS. It follows the standard structure for a WBS given in Figs. 4–6a and b. The total CEMICS development and implementa-

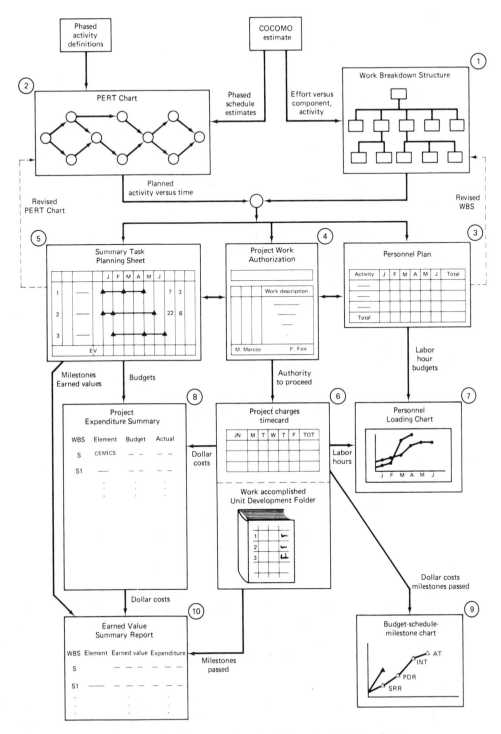

FIGURE 32–16 Software project planning and control framework

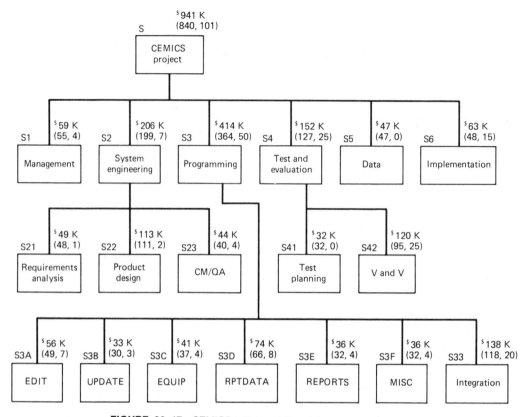

FIGURE 32–17 CEMICS initial work breakdown structure (WBS)

tion budget of $941K covered by the WBS includes the following costs estimated in Section 31.8:

Labor costs	$840K
Development	792K
Implementation	48K
Computer costs	101K
Development	86K
Implementation	15K
Total	$941K

The implementation costs are covered in WBS element S6; Implementation, as shown in Fig. 32–17. (Each WBS element in Fig. 32–17 has three associated budget items: the total budget on top, and the labor and computer costs in parentheses below.) The development budget, by definition, does not include the plans and requirements phase costs.

Allocating Software Development WBS Element Budgets. To allocate the $792K of software development labor costs into initial WBS elements, we first break it down into the percentages of total development effort given in Table 7–3 for organic-mode projects (for size-dependent percentages, we consider the 48-KDSI CEMICS product as medium size).

Activity	Percent of Effort (from Table 7–3)	Budget
Requirements analysis	6%	$ 48K
Product design	14	111
Programming	46	364
Test planning	4	32
V & V	12	95
Project office	7	55
CM/QA	5	39
Manuals	6	48
Total	100%	$792K

We then collect the system engineering-related budgets and the test and evaluation-related budgets into their second level WBS elements, leaving the individual activities at the third level of the WBS as shown in Fig. 32–17. The specific task responsibilities associated with these budgets are those identified in the phase and activity definitions given in Table 4–3.

The $364K of programming budget is too large to be left as an individual WBS element (generally, a $50 to 100K WBS element is the best compromise between having good control and having too much detail). It is best broken down into individual budgets for the major CEMICS program components used in the COCOMO cost estimate in Fig. 31–5, plus a WBS element for Integration, which includes both integration activities and the overall programming activities performed before unit development and after integration.

A good budget estimate for the integration task is to allocate it twice the fraction of the programming budget expended during the integration and test phase. From Table 7–3, this is

$$2(\$792K)(0.22)(0.34) = \$118K$$

This leaves $246K for the programming of the individual components. This budget is best broken down according to the contribution of each component to the overall COCOMO development cost estimate in column ㉓ of Fig. 31–10, as shown below.

Component	Total Cost Contribution (Fig. 31–10)	Percentage Contribution	Programming Budget
EDIT	$160K	20%	$ 49K
UPDATE	90	12	30
EQUIP	120	15	37
RPTDATA	214	27	66
REPORTS	104	13	32
MISC	104	13	32
Total	$792K	100%	$246K

The allocation of computer time to the various WBS elements is in proportion to general experience on computer time distribution. The resulting overall WBS budget allocations are as shown in Fig. 32–17.

Step 2. PERT Charts

The simple software development project PERT chart we discussed in Section 32.3 becomes more complex in CEMICS because of the project's plan to develop the software in three increments. The first increment performs the core UPDATE and EQUIP functions involving the master equipment data base, and includes only the basic I/O functions from the other components. The second and third increments add further functional capabilities; Table 32–4 indicates the number of instructions in each CEMICS component to be developed in each increment. Thus, for example, the 6000-DSI UPDATE program will have 4000 DSI developed in Increment 1, 2000 DSI in Increment 2, and none in Increment 3.

TABLE 32–4 CEMICS Development Increments

Component / Increment	Size in DSI						
	EDIT	UPDATE	EQUIP	RPTDATA	REPORTS	MISC	Total
1	1000	4000	4000	2000	2000	0	13,000
2	3000	2000	4000	4000	2000	2000	17,000
3	6000	0	0	6000	2000	4000	18,000
Total	10,000	6000	8000	12,000	6000	6000	48,000

Figure 32–18 shows the PERT chart for the CEMICS project. Its form and method of construction are basically the same as for the PERT charts in Section 32.3, with one addition: Here, we have employed a time-phased PERT chart to show specific calendar times for the various project tasks. The time phasing of the three development increments creates a situation with multiple critical paths. The schedule is well-balanced, but a schedule slip on any of the critical paths implies a slip in the overall project schedule.

In this case, the overall COCOMO 16½-month development schedule estimate is preserved, as have been the lengths of the first two phases, but the phase boundary between programming and integration-and-test has become staggered.

Step 3. Personnel Plan

In order to develop a detailed month by month personnel plan, we need to calculate from our COCOMO estimates the average number of people devoted to each activity during each phase. We can do this using the COCOMO estimates of phase distribution of effort and schedule given in Table 6–8, and the estimates of effort distribution by phase and activity in Table 7–3.

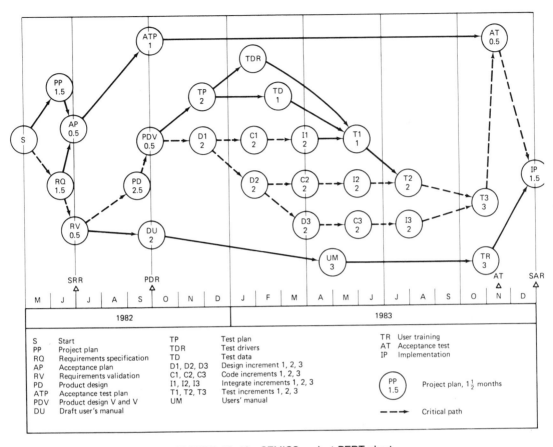

FIGURE 32–18 CEMICS project PERT chart

Table 32–5 shows the resulting estimated personnel levels for each phase and activity of the CEMICS projects. For example, the quantities in the lefthand column (for the plans and requirements phase) are derived as follows:

- From Table 6–8, 6% in addition to the 144-MM CEMICS development effort (or 9 MM) is devoted to Plans and Requirements
- From Table 6–8, 12% in addition to the 16½-month CEMICS development schedule (or 2 months) is devoted to Plans and Requirements
- The resulting average project personnel level in the Plans and Requirements phase is 9MM/2 months = 4.5 FSP.
- Of this 4.5 FSP, by Table 7–3, 46% is devoted to requirements analysis activities, or 2.1 FSP. Similarly, 20% is devoted to product design activities, or 0.9 FSP, etc.

Given these average personnel levels by phase and activity, given the PERT chart connecting phase, activity and calendar time, and given the initial WBS providing

TABLE 32–5 CEMICS Phase and Activity Distribution

Phase / Quantity		Plans and Requirements		Product Design		Programming		Integration and Test	
Effort	%	6		16		61.5		22.5	
	MM	9		23		89		32	
Schedule	%	12		19		54.3		26.7	
	Mo	2		3		9		4.5	
$FSP = \dfrac{MM}{Mo}$		4.5		7.7		9.9		7.1	

Phase / Activity	%	FSP	%	FSP	%	FSP	%	FSP
Requirements analysis	46	2.1	15	1.1	5	0.5	3	0.2
Product design	20	0.9	40	3.1	10	1.0	6	0.4
Programming	3	0.1	14	1.1	58	5.7	34	2.4
Test planning	3	0.1	5	0.4	4	0.4	2	0.2
Verification and validation	6	0.3	6	0.5	6	0.6	34	2.4
Project office	15	0.7	11	0.8	6	0.6	7	0.5
CM/QA	2	0.1	2	0.2	6	0.6	7	0.5
Manuals	5	0.2	7	0.5	5	0.5	7	0.5

a more detailed breakdown of activities by task, we can construct a detailed personnel plan indicating how many people will be needed for each task during each month of the project.

Such a personnel plan is shown in Table 32–6. The total of 159 MM in the plan consists of the 144 MM estimated by COCOMO for software development, plus an additional 9 MM estimated for the plans and requirements phase in Table 32–5, and 6 MM estimated in Section 31.8 for the implementation activity. Some additional comments on the plan are given below:

1. The personnel distribution by WBS element will generally vary somewhat from the initial WBS budgets. For example, since the CEMICS Project Office and CM/QA FSP levels in Table 32.5 generally add up to about 1 FSP, the CEMICS project manager, Maria Marcos, has decided to include the CM/QA function as part of her project management activity, and to have her secretary perform the administrative CM/QA functions. Since clerical personnel are not included in the COCOMO man-month estimates or included in the personnel plan (at PPI, the secretarial pool is charged to projects via the overhead rate), a note to this effect is included in the personnel plan. A similar note explains that the training task is covered within the system engineering activity. Also, actual programming personnel assignments will create some variance from the initial WBS estimates. Therefore, a revised WBS must be developed which reflects the realities of detailed personnel planning.

2. The personnel plan should not be overly precise. It is generally not worthwhile to try to specify personnel levels to more than a half-FSP level of precision.

TABLE 32–6 CEMICS Personnel Plan

Milestones (△): SRR and PDR in 1982; I1, I2, I3, and PT / AT / IP (△△△) in 1983.

Months: columns M–D (first 8) are 1982; columns J–D (next 12) are 1983.

WBS Element	Activity	M	J	J	A	S	O	N	D	J	F	M	A	M	J	J	A	S	O	N	D	Total
S1,S23	Project management, CM/QA[a]	1	1	1	1	1	1	1	1	1	1	1	1	1	1	1	1	1	1	1	1	20
S2,S5, S63	System engineering	2.5	3.5	4	5	5	3	3	2.5	2	1	1	1	1	2	2	1	1	1	.5		42
S3	Programming				.5	1	2	4	4.5	5	5.5	8	7.5	7.5	7	4.5	4	3	2	1.5	1	68.5
S3A	EDIT										1	1	1	1	2	2	2	1	.5	.5		12
S3B	UPDATE											1	1	1	.5	.5	.5	.5	.5			5.5
S3C	EQUIP											1	1	1	1	1	.5	.5	.5			6.5
S3D	RPTDATA								.5	1	1	1	2	2	2	2	1	.5				13
S3E	REPORTS								.5	.5	.5	.5	1	1	.5	.5	.5	.5				6
S3F	MISC											.5	.5	.5	.5	1	1	.5	.5			5
S33	Integration											1	1	1	1	1.5	2	2				9.5
S4	Verification and validation	.5	.5	.5	1	1	1	.5	.5	.5	.5	1	1	1	2	2	3	3	3	1.5		24
S6	Implementation																[b]			1.5	3	4.5
S	Total	4	5	6	8	9	9	9	9	9	10.5	10.5	10.5	10	9.5	9	8	7	6.5	5.5	4	159
	Computer cost ($K)		1	1	1	1	2	2	3	4	5	6	7	7	7	8	9	9	9	9	10	101

NOTES: [a] CM/QA administrative functions to be handled by Project Manager's secretary
[b] Training activities performed as part of system engineering

3. Typically, the personnel plan will take 3 or 4 iterations to converge; to smooth out the loading, reconcile the plan's totals to the previous estimates, and to define nonstandard task interfaces such as those in item 1 above.

4. The use of incremental development leads to a very flat personnel distribution for the CEMICS project. This is good in that it avoids major project staffing peaks and valleys, but note that it is considerably different from a Rayleigh distribution.

5. For convenience, the time distribution of computer costs has been estimated along with the personnel distribution. The CEMICS incremental development approach leads to a computer time distribution which is somewhat flatter than the curve given in Fig. 31–5.

6. Probably the most valuable feature of the personnel plan is that it stimulates the project manager's thinking about who will be performing the various tasks on her project. This adds a further element of realism to the planning activity, and also gives the project manager a chance to get future performers involved in the project early, giving them a higher level of influence over and identification with the project's objectives, rather than pulling in performers on a few days' notice, after the project plans have been cast in concrete.

The Revised WBS. Figure 32–19 shows the revised CEMICS WBS, based on the detailed personnel plan given in Table 32–6. The WBS personnel budget figures were obtained by multiplying the number of man-months in the personnel plan (the rightmost column) by $5.5K per MM, except for the management element, where

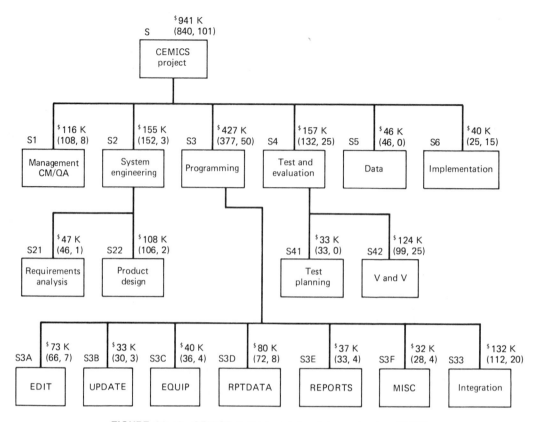

FIGURE 32–19 CEMICS revised work breakdown structure (WBS)

$6K per MM was used. The computer time budgets remained the same. Some further remarks on the detailed derivation of the revised WBS budgets are

1. The changes in the test and evaluation components and the system engineering components (including data and excluding CM/QA) were allocated proportionally to the initial WBS component budget distributions. For example, $4K of the $5K test and evaluation increase was allocated to V & V, and $1K to test planning.
2. The implementation budget is reduced because part of it is properly allocated to the management function during the implementation phase.
3. The CM/QA budget becomes submerged in the management WBS element. This is an example of the difficulties in exact cost data recovery caused by differing organizational procedures. Most of the CM/QA activity will be performed by the project manager's secretary, whose time is not charged directly to the project in the PPI, Inc., accounting system. Various special procedures could be developed to track CM/QA costs, but each would involve some inaccuracies and would generally not be worth the extra effort.

Step 4. The Project Work Authorization (PWA)

The project work authorization (PWA) is an informal contract under which a project manager provides a specified amount of money (and perhaps other resources) to a performer organization in return for a specified set of services defined by the PWA. It is an effective means for establishing that each project group has a level of funding authority commensurate with its performance responsibility. It is also an effective way to establish the commitment of each project group to a set of project goals consistent with the project's overall objectives.

Figure 32–20 shows an example PWA authorized by the CEMICS project manager, Maria Marcos, and accepted by the CEMICS programming team leader, Fred Fox. Most of the entries in the PWA are self-explanatory; further comments on some of the more significant features of the PWA are given below.

PROJECT TITLE CEMICS	PROJ. NO. B142	PWA ORIGINATOR J. P. Jones	ORIG. DATE 9/15/82
PWA TITLE CEMICS programming	PWA NO. B142-022	TOTAL COST $427, 000	LABOR COST $377,000

REFERENCES
   1. Document B142-D002.   CEMICS requirements and design spec., Sept. 10, 1982.
   2. Document B142-D005A. CEMICS project plan, revision A, Sept. 1, 1982

WBS element	Cost	Due date	Work description
S3	$427,000		• Detailed design, programming, integration, and as-built documentation of the CEMICS software specified in reference 1, subject to the conditions specified in reference 2.
		4/1/83 6/1/83 8/1/83 11/1/83	— complete integration of increment 1 — complete integration of increment 2 — complete integration of increment 3 — complete as-built documentation
			• Correction of programming errors found in product test and acceptance test

REVISION NO., DATE	MAJOR CHANGES					

AUTHORIZED BY Maria Marcos	ORG MSD	DATE 9/22/82	ACCEPTED BY Fred Fox	ORG BSD	DATE 9/24/82

FIGURE 32–20 Project work authorization (PWA) for CEMICS programming

1. If the project's plans and specifications are well-documented, the generation of a PWA requires very little additional documentation, as the tasks, products, assumptions, etc., can be defined by reference to existing documents.
2. The best time to define and negotiate a PWA is during the period between the initial draft task definition and the full refinement of the task definition, as this allows the performer to help define the parameters of the task to be performed, and gives an additional validation of the producibility of the specified products within the allocated budgets. In the CEMICS example in Fig. 32–20, the PWA has been defined and negotiated during the latter half of September, 1982, in the two weeks before the product design review (PDR) and the initiation of the Programming activity.
3. The PWA identifies major schedule milestones as well as funds allocated and work to be performed.
4. The PWA does not go into too much detail on the fund allocations to individual task elements. The programming team leader should not have to renegotiate the PWA each time resources are reallocated between tasks (such as using an underrun in the EDIT program to underwrite some on the job training for an upcoming programmer on the UPDATE program).
5. The PWA does have a section for easily defining incremental changes to the PWA, as these are fairly common.

Step 5. The Summary Task Planning Sheet (STPS)

The summary task planning sheet (STPS) has been discussed in detail in Section 32.5, where an example STPS for the CEMICS EDIT, UPDATE, and EQUIP programming tasks was shown as Fig. 32–14 (reproduced here for convenience as Fig. 32–21). STPSs provide the following further project planning and control capabilities:

- Detailed Gantt charts for the individual project tasks
- Earned-value allocations for the individual task milestones, to serve as a basis for continuing assessment of the project's earned value versus its expenditures
- Milestone and earned-value tracking of each project task

The STPS and the Earned Value System discussed in Section 32.5 provide the bridge between the cost and personnel tracking techniques provided by the WBS (step 1 above) and the personnel plan (step 3); and the progress tracking techniques provided by the PERT chart (step 2) and the Unit Development Folder (step 6 below). The PWA (step 4) provides the identification of responsibility for corrective action if any of the tracking systems identify problems.

Step 6. The Time Card and The Unit Development Folder

Once work on the project begins, we need two basic tracking capabilities: one for tracking expenditures, the other for tracking progress. The first, generally implemented via a time card or its equivalent, records how much of a project member's

Summary Task Planning Sheet

Sheet 1 of 3

(1) Project number: B142 (2) Project: CEMICS (3) Component: Programming (4) Date: 1/1/83

(5) WBS element: S3A, S3B, S3C (6) Responsible organization: BSD (7) Manager: F. Fox (8) PWA number: B142-022

(9) (10) (11) (12) (13) (14) (15) (16) (17)

Task number	WBS element	Task description	EV type	Year			1982	1983											Earned value			Expenditure
				Month	O	N	D	J	F	M	A	M	J	J	A	S	O	N	D	Total	To date	WBS to date	
1	S3A	EDIT programming, incr 1	MS		▲	2 ▲ D	1 ▲ C	2 △ T			2 △ I									7.0	3.0		
2	S3A	EDIT programming, incr 2	MS				▲	6 ▲ D		5 △ C	5 △ T		6 △ I							22.0	6.0		
3	S3A	EDIT programming, incr 3	MS						△		12 △ D	10 △ C	10 △ T		12 △ I					44.0	0.0	9.0	13.1
4	S3B	UPDATE programming, incr 1	MS		▲	6 ▲ D		5 ▲ C	5 ▲ T		6 △ I									22.0	16.0		
5	S3B	UPDATE programming, incr 2	MS				▲		3 ▲ D	2 △ C	3 △ T		3 △ I							11.0	3.0	19.0	16.2
6	S3C	EQUIP programming, incr 1	MS		▲	5 ▲ D	5 ▲ C	5 ▲ T			5 △ I									20.0	15.0		
7	S3C	EQUIP programming, incr 2	MS				▲		5 △ D	4 △ C	5 △ T		6 △ I							20.0	0.0	15.0	20.3
8																							
9																							
Totals:		(18) Earned value			13.0	11.0	19.0													146.0		43.0	
		(19) Expenditures			14.8	12.2	17.6																49.6

(20) (21) (22)

FIGURE 32–21 Summary task planning sheet: CEMICS programming

time has been devoted to the project's various WBS elements, each of which is typically identified by a unique accounting system job number. (Similar instruments such as purchase orders cover expenditure of other resources.)

Figure 32–22 shows an example CEMICS time card for the programmer-analyst on the EDIT program, Bill Jones. The time card shows that Bill spent a total of 34 hours during the week on Job Number (JN) B14204, which was identified on the earned value summary report (Fig. 32–15) as the JN for the programming of the EDIT program (work breakdown structure element S3A). Bill charged another 4 hours to JN B14206, representing his work on a code inspection of the EQUIP program, and a final 4 hours to the training (TRNG) JN for time spent in a PPI training course on advanced DBMS techniques.

EMPLOYEE W. P. Jones		DEPT BSD					WK. ENDING 12 – 3 – 82		
JOB NO.	SAT	SUN	MON	TUE	WED	THU	FRI	TOTAL	COMMENT
B14204			6	10	4	6	8	34	
B14206					4			4	
TRNG						4		4	
Total			6	10	8	10	8	42	

EMPLOYEE SIGNATURE *Bill Jones*   SUPERVISOR *Fred Fox*

FIGURE 32–22 CEMICS project time card

The information on each employee's time card is then entered into a computerized accounting system, which can then produce summary reports on

- the number of man-hours spent on each task
- the number of dollars charged to the task as a result
- various cumulative and aggregate totals by phase, by activity, and by product component
- comparisons of actual expenditures to allocated budgets

These are illustrated below by the personnel loading chart (step 7), the project expenditure summary (step 8), and the budget-schedule-milestone chart (step 9).

UNIT: EDIT (Increment 1)			CUSTODIAN: W.P. Jones		

ROUTINES INCLUDED: EDIN, EDSCAN, EDTAS, EDADD, EDDEL, EDMOD, EDERR

Section	Description		Due date	Date complete	Originator	Reviewer
1	Unit requirements		10/1/82	10/1/82	W.P. Jones _W.P.J._	R.E. Lee _R.E.L_
2	Unit design	2a. Prelim	10/1/82	10/1/82	_W.P.J._	_R.E.L_
		2b. Code-to	11/1/82	10/29/82	_W.P.J._	_R.E.L. "/1_
		2c. As-built	4/1/83			
3	Test plan		11/15/82	11/18/82	_W.P.J._	_R.E.L. "/9_
4	Unit code		12/1/82	11/29/82	_W.P.J._	_R.E.L. 12/2_
5	Test results		1/1/83			
6	Problem reports					
7	Notes					
8	Reviewers' comments					

FIGURE 32–23 Unit development folder cover sheet: CEMICS EDIT program

The Unit Development Folder (UDF). As the time card registers increments of expenditure on various project tasks, so the Unit Development Folder (UDF) registers increments of progress in completing the tasks. The UDF was discussed in detail in Section 32.4, where an example UDF cover sheet for the programming of Increment 1 of the EDIT program was shown as Fig. 32–13, reproduced here for convenience as Fig. 32–23. It indicates that the 34 hours spent on the EDIT program by Bill Jones during the week ending December 3, 1982, resulted in (among other things) the completion of the unit code milestone for Increment 1 of the EDIT program. The resulting combination of expenditure information from the time cards and progress information from the UDF's provides the basis for the earned value cost-versus-progress tracking system (item 10) for overall project management.

Step 7. The Personnel Loading Chart

Figure 32–24 shows the personnel loading chart for the CEMICS project as of January 1, 1983, obtained from the CEMICS time card data. The upper graph shows the comparison between the budgeted and actual personnel levels in full-time software personnel (FSP); the lower graph shows the cumulative comparison of budgets vs. actuals. It is evident from Fig. 32–24 that the CEMICS project experienced staffing

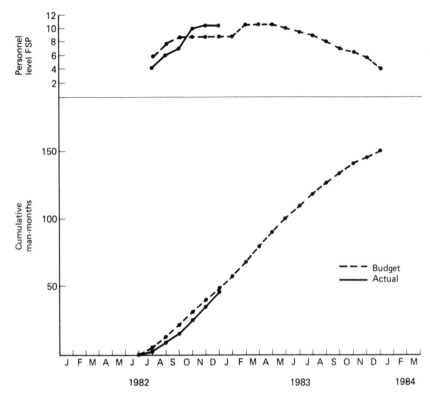

FIGURE 32-24 CEMICS manpower loading chart

difficulties at the beginning, but after PDR (October 1, 1982) was able to staff up to its peak level somewhat early, so that the cumulative man-month deficit is being reduced.

The personnel loading chart is a good indicator of overall project labor problems, but it provides no information on the effect of these problems on project progress or on individual task elements. Such information is provided by the three capabilities given below.

Step 8. The Project Expenditure Summary

The project expenditure summary is a generic name for a class of reports which provide summaries of current and cumulative project expenditures based on such expenditure records as time cards, purchase orders, computer time charges, etc. Figure 32-25 shows an example project expenditure summary generated for the manager of the CEMICS Project, Maria Marcos. For each work breakdown structure element within the CEMICS project, the project expenditure summary provides the following information:

Columns	Information
1, 2, 3	WBS element number, job number (JN), and WBS element name
4, 5	Budgeted and actual expenditures for the previous month (here, December 1982)
6, 7	Cumulative budgeted and actual expenditures since the beginning of the project
8	Percentage underrun (minus sign) or overrun of cumulative budget to date
9	To-date underrun/overrun exception report (*:20–40%; **:40–60%; ***: over 60%)
10	Total budget for the WBS element
11, 12	Percentage of WBS element total budget budgeted and spent to date
13	Percentage of WBS element total budget underrun (minus sign) or overrun to date
14	Total budget underrun/overrun exception report (*:10–20%; **:20–30%; ***:over 30%)

Project Expenditure Summary

Project: CEMICS   Project number: B142   Date: 1/1/83

Budget: $941,000   From: 7/1/82   To: 12/31/83   Manager: M. Marcos

WBS Number	Job Number	WBS Element	Last Mo $K Budget	Last Mo $K Actual	To date $K Budget	To date $K Actual	$\frac{A-B}{B}$	E20	Total Budget $K	Percent of total budget Budget	Percent of total budget Actual	Percent of total budget Diff.	E10
S		CEMICS	50.5	61.8	292.0	272.4	−7		941.0	31	29	−2	
S1	B14201	Management	6.5	6.2	39.0	37.1	−5		116.0	34	32	−2	
S2		Systems engr.	8.0	9.6	111.0	91.7	−17		155.0	72	59	−13	*
S21	B14202	Requirements	2.0	2.5	32.0	24.1	−25	*	47.0	68	51	−17	*
S22	B14203	Product design	6.0	7.1	79.0	67.6	−14		108.0	73	63	−10	*
S3		Programming	30.0	34.0	100.0	92.7	−7		427.0	23	22	−1	
S3A	B14204	EDIT	6.0	4.8	18.0	13.1	−27	*	73.0	25	18	−7	
S3B	B14205	UPDATE	6.0	5.7	18.0	16.2	−10		33.0	55	49	−6	
S3C	B14206	EQUIP	6.0	7.1	18.0	20.3	13		40.0	45	51	6	
S3D	B14207	RPTDATA	6.0	6.0	15.0	12.2	−19		80.0	19	15	−4	
S3E	B14208	REPORTS	3.0	4.6	9.0	10.6	18		37.0	24	'29	5	
S3F	B14209	MISC	3.0	5.8	3.0	5.8	93	***	32.0	9	18	9	
S33	B14210	Integration	0.0	0.0	19.0	13.5	−29	*	132.0	14	10	−4	
S4		TEST	3.0	9.6	25.0	37.0	48	**	157.0	16	24	8	
S41	B14211	Test planning	3.0	9.6	16.0	29.7	86	***	33.0	48	90	42	***
S42	B14212	V&V	0.0	0.0	9.0	7.3	−19		124.0	7	6	−1	
S5	B14213	Documentation	3.0	2.4	16.0	13.9	−13		46.0	35	30	−5	
S6	B14214	Implementation	0.0	0.0	0.0	0.0	−		40.0	0	0	0	

FIGURE 32–25 CEMICS project expenditure summary

The management value of such reports is heightened significantly by the use of the exception reporting capabilities in columns 9 and 14, which allow the manager to focus on the most likely trouble spots directly, rather than having to hunt for them in the mass of detail provided by the overall summary report.

The to-date underrun/overrun exception report (Column 9) tends to highlight those WBS elements which are getting off to a too slow or a too fast start. For example, the MISC programming effort rates a three-star exception report in column 9, but its small $2.8K overrun does not even rate a one-star exception report in column 14, which tends to highlight those WBS elements with potential problems in meeting their total budgets. If a WBS element has serious problems in both exception reports, particularly with overruns, such as with the test planning element, it should be the subject of a major management review.

Of course, the budget may be overrun because the work is being done more quickly, in which case there might not be a need for corrective action. (Similarly, the doubly flagged underrun in the requirements WBS element may not be a problem if the work is being done satisfactorily but with less effort.) The earned value summary report discussed below as step 10 provides a way for the project manager to determine whether or not the work done is keeping pace with the expenditures.

Step 9. The Cost-Schedule-Milestone Chart

Figure 32–26 shows a cost-schedule-milestone chart for the CEMICS project. It shows the planned times and budgets associated with the six major CEMICS development and implementation milestones: product design review (PDR); completion of integration of the three CEMICS development increments (INT 1, 2, 3); software acceptance review (SAR); and computer system acceptance review (CSAR). The milestone completion times are obtained from the project PERT Chart (step 2, Fig. 32–18); the associated budgets are obtained from the budget inputs prepared for the project expenditure summary (step 8, Fig. 32–25), based on the information in the personnel plan (step 3, Table 32–6).

The information in the cost-schedule-milestone chart that the CEMICS project was underspending during the product design phase (July–September 1982) was also available from the personnel loading chart (step 7, Fig. 32–24) and the September 1982 project expenditure summary (step 8, Fig. 32–25). The added information provided by the cost-schedule-milestone chart is that the underspending did not delay the successful completion of the product design review, and that therefore the underspending was good news rather than bad.

The cost-schedule-milestone chart is simple and straightforward to use, but it only covers the major overall project milestones in comparing progress to expenditures. The earned value summary report below provides more detailed visibility, both in terms of individual WBS elements and in terms of tracking progress versus expenditures between the major project milestones.

Step 10. The Earned Value Summary Report

The earned value summary report has been discussed in detail in Section 32.5, where an example report for the CEMICS project was shown as Fig. 32–15, which

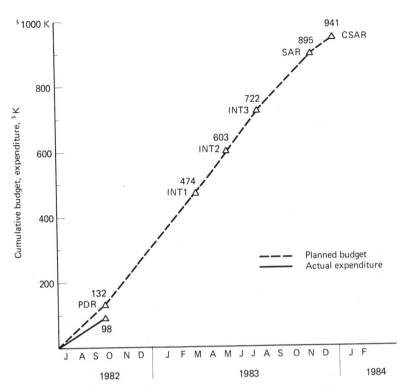

FIGURE 32–26 CEMICS cost-schedule-milestone chart

is reproduced here for convenience as Fig. 32–27. This report summarizes the detailed cost- and milestone-achievement tracking performed with the summary task planning sheets (STPSs) also discussed in Section 32.5 and as step 5 in this section. Like the STPSs, the earned value summary report provides a bridge between the cost and labor tracking techniques provided by the WBS, the personnel plan, the time cards, the personnel loading chart, and the project expenditure summary; and the progress tracking techniques provided by the PERT chart and the Unit Development Folder.

The earned value status report provides both an overall up to date indicator of the project's status and cost-to-complete prospects, and a detailed indiciator of the status and cost-to-complete prospects of each WBS element. Its exception-reporting capabilities (the starred To-Date E20 column and Total-EV E10 column) identify for the project manager the WBS elements most needing management attention. In Fig. 32–27, the most critical problem flagged by the earned value summary report is on the test planning WBS element, which has spent 90% of its budget and accumulated only 30% of its earned value, producing a three-star overexpenditure rating in both the To-Date E20 and the Total-EV E10 columns.

On investigating the source of this problem, the project manager, Maria Marcos, found that the V & V team had signed up two available programmers to write test drivers, but that their design of the test drivers was much more elaborate than the project needed. Further, the two programmers were still working about halftime on their previous project while charging her project fulltime. By quickly diagnosing

Earned Value Summary Report

PROJECT: CEMICS PROJECT NUMBER: B142 DATE: 1/1/83

BUDGET: $941,000 FROM: 7/1/82 TO 12/31/83 MANAGER: M. Marcos

WBS Number	Job Number	WBS Element	EV Type	Last Mo $K		To Date $K				TOT EV $K	Percent of total EV			
				EV	Actual	EV	Actual	$\frac{A-E}{E}$	E20		EV	Actual	Diff.	E10
S		CEMICS		51.2	61.8	269.0	272.4	1		941.0	29	29	0	
S1	B14201	Mangement	LM	6.2	6.2	38.5	37.1	-4		116.0	33	32	-1	
S2		System engr.		9.6	9.6	107.7	91.7	-15		155.0	69	59	-10	*
S21	B14202	Requirements	LM	2.5	2.5	32.4	24.1	-26	*	47.0	69	51	-18	*
S22	B14203	Product design	LM	7.1	7.1	75.3	67.6	-10		108.0	70	63	-7	
S3		Programming		28.0	34.0	89.0	92.7	4		427.0	21	22	1	
S3A	B14204	EDIT	MS	6.0	4.8	9.0	13.1	46	**	73.0	12	18	6	
S3B	B14205	UPDATE	MS	5.0	5.7	19.0	16.2	-15		33.0	58	49	-9	
S3C	B14206	EQUIP	MS	6.0	7.1	15.0	20.3	35	*	40.0	38	51	13	*
S3D	B14207	RPTDATA	MS	6.0	6.0	16.0	12.2	-24	*	80.0	20	15	-5	
S3E	B14208	Reports	MS	3.0	4.6	12.0	10.6	-12		37.0	32	29	-3	
S3F	B14209	MISC	MS	2.0	5.8	2.0	5.8	190	***	32.0	6	18	12	*
S33	B14210	Integration	MS	0.0	0.0	19.0	13.5	-29	*	132.0	14	10	-4	
S4		test		5.0	9.6	19.0	37.0	95	***	157.0	12	24	12	*
S41	B14211	Test plan	MS	5.0	9.6	10.0	29.7	197	***	33.0	30	90	60	***
S42	B14212	V&V	MS	0.0	0.0	9.0	7.3	-19		124.0	7	6	-1	
S5	B14213	Documentation	LM	2.4	2.4	14.8	13.9	-6		46.0	32	30	-2	
S6	B14214	Implementation	LM	0.0	0.0	0.0	0.0	-		40.0	0	0	0	

FIGURE 32–27 CEMICS earned value summary report

the problems, simplifying the test-driver objectives, and renegotiating the time charges with the manager of the other project, Maria was able to bring this portion of her project back under control before it could seriously compromise the project's success. By the end of the project, the test planning activity was about $10K overspent, but this was evened out by the underexpenditures in requirements analysis and product design. As a result, the project successfully passed its acceptance test and pilot operation with no serious defects, and within budget and schedule.

Of course, on a nine-person project, there is generally enough personal contact for the project manager to discover such problems without the aid of an Earned Value System. Their major value is on large projects, on which the managers cannot keep in close personal touch with each detailed activity. But even on smaller projects, the Earned Value System can be very helpful in keeping the project manager in touch with progress across vacation periods (as was the case here) or across periods of fire-fighting on another part of the project.

32.7 BUILDING A SOFTWARE COST DATA BASE

Although the prime objective of a software planning and control system is to support effective project management, its existence provides a powerful side benefit for the organization's long-range cost-estimation capability. The data collected via planning and control activities over several projects can be analyzed to determine how the distribution of actual software costs in the organization differs from the COCOMO estimates, and the differences fed back into an improved cost-estimation model calibrated to the organization's experience. (Section 29.9 contains some basic calibration techniques.)

Besides collecting data on the evolution of a project's expenditures and progress, it is also important to collect data on the evolution of the project's cost driver attributes and resulting revised COCOMO estimates throughout the development period. A good practice is to rerun the COCOMO model at each major project milestone (and, of course, at each revision of product requirements having budget and schedule consequences), using appropriately updated estimates of component sizes and cost driver attribute ratings. With this information, the organization can also determine typical trends in the growth of estimates of software product size, complexity, etc., across the product's life-cycle. These can then be used to better assess the cost-growth risks involved in initial project estimates.

The data thus collected is a great deal more valuable if it is organized into a data base for effective query and analysis, and if a specific person is given responsibility for managing it as an organizational resource. A recommended approach is to combine this cost data base responsibility with the responsibility for providing software cost analysis and productivity improvement services to the organization, as will be discussed further in Section 33.8.

Forms and further guidelines for performing such software cost data collection are provided in Appendix A.

32.8 SOFTWARE PLANNING AND CONTROL: SUMMARY DISCUSSION

1. The ten basic planning and control techniques given in this chapter provide the essential capabilities needed to steer a software project, and to turn a reasonably close COCOMO cost and schedule estimate into a self-fulfilling prophecy. The techniques are essential for large projects, but also very valuable for small projects. One of the biggest payoffs in using them is the increased understanding of project interactions we gain by thinking through the project plans.

2. The techniques given here are only a small part of a wide variety of further useful planning and control techniques. A good introduction to these techniques is given in [Maciariello, 1978].

3. A project plan is a living entity. Planning and control techniques must therefore accommodate changes in the plans. Although the examples in this chapter did not involve much change, in the interests of simplicity, be prepared to update project plans frequently.

4. The planning and control techniques given here can and should be extended through the operations and maintenance portion of the life-cycle. In particular, it is important to employ benefit-tracking capabilities to assess the extent to which estimated benefits were actually realized.

5. There is a strong temptation to use planning and control results, particularly those of the Earned Value System, as a performance-appraisal device. As with other "personnel management by the numbers" schemes, this is not recommended. It can lead to people gaming the system in ways which de-emphasize team cooperation and emphasize a minimal interpretation of project responsibilities. However, earned value and other planning and control data do provide some useful perspectives which should not be neglected as part of an overall, primarily subjective, performance appraisal approach.

6. To some people, the planning and control techniques presented here may seem to lead directly to routinization and deskilling of software people's jobs, and to exploitation of performers in the interest of making low-ball cost estimates into self-fulfilling prophecies. I have to admit that with some short-sighted, heavy-handed software managers, this will happen. But I have also seen these techniques work successfully under more enlightened managers, producing organizations with satisfied, creative people and very low turnover rates. Software is still sufficiently complex that our attempts to organize parts of it still leave more than enough challenging jobs to go around.

32.9 QUESTIONS

32.1. Do programmers spend more time writing programs, reading programs, or talking and listening?

32.2. How well do Parkinson's Law and the Deadline Effect describe your approach to software development? To studying for courses and writing term papers?

32.3. Express the sequence of courses and prerequisites for graduating from your university with a BA in computer science (or a related subject) as a PERT chart.

32.4. Du Bridge Chemical, Inc., is planning and specifying the requirements for a real-time chemical process control system, including the development of a model of the system to verify that the software will handle the workload in real time. Figure 32–28 is a PERT chart for the plans and requirements phase, with activity durations expressed in weeks. Determine the critical path, the early start and late start times, and the slack time for each activity.

32.5. In the Du Bridge PERT Chart of Fig. 32–28, by how much is the minimum completion time reduced if we reduce the duration of the develop-model activity to 7 weeks? to 6 weeks? to 5 weeks?

32.6. A schedule–risk analysis of the Du Bridge project of Fig. 32–28 indicates a worst case estimate of 10 weeks each for the draft-requirements and develop-model activities. With these changes, determine the resulting minimum completion time and critical path.

32.7. Develop a PERT chart of the activities involved between a Start of waking up in the morning and a Finish of arriving at your first class. Determine the critical path and minimum time.

32.8. Develop a Gantt chart for the Du Bridge Chemical activities in Question 32.4.

32.9. What are the items generally contained in a Unit Development Folder? Which of them have schedule deadlines on the cover sheet?

32.10. In the CEMICS Unit Development Folder example in Fig. 32–13, suppose that on January 1, 1983, the Federal Government informs PPI that a new set of OSHA safety categories must be established for all PPI equipment, requiring a significant set of changes in the EDIT program. How should the changed situation be accommodated via the UDF cover sheet?

32.11. Update the CEMICS summary task planning sheet in Fig. 32–14 to reflect the following progress during January, 1983:
  EDIT: Complete Increment 1 test and Increment 2 code, begin Increment 3, spend $8.8K.

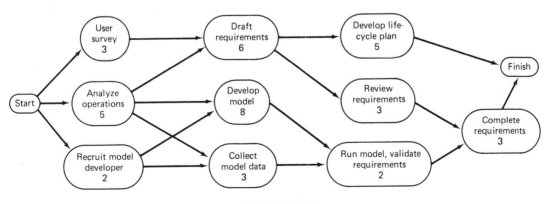

FIGURE 32–28

UPDATE: Complete Increment 1 integration and Increment 2 code, spend $6.5K.
EQUIP: Complete Increment 2 design and code, spend $5.8K.

32.12. Develop a summary task planning sheet for the **Du Bridge Chemical** project in Question 32.4. Break the develop-model activity into at least three stages. Use $1K per week to determine dollar costs and earned values.

32.13. In the earned value summary report in Fig. 32–15, rank the exceptions flagged in the E20 and E10 columns in order of their relative criticality as threats to the project's success. Can you express a rule which you used to determine priorities? Could it be made part of the exception reporting capability?

32.14. In Section 31.8, we determined the following conservative estimates for the sizes of the CEMICS components:

EDIT: 13 KDSI   RPTDATA: 16 KDSI
UPDATE: 8 KDSI   REPORTS: 7 KDSI
EQUIP: 10 KDSI   MISC: 9 KDSI

Develop a revised COCOMO estimate and initial work-breakdown-structure budgets for this version of CEMICS.

32.15. Develop a PERT chart and a personnel plan for developing CEMICS in a single increment, rather than in three increments.

32.16. In the CEMICS PERT chart of Fig. 32–18, suppose three activities take longer than expected:

Product design: 3.5 months
Test plan: 3 months
Design of increment 3: 3 months

By how much time is the overall project schedule lengthened?

32.17. In the revised CEMICS WBS in Fig. 32–19, the CM/QA costs have become invisible, as they are being done largely by the project manager's secretary, whose time is not charged directly to the project in the PPI accounting system. Identify some ways in which the CEMICS project might still track its CM/QA costs.

32.18. Of the ten planning and control capabilities identified in Fig. 32–3, which appear to be the most dispensable? Which appear to be indispensable? What additional reports might enhance people's visibility into the project's status?

32.19. In Fig. 21–1, we indicated that a project generally cannot estimate the cost of a software product to within a factor of 1.25 until the product design is completed. In this chapter, we indicated that a good project manager can make a software cost estimate into a self-fulfilling prophecy only when the initial estimate is within a factor of 1.25 of the "ideal" cost estimate. What does this imply about the advisability of entering into fixed-price contracts for software development before the product design is complete?

32.20. What guidelines should be established on the use of planning and control techniques to avoid over-routinization of software jobs?

Chapter 33

Improving Software
Productivity

33.1 INTRODUCTION

The insights we have obtained in attempting to solve the problem of software cost estimation can also be used to address the even more critical problem of improving software productivity. Frequently, and somewhat misguidedly, the subject of improving software productivity is interpreted as the process of introducing modern programming practices (MPPs), and productivity improvements of up to 50% are considered achievable through implementing MPPs. In this chapter, we show that

- An effective software productivity improvement program involves much more than introducing MPPs.
- The COCOMO cost driver attributes and effort multipliers provide a natural framework for identifying the high leverage productivity improvement factors and estimating their likely payoff for a given installation.
- Most data processing installations can increase their software development and maintenance productivity by an additional 100% in three to four years, and by an additional 400% in six to eight years.

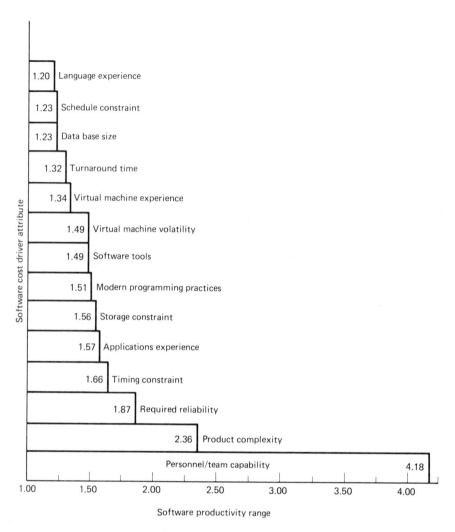

FIGURE 33–1 COCOMO software cost driver productivity ranges

- Software productivity can be improved by a great deal more than the above factors via increased use of already developed software.

Figure 33–1 gives us an overall perspective of the relative software productivity leverage provided by the various COCOMO cost driver attributes. It shows each attribute's *Software Productivity Range:* the ratio between the overall COCOMO effort multipliers for the least productive attribute rating and for the most productive attribute rating. Thus, for example, all other factors being equal, a 90th-percentile team of programmers and analysts will be about four times as productive in DSI/MM as a 15th-percentile team.*

* Here, we have combined the productivity ranges from analyst capability (2.06) and programmer capability (2.03) into an overall personnel/team capability productivity range of 4.18.

These productivity ranges provide us a means of identifying the high payoff areas to emphasize in a software productivity improvement activity. Further, since the COCOMO cost driver effort multipliers are multiplicative, an integrated productivity improvement strategy involving the improvement of several cost driver attributes will yield multiplicative benefits. This synergetic effect is the key to the high productivity improvement figures cited above.

Importance of Improving Software Productivity

The primary reason that software productivity is such a critical problem is that the demand for new software is increasing faster than our ability to supply it, using traditional approaches. The increased demand for software stems largely from pressures throughout the economy to improve commercial, industrial, and service productivity via automation.

For example, Fig. 33–2 shows the growth in software demand, in millions of object instructions generated, across four generations of the U.S. manned spaceflight program, from about 1,000,000 instructions to support Project Mercury to the present 40,000,000 instructions to support Space Shuttle operations [Stokes, 1970; Reifer, 1977].

The reasons for this increased demand are basically the same reasons encountered by other sectors of the economy as they attempt to increase productivity via automation. The major component of growth in the Space Shuttle software has been in the checkout and launch support area, in which the National Aeronautics and Space Administration (NASA) automated many functions in order to avoid the requirement for 20,000 people to support each launch, as in previous manned spaceflight operations.

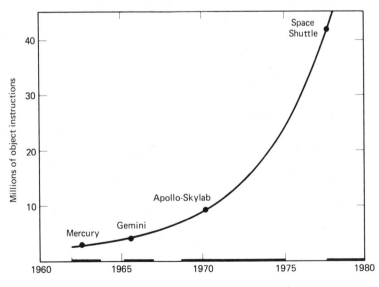

FIGURE 33–2 Growth in software demand

The result has been a significant reduction in required launch support personnel, but a significant increase in the required amount of software.

The annual growth rate in demand for new software over the 16 to 20 years of the manned spaceflight program is thus about 20 to 26%. This figure is probably considerably higher than the overall growth rate in software demand, although the 24% annual growth rate in the total number of computers reported in [Phister, 1979] would suggest a proportionally high annual growth rate in the demand for new software. [Business Week, 1980] indicated that the need for programmers could reach 1,500,000 by 1990, more than triple the number working in 1980. This corresponds to a 12% annual growth in demand for software personnel.

At any rate, the current excess in demand over supply of software personnel would indicate that the growth rate in our ability to supply new software is not keeping up with the demand. The current annual growth rate in software personnel is generally estimated at about 3 to 4% [Dolotta and others, 1976; Morrisey–Wu, 1979], although the estimates in [Phister, 1979] indicate a growth rate of more like 13 to 14%. The annual growth rate in software productivity in new object instructions per man-month averaged about 8 to 9% during the 1960s [Boehm, 1973], due largely to the transition from assembly language to higher order language software development. However, the prediction in [Boehm, 1973] that the 8 to 9% growth rate would continue through 1985 has not been borne out; later estimates have ranged from 3% in [Dolotta and others, 1976] to 5 to 6% in [Morrisey–Wu, 1979].

Relation to Software Cost Estimation

A strong capability to estimate software costs provides two primary keys for improving software productivity. One is a sounder baseline for management planning and control of software projects, as discussed in the previous chapter. The other, which is discussed in detail in this chapter, is that many of the software cost driver attributes are project *controllables;* figuratively, they are control knobs which can be set to positions which improve software productivity. Clearly, some cost driver attributes, such as the type of software being developed, are uncontrollable, but most of the cost drivers are at least partly controllable in ways which increase software productivity.

Thus, for example, even the size of the software to be developed is a major controllable which may yield impressive savings in software costs by choosing options which reduce the number of instructions we need to develop, and that, in some cases, avoid the requirement to develop software at all. For example, we may choose instead to purchase a software product or to adapt a number of existing software routines or subsystems as part of our software product.

In doing so, we provide the required software functions, but we do not create many new software instructions. Thus, we need again to keep our concepts of software productivity in perspective; producing a great many new Delivered Source Instructions/MM may be much less productive in terms of Needed Software Functions/MM than an alternate strategy of buying a software product which already furnishes the needed functions.* On the other hand, we cannot simply use the number of DSI in a purchased software product as an index of productivity; for one thing, we will often find that many of the functions provided in the software product are not needed for our application.

Development versus Life-Cycle Productivity

Another valuable perspective on software productivity provided by software cost-estimation technology is the distinction between software development productivity and software life-cycle productivity. The tradeoffs between lower development costs and lower life-cycle costs are characterized by the modern programming practices and required realiability cost-estimating relationships for software development and maintenance. These emphasize the reduction in maintenance costs possible via better structured and documented software, program support library procedures, and reliability-oriented aids such as diagnostics, environmental simulators, and test data management systems. Even though some of these latter steps may increase development costs, they will pay off in reduced maintenance costs, particularly for software products with long lifetimes.

Software Productivity and Human Economics

A further perspective we need to consider in improving software productivity is that our concern for the life-cycle of the software *product* needs to be balanced by our concern for the life-cycle of the software *people* involved. Thus, we need to balance the material-economics concept of work as an activity which adds monetary value to a product with such human-economics concepts of work as an activity which helps people develop character. We can't allow ourselves to routinize software development along the lines of the scenario developed in [Kraft, 1977], by fragmenting software jobs into small, meaningless pieces, or by binding a programmer in perpetuity to a boring maintenance job in much the same way that the medieval serf was bound to a feudal estate.

Such routinizing methods of organizing software projects may appear to increase software productivity in the near term, but they have a larger negative impact on productivity in the long term. Besides producing uninspired software, such methods produce people who lose their interest in professional growth, lose their interest in the organization's objectives, lose their ability to cope with new situations, and lose their self-confidence as software engineers.

Fortunately, the objectives of effective software development and effective software career development are not necessarily in conflict. Methods such as the GOALS approach described in Chapter 3, particularly with respect to the portion of the Software Engineering Goal Structure devoted to human relations throughout the

---

* It would be highly valuable for the software field if we could develop a software productivity metric in terms of desired product functionality rather than in terms of DSI. Unfortunately, due to the reasons discussed in Sections 28.3 and 21.4, this ideal has been and will be very difficult to achieve.

software process, provides a means by which we can integrate these concerns into our software life-cycle plans and activities. Some specific principles and guidelines for performing this integration are provided in Section 33.6.

The Major Controllable Factors in Software Productivity

As we pointed out above, one of the primary controllable factors we have for improving software productivity is the number of instructions we choose not to develop, either by deferring the development on marginally useful features or by using already available software via such options as

• Commercial software packages
• Adaptation of existing in-house software
• Program generators (program libraries, software piece-parts, application generators, very high level languages, automatic programming)

Section 32.2 covers specific considerations on the use of software packages. It presents and discusses a general balance sheet of advantages and difficulties in using software packages. It also discusses adaptation of existing in-house software as a special case of an internally available software package. Section 33.3 similarly discusses the nature and usage considerations of the various kinds of program generators.

Sections 33.4 through 33.7 cover the other main controllable factors in improving software productivity. The factors are organized along the same lines used in discussing the COCOMO cost driver attributes in Chapters 24 to 27.

• Section 33.4 covers controllable software product attributes, such as use of higher order languages and avoiding development of overly complex software.
• Section 33.5 covers controllable computer attributes, such as acquiring additional hardware capacity in order to reduce execution time and main storage constraints.
• Section 33.6 covers controllable personnel attributes, such as staffing, motivation, and effective management.
• Section 33.7 covers controllable project attributes, such as the long-range improvements in productivity available via investments in software tools and modern programming practices.

Section 33.8 provides guidelines for using the information in Sections 33.2 to 33.7 to tailor and implement a strategy for improving software productivity within a given installation. It first discusses techniques and considerations involved in performing a software productivity study, then presents guidelines for implementing the resulting study recommendations. Section 33.9 concludes with a final set of conclusions and recommendations on improving software productivity and on keeping productivity improvements in the right perspective.

33.2 NONPROGRAMMING OPTIONS: SOFTWARE PACKAGES

Improving software productivity by the use of nonprogramming options can be achieved via the following major alternatives:

- Commercial software packages
- Adaptation of existing in-house software
- Program generators

In this section, we will discuss the commercial package option in some detail, as its relative advantages and difficulties are fairly typical of the other options. This section will also cover the option of adapting existing software as a special case of an internally available software package.

Nature of Software Packages

Software packages are commercially offered products which typically provide solutions to a particular range of software development or applications problems. As they have been developed for commercial sale in a competitive market, and used by a wide variety of customers, their vendors generally have invested a fair amount of effort into making them reliable and easy to use.

Software packages have been developed for a wide variety of *uses*, including the following major usage categories:

- Management information systems applications (payroll, general ledger, personnel)
- Industrial support systems (inventory control, process control, production control, order processing)
- Office automation (word processing, correspondence control, electronic mail)
- Utilities (sorting, report generation, file processing)
- Software tools

The software tools available as software packages cover practically all of the tools described in Section 27.2, ranging from basic programming aids (assemblers, compilers, debuggers) through integrated "programmers' workbench" support environments to advanced requirements language processors and special-purpose support systems for data base management, data communications processing, and display processing.

Software packages also come in a wide variety of *forms*. The major options are

- Small, single-purpose modules (for example, sorting)
- Integrated software subsystems (for example, data base management systems, programmers' workbench systems)
- Integrated hardware–software turnkey application systems (for example, word processing, process control)

Also, software packages are made available in a wide variety of *arrangements,* including the following major categories:

- Nature of software package or service (source code, object code, access to remote timeshare service)
- Range of options available (single total package, menu of options, tailored subsystems)
- Range of services provided (none, program tailoring, program maintenance, training, consulting, facilities management)
- Acquisition financing (purchase, lease, rental, license to use, single charge versus multiple charge for use on several computers, payment options on other services provided)

Software Package Cost-Benefit Considerations

Clearly, the vendor of the software package has developed it based on the conviction that its purchase by users will be more cost-effective for them than would be any alternatives. Often, the vendor will provide a cost-benefit analysis which shows why the acquisition of the software package will furnish a significant cost-effectiveness gain for the user. Even though this cost-benefit analysis may be somewhat slanted toward acquisition of the vendor's product, it provides a good starting point for the decision analysis on whether or not to acquire the software package.*

Some of the major advantages and difficulties in using commercial software packages which should be considered in performing a cost-benefit analysis for a software package are summarized in Table 33–1. Each of the items in the table are discussed in more detail below.

Advantages of Software Packages

Cost savings. A commercial software package is developed once, and the development cost is amortized over a large number of users, rather than being totally absorbed by a developer-user organization. For example, [Frank, 1979] indicates that a typical large commercial data base management system will cost about $100,000 to purchase and over $1,000,000 to develop. The 400-KDSI Mark IV software package discussed in [Frank, 1979] has cost about $10 million to date, but the current base price for the top-of-the-line system is $42,000.

One good way of assessing the relative costs of developing a software product, in comparison to acquiring an already-developed software package, is to use a software cost-estimation model such as COCOMO. In general, a vendor will be willing to provide approximate sizing information on the components of his software package. We can use this information to develop sizing estimates for the corresponding components we wish in our software application, supply the associated cost driver attribute ratings for each component, and derive a COCOMO software development cost estimate to compare with the cost of the vendor's package.

---

* If the vendor cannot provide any sort of cost-benefit analysis for a software package, one should have serious reservations about its likely cost-effectiveness.

TABLE 33–1 Software Packages: Advantages and Difficulties

Advantages	Difficulties
• Cost savings	• Application incompatibilities
• Earlier payback	• Procurement delays
• Manpower savings	• In-house expertise
• Range of capabilities	• In-house improvements
• Technology leverage and risk	• Controllability
• Reliability	
• User engineering	
• Documentation	
• Training	
• User group	

Earlier payback. A software package is available for service as soon as it is acquired. It thus has a considerable head start in providing benefits to the user organization, compared to the in-house software development option, which does not provide any usage benefits to the organization during the time required to develop the product.

An example of the joint effect of the cost-savings and earlier-payback advantages is shown in Fig. 33–3 and Table 33–2, which provide a comparison between the development of a 15-KDSI software product whose use provides a $15K per month benefit to the organization, and the purchase of a comparable software package for $100K whose use provides a $10K per month benefit to the organization. The in-house development of a 15-KDSI product would typically require 50 man-months, or $300K at an average labor cost of $6K per MM, and would typically require about 11 months to complete. This means that it would take a long time before the higher benefit rate of the in-house product pays off in terms of net benefit to the user organization, and an even longer time before the net benefit of the in-house product exceeds that of the purchased software product.

As shown in Fig. 33–3, the purchased software package reaches a breakeven point at 12 months after the decision to proceed, assuming a two-month acquisition

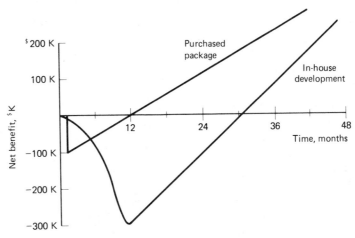

FIGURE 33–3 Net benefit history of purchased package and in-house product

TABLE 33–2 Comparison of Purchased Package and In-House Development

Quantity	Purchased Package	In-House Development
Cost to acquire	$100K	$300K
Available for use	2 months	11 months
Benefit via use	$10K/month	$15K/month
Undiscounted Calculation		
Net Benefit ($K)		
after M months	$10(M-2)-100$	$15(M-11)-300$
Breakeven Point	12 months	31 months
Crossover Point	69 months	69 months
Present Value Calc. ($D=.99$)		
Net Benefit ($K)		
after M months	$\dfrac{10(1-.99^{M-2})}{.01}-98$	$\dfrac{15(1-.99^{M-11})}{.01}-286$
Breakeven Point	12.3 months	32 months
Crossover Point	74 months	74 months

period. The in-house product only reaches a breakeven point after 31 months. It takes 69 months, or almost 6 years, before the net benefit of the in-house product exceeds that of the purchased package. If this is longer than the useful lifetime of the product, as is often the case, then the preferred option would clearly be to choose the purchased software package.

The purchased package is even more competitive if we use present-value calculations rather than undiscounted dollars as our basis of comparison. Table 33–2 also shows the present value calculations for the two alternatives, based on the formulas given in Section 14.2, using a monthly discount rate of $D=.99$, roughly corresponding to an interest rate of 1% per month or 12% per year. The resulting crossover point at which the net present value of the in-house product exceeds that of the purchased package occurs at 74 months, as compared to 69 months using the undiscounted calculations.

Personnel savings. Another advantage of the commercial software package is that it requires no in-house personnel to develop. Thus, in the example above, an average of four to five people are available for 11 months to perform other software functions needed by the organization. This advantage is particularly important to the increasing number of software organizations which find that sheer availability of software personnel is their limiting factor in achieving organizational information processing objectives.

Range of capabilities. A commercial software package, particularly a mature one which has been used by many organizations, will often have additional unanticipated capabilities which other organizations have found useful as their operational needs have evolved. An organization initially acquiring the software package may not be able to use all of these capabilities at once, but they provide an experience-based set of growth options once the basic system has been integrated into the organization's operations.

Technology leverage and risk. A commercial software package has generally been developed by people who are already highly experienced in the applications and computer science disciplines required by the product. The purchasing organization thus obtains a technology boost which would often be very difficult to match in-house. Also, there is always a risk that less experienced in-house personnel might not develop a successful product, while the commercial product has already overcome this risk. A related advantage is that the software package vendor is often able to provide consulting assistance to speed the in-house organization's progress along the learning curve for a new applications area.

Reliability, user engineering, documentation, and training. In terms of product qualities, particularly for mature software packages, the purchaser again gains the benefit of the previous experience of a number of users in working with the package. This experience provides significant advantages in eliminating errors, refining the product's human-machine interface, improving its documentation, and enhancing the effectiveness of user training. Even for a new software package, competitive pressures require vendors to provide a high level of quality in these respects.

User group. Another significant advantage often found with highly complex or sophisticated software packages is the existence of a user group, allowing the organization to compare experiences with other organizations on ways to make the package best serve the organization's needs. The resulting benefits may include improved strategies and techniques for using the package, evaluation of existing or proposed package extensions, applications of the package in additional areas, and insights into general information processing issues related to the package and its use.

Difficulties with Commercial Software Packages

Application incompatibilities. In many cases, a commercial software package will have a number of built-in assumptions about the users (their education level, motivation level, computer science expertise, etc.), about the organization's operational philosophy (centralized or decentralized, authoritarian or permissive, profit or service-oriented, etc.), or about the user's organizational structure (project-oriented, skill-centered, or matrixed). Modifying a software package to change or eliminate these assumptions is generally a much bigger job than just putting in a few front-end or back-end fixes. Several examples have involved unsuccessful attempts to use a project management information system package developed for one type of organizational structure in a user installation having a different type of organizational structure (for example, applying a matrix-management information system to a project-oriented organization).

The best way to determine whether in-house incompatibility may be a problem is to contact other previous and present users of the package with similar usage profiles to your own, and to discuss their experiences with respect to compatibility issues.

In other situations, the incompatibility may be simply that the software package solves a somewhat different application problem than the one we need to solve. Thus, acquiring an aircraft structural analysis package to perform structural analysis for bridges is a good idea only if we know that the algorithms in the aircraft program are a good match for our class of bridge analyses.

Procurement delays. The fact that a software package is available for use immediately upon acquisition does not mean that it is available immediately. Many organizations have long, cumbersome authorization and acquisition procedures which may take longer to surmount than it would take to develop a small product in-house.

In-house expertise. Although acquiring a commercial software package frees up people for other tasks, it also means that in-house software people lose the opportunity to gain development experience in the technical area covered by the software package. Often, a short-term decision to acquire a software package becomes a long-term decision to rely on outside expertise for a given class of software capabilities. Thus, an organization's long-term needs for in-house expertise in such areas as microprocessors, process control systems, computer aided design, tax calculations, etc., need to be considered as well as the near-term benefits of purchasing the software package.

In-house improvements; controllability. For most software products, it is inevitable that users will request new or modified capabilities to reflect patterns of growth or change in their organization, operational mission, technological capabilities, external environment, etc. Requests made to software package vendors to provide such improvements will meet with a good deal of vendor interest if the improvements will give them a more competitive product, or if they have some underemployed people available. Otherwise, a user organization may find it very difficult to negotiate an acceptable cost and schedule for the vendor to make the desired improvements. The situation is even more difficult if the product comes only as a set of object code or as a dial-up timesharing service, with no in-house modification options available at all. Here again, the best way to determine whether there will be an acceptable degree of controllability over the situation is to consult with current or previous users of the software package.

Having now discussed the major advantages and difficulties of software packages, let us now summarize the special considerations involved in making software package make-or-buy decisions.

Software Packages: Special Considerations for Make-or-Buy Decisions

The overall principles for performing a make-or-buy decision analysis are the same cost-effectiveness decision analysis principles we covered in Part III. In fact, a particular make-or-buy decision analysis example involving an in-house versus vendor operating system decision is provided in Section 18.1. Here, we identify some of the primary special considerations involved in performing a make-or-buy decision analysis for a commercial software package.

- *Available In-House Personnel.* If qualified in-house people are scarce, the software package is more attractive than if qualified in-house people are looking for useful things to do.
- *Organizational Growth Pattern.* If an organization anticipates a large number of future applications in, say, process control using microprocessors, it may consider the purchase rather than in-house development of a microprocessor energy-management package less attractive than will an organization doing primarily business data processing.
- *Compatibility with In-House Products.* If a software package is developed in a special programming language incompatible with an organization's primary programming language, for example, the package will be less attractive.
- *Controllability and Cost of Maintenance.* If a vendor has a good track record in providing specially tailored options for customers, the package will be more attractive than if not.
- *Vendor Service, Reputation, and Stability.* A software package will be more attractive to the extent that the vendor has a strong service record, a reputation for following through on commitments, and a strong likelihood of being in business next year to service the package.

Sources of Information on Software Packages

Here are several sources of information on commercially available software packages

- *A Directory of Computer Software and Related Technical Reports 1980,* U.S. Department of Commerce, National Technical Information Service [NTIS, 1980].
- "Computer Program Abstracts," NASA-COSMIC (Univ. of Georgia), [NASA, 1980].
- International Computer Programs, Inc. software product catalog [ICP, 1980].
- "Auerbach Computer Technology Reports" [Auerbach, 1980].
- *Datapro Directory of Software* [Datapro, 1980].
- Vendor catalogs, such as the IBM "Auditability and Productivity Information Catalog: System 370" [IBM, 1977].

Some further useful information on software packages is given in [Shoor, 1981].

Adaptation of Existing In-House Software

Adaptation of existing in-house software may be considered as a special case of acquiring an external software package. Practically all of the advantages remain (cost savings, earlier payback, labor savings, etc.), and many of the difficulties disappear (procurement delays, in-house expertise, controllability). Adaptation cost-estimation considerations are covered in Section 8.8, and Section 31.2 covers conversion cost estimation.

33.3 NONPROGRAMMING OPTIONS: PROGRAM GENERATORS

Another class of nonprogramming options for improving software productivity are the program generators, which are systems for constructing (or aiding in the construction of) programs out of pre-existing pieces.

Various types of program generators exist, such as program libraries, applications generators, and Very High Level Languages (VHLLs). In fact, relative to the initial usage of absolute binary code for programming, one can consider assemblers, macroassemblers, and current higher order languages (HOLs) as initial successful steps in developing program generators.

We can use current HOL technology as a means of illustrating the four main elements of a program generator.

1. *A set of components.* For HOLs, these include assembly language instructions, call and return macros, and standard functions such as square root, successor, end-of-file, etc.
2. *A set of conventions for joining the components.* For HOLs, these include conventions on use of registers for call and return sequences, and handling of exception conditions (negative square root, divide by zero, etc.).
3. *A language for users to specify desired applications.* For HOLs, these include FORTRAN, COBOL, Pascal, etc.
4. *A set of capabilities for interpreting user specifications, configuring the appropriate set of components, and executing the resulting program.* For HOLs, these include compilers, linkers, loaders, and execution monitors.

The main classes of program generator capabilities are summarized below, in terms of their distinguishing characteristic sets of components, sets of conventions for joining components, user languages, and sets of interpretation, configuration and execution capabilities.

1. *Software Piece Parts.* These are largely extensions of the standard functions provided within HOLs. They perform elementary functions in such areas as text processing, matrix-vector manipulations, input editing, etc., usually in the form of in-line code generated by an extension of an assembler or HOL compiler.
2. *Program Libraries.* These generally refer to collections of more extensive data processing capabilities, such as statistical analysis, financial calculations, graphics display generation, etc. These again are typically called as subroutines or external procedures from an HOL program.
3. *Application Generators.* These typically consist of a program library which operates in a prestructured context, based on knowledge of a particular applica-

tion area (display management, inventory control, aircraft flight mechanics, etc.). The structure imposed by the particular knowledge domain allows users to generate application programs simply by specifying options, sequences, and parameters in a special application-oriented language. Some particularly powerful application generators are becoming available for business applications, such as Mathematica's RAMIS, National CSS's NOMAD [McCracken, 1980], Information Builders' FOCUS, and IBM's Application Development Facility.

4. *Very High Level Languages.* These typically combine the special knowledge-domain structure and program library of the application generator with the power of a HOL and its compiler. Examples are simulation languages, automatic test equipment languages, query languages, etc.

5. *Automatic Programming.* This refers to the ultimate in program generation capability, in which a user begins to specify his desired information processing activity to an automatic programming system, which then asks the user questions to resolve ambiguities, clarify relationships, etc., and to converge on a particular program specification. The system then automatically generates a program which implements the specification. Outside of some very restricted-domain systems which are more accurately termed application generators or very high level languages, automatic programming systems are still somewhat beyond the current frontier of the state of the art.

Productivity Advantages of Program Generators

The major productivity advantage of program generators is that sizable computer applications can be generated using a very small number of user-language directives. Developing software via program generators can certainly be a far more cost-effective pursuit than developing software one instruction at a time.*

However, in doing so, it is essential to consider whether the generated program is actually going to solve your problem. If it does, you reap the benefit of a large labor savings. If it does not, though, you may simply reap larger problems. As an example, suppose that the initial program described in the *Scientific American* case study in Chapter 1 could have been developed with a program generator. Although this would have reduced the amount of software development effort, the end result would still have been to increase operating costs, decrease reliability and quality of service, and decrease staff morale. Thus, the existence of a program generator for a given application area does not imply that all of our software problems in that area are solved. We still need a good deal of front-end effort in applying such techniques as cost-benefit analysis and the GOALS approach, to ensure that our program generator will generate the right program.

One clear advantage of the program generator is this regard is its value in developing quick prototypes of a desired software capability, on which our assumptions about system usage can be tested by actual use. If the resulting software is somewhat

---

* Another attractive option in this direction is the implementation of software componentry in hardware chips. See [Boehm, 1980] for a discussion of the potential capabilities and limitations of this option.

off the mark, but can be corrected within the domain of the program generator, we still achieve a significant labor savings. And even if the use of the prototype convinces us that we need to build a new product, we have learned that lesson much more cheaply than we would by building the software from scratch based on faulty assumptions.

In sum, although it is inadvisable to apply a program generator without some initial analysis of its applicability, it is equally inadvisable to reject the program generator option (or the software package option) with a wave of the hand and an assertion that "our problems are so special that we need custom software." More and more frequently, this will not be the case. Often, just a few inessential compromises in our mode of operation will make a program generator product or software package an adequate match for our needs.

On Rapid Prototyping and Evolutionary Design

The emergence of application generators oriented around a data base management system and report-generation capability has created an attractive approach for software development; the rapid-prototyping/evolutionary-design (RP/ED) approach. The basic RP/ED approach is as follows [McCracken, 1980a; 1981]:

1. Use the application generator to develop a rapid prototype of key portions of the user's desired capability.
2. Have the user try the prototype and determine where it needs improvement.
3. Use the application generator to iterate and evolve the prototype until the user is satisfied with the results.
4. If the performance of the resulting system is adequate, establish it as the user's system and continue to update and maintain it via the application generator. If higher performance is required, either tune the prototype or use the prototype as the *de facto* specification for developing a high-performance system.

Advantages of the RP/ED Approach

The RP/ED approach provides an alternative to the generation and validation of written requirements specifications and draft users' manuals as a way of ensuring that a software product will be responsive to the user's needs. The main advantages of the RP/ED approach are:

- Exercising the prototype provides a much more realistic validation of user requirements than does the review of a set of specifications and manuals.
- Using the prototype surfaces a number of second-order impacts that the system will have on the user's mode of operation.
- The rapid development minimizes the problems of accommodating the inevitable stream of requirements changes which surface during a long development period.
- The rapid-prototyping capability makes it possible to generate several alternative systems for comparative trials, and to provide quick-response solutions for user difficulties.

Difficulties with the RP/ED Approach

The above advantages have caused some people to claim that written requirements specifications have become completely outmoded by the RP/ED approach. This is a good goal for the RP/ED approach, and one which may be realizable in some problem domains. However, at present, the RP/ED approach has some difficulties which limit its general applicability:

- Although fairly good rapid-prototyping capabilities exist for some problem domains (notably small business applications, inventory control, and some scientific application areas), they do not currently exist for other problem areas (notably for most real-time distributed processing systems, command and control systems, and large, integrated, corporate information systems).
- The flexibility of prototypes is often negated by organizational inertias. (A typical example: "It's nice that you could change those equipment codes to make them more intelligible for us, but the Codes Committee just met and established the current codes as company standards. There's no way we can change them now.")
- If the initial prototype is too far off the mark, it may lead to disastrous results, such as:
  a. Fielding such an unresponsive system that users are turned off completely.
  b. Concentrating on near-term user needs and neglecting foreseeable longer-term needs until too late. ("Oops! It's tax-return time next month and we haven't been entering a lot of the data we need to generate the returns.")
  c. Developing a suboptimal system which requires a great deal of rework to correct its negative effects on the overall system (for example, the initial *Scientific American* system).

Because of these difficulties, the RP/ED approach cannot be considered as a universal replacement for specifications, scenarios, protocols, and draft users' manuals as a way to establish user requirements. Most centainly, RP/ED is not a substitute for careful examination of the user's overall problem before plunging into code.

However, these difficulties are *not* presented as reasons for avoiding the RP/ED approach. Where it is supported by application-generator capabilities, it provides an extremely powerful avenue for improving software life-cycle productivity and for developing more responsive software systems. And its major current strengths lie in the most common area of software endeavor: the development and maintenance of small business-oriented applications.

On the Use of DSI/MM As a Productivity Metric

Along with the program generators have come advertising claims of extremely high productivity rates in terms of delivered source instructions per man-month (DSI/MM). These claims may be literally true, but they need to be interpreted with a good deal of perspective and caution.

As early as the mid-1950s, it was possible to use an aerospace trajectory-simulation program generator to generate a 10-KDSI program within 10 mintues of effort [Boehm, 1973]. The literal productivity rate for such a program is

$$\left(\frac{10,000 \text{ DSI}}{10 \text{ min}}\right)\left(\frac{60 \text{ min}}{\text{hr}}\right)\left(\frac{152 \text{ hr}}{\text{MM}}\right) = 9,120,000 \text{ DSI/MM}$$

Figures such as this cause people to claim that the whole concept of DSI/MM as a productivity metric is meaningless. And certainly it is, if it is taken completely out of context—as it is here, since the 10,000 instructions will be generated whether we need them all, need only a small part of them, or don't need them at all to perform our mission.

In general, in dealing with software packages or program generators, the DSI/MM metric is not of much help in analyzing decision situations. The cost-effectiveness comparisons involved in software-package or program-generator decisions are better expressed in terms of mission-relevant benefits provided versus overall contribution to cost, and DSI/MM considerations do not enter the picture.

In dealing with software *development* decisions, however, the DSI/MM metric is very helpful in providing a basis for analyzing decisions on such issues as hardware capacity versus software productivity tradeoffs, effort versus schedule tradeoffs, software tool investment, and incremental development options. It is clearly not an ideal productivity metric even for software development issues, but as we have discussed in Section 28.3, it is better than any other candidates which are currently available.

Some conclusions from this discussion are that

- The best criterion for the value of a metric is the degree to which it helps us make decisions
- The value of a metric thus varies, depending on the decisionmaking situation in which it is applied

In the following several sections, we will be assessing the effect of various cost driver attributes on software development productivity, to provide a basis for decisions on improving productivity on software development projects. Within this context, the use of DSI/MM as a productivity metric will be quite helpful.

33.4 SOFTWARE PRODUCTIVITY CONTROLLABLES: PRODUCT ATTRIBUTES

Sections 33.4 through 33.7 discuss the major controllable factors in improving software development productivity (expressed in DSI/MM), using the same categorization of cost driver attributes (product attributes, computer attributes, personnel attributes, project attributes) that was used in Chapters 24 to 27 to discuss the COCOMO cost driver attributes. The discussions cover the productivity improvement implications of each of the COCOMO cost driver attributes, plus other related factors (language level, management, requirements volatility) which are not included in COCOMO but which are often significant productivity influence factors.

Required Reliability

In general, a software project has little control over the required reliability of the desired product. The main productivity considerations involve

- Not devoting effort to providing more reliability than the product needs. For example, although aircraft flight software may require very high reliability, this does not imply that the same level of reliability assurance effort be applied to the postflight data reduction software.
- Not attempting false economies such as eliminating software requirements and design V & V activities; the resulting errors will simply be more expensive to fix later on.

Where it is feasible to relax reliability requirements, the payoff can be fairly high. The overall COCOMO productivity range for required reliability is 1.87; a difference of one step on the five-step rating scale can make a productivity difference of about 15% in productivity.

On the other hand, for long-life software products, relaxing reliability requirements simply leads to higher life-cycle costs. The 15% savings in development effort gained by relaxing required reliability from nominal to low is eventually paid for by a 15% increase in annual maintenance costs. Thus, if life-cycle maintenance costs will eventually exceed development costs (as they generally do for large products), we should not attempt to relax our reliability requirements. Further examples of life-cycle reliability tradeoff analyses are given in Section 8.5.

Data Base Size

Again, there is very little control that a project has over the required data base size. As with required reliability, the major control activity influencing productivity is a series of reviews; here, to ensure that the product's data base size reflects actual operational needs.

However, overall project productivity is relatively insensitive to moderate changes in data base size. The overall COCOMO productivity range for data base size is only 1.23; reducing the data base size by a factor of 10 yields a productivity improvement of only around 6 to 8%.

Software Product Complexity

Although the inherent complexity of a software product is beyond the control of a software project, there are many temptations to reduce productivity by making the product more complex than it needs to be. A number of examples (instant response time, pinpoint accuracy, unbalanced systems, multicolor vector graphics) are discussed in Section 11.2 under the topic of software gold-plating.

Where it is feasible to reduce the product's complexity by such means as eliminating sources of unnecessary gold-plating or by simplifying processing functions, the payoff can again be significant. The overall COCOMO productivity range for product complexity is 2.36; a difference of one step on the six-step rating scale can make a difference of about 15% in productivity.

It is appropriate to be concerned here about whether we are overly concerned about productivity. Are we achieving productivity gains at the price of taking the fun parts out of programming? This is certainly not the intent. The primary intent is to avoid the frequent "agonizing reappraisals" which occur when a software project finally admits that it has blown its budget and schedule by trying to complete unnecessary advanced *research* activities on the critical path of a software *development* project. People who have lived through any of these agonizing reappraisals and their aftermath will generally agree that the back-end agony was not worth the front-end fun.

On the other hand, a good manager can generally convince his customer to fund some noncritical-path research activities out of the savings achieved by keeping the development project simple. This provides some opportunity for stimulating research activities, but in the right place. Also, as some of our best software products in the field have shown, achieving elegant simplicity in a software product is even more challenging and satisfying than achieving baroque complexity.

Programming Language

Most recent software cost estimation and productivity studies, such as the COCOMO studies and the IBM [Walston–Felix, 1977] studies, have found that software productivity per source statement is relatively independent of the level of the source language (HOL versus MOL), as long as a project has used an MOL only where necessary. That is, as long as the project follows the guidelines

- Whenever a software function can be conveniently expressed in HOL, use HOL.
- Use MOL for reasons of efficiency only after programming the function in HOL, determining the sources of inefficiency, and then selectively reprogramming these in MOL.

By using these guidelines, organizations which had previously been using MOL for many HOL-expressable functions have experienced significant productivity gains. It is difficult to use the COCOMO model to predict the magnitude of these gains, as the COCOMO productivity rates are based on the assumption that the project is following the guidelines above. However, some recent German studies comparing projects using MOL versus the HOL PEARL report savings of 25 to 37% (or productivity gains of 33 to 59%) across the overall development cycle due to the use of HOL [Martin, 1979]; these figures are consistent with most previous studies.

Even larger productivity gains are achieved during the maintenance phase by using HOLs, as shown by the [Graver and others, 1977] study results discussed in Section 30.4. Typically in that study, four times as many people were required to maintain a given number of object instructions on MOL products as compared to HOL products.

Assessing the relative effects on software productivity of different HOLs (such as FORTRAN versus Pascal) is a much more difficult task.

The results in Section 28.2 do not indicate any strong variations in productivity between HOLs, but the sample size is too small on such languages as Pascal to support any definitive conclusions. The results of the [Boehm, 1980] experiment, in which two teams used FORTRAN and Pascal to develop the same small applications software product, indicated that the choice of programming language was not a major determinant of the projects' outcomes or of their productivity. However, the study also concluded that

- The choice of programming language would be a more significant factor in developing more complex and ambitious software products.
- The choice of programming language would be a more significant factor over an organization with many products to develop than it is for a single stand-alone product.

Further, the choice of HOL is likely to have a significant influence on the maintenance productivity of an entire organization. Another consideration is the suitability of the HOL for the applications area (e.g., COBOL for business vs. scientific software). In general, an HOL which facilitates the use of modern programming practices (such as Pascal and Ada), and which is strongly supported by software tools, is the strongest choice for enhancing productivity in the long run.

Product Size

As we discussed in Sections 33.2 and 33.3, one of the best ways of reducing software costs is to reduce the number of DSI we must develop. We can do this by using already-developed software, as with software packages, adapted software, or program generators; or we can devote more attention to *avoiding the development of unnecessary software*. In many cases, a significant amount of effort has gone into developing software that was never put to use by its prospective users [Boehm, 1973; GAO, 1979].

In general, the best way to avoid developing unnecessary software is to perform thorough requirements and design verification and validation activities with extensive involvement of the prospective users, employing early usage scenarios, protocols, and users' manuals to ensure that the users understand what the software will be doing for them in their own terms. If these activities establish that some software functions are not needed by the users, these functions can be eliminated, resulting in significant software development savings, and less frustration in seeing the fruit of a lot of hard work going unused. If there is some doubt after the V & V activity as to whether a software function will be needed, its development can be deferred to a later stage of incremental development, or it can be put on a user "wish list" for future consideration as a product component. Many organizations have found that the formal use of such a "wish list" is an effective way of recording and managing its backlog of desired product enhancements.

33.5 SOFTWARE PRODUCTIVITY CONTROLLABLES: COMPUTER ATTRIBUTES

Execution Time and Main Storage Constraints

Software productivity can be improved considerably by acquiring enough computer speed and main storage capacity to free the software development from the excess effort required to shoehorn the software within tight execution time and main storage constraints.

Figures 33–4a and b show how the COCOMO effort adjustment factors for execution time constraint and main storage constraint can be used to determine how much excess hardware capacity to procure in order to minimize total system (hardware plus software) acquisition cost. The total system cost curves are given in terms of the ratio

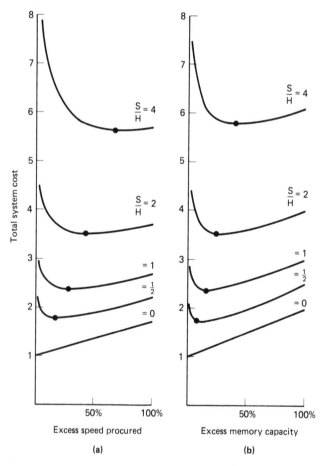

FIGURE 33–4a Hardware-software cost versus speed; **b** cost versus memory

$$\frac{S}{H} = \frac{\text{Ideal software cost}}{\text{Ideal hardware cost}}$$

where the ideal software cost excludes any extra costs due to hardware constraints, and the ideal hardware cost excludes any extra costs for acquiring excess hardware capacity over the minimal capacity required to support the application.

The tradeoff curves in Fig. 33–4a are based on the COCOMO curve of software productivity versus execution time constraint given in Fig. 25–4, and a model of central processing unit cost as a function of execution time performance of the form

$$\text{Performance} = c(\text{Cost})^{1.3} \qquad (33\text{–}1)$$

based on the analyses in [Phister, 1979] of the cost-performance ratios of recent IBM 360, 370, 303X, and 43X1 product lines. The tradeoff curves in Fig. 33–4b are based on the COCOMO curve of software productivity versus main storage constraint given in Fig. 25–4, and a linear model of main memory cost versus capacity

$$\text{Capacity} = c(\text{Cost}) \qquad (33\text{–}2)$$

here based on the analysis of the more recent IBM 370, 303X, and 43X1 product lines given in [Phister, 1979].

It is clear from Figs. 33–4a and b that the procurement of additional speed and storage capacity can lead to significant overall system cost savings. Specifically, we can infer the following guidelines from Figs. 33–4a and b

1. Overall system cost is generally minimized by procuring computer hardware with 30 to 50% more capacity than is absolutely necessary.
2. The more the ratio of software-to-hardware cost increases, the more excess capacity one should procure.
3. It is far more risky to err by procuring too little hardware capacity than by procuring too much. This is especially important, given the tendencies discussed elsewhere for sizing estimates to be low and for software products to expand during development and maintenance. Thus, the preferred amount of hardware capacity procured should be even higher than the minimum system cost level.

Example: A Process Control System

Montana Mining and Manufacturing Corporation is planning to develop a number of minicomputer-based process control systems for surface coal processing. The ideal software cost for the system is estimated at $400K; the cost of the hardware will depend on the number of systems installed and the hardware speed in millions of instructions per second (MIPS). The required speed for performing the process control functions is 1.0 MIPS; the ideal hardware cost for such a processor is $20K; and the cost for additional hardware speed roughly follows the relation in Eq. (33–1).

TABLE 33–3 Process Control Example: Optimal Cost versus Number of Systems

Number of Systems	Ideal Hardware Cost	$\frac{S}{H}$	Optimal MIPS	Optimal Hardware Cost	Time Constraint	Software Cost	Optimal Cost
5	$100K	4	1.69	$150K	59%	$418K	$ 568K
10	200	2	1.43	264	70	444	708
20	400	1	1.29	488	$77\frac{1}{2}$	476	964
40	800	$\frac{1}{2}$	1.18	912	85	520	1432

Table 33–3 shows how the optimal amount of excess processor speed varies with the number of process control systems to be installed. If the software cost is spread over only five copies of the system ($H = 5 \times \$20K = \$100K$), we have a high software–hardware cost ratio ($S/H = 4$). Applying Fig. 33–4a, it is best to acquire 1.69 MIPS of processor speed and reduce the execution time constraint of 59% in order to conserve software costs. On the other hand, if the software cost is spread over 40 copies of the system, we have a low software–hardware cost ratio ($S/H = \frac{1}{2}$), and it is best to acquire only 1.18 MIPS of processor speed. This reduces the execution time constraint to only 85%, but the growth in software cost is more than balanced by reduced hardware costs.

Resource Control

Quite a few projects have procured an appropriate level of extra speed or storage capacity, but have still come to grief by allowing Parkinsonian tendencies to absorb all the excess capacity (and sometimes even more) during the development period. The best way to avoid such a situation is to employ an execution time and core-budget control device such as the *computer program assembly list* shown in Fig. 33–5. With such a system, the resources spent on each computer program component can be compared with their allocated budgets, and appropriate control actions taken if a component's size or execution time becomes unacceptably large. Thus, for example, in Fig. 33–5, the size of the Pulse Rate Control routine as coded is over twice as large as was estimated. Thus, the routine needs further investigation to determine whether some alternate approach could be found to perform the necessary functions within the available core budget. Surprisingly often, this can be done if the problem is discovered early and understood to be important.

Relaxing Performance Requirements

If a project is faced with potential software productivity losses because of hardware speed or storage constraints, and none of the above techniques will provide an appropriate margin for effective software development and maintenance, there is one additional option remaining. The system performance requirements can be relaxed. Relaxing required response time from 2 sec to 3 sec, for example, has the effect of transforming a 95% execution time constraint and a 66% software productivity penalty into a 63% execution time constraint and a 7% software productivity penalty. Given

MNEMONIC	DESCRIPTION	Machine Instructions		Source statements coded
		Estimated	Coded	
TOTT	Object track return processing	8335	4722	787
ROUTINES:				
TTOTT	Task control routine	550	540	90
TMAJR	Track filtering	145	90	15
TPRED	State and covariance prediction	600	498	83
TEDTA	Editing of single detections	455	468	78
TCORR	State and covariance update	551	318	53
TLFML	LFM waveform selection	105	132	22
TXMRC	Radar transmit and receive	330	342	57
TRADQ	Pulse rate control routine	240	558	93

FIGURE 33-5 CPAL: a core budget planning and control tool

the relatively high COCOMO productivity ranges for the hardware constraint factors—1.66 for the execution time constraint and 1.56 for main storage constraint—this option is well worth investigating.

Virtual Machine Volatility

Frequently, a project or an installation can achieve an appreciable software productivity gain simply by realizing the negative effect of virtual machine volatility—the rate of change in the underlying computer hardware, operating system, and/or data base management system on which foundation a software product is being developed—and by taking several fairly straightforward steps to reduce the volatility level. One such step is to package changes in periodic releases instead of feeding them in continuously. Another is simply to establish a higher threshold of cost-effectiveness in authorizing changes to the underlying system. Another is to choose more mature and stable underlying support systems. A further technique which can be effectively applied to both the software under development and its underlying virtual machine is to use the information-hiding techniques in [Parnas, 1979] to contain the adverse effects of changes within individual modules.

Compared to the software productivity leverage provided by other COCOMO cost driver attributes, virtual machine volatility is at an intermediate level. Its COCOMO productivity range is 1.49. A difference of one step on its four-step rating scale (such as reducing the frequency of major changes from 2 weeks to 2 months and the frequency of minor changes from 2 days to 1 week) can make a difference of about 15% in productivity.

Computer Turnaround Time

The COCOMO productivity range for computer turnaround time is 1.32. This is one of the smaller ranges as compared to the other COCOMO cost driver attributes, but on the other hand, computer turnaround time is often a more controllable factor than most of the other factors. Further, the 15% productivity gain typically realized by going to interactive software development is significant. Below are some major do's and don'ts to consider in using turnaround time to improve software productivity.

- *Do* reinforce the use of interactive software development with the use of software tools and modern programming practices. The use of powerful interactive text editors and modular software structures, for example, will strongly enhance the productivity benefits of interactive development.
- *Do* provide a balanced set of available resources. Providing interactive operation on an inadequate number of available terminals or microprocessor development systems, for example, can cause even worse delays and inefficiencies than slow turnaround batch processing.
- *Do* provide turnaround priority for software development, especially for critical-path items. Delays in critical-path items simply magnify the productivity losses on other dependent components.
- *Don't* just provide interactive development facilities without some training and discipline in how to use them. For example, using a terminal to perform batch-style debugging or to propagate an uncontrolled proliferation of versions can negate all the potential benefits of interactive operation.
- *Don't* carry top-down development and test to extremes. Pure top-down testing recommends the use of the entire system as a test driver for later program units as they are developed. This may require very elaborate runs, with associated long turnaround times, when the testing could be accomplished more quickly at the unit or subsystem level.
- *Don't* overemphasize computer throughput and CPU utilization as primary goals in an installation supporting software development. Extremely high CPU utilization almost inevitably leads to long job queues, increased turnaround time, and lower software productivity.

Finally, for any installation decisions affecting turnaround time, *do* precede the decision with a suitable cost-benefit analysis of the options. Such an analysis can establish the right balance of throughput and turnaround time in situations such as the ones above, and can help avoid some of the excesses sometimes practiced in the name of software productivity. For example, one installation with a largely production workload and with very little software development activity was sold a high-overhead interactive software development system for its four programmers. This system slowed down the production workload so much that a larger computer, costing $2 million more, had to be purchased. For a cost of $500,000 per programmer, a number of more effective steps could have been taken to improve software productivity.

33.6 SOFTWARE PRODUCTIVITY CONTROLLABLES: PERSONNEL ATTRIBUTES

Personnel attributes and human relations activities provide by far the largest source of opportunity for improving software productivity. The combined COCOMO productivity range for analyst capability and programmer capability is 4.18 (that is, all other factors being equal, a 90th-percentile team of analysts and programmers will be about four times as productive as a 15th-percentile team of people). The combined COCOMO productivity range for applications experience, virtual machine experience, and programming language experience is 2.52, also very high.

Further, there are a good many different ways in which an organization can capitalize on these high productivity ranges in order to improve software productivity. These are discussed below within the primary categories of staffing, motivation, and management.

Most importantly, these "people factors" provide us with a means for keeping software productivity in context with respect to our overall human relations goals, which emphasize a concern for the objectives of the people involved in the software process as well as a concern for the objectives of the software process itself. Fortunately, as we will see below, these objectives are not in much conflict when we take a long-term view. Actions which advance people's long-range career objectives are also actions which enhance an organization's long-term software productivity.

Staffing

The tremendous range of variability between individuals in software productivity (up to 26:1 in the [Grant–Sackman, 1966] study) provides an outstanding opportunity for an organization to improve its software productivity via staffing initiatives. Most organizations do not take much advantage of this opportunity, as evidenced by the [Cooper, 1975] survey of 14 large industrial and government software installations. This survey produced the following profile of the average coder at these installations:

- Two years' college-level education
- Two years' software experience
- Familiar with two programming languages
- Familiar with two software products
- Generally sloppy, inflexible, introverted, "in over his head," and undermanaged

With a little initiative, any software installation should be able to improve its staffing situation considerably above this level, with significant gains in productivity.

Staffing Principles

Following the pattern in [Koontz–O'Donnell, 1972] of organizing management guidelines along the lines of basic principles, five basic principles of software staffing are presented and discussed below. These are

- The Principle of Top Talent
- The Principle of Job Matching
- The Principle of Career Progression
- The Principle of Team Balance
- The Principle of Phaseout

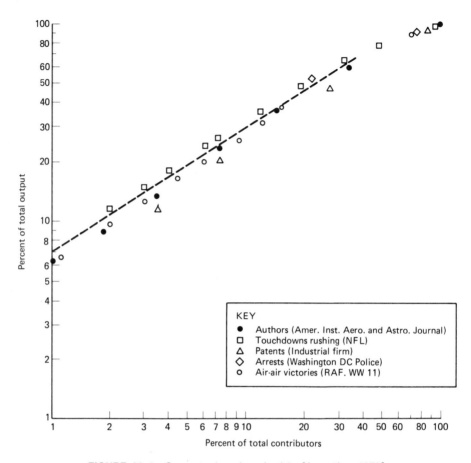

Percent of total output

KEY
● Authors (Amer. Inst. Aero. and Astro. Journal)
□ Touchdowns rushing (NFL)
△ Patents (Industrial firm)
◇ Arrests (Washington DC Police)
○ Air-air victories (RAF. WW 11)

Percent of total contributors

FIGURE 33–6 Concentration of productivity [Augustine, 1979]

1. *The Principle of Top Talent. Use better and fewer people.* The wide productivity ranges among software personnel shown by the [Grant–Sackman, 1966] study and other studies are simply special cases of a well-known human phenomenon: The bulk of the productivity comes from a relatively small number of participants. Figure 33–6, from [Augustine, 1979], shows the remarkably similar concentrations of productivity found among authors, football players, inventors, policemen, and pilots. The top 20% of the people produce about 50% of the output; the bottom 50% of the people produce about 20% of the output.*

Given this concentration of productivity in a relatively small fraction of people, and the additional productivity bonus of reducing project communications overhead by using fewer, more productive people, one would expect every software manager to follow the Principle of Top Talent. But surprisingly,

---

* As Augustine points out, the concentration of productivity is probably understated, as the data exclude participants who made no contributions (patents, touchdowns, etc.).

very many do not. Given a choice between a $40,000 per year analyst and a $25,000 per year analyst, they will inevitably choose the latter, because

"I can't afford those high-priced people," or

"I can't take a risk on somebody that expensive";

independently of any considerations of the analysts' relative talent.

2. *The Principle of Job Matching: Fit the tasks to the skills and motivation of the people available.* One of the common violations of this principle is

The Peter Principle [Peter-Hull, 1969]: "In a hierarchy, every employee tends to rise to his level of incompetence."

The most common realization of the Peter Principle in software engineering is the practice of "advancing" good programmers by promoting them into management. Sometimes this works well, but overall it produces more mismatches, frustrations, and damaged careers in software engineering than in other fields. The reason for this is shown in Fig. 33–7, adapted from [Couger-Zawacki, 78]. This figure compares the relative growth need (for skill growth in one's professional discipline) and social need, for people in data processing and people in other job categories such as clerical, sales, service, management, and other professions (legal, medical, etc.). It is clear from Fig. 33–7 that (on the average) the data processing professional's social need is extremely low in comparison to his growth need, while the relative ranking of these needs is in the opposite direction for managerial people.

This comparison indicates that the practice of rewarding good performers by making them managers is more likely to invoke the Peter Principle in

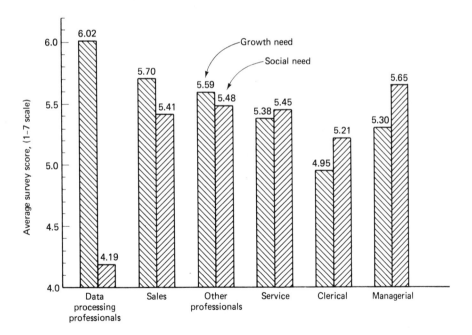

FIGURE 33–7 Comparative growth needs and social needs, DP and other professions [Couger-Zawacki, 1978]

the data processing field than elsewhere. This point has been realized by a number of organizations, which have instituted dual or multiple career paths culminating in "superprogrammer" or "superanalyst" as well as "supermanager" jobs. However, one still sees advice counseling exactly the opposite. For example, *Data Processing Organization and Manpower Planning* [Brandon, 1974] contains a number of the old career progression diagrams which equate career advancement with transition into management.

Of course, the principle of job matching applies to other dimensions as well, such as in matching programming, debugging, customer relations, and communications skills to programmer and system-analyst jobs, see, for example, [Arvey–Hoyle, 1973].

3. *The Principle of Career Progression. An organization does best in the long run by helping its people to self-actualize.* Self-actualization, or bringing out the best in oneself, is the highest level in the human needs hierarchy (Fig. 33–8) formulated by [Maslow, 1954] as a guide to understanding human motivation and behavior. Maslow's main conclusions with respect to the needs hierarchy are

- People will not be strongly motivated by higher level needs if lower level needs are unfulfilled. Thus, if we are starving, we will not be concerned about extending our computer science skills while remaining in need of food and drink.
- On the other hand, satisfied needs are not motivators. Thus, once we have satisfied our physiological and intermediate level needs, we will not be much interested in eating more food, but we will still have a strong remaining urge to realize some untapped potential we feel in ourselves as software engineers, poets, teachers, etc.

People self-actualize in many different ways, but for many software people, a good deal of self-actualization is involved with becoming a better software professional. The principle of career progression indicates that it is in an organization's best interest to help people determine how they wish to grow professionally, and to provide them with career development opportunities in those directions. This may seem like a somewhat obvious principle, but in practice there are many software organizations which follow strongly opposing principles. Two such opposing principles related to the Peter Principle are the Inverse Peter Principle and the Paul Principle.

FIGURE 33–8 Maslow human need hierarchy

- *The Inverse Peter Principle:* "People rise to an organizational position in which they become irreplaceable, and get stuck there forever." This is most often encountered in software maintenance, where a programmer becomes so uniquely expert on the inner complexities and operating rituals of a piece of software that the organization refuses to let the person work on anything else. The usual outcome is for the programmer to leave the organization entirely, leaving an even worse situation.
- *The Paul Principle* [Armer, 1966]: "People rise to an organizational position in which their technical skills become obsolete in five years." Given the rapid evolution of the computer field, it is important for organizations to provide opportunities for their people to grow with the field. Otherwise, they can run themselves into major disasters, as several organizations attempting to implement large real-time distributed data processing systems with armies of second-generation, tape-oriented COBOL programmers have found. Again, this advice may appear obvious, but one can still find books such as *Data Processing Cost Reduction and Control* [Brandon, 1978] counseling organizations to do just the opposite: to reduce training and conference budgets, limit professional society memberships to one person per society, and similar short-term cost-cutting actions which are likely to be long-run false economies.

Some good examples of the application of the Maslow need hierarchy to software engineering situations, and some additional valuable principles in the spirit of the Peter and Paul Principles, are given in [Weinberg, 1979].

4. *The Principle of Team Balance. Select people who will complement and harmonize with each other.* As with the other principles, this principle acts as a moderating force on the principle of top talent, which by itself might lead us to recruit a group of incompatible, overqualified technical superstars. In this regard, your software team is similar to a football team: if you want a team which will score a lot of touchdowns, you will not do very well by going to Fig. 33–6 and picking the 11 individuals who made the most touchdowns as the members of your team.

Team balance involves not just balancing the many components of technical skill but also balancing the many psychological components of the team and its members. It is difficult to provide much valuable insight on the topic in a few paragraphs or pages, but the best advice of all takes only one sentence in this book. Read Gerald Weinberg's *The Psychology of Computer Programming* [Weinberg, 1971].

5. *The Principle of Phaseout. Keeping a misfit on the team doesn't benefit anyone.* No matter how carefully you select the members of your software team, inevitably you will find some people who do not contribute anywhere near their fair share to the team's objectives, even after several attempts to find a suitable role for them on the team. In such a situation, you will be tempted to postpone dealing with the problem, to profess not to notice it, to smooth it over with words, or to ask the other team members to do extra tasks. This may be

the easy way out in the short run, but invariably it produces unhealthy results in the long run.

Phasing people out isn't easy. But if you contribute enough time, thought, and sympathy, you can often create a situation in which the phaseout becomes a positive rather than a negative experience, and the person concerned finds a new line of work which suits him or her much better than a group-oriented software project. If this doesn't work, and you are left with a definite misfit, don't back away from the problem. Get rid of the misfit as quickly as possible.

But be very careful in determining what constitutes a positive contribution to a software team. As with the football team, people's contributions are not solely measured by the number of touchdowns or delivered source instructions they produce as individuals. Often someone who doesn't look very productive in DSI/MM is providing an irreplaceable function in understanding and interpreting the users' requirements or in keeping up team morale. Again, [Weinberg, 1971] is an outstanding source of help in addressing this problem.

Motivation

Motivation is the means by which the potent wellsprings of human energy and creativity are directed toward people's desired goals. Most productivity studies have found that motivation is a stronger influence of productivity than any other contributing factor [Gellerman, 1963].

The classic experiments concerning motivation and productivity were conducted by Elton Mayo and his associates from 1927 to 1932 at the Hawthorne Works of the Western Electric Company in Chicago, giving rise to the term "Hawthorne effect." The initial experiments attempted to determine the effect of lighting and illumination on productivity. The results of the experimental groups were as follows:

- When illumination was increased, productivity went up.
- When illumination was decreased, productivity went up.
- When illumination was held constant, productivity went up.

After a long series of further experiments which tried to explain this effect by factoring out motivational considerations and varying other environmental factors, Mayo finally concluded [Mayo, 1945]:

The major experimental change was introduced when those in charge tried to hold the situation humanly steady . . . by getting the cooperation of the workers. What actually happened was that six individuals became a team and the team gave itself wholeheartedly and spontaneously to cooperation in the experiment.

The Hawthorne effect has been subsequently observed in many productivity experiments, including a number of structured programming experiments. A related effect in software engineering is the effect demonstrated in the [Weinberg, 1972] experiment discussed in Section 3.6, in which teams given several different objectives (finish quickly, conserve memory, etc.) each finished first (or, in one case, second) with respect to the objective they were asked to optimize.

Motivating Factors: General

Given the strength of these effects, we would like to find ways to "motivate people" to improve their software productivity. Unfortunately, motivation doesn't work that way. In the words of [Townsend, 1970]:

"You can't motivate people. That door is locked from the inside. You can create a climate in which most of your people will motivate themselves to help the company reach its objectives."

A good principle for creating such a climate is [Koontz–O'Donnell, 1972]:

• *The Principle of Harmony of Objectives.* The more that people perceive that their personal goals are in harmony with organizational goals, the greater will be their contribution to organizational goals.

This principle has two major implications for any of our efforts to improve software productivity via motivation

1. We need to understand software people's objectives.
2. We need to incorporate software people's objectives into our organizational decisions.

There is a good deal of general knowledge about people's objectives and their relation to organizational objectives and decisions. The Maslow need hierarchy in Fig. 33–8 provides some basic illumination. The [McGregor, 1960] Theory X (authoritarian)–Theory Y (cooperative) distinction of organizational management styles provides further valuable insights. The [Herzberg and others, 1959] distinction between motivating factors (which stimulate performance) and hygiene factors (which prevent losses of performance) is another good source of general understanding.

Motivating Factors: Software People

In addition, though, we need specific understanding of how the motivating factors of software people may differ from those of other groups of people. The [Couger–Zawacki, 1978] results in Fig. 33–7, for example, show that data processing people are more highly motivated by growth needs than by social needs. Another significant study reported in [Fitz-Enz, 1978] showed that, although the Herzberg distinctions between motivating factors and hygiene factors generally held for data processing professionals, there were significant differences between the factor profiles of data processing professionals and those of Herzberg's overall population of subjects.

These differences are summarized in Table 33–4, which compares the rank order of the motivational factors in the general Herzberg survey and the Fitz-Enz survey

TABLE 33–4 Comparison of First-Level Motivating Factors, Data Processing Professionals versus General Population

General Population [Herzberg and others, 1959]	Data Processing Professionals [Fitz-Enz, 1978]
1. Achievement	1. Achievement
2. Recognition	2. Possibility for growth
3. Work itself	3. Work itself
4. Responsibility	4. Recognition
5. Advancement	5. Advancement
6. Salary	6. Supervision, technical
7. Possibility for growth	7. Responsibility
8. Interpersonal relations, subordinate	8. Interpersonal relations, peers
9. Status	9. Interpersonal relations, subordinate
10. Interpersonal relations, superior	10. Salary
11. Interpersonal relations, peers	11. Personal life
12. Supervision, technical	12. Interpersonal relations, superior
13. Company policy and administration	13. Job security
14. Working conditions	14. Status
15. Personal life	15. Company policy and administration
16. Job security	16. Working conditions

of data processing professionals. The main result corroborates the Couger–Zawacki findings: the possibility for growth factor, which was a seventh-ranked hygiene factor in the general Herzberg survey, was a strong second-ranked motivating factor in the Fitz-Enz data processing survey. Other significant differences were that data processing professionals are

- More strongly motivated by opportunities for technical supervision, by peer relations, and by personal life
- Less strongly motivated by recognition, responsibility, salary, and status

These differences were significantly more pronounced among programmer-analysts than they were among data processing project leaders and managers, as is shown in Fig. 33–9, a comparative distribution of the motivating factors by job level from [Fitz-Enz, 1978]. These results carry an additional lesson for data processing managers. They should not expect their subordinates to be motivated by the same factors that they are, especially in the areas of recognition, responsibility, technical supervision, and personal life.

Given the significantly higher levels of software productivity exhibited by highly motivated people and teams, we should expect data processing managers and books on data processing personnel management to emphasize staff motivation as one of an organization's highest priorities. Yet many data processing managers pay very little attention to staff motivation factors, and some books emphasize exactly the opposite, as exemplified by [Brandon, 1974] (emphasis Brandon's):

> "Thus, [the systems analyst] must display a certain amount of creativity and imagination, by sharp contrast to the programmer whose creative instincts should be totally dulled to insure uniform and understandable programming."

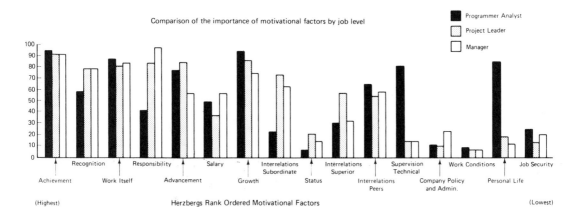

Given what we now know about programmers and their growth motivation, such advice is a clear recipe for disaster.

Management

As we discussed in Section 28.6, poor management can increase software costs more rapidly than any other factor. Conversely, good management can promote both an efficient, well-coordinated software process and the high levels of staff capability, motivation and teamwork which lead to outstanding software productivity. Here also, it is difficult to summarize the many principles of good overall software management. The best sources for such information are [Koontz–O'Donnell, 1972], [Metzger, 1973], and [Brooks, 1975].

However, we need to emphasize one point about software management and productivity which dominates all the others:

> *If managers do not genuinely want improved software productivity, the organization will not get improved software productivity.*

No matter how big the ballyhoo at the beginning of a productivity improvement effort, if the managers do not demonstrate continued commitment to the effort by means of investment in better tools, recognition and rewards for outstanding performance, and enforcement of standard practices, or if managers continue to say, "I know you need three months to do the top-down design right, but the customer wants to see some early progress, so we're scheduling the product design review in a month," then the entire productivity effort will degrade into an empty exercise.

Software Personnel and Productivity: Summary

This section has covered a good many considerations with respect to software personnel and productivity. To summarize

1. *Personnel factors are very significant.* A strictly programming-oriented or material–economics-oriented approach to improving software productivity will miss the biggest opportunity of all.
2. *Personnel factors are not a total mystery.* Although activities involving people are never completely predictable, a good deal of information is becoming available which helps us understand what makes a group of software personnel more productive.
3. *Personnel factors are personal.* Although quantitative information can help, strictly quantitative and manipulative approaches to structuring people's software roles will be counterproductive in the long run.

33.7 SOFTWARE PRODUCTIVITY CONTROLLABLES: PROJECT ATTRIBUTES

In this section, we return to the sequence of discussing the software productivity leverage opportunities for individual cost driver attributes as in Sections 33.4 and 33.5. We will cover the three COCOMO project attributes discussed in Chapter 27: modern programming practices, use of software tools, and schedule constraint, along with two additional project attributes: requirements volatility and work environment.

Modern Programming Practices (MPPs)

As described in Section 27.1, modern programming practices (MPPs) included the following:

- Top-down requirements analysis and design
- Structured design notation
- Top-down incremental development
- Design and code walkthroughs or inspections
- Structured code
- Program librarian

In addition, the program support library, covered under Tools in Chapter 27, is an integral part of the program librarian function. The Chief Programmer Team concept, which is often associated with the above techniques but which has had highly mixed results, is not included. Other modern techniques such as ISDOS [Teichroew–Hershey, 1977], SREM [Alford, 1977; Bell and others, 1977], SADT [Ross–Schoman, 1972], information hiding [Parnas, 1979], data-directed design [Warnier, 1974; Jackson, 1975], and structured design [Yourdon–Constantine, 1978] are considered as extensions to top-down requirements analysis and design and structured design notation.

Frequently, and somewhat misguidedly, the entire subject of software productivity improvement is identified with the implementation of MPPs. As we have seen, there are numerous other ways to improve software productivity, many of which have a greater productivity range than the COCOMO productivity range of 1.51 associated with MPPs. However, the introduction of MPPs makes it easier to realize many of the productivity improvements from other sources (for example, tools, interactive development, motivation, management). Also, the COCOMO maintenance productivity ranges for MPPs are considerably greater, varying from 1.54 for small (2-KDSI) projects to 2.07 for very large (512-KDSI) projects.

MPP Implementation Guidelines

The best sets of guidelines on how to implement MPPs in an organization are those in [Yourdon, 1979] and [Infotech, 1978]. Detailed checklists and representative experiences can best be obtained from these sources; below is a set of general guidelines for MPP implementation.

1. Ensure that management is committed to the MPP implementation effort.
2. Embed the MPP implementation within an overall strategy for improving software productivity.

   • Include other options such as computer capabilities, work environment, staffing, career development;
   • Include such features as a productivity agent, an implementation study, a productivity plan, a training program, a pilot project, an incremental implementation approach, and an evaluation and improvement activity (see Section 33.8).

3. Make sure that both managers and performers agree on an appropriate set of objectives and performance criteria, such as

   • Clear, adaptable software rather than complex, hyperefficient software
   • Public rather than private software
   • Thorough, validated requirements and design specifications rather than early code

4. Don't implement all the MPPs at once. One effective three-step approach is the following:
   (a) Structured code and walkthroughs
   (b) Top-down requirements analysis and design, structured design notation, and top-down incremental development
   (c) Program library, librarian, and other team and organizational changes.
5. Allow enough time for training. Make sure that performers understand the objectives and principles of the new techniques as well as the rules.
6. Make sure that the techniques are consistently applied. Verify compliance and reject noncompliant work.
7. However, avoid structured purism. Occasionally, a GOTO or an extra-large module is the best way to do the job. Don't confuse means and ends.
8. Don't be afraid of mistakes and false starts. They are part of the learning and assimilation experience.

9. Don't expect instant results. In fact, be prepared for some reduction in productivity during the training and assimilation period.
10. Establish a continuing evaluation activity with feedback into improving the techniques used.

Use of Software Tools

The COCOMO productivity range for use of software tools is 1.49. Thus, tools provide a significant opportunity to improve productivity, particularly since an organization's tool support is one of its more controllable factors. A difference of one step on the five-step COCOMO tools rating scale can make a difference of about 10% in productivity. For a large organization with, say, 200 software people, this means freeing up 20 software people for new activities, a payoff worth a significant level of investment.

Further, as with modern programming practices, the use of software tools can make it easier to realize productivity improvements from other sources (such as from MPPs, interactive development, motivation, or management). Below are some guidelines for various situations in which the level of tool support may provide a good opportunity for improving software productivity.

- If your current facility is strongly tool-deficient, consider acquiring an integrated software tools capability. For example, several versions of the Unix-Programmers' Workbench capability [Ivie, 1977] are available as commercial products.
- If your current facility has a well-integrated set of tools, be on the lookout for additional cost-effective tools. Sources of information on available tools are given below.
- If you are planning to develop a new tool, look carefully at your expected costs and benefits (most tools will provide only a fraction of the 10% productivity gain associated with a one-step improvement on the COCOMO scale), and consider any commercial tools which may provide similar capabilities.
- If you are choosing a new computer system, particularly a microcomputer, make a thorough cost-benefit analysis of the candidate system's relative tool capabilities. Table 33–5 shows that the tools differential for even a small (20 MM) total software effort will outweigh a factor-of-two difference ($5K versus $10K) in the purchase price of the computer system.

TABLE 33–5 Effect of Tools on Computer Selection

Quantity	Computer A	Computer B
Purchase price	$ 5K	$ 10K
Tools level	Very low	Low
Tools effort multiplier	1.24	1.10
Nominal software effort	20 MM	20 MM
Software effort with tools	25 MM	22 MM
Labor cost at $5K/MM	$125K	$110K
Total cost	$130K	$120K

- If you are developing a new computer system for sale, be prepared to commit a significant level of investment in software tools, as customers are becoming more aware of tools effects such as shown in Table 33–5.

The list of sources of information on commercially available software packages in Section 33.2 provides a way to obtain further information on software tools. Another good source is [Reifer, 1981].

Schedule Constraint

The main productivity concern with respect to schedule constraint is not with improving productivity, but with keeping it from degrading due to unrealistic scheduling or unnecessary slippage. The most significant concerns and guidelines are given below.

1. *Use the COCOMO schedule equations to determine a realistic schedule.* Many projects get into trouble because they don't know what a realistic schedule should be. The COCOMO equations (in Table 8–1 or Table 23–1) are not precise, but they give reasonably realistic estimates. For incremental development, use the extension provided in Section 29.4.
2. *If a shorter schedule is desired, make sure it is worth the cost.* A 25% reduction in the nominal schedule will cost an additional 23% in development effort.
3. *Never schedule a software development effort for less than 75% of the nominal schedule.*
4. *If the size or nature of the job changes during development, change the schedule also.* A variation on the incremental development schedule estimation technique in Section 29.4 can be used for rescheduling estimates.
5. *Don't let the development schedule slip unnecessarily.* In particular, monitor and control your critical-path development activities very closely.
6. *Don't waste time up front.* Below is a typical example of the inexcusable type of front-end behavior which all too frequently plagues software projects:

Jan. 1, 1984	"We should finish up the plans and requirements by April 1, and the development schedule is estimated at 21 months, so we'll schedule the system delivery for December 1985."
April 1, 1984	"We haven't quite finished surveying some of the off-site users. We should have the spec ready in about a month."
July 1, 1984	"We're just about ready on the spec. Some of the Codes Committee people are out on vacation, but we don't expect any delays from them once we get them all together."
Sept. 1,1984	"We have everything pretty well specified, but somebody said we should get a legal opinion on some of the data items. We'd better not proceed until Legal gives us their blessing."
Dec. 1, 1984	"Well, here's the spec. It's still got a lot of holes in the user interface area, but we've really got to get moving now because the system is still scheduled for cutover in December 1985. You'd better cancel some Christmas vacations, because we've

scheduled PDR on January 10 in order to start catching up on schedule."

The inevitable outcome of this scenario has been replayed many times

- An initial burst of enthusiasm while the team sincerely believes it can do the impossible.
- Total disillusionment as the team members come to fully understand the size and complexity of the job.
- The agonizing reappraisal when management finally realizes the schedule is not going to be met.
- Often, an attempt to catch up on schedule by adding more people, doomed to failure by Brooks' Law.
- In the end, an unsatisfactory compromise product which took much more time and effort than the original development estimates.

The real tragedy is that software managers and performers continue to accept such unrealistic schedules. One of the main reasons for this has been that software people have not had much solid experience data to convince their customers of the unrealism of their schedule demands. Before you agree to a tight schedule, look at Figs. 27–8 and 27–9, and their associated discussion in Section 27.3. Think carefully: Do you want to be responsible for Mission Impossible?

Requirements Volatility

In Section 28.4, we noted that

- Some requirements volatility on software projects is unavoidable (IBM's experience averages 25%)
- The COCOMO productivity range for requirements volatility is a significant 1.78
- Some large projects with frequent redirection have experienced productivity penalties of factors greater than four due to requirements volatility

Thus, reducing requirements volatility is a major avenue for improving software productivity.

The usual source of requirements volatility is a scenario such as the following:

Customer: "We've got to reorganize the exception reporting module to feature an Outcome Prediction capability. We've just heard that the new chief is very big on outcome prediction."

Software Manager: "Gee, that sounds interesting. We should be able to put something good in for you there. Let's see—George is working on the exception reporting module. We'll have Joan help him take a crack at it. Joan is currently working on the scheduler. She's very good at problems like this."

Particularly if Joan's scheduler is on everybody else's critical path, the software manager has just introduced a major slowdown into his project without any renegotiation of budget and schedules.

The best way to keep the sources of requirements volatility down to the necessary ones is to

1. Establish a formal or informal contract between the customer and the software developer, such that any proposed change with budget and schedule impact requires a budget and schedule renegotiation.
2. Establish a user "wish list" for recording candidate improvements to be considered for future releases of the software product, and a means of establishing the cost-benefit priority of wish list items for future releases.

It is remarkable how frequently the prospect of a budget and schedule renegotiation turns a "must have" change request into a "nice to have" wish list entry.

Work Environment

Besides the psychological work environment we discussed in Section 33.6, the physical work environment is a significant influence on software productivity. Anyone who has attempted to develop good software efficiently in a hot, noisy, overcrowded programming bullpen with poor clerical and telephone support, awkward work procedures and computer access, inadequate supplies and conference facilities, and frequent moves will certify that these have a strong negative effect on both motivation and productivity. As indicated in Fig. 33–6, work conditions tend to act as a Herzberg hygiene factor. Above a certain threshold, they are not a powerful motivator, but below that threshold, they are a powerful demotivator. If conditions become too bad, people will quit, leaving the organization with a personnel continuity problem as well.

The most significant attempt to provide a work environment suited to the needs of software people has been the architectural design and development of the IBM Santa Teresa Laboratory [McCue, 1978]. The buildings, offices, furnishing, electrical and telephone connections of the Santa Teresa Laboratory were designed to meet, as much as possible, a set of requirements derived from studies of software development activities, including such items as

- *Communication.* Facilities for intraproject communication (such as office proximity, conference rooms) and external communication (such as voice and data telecommunications).
- *Privacy.* Personal offices with acoustical isolation, adequate ventilation, external awareness (windows), and individual control of the office environment.
- *Furniture.* In particular, work surfaces and storage compartments which accommodate the use of computer listings and interactive terminals.
- *Computer connections.* Terminal connections for every office, and easy project access to video, high-speed, and low-speed communications, to remote job entry stations, and to hardcopy devices.

- *Security.* Controlled access to the site, to data processing facilities, and to project facilities.
- *Technology.* Flexibility to accommodate future computer and software technology advances (such as broadband teleconferencing, powerful personal terminals).

Several other organizations have recently established similar work environments, and have concluded that the new environment is proving to be a positive influence on productivity, personnel satisfaction, and personnel retention. Not every organization will have a chance to specify an entire building complex to meet software personnel needs, but every organization will have some opportunities to evolve toward a better matched software work environment. At the very least, we should be able to match our level of concern for providing a suitable work environment for our software people to our level of concern for providing a suitable work environment for our computer equipment.

33.8 ESTABLISHING A SOFTWARE PRODUCTIVITY IMPROVEMENT PROGRAM

Software productivity improvement programs for different organizations will generally be fairly similar, but an effective program for a given organization will require some specific tailoring to the organization's unique characteristics. The major steps involved in establishing and tailoring a software productivity improvement program are

1. Obtain top management commitment
2. Establish a software productivity agent
3. Arrange broad-based participation
4. Identify objectives, alternatives, constraints
5. Evaluate alternatives
6. Choose best combination of alternatives
7. Prepare phased implementation plan
8. Obtain authority to proceed
9. Implement plan
10. Followup, iterate plan

Each of these steps is elaborated below.

1. *Obtain Top Management Commitment.* We discussed the need for this step in Section 33.6. The major conclusion there was

   - If managers do not genuinely want improved software productivity, the organization will not get improved software productivity.

2. *Establish a Software Productivity Agent.* This step follows a basic management principle: *If you want to get something to happen, make somebody specifically responsible for it.* The productivity agent serves as a dedicated focal point for productivity-related activities. Due to their close interrelationships, it is

generally a good idea to include software cost estimation and software data collection and analysis activities as part of the productivity agent's charter. Under such a charter, the productivity agent's primary responsibilities would be to

- Identify potential productivity improvement avenues
- Evaluate candidate productivity improvement proposals
- Evaluate external productivity aids
- Perform or review software cost estimates
- Collect and analyze software cost and productivity data
- Serve as a corporate memory and consultant on productivity-related issues

The major job qualifications for a software productivity agent are a good knowledge of software and the organization, quantitative analysis skills, and a strong desire to help people improve their productivity. Organizationally, the best location for the productivity agent is in a staff position reporting to the highest level manager responsible for software development. Again, however, without this manager's strong commitment to improving productivity, the agent's effect will be minimal.

3. *Arrange Broad-based Participation.* Improving software productivity inevitably involves making changes. If you arrange for everyone to be affected by these changes to become a part of the definition and planning of the changes, you achieve two main advantages.

- *You stimulate people's enthusiasm rather than their resistance.*
- *You get a more accurate assessment of the environment.* Figure 33–10 shows the results of a recent survey conducted as part of a software productivity improvement effort. A sample of upper level managers, middle managers, and performers were asked, "What should we do to improve software productivity?" Their answers were classified as to whether the suggestions involved project management actions (better planning, organization, etc.), work environment and compensation (better office space, facilities, performance bonuses, etc.), education and training (in modern programming practices, management, etc.), or acquisition of software tools.

  It is evident from Fig. 33–10 that the upper managers' world view conditions them to see management actions as the high-leverage items, while the performers' world view conditions them to see tools as the high-leverage items. The important point is not which group is more correct, but that each group brings a valid set of perceptions to bear on the problem. Further, since motivation is such a key factor in software productivity, people's perceptions are an important consideration. If the upper managers in the organization had proceeded with a big campaign to improve project planning, organization, reporting, etc., without providing the performers with improved tools, the organization's resulting productivity gains would not have been anywhere near their potential.

4. *Identify Objectives, Alternatives, Constraints.* This step involves the systems

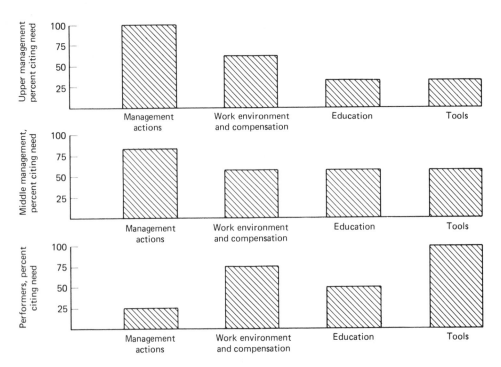

FIGURE 33-10 Software productivity—perceptions of major needs

analysis techniques treated in Part III of this book, particularly in Chapter 17. A good statement of an overall productivity improvement objective is

- Find ways of producing an equivalent level of desired software functionality at a reduced cost, with no loss in product quality, and with an improved set of staff career options.

Besides this basic objective, installations may have specific objectives reflecting greater needs to improve productivity on large projects, to improve computer center services concurrently, etc. The alternatives to be considered are all those controllable factors discussed in Sections 33.2 to 33.7. The organization's constraints may include personnel ceilings, investments in existing hardware and software inventory, office space limitations, government regulations, etc.

5. *Evaluate Alternatives.* Here, the COCOMO tables can be of great value in assessing both the organization's current status and the likely productivity impact of various candidate improvements. For example, Table 33–6 shows an evaluation of the long-range effects of a plan to improve software tools availability and usage within a given organization. It shows, for each COCOMO level of tool usage, the organization's current (1981) situation in terms of products operating at that tools level and the overall percentage of the organization's software activity operating at that tools level (here, for example, 15% of the organization's 1981 effort is devoted to projects

TABLE 33–6 Evaluation of Tools Improvement Strategy

COCOMO Tools Rating		1981 Projects	Percent of Projects		
Level	Multiplier		1981	1985	1990
Very low	1.24	Lab auto, Test equipment	15%	0%	0%
Low	1.10	Process control, Communications	25	10	5
Nominal	1.00	MIS, Inventory	50	25	10
High	.91	Scientific	10	50	25
Very high	.83			15	60
Weighted average multiplier			1.05	.94	.88
Productivity gain				12%	19%

with very low tools support, primarily in the laboratory automation and test equipment software areas). Further, it shows how this percentage profile is likely to change as the long-range tools improvement program is implemented. From these profiles, the weighted average COCOMO TOOL multiplier for each representative year can be calculated. It shows the organization's average TOOL factor being reduced from 1.05 to .94 (a 12% productivity gain) in 4 years and from 1.05 to .88 (a 19% productivity gain) after another 5 years of tool enhancement.

Of course, as with the other evaluations we studied in Part III, the more subjective effects must be evaluated as well as the easily quantifiable ones. Thus, the effects of improved tools on people's motivation (remember Fig. 33–10) and their career goals should be assessed as well.

6. *Choose Best Combination of Alternatives.* Again, by far the best results in productivity improvement are obtained by working the whole problem. Simply concentrating on modern programming practices, or on management actions, or on tools will lose a great deal of the potential productivity synergy of an integrated combination of alternatives. The evident validity of the COCOMO multiplicative model indicates that the cumulative effects of implementing several alternatives will multiply together the individual productivity improvements such as those calculated for tools in Table 33–6. Table 33–7 shows the result of such a calculation, based on an integrated effort to improve an organization's use of tools, MPPs, interactive software development, staffing, work environment and compensation, management procedures, and use of already developed software.

Several significant points can be made about Table 33–7.

- *An integrated software productivity improvement program can have an extremely large payoff.* Productivity gains by factors of three in 4 years and factors of eight in 9 years are possible for some organizations to achieve, and are worth a good deal of planning and investment. Most organizations will not be able to achieve quite so high a productivity

TABLE 33-7 Evaluation of Overall Productivity Strategy

	Weighted Average Multiplier		
COCOMO Attribute	1981	1985	1990
Use of software tools	1.05	.94	.88
Modern programming practices	1.07	.89	.83
Computer response time	1.02	.91	.89
Analyst capability	1.00	.88	.80
Programmer capability	1.05	.90	.80
Virtual machine volatility	1.06	.95	.90
Requirements volatility	1.27	1.08	1.00
Use of existing software	.90	.70	.50
Cumulative multiplier	1.46	0.43	0.19
Productivity gain		3.4	7.8

gain, but could achieve gains of a factor of two in 3 to 4 years, and a factor of five in 6 to 8 years with an integrated long-range program.

- *Improving software productivity involves a long, sustained effort.* The payoffs are large, but they require a long-range commitment. There are no easy, instant panaceas.
- *An effective productivity improvement program involves much more than introducing MPPs.* In the situation shown in Table 33-7, only a 29% productivity gain would be achieved just from introducing MPPs.
- *Evaluating potential productivity gains requires a sound assessment of the organization's current practices.* As seen in Table 33-6,* the fact that the COCOMO tools productivity range is 1.49 does not mean that an organization will get a 49% productivity gain by fully tooling up.
- *Table 33-7 actually underestimates the organization's likely productivity improvement.* It does not include gains which would likely be made independently of the productivity program, such as those due to increases in the applications, language, and virtual machine experience factors; it underestimates the maintenance benefits of using MPPs; it assumes that no improvements are possible from the hardware constraint and schedule constraint factors.
- *In the very long run, the biggest productivity gains will come from increasing use of existing software.*
- *Even without the gains from using existing software, software development and maintenance productivity gains can be very high.* Figure 33-11 shows the calculated software development productivity gains from Table 33-7, excluding the use of existing software factor. Starting from an assumed base of 250 DSI/MM in 1981, development productivity is calculated

---

* Note that Table 33-6 provides an effective framework for performing such an assessment, if extended to the other COCOMO cost driver attributes as well. A good complementary checklist for performing a software productivity assessment is given in [Patrick, 1980].

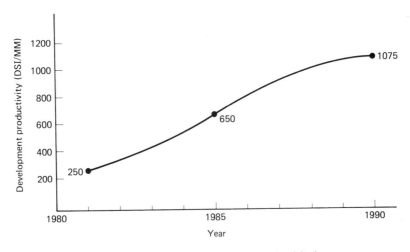

FIGURE 33–11 Estimated development productivity increase

to reach 650 DSI/MM (a factor of 2.6) by 1985 and 1075 DSI/MM (a factor of 4.3) by 1990. The improvement for maintenance would actually be greater, due to the increased maintenance benefit from MPPs.

7. *Prepare Phased Implementation Plan.* The plan should be incremental, with the early phases concentrating on the more straightforward, easy to implement, high payoff items (such as structured code, walkthroughs, stabilizing requirements and virtual machine support). The plan should follow the "why, what, when, who, where, how, how much" format illustrated in Table 21–1, and should contain provisions for addressing the entire range of improvements upon which the productivity improvement calculations were based.

8. *Obtain Authority to Proceed.* The "how much" portion of the implementation plan should identify the resources required for increased salaries, facilities, tool acquisition, training, software product acquisition, etc. Authority to proceed includes authority to commit funds for these items. One shouldn't expect threefold or eightfold productivity improvements without the expenditure of some resources to achieve them.

9. *Implement the Plan.* This means implement the whole plan, not just the fun parts. Improving productivity by phasing out misfit staff members is not fun, but if you plan to do it and then back off, it will erode the progress you may have been making elsewhere, as people begin to wonder what other parts of the program are not for real.

10. *Followup and Iterate Plans.* The COCOMO model and the software project data collection instruments given in Appendix A provide a good framework for followup. If each project collects and tracks data on its attribute ratings and its productivity, we will gain a set of records for determining whether our plans are being implemented, whether the implementation is actually realizing the predicted improvements in cost driver attribute ratings, and whether the improvements in attribute ratings are producing improvements

in productivity. Since no long-range plan is perfect, we will undoubtedly find some situations in which plan improvements will be necessary.

It is clear that the implementation of this plan requires a great deal of organizational will power and staying power. A good source of encouragement and insight is [SHARE-GUIDE, 1979], which contains histories of some organizations which have implemented subsets of this plan, with highly successful results. Another encouraging case history is given in [Paster, 1981].

33.9 CONCLUSIONS

What can we conclude from the material presented in this chapter? Here are the key points.

- *For most data processing installations, software productivity will be the critical problem of the 1980s.* The demand for new software is rising much more rapidly than the supply of capable software people.
- *Most data processing installations can increase their software development and maintenance productivity by a factor of two in 3 to 4 years, and by a factor of five in 6 to 8 years.* With such large potential payoffs, every good sized installation should establish a software productivity improvement program. However, nobody should expect instant results.
- *The COCOMO cost driver attributes and effort multipliers provide a natural framework for establishing and implementing a software productivity improvement strategy.* As was seen in Fig. 33–1, which summarized the productivity ranges of the COCOMO cost driver attributes, improving software productivity involves pursuing many more opportunity areas besides introducing modern programming practices. In particular, the personnel areas of staffing, motivation, and management offer the biggest payoffs.
- *In the long run, the best productivity program is one which considers both the life cycle of the software product and the life-cycle of the software people involved.* For example, this means avoiding such common pitfalls as the Peter Principle, the Inverse Peter Principle, and the Paul Principle.
- *Software productivity can be improved by a great deal more than the factors cited above via increased use of existing software.* In fact, a more appropriate criterion than DSI/MM for assessing software productivity improvements would be one expressed in desired software functionality per unit cost.
- *Significant software productivity improvements are not achievable without the full commitment of higher management.* Some example situations involve establishing significant salary increase differentials for top performers, phasing out misfits, enforcing disciplined practices, holding the line with customers on unrealistic schedule demands or requirements changes, and stimulating a higher proportion of "not invented here" software.
- *The best way to get started on a sustained software productivity improvement program is to establish a software productivity agent.* This agent should be responsible for

identifying, evaluating and preparing the way for proposed productivity improvements. Usually, the agent can also serve as the organization's focal point and corporate memory on software cost estimation, data collection and analysis activities.

One final point deserves particular emphasis. In pursuing improvements in software productivity, we need to be careful not to confuse means with ends. Improved software productivity is not an end in itself; it is a means of helping people better expand their capabilities to deal with data, information, and decisions.

Often, helping people to do this will involve us in activities—for example, spending two weeks helping someone find an effective non-software solution to their problem—which don't add points to our software productivity scoreboard. At such times, we need to recall that the software productivity scoreboard is just one of the many ways we have to gauge our progress toward becoming more effective data processing professionals.

Appendix A

Software Cost Data Collection Forms and Procedures

INTRODUCTION

Appendix A provides a set of forms and procedures for cost data collection throughout the life-cycle of a software product. The procedures are oriented around the collection of information and the updating of the software product's COCOMO estimates at the project's major life-cycle milestones.* The revised COCOMO estimates provide immediate project management benefits by furnishing improved cost-to-complete estimates for use in revising schedules and personnel requirements, and by providing improved estimates to compare with project costs to date. They also provide an opportunity to perform up-to-date sensitivity analyses and cost-risk analyses of project options. Thus, the data collection activities specified below are not an added cost burden to the project for historical purposes, but an integral part of the process of keeping the project's management plan up to date.

---

* Thus, the forms provided include the Intermediate COCOMO CLEF form introduced in Chapter 9 and the Detailed COCOMO SHEF forms introduced in Chapter 23.

Procedures for an Ongoing Project

The Software Project Data (SPD) forms provided here can be used either for ongoing projects or for completed projects. The forms and their use for ongoing projects are explained and illustrated below, using the CEMICS inventory control project of Chapters 31 and 32 as an example.

Form SPD-1: General Information (Figure A–1 and Table A–1). Originated at the start of the project and completed at the end of software development.

Form SPD-2: Phase Summaries (Figure A–2 and Table A–2). Phase data entered at the end of each phase (Figure A–2 shows its status at the end of the Product Design Phase). Completed at the end of development.

Form SPD-3: Subsystem Summaries (Figure A–3 and Table A–3). Filled out at the end of development.

Form SPD-4: COCOMO Milestone Runs (Figure A–4 and Table A–4). Milestone information entered at each major development milestone, along with completion of either an Intermediate COCOMO CLEF form (Figure A–5) or Detailed COCOMO SHEF forms.

COCOMO Maintenance Estimates. Performed at the beginning and end of each year of annual maintenance (thus, for example, at the end of Year 2, one would perform a revised estimate of Year 2 costs and an estimate of anticipated Year 3 costs). These estimates also involve using either the Intermediate COCOMO CLEF form (Figure A–6) or the Detailed COCOMO SHEF forms.

Form SPD-M: Annual Maintenance (Figure A–7 and Table A–5). Filled out at the end of each year of annual maintenance.

TABLE A–1a. Explanation of Form SPD-1: Definitions

Customer Experience: Application. The customer's overall degree of familiarity and experience with the type of application system (inventory control, energy management, investment analysis, etc.) being developed.

Customer Experience: Data Processing. The customer's overall degree of familiarity and experience with data processing.

Customer Interface Complexity. The degree of complexity involved in obtaining customer cooperation on reviews, approvals, obtaining data, specifying interfaces, etc.

Detailed Project Plan. The degree to which the project is guided by a detailed plan specifying products, schedules, milestones, responsibilities, techniques, resources, and project assumptions.

Full Requirements Specification. The degree to which the project completes a requirements specification detailing functional, performance, and interface requirements during the Plans and Requirements phase and the Product Design phase.

Early Verification and Validation. The thoroughness with which the project performs V&V activities on its requirements and design specifications.

Thorough Baseline Configuration Management. The thoroughness with which the project establishes baseline versions of specifications and code, and performs change control and status accounting functions to ensure effective software version control.

Unit Development Folders or Equivalent. The degree to which the project employs the Unit Development Folder technique presented in Section 32.4, or its equivalent.

Thorough Test Plans and Procedures. The degree to which the project's test activities are guided by detailed test plans and procedures establishing test concepts, criteria, input data, output data, facilities, schedules, resources, support software, responsibilities and operational procedures.

Standards and Quality Assurance. The degree to which the project establishes standards for programming, documentation, test completeness, etc., and monitors the project for compliance with the standards.

Resource Planning and Control System. The degree to which the project's resource management is guided by a planning and control system similar to that presented in Chapter 32.

Good Work Environment. The degree to which the project's work environment provides quiet, pleasant, stable, uncrowded facilities with good clerical and telephone support, supplies, work procedures, etc.

Privacy, Security Constraints. The degree to which the project is constrained by extra procedures, restricted access to information, and added security or privacy protection requirements.

TABLE A-1b. Explanation of Form SPD-1: General Information

1. *Project Title.* A short title of the project or product
2. *ID Number.* A unique identifying number for the project
3. *Revision Number.* Sequence number of latest revision (if any)
4. *Date.* Date of origin or latest revision
5. *Development Organization.* The organization primarily responsible for developing the product
6. *Project Manager.* Name of the person primarily responsible for developing the product
7. *Originator.* Name of the person responsible for completing this form
8. *Customer Organization.* The organization primarily responsible for acquiring and using the product
9. *Project Type.* BUS: Business; CTL: Process Control; HMI: Human-Machine Interactive; SCI: Scientific; SUP: Support; SYS: Systems
10. *Hardware Configuration.* A brief summary of the computer hardware configurations used for development and operation.
11. *Brief Project Description.* A brief summary of the major distinguishing features of the project
12. *References to Detailed Description.* Reports, memos, or other documents describing the project
13. *Project Attributes.* Ratings on the scale [Very low; low, nominal, high, very high] of project attributes in addition to those specified as COCOMO attribute ratings. Attribute definitions are given in Table A–1a. Four blank spaces are provided for additional significant attributes
14. *Comments.* Explanatory comments on any of the attribute ratings
15. *Special Factors Increasing or Decreasing Cost.* Identification of factors considered particularly significant project cost drivers. This, or any of the other entries, may be elaborated by continuing comments on additional pages or by referencing other documents.

(1) Project title __CEMICS__ (2) ID NO. __B142__ (3) Rev. no. __3__ (4) Date __9/19/82__

(5) Development org. __BSD__ (6) Project MGR. __M. MARCOS__ (7) Originator __R. LEE__

(8) Customer org. __MSD__ (9) Project type __Bus__

(10) Hardware configuration __IBM 3032 using MVS__

(11) Brief project description

Inventory control system for PPI central Equipment Management Operation

(12) References to detailed description

Document B142-D002, "CEMICS Rqts./Design Spec", 9/10/82
B142-D005A, "CEMICS Plan", 9/1/82

(13) Project attributes

	Rating					(14) Comments
	VLO	LO	N	HI	VHI	
Customer Experience: Application					X	
Customer Experience: Data Processing				X		_Early V & V would have been "very high"_
Customer Interface Complexity		X			X	_if we hadn't accepted existing documenta-_
Detailed Project Plan						_tion without question._
Full Requirements Specification				X		
Early Verification and Validation				X		
Thorough Baseline Config. Mgmt.				X		
Unit Development Folders or Equivalent				X		
Thorough Test Plans and Procedures				X		
Standards and Quality Assurance				X		
Resource Planning and Control System					X	
Good Work Environment				X		
Privacy, Security Constraints	X					
Quality of existing Documentation.	X					

(15) Special factors increasing or decreasing cost

About 5% added effort due to misleading information in documentation of previous system. See memo B142-M17, 7/16/82.

FIGURE A-1: Form SPD-1

TABLE A-2. Explanation of Form SPD-2: Phase Summaries

1. *Project Title.* A short title of the project or product
2. *ID Number.* A unique identifying number for the project
3. *Originator.* Name of the person responsible for completing this form
4. *Date.* Date of origin or latest revision
5. *Phase.* The major development phases as defined in Table 4–1
6. *Start Date, End Date.* The dates each phase is initiated and completed
7. *Man-Months by Activity.* The number of man-months devoted during each phase to the major project activities (Requirements analysis, product design, etc.) as defined in Tables 4–2 and 4–3
8. *Total $K.* The total cost of completing each phase in thousands of dollars
9. *Computer Hours, $.* The number of computer hours and dollars expended during each phase.
10. *PP Documents.* The number of *new* pages of specifications, plans, and manuals produced during each phase.
11. *Errors: This Phase, Previous.* The number of nontrivial, distinct errors detected during each phase which originated in the same phase or in a previous phase.
12–14. Three blank columns available to specify other phase attributes (e.g., number of new requirements introduced during the phase)
15. *Other Project Costs.* The number of man-months and dollars expended over the development cycle (excluding the plans and requirements phase and the implementation phase) on training, installation, etc., and the number of dollars expended over the same period on travel, communications, etc.
16. *Type of Funding.* FP: Fixed-price contract Int-User: Internal funding, paid by user organization
    CPFF: Cost plus fixed fee contract Int-Devel: Internal funding, paid by developer organization
    CPIF: Cost plus incentive fee contract Other: (specify)
17. *Burden Rate:* The ratio: Total personnel costs to the customer organization / Total personnel salaries paid by the developer organization

    Besides salaries, total personnel costs include fringe benefits, facility and support costs, general and administrative expenses, profits, and other expenditures included in the organization's overhead.
18. *% Uncompensated Overtime.* Relative to the standard 152-hour man-month, the average percentage of additional uncompensated effort expended by project personnel on project tasks.

① Project title __CEMICS__ ② ID NO. __B142__ ③ Originator __R. LEE__ ④ Date __9/28/82__

⑤ Phase	⑥ Start date	End date	⑦ Man-months by activity									⑧ Total $K	⑨ Computer		⑩ PP. Documents			⑪ Errors		⑫ New Rqts.	⑬	⑭
			RA	PD	PG	TP	VV	PO	CQ	MN	Total		HR	$	SPEC	PLAN	MAN.	This phase	PREV			
Plans and Requirements	5/1/82	7/2/82	3.0	1.0	0.1	–	0.5	1.0	⎫	–	5.6	33.9	0.6	130	120	70		131				
Product Design	7/3/82	9/27/82	2.0	9.1	0.7	0.6	1.0	2.0		1.9	17.3	101.4	2.1	460	550	110	60	304	29	12		
Detailed Design																						
Code and Unit Test																						
Integration and Test																						
Development Total																						
Totals																						

⑮ Other project costs

Item	MAN-MO.	$K
Training		
Installation		
Program Conversion		
Data Base Conversion		
Clerical		

Item	$K
Travel	
Communications	
Publications	
Software Products	

⑯ Type of Funding

⑰ Burden Rate

⑱ % Uncompensated Overtime

FIGURE A-2: Form SPD-2

TABLE A-3. Explanation of Form SPD-3: Subsystem Summaries

1. *Project Title.* A short title of the project or product
2. *ID Number.* A unique identifying number for the project
3. *Originator.* Name of the person responsible for completing this form
4. *Date.* Date of origin or of latest revision
5. *SS Number.* Number of the software subsystem being described
6. *Subsystem.* Name of the software subsystem being described
7. *KDSI: Exec, Non-Exec.* Thousands of executable and non-executable delivered source instructions in the subsystem
8. *KDMI: Exec, Non-Exec.* Thousands of executable and non-executable delivered machine instructions in the subsystem
9. *Adapt.* The COCOMO parameters describing to what extent the subsystem was adapted from existing software (see Section 8.8 for details):

    DM: Percent design modified
    CM: Percent code modified
    IM: Percent of integration required for modified software
    Completely new software can be indicated either by 100's or by dashes, as in the example.

10. *Requirements Definition.* The thoroughness with which the software requirements have been specified by the time of the Product Design Review milestone (rated on a scale of Very High, High, Nominal, Low, Very Low).
11. *Requirements Volatility.* The extent to which changes in the software requirements cause the software cost to increase due to the required rework of plans, specifications, manuals, code, etc. A rating scale is given below with corresponding effort multipliers; it is best to key the rating to your estimate of the effort multiplier experienced by the project.

Rating	Project Rework due to Requirements Changes	Effort Multiplier
LOW	Essentially none	0.91
NOMINAL	Small, non-critical redirections	1.00
HIGH	Occasional moderate redirections	1.19
VERY HIGH	Frequent moderate or occasional major redirections	1.38
EXTRA HIGH	Frequent major redirections	1.62

12. *Language.* The languages used in the subsystem and the percentages of source instructions in each language (COB = COBOL in the example)
13. *Personnel Continuity.* The degree to which the project avoids undesired personnel turnover. The rating scale is based on the percentage of undesired turnovers to total personnel on the project:

    Very Low—100%   High—5%
    Low— 30%   Very High—0%
    Nominal— 10%

14. *Average Personnel.* The average number of full-time software personnel (FSP) working on the subsystem
15. *Maximum Personnel.* The maximum number of full-time software personnel (FSP) working on the subsystem
16. *Man-Months by Phase.* The number of man-months expended on the subsystem during each phase. (In the example, man-months expended on entire-system activities such as project management, requirements analysis, and product design are entered on the SYSTEM line)

17. *Total Development Man-Months.* The number of man-months expended on the subsystem—or on system-level activities—during development (excluding Plans and Requirements phase effort)

18. *Development Labor Costs ($K).* Thousands of dollars expended on labor costs during development.

19–22. Four blank columns available to specify other subsystem attributes (the example shows thousands of lines of Program Design language; other possibilities include complexity measures, number of errors, number of inputs, outputs, files, reports, etc.)

23. *Total.* A line for the totals of appropriate columns.

① Project title Cowie S　　② ID NO. B142　　③ Originator R Lee　　④ Date 1/15/84

⑤ SS No.	⑥ SUBSYSTEM	⑦ EXEC	⑦ NON-EXEC	⑧ EXEC	⑧ NON-EXEC	⑨ Adapt DM	CM	IM	⑩ RQTS DEF	⑪ RQTS VOL	⑫ Language COB	⑬ PERS. CONT.	⑭ AVE. PERS.	⑮ MAX. PERS.	⑯ PR	PD	DD	CUT	IT	⑰ TOT DEVEL	⑱ 'K DEVEL	⑲ PDL K	⑳	㉑	㉒
0	SYSTEM								HI	N		VHI	3 8	7	6	17		57	37	117	625				
1	EDIT	8 1	7 8	25	17	—	—	—	HI	N	100	VHI	1 5	2				11		11	52	2 1			
2	UPDATE	5 2	15	18	7	—	—	—	HI	LO	100	VHI	0 5	1				5		5	31	2 4			
3	EQUIP	7 0	4 2	26	10	—	—	—	HI	LO	100	VHI	0 6	1				6		6	39	2 9			
4	RPT DATA	12 5	8 4	41	34	—	—	—	HI	HI	100	N	1 2	2				18		18	81	4 0			
5	REPORTS	7 0	8 0	23	20	—	—	—	HI	HI	100	N	0 8	1				8		8	39	1 9			
6	MISC	7 6	2 4	27	14	—	—	—	N	HI	100	N	0 5	1				7		7	30	1 7			
㉓	TOTAL	47 4	32 3	160	102								8 9		6	17		112	37	172	897	15			

FIGURE A-3: Form SPD-3

TABLE A–4. Explanation of Form SPD-4: COCOMO Milestone Runs

1. *Project Title.* A short title of the project or product
2. *ID Number.* A unique identifying number for the project
3. *Originator.* Name of the person responsible for completing this form
4. *Date.* Date of origin or latest revision
5. *Milestone.* Project milestone of COCOMO run as defined in Table 4–1. Two blank rows are provided for intermediate milestones (In the example, these will be on completion of testing for CEMICS increments 1 and 2).
6. *COCOMO Run: Type.* BAS.= Basic COCOMO; INT = Intermediate COCOMO; DET = Detailed COCOMO
7. *COCOMO Run: Date.* Date of COCOMO run
8. *Qualifying Remarks on COCOMO Inputs.* Comments on assumptions made in preparing COCOMO inputs, or on the reasons for changes from the inputs used in previous runs
9. *Major Project Lessons Learned During Phase.* A summary of lessons learned—things one should do differently on similar projects in the future—or references to documents providing more detail

① Project title __Cemics__   ② ID NO. __B142__   ③ Originator __R. Lee__   ④ Date __2/22/82__

⑤ Milestone	COCOMO run ⑥ Type	⑦ Name	⑧ Qualifying remarks on COCOMO inputs	⑨ Major project lessons learned during phase
Life cycle concept review	INT	2/22/82	Sizing estimate: 48 ± 15 KDSI	
Software requirements review		4/26/82	No run made: no significant changes	
Product design review	INT	9/24/82	Turn rating: partly interactive, partly 8-hour turnaround. Less experienced programmers available for RPTDATA, REPORTS, MISC	Don't assume existing documentation is accurate. Here it was tragically out of date. Include a document verification activity in requirements V & V. See memo B142 - M-7, 7/16/82.
Increment 1 test review				
Increment 2 test review				
Software acceptance review				
System acceptance review				

FIGURE A-4: Form SPD-4

(1) COMPONENT	(2) EDSI	(3) AAF	Product (4) RELY	(5) DATA	(6) CPLX	Computer (7) TIME	(8) STOR	(9) VIRT	(10) TURN	Personnel (11) ACAP	(12) AEXP	(13) PCAP	(14) VEXP	(15) LEXP	(16) MODP	(17) TODL	(18) SCED	(19) EAF	(20) MM NOM	(21) MM DEN/AM	(22) EDSI/MM ACT	(23) $K	(24) S/EDSI
(nominal)			N	VHI	LO	N	N	N	N	N	HI	N	N	HI	HI	N	N						
(factor)			1.0	1.16	0.85	1.0	1.0	1.0	1.0	1.0	0.91	1.0	1.0	0.95	0.91	1.0	1.0						
1. EDIT	4450																	0.78	37	29	326	5.0 / 145	15
2. UPDATE	5200				N 1.0					HI 0.86		HI 0.86	HI 0.90					0.61	20	12	433	6.0 / 72	14
3. EQUIP	7800											HI 0.86	HI 0.90					0.61	30	18	433	6.0 / 108	14
4. RPTDATA	12850											N 1.0	1.0	1.0				0.97	50	48	268	5.0 / 240	19
5. REPORTS	7100																	0.97	28	27	268	5.0 / 135	19
6. MISC	6300												1.10	1.07				0.97	24	23	268	5.0 / 115	19
7.																							
8.																							
9.																							
10.																							
11. Total EDSI	48700																						
12. (MM)NOM	189																						
13. (EDSI/MM)NOM	258																						

Totals: 157   310   815   17

Schedule (Mo): 17

Development mode: Organic

FIGURE A-5

COCOMO software cost model: component-level estimating form (CLEF)

Project: Comics – 1984 Maintenance Analyst: T. Tanaka Date: 1/4/84

Project:

(1) COMPONENT	(2) EDSI	(3) AAF	Product (4) RELY	(5) DATA	(6) CPLX	Computer (7) TIME	(8) STOR	(9) VIRT	(10) TURN	Personnel attributes (11) ACAP	(12) AEXP	(13) PCAP	(14) VEXP	(15) LEXP	Project (16) MODP	(17) TODL	(18) SCED	(19) EAF	(20) MM NOM	(21) MM DEN /AM	(22) EDSI/MM ACT	(23) $K	(24) $/EDSI
1. EDIT	10744														0.86			0.74	42	5.3	17	5.9	
															0.91			0.78				31	
2. UPDATE	5731														0.86			0.58	22	0.9	7	6.5	
															0.91			0.61				6	
3. EQUIP	8426														0.86			0.58	33	2.3	12	6.5	
															0.91			0.61				15	
4. RPTDATA	15237									1.0			1.0	1.0	0.86			0.91	60	12.0	22	5.9	
										0.86			1.10	1.07	0.91			0.97				71	
5. REPORTS	9676									1.0			1.0	1.0	0.86			0.91	38	6.2	18	5.9	
										0.86			1.10	1.07	0.91			0.97				37	
6. MISC	8424									1.0			1.0	1.0	0.86			0.91	33	6.0	20	5.9	
										0.86			1.10	1.07	0.91			0.97				35	
7.																							
8.																							
9.																							
10.																							
11.	58238	Total EDSI																	Totals	32.7		195	
12.	228	(MM)ₙₒₘ																					
13.	255	(EDSI/MM)ₙₒₘ																	Schedule (Mo)				

Development mode: Organic

COCOMO software cost model: component-level estimating form (CLEF)

FIGURE A-6

TABLE A–5. Explanation of Form SPD-M: Annual Maintenance

1. *Project Title.* A short title of the project or product
2. *ID Number.* A unique identifying number for the project
3. *Originator.* Name of the person responsible for completing this form
4. *Date.* Date of origin or latest revision
5. *Distribution of Labor by Subsystem.* Estimated and actual man-months expended on maintenance of each subsystem during the year
6. *Distribution of Labor by Function.* Percentage of the year's maintenance effort expended on each of the functions indicated
7. *Distribution of Labor by Activity.* Percentage of the year's maintenance effort expended on each of the activities indicated
8. *Labor $K.* Thousands of dollars expended on the year's maintenance labor.
9. *Computer $K.* Thousands of dollars expended on the year's maintenance computer costs
10,11. Two blank entries for other maintenance costs
12. *Total $K.* Thousands of dollars expended on the year's maintenance of the software product
13. *Percent of Code Added, Modified, Deleted.* Percentage of the year's original source instructions added to the product, modified, or deleted from the product
14. *Special Factors Increasing or Decreasing Cost.* Identification of factors considered particularly significant maintenance cost drivers

Project title Cemics - 1984 maint ID NO. B142 Originator T. Tanaka Date 1/5/85

Distribution of labor

By subsystem

Subsystem	Est. MM	Act. MM
EDIT	5.3	5.0
Update	0.9	0.7
Equip	2.3	1.9
Rptdata	12.0	14.6
Reports	6.2	8.1
Misc	6.0	5.4
Total	32.7	35.7

Labor $K 244
Computer $K 67

Total $K 311

By function

Emergency program fixes	6 %
Routine debugging	7 %
Accommodating changes to data inputs, files	22%
Accommodating changes to hardware, system software	3 %
Enhancements for users	52 %
Improving documentation	4 %
Improving code efficiency	2 %
Other (studies)	4 %
Total	100 %

% Code Added 12
% Code Modified 14
% Code Deleted 2

By activity

Rqts. analysis	10 %
Product design	16 %
Programming	31 %
Test planning	2 %
V&V	20 %
Project office	8 %
CM/QA	6 %
Manuals	7%
Other	%
Total	100 %

Special factors increasing or decreasing cost
Higher level of modification than estimated in Rptdata (ACT = 28 versus 22)
and Reports (ACT = 30 versus 18)

FIGURE A-7: Form SPD-M

Procedures for a Completed Project

In general, it is not possible to reconstruct COCOMO milestone runs and detailed phase/activity data from completed projects. The procedures for a completed project still try to capture as much cost-relevant information as possible.

Form SPD-1: General Information. Filled out completely.

Form SPD-2: Phase Summaries. Items 7–14 filled out at least for Development Totals, and as much as possible for each phase. Other items filled out completely.

Form SPD-3: Subsystem Summaries. Filled out completely, except where data does not support such items as man-months by phase and subsystem (item 16).

Form SPD-4: COCOMO Milestone Runs. Filled out only for Software or System Acceptance Review, with a single end-of-project COCOMO estimate.

Data Conditioning

Data conditioning is an essential activity in the software data collection and analysis process. Even when people try to provide the best data they can, there are a number of subtle sources of misunderstanding which can inject a severe bias into their data. Other problems arise when people compile their data from a number of inconsistent sources. If these and other common sources of data contamination are not removed, such analyses as the recalibration of a software cost model or the evaluation of new development techniques become highly confounded. Some of the major software data collection problem sources and the primary data conditioning guidelines for dealing with the problems are given below.

Data Collection Problem Sources

Besides the problems of missing data and the inevitable clerical errors, here are some of the most frequent sources of software data collection problems.

1. *Inconsistent Definitions.* Some of the common symptoms here are:
   - Using nonstandard conversion factors (for example, using 176 man-hours/MM rather than 152)
   - Using inconsistent phase definitions
   - Using different definitions of "delivered" instructions (sometimes including support software, sometimes not)

2. *Observational Bias.* Common problems here include the optimist/pessimist phenomenon (people who are fundamentally very generous or critical when making subjective ratings) and the success-orientation phenomenon (people whose ratings are conditioned by their desire for the project to succeed, or at least to appear successful).

3. *Local vs. Global Frame of Reference.* An example of this problem came from a field site consisting exclusively of highly experienced and talented personnel. Their project ratings for personnel experience and capability were originally given as Nominal, because they were at the average with respect to the field site. However, with respect to the entire population of software personnel in the organization (or in general), they would certainly be rated Very High.

4. *Averaging and Size Effects.* Frequently, project or subsystem data submittals establish their ratings of complexity, required reliability, timing constraint, etc., as being the rating of the most highly-stressed portion rather than the average rating across the project or subsystem. Also, people tend to give large software products higher complexity ratings than small projects, when their intrinsic complexity on the COCOMO scale is actually the same.

5. *Double Counting.* One common problem here involves counting management man-hours twice (both in the Project Office and Programming activities), particularly for first-level chief-programmer personnel performing both programming and management functions. Another involves counting the same software or software effort twice if it is used in two subsystems.

Data Conditioning Guidelines

The best defense against these problems is to provide a clear set of data collection definitions, procedures, and examples. Even if these are available, though, it is unwise to assume that people will read them or remember them while preparing their data. More frequently, people will follow what [Cozzens, 1980] calls The American Way: "When all else fails, read the instructions." The following additional data conditioning activities and guidelines are thus recommended.

1. *Initial Screening.* Each form submitted should be quickly screened to ensure that all entries have been completed, and that each entry is acceptable with respect to type, units, and range of acceptable values.

2. *Redundancy and Consistency Checking.* One way to reduce observational bias is to include some overlap in the inputs submitted by different individuals. This provides an opportunity to calibrate each respondent with respect to optimism, reliability standards, personnel rating scales, etc.

As another aid, the forms provided here incorporate some redundancy which can be used for consistency checking in the following ways:

- Comparing the figures given for average personnel (Form SPD-3) with those obtained by dividing total man-months by project duration.
- Comparing the required reliability ratings with the percentage of effort devoted to testing.
- Comparing the figures given for total man-months by phase on Forms SPD-2 and SPD-3.
- Comparing the labor dollar expenditures with man-month expenditures to determine consistency of labor costs.

- Comparing the Modern Programming Practices rating with the amount of documentation produced in each phase.

   3. *Reference Projects.* For some of the more subjective ratings within an installation, it is extremely valuable to have a number of common-experience reference projects to serve as base points for attribute ratings. For example, a discussion of a High required reliability rating can then begin from a question such as, "What is it about this project that makes its required reliability higher than CEMICS, equal to Aircraft Autopilot, etc.?"
   4. *Work Breakdown Structure Definition and Monitoring.* Data collection is much easier if the accounting system is automatically keeping track of expenditures in the right categories. Assigning job numbers along the lines of the COCOMO Work Breakdown Structure (as is done in the CEMICS example in Section 32.6) will be far more helpful than establishing job numbers along organizational lines, when each organization may contain people performing several different project functions.
   5. *Followup Interviews by Experienced Personnel.* Many of the problems above can be detected and eliminated by having an experienced person review the data submitted, followed by a discussion of possible problem data items with the originators. While the initial screening above can be performed by clerical personnel (and to some extent by a computer program), this step requires an experienced person for success.

Given the need for expert personnel to perform data conditioning, complete verification of every data item on every project is too expensive to be feasible. However, a program of selective spot-checking will produce significant payoffs, not only by making present data more accurate, but also by providing feedback to data originators which will make future data more accurate.

Complementary Data Collection

A well-conditioned software cost data base provides an invaluable corporate memory on the cost aspects of previous projects. This corporate memory is further enhanced if complementary data are collected on other project phenomena such as error rates and project completion summaries.

Providing guidelines for these activities is outside the scope of this book. Two good sets of forms and procedures for software error data collection and analysis are given in [Thayer and others, 1978] and [Basili, 1980]. An example of a project completion summary is provided within [Boehm, 1981]. It includes such items as:

- A summary of project and product objectives, and how well they were met
- Highlights of each development phase
- A summary of software attribute, cost, and error data
- A summary of the participants' major lessons learned, and recommendations for future projects.

BLANK FORMS

The following pages contain blank copies of the data collection forms and COCOMO estimation forms:

- Form SPD-1. Software Project Data: General Information
- Form SPD-2. Software Project Data: Phase Summaries
- Form SPD-3. Software Project Data: Subsystem Summaries
- Form SPD-4. Software Project Data: COCOMO Milestone Runs
- Form SPD-M. Software Project Data: Annual Maintenance
- Intermediate COCOMO Component-Level Estimation Form (CLEF)
- Detailed COCOMO Software Hierarchy Estimation Form (SHEF): Subsystem Level
- Detailed COCOMO Software Hierarchy Estimation Form (SHEF): Module Level.

Project title _____   ID NO. _____   Rev. no. _____   Date _____

Development org. _____   Project mgr. _____   Originator _____

Customer org. _____   Project type _____

Hardware configuration _____

Brief project description	References to detailed description

Project attributes	Rating					Comments
	VLO	LO	N	HI	VHI	
Customer Experience: Application						
Customer Experience: Data Processing						
Customer Interface Complexity						
Detailed Project Plan						
Full Requirements Specification						
Early Verification and Validation						
Thorough Baseline Config. Mgmt.						
Unit Development Folders or Equivalent						
Thorough Test Plans and Procedures						
Standards and Quality Assurance						
Resource Planning and Control System						
Good Work Environment						
Privacy, Security Constraints						Special factors increasing or decreasing cost

Form SPD-1. Software Project Data: General Information

Project title _____ ID NO. _____ Originator _____ Date _____

| Phase | Start date | End date | Man-months by activity | | | | | | | | | Total $K | Computer | | PP documents | | | Errors | | | |
			RA	PD	PG	TP	VV	PO	CQ	MN	Total		HR	$	SPEC	PLAN	MAN.	This phase	PREV		
Plans and Requirements																						
Product Design																						
Detailed Design																						
Code and Unit Test																						
Integration and Test																						
Development Total																						
Totals																						

Other Project Costs

Item	MAN-MO.	$K
Training		
Installation		
Program Conversion		
Data Base Conversion		
Clerical		

Item	$K
Travel	
Communications	
Publications	
Software Products	

Type Of Funding	
Burden Rate	
% Uncompensated Overtime	

Form SPD-2. Software Project Data: Phase Summaries

| SS NO. | SUBSYSTEM | KDSI | | KDMI | | Adapt | | | RQTS. DEF | RQTS. VOL. | Language | | PERS. CONT. | AVE. PERS. | MAX PERS | Man-months | | | | | TOT DEVEL | K DEVEL | | | |
| | | EXEC | NON-EXEC | ECEX | NON-EXEC | DM | CM | IM | | | | | | | | PR | PD | DD | CUT | IT | | | | | |

Form SPD-3. Software Project Data: Subsystem Summaries

Project title _____   ID NO. _____   Originator _____   Date _____

Milestone	COCOMO run		Qualifying remarks on COCOMO inputs	Major project lessons learned during phase
	Type	Date		
Life cycle concept review				
Software requirements review				
Product design review				
Software acceptance review				
System acceptance review				

Form SPD-4. Software Project Data: COCOMO Milestone Runs

Project title _____   ID NO. _____   Originator _____   Date _____

Distribution of labor

By subsystem

Subsystem	Est. MM	Act. MM
_____	_____	_____
_____	_____	_____
_____	_____	_____
_____	_____	_____
_____	_____	_____
_____	_____	_____
_____	_____	_____
_____	_____	_____
Total ___	_____	_____

By function

Emergency program fixes	___ %
Routine debugging	___ %
Accommodating changes to data inputs, files	___ %
Accommodating changes to hardware, system software	___ %
Enhancements for users	___ %
Improving documentation	___ %
Improving code efficiency	___ %
Other	___ %
Total	100 %

By activity

Rqts. analysis	___ %
Product design	___ %
Programming	___ %
Test planning	___ %
V&V	___ %
Project office	___ %
CM/QA	___ %
Manuals	___ %
Other	___ %
Total	100 %

Labor $K   _____   % Code Added   _____
Computer $K   _____   % Code Modified _____
              _____   % Code Deleted _____
TOTAL $K   _____

Special factors increasing or decreasing cost

Form SPD-M. Software Project Data: Annual Maintenance

Intermediate COCOMO Component-Level Estimation Form (CLEF)

(1)	(2)	(3)	Product (4)	(5)	(6)	Computer (7)	(8)	(9)	(10)	Personnel attrib. (11)	(12)	(13)	(14)	(15)	Project (16)	(17)	(18)	(19)	(20)	(21)	(22)	(23)	(24)
COMPONENT	EDSI	AAF	RELY	DATA	CPLX	TIME	STOR	VIRT	TURN	ACAP	AEXP	PCAP	VEXP	LEXP	MODP	TODL	SCED	EAF	MM NOM	MM DEN/AM	EDSI/MM ACT	^{s}K	$^s\overline{EDSI}$
1.																							
2.																							
3.																							
4.																							
5.																							
6.																							
7.																							
8.																							
9.																							
10.																							
11. TOTAL EDSI																			Totals				
12. (MM)$_{NOM}$																							
13. (EDSI/MM)$_{NOM}$																			Schedule (Mo)				

Development mode: _____

COCOMO software cost model: Component-level estimating form (CLEF)

Project: _____ Analyst: _____ Date: _____

① SS NO	② SUBSYSTEM	③ EDSI	Product		Computer attributes				Personnel		Project			㉜ EAF SS	⑳ MM MOD	㉝ MM EST	㉞ $K/MM	㉟ $K	㊱ TOTALS/ANGS
			㉑ RELY	㉒ DATA	㉓ TIME	㉔ STOR	㉕ VIRT	㉖ TURN	㉗ ACAP	㉘ AEXP	㉙ MODP	㉚ TOOL	㉛ SCED						
PD DD CUT IT																			

⑨ TOTAL EDSI

⑩ (MM)NOM

⑪ (EDSI/MM)NOM

Mode: _____

⑫ Phase frac: PD DD CUT IT

Right-side summary: PD DD CUT IT TOT — MM SCHED $K

MM $K → $K/DSI DSI/MM

Software hierarchy estimation form (SHEF): Subsystem level

Detailed COCOMO Software Hierarchy Estimation Form (SHEF): Subsystem Level

Project: _____   Analyst: _____   Date: _____

③	④	⑤	⑥	⑦	⑭	⑮	⑯	⑰	⑱	⑬	⑲	㊲
SS NO	MOD NO.	MODULE	EDSI	AAF	CPLX	PCAP	VEXP	LEXP	EAF M	MM NOM	MM MOD	MM EST
PD DD CUT IT												

Software hierarchy estimation form (SHEF): Module level

Detailed COCOMO Software Hierarchy Estimation Form (SHEF): Module Level.

Appendix B

The Software Engineering Goal Structure

Figure B–1 presents a hierarchical goal structure for successful software engineering. It indicates that if we wish to be fully successful in software engineering, we need to pay attention to two primary subgoals

1. Achieving a successful software *product;*
2. Conducting a successful software development and maintenance *process.*

Each of these two subgoals has three similar components

1. *Human relations.* The application of science and human judgment to the development of systems which enable people to satisfy their human needs, and to fulfill their human potential.
2. *Resource engineering.* The application of science and mathematics to the development of cost-effective systems.
3. *Program engineering.* The application of science and mathematics to the development of computer programs.

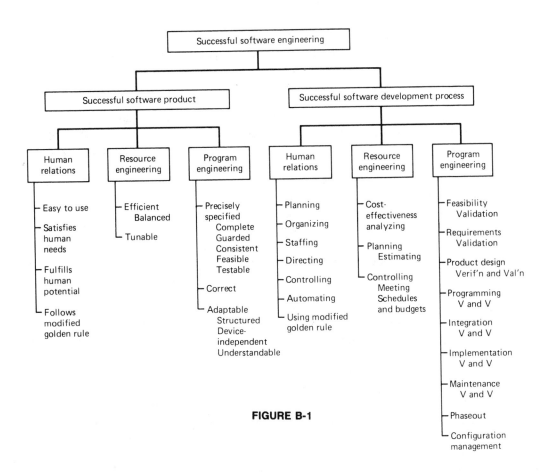

FIGURE B-1

Successful software engineering is the result of achieving an appropriate balance between these component subgoals, for both the software product and the software process. This appendix will discuss these components in terms of a number of software examples, which illustrate why each of the components is indispensible to successful software engineering.

Below each component subgoal in Fig. B-1 is listed a number of more specific subgoals. Each of these subgoals is defined, discussed, and briefly illustrated below.

SOFTWARE PRODUCT GOALS

Human Relations Goals for the Software Product

Easy to Use. Successful achievement of this subgoal implies that the software product's inputs, outputs, documentation, and user controls are such that the product is convenient, natural, flexible, and straightforward for people to use. *Good examples* are the provision of "help" messages and diagnostic messages in the users' language, and exception reporting capabilities for user outputs. *Counterexamples* are inflexible, "lock-step" user inputs and controls, which are easy to program but frustrating to use; and software which is easy to misuse, where a small typographical error or user misunderstanding can lead the software to crash the system, wreck a person's credit rating, or issue fatal prescriptions to medical patients.

Satisfies Human Needs. Successful achievement of this subgoal implies that the software product is well-tuned to the human needs for information or computer-produced instruments (tickets, paychecks, forms, procedures) that it is intended to satisfy. A *good example* is a decision-oriented inventory control system, which presents its results in terms of the likely inventory control decisions that need to be made: reorder, transship, expedite, etc. A type of *counterexample* is a model developed to find an optimal solution in terms that could never be implemented. One such model, developed at considerable government expense, was an optimal urban traffic model whose solutions would have required the sponsoring agency to tear down and reroute freeways, and impose controls on when and where people could travel. The agency people had no need for such recommendations, because they had no practical way to implement them.

Fulfills Human Potential. Successful achievement of this subgoal implies that the software product provides greater human challenge and job satisfaction for the people using and operating it. A good example is the warehouse management system that allows the person operating it to act like a warehouse manager: receiving information from the computer, and using it to decide what, when, and how much to reorder; when to check on the progress of shipments, etc. In many cases, such systems were only developed after some bad experiences with *counterexample* systems, which caused the persons operating them to act like mindless computer peripherals, while the computer systems made all the reordering decisions. Not only were such systems human failures, but they caused economic problems as well, because of high personnel turnover and little contribution from the operators in sensing and compensating for shortcomings in the automatic reordering process.

Follows the Modified Golden Rule. This rule says

> *Do unto others as you would*
> *have others do unto you—*
> *if you were like them.*

One of the biggest pitfalls in software engineering is a well-intentioned but unfortunate tendency to apply the Unmodified Golden Rule

| *To do unto others,* | *To develop a computer system to serve users and operators,* |
| *as you would have others do unto you.* | *assuming that the users and operators like to write computer programs, and know a good deal about computer science.* |

In the world of systems software, compilers, and operating systems that is largely the province of university computer science departments, this latter assumption is not too bad. Users of compilers and operating systems are programmers, who like to program and know a good deal about computer science.

However, this assumption is extremely dangerous in the world of applications software. There, the users and operators are typically aircraft pilots, retail store clerks, doctors, bank tellers, and fire department dispatchers. They don't generally know much about programming and computer science, and are much more concerned about flying the airplane safely, keeping the customers satisfied, and making their patients well quickly than they are in learning a little computer science as they work with the computer system we have developed for them.

Successfully achieving the Modified Golden Rule subgoal implies that the users' skills, needs, and functions are well understood, and that the software product's inputs, outputs, controls, and documentation reflect this understanding. A fairly familiar *good example* is the point-of-sale terminal used in a fast-food hamburger stand, with its special buttons labeled "Double Burger," "Chocolate Milkshake," etc., directly tailored to the operator's world of quick customer service. *Counterexamples* include a number of systems built to aid medical doctors, which were eventually scrapped because their complex control syntax, frequent use of unfamiliar computer science terminology, and machine-oriented diagnostic messages were simply unacceptable to the doctors.

Resource Engineering Goals for the Software Product

Efficient. Successful achievement of this subgoal implies that the software product fulfills its purpose without waste of resources. *Resources* include any quantities whose supply is limited: dollars, calendar time, computer time, main computer memory, communications channel capacity, etc. *Good examples* include systems which are well *balanced;* that is, each component spends only enough resources to be able to meet the needs of the other components, such as the urban emergency services example discussed in Section 11.7.

A striking *counterexample* was a program which for 2 years consumed over 10% of a $6,000,000 computer executing the following instruction in an inner loop:

$$A = B * SQRT(2.)$$

The programmer on the job had intended to go back and replace the SQRT(2.) with 1.4140678, but forgot, and the waste of resources was not picked up until a computer performance audit 2 years later.

Tunable. Successful achievement of this subgoal implies that the software product can be easily instrumented and measured to identify bottlenecks and inefficiencies, and can be easily modified or retuned to account for changes in workload characteristics, hardware components, or external interfaces. A *good example* is the control software for the ARPANET Interface Message Processor (IMP) [Heart and others, 1970]. A *counterexample* was the design originally proposed for the IMP software, which featured a very tight inner loop which would have run very fast for the originally anticipated traffic patterns, but which would have been extremely difficult to instrument and modify as other traffic patterns developed.

Program Engineering Goals for the Software Product

Precisely Specified. Successful achievement of this subgoal implies that the software product's functional, performance, and interface requirements have been thoroughly and unambiguously specified as a prerequisite to program development. As with the other goals, this is an objective to be balanced with other objectives, such as meeting schedules and budgets, or such as developing and exercising a prototype to ensure that the product's human relations goals will be met. It is not an absolute requirement to refrain from program development until every last detail has been worked out in the requirements specification.

The basic characteristics of a precise specification (complete, guarded, consistent, feasible, testable) are

- *Complete.* A specification is complete to the extent that all of its parts are present and each part is fully developed. A *good example* is a specification which has no references to nonexistent functions, inputs, outputs, or interfaces. A *counterexample* is a specification which fails to provide for backup and recovery functions or audit trail functions where these are needed.
- *Guarded.* A specification is guarded to the extent that it specifies how the software shall perform under all conditions, particularly off-nominal conditions. A *good example* is a specification which guards against singularities, empty sets, potential buffer overflows, input errors, or attempts to compromise information security and privacy. A *counterexample* is a specification which leaves many of these issues to be hopefully discovered by programmers, and which leads to catastrophic failure if they are not. One such example involved the software aboard a French meteorological satellite, in which an erroneous attempt to interrogate 141 high-altitude weather balloons caused the software to emergency destruct 73 of the balloons instead! The predicate-transformation approach in [Dijkstra, 1976] provides a constructive method of achieving guardedness.
- *Consistent.* A specification is consistent to the extent that its provisions do not conflict with each other or with other governing specifications and objectives. A *good example* is a specification which has been thoroughly validated via cross reference tables or an automated consistency checker. A *counterexample* was a specification requiring extensive access-control security features in the data base management subsystem, but specifying full access to all information, including passwords, in the terminal handling subsystem specification. The resulting system satisfied neither desire.
- *Feasible.* A specification is feasible to the extent that the life-cycle benefits of the system specified will exceed the life-cycle costs. A *good example* of a feasible specification is one for which all potential high-risk items have been identified and resolved via modeling, simulation, prototyping, user survey, etc. A *counterexample* is provided by the Univac/United Air Lines passenger reservation system, which was finally scrapped as infeasible after the number of instructions required to process a transaction had grown from 9000 originally up to 146,000 [Aviation Week, 1970].
- *Testable.* A specification is testable to the extent that one can identify an economi-

cally feasible technique for determining whether or not the developed software will satisfy the specification. Some *counterexamples* are

* The software shall degrade gracefully under stress
* The software shall provide the necessary processing under all modes of operation
* The software shall provide accuracy sufficient to support effective flight control
* The software shall provide real-time response to sales activity queries

A *good example* corresponding to the last counterexample is the following

* The system shall respond to
    Type A queries in ≤ 2 sec
    Type B queries in ≤ 10 sec
    Type C queries in ≤ 2 min

where Type A, B, and C queries are defined in detail in the specification, as are the endpoints associated with the definition of "response time."

The best example of a large specification embodying all of the above precise-specification properties is the A-7 aircraft software specification given in [Heninger and others, 1978]. A more detailed discussion of the properties is given in [Boehm, 1979].

Correct. Successfully achieving this subgoal implies that the software product exactly satisfies the functional and interface specifications, and meets all performance specifications within the required tolerances. A number of *good examples* of correct programs are given in [Dijkstra, 1976]. A number of *counterexamples:* examples of errors discovered in published "correct" programs, are given in [Gerhart-Yelowitz, 1976]. Again, complete correctness is a goal to be balanced with other goals, and not an absolute necessity for all programs.

Adaptable. Successful achievement of this subgoal implies that the software product or its components can be easily used or modified to serve another purpose. Adaptability includes

* *Modifiability.* The product facilitates the incorporation of changes.
* *Portability.* The product can be operated easily and well on computer configurations other than the current one.
* *Interoperability.* The product or its components can be easily incorporated as components of other systems.

It also includes combinations of these properties, for example, the ability to incorporate a modified version of a product component as a component of a system operating on another computer configuration.

The basic characteristics of adaptable software (structured, independent, and understandable) are

- *Structured.* A software product is structured to the extent that it is organized according to the following principles:

    1. *Abstraction.* The product is organized into a hierarchy of "levels of abstraction," each of which has no information about the properties of higher levels, and hides its own internal information from higher levels.

    2. *Modularity.* The product is organized into small, coherent, independent modules. See [Yourdon-Constantine, 1978] for some useful guidelines on modularization.

    3. *Parsimony of Components.* The product is built from the smallest practicable number of components (for example, sequence, if-then-else, case, do-while, do-until, and undo for sequential control structures).

    Some well-known *good examples* are the THE [Dijkstra, 1968], operating system, and the IBM-New York Times information retrieval system [Baker, 1972]. Some *counterexamples* are given in Chapter 3 of [Kernighan–Plauger, 1974]. It should be noted that structuredness principles apply to documentation as well as programming.

- *Device-Independent.* A software product is device-independent to the extent that its performance is unaffected by changes in underlying devices. "Devices" here include underlying software devices such as operating systems or data base management systems. A *good example* is the address processing system discussed in [Parnas, 1979], which shows the power of the abstraction or information-hiding principle in enhancing device-independence. A *counterexample* is a text-processing program given as a textbook example of good structured programming, which referred to input and output linewidths, device numbers, etc., as embedded literals throughout the code.

- *Understandable.* A software product is understandable to the extent that its purpose and operation are clear to the people who must work with it. A *good example* is a software product with meaningful variable and procedure names; well-formatted, segmented, and indented code; cross reference information; and reader-oriented documentation and program commentary which allows the reader to determine each component's objectives, assumptions, constraints, inputs, outputs, components, and status. *Counterexamples* are systems which do not provide the above.

SOFTWARE PROCESS GOALS

The software product goals discussed above characterize desired *properties* of the product. The goals for the software development and maintenance process involve a number of *activities* which are carried out—some concurrently, some largely sequentially—during the software life-cycle.

As with the realization of the software product, the management of the software process involves a balance between the human relations objectives of fostering human achievement and growth, the basic resource engineering objectives of holding down development and maintenance costs, and the basic program engineering objectives of sequentially producing a precise, valid requirements specification; a precise, verified product design; etc.

Human Relations Goals for the Software Process

The human relations goals for the software development and maintenance process have to do with the management of people's activities in a way which satisfies the human needs and fulfills the human potential of the people involved in the process. Thus, they are largely management activities. In this appendix, we will use the widely accepted structuring of management activities into the basic functions of planning, organizing, staffing, directing, and controlling [Koontz–O'Donnell, 1972]. In addition, we will include the goal of automating appropriate portions of the software job, and our guiding principle of the Modified Golden Rule, which applies as well to the software process as it does to the software product.

Planning. Successful achievement of this subgoal involves the development and continuing maintenance of a software life-cycle project plan, which tells

- *Why* the project is being undertaken
- *What* results the project will achieve
- *When* the results will be achieved
- *Who* is responsible for achieving them
- *Where* they will achieve them
- *How* they will achieve them
- *How much* (in resources) it will take to achieve them
- *Whereas* or *assuming* the following conditions hold

Organizing. Successful achievement of this subgoal involves the development and continuing maintenance of a structure of project roles and responsibilities throughout the software life-cycle. The main components of organizing are the functions of

- delegation of authority
- division of work

Some of the principles of structuring a project organization are similar to the principles of structuring the software product (for example, modularity, information-hiding). This has given rise to a fairly valid piece of software engineering folklore, often called Conway's Law [Conway, 1968], which says that

> *"The structure of a software product is isomorphic to the structure of the project which developed it."*

Some further similarities are discussed in [Daly, 1979].

Staffing. Successful achievement of this subgoal involves the *selection, recruiting,* and *retention* of appropriate people to fill the organizational roles. Particularly in staffing, the manager is concerned with balancing the needs of two different life-cycles

- The life-cycle of the software product
- The life-cycle or career path of each person involved in the project

This balance often implies a sacrifice of short-term project goals in favor of more long-term career path goals for the people involved.

Directing. Successfully achieving this subgoal involves the following pursuits

- *Motivation.* The creation and maintenance of challenges and incentives which motivate people to contribute their best efforts toward the success of the project.
- *Communication.* The creation and maintenance of a flow of information about the project and its environment which satisfies the information needs of each project participant.
- *Leadership.* The understanding by the manager of the factors that motivate subordinates, and the continuing reflection of this understanding in management actions and decisions.

Clearly, successful directing requires that we understand what factors primarily motivate software people. As seen in [Couger–Zawacki, 1978] and [Fitz-Enz, 1978], the primary motivating factors for programmers (for example, a relatively high need for professional growth, a relatively low social need, a relative indifference toward status factors) are significantly different from those of software managers, or from those of professionals in other fields.

Controlling. Successful achievement of this subgoal involves the measurement of project accomplishments with respect to the standard of project goals and plans, and the correction of deviations to assure the attainment of project goals according to plans. Planning and controlling are complementary subgoals. Without a well-defined plan, there is no standard on which to base controls. And unless the manager actually exerts the controls, the plans are virtually useless.

Automating. Successful achievement of this subgoal involves the use of computer power to free software people from the drudgery of performing a number of tedious, error-prone manual tasks. The development of assemblers and compilers eliminated a great deal of this kind of effort in the past. Nowadays, there are a large number of additional software tools which can similarly eliminate or reduce the amount of manual effort required to perform such functions as requirements and design consistency checking, standard compliance checking, test data management, test case monitoring and exception reporting, documentation update, and product status accounting. These and other tools are discussed throughout the text, particularly in Section 27.2.

Using the Modified Golden Rule. As we have seen, the factors that primarily motivate programmers are often significantly different from the factors that primarily motivate software managers. Therefore, if we manage by doing unto our programmers as we would have them do unto us (that is, by offering rewards in terms of status or promotion to management), we will often be very disappointed in the results.

Resource Engineering Goals for the Software Process

Cost-Effectiveness Analysis. Successful achievement of this subgoal involves thorough analysis of the costs and benefits of alternative software project approaches, so as to select the most appropriate one. Here again, software project "costs" cover a number of resources besides dollars, for example, calendar time, computer time, main memory capacity, and communications bandwidth. Techniques of cost-effectiveness analysis are discussed in detail in Part III of this book.

Planning and Controlling. These functions are important in both human relations and resource engineering. The resource engineering component covers the establishment and control of project schedules and resource budgets.

As control cannot satisfactorily proceed without good plans, so planning cannot satisfactorily proceed without good resource estimates. Techniques for software project manpower and resource estimation are provided via the Constructive Cost Model (COCOMO) presented in Part II and Part IV of this book.

An indication of the importance of planning and control in software engineering is given in Fig. B–2, which summarizes the results of 151 management audits of problems in the acquisition and use of computer systems in the U.S. Government [GAO, 1977a]. The audits, performed by the General Accounting Office over the years 1965 to 1976, showed that deficiencies in management planning and control were significantly larger sources of problems than were technology factors. Over 50% of the audits identified significant problems due to poor planning, and about 34% identified significant deficiencies in project control, while technology factors were identified as significant problem sources in only about 15% of the audits. Techniques for software project resource planning and control are covered in Chapter 32.

FIGURE B-2

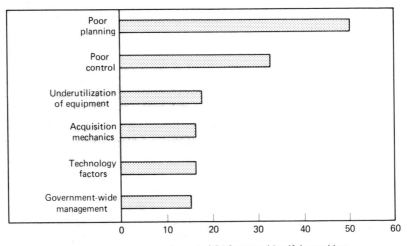

Percent of GAO reports identifying problem

Program Engineering Goals for the Software Process

The goal structure for successful program engineering of the software development and maintenance process is different from the other goal structures, in that most of the subgoals are ideally approached sequentially rather than concurrently. (In practice, however, consideration of the other goals discussed above will cause deviations from a pure sequential approach.) The eight major sequential subgoals are

1. *Feasibility.* Achieving the definition of a preferred concept of operation for the software product, and determining its life-cycle feasibility and superiority to alternative concepts
2. *Requirements.* Achieving a precisely specified statement of the required functions, interfaces, and performance for the software product
3. *Product Design.* Achieving a precisely specified statement of the overall hardware–software architecture, control structure, and data structure for the product, along with such other necessary components as draft users' manuals and test plans
4. *Programming.* Achieving a complete set of software components
5. *Integration.* Achieving a properly functioning software product composed of the software components
6. *Implementation.* Achieving a fully functioning operational hardware–software system, including such objectives as program and data conversion, installation, and training
7. *Maintenance.* Achieving a fully functioning update of the hardware–software system (repeated for each update)
8. *Phase out.* Achieving a clean transition of the functions performed by the product to its successors (if any)

Again, as with the other goals, the achievement of these subgoals in sequence is not an absolute requirement, but an objective to be balanced with other goals. These subgoals, the rationale for approaching them sequentially, and the rationale for common variations such as prototyping and incremental development, are discussed in detail in Chapter 4.

9. *Verification and Validation.* An integral part of the achievement of each program engineering life-cycle subgoal is the verification and validation (V&V) that the intermediate software products do indeed satisfy their objectives. We define them as follows:

   Verification: To establish the truth of correspondence between a software product and its specification (from the Latin *veritas,* "truth")

   Validation: To establish the fitness or worth of a software product for its operational mission (from the Latin *valere,* "to be worth")

   Informally, these definitions translate to

   Verification: "Are we building the product right?"

   Validation: "Are we building the right product?"

   Chapter 4 also provides a rationale for performing V&V during each life-cycle phase.

10. *Configuration Management.* Successful achievement of this subgoal implies that the project is able at any time to provide a definitive version of the software product, or of any of the controlled intermediate products (called *baselines*) such as the requirements specification. These baselines and the life-cycle *milestones* at which they are established are fundamental to the GOALS approach. They form a vital unifying link between the management and control of the software *process,* and the management and control of the software *product.* The milestone–baseline process generally works in the following way [TRW, 1973]:

1. An initial version of the intermediate or final software product is developed.

2. This initial version is verified and validated, and iterated as necessary.

3. A formal product review (such as a Software Requirements Review) determines whether or not the product is in satisfactory shape to proceed to the next phase (that is, whether or not the milestone has been reached). If not, the process reverts to step 1.

4. If the product is satisfactory, it is baselined (that is, put under a formal change control process).

The baselining of the product has the following three main advantages

1. No changes are made thereafter without the agreement of all interested parties.

2. The higher threshhold for change tends to stabilize the product.

3. The controller of the configuration management process achieves the goal of having at any time a definitive version of the product.

The configuration management subgoal is pursued concurrently with the other sequential program engineering life-cycle subgoals.

Appendix C

List of Acronyms

References

[Adams, 1980]. E.N. ADAMS, "Minimizing Cost Impact of Software Defects," IBM Research Report RC 8228, April 1980.

[ADPESO, 1976]. U.S. Navy ADP Equipment Selection Office, "1977 Fortran Compiler Validation System—Version 1.0: Project History," Department of the Navy, Washington, DC, September 1976.

[AFIPS–Time, 1971]. *A National Survey of the Public's Attitudes Toward Computers,* AFIPS and Time, Inc., November 1971.

[AFIPS, 1973]. "AFIPS Programmer Job Description Survey Booklet," AFIPS, 1973.

[Air Force, 1966]. Air Force Space and Missile Systems Organization, "Computer Program Subsystem Development Milestones," SSD Exhibit 61–47b, April 1, 1966.

[Air Force, 1974]. *Proceedings, Government/Industry Software Sizing and Costing Workshop,* U.S. Air Force Electronic Systems Div., Bedford, MA, October 1974.

[Air Force, 1978]. *Cost-Schedule Management of Non-Major Contracts,* AFSCP 173–3, U.S. Air Force Systems Command, Andrews AFB, MD, November 1978.

[Albrecht, 1979]. A.J. ALBRECHT, "Measuring Application Development Productivity," in [SHARE–GUIDE, 1979], pp. 83–92.

[Alford, 1977]. M.W. ALFORD, "A Requirements Engineering Methodology for Real-Time Processing Requirements," *IEEE Trans. Software Engr.,* January 1977, pp. 60–68.

[Armer, 1966]. P. ARMER, "Computer Aspects of Technological Change, Automation, and Economic Progress," P-3478, The Rand Corp., November 1966.

[Aron, 1969]. J.D. ARON, *Estimating Resources for Large Programming Systems,* NATO Science Committee, Rome, Italy, October 1969.

[Aron, 1974]. J.D. ARON, *The Program Development Process: The Individual Programmer,* Addison-Wesley, Reading, MA, 1974.

[Aron–Arthur, 1975]. J.D. ARON and R.W. ARTHUR, "Computing Resource Requirements for Programming Development," IBM-FSD, Gaithersburg, MD, 1975.

[Arvey–Hoyle, 1973]. R.D. ARVEY and J.C. HOYLE, "Evaluating Computing Personnel," *Datamation,* July 1973, pp. 69–73.

[Asch and others, 1975]. A. ASCH and others, *DoD Weapon System Software Acquisition and Management Study,* Report MTR-6908, MITRE Corp., Bedford, MA., June 1975.

[Auerbach, 1980]. *Auerbach Computer Technology Reports,* Auerbach Publishers, Inc., 6560 No. Park Dr., Pennsauken, NJ 08109, periodical.

[Augustine, 1979]. N.R. AUGUSTINE, "Augustine's Laws and Major System Development Programs," *Defense Systems Management Review,* 1979, pp. 50–76.

[Aviation Week, 1970]. "United Drops Univac Contract for $56 Million Data System," *Aviation Week,* Feb. 9, 1970, p. 31.

[Bailey–Basili, 1981]. J.W. BAILEY and V.R. BASILI, "A Meta-Model for Software Development Resource Expenditures," *Proceedings, Fifth International Conference on Software Engineering,* IEEE/ACM/NBS, March, 1981, pp. 107–116.

[Bairdain, 1964]. E.F. BAIRDAIN, "Research Studies of Programmers and Programming," 1964. Unpublished studies, pp. 62, 78, 136, New York.

[Baker, 1972]. F.T. BAKER, "Chief Programmer Team," *IBM Syst. J.,* **11**, *1,* 1972.

[Basili–Turner, 1975]. V. BASILI and A. TURNER, "Iterative Enhancement: A Practical Technique for Software Engineering," *IEEE Trans. Software Engr.,* December 1975, pp. 390–396.

[Basili and others, 1977]. V.R. BASILI, M.V. ZELKOWITZ, F.E. MCGARRY, R.W. REITER, JR., W.F. TRUSZKOWSKI, and D.L. WEISS, "The Software Engineering Laboratory," TR-535, University of Maryland, May 1977.

[Basili–Zelkowitz, 1978]. V.R. BASILI and M.V. ZELKOWITZ, "Analyzing Medium-Scale Software Development," *Proceedings, Third International Conference on Software Engineering,* IEEE/ACM/NBS, May 1978, pp. 116–123.

[Basili–Reiter, 1979]. V.R. BASILI and R.W. REITTER, JR., "An Investigation of Human Factors in Software Development," *Computer,* December 1979, pp. 21–38.

[Basili, 1980]. V.R. BASILI, *Tutorial on Models and Metrics for Software Management and Engineering,* IEEE Catalog No. EHO-167-7, October 1980.

[Basili–Beane, 1980]. V.R. BASILI and J. BEANE, "Can the Par Curve Help with the Manpower Distribution and Resource Estimation Problems?" Univ. of Maryland, July 1980.

[Basili–Weiss, 1981]. V.R. BASILI and D.M. WEISS, "Evaluation of a Software Requirements Document by Means of Change Data," *Proceedings, Fifth International Conference on Software Engineering,* IEEE, March 1981, pp. 314–323.

[Belady–Lehman, 1979]. L.A. BELADY and M.M. LEHMAN, "Characteristics of Large Systems," in P. Wegner (ed), *Research Directions in Software Technology,* M.I.T. Press, Cambridge, MA, 1979.

[Bell and others, 1975]. T.E. BELL, B.W. BOEHM, and S. JEFFERY (ed), *Computer Performance Evaluation: Report of the 1973 NBS/ACM Workshop,* NBS Special Publication 406, U.S. Government Printing Office, Washington, DC, 1975.

[Bell–Thayer, 1976]. T.E. BELL and T.A. THAYER, "Software Requirements: Are They Really a Problem?", *IEEE Proceedings, Second International Conference on Software Engineering,* October 1976, pp. 61–68.

[Bell and others, 1977]. T.E. BELL, D.C. BIXLER, and M.E. DYER, "An Extendable Approach to Computer-Aided Software Requirements Engineering," *IEEE Trans. Software Engr.,* January 1977, pp. 49–59.

[Black and others, 1977]. R.K.D. BLACK, R.P. CURNOW, R. KATZ, and M.D. GRAY, *BCS Software Production Data,* Final Technical Report, RADC-TR-77-116, Boeing Computer Services, Inc., March 1977. NTIS No. AD-A039852.

[Bloodworth and others, 1979]. J.E. BLOODWORTH, J.R. ELSTON, and M.H. STIEGLITZ, "Minimizing ALCM Software Life Cycle Cost," *Proceedings, AIAA Second Computers in Aerospace Conference,* October 1979, pp. 23–32.

[Boehm, 1970]. B.W. BOEHM, "Some Information Processing Implications of Air Force Space Missions: 1970–1980," The Rand Corp., RM-6213-PR, January 1970.

[Boehm and others, 1971]. B.W. BOEHM, M.J. SEVEN, and R.A. WATSON, "Interactive Problem Solving—An Experimental Study of 'Lockout' Effects," *Proceedings, 1971 SJCC,* AFIPS, pp. 205–210.

[Boehm–Haile, 1972]. B.W. BOEHM and A.C. HAILE, *Information Processing/Data Automation Implications of Air Force Command and Control Requirements in the 1980's (CCIP-85), Vol. I: Highlights,* Report SAMSO/XRS-71-1, U.S. Air Force Systems Command (NTIS: AD 900031L), Los Angeles, CA, April 1972.

[Boehm, 1973]. B.W. BOEHM, "Software and its Impact: A Quantitative Assessment," *Datamation,* May 1973, pp. 48–59.

[Boehm and others, 1974]. B.W. BOEHM, C.A. BOSCH, A.S. LIDDLE, and R.W. WOLVERTON, *The Impact of New Technologies on Software Configuration Management,* TRW Report to USAF-ESD, Contract F19628-74-C-0154, 10 June 1974.

[Boehm and others, 1975]. B.W. BOEHM, C.E. HOLMES, G.R. KATKUS, J.P. ROMANOS, R.C. MCHENRY, and E.K. GORDON, "Structured Programming: A Quantitative Assessment," *Computer,* June 1975, pp. 38–54.

[Boehm, 1976]. B.W. BOEHM, "Software Engineering," *IEEE Trans. Computers,* December 1976, pp. 1226–1241.

[Boehm and others, 1978]. B.W. BOEHM, J.R. BROWN, H. KASPAR, M. LIPOW, G.J. MACLEOD, and M.J. MERRITT, *Characteristics of Software Quality,* North-Holland, New York, 1978.

[Boehm–Wolverton, 1978]. B.W. BOEHM, and R.W. WOLVERTON, "Software Cost Modeling: Some Lessons Learned," *Proceedings, Second Software Life-Cycle Management Workshop,* U.S. Army Computer Systems Command, Atlanta, August 1978. Also in *Journal of Systems and Software,* 1, 3, 1980, pp. 195–201.

[Boehm, 1979]. B.W. BOEHM, "Guidelines for Verifying and Validating Software Requirements and Design Specifications," *Proceedings, EuroIFIP Congress,* September 1979, pp. 711–720.

[Boehm, 1980]. B.W. BOEHM, "Developing Small-Scale Application Software Products: Some Experimental Results," *Proceedings, IFIP 8th World Computer Congress,* October 1980, pp. 321–326. See also [Boehm, 1981].

[Boehm, 1981]. B.W. BOEHM, "An Experiment in Small-Scale Application Software Engineering," *IEEE Trans. Software Engr.,* 1981 (to appear).

[Boeing, 1979]. Boeing Co., "Software Cost Measuring and Reporting," U.S. Air Force-ASD Document D180-22813-1, January 1979.

[Boies–Spiegel, 1973]. S.J. BOIES and M.J. SPIEGEL, "A Behavioral Analysis of Programming: On the Use of Interactive Debugging Facilities," IBM Technical Report RC-4472, August 1973. (NTIS AD-772127).

[Brandon, 1974]. D.H. BRANDON, *Data Processing Organization and Manpower Planning,* Petrocelli Books, New York, 1974.

[Brandon, 1978]. D.H. BRANDON, *Data Processing Cost Reduction and Control,* Van Nostrand Reinhold, New York, 1978.

[Brooks, 1975]. F.P. BROOKS, JR., *The Mythical Man-Month,* Addison-Wesley, Reading, MA, 1975.

[Brooks, 1980]. W.D. BROOKS, "Software Technology Payoff: Some Statistical Evidence," IBM-FSD, Bethesda, MD, April 1980, pp. 2–7.

[Brown–Lipow, 1975]. J.R. BROWN and M. LIPOW, "Testing for Software Reliability," *Proceedings, 1975 International Conference on Reliable Software,* April 1975, pp. 518–527.

[Brown, 1977]. J.R. BROWN, "The Impact of Modern Programming Practices on System Development," TRW, Inc., Final Technical Report, RADC-TR-77-121, Griffiss AFB, NY, May 1977.

[Brustman, 1978]. K. BRUSTMAN, "Software Cost Estimation: Two Management Perspectives," *Proceedings, AIAA/TMSA/DPMA Software Management Conference III,* 1978, pp. 103–108.

[Business Week, 1980]. "Missing Computer Software," *Business Week,* September 1, 1980, pp. 46–53.

[Buxton, 1980]. J. BUXTON, "Requirements for Ada Programming Support Environments: 'Stoneman'," U.S. Department of Defense, OSD/R&E, Washington, DC, February 1980.

[Canada, 1971]. J.R. CANADA, *Intermediate Economic Analysis for Management and Engineering,* Prentice-Hall, Englewood Cliffs, NJ, 1971.

[Carriere–Thibodeau, 1979]. W.M. CARRIERE and R. THIBODEAU, "Development of a Logistics Software Cost Estimating Technique for Foreign Military Sales," Report CR-3-839, General Research Corp., June 1979.

[Chapanis, 1959]. A. CHAPANIS, *Research Techniques in Human Engineering,* Johns Hopkins Press, Baltimore, MD, 1959.

[Chen-Zelkowitz, 1981]. E. CHEN and M.V. ZELKOWITZ, "Use of Cluster Analysis to Evaluate Software Engineering Methodologies," *Proceedings, Fifth International Conference on Software Engineering,* IEEE, March 1981, pp. 117–123.

[Christensen, 1980]. K. CHRISTENSEN, "Programming Productivity and the Development Process," IBM Santa Teresa Laboratory, TR 03.083, January 1980.

[Chrysler, 1978]. E. CHRYSLER, "Some Basic Determinants of Computer Programming Productivity," *Comm. ACM,* June 1978, pp. 472–483.

[Climis, 1979]. T. CLIMIS, "Software Cost Estimation," presentation at NSIA Software Workshop, Buena Park, CA, February 1979.

[CODASYL, 1976]. CODASYL Systems Committee, *Selection and Acquisition of Data Base Management Systems,* ACM, New York, March 1976.

[Comper, 1979]. F.A. COMPER, "Project Management for System Quality and Development

Productivity," Bank of Montreal, Montreal, Quebec, 1979. Also in [SHARE–GUIDE, 1979], pp. 17–23.

[Congress, 1976]. U.S. Congress, House of Representatives, "Advanced Logistic (ADP) System," Dept. of Defense Appropriation Bill, 1976, Report No. 94–517, September 25, 1975, pp. 163–165.

[Conway, 1968]. M.E. CONWAY, "How Do Committees Invent?" *Datamation,* April 1968, pp. 28–31.

[Cooper, 1975]. J.D. COOPER, "Characteristics of the Average Coder," personal communication, May 1975.

[Cortada, 1980]. J.W. CORTADA, *EDP Costs and Charges,* Prentice-Hall, Englewood Cliffs, NJ, 1980.

[Couger–Knapp, 1974]. J.D. COUGER and R.W. KNAPP, *System Analysis Techniques,* John Wiley & Sons, New York, 1974.

[Couger–Zawacki, 1978]. J.D. COUGER and R.A. ZAWACKI, "What Motivates DP Professionals?", *Datamation,* September 1978, pp. 116–123.

[Cozzens, 1980]. M. COZZENS, "Cost Data Definitions and Collection Program: Final Report," TRW, Inc., prepared for National Bureau of Standards, Contract No. EO-A01-78-3622, August, 1980.

[Crossman, 1979]. T.D. CROSSMAN, "Some Experiences in the Use of Inspection Teams in Applications Development," in [SHARE–GUIDE, 1979], pp. 163–168.

[Curtis and others, 1978]. B. CURTIS, S.P. SHEPPARD, M.A. BORST, P. MILLIMAN, and T. LOVE, "Some Distinctions Between the Psychological and Computational Complexity of Software," *Proceedings, U.S. Army/IEEE Second Software Life Cycle Management Conference,* Atlanta, August 1978, pp. 166–71.

[Curtis, 1979]. B. CURTIS, "In Search of Software Complexity," *Proceedings, IEEE/PINY Workshop on Quantitative Software Models,* IEEE Catalog No. TH0067-9, October 1979, pp. 95–106.

[Curtis and others, 1979a]. B. CURTIS, S.B. SHEPPARD, P. MILLIMAN, M.A. BORST, and T. LOVE, "Measuring the Psychological Complexity of Software Maintenance Tasks with the Halstead and McCabe Metrics," *IEEE Trans. Software Engr.,* March 1979, pp. 96–104.

[Curtis and others, 1979b]. B. CURTIS, S.B. SHEPPARD, and P. MILLIMAN, "Third Time Charm: Stronger Prediction of Programmer Performance by Software Complexity Metrics," *Proceedings, Fourth International Conference on Software Engineering,* September 1979, pp. 356–360.

[Daly, 1977]. E.B. DALY, "Management of Software Engineering," *IEEE Trans. Software Engineering,* May 1977, pp. 229–242.

[Daly, 1979]. E.B. DALY, "Organizing for Successful Software Development," *Datamation,* December 1979, pp. 107–120.

[Dantzig, 1963]. G.B. DANTZIG, *Linear Programming and Extensions,* Princeton University Press, Princeton, NJ, 1963.

[Datapro, 1980]. *Datapro Directory of Software,* Datapro Research Corp., 1805 Underwood Blvd., Delran, NJ 08075, periodical.

[Dearden, 1972]. J. DEARDEN, "MIS Is A Mirage," *Harvard Business Review,* January–February, pp. 90–99.

[Devenny, 1976]. T.J. DEVENNY, "An Exploratory Study of Software Cost Estimating at the Electronic Systems Division," Thesis No. GSM/SM/765-4, Air Force Institute of Technology, Dayton, OH, July 1976.

[Dijkstra, 1968]. E.W. DIJKSTRA, "The Structure of the 'THE' Multiprogramming System," *ACM Communications,* May 1968, pp. 341–346.

[Dijkstra, 1976]. E.W. DIJKSTRA, *A Discipline of Programming,* Prentice-Hall, Englewood Cliffs, NJ, 1976.

[DiNardo, 1975]. G.P. DINARDO, "Computer System Performance Factors at Mellon Bank," in [Bell and others, 1975].

[Distaso and others, 1979]. J.R. DISTASO, B.F. KOHL, K.R. KRAUSE, J.W. SHIVELY, E.D. STUCKLE, J.T. ULMER, and L.R. VALLEMBOIS, "Developing Large-Scale Software: The BMD-STP Experience," TRW Software Series TRW-SS-79-01, February 1979.

[Dittman, 1980]. J.T. DITTMAN, *Transferability Factor Manual,* Veterans Administration, Columbia, MO 65201, March 1980.

[Docherty, 1977]. P. DOCHERTY, IFIP 77 panel remarks, in N. French, "DP Deprives Workers of Job Satisfaction, Europe Studies Show," *Computerworld,* August 22, 1977, p. 1.

[Doherty, 1970]. W. DOHERTY, "Scheduling TSS/360 for Responsiveness," *Proceedings, 1970 FJCC,* AFIPS, 1970, pp. 97–111.

[Doherty-Kelisky, 1979]. W.J. DOHERTY and R.P. KELISKY, "Managing VM/CMS for User Effectiveness," *IBM Syst. J.* **18,** *1,* 1979, pp. 143–163.

[Dolotta and others, 1976]. T.A. DOLOTTA and others, *Data Processing in 1980–85,* John Wiley & Sons, New York, 1976.

[Dolotta and others, 1978]. T.A. DOLOTTA, R.C. HAIGHT, and J.R. MASHEY, "The Programmers' Workbench," *Bell System Technical Journal,* July–August 1978, pp. 2177–2200.

[Dowkont and others, 1967]. A.J. DOWKONT, W.A. MORRIS, and T.D. BUETTELL, *A Methodology for Comparison of Generalized Data Base Management Systems: PEGS,* Informatics, Inc., March 1967.

[Drucker, 1954]. P.F. DRUCKER, *The Practice of Management,* Harper & Row, New York, 1954.

[Dunsmore–Gannon, 1979]. H.E. DUNSMORE and J.D. GANNON, "Data Referencing: An Empirical Investigation," *Computer,* December 1979, pp. 50–59.

[Duvall, 1979]. L. DUVALL, "Quantitative Software Models," Report SRR-1, Data and Analysis Center for Software, Rome, NY, March 1979.

[Elbing, 1978]. A.O. ELBING, *Behavioral Decisions in Organizations,* Scott, Foresman, and Co., Glenview, IL, 1978.

[Elliott, 1977]. I.R. ELLIOTT, "Life-Cycle Planning for a Large Mix of Commercial Systems," *Proceedings, U.S. Army ISRAD Software Phenomenology Workshop,* August 1977, pp. 203–216.

[Elshoff, 1976]. J.L. ELSHOFF, "An Analysis of Some Commercial PL/I Programs," *IEEE Trans. Software Engr.,* June 1976, pp. 113–120.

[Elshoff, 1978]. J.L. ELSHOFF, "A Review of Software Measurement Studies at General Motors Research Laboratories," *Proceedings, U.S. Army/IEEE Second Software Life Cycle Management Conference,* Atlanta, August 1978, pp. 172–73.

[Emery, 1971]. J. EMERY, "Cost-Benefit Analysis of Information Systems," *J. SMIS,* 1971, pp. 16–46. Reprinted in [Couger–Knapp, 1974], pp. 395–425.

[Endres, 1975]. A.B. ENDRES, "An Analysis of Errors and Their Causes in System Programs," *IEEE Trans. Software Engr.,* June 1975, pp. 140–149.

[Esterling, 1980]. B. ESTERLING, "Software Manpower Costs: A Model," *Datamation,* March 1980, pp. 164–170.

[Fagan, 1976]. M.E. FAGAN, "Design and Code Inspections to Reduce Errors in Program Development," *IBM Syst. J.*, **15**, *3*, 1976, pp. 182–211.

[Farquhar, 1970]. J.A. FARQUHAR, "A Preliminary Inquiry Into the Software Estimation Process," RM-6271-PR, The Rand Corp., August 1970.

[Farr and others, 1965]. L. FARR, V. LA BOLLE, and N.E. WILLMORTH, "Planning Guide for Computer Program Development," TM-2314/00/00, System Development Corp, May 1965.

[Ferens–Harris, 1979]. D.V. FERENS and R.L. HARRIS, "Avionics Computer Software Operation and Support Cost Estimation," *Proceedings, NAECON 79*, Dayton OH, May 1979.

[Ferrari, 1978]. D. FERRARI, *Computer Systems Performance Evaluation*, Prentice-Hall, Englewood Cliffs, NJ, 1978.

[Fisher, 1971]. G.H. FISHER, *Cost Considerations in Systems Analysis*, American Elsevier, New York, 1971.

[Fitz-Enz, 1978]. J. FITZ-ENZ, "Who is the DP Professional?", *Datamation*, September 1978, pp. 124–129.

[Fordyce–Weil, 1971]. J.K. FORDYCE and R. WEIL, *Managing With People*, Addison-Wesley, Reading, MA, 1971.

[Formica, 1978]. G. FORMICA, "Software Management by the European Space Agency: Lessons Learned and Future Plans," *Proceedings, Third International Software Management Conference*, AIAA/RAeS, London, October 1978, pp. 15–35.

[Frank, 1979]. W.L. FRANK, "The New Software Economics,: Parts 1–4," *Computerworld*, January 1979. Also available in book form from the United States Professional Development Institute, Inc., Silver Spring, MD, 1979.

[Freburger–Basili, 1979]. K. FREBURGER and V.R. BASILI, "The Software Engineering Laboratory: Relationship Equations," Report TR-764, University of Maryland, May 1979.

[Frederic, 1974]. B.C. FREDERIC, "A Provisional Model for Estimating Computer Program Development Costs," Tecolote Research, Inc., December 1974.

[Freiman–Park, 1979]. F.R. FREIMAN and R.E. PARK, "PRICE Software Model—Version 3: An Overview," *Proceedings, IEEE-PINY Workshop on Quantitative Software Models*, IEEE Catalog No. TH0067-9, October 1979, pp. 32–41.

[Galinier, 1978]. Personal communication from M. Galinier, Univ. of Toulouse, 1978.

[GAO, 1977]. General Accounting Office, "Problems Found with Government Acquisition and Use of Computers from November 1965 to December 1976," Report FGMSD-77-14, GAO, Washington DC, March 1977.

[GAO, 1977a]. General Accounting Office, "Millions in Savings Possible in Converting Programs from One Computer to Another," Report FGMSD-77-34, GAO, Washington, DC, September 1977.

[GAO, 1979]. General Accounting Office, "Contracting for Software Development—Serious Problems Require Management Attention to Avoid Wasting Additional Millions," Report FGMSD-80-4, GAO, Washington, DC, Nov. 9, 1979.

[Gayle, 1971]. J.B. GAYLE, "Multiple Regression Techniques for Estimating Computer Programming Cost," *J. Systems Mgmt.*, February 1971, pp. 13–16.

[Gehring, 1976]. P.F. GEHRING, JR., "A Quantitative Analysis of Estimating Accuracy in Software Development," Ph.D. Dissertation, Texas A&M University, August 1976.

[Gellerman, 1963]. S.W. GELLERMAN, *Motivation and Productivity*, American Management Association Executive Books, New York, 1963.

[Gerhart–Yelowitz, 1976]. S.L. GERHART and L. YELOWITZ, "Observations of Fallibility in Applications of Modern Programming Methodologies," *IEEE Trans. Software Engr.,* September 1976, pp. 195–207.

[Gilb, 1969]. T. SCHARF (GILB), "Weighted Ranking by Levels," *IAG Journal, 2,* 1969, pp. 7–23.

[Gilb, 1977]. T. GILB, *Software Metrics,* Winthrop Publishers, Cambridge, MA, 1977.

[Gilb–Weinberg, 1977]. T. GILB and G.M. WEINBERG, *Humanized Input,* Winthrop Publishers, Cambridge, MA, 1977.

[Gilb, 1979]. Personal Communication from T. Gilb, 1979.

[Glass–Noiseux, 1981]. R.L. GLASS and R.A. NOISEUX, *Software Maintenance Guidebook,* Prentice–Hall, Englewood Cliffs, NJ, 1981.

[Goodenough–Gerhart, 1975]. J.B. GOODENOUGH and S.L. GERHART, "Toward a Theory of Test Data Selection," *IEEE Trans. Software Engr.,* June 1975, pp. 156–173.

[Gordon–Lamb, 1977]. R.L. GORDON and J.C. LAMB, "A Close Look at Brooks' Law," *Datamation,* June 1977, pp. 81–86.

[Graham, 1978]. G.S. GRAHAM (ed), "Special Issue: Queuing Network Models of Computer System Performance," *ACM Computing Surveys,* September 1978, pp. 219–360.

[Grant–Sackman, 1966]. E. GRANT and H. SACKMAN, "An Exploratory Investigation of Programmer Performance Under On-Line and Off-Line Conditions," Report SP-2581, System Development Corp., September 1966.

[Graver and others, 1977]. C.A. GRAVER and others, *Cost Reporting Elements and Activity Cost Tradeoffs for Defense System Software,* General Research Corp., Santa Barbara, CA, March 1977.

[Gregory–Atwater, 1957]. R.H. GREGORY and T.V. ATWATER, JR., "Cost and Value of Management Information as Functions of Age," *Accounting Research,* January 1957, pp. 42–70.

[Grether–Baker, 1972]. W.F. GRETHER and C.A. BAKER, "Visual Presentation of Information," in *Human Engineering Guide to Equipment Design,* H.P. van Cott and R.G. Kinkade (ed), Government Printing Office, Washington, DC, 1972.

[Griffin, 1980]. E.L. GRIFFIN, "Real-Time Estimating," *Datamation,* June 1980, pp. 188–198.

[GUIDE, 1979]. "GUIDE Survey of New Programming Technologies," *GUIDE Proceedings,* GUIDE, Inc., Chicago, IL, 1979, pp. 306–308.

[Halstead, 1977]. M.H. HALSTEAD, *Elements of Software Science,* Elsevier, New York 1977.

[Halstead, 1978]. M.H. HALSTEAD, "Software Science: A Progress Report," *Proceedings, U.S. Army/IEEE Second Software Life Cycle Management Conference,* Atlanta, August 1978, pp. 174–79.

[Hartwick, 1977]. R.D. HARTWICK, "Software Verification and Validation," *Proceedings, AIAA Third Software Management Conference,* Washington, DC, 1977.

[Heart and others, 1970]. F.E. HEART, R.E. KAHN, S.M. ORNSTEIN, W.R. CROWTHER, and D.C. WALDEN, "The Interface Message Processor for the ARPA Computer Network," *Proceedings, SJCC 1970,* AFIPS, 1970.

[Helmer, 1966]. O. HELMER, *Social Technology,* Basic Books, New York, 1966.

[Heninger and others, 1978]. K.L. HENINGER, J.W. KALLANDER, D.L. PARNAS, and J.E. SHORE, *Software Requirements for the A-7E Aircraft,* Report 3876, Naval Research Lab., Washington, DC, November 1978.

[Herd and others, 1977]. J.R. HERD, J.N. POSTAK, W.E. RUSSELL, and K.R. STEWART, *Software Cost Estimation Study—Study Results,* Final Technical Report, RADC-TR-77-220, Vol. I (of two), Doty Associates, Inc., Rockville, MD, June 1977.

[Herzberg and others, 1959]. F. HERZBERG, B. MAUSNER, and B.B. SNYDERMAN, *The Motivation to Work,* John Wiley & Sons, New York, 1959.

[Hice and others, 1974]. G.F. HICE, W.S. TURNER, and L.F. CASHWELL, *System Development Methodology,* North-Holland, 1974.

[Horowitz–Sahni, 1976]. E. HOROWITZ and S. SAHNI, *Fundamentals of Data Structures,* Computer Science Press, Woodland Hills, CA, 1976.

[Horowitz–Sahni, 1978]. E. HOROWITZ and S. SAHNI, *Fundamentals of Computer Algorithms,* Computer Science Press, Woodland Hills, CA, 1978.

[Houtz–Buschbach, 1981]. C. HOUTZ and T. BUSCHBACH, "Review and Analysis of Conversion Cost-Estimating Techniques," GSA Federal Conversion Support Center Report No. GSA/FCSC-81/001, Falls Church, VA, March 1981.

[Howden, 1978]. W.E. HOWDEN, "Theoretical and Empirical Studies of Program Testing," *IEEE Trans. Software Engr.,* July 1978, pp. 293–297.

[IBM, 1977]. IBM Corp., "Auditability and Productivity Information Catalog: System 370," IBM, September 1977.

[ICP, 1980]. *ICP Directory: Data Processing Management,* International Computer Programs, Inc., 9000 Keystone Crossing, Indianapolis, IN 46240, periodical.

[Infotech, 1978]. *Structured Programming: Practice and Experience,* Infotech International Ltd., Maidenhead, England, 1978.

[Ingrassia, 1978]. F.S. INGRASSIA, "Combating the 90% Syndrome," *Datamation,* January 1978, pp. 171–176.

[Ivie, 1977]. E.L. IVIE, "The Programmer's Workbench: A Machine for Software Development," *Comm. ACM,* October 1977, pp. 746–753.

[Jackson, 1975]. M.A. JACKSON, *Principles of Program Design,* Academic Press, New York, 1975.

[Jeffery–Lawrence, 1979]. D.R. JEFFERY and M.J. LAWRENCE, "An Inter-Organizational Comparison of Programming Productivity," *Proceedings, Fourth International Conference on Software Engineering,* IEEE Catalog No. 79 CH 1479-5C, September 1979, pp. 369–377.

[Jensen–Tonies, 1979]. R.W. JENSEN and C.C. TONIES, *Software Engineering,* Prentice-Hall, Englewood Cliffs, NJ, 1979.

[Jones–Nelson, 1976]. L.C. JONES and D.A. NELSON, "A Quantitative Assessment of IBM's Programming Productivity Techniques," *Proceedings, ACM/IEEE 13th Design Automation Conference,* June 1976.

[Jones, 1975]. T.C. JONES, "Programming Defect Removal," *Proceedings, GUIDE 40,* Miami, FL, May 1975.

[Jones, 1977]. T.C. JONES, "Program Quality and Programmer Productivity," IBM TR 02.764, 28 January 1977.

[Jones, 1978]. T.C. JONES, "Measuring Programming Quality and Productivity," *IBM Syst. J.,* **17,** *1,* 1978, pp. 39–63.

[Jones, 1979]. T.C. JONES, "A Survey of Programming Design and Specification Techniques," *Proceedings, IEEE Specifications of Reliable Software Conference,* March, 1979, pp. 91–103.

[Joslin, 1968]. E.D. JOSLIN, *Computer Selection,* Addison-Wesley, Reading, MA, 1968.

[Kanter, 1972]. J. KANTER, *Management-Oriented Management Information Systems,* Prentice-Hall, Englewood Cliffs, NJ, 1972.

[Kendall–Lamb, 1977]. R.C. KENDALL and E.C. LAMB, "Program Usage Studies," *Proceedings, GUIDE,* May 1977.

[Kernighan–Plauger, 1974]. B.W. KERNIGHAN and P.J. PLAUGER, *The Elements of Programming Style,* McGraw-Hill, New York, 1974.

[Kernighan–Plauger, 1976]. B.W. KERNIGHAN and P.J. PLAUGER, *Software Tools,* Addison-Wesley, Reading, MA, 1976.

[King–Schrems, 1978]. J.L. KING and E.L. SCHREMS, "Cost-Benefit Analysis in Information Systems Development and Operation," *ACM Computing Surveys,* March 1978, pp. 19–34.

[Kleijnen, 1980]. J.P.C. KLEIJNEN, *Computers and Profits: Quantifying Financial Benefits of Information,* Addison-Wesley, Reading, MA, 1980.

[Kleinrock, 1976]. L. KLEINROCK, *Queuing Systems, Vol. 2: Computer Applications,* John Wiley & Sons, 1976.

[Knuth, 1969]. D.E. KNUTH, *The Art of Computer Programming, Vol. II: Seminumerical Algorithms,* Addison-Wesley, Reading, MA, 1969.

[Knuth, 1973]. D.E. KNUTH, *The Art of Computer Programming, Vol. III: Sorting and Searching,* Addison-Wesley, Reading, MA, 1973.

[Knuth, 1973a]. D.E. KNUTH, *The Art of Computer Programming, Vol. I: Fundamental Algorithms,* (2nd ed), Addison-Wesley, Reading, MA, 1973.

[Koontz–O'Donnell, 1972]. H. KOONTZ and C. O'DONNELL, *Principles of Management: An Analysis of Managerial Functions* (5th ed), McGraw-Hill, New York, 1972.

[Kossiakoff and others, 1975]. A. KOSSIAKOFF, "DoD Weapon Systems Software Management Study," Applied Physics Laboratory, The Johns Hopkins Univ., Laurel, MD, Rep. SR-75-3, June 1975.

[Kraft, 1977]. P. KRAFT, *Programmers and Managers: The Routinization of Computer Programming in the United States,* Springer-Verlag, New York, 1977.

[Lanergan–Poynton, 1979]. R.G. LANERGAN and B.A. POYNTON, "Reusable Code—The Application Development Technique of the Future," in [SHARE–GUIDE, 1979], pp. 127–138.

[Lasher, 1979]. W. LASHER, "Software Cost Evaluation and Estimation: A Government Source Selection Case Study," *Proceedings, IEEE/PINY Workshop on Quantitative Software Models,* IEEE Catalog No. TH0067-9, October, 1979, pp. 42–55.

[Lehman, 1978]. M.M. LEHMAN, "Laws and Conservation in Large-Program Evolution," *Proceedings, U.S. Army Second Software Life-Cycle Management Workshop,* IEEE Report 78CH-1390-4C, August 1978, pp. 140–145.

[Lientz–Swanson, 1978]. B.P. LIENTZ and E.B. SWANSON, "Software Maintenance: A User/Management Tug-of-War," *Data Management,* April 1979, pp. 26–30.

[Lientz–Swanson, 1980]. B.P. LIENTZ and E.B. SWANSON, *Software Maintenance Management: A Study of the Maintenance of Computer Application Software in 487 Data Processing Organizations,* Addison-Wesley, Reading, MA, 1980.

[Lipow and others, 1977]. M. LIPOW, B.B. WHITE, and B.W. BOEHM, "Software Quality Assurance: An Acquisition Guidebook," TRW Software Series, TRW-SS-77-07, November 1977.

[Lipow, 1979]. M. LIPOW, "Prediction of Software Failures," *Journal of Systems and Software,* **1,** *1,* 1979, pp. 71–76.

[Luce–Raiffa, 1957]. R.D. LUCE and H. RAIFFA, *Games and Decisions,* John Wiley & Sons, 1957.

[Lundell 1979]. E.D. LUNDELL, JR., "Software for IBM 4300 May Cost More Than Hardware," *Computerworld,* April 30, 1979, p. 1.

[Maciariello, 1978]. J.A. MACIARIELLO, *Program-Management Control Systems,* John Wiley & Sons, New York, 1978.

[Martin, 1973]. J. MARTIN, *Design of Man-Computer Dialogues,* Prentice-Hall, Englewood Cliffs, NJ, 1973.

[Martin, 1979]. T. MARTIN, "PEARL at the Age of Three," *Proceedings, Fourth International Conference on Software Engineering,* IEEE, September 1979, pp. 100–109.

[Maslow, 1954]. A.H. MASLOW, *Motivation and Personality,* Harper and Row, New York, 1954.

[Mayer–Stalnaker, 1968]. D.B. MAYER and A.W. STALNAKER, "Selection and Evaluation of Computer Personnel," *Proceedings, ACM National Conference 1968,* ACM, 1968, pp. 657–670. Also in [Weinwurm, 1970], pp. 133–157.

[Mayo, 1945]. E. MAYO, *The Social Problems of an Industrial Civilization,* Harvard University Press, Cambridge, MA, 1945.

[McCabe, 1976]. T.J. MCCABE, "A Complexity Measure," *IEEE Trans. Software Engr.,* December 1976, pp. 308–320.

[McCracken, 1980]. D.D. MCCRACKEN, *A Guide to NOMAD for Applications Development,* National CSS, Inc., Wilton, CT, 1980.

[McCracken, 1980a]. D.D. MCCRACKEN, "Software in the 80s: Perils and Promises," *Computerworld,* September 17, 1980, pp. 5–10.

[McCracken, 1981]. D.D. MCCRACKEN, "A Maverick Approach to Systems Analysis and Design," in *Systems Analysis and Design: A Foundation for the 1980s,* Elsevier-North Holland, 1981.

[McCue, 1978]. G.M. MCCUE, "IBM Santa Teresa Laboratory—Architectural Design for Program Development," *IBM Syst. J.,* **17,** *1,* 1978, pp. 4–25.

[McGarry, 1979]. F. MCGARRY, "Overview of the Software Engineering Laboratory," *Proceedings, Fourth Summer Software Engineering Workshop,* NASA-Goddard, Greenbelt, MD, November, 1979, pp. 3–16.

[McGregor, 1960]. D. MCGREGOR, *The Human Side of Enterprise,* McGraw-Hill, New York, 1960.

[Meister, 1976]. D. MEISTER, *Behavioral Foundations of System Development,* John Wiley & Sons, 1976.

[Merwin, 1978]. R.E. MERWIN, (ed), "Special Section on Software Management," *IEEE Trans. Software Engr.,* July 1978, pp. 307–361.

[Metzger, 1973]. P.J. METZGER, *Managing a Programming Project,* Prentice-Hall, Englewood Cliffs, NJ, 1973.

[Miller, 1956]. G.A. MILLER, "The Magical Number Seven, Plus or Minus Two: Some Limits on Our Capability for Processing Information," *Psych. Review,* March 1956, pp. 81–97.

[Miller, 1968]. R.B. MILLER, "Response Time in Man-Computer Conversational Transactions," *Proceedings, 1968 SJCC,* AFIPS, 1968, pp. 267–277.

[Miller, 1980]. E.F. MILLER, JR., "Survey of Verification and Validation Technology," *Proceedings, NRC/IEEE Conference on Advanced Electrotechnology Applications to Nuclear Power Plants,* IEEE, January 1980.

[Milliman–Curtis, 1980]. P. MILLIMAN and B. CURTIS, "A Matched Project Evaluation of Modern Programming Practices," General Electric Co., RADC-TR-80-6, February 1980.

[Mills, 1970]. H.D. MILLS, "Structured Programming in Large Systems," IBM-FSD, 1970.

[Millstein and others, 1976]. R. MILLSTEIN and others, "National Software Works, Status Report No. 1," RADC-TR-76-276, U.S. Air Force, September 1976.

[Moher–Schneider, 1981]. T. MOHER and G.M. SCHNEIDER, "Methods for Improving Controlled Experimentation in Software Engineering," *Proceedings, Fifth International Conference on Software Engineering,* IEEE, March 1981, pp. 224–233.

[Morin, 1973]. L.H. MORIN, "Estimation of Resources for Computer Programming Projects," Master's Thesis, University of North Carolina, 1973.

[Morrisey–Wu, 1979]. J. MORRISEY and S.Y. WU, "Software Engineering: An Economic Perspective," *Proceedings, Fourth International Conference on Software Engineering,* IEEE Catalog No. 79 Ch 1479-5C, September 1979, pp. 412–422.

[Musa, 1975]. J.D. MUSA, "A Theory of Software Reliability and Its Application," *IEEE Trans. Software Engr.,* September 1975, pp. 312–327.

[Musa, 1979]. J.D. MUSA, "Validity of Execution Time Theory of Software Reliability," *IEEE Trans. Reliability,* August 1979, pp. 181–191.

[Musa, 1980]. J.D. MUSA, "The Measurement and Management of Software Reliability," *IEEE Trans. Software Engr.,* to appear, 1981.

[Myers, 1976]. G.J. MYERS, *Software Reliability,* John Wiley & Sons, Inc. New York, 1976.

[Myers, 1978]. G.J. MYERS, "A Controlled Experiment in Program Testing and Code Walk-throughs/Inspections," *Comm., ACM,* September 1978, pp. 760–768.

[NASA, 1980]. *"Computer Program Abstracts,"* NASA-COSMIC, Univ. of Georgia, Athens, GA 30602, periodical.

[Naur, 1969]. P. NAUR, "Programming by Action Clusters," *BIT* **9,** *3,* 1969, pp. 250–258.

[Naur–Randell, 1968]. P. NAUR and B. RANDELL, *Software Engineering,* NATO Scientific Affairs Division, Brussels, Belgium, 1968.

[Nelson, 1966]. E.A. NELSON, *Management Handbook for the Estimation of Computer Programming Costs,* AD-A648750, Systems Development Corp., Oct. 31, 1966.

[Nelson, 1978]. R. NELSON, *Software Data Collection and Analysis at RADC,* Rome Air Development Center, Rome, NY, 1978.

[Norden, 1958]. P.V. NORDEN, "Curve Fitting for a Model of Applied Research and Development Scheduling," *IBM J. Rsch. Dev.,* Vol. 2, No. 3, July 1958.

[Norden, 1970]. P.V. NORDEN, "Useful Tools for Project Management," in *Management of Production,* M.K. Starr, ed. Penguin Books, Baltimore MD, 1970, pp. 71–101.

[NTIS, 1980]. National Technical Information Service (NTIS), *A Directory of Computer Software and Related Technical Reports 1980,* NTIS, Dept. of Commerce, 5285 Port Royal Rd., Springfield, VA 22161, 1980.

[Oliver, 1979]. P. OLIVER, "Handbook for Estimating Conversion Costs of Large Business Programs," ADPESO, U.S. Navy, Washington, DC 20376, February 1979.

[Parikh, 1980]. G. PARIKH (ed), *Techniques of Program and System Maintenance,* Ethno-tech, Inc., Lincoln, NB, 1980.

[Parker, 1976]. D.B. PARKER, *Crime by Computer,* Scribner's, New York, 1976.

[Parkinson, 1957]. G.N. PARKINSON, *Parkinson's Law and Other Studies in Administration,* Houghton-Mifflin, Boston, 1957.

[Parnas, 1976]. D.L. PARNAS, "On the Design and Development of Program Families," *IEEE Trans. Software Engr.,* March 1976, pp. 1–9.

[Parnas, 1979]. D.L. PARNAS, "Designing Software for Ease of Extension and Contraction," *IEEE Trans. Software Engr.,* March 1979, pp. 128–137.

[Parr, 1980]. F.N. PARR, "An Alternative to the Rayleigh Curve Model for Software Development Effort," *IEEE Trans. Software Engr.,* May 1980, pp. 291–296.

[Paster, 1981]. D.L. PASTER, "Experience with Application of Modern Software Management Controls," *Proceedings, Fifth International Conference on Software Engineering,* IEEE, March 1981, pp. 18–26.

[Patrick, 1980]. R.L. PATRICK, "Probing Productivity," *Datamation,* September 1980, pp. 207–210.

[Peter–Hull, 1969]. L.J. PETER and R. HULL, *The Peter Principle,* William Morrow, New York, 1969.

[Phister, 1979]. M. PHISTER, JR., *Data Processing Technology and Economics,* Digital Press, Bedford, MA, 1979.

[Pietrasanta, 1970]. A.M. PIETRASANTA, "Resource Analysis of Computer Program System Development," in [Weinwurm, 1970].

[Pitchell, 1979]. R. PITCHELL, "The GUIDE Productivity Program," *GUIDE Proceedings,* GUIDE, Inc., Chicago, IL, 1979, pp. 783–794.

[Putnam, 1976]. L.H. PUTNAM, "A Macro-Estimating Methodology for Software Development," *Proceedings, IEEE COMPCON 76 Fall,* September 1976, pp. 138–143.

[Putnam–Wolverton, 1977]. L.H. PUTNAM and R.W. WOLVERTON, "Quantitative Management: Software Cost Estimating," *IEEE Comp. Soc. First Int'l. Computer Software and Applications Conf.* (COMPSAC 77), IEEE Catalog No. EHO 129–7, Chicago, IL, November 8–11, 1977.

[Putnam, 1978]. L.H. PUTNAM, "A General Empirical Solution to the Macro Software Sizing and Estimating Problem," *IEEE Trans. Software Engr.,* July 1978, pp. 345–361.

[Putnam–Fitzsimmons, 1979]. L.H. PUTNAM and A. FITZSIMMONS, "Estimating Software Costs," *Datamation,* September 1979, pp. 189–198. Continued in *Datamation,* October 1979, pp. 171–178 and November 1979, pp. 137–140.

[Putnam, 1980]. "SLIM System Description," Quantitative Software Management, Inc., McLean, VA, 1980.

[Quade, 1968]. E.S. QUADE, "Principles and Procedures of Systems Analysis," in *Systems Analysis and Policy Planning: Applications in Defense,* E.S. Quade and W.I. Boucher (ed), Elsevier, New York, 1968.

[Rand, 1957]. A. RAND, *Atlas Shrugged,* Random House, Inc., New York, 1957.

[Raskin, 1978]. L. RASKIN, *Performance Evaluation of Multiple Processor Systems,* Report CMU-CS-78-141, Carnegie Mellon Univ., Pittsburgh, PA, August 1978.

[RCA, 1978]. RCA PRICE Systems, "PRICE Software Model: Supplemental Information," RCA, Cherry Hill, NJ, March 1978.

[Reaser–Carrow, 1975]. J.M. REASER and J.C. CARROW, "Interactive Programming: Summary of an Evaluation and Some Management Considerations," Report USACSC-AT-74-03, U.S. Army Computer Systems Command, March 1975.

[Reifer, 1977]. D.J. REIFER, "Software Acquisition Planning for the DoD Space Transportation System (Space Shuttle)," *Proceedings, AIAA/DPMA Third Software Management Conference,* Washington, DC, December 1977, pp. 81–90.

[Reifer–Trattner, 1977]. D.J. REIFER and S. TRATTNER, "A Glossary of Software Tools and Techniques," *Computer,* July 1977, pp. 52–60.

[Reifer, 1978]. D.J. REIFER, *Verification, Validation, and Certification: A Software Acquisition Guidebook,* TRW-SS-78-05, TRW Software Series, September 1978.

[Reifer, 1981]. D.J. REIFER, "The Software Tools Directory," Reifer Consultants, Inc., Torrance, CA, 1981.

[Remus–Zilles, 1979]. H. REMUS and S. ZILLES, "Prediction and Management of Program Quality," *Proceedings, Fourth International Conference on Software Engineering,* IEEE, September 1979, pp. 341–350.

[Ross–Schoman, 1977]. D.T. ROSS and K.E. SCHOMAN JR., "Structured Analysis for Requirements Definition," *IEEE Trans. Software Engr.,* January 1977, pp. 6–15.

[Rosove, 1967]. P.E. ROSOVE, *Developing Computer-Based Information Systems,* John Wiley & Sons, New York, 1967.

[Royce, 1970]. W.W. ROYCE, "Managing the Development of Large Software Systems: Concepts and Techniques," *Proceedings, WESCON,* August 1970.

[Rubey and others, 1975]. R.J. RUBEY, J.A. DANA, and P.W. BICHE, "Quantitative Aspects of Software Validation," *IEEE Trans. Software Engr.,* June 1975, pp. 150–155.

[Sackman, 1967]. H. SACKMAN, *Computers, System Science, and Evolving Society,* John Wiley & Sons, New York, 1967.

[Sackman, 1969]. H. SACKMAN, "Experimental Evaluation of Time-Sharing and Batch Processing in Teaching Computer Science," System Development Corp., SP-3411, October 1969.

[Sackman, 1970]. H. SACKMAN, *Man-Computer Problem Solving,* Auerbach, Philadelphia, PA, 1970.

[Schluter, 1977]. R.G. SCHLUTER, "Experience in Managing the Development of Large Real-Time BMD Software Systems," *Proceedings, AIAA/NASA/IEEE/ACM Computers in Aerospace Conference,* Los Angeles, October–November 1977, pp. 168–173.

[Schneider, 1977]. JOHN SCHNEIDER, IV, *A Preliminary Calibration of the RCA PRICE/S Software Cost Estimation Model,* Air Force Institute of Technology, Dayton, OH, Thesis No. GSM/SM/77S-15, NTIS No. AD-A046808, September 1977.

[Schneider, 1978]. V. SCHNEIDER, "Prediction of Software Effort and Project Duration: Four New Formulas," *ACM SIGPLAN Notices,* June 1978, pp. 49–59.

[Schumacher, 1973]. E.F. SCHUMACHER, *Small Is Beautiful: Economics as if People Mattered,* Harper and Row, New York, 1973.

[Scott–Simmons, 1974]. R.F. SCOTT and D.B. SIMMONS, "Programmer Productivity and the Delphi Technique," *Datamation,* May 1974, pp. 71–73.

[SHARE–GUIDE, 1979]. SHARE, Inc., and GUIDE International, *Proceedings, Application Development Symposium,* October 1979, available through either SHARE or GUIDE Secretary, 111 E. Wacker Dr., Chicago IL 60601.

[Sharpe, 1969]. W.F. SHARPE, *The Economics of Computers,* Columbia University Press, New York, 1969.

[Sheppard and others, 1980]. S.B. SHEPPARD, P. MILLIMAN, and B. CURTIS, "Experimental Evaluation of On-Line Program Construction," *Proceedings, IEEE COMPSAC 80,* October 1980, pp. 505–510.

[Sheppard and others, 1981]. S.B. SHEPPARD, E. KREVESI, and B. CURTIS, "The Effects of Symbology and Spatial Arrangement on the Comprehension of Software Specifications," *Proceedings, Fifth International Conference on Software Engineering,* IEEE, March 1981, pp. 207–214.

[Shneiderman and others, 1977]. B. SHNEIDERMAN, R. MAYER, D. MCKAY, and P. HELLER, "Experimental Investigations of the Utility of Detailed Flowcharts in Programming," *Comm. ACM,* **20,** 1977, pp. 373–381.

[Shneiderman, 1979]. B. SHNEIDERMAN, "Human Factors Experiments in Designing Interactive Systems," *Computer,* December 1979, pp. 9–19.

[Shneiderman, 1980]. B. SHNEIDERMAN, *Software Psychology: Human Factors in Computer and Information Systems,* Winthrop Press, Cambridge, MA, 1980.

[Shoor, 1981]. R. SHOOR, ed., "Application Packages: Getting the Right Fit," *Computerworld,* January 26, 1981, pp. SR/1–31.

[Steel, 1977]. T.B. STEEL JR., "A Note on Future Trends," in P.S. Nyborg (ed), *Information Processing in the United States: A Quantitative Summary,* AFIPS, Montvale, NJ, 1977.

[Stephenson, 1976]. W.E. STEPHENSON, *An Analysis of the Resources Used in Safeguard System Software Development,* Bell Labs., draft paper, August 1976.

[Stokes, 1970]. J.C. STOKES, "Managing the Developing of Large Software Systems: Apollo Real-Time Control Center," *Proceedings, WESCON 70,* August 1970.

[Stone, 1978]. H.S. STONE, "Final Report: Life-Cycle Cost Analysis of Instruction Set Architecture Standardization for Military Computer-Based Systems," U.S. Army Research Office, January 1978.

[Stone–Coleman, 1979]. H.S. STONE and A. COLEMAN, "Life-Cycle Cost Analysis of Instruction-Set Architecture Standardization for Military Computer-Based Systems," *Computer,* April 1979, pp. 35–47.

[Sukert, 1978]. A.N. SUKERT, "A Four-Project Empirical Study of Software Error Prediction Models," *Proceedings, COMPSAC 78,* Chicago, November 1978.

[Sunohara and others, 1981]. T. SUNOHARA, A. TAKANO, K. UEHARA, and T. OHKAWA, "Program Complexity Measure for Software Development Management," *Proceedings, Fifth International Conference on Software Engineering,* IEEE, March 1981, pp. 100–106.

[Swanson, 1976]. E.B. SWANSON, "The Dimensions of Maintenance," *Proceedings, IEEE/ACM Second International Conference on Software Engineering,* October 1976.

[Teichroew–Hershey, 1977]. D. TEICHROEW and E.A. HERSHEY III, "PSL/PSA: A Computer-Aided Technique for Structured Documentation and Analysis of Information Processing Systems," *IEEE Trans. Software Engr.,* January 1977, pp. 41–48.

[Thacker and others, 1979]. C.P. THACKER, E.M. MCCREIGHT, B.W. LAMPSON, R.F. SPROULL, and D.R. BOGGS, "Alto: A Personal Computer," Xerox Palo Alto Research Center Report CSL–79–11, 1979.

[Thayer and others, 1978]. T.A. THAYER, M. LIPOW, and E.C. NELSON, *Software Reliability: A Study of Large Project Reality,* North-Holland, New York, 1978.

[Thurber, 1976]. K.J. THURBER, *Large Scale Computer Architecture: Parallel and Associative Processors,* Haydon, Rochelle Park, NJ, 1976.

[Townsend, 1970]. R. TOWNSEND, *Up the Organization,* Fawcett Publications, Greenwich, CT, 1970.

[TRW, 1973]. TRW, Inc., *Software Development and Configuration Management Manual,* TRW-SS-73-07, December 1973.

[Wagner, 1977]. H.M. WAGNER, *Principles of Operations Research,* (2nd ed) Prentice-Hall, Englewood Cliffs, NJ 1977.

[Walston–Felix, 1977]. C.E. WALSTON and C.P. FELIX, "A Method of Programming Measurement and Estimation," *IBM Syst. J.,* 16, 1, 1977, pp. 54–73.

[Walston–Felix, 1977a]. C.E. WALSTON and C.P. FELIX, "Authors' Response," *IBM Syst. J.* No. 4, 1977, pp. 422–423.

[Ware and others, 1974]. W.H. WARE and others, *Records, Computers, and the Rights of Citizens,* M.I.T. Press, Cambridge, MA, 1974.

[Warnier, 1974]. J.D. WARNIER, *Logical Construction of Programs,* Van Nostrand Reinhold, New York, 1974.

[Webster, 1979]. *Webster's New Collegiate Dictionary,* G.&C. Merriam Co., Springfield, MA, 1979.

[Weinberg, 1971]. G.M. WEINBERG, *The Psychology of Computer Programming,* Van Nostrand Reinhold, New York, 1971.

[Weinberg, 1972]. G.M. WEINBERG, "The Psychology of Improved Programming Performance," *Datamation,* November 1972, pp. 82–85.

[Weinberg–Schulman, 1974]. G.M. WEINBERG and E.L. SCHULMAN, "Goals and Performance in Computer Programming," *Human Factors,* 1974, 16 (1), 70–77.

[Weinberg, 1979]. G.M. WEINBERG, "The Psychology of Change in Development Methodology," in [SHARE–GUIDE, 1979], pp. 93–100.

[Weinwurm, 1970]. G.F. WEINWURM (ed), *On the Management of Computer Programming,* Auerbach, New York, 1970.

[Weiss, 1979]. D.M. WEISS, "Evaluating Software Development by Error Analysis: The Data from the Architecture Research Facility," *Journal of Systems and Software,* **1,** *1,* 1979, pp. 57–70.

[Weissman, 1974]. L. WEISSMAN, "A Methodology for Studying the Psychological Complexity of Computer Programs," Technical Report TR-CSRG-37, Computer Systems Research Group, Univ. of Toronto, 1974. See also *ACM SIGPLAN Notices,* June 1974, pp. 25–36.

[Weizenbaum, 1976]. J. WEIZENBAUM, *Computer Power and Human Reason,* W.H. Freeman, San Francisco, 1976.

[Westin–Baker, 1972]. A.F. WESTIN and M.A. BAKER, *Databanks in a Free Society,* Quadrangle Books, New York, 1972.

[Wiest–Levy, 1977]. J.D. WIEST and F.K. LEVY, *A Management Guide to PERT/CPM,* Prentice-Hall, Englewood Cliffs, NJ, 1977.

[Williams, 1975]. R.D. WILLIAMS, "Managing the Development of Reliable Software," *Proceedings, 1975 International Conference on Reliable Software,* IEEE/ACM, April 1975, pp. 3–8.

[Williamson, 1979]. I.M. WILLIAMSON, "NARDAC Model," NRL Technical Memorandum 7503-XXX, July 16, 1979.

[Williman, 1969]. A.O. WILLIMAN, "Autonetics Programming Cost Data, 1969," personal communication from A.O. Williman, October 1971.

[Williman–O'Donnell, 1970]. A.O. WILLIMAN and C. O'DONNELL, "Through the Central 'Multiprocessor' Avionics Enters the Computer Era," *Astronautics and Aeronautics,* July 1970.

[Wirth, 1981]. N. WIRTH, "Lilith: A Personal Computer for the Software Engineer," *Proceedings, Fifth International Conference on Software Engineering,* IEEE, March 1981, pp. 2–15.

[Withington, 1972]. F.G. WITHINGTON, *The Organization of the Data Processing Function,* Wiley-Interscience, New York, 1972.

[Wolff, 1970]. H.T. WOLFF, "The Hospital Ward—A Technological Desert," in *Instruments in Working Environments,* Adam Hilger, London, 1970.

[Wolverton, 1974]. R.W. WOLVERTON, "The Cost of Developing Large-Scale Software," *IEEE Trans. Computers,* June 1974, pp. 615–636.

[Wolverton, 1980]. R.W. WOLVERTON, "Airborne Systems Software Acquisition Engineering Guidebook: Software Cost Analysis and Estimating," U.S. Air Force ASD/EN, Wright-Patterson AFB, OH, February 1980.

[Woodfield and others, 1981]. S.N. WOODFIELD, H.E. DUNSMORE, and V.Y. SHEN, "The Effect of Modularization on Program Comprehension," *Proceedings, Fifth International Conference on Software Engineering,* IEEE, March 1981, pp. 215–223.

[Woodside, 1980]. C.M. WOODSIDE, "A Mathematical Model for the Evolution of Software," *J. Systems and Software,* Vol. 1, No. 4, 1980, pp. 337–345.

[Yourdon, 1975]. E. YOURDON, *Techniques of Program Structure and Design,* Prentice-Hall, 1975.

[Yourdon–Constantine, 1978]. E. YOURDON and L.L. CONSTANTINE, *Structured Design* (2nd ed), Prentice-Hall, Englewood Cliffs, NJ, 1978.

[Yourdon, 1979]. E.N. YOURDON, *Managing the Structured Technologies,* Prentice-Hall, Englewood Cliffs, NJ, 1979.

[Yourdon, 1979a]. E. YOURDON, *Structured Walkthroughs,* Prentice-Hall, Englewood Cliffs, NJ, 1979.

AUTHOR INDEX

SUBJECT INDEX

A

Customer interface quality:
    effect on software cost, 488

D

Data base size (DATA), 119–20, 354, 386–390, 642, 659
    ideal effort multiplier, 389–90
    project activity effects, 388–89
    project data, 496
    ratings and effort multipliers, 387
    related studies, 390
    research topics, 398
    software productivity leverage, 642, 659
Data collection, 326–28, 447–48, 637, 691–709
    problem sources, 706
Data conditioning, 706–8
Deadline effect, 593
Decision criteria:
    cost-effectiveness, 197–204
Decision guidelines:
    value-of-information, 298–300, 302
Decision-making:
    under complete uncertainty, 280–84, 289–90
    under uncertainty, 294–96
Decision-oriented software system, 720
Decision point, 249
Decision space, 246–49, 259–62
Decision theory:
    statistical, 289–303
Decision variables, 248–53
Decisions:
    identifying controllables, 6, 251–52, 259–260
Definition of cost model, 476, 482, 484, 486, 487, 520–21
Deliverable executable machine instructions (DEMI), 477–79
Delivered capacity, 237–39
Delivered source instructions, 58–59, 477–79, 482–84
Delivered system capability, 236–42
    advantages, 237, 240
    definition, 237
    problems, 240, 245
Delphi technique, 266, 282, 333–35, 342–43
    of COCOMO, 521
Detail of cost model, 476, 522
    of COCOMO, 522
Detailed COCOMO model, 344
    accuracy, 495, 497, 501–2
    activity distribution, 366
    distinguishing features, 344–45
    phase distribution of effort, 351–53, 356–58, 360, 361–65
        accuracy, 504–7
    phase distribution of schedule, 359, 361
    procedures, 348–61
    product hierarchy, 347–48, 349–52, 356–58

schedule estimation, 352–53, 358, 359, 361
    Software Hierarchy Estimating Form (SHEF), 348–358, 369–70
    summary of formulas, 366
Detailed design phase, 36–37, 46–50
Diminishing returns segment, 189
    software maintenance, 545–50
    software product, 193–94
Discount rate, 217–21
    composite, 221–22
Diseconomies of scale, 65–67, 86–87, 190–95
Documentation:
    anticipatory, 44–45, 452, 489
    cost estimation, 571, 574
    effect on software cost, 488–89
    effort distribution, 572–74
    project data, 497, 571–75
    project effort producing, 575–76
Documentation rate, 571–75, 590
    definition, 571
    project data, 571–75
    variation with project type, 572, 574
    variation with required reliability, 572–73, 575
Dollar estimates, 61, 148, 150, 353, 358
Doty 1977 cost model, 511, 514–15, 522
Double counting, 275–76, 282

E

Earned value summary report, 595, 597, 615–17, 634–36
Earned value system, 597, 612–18, 628–29, 634–37
    allocation problems, 617–18
    benefits, 618, 637
Ease of use of cost model, 476, 481, 523
    of COCOMO, 523
Economic-programming approach, 6
    Scientific American case study, 6–8
Economics:
    human, 12, 212, 214
    material, 12, 212, 214
Economies of scale, 189–90, 254
Effectiveness-cost difference, 199–200
Effectiveness/cost ratio, 199
Effectiveness criteria, 270, 585, 587–88
Effort adjustment factor, 125, 148–49, 156–59
    module level, 350–52, 357
    subsystem level, 349, 352, 357
Effort equations:
    comparison among models, 86–87
Effort estimates:
    conversion to cost estimates, 61, 148, 150, 352, 358
Effort multipliers, 117–24, 129–30, 148–49, 156–59
    phase sensitive, 348, 353–55, 356–57
Embedded mode:
    activity distribution by phase, 99
    definition, 79–82

Ideal effort multiplier *(cont.)*
    Programming language experience (LEXP), 443–44
    Required development schedule (SCED), 468–69
    Required software reliability (RELY), 377–80
    Requirements volatility (RVOL), 484–86
    Use of software tools (TOOL), 459–60, 463
    Virtual machine experience (VEXP), 439, 441
    Virtual machine volatility (VIRT), 414–16
Imperfect information, 290–96
Implementation phase, 36–37, 46–50
Incremental development, 41–44, 56, 191, 194, 452
    schedule estimation, 500, 504
Independent cost estimates, 323–24, 582
Independent verification and validation, 380–81
Infeasible decision problem, 250
Infeasible point, 247–49
Information:
    value of, 212–13, 270, 283–84, 290–303
Information hiding, 192, 425, 474, 491, 665, 724
Information system benefits, 270, 585, 587–88
Inspections, 452, 457, 474
    error removal effectiveness, 383–85
Installation, software:
    cost estimation, 565–66, 582, 584
    definitions, 565
    project data, 565–66
Instant response time, 191
Instruction counting, 58–59, 73, 477–79, 484
Integration and test phase, 36–37, 46–50
Interactive software development, 415–21, 423–25, 457
Interest calculations, 216
Interest rate, 216–22
Intermediate COCOMO model, 114–63
    accuracy, 138–40, 495, 497, 500, 502
    activity and phase distribution, 124, 159–60
        accuracy, 504–10
    adaptation effort estimation, 133–38
    component-level estimation, 145–163, 559–61
    cost driver attributes, 115–124
    effort multipliers, 117–124
    limitations, 344
    maintenance effort estimation, 129–32, 142–43, 156–59
    nominal effort equations, 117–18, 148
    schedule estimation, 124, 148
    summary of formulas, 366
Interpolation, 69–71, 132–33
Inverse Peter Principle, 671
Investment segment, 189
    software maintenance, 545–50
    software product, 193–94
Isoquants, 249, 253, 261
Iteration:
    of solution approach, 254, 262–63

K

Kiviat graph, 274–75

L

Labor distribution:
    Basic COCOMO, 65–69, 92–94, 111
    detailed project plan, 622–25
    incremental development, 42–43
    Rayleigh distribution, 42–43, 67–69, 92–94, 110, 625
Language *(see* Programming language)
Language experience *(see* Programming language experience)
Laplace rule, 281–83, 286–88
Laws of large-program evolution, 546–47
Lease-squares approximation, 525–28
Librarian, 452, 457
Libraries of programs, 654 *(see also* Program generators)
Lientz-Swanson maintenance data base, 533–35, 543, 548–49
Life-cycle:
    cost-benefit analysis *(see* CEMICS cost-benefit analysis)
Life-cycle concept review, 48
Life-cycle cost estimation, 132, 142–43, 273, 556–90
    CEMICS example, 579–86
Linear function, 250
Linear programming, 250–54, 257
    validity of assumptions, 254
Local maximum, 174, 255

M

Macroeconomics, 166
Main storage constraint (STOR), 119–20, 141, 142, 160, 163, 354, 410–13, 422–23, 642, 662–65
    ideal effort multiplier, 412–13
    project activity effects, 411–12
    project data, 496
    ratings and effort multipliers, 410
    related studies, 404–6
    research topics, 424–25
    software productivity leverage, 642, 662–65
Maintenance, 54–55, 71, 99–101, 109–10, 129–32, 156–59, 267, 533–55, 585–86
    activity distribution, 99–101, 105, 109–10, 548–50
    adaptive, 55, 536, 548–50
    Annual change traffic, 71, 536, 538–40, 543–45, 550–52, 555
    cards-per-person ratio, 541, 543–45
    COCOMO model accuracy, 539–40, 550–53
    corrective, 54, 536, 548–50
    cost estimation, 71, 129–32, 142–43, 156–59, 366, 536, 538–39, 585–86
    cost trends, 18
    definition, 49, 54–55, 534–47
    dynamics, 545–47, 554–55

effort estimation, 71, 129–32, 142–43, 156–59, 366, 536, 538–39
fraction of life-cycle cost, 18, 533–34, 540–41
HOL-MOL effects, 542
MODP effort multipliers, 130, 538–39
necessity of, 550
OS/360 evolution, 547
perfective, 55, 536, 548–50
phenomenology, 545–50
production function, 545–50, 553, 555
productivity, 542–44, 548–50, 657, 659, 677, 687
project data, 550–53
RELY effort multipliers, 129, 538–39
research topics, 554–55
techniques, 550
Maintenance/development cost ratio, 540–41
Maintenance phase, 36–37, 46–50, 54–55
Maintenance productivity ratio, 542
Make-or-buy analysis, 312
value of information, 297
Management:
effect on software cost, 486–88
Management reserve, 488
Man-month, 59, 61
Manuals, 46, 49–50, 98–110
Marginal analysis, 207–14
decision rules, 209–10
Marginal cost, 210–11
Marginal net value, 209–10
Marginal value, 210–11
Maslow need hierarchy, 670–71
Material economics, 12, 212, 214
Mathematical optimization techniques, 250–56, 262–63
Maximax rule, 281, 283, 286–88
Maximin rule, 280–81, 283, 286–88
Measurement, 318, 447–48, 479–84, 493–94, 638, 644–45, 657–58
Microeconomics, 166, 169–303
Milestone, 38, 326–28, 593, 595, 597, 610–12, 613–15, 623, 628
Military Computer Family:
software tool analysis, 461–64
Modern programming practices (MODP), 119–20, 130, 355, 451–58, 473, 641–42, 676–78
GUIDE survey, 456–58
ideal effort multiplier, 453, 455
implementation guidelines, 677–78
project activity effects, 453–54
project data, 497
ratings and effort multipliers, 452–53
related studies, 453, 455–58, 474
research topics, 473–74
routinization effects, 458
software productivity leverage, 641–42, 676–78
Modified Golden Rule, 24, 720, 721, 725, 726
Modularity, 192, 194–95, 425, 474, 491, 724
Motivation:
growth vs. social needs, 669
harmony of objectives, 673–75
Hawthorne effect, 672–73

Herzberg motivation factors, 673–74
Maslow need hierarchy, 670–71
of software personnel, 21, 266, 318, 484, 638, 645, 669–75
Multiple goals:
decision analysis, 205–77
in software engineering, 20–21
Multiprocessor overhead, 171–72, 177–78, 190

N

National Software Works, 461
Net expected value, 293–94, 297
of prototype, 293–94
Net Value, 207–11, 224–25, 245, 248, 280
90% syndrome, 607–8
Nonlinear programming, 254–55
Number of program entities:
as sizing metric, 481–82
Number of specification elements:
as sizing metric, 481–82

O

Object instructions, 478–79
Objective function, 248–55, 260–63
Objective function isoquants, 249, 253, 261
Objectives, 6, 251, 259–63
global, 259
system, 259
Objectivity of cost model, 476, 482, 484, 521–22
of COCOMO, 521–22
Obsolescence, 671
Operational profile, 372
Optimal performance, 173–75, 183–84
Optimal solution, 248–49, 253–54, 261–63
necessary and sufficient conditions, 249, 253
Optimism, 320–21, 324, 325, 340–41
Optimization, 173–76, 209–11, 246–57, 262–63
software engineering applications, 250
Organic mode:
activity distribution by phase, 101
definition, 78–82
effort and schedule equations:
Basic COCOMO, 57, 61–64, 75–77
Intermediate COCOMO, 117
phase distribution of effort and schedule:
Basic and Intermediate COCOMO, 64–69, 89–94
Organization charts, 104–10, 190
OS/360 maintenance evolution, 547
Overruns, 30–32, 633–37

P

Q

R

Software productivity *(cont.)*
   means and ends, 689
   measurement, 318, 447–48, 479–84, 493–94, 638, 644–45, 657–58
   metrics, 318, 479–84, 493–94, 638, 644–45, 657–58
   modern programming practices, 641–42, 676–78
   motivation, 672–75
   nonprogramming options, 644, 647–58, 661, 686, 688
   payoff estimates, 684–87
   personnel/team capability, 642, 666–76
      management, 486–88, 675
      motivation, 672–75
      staffing, 667–72
   possible improvement, 641, 686–88
   product complexity, 642, 659–60
   program generators, 654–58 *(see also* Program generators)
   programming language experience, 642
   programming language level, 644, 660
   project data, 497
   required reliability, 642, 659
   requirements volatility, 680–81
   schedule constraint, 642, 679–80
   sensitivity to definitions, 73, 140–41, 318, 644–45, 657–58
   software packages, 647–53 *(see* Software packages)
   staffing, 667–72
   status assessment, 684–86
   use of existing software, 644, 647–58, 661, 686, 688
   use of software tools, 642, 678–79
   virtual machine experience, 642
   virtual machine volatility, 642, 665
   weighted, 493–94
   wish list, 661, 681
   work environment, 681–82
Software Productivity Range, 642
Software Project Data (SPD) forms, 691–717
Software psychology, 446–48
Software reliability:
   definition, 372
   estimation, 372–73, 384
   production function, 381–86
Software requirements review, 48
Software sizing, 316–23, 328, 479–84, 579–81
Software tools, 459–66 *(see also* Use of software tools)
   production function, 462–65
Software training:
   cost estimation, 565–66, 584
   definitions, 565
   project data, 565–66
Soundness of cost estimates, 325, 341–42
Source instructions, 58–59, 477–79
Spaceflight program:
   growth in software demand, 643–44
Specifications:
   testable, 315–16
Stability of cost model, 476, 522–23
   of COCOMO, 523

Staffing principles, 667–72
   career progression, 670–71
   job matching, 669–70
   phaseout, 671
   team balance, 671–72
   top talent, 668–69
State of nature, 280–84, 289–98
Statistical decision theory, 289–303
Stoneman, 465–66
Structured code, 452, 457
Structured design, 452
Structured purism, 677
Structured walkthroughs *(see* Inspections)
Subjective probabilities, 282, 284, 294
Summary task planning sheet, 595–96, 613–15, 628–29, 635
Supply and demand:
   for software, 643–44
Support software:
   relative size, 321–23
Swedish bank case study, 13, 212
System acceptance review, 49
System alternatives, 260
System capability, 237–39
System objectives, 259
Systems analysis, 258–64
   Scientific American case study, 6–8, 258

T

Tabular methods:
   for presenting mixed criteria, 272–3
Tailoring:
   of COCOMO model, 524–30
      installation differences, 524
      modifying cost drivers, 529–30
Tall pole in the tent, 324
Task Unit Planning Sheet, 339–40
Technologically efficient, 188
Test planning, 46, 49–50, 98–110
Testing:
   value of information, 298, 300
Test-unit cost estimation, 339–41
Theory of the firm, 212
Time and motion studies:
   Bell Laboratories, 340–41, 591–92
Time card, 595–96, 628, 630
Tools *(see* Software tools, Use of software tools)
Top-down cost estimation, 323–24, 337–38
Top-down development, 4–8, 299, 452, 457, 666
   programming-oriented, 4–5
   user-oriented, 6–8
Total Value, 207–11, 248
Training, software:
   cost estimation, 565–66, 584
   definitions, 565
   project data, 565–66

Transaction processing system (TPS)
  cost-effectiveness decision criteria, 197–201
  cost-effectiveness model, 178–81
  delivered system capability, 238–39, 244–45
  description, 153–54
  make-or-buy analysis, 266–69
  net value and marginal analysis, 207–8, 210–11, 224–25
  operating constraints, 243–48
  performance model, 171–74, 177–78
  present value analysis, 215–22
  production function, 187–89
  reducing scale, 194–95
  reliability and availability, 243–47
  rental vs. purchase analysis, 215–22
  risk analysis: OS options, 279–83, 289–95
  software cost estimation, 154–60
  software package selection, 223–27, 238–39
  systems analysis of airline reservation TPS, 259–262, 264
  unquantifiable factors, 261–62, 266–69
  value of information, 199–200, 207–8, 212–13
  weighted sum analysis, 225–27, 239–40
TRW Wolverton cost model, 511–13, 522
Turnaround time (*see also* Computer turnaround time)
Type of application (TYPE), 476–78
  ideal effort multiplier, 477–78
  project data, 496
  related studies, 477

U

Unbalanced system, 192
Uncertainties, 278–303
Underestimation, 320–23, 340–41
Unit development folder, 595–96, 607–12, 631
  contents, 609–10
  cover sheet, 610–12
  objectives, 608
  procedures, 609–12
Unit test:
  error removal effectiveness, 383–85
Unix programmers' workbench, 466, 678
Unquantifiable goals, 261–62, 265–77, 598
Urban school attendance system case study, 10–11, 25–26, 263
Use of software tools (TOOL), 119–20, 126–27, 355, 459–66, 473, 642, 678–79, 726
  ideal effort multiplier, 459–60, 463
  project activity effects, 459, 462
  project data, 497
  ratings and effort multipliers, 459–61
  related studies, 460–66, 474

research topics, 473–74
  software productivity leverage, 642, 678–79
User costs, 584
Utility function, 284–88, 290, 293, 294

V

Value, 212, 219, 270
Value of information, 212–13, 270, 283–84, 290–303
Value-of-information procedure, 296–300, 302
Verification and Validation, 37, 46–50, 98–110, 728
  value of information, 298–300, 302–3
Very high level languages, 655 (*see also* Program generators)
Virtual machine experience (VEXP), 119–20, 353, 439–441, 642
  ideal effort multiplier, 439, 441
  project activity effects, 439–40
  project data, 496,
  ratings and effort multipliers, 439–40
  related studies, 441, 446–47
  research topics, 449–50
  software productivity leverage, 642
Virtual machine volatility (VIRT), 119–20, 354, 413–16, 423, 642, 665
  ideal effort multiplier, 414–16
  project activity effects, 414–15
  project data, 496
  ratings and effort multipliers, 413–14
  related studies, 415
  research topics, 425
  software productivity leverage, 642, 665
Visibility, 607–12, 634–37

W

Walkthroughs (*see* Inspections)
Waterfall model of software life cycle, 35–46
  economic rationale, 38–41, 55–56
  refinements, 41–46, 55–56
Weighted delivered source instructions, 140–41, 479, 493
Weighted productivity, 493–94
Weighted sum analysis, 225–36, 239–42
  advantages, 236, 240
  problems, 234–36
Weinberg experiment, 20–21, 318, 484, 672–73
Wideband Delphi technique, 335, 582
Wish list, 661, 681
Work breakdown structure, 46, 49, 51–54, 59, 338, 536–37, 595–96, 616–17, 618–26, 632–36
Work package, 596